Geoeconomics of the Sustainable Development Goals

In 2015, the United Nations introduced its very ambitious 2030 Agenda, known as the Sustainable Developmental Goals or SDGs. The SDGs provide a comprehensive list of goals and targets to address social, economic and environmental issues. In this book, different areas of expertise are brought together, examining the main challenges associated with the effects of "*climate change*" and the broader scope of the SDGs through the lenses of the geoeconomics and geopolitics of sustainability. The book sheds light on the growing connections between the economic and financial fields and their impact on defining the international order and its economy. It examines the importance of trade and economic integration in promoting sustainable development and achieving the SDGs.

The role of supranational organisations like the United Nations, the World Trade Organisation and the IMF in supporting the SDGs within the context of the world's most advanced economies and those less developed; the influence of economic diplomacy and geopolitical rivalries on progress towards the SDGs; the changing global balance of power and the significance of technology and innovation; as well as the role of emerging and less developed economies in enabling sustainable development. The book offers insights into practical issues linked to theory and applied frameworks, underscoring the significant challenges associated with sustainable development, the global economic and political reality, and how political tensions affect the global economy.

The book supports students through the established disciplines of economics, finance, political science, and law and provides academics with new research and theory-building tools.

Lucía Morales is an academic and active researcher at the Faculty of Business, Technological University Dublin, Ireland and the European University of Technology (EUt+).

Bernadette Andreosso-O'Callaghan is Jean Monnet Professor of Economics at the Kemmy Business School, University of Limerick Ireland and Visiting Professor at the Ruhr Universität Bochum, Germany.

Daniel Rajmil is Associate Professor in the School of Law and Political Science, Universitat Oberta de Catalunya (UOC), Barcelona, Spain.

Frontiers of Geoeconomics, Geopolitics and Sustainability

Series editors: Bernadette Andreosso-O'Callaghan, Jacques Jaussaud, Robert Taylor, Sam Dzever, Jöern Carsten Gottwald and Lucía Morales

Frontiers of Geoeconomics, Geopolitics and Sustainability" delves into the intricate relationship between sustainable development, geoeconomics, and geopolitics. Written and guided by experts in the field, the series integrates novel contributions, and fosters collaboration between young researchers, practitioners, and doctoral students, who bring critical and reflective insights into the pressing issues emerging due to our changing political and economic landscape. The series offers a multidimensional framework of scientific academic research to understand and analyse the complex interplay between economic factors, political dynamics, and sustainability on a global scale. The field of international relations takes prominent role as the series brings together geoeconomics, geopolitics and globalisation; these three distinct areas are interconnected and the association between the three helps shed some light on the complexities associated with the concept of sustainability and its paramount implications. At the centre of the debate, the Editors identify the significance of human resource management, the implications of corporate social responsibility and how they should be considered in the context of the three Pillars of Sustainability: Environment, Society and Economics. Governance is poised to play a critical role in the international context as we seek to better understand economic activities and existing business models. The Social Pillar of Sustainability emerges as a critical one as we are facing a significant challenge in how our global economy is evolving towards increasing economic and political polarisation. With its interdisciplinary perspective, this book series offers fresh insights and innovative perspectives, paving the way for a more holistic and integrated approach to addressing the sustainability imperative.

Geoeconomics of the Sustainable Development Goals
Edited by Lucía Morales, Bernadette Andreosso-O'Callaghan and Daniel Rajmil

For more information about this series, please visit: https://www.routledge.com/our-products/book-series/GEOECONSUST

Geoeconomics of the Sustainable Development Goals

Edited by Lucía Morales,
Bernadette Andreosso-O'Callaghan and
Daniel Rajmil

Routledge
Taylor & Francis Group
LONDON AND NEW YORK

First published 2025
by Routledge
4 Park Square, Milton Park, Abingdon, Oxon OX14 4RN

and by Routledge
605 Third Avenue, New York, NY 10158

Routledge is an imprint of the Taylor & Francis Group, an informa business

British Library Cataloguing-in-Publication Data
A catalogue record for this book is available from the British Library

ISBN: 978-1-032-65580-2 (hbk)
ISBN: 978-1-032-65584-0 (pbk)
ISBN: 978-1-032-65585-7 (ebk)

DOI: 10.4324/9781032655857

Typeset in Times New Roman
by SPi Technologies India Pvt Ltd (Straive)

Contents

Figures

Tables

Contributors

Abrar Alzankawi is a PhD student and active researcher in the School of Accounting Economics and Finance at Technological University Dublin (TU Dublin). Abrar's subject areas and research interests include Geopolitics & Geoeconomics, Economic sustainability, and Education for sustainability. Abrar is interested in education and research and seeks an academic career in economics and finance.

Amal Abu-Warda Perez is a Lawyer and political scientist and holds a PhD in International Law and International Relations. Abu-Warda is an international relations lecturer at the Complutense University of Madrid. Her areas of expertise include politics, security and human rights in the Middle East and Africa, political Islam, and international terrorism. She has published articles and participated in national and international conferences on these topics. She has worked in the field of international cooperation for development in Egypt and as a visiting researcher at Cairo University through the Spanish Agency for International Development Cooperation.

Bernadette Andreosso-O'Callaghan is Professor of Economic Integration at the University of Limerick (Ireland) and visiting Professor at the Ruhr University (Germany). She has written in the areas of comparative economic integration (Europe and Asia) and of economic growth, structural change, crises, and financialisation with a specific focus on East Asian countries. Bernadette's most recent articles have been published in the *Journal of Emerging Market Finance*, *China Report*, *Peace Review*, *Asia Pacific Business Review*, *International Review of Economics and Finance*, *Journal of Economics and Finance*, *The World Economy*, and *International Journal of Financial Studies*. She is also the co-editor of *Sustainable Development in Asia: Socio-economic, Financial, and Economic Perspectives*, with Serge Rey and Robert Taylor (2022) (Springer: Cham, Switzerland); of *Economic Policy and the Covid-19 Crisis: The Macroeconomic Response in the US, Europe and East Asia*, with Woosik Moon and Wook Sohn (2022) (Routledge: London); and of *Geopolitical Uncertainty and International Business – Shaping our Future World*, with Daniel Rajmil (in press, 2024) (Edward Elgar: Cheltenham).

Jon-Hans Coetzer is a senior higher education leader with over 15 years of experience. He served as Academic Dean of IHTTI, Neuchâtel, and most recently Academic Dean of the European University's Swiss Campuses. He also served as a member of the strategic management team. He designed and led academic programs in Germany, Australia, Thailand, Japan, China, Vietnam, Bosnia and Herzegovina, Croatia, South Korea, and Kazakhstan. He forged collaborative partnerships with prestigious global and regional institutions and organizations. Jon-Hans has further developed a solid experience of managing collaborative partnerships with UK partners; Bournemouth University, Derby University, and Roehampton University. These also include academic partnerships in the USA; Boston University and Pace University. Strong intercultural competencies, and experience working with students, colleagues and external constituencies from 35+ countries. He also worked as Project Coordinator in Strategic Crisis Management Training for the Federal Chancellery in Bern. Jon-Hans has also worked as a senior delegate of the International Committee of the Red Cross (ICRC) in more than 15 countries and project coordinator for the United Nations Institute for Training and Research (UNITAR).

Ilaria De Vita is an independent researcher and practitioner. She graduated with a MEng in Chemical Engineering from the University of Manchester, followed by an MSc in Interdisciplinary Sustainability Studies from the Universitat Autònoma de Barcelona. As a practitioner, Ilaria has extensive experience in the agricultural sector. She initially worked in support of the European Commission as Programme Officer Assistant on the Common Agricultural Policy (CAP) 2023-27 Stategic Plan for Italy, focusing specifically on rural areas and environmental measures. Subsequently, she engaged in fieldwork with local communities and NGOs; first in Bolivia, contributing to environmental and water management activities in rural projects, and then in the Dominican Republic, at the border with Haiti, supporting an agroforestry and ecosystem restoration project. Currently, Ilaria's research focuses on the sustainable transition of the agri-food sector.

Ana García-Juanatey is a lecturer at the CEI International Affairs, center affiliated to the Universitat de Barcelona. She is a political scientist and holds a PhD in Law from the Universitat Pompeu Fabra (2016). She has been a post-doc researcher at the Institut Barcelona d'Estudis Internacionals, as well as a visiting researcher at the UN Organization of Food And Agriculture and the Universidade da Coruña. Her research interests focus on the relationship between human rights and the environment; foods systems from a human rights perspective; the challenges of human rights law in the age of internet; and the transparency and accountability of public entities. She has published her research work in several international journals, such as *Peace Review, South European Society and Politics*, *Administration and Society*, and the *European Journal of Higher Education*, among others.

Murat Gulmez currently serves as the Associate Dean of the Faculty of Economics and Administrative Sciences at Çağ University since 2013 and has been instrumental in driving forward developments and innovations within the faculty. Additionally, he has held the position of IACBE Accreditation Coordinator since 2017, ensuring academic programs meet international standards of excellence. He is also the founder and the director of VR Lab that coordinates the immersive learning and VR initiatives at Çağ University. Dr. Gülmez lectures on Virtual Reality and Virtual Worlds, including courses on Virtual World/International Student Project and Metaentrepreneurship, showcasing his commitment to integrating cutting-edge technologies into education.

Intesar Madi is Assistant Lecturer in Economics in the School of Accounting, Economics, and Finance at Technological University Dublin (TU Dublin). Her research areas of interest are economic sustainability, energy sustainability, the MENA region, and Asian Studies.

Daniel Kamphambale, based on a rich mix of banking and entrepreneurship for more than 15 years, Daniel is currently focused on academic activities as a researcher, pursuing a PhD in Economics at Dublin University of Technology, Ireland. Currently, research is focused on the crossroads between education and sustainable development, a topic that Daniel is passionately investigating.

Erja Kettunen-Matilainen, D.Sc.(Econ.) is Senior Research Fellow and holds the title of Docent in Economic Geography at Turku School of Economics, University of Turku. Her research focuses on European Union – Asia trade and trade policy, sustainable development, responsible society, and regionalism in Asia. Recently, she has also studied social innovation in diversity, inclusion, and decent work in Finland and Japan. She leads the project "Good and Bad Palm Oil", and was Visiting Scholar at Ca' Foscari University of Venice and Guest Researcher at Nordic Institute of Asian Studies, Copenhagen, to study sustainability in Finland–China food exports and EU–Indonesia bargaining on palm oil policy, respectively. Previously, she was Research Manager at Aalto University School of Business, Finland, and Senior Lecturer at the University of Gothenburg, School of Business, Economics and Law, Sweden.

Guenwoo Lee, PhD, is a development economist and researcher at the Japan International Research Center for Agricultural Sciences (JIRCAS). With a focus on small-scale farmers in developing countries, his empirical research spans across Indonesia, India, Vietnam, Thailand, Ethiopia, Ghana, and Burkina Faso, aiming to devise effective economic development strategies for poverty reduction. He previously served as an Assistant Professor at the Institute of Economic Research, Hitotsubashi University, from 2019 to 2021. He earned his PhD and M.A. in International Studies from the University of

Tokyo. His work is widely published, including articles in *World Development*, *Aquaculture*, and *Aquaculture Economics and Management*.

Heli Marjanen, D.Sc. (Econ. & Bus. Adm.), professor, has held the chair in Economic Geography at the Department of Marketing and International Business at the Turku School of Economics, University of Turku, since 1999. Throughout her academic career, she has been involved in consumer behaviour and regional development in various contexts. Her particular focus is on long-term structural and spatial changes in consumption, especially in the fields of retail location and place management. She and her team have a solid track record for their dedication and teamwork in projects focused on development and future planning. In addition to retail-focused journals, her research has appeared in publications such as Food Studies and Urban, Planning, and Transport Research.

Deirdre McQuillan is a senior researcher at TU Dublin and is currently a project team lead at European University of Technology (EUt+). Prior to this, she was Head of Research in the Faculty of Business, and before this a lecturer in strategy and international business at the University of Bradford in the UK. Her research interests are in entrepreneurship and creative sector strategy and work contexts. Her work is published in leading international journals including *International Marketing Review*, *Advances in Strategic Management*, and *Journal of Business Strategy*.

Lucía Morales holds a PhD in Economics and is an educator, academic innovator, and active researcher in the School of Accounting, Economics and Finance at Technological University Dublin (TU Dublin) in Ireland and a researcher at the European University of Technology (EUt+). Before her academic career, Lucía worked in the private sector, holding different roles: Financial Manager, Assistant Financial Manager, and Foreign Department Risk Analyst (Bank). Lucía has worked at various Higher Education Institutions in Ireland, Spain, the UK, and Switzerland, among others, gaining an in-depth understanding of the main challenges faced by Third Level Institutions in the fields of Economics, Finance, Data Analytics, and Education at the undergraduate and postgraduate levels. Lucía is passionate about education, its importance for economic development, and the significance of quality research to drive change and impact, as she has published extensively in Economics, Data Analysis, Finance and Education.

Sophie Nivoix is Professor of Finance at the University of Poitiers (France) and a member of the CEREGE (UR 13564) laboratory. She has been treasurer of Atlas-AFMI (French Association of International Business) since 2008 and was responsible for the master's in law and marketing at the Faculty of Law and Social Sciences of Poitiers from 2004 to 2020. Her work focuses, in particular, on profitability and risks, financial equity markets, in Europe and Asia, and on banks. He has published in many academic reviews such as Asian Business and Management, Peace Review, Bankers Markets and Investors, Accounting and Finance, Applied Financial Economics, and Asian Pacific Business Review. She is also the co-editor of: "Economic transitions and international business", with Eric Milliot (2019, eds) (Routledge: London); "Firm Internationalization, Intangible Resources and Development", with Christian Marcon (2023, eds) (Routledge: London); and of "Internationalization and organizations", with Eric Davoine and Olivier Furrer (2024, eds) (Routledge: London).

Olubunmi Oludipe is a Human Resources Independent Management Consultant and a certified John Maxwell Coach, Speaker and Trainer, with over 3 decades leaning towards the Learning and Development function. She has designed and facilitated several programmes both for employees and C-Suite executives. She is a fellow of the Chartered Institute of Personnel Development, UK; Institute of Management Consultants, Nigerian Institute of Management (Chartered); and Nigerian Institute of Training & Development (NITAD). She holds a Masters of Research from the University of Liverpool, UK; M.Sc. Human Resources Management from Robert Gordon University, Aberdeen; and a B.Sc. in Business Administration from the University of Lagos, Nigeria. She is currently a PhD student with the School of Accounting, Economics, and Finance at the Technological University, Dublin. Her research focuses on "E-learning – An Essential Learning Method in Developing Economies in the 21st Century : The Nigerian Stakeholders' Perspectives", and has presented her works at various conferences. Olubunmi is an alumna of the Fate Foundation, Nigeria, and a Life Member of Women in Management, Business and Public Service (WIMBIZ). As part of her social responsibility, she serves as a Mentor to women in the corporate world under the WIMBIZ Mentoring Programme.

Maria (Mary) Papageorgiou is a Leverhulme Early Career Scholar at Newcastle University, UK, investigating the Sino-Russian relationship. Before this role, she was a Lecturer in Politics and International Relations at the University of Exeter, UK, while having also taught at University College London (UCL), SOAS University, and the University of Bradford. She has been a visiting researcher at King's College London, Newcastle University, and Saint Petersburg State University in Russia (online). Her expertise includes international relations theory and the foreign policy behaviour of great powers, particularly China, Russia, and the US focusing more specifically on China's engagement in the Middle East, Sino-Russian relations, and China's economic coercion as a foreign policy tool. She has testified before the U.S.-China Economic and Security Review Commission on China's arms transfers and security activities in the Middle East and her work is published in leading international relations journals, and she has contributed to international think tanks and media.

Ivaylo Peev, Assoc. Prof. PhD. *Professional background*: PhD in Philology, an Associate Professor of Pedagogy at the Department of Foreign Languages and Applied Linguistics of the Technical University of Sofia. Lecturer in Bulgarian language to foreign students at the Technical University of Sofia and the National Academy of Art. An author of 3 monographs, 3 university course books, and of over 40 publications (scientific articles and studies) in the field of pedagogy, linguistics, theory of literature, and theory of art. *Research direction and/or research interests*: new methods in foreign language teaching, academic communication and academic writing, body language and verbal language, pedagogy, and digital technologies.

Lia Pop has been an assistant professor at Cluj Napoca Technical University since 2019. Previously, she was a psycho-pedagogue for more than 13 years, working especially with students with autism spectrum disorders and associated disabilities in the public special education system from Romania. Passionate about high-quality education for all, with a PhD in Educational Sciences and specialisations in the domains of Management (Management styles), Psychology (clinical psychology, educational psychology, developmental psychology, personal and professional coaching), Pedagogy, Special Education and over 32 relevant publications in the Educational Science field, her academic interests are closely related to Full Inclusive Education and Equity as Pedagogy, Alternative and Augmentative Communication, Assistive Technology and Universal Design of Learning, Creativity and Innovative Pedagogy, Moral Inclusion and Transdisciplinarity, Proactive Learning Environments and Challenge Based Learning, GRIT and Lifelong Learning, Educational Policies, and Teaching & Research parity of esteem.

Ayu Pratiwi, PhD, is a postdoctoral researcher in the Economic Geography unit of the Turku School of Economics, University of Turku, Finland. She is a development economist by training and obtained her doctorate from the University of Tokyo, Japan. Her research interests primarily lie in the diffusion of innovation in agriculture, aquaculture, and forestry, with empirical investigation covering Ethiopia, Indonesia, Ghana, and Namibia. She previously worked with the World Bank and the United Nations University World Institute for Development Economics Research (UNU-WIDER) and held visiting fellowship positions at the Australian National University and the Japan International Research Center for Agricultural Sciences (JIRCAS). She has also published in the Journal of Rural Studies, Transportation, Journal of Economic Structures, and Agricultural and Food Economics, among others.

Daniel Rajmil is an International Relations Assoc. Prof. PhD. at the Universitat Oberta de Catalunya (UOC) School of Law and Political Science and an adjunct lecturer at the Political Sciences Faculty of Pompeu Fabra University (UPF). He holds a PhD in Political Sciences from the Economics and Social Sciences Doctoral Program of the University of Vienna, an MA in Middle East studies, an MA in Applied Statistics, a BA in Political Sciences, and a BA in Market Research. His lines of research are International Relations, Comparative Politics, Nuclear Politics, Geopolitics and Geoeconomics. He is the director of the UOC-UNITAR (UN Institute for Training and Research) master in Conflict, Peace and Security and he is the Research Coordinator and IP of the Catalan Government recognized research group in Geopolitics, Conflict and Human Rights (GEOCONDAH). Daniel has published extensively in the fields of International Relations, Geopolitics, Middle East studies and Conflict Studies. He is passionate about education, its importance for social development and conflict transformation.

Wael Rashwan holds a B.Sc. and M.Sc. degrees in Computer Science from Cairo University, Egypt, and a PhD in applied data analytics from Technological University Dublin (TU Dublin), Ireland. He currently serves as a Lecturer in Data Analytics and a research leader at the Explainable AI Group (XAG) and 3S Group at TU Dublin. His research focuses on predictive analytics, explainable artificial intelligence (XAI), and healthcare analytics. As a Principal Investigator and Technical Lead, he has significantly contributed to diverse applied data analytics and AI projects. Dr. Rashwan focuses on applied research by developing innovative solutions and theories to support decision-making in uncertain and complex environments, particularly through predictive/prescriptive modelling, XAI, and simulation/optimisation. He actively engages in various business and industry projects to improve operations, increase efficiency, and create societal impact.

Serge Rey is Professor of Economics at the University of Pau & Pays de l'Adour France) and former Director of the Social Sciences and Humanities College. His research interests are in international macroeconomics, economic convergence, the economics of the exchange rate and applied econometrics. He has published on these issues in leading academic journals, such as *The Annals of Regional Science*, *Applied Economics*, *Economica*, *Economics Bulletin*, *Economics and Statistics*, *Economic Modelling*, *International Economics*, *Journal of Economic Integration*, *Pacific Economic Review*, etc, with a focus on the following territories/countries: MENA countries, European Union, Pacific economies and in particular Japan, French Overseas territories. He is also the co-editor of *Sustainable Development in Asia: Socio-economic, Financial, and Economic Perspectives*, with Bernadette Andreosso-O'Callaghan and Robert Taylor (2022, eds) (Springer: Cham, Switzerland).

Ozéias Rodrigues da Rocha has over two decades of corporate finance expertise, and excelled in financial management for large and medium-sized companies, consistently driving growth and maximizing value. Currently, as a PhD student in Economics at Technological University Dublin, he channels his passion for knowledge and innovation. His research focuses on Education for Sustainable Development and Economic Growth, aiming to contribute insights for a sustainable future. With several publications, he advances dialogue on these critical issues and inspires actionable change. Beyond the boardroom and academia, he advocates for sustainable practices and believes in education's power to drive positive transformation.

Elena Sánchez-Montijano. Research Professor and Director of the Interdisciplinary Group on Migration Studies at the Centro de Investigación y Docencia Económicas (CIDE, Mexico). She holds a PhD in Political and Social Sciences from the Pompeu Fabra University (Barcelona) and a Masters in International Cooperation and Development from the University of Granada. For ten years she was Senior Research Fellow at CIDOB (Barcelona). Her main areas of interest are migrant integration policies and transnational relations of migrants with their countries of origin. She has participated in dozens of international academic projects (as scientific coordinator and researcher) and has published more than 100 academic and public policy documents in this area. She was a visiting researcher at the Centre on Migration, Policy and Society (COMPAS), Oxford University; at the Centre for Ethnic and Migration Studies (CEDEM), Université de Liège; and at the Research and Expertise Centre for Survey Methodology (RECSM), Universitat Pompeu Fabra.

Suleman Sarwar is offering his services as Associate Professor in Finance and Economics Department, College of Business, University of Jeddah, Saudi Arabia. He holds a PhD in Economics and Finance. Their area of interest is financial economics, energy economics, environmental economics, etc., and he has multiple research articles in diverse journals, such as *Energy Economics*, *Energy Policy*, *Journal of Cleaner Production*, and *Technological Forecasting and Social Change*.

Robert Taylor was formerly Director of the Centre for Chinese Studies and Reader in Modern Chinese Studies at the University of Sheffield. His research interests focus on China's domestic and foreign policy, especially Chinese business management and foreign economic relations. He has published widely in academic journals. His publications include *China's Intellectual Dilemma* (University of British Columbia, 1981) and *Greater China and Japan* (1996). He has also engaged in management consultancy.

Anna Zherdeva is an assistant lecturer and an active researcher in the School of Management, People, and Organisations at Technological University Dublin. Her research interests include economy and politics, business education, entrepreneurship, human resource management, leadership and development, digital skills, AI and VR, and sustainable practices in SMEs and corporations. Before her academic career, Anna held leadership roles in Training and Development and HR Departments. She holds Master's Degrees in Economics, Management, and HRM and is currently actively working on her PhD.

Acknowledgements

We would like to extend our heartfelt gratitude to all the coauthors and contributors for their invaluable work on the book *Geoeconomics of the Sustainable Development Goals*. Your insightful chapters have significantly enriched the content and provided diverse perspectives on this critical subject. Each contribution reflects your dedication, expertise, and commitment to advancing sustainable development through geoeconomics and your critical reflections. Your collaborative efforts have been instrumental in making this book a comprehensive resource. Thank you for your unwavering support, meticulous research, and shared passion, which have made this project a success. Your contributions are deeply appreciated.

Abbreviations

AFROCOM	Coordinating Committee for Economic Cooperation with African Countries
AI	Artificial Intelligence
AIEd	Artificial Intelligence in Education
APEC	Asia Pacific Economic Cooperation
APS	Announced Pledges System
ASEAN	Association of South East Asian Nations
ATT	Arms Trade Treaty
BRI	Belt and Road Initiative
BRICs	Brazil Russia India China
CCP	China Communist Party
CCUS	Carbon Capture Utilization and Storage
CEPAL	Comisión Económica para América Latina y el Caribe
ChatGPT	Chat Generative Pre-Trained Transformer
C*HN*	China
CIA	Central Intelligence Agency
COP*28*	28th Conference of Parties
COVID-*19*	Corona Virus Immuno-Deficiency Disease
CO_2	Carbon Dioxide
CSO	Central Statistics Office (Dublin)
CSR	Corporate Social Responsibility
DESI	Digital Economy and Society Index
DETE	Department of Enterprise, Trade and Employment
DR Congo	Democratic Republic of Congo
DSR	Digital Silk Road
ECLAC	Economic Commission for Latin America and the Caribbean
EPU	Economic and Political Uncertainty
ESD	Education for Sustainable Development
ESG	Environmental Social and Governance
ETS	Emissions Trading System
EU	Economic Union
FAO	Food Agriculture Organization
FDI	Foreign Direct Investment

FED	Federal Reserve
FOCAC	Forum on China–Africa Cooperation
FYP	Five-Year Plan
J*PN*	Japan
GDI	Gross Domestic Income
GDP	Gross Domestic Product
GEFC	Global Economic and Financial Crisis
GenAI	Generative Artificial Intelligence
GHG	Greenhouse Gas
G*7*	Group of Seven (countries)
G-*77*	Group of 77 (developing and emerging countries)
HLPE	High-Level Panel of Experts (on Food Security and Nutrition)
IDA Ireland	Industrial Development Authority Ireland
IDFC	International Development and Financial Cooperation
IFAD	International Fund for Agricultural Development
IMF	International Monetary System
IOM	International Organization for Migration
IPSS	Institute of Population and Social Security (Tokyo)
IPCC	Intergovernmental Panel on Climate Change
IPEF	Indo-Pacific Economic Framework
LLMs	Large Language Models
MDGs	Millenium Development Goals
MENA	Middle-East and North Africa (Region)
METI	Ministry of Economy, Trade and Industry
MNCs	Muti-National Corporations
MOU	Memorandum of Understanding
NDC	Nationally Determined Contribution
ODA	Official Development Assistance
OECD	Organization for Economic Cooperation and Development
QUAD	Quadrilateral Security Dialogue
RCEP	Regional Comprehensive Economic Partnership
R&D	Research and Development
SDGs	Sustainable Development Goals
SMEs	Small and Medium-Sized Enterprises
UK	United Kingdom
UN	United Nations
UNCED	United Nations Conference on Environment and Development
UNCLOS	United Nations Convention on the Law of the Sea
UN DESA	United Nations Department of Economics and Social Affairs
UNDP	United Nations Development Program
UNESCO	United Nations Educational, Scientific and Cultural Organization
UNGA	United Nations General Assembly
UNICEF	United Nations Children's Fund
USA	United States of America
USD	US Dollar

VAR	Vector Autoregressive (model)
WEF	World Economic Forum
WFP	World Food Program
WHO	World Health Organization
WWII	World War 2
XAI	Explainable Artificial Intelligence

Introduction

Lucía Morales, Bernadette Andreosso-O'Callaghan and Daniel Rajmil

This book emerges from the editors' growing concerns, deep reflections, ongoing discussions and international collaborative research activity regarding socio-economic and environmental complexities at the international level and their mounting economic and political significance and pressures. We are facing uncertain and fast-evolving times defined by rising levels of war, conflict, lack of cooperation, and a sharp, inward-looking economic shift exacerbated by the continuous deterioration of our democratic systems and governing institutions. The post-World War II economic and political systems have gradually become outdated and detached from the global reality, missing opportunities to adapt and stubbornly replicating historical mistakes through the establishment of new forms of "*colonialism and power dominance*" seeking to gain access and control to natural resources while dictating the global economic agenda. This new "*old*" system shows that in an integrated global economy, there is a need to change economic and political patterns as the world's largest emerging markets are pushing for new access to international decision-making processes as they are becoming prominent contributors to global growth and progress. The risks and unpredictability of emerging markets are also associated with potential adverse spillover effects on the global economy. The growing representation of riskier economies can become a conducive channel for the propagation of domestic shocks that can drag economic growth due to the increasing influence of the largest emerging markets, which can trigger global economic instability and challenge political stability. We are immersed in a global landscape where wealth and privilege dictate the need to safeguard and preserve the privileges enjoyed by the few to the detriment of the most vulnerable. At the same time, the world's poorest and most vulnerable are falling deeper into a vicious cycle of marginalisation and exclusion as a result of growing economic imbalances that are now visualised within the world's most affluent economies as internal. The scrappiness of the reshaping global economic and political order is preventing open dialogue and hindering support for developing multidimensional, collaborative, agile and adaptable working frameworks that are cognisant of the differences between the world's most advanced and less developed economies.

DOI: 10.4324/9781032655857-1

Our international landscape is convoluted and in a profound state of flux, still significantly affected and damaged by the lagging effects of the 2008 Global Economic and Financial Crisis that acted as a breakpoint, signalling the growing divide between socio-economic and political cleavages. In parallel, in an interconnected world, our global society has become more aware of the unstoppable deterioration of international cooperation, the dominance of political and economic agendas and our inability to engage in knowledge-sharing processes resulting from stringent competition and countries' self-centric goals. This has created a polarised society, whereby a shift towards protectionism, bilateralism and the advance of extremism, racism and xenophobia accentuates the decline of the global economic and political landscape. The consolidation of populist movements by the hand of the steadily marching of the far-right that has consistently gained support has facilitated access to countries' ministerial roles and becoming active players in coalition governments cemented on weaker and debilitating institutions and educational systems. They are guided by countries' individualistic agendas that seek to secure rapid economic and political gains and create a very different culture that significantly influences political systems and how they operate. Further, the 2020 Global Health Crisis has been considered a wake-up call, as it revealed a painful reality where the world's most advanced economies failed to show leadership through a united front that helped to confront and counteract the effects of the shock. Initially started as a health crisis, it rapidly showed how our society's socio-economic and political basis were not ready to proactively respond to a crisis as it was foreseen. While some of the world's most advanced economies entered into an economic hibernation state – as their relatively affluent economies could afford the costs of social distancing measures guided by health fears – those less developed just witnessed the dramatic effects of the virus defined by their inability to offer any essential supports to their population. The global health shock unfolded due to high levels of competition to profit from developing a vaccine that could be commercialised and accessible to the world's wealthiest economies. At the same time, countries' frontiers were closed during a time that required closer cooperation and collaboration. Moreover, the world's poorest economies witnessed the accelerated deterioration of their fragile economic systems and dysfunctional institutions and their lack of access to health services as they insufficient economic means to fulfil their population's most basic needs, including access to health, sanitation, water and education. The world's poorest were left to their fortunes as the economic recovery process has been defined as being very slow and uneven, and growing levels of conflict have created a significant disruption in terms of global trade, adverse impact on global value chains, and increasing living costs characterised by high levels of inflation that have had a disproportionate effect on the world's poorest.

In addition, as the world was trying to recompose from the effects of the health crisis, international tensions kept mounting as a result of different international geopolitical events that have shown how interconnected political interests, resources and military goals are. In this context, the Russian war in

Ukraine, at the time of writing, has consolidated into a long-lasting war with severe financial and economic effects and with the always-present nuclear threat of unpredictable effects. Thus, the international fragile geopolitical equilibrium has further deteriorated by the dramatic situation in the Middle East whereby the current war in Gaza has reframed the international political agenda, leaving behind the civil population that are suffering the cruelty of the war in favour of geopolitical interests and the reshaping of the global balance of power whilst leaving the sustainability agenda to a secondary level. Once more, the international community is identified as inefficient and unable to respond to emerging risks and threats, adding more complexities to the frail international world order.

Current geopolitical and geoeconomic scenarios emerge from a complex interplay between economic factors, political dynamics and the pressing need for sustainable economic development on a global scale that goes beyond mere climate change rhetoric. The editors' profound concerns regarding the multiplex relationship between geoeconomics and geopolitics require a critical overview of the sustainability agenda, its needs, and the pressing mounting dynamics that push for a new balance of power. In this context, there is a need to bring in novel research contributions that accommodate young researchers, practitioners and early career researchers to foster critical and reflective thinking that ignites the debate about the ever-evolving nature of our global economic and political landscape. This book offers a much-needed space to initiate in-depth reflection, analysis and critical insights that examine the United Nations 2030 Agenda and its progress as the historical context of sustainable development is explored and supported by insights that connect education and economic progress while looking at corporate social responsibility amidst geopolitical rivalries and multifaceted crisis. The energy dilemma and the paradox faced by a world dependent on fossil fuels and the need to secure access to natural resources are carefully considered throughout the book chapters as the current and more prominent challenge that human civilisation will face in the coming decades. The need for a change of direction, as we examine the importance of business productivity and the resistance to climate action, changing demographic patterns, and its effects on human mobility and displacement, helps us to understand the challenges ahead and the difficulties in coordinating actions that drive change as we do not have a guiding compass towards functional, sustainable economic models that integrate the realities of the world's less developed economies.

Migration and human rights dynamics are often not included in political and economic agendas, neglecting complementary security spectrums as the human security perspective that clashes with the renewed state-centric approach. While the 2030 Agenda and its concatenated Sustainable Development Goals (SDGs) were meant to become a step forward emerging from the collective political negotiation spectrum of the Millennium Development Goals (MDGs) agenda, the new bottom-up paradigm embraced by the 2030 Agenda seems to have failed to be conclusively materialised, not a surprising outcome, as the economic and financial implications of the agenda have not been considered within a context that lacks international cooperation, and countries' leadership and commitment to work together. Having already bypassed the temporary equator of the SDGs timeframe, it seems that the world's economic, political and business leaders have not managed to create a collaborative working environment that provides an actionable framework that drives change and positive impact on redesigning a new global economic and political order. Global inequality and imbalances are accentuated and encompassed by the rapid deterioration of our ecosystems, which cannot cope with the demands of our neoliberal, market-driven and capital-centric models. Meanwhile, crisis and globalisation trends are clashing, hindering change opportunities and bringing back to the front line old political ideas that are even more of an obstacle to a global, equal, equitative and conclusive green transition. In this book, and with the esteemed collaboration of our authors and co-authors, we give the first steps aiming to provide an in-depth analysis of Geoeconomic and Geopolitical tensions through the lens of the United Nations 2030 Agenda and its ambitious SDGs. The book critically assesses the International Political Economy and its current social, economic and political consequences. It sheds some light on the growing connections between the economic and political systems and their impact on defining the international order and its economic trends. This book is the first of a series that offers a critical space for scholarly, professional and creative thinking to explore the complexities surrounding Sustainable Economic Development from a multidimensional perspective. With its interdisciplinary perspective, this book offers fresh insights and innovative critical thinking, paving the way for a more holistic and integrated approach to addressing the sustainability imperative in the face of geoeconomic and geopolitical realities and their interrelated consequences. The many sides of history need resourceful analysis and open discussions; otherwise, we will fail to address the needs of our current generation, which will significantly undermine our legacy for future generations to work together and thrive.

Part 1

Geoeconomics and Geopolitics Landscape

1 Historical Context and Epistemology of the Concept of Sustainable Development

Amal Abu Warda Perez, Daniel Rajmil, Bernadette Andreosso-O'Callaghan and Lucía Morales

Introduction

For decades, the international community has been engaging in the search for a path toward what could be considered global "sustainable development". This has been a non-linear process whereby different historical moments have been shaped by geoeconomic and geopolitical rivalries and often, by political agendas. The division between the Global North and the Global South is far less pronounced today than before while the global community strives to find a definition for "sustainable development" that could be accommodated in the ambit of practical policies. An important milestone came in when, on September 25, 2015, during the 70th General Assembly of the United Nations (UN), 193 heads of states unanimously approved a document entitled "*Transforming our World: the 2030 Agenda for Sustainable Development*" (UNGA, 2015); this document has the ambition to set the diplomatic framework related to the sustainability agenda for the years to come.

The *2030 Agenda* is a natural successor to the Millennium Development Goals (MDGs), which, from 2000 to 2015, encompassed eight UN development goals centered on poverty reduction along with other priorities that ranged from universal primary education to a global partnership for development (Hickmann et al., 2023). Building on very lukewarm and non-impressive results achieved by the MDGs,[1] further steps for development policies, programs, and projects at the global and local levels are now being enshrined in measurable Sustainable Development Goals (SDGs). Specifically, the SDGs are defined as a global development action plan composed of 17 goals and 169 targets of an economic, social, and environmental nature, which revolve around the concept of "sustainability" (UNGA, 2015).

Despite the popularity that the concept of sustainable development has acquired over the recent past, a concept used extensively as an iconic slogan in contemporary development discourse, especially at the political level and particularly in the developed world, there is, paradoxically, little consensus on the definition of the concept, with numerous controversies and debates regarding its scope and content. With this background in mind, this chapter intends to unveil and offer the reader a review of the concept and its scope; it will suggest

DOI: 10.4324/9781032655857-3

a critical assessment of the historical context that surrounded the appearance of "sustainability", and more importantly, of how it could be understood in order to comprehend its current applications. A critical approach is required so as to avoid it being used as a merely empty slogan for political correctness, or as a mere fashionable expression that is used exaggeratedly without paying attention to its meaning as argued for example by Hull (2008), Ala-Uddin (2019) and Du Pisani (2006).

The main goal of this chapter is to bring some clarity to the meaning and main characteristics of the concept of "sustainable development", starting from the problems surrounding the preciseness of its definition. To this end, we will review the main milestones that have been shaping and giving content to the concept up to the approval of the 2030 Agenda, as well as the main criticisms that have arisen around them, which translate into the challenges facing the concept. The chapter is developed into two main sections; the first section presents critically its evolving definition over time; this will be followed by a critical thoughts section based on the epistemology of the concept, and finally some conclusions will be proffered.

Milestones in the evolving sustainable development concept

This section provides a review of the historical context that saw the evolving definition of the so-called "sustainable development" concept. It explores the genealogy of the concept of sustainable development by introducing first some preliminary observations that need to be carefully explored in order to offer a proper definition of the concept and to understand its epistemological limitations, which will be contextualized in the ensuing section.

There are several historical episodes that can be highlighted as important markers of the beginning of the sustainable development agenda as is known today. On the economic level, the post-World War II (WWII) period – up until the early 1970s – witnessed levels of unprecedented economic growth, coupled with economic development and prosperity.[2] Referred to as the "Golden Age of capitalism",[3] this happened mainly in the West, although parts of Asia also experienced significant economic growth (UN, 2017). This translated into a sharp rise in economic growth, in living standards, as well as in life expectancy, enabling societies to experience a development period, the latter being understood as an improvement in socioeconomic and life conditions in industrialized societies. During the Golden Age, the macroeconomic structure of individual countries was founded on, and could reproduce itself by, a specific system of production within a particular international order (Glyn et al., 1988: 4). These growth benefits were largely achieved without much questioning or criticism of the costs inflicted to the environment (negative externalities), and even to people's health, given the new production methods that developed new products (such as a proliferation of plastics, synthetic and chemical products, pesticides in agriculture and/or fossil fuels) and its resultant consumption and production behavior (consumerism and wastefulness among others).[4] The then-chosen development model was not exempt from challenges and negative consequences; these would become decisive in the building-up of major structural problems that are still present in the current globalization scenario, bringing new complexities to the multifaceted reality of crises. The oil shocks of the early 1970s led to a major economic crisis that triggered significant industrial/structural and political change. As we will discuss later, this crisis was instrumental in allowing a general acceptance of a new environmental agenda enshrined in a new international order. It shows that today, more than ever since WWII, new uncertainty levels have led us to embrace the multidimensionality of the current financial and economic reality by including the geopolitical dimension (Andreosso-O'Callaghan and Rajmil, 2024).

Just before and particularly since the end of WWII, a series of scientific works had been published concerning the interference and negative effects of human activity on ecosystems.[5] For example, many of these early works encompassed the studies of Aldo Leopold or Rachel Carson, whose work *Silent Spring* (1962) was a turning point in the consolidation of the environmentalist movement (Harry & Harry, 1974). Some of these studies would start to transcend the areas of physics, biology, chemistry, etc., and to be appraised by economists; in particular, the work of Prigogine and Henin (1966) on entropy and systems would then be applied to the sphere of economics, leading to the concepts of economic systems encompassing the environmental dimension.

In the 1960s, when global economic growth came to exceed even that of the previous decade (UN, 2017), an awareness about the unsustainability and inoperability of the neoliberal growth model that had prevailed since the end of WWII began to crystallize (Bustillo-García & Martínez-Dávila, 2008). The rise of the wave of environmentalism occurred therefore in the late 1960s and early 1970s. In the 1960s, an important trigger of this new movement was the use, during the Vietnam War, of napalm – a weaponized chemical produced by a prominent US multinational company – onto the population of Vietnam by the US military. Consequently, student activists disavowed different facets of modern American society, and they used those concerns as a radical critique of the post-WWII United States (Woodhouse, 2009). Although important within the movement, the student movement should not however be interpreted as the main trigger for the environmentalist movement according to Harry and Harry (1974).

It is clear nevertheless that environmentalist movements started from a genuine, scientifically uncontested basis and a true concern for the environment in the 1960s; what would happen later was a radically new step in the movement.

Indeed, in the 1970s, the movement became politicized. Funded by large oil and finance interests (Raymond, 1988), it produced a number of pseudo-scientific publications and reports; one such report is the Club of Rome's report entitled *The Limits to Growth* (1972).[6]

Consequently, what was especially relevant in these years was the leap from scientifically based environmental issues to the international political/diplomatic sphere which focused on the relationship between population growth, development and the need to preserve nature and its resources. One can easily say that the Club of Rome 1972 report is, not surprisingly, fundamentally Malthusian in essence.[7] It states for example on page 48 that "food production per capita in the non-industrialized world is barely holding constant at its present inadequate level". It should be noted that most of the predictions in terms of looming shortages did not materialize. In this context, a stand-out event was the celebration in Stockholm of the 1972 United Nations Conference on Human Environment, where, for the first time, the environmental issue was recognized as a global issue, and the connection between economic development and deterioration was addressed (Ala-Uddin, 2019; Lebada & Chasek, 2021).[8] The 1980s will be particularly relevant as they witnessed an increasing pace in the momentum given to sustainable development, a concept that became the central axis of development debates in the following decades. In 1983, the UN General Assembly created the World Commission on Environment and Development with the task of proposing "long-term environmental strategies for achieving sustainable development to the year 2000 and beyond" (UNGA, 1983). The work of the Commission ended with the publication in 1987 of the report *Our Common Future*, popularly known as the *Brundtland Report*.[9] The main contribution of the Commission's work and the final report was the popularization of the concept of "sustainable development" with the adoption of a definition according to which "Sustainable development is the development that meets the needs of the present without compromising the ability of future generations to meet their own needs" (WCED, 1987, p.43). This definition describes sustainable development as a process in which different dimensions of sustainability are involved: political, economic, social, and cultural.

Consequently, starting from a pessimistic scenario about the critical situation of the planet and recognizing the limits to growth, the report highlights the need for a change in human behavior and points to instruments such as research and international cooperation as the keys to avoiding giving up on development (WECD, 1987).

Since the *Brundtland Report*, the concept of sustainable development has spread widely and rapidly, and it became the new globally accepted and unchallengeable paradigm and doctrine on development; it is clear that the economic dimension is increasingly dwarfed leaving room for the area of geopolitics whereby nations' branding strategies and "green diplomacy" are deployed.

Subsequent years were marked by the leading role played by the holding of international conferences related to the environment, and these contributed to the implementation and evolution of the concept of sustainable development. Among the most important of these was the United Nations Conference on Environment and Development (UNCED), also known as the Rio Summit or Earth Summit, held in Rio de Janeiro in 1992, coinciding with the 20th anniversary of the Stockholm Conference. Sustainable development was formally endorsed and institutionalized internationally through the so-called "Agenda 21" (UNCED, 1992a), which contained an action plan for the achievement and promotion of sustainability and a set of 27 universal principles that were included in the Rio Declaration; these were to guide national conduct on environmental protection and development (UNCED, 1992b). At this summit, the definition of development was expanded again, adding a new component to it so that, along with the economic and social components, environmental protection and restoration were included. The conference introduced an expanding scope of the understanding of sustainable development whereby "there was hardly an issue that did not fall in some way under the rubric of sustainable development" (Lebada & Chasek, 2021: 2).

The beginning of the 21st century will be marked by a new milestone in this area, with the adoption in 2000 of the so-called Millennium Development Goals (MDGs), predecessors of the Sustainable Development Goals (SDGs). These consisted of eight fundamental goals aimed primarily at combating poverty, to be achieved by 2015 (UN, 2015). Several important international conferences were held, such as the 2002 World Summit on Sustainable Development in Johannesburg and the United Nations Conference on Sustainable Development, held again in Rio de Janeiro in 2021, also known as Rio+20.

As the MDGs period was coming to an end, all countries agreed to reform and propose a more comprehensive, inclusive and reflective set of development goals. Following rather disappointing results achieved by the MDGs (Kabiru and Batsari, 2020), the SDGs emerged and were adopted in 2015 as a new attempt to address, yet again, the challenges faced by countries in the next 15 years and beyond.

At this juncture, one is bound to reflect critically upon the limitations of the sustainable development concept and also on the pertinence of the sustainable development strategy.

Challenges and epistemological limitations of the sustainable development concept

This section will first introduce the limitations of the sustainable development concept *per se*; by reviewing its epistemological limits, the understanding of the sustainability development concept will be more complete.

First of all, an important clarification has to do with the need of not losing sight of the fact that sustainable development is not such a novel idea as argued by Du Pisani (2006). From the beginning, the survival and well-being of societies have always depended, directly or indirectly, upon their natural environment. From this perspective, if we go back in history, we can find elements and practices of sustainability that were naturally embedded in the lives of many peoples and societies throughout the world; these were intrinsically connected with deep knowledge about natural assets and with the need for harmony with their natural environment for the sake of their own survival and well-being (Washington, 2015). Therefore, it can be reminded that "to pursue sustainability is to create and maintain the conditions under which humans and nature can exist in productive harmony to support present and future generations" (National Research Council, 2011; 16).

Even at the level of values, very diverse and ancient religious and philosophical traditions have historically contemplated the responsibility of human beings in managing not only their own life on earth but also that of the rest of its inhabitants and creatures; it is thus "vital for the security and survival of the human species to maintain the code found in nature and in the laws that govern life on earth. This code defines the environment as a sacred 'gift' given by God" (Razak & Sanusi, 2010: 29). This is one of many quotes that highlight the indissoluble link existing between mankind and nature through a superior entity.

Consequently, the foundations underlying the idea of sustainable development have historically been embedded in most cultures and societies. But since the Industrial Revolution, the surge of materially based industrial societies has filled the void of a gradual withdrawal of spirituality and philosophy. This surge has seen possibly the worst form of industrialization conceivable, with, for example, high pollution levels; "commodification" of the individual reduced to selling the only asset available to him – his labor power; increased income disparity levels and widespread poverty. Eventually, the advent of more affluent societies after WWII pushed the issue of environmental degradation to the top of individuals' priorities. After a brief interlude during which environmentalism gained the consideration of concerned scientists – as discussed earlier – we are witnessing now a new stage in the evolution of the concept. Therefore, the questions would be: what are the novelties intended to be introduced with this new concept of sustainable development, what contributions have been made, and what is being questioned by this concept? In line with the above, another important consideration when analyzing the emergence and evolution of the concept of sustainable development is the need to take into account and adequately understand the particular historical contexts: political, economic, social, and cultural. This is not only related to the moment when the idea was initially shaped but also with respect to the main milestones in its evolution and development. The idea of sustainable development does not emerge, evolve, or reorient itself spontaneously. If attention is not paid to the fact that the historical contexts in which it emerges and evolves, especially at the political level, are not neutral (Redclift, 1987; Williams, 1998), it will not be possible to address the understanding of the concept adequately nor to analyze the causes and scope of its successes or failures. In this sense, it is important to bear in mind the fact that both environmentalism and the concept of sustainable development began to take shape as a response to a genuine development problem, which again, has been intimately connected to the chosen industrial development model established after WWII. After several decades, the postwar model, especially in the Western world, began to show its limits and, as a consequence, began to be questioned.

It is also appropriate to mention that the development of the concept in the different spheres or contexts that have contributed to its configuration and evolution – from research and academia through the political and institutional spheres, as well as the business sectors and civil society organizations – has generally not occurred at the same time or in a consensual manner. This has given rise to criticism, especially from civil society organizations and social movements, regarding the positions and decisions adopted by governmental entities and institutions. This has been evidenced, for example, by the events that have been held in parallel to governmental conferences and fora, as was the case of the so-called Global Forum 92, organized by non-governmental organizations and social movements from different parts of the world, which was held simultaneously with the Rio 1992 Summit in order to provide a critical point of view to the positions defended by governments at the official summit.

Neither of the two terms that make up the concept of "sustainable development" was a novelty at the time of its adoption, and even much less were the issues and ideas that underlie it, such as the idea of progress (Du Pisani, 2006) or the idea of sustainability, as explained earlier. However, the conjunction and interaction of the two is relatively recent. It began to take shape in the historical context of the second half of the 20th century.

Since the beginning of this century, although sustainability seems to have become the "buzzword" in international political circles working or touching on development, the concept continues to pose problems and challenges, both at the theoretical and practical levels. Understanding these issues is a major part of the solution.

More than three decades after the 1987 *Brundtland Report*, and although the concept of sustainable development is now fully integrated into the vocabulary of international political actors, the debate over its meaning remains open. Despite this, we can identify some characteristics that, to a large extent, serve to explain the keys to the main challenges that confront the operability of the notion itself. Among these challenges, in many cases intertwined, some have been a constant since the emergence of the concept of sustainable development, while others have arisen as a result of the transformations that the term itself has undergone over time.

Among the most outstanding characteristics of the concept of sustainable development, which has accompanied the term since its inception, is its ambiguity. This feature is the result of the difficulty in specifying and agreeing on an essential meaning of the term (Dernbach & Cheever, 2015), which is largely explained by two circumstances: on the one hand, the fact that the elements that integrate it (sustainable and development) face the same problem, both are equally equivocal and polysemic (Mensah, 2019). Thus, in order to properly understand the concept of sustainable development, it is necessary first to investigate the origin and evolution of the notions of development and sustainability as has been attempted in this chapter. On the other hand, especially since the incorporation of the Brundtland Report definition, the concept of sustainable development has experienced an accelerated expansion of its popularity, as well as of its interpretations and uses of the notion with which it has been associated. Although, in general terms, it tends to be taken for granted that the concept "is an attempt to combine growing concerns about a variety of environmental issues with socioeconomic issues" (Hopwood et al., 2005: 38), we can see it acquiring different meanings, depending on the context or forum in which it is used.

The fact that the term has ended up alluding to very varied or different things depending on the fields and contexts in which it is used – environmentalism, economics, politics, etc. – has been exacerbated by the additional tendency that seems to have turned the polysemic flexibility of sustainable development into "a panacea for all modern ills or as a catch-all theme to which all policy challenges (no matter of what complexion) are somehow inextricably linked" (Atkinson et al., 2014: xxvii).

All of the above requires a constant exercise of interpretation of the objectives, visions, and interests that underlie each case in which the term is used. Along the same lines, it is also pointed out that its broad or vague nature, sometimes even empty of meaning, which is also transferred to the proposals for defining the concept further, as is the case with the classic Brundtland definition, would have the ultimate intention to cover up "a tacit agreement" by not specifying a definition that otherwise would have ended up being an obstacle to the adoption of international agreements on the subject (Elizalde, 2003:2). In other words, the key to its success and strength would have been due to this ambiguity since, as it has been used, it can mean anything (Redclift, 1991; Montes, 2007).

As a result of this ambiguity, it is worth pointing out other features of which sustainable development suffers or is accused of, such as its confusability with other concepts to which it is related; its contradictory nature (for some, even controversial); or the overexposure of the term are cases in point.

Regarding the confusion that can be generated with respect to other concepts, sometimes these have been produced by the added use or interchange with other terms and concepts that have been considered synonyms. At other times, the concept has been supplanted by other new notions with which it has entered into competition, in either trying to reinforce specific aspects of sustainable development or in even seeking to highlight its limitations; this is the case for concepts such as "green economy", "green growth", or even "resilience" (Bermejo, 2014; Dernbach & Cheever, 2015). In this sense, neither the variety of disciplines that have adopted and addressed the concept of sustainable development nor the multiplicity of fields that have echoed the wide range of topics in which the term has ended up evolving should be lost sight of.

Regarding its alleged contradictory nature, this derives from considering the concept as an oxymoron (Daly, 1993; Redclift, 2005); the concept suffers from an intrinsic and insurmountable contradiction due to its two essential components: development and sustainability, in the sense of the unfeasibility of an economic growth that can converge in a balanced way with the preservation of nature or, as Du Pisani points out in his analysis of the historical roots of the concept, "the idea of sustainability evolved over the centuries as a counterpoint to the notions of progress" (2006: 83).

To the above, and partly as a consequence, it should be added that some refer to sustainable development as an idea worn out by the overuse to which it has been subjected. Despite having become a hegemonic concept in all development discourses, especially at the political level, the scarce effectiveness in the implementation of solutions to the problems that have been recognized in recent decades has not only contributed to accentuating the other features mentioned but has also favored the lack of credibility (Montes, 2007).

In addition to these challenges posed by the conceptual level of the term, there are other controversies surrounding the implications of its implementation. These include the concerns of developing countries regarding the consequences that the adoption of sustainable development as a normative and political conceptual framework may have for them in particular. These concerns, raised since the initial endorsement of the sustainable development agenda as a new paradigm of development model, have to do with the conflicting interests between the more- and the less-developed countries and regions. On the one hand, the latter understood that it would affect their right to development and they claimed that their responsibilities were not the same as those of the developed countries. On the other hand, the less developed countries' concerns also come from their perception of facing a new excuse on the part of Western countries to perpetuate their domination over non-Western people. The sustainable development agenda is thus perceived as a renewed form of intervention; by encompassing a set of new modalities in terms of political conditionality such as "good governance" and "democratization", it is ultimately only a "disguised" concern for the environment (Williams, 1998).

Conclusions

In a constantly changing world shaped by geoeconomics and geopolitics, the optimization of natural resources does affect the prospects of human development. This implies that, since the era of industrialization, the chosen system of economic activity has led to levels of environmental degradation incompatible with human well-being in the long term. Eventually, the rise of affluent societies after WWII has unbridled the environmental concern in the Western world, leading to the first environmentalist movements in the 1960s. Born from a genuine concern for the environment and with solid scientific evidence, these movements became subsequently politicized, radicalized, and increasingly detached from a scientific base as testified, for example, by the Club of Rome Report and by Mann's "hockey stick" to justify the current "climate change" narrative, which is another variation on the same theme.[10]

The 1960s genuine concern for the environment at grassroot levels turned increasingly into a new doctrine spawned through a top-down approach. At that stage, financial interests and "environmental diplomacy" set in, the latter being tasked with the necessity to rally all forces around a new uncontestable environment paradigm. The oil shocks of the 1970s cannot be disassociated from the 1972 Club of Rome report, as the two phenomena are intrinsically intertwined. The subsequent "sustainable development" concept emerged and gave rise to a number of policy documents and initiatives such as the

UN-driven 2000 MDGs and its 2015 SDGs. An example of an outcome arising from these doctrinal policy moves is the urge for the widespread use of electric vehicles; but mining for electric vehicles battery ingredients, such as lithium, is not eco-friendly and is thus not sustainable.

This chapter has unveiled a review of the concept of sustainable development from both a historical and epistemological perspective. Interestingly, the concept of sustainable development is grounded in economic theory at two levels: (i) In terms of economic efficiency theory, the non-optimization of scarce resources, and their ensuing environmental problems, has meant that factor-price efficiency rather than technical efficiency has been favored. This means that more effort should have been (and should be) deployed in adapting new and suppressed technologies to the production of energy, for example. (ii) The concept is also firmly rooted in the Malthusian "pessimistic" view of world population control; the UN documents infer that economic development is not sustainable because it is anthropogenic. In response to this, it can be said that this is rather *because of policy choices* driven precisely by these same (global) institutions.

At this juncture, other questions that remain and that could be explored are the following: (i) Why is there such an obsession, in the conception and drafting of the policies, with the phenomenon of population growth? (ii) the lack of *independent* assessments or evaluations of the progress in terms of MDGs and SDGs; (iii) the mitigated success of the MDGs given, *inter al.*, that "extreme poverty eradication", a grandiose objective for the year 2015 has far from been achieved; and finally (iv) one needs to question why financial and oil interests are so prominently represented in a global discourse on sustainable development given that, yet again, factor-price efficiency and returns on investment are the driving principles of investors, irrespective of their impact on the environment and despite the many efforts deployed in terms of corporate social responsibility.

Notes

1 The reader interested in this issue can refer, for example, to Kabiru and Batsari (2020) who show, for example, that progress in terms of eradicating extreme forms of poverty in Africa and South America did not materialize.

2 One should be aware of the difference existing between economic growth and economic development as warned already by authors such as F. Perroux in the 1980s (Perroux, 1983). Economic growth can indeed take place without much (socioeconomic) development. See also Andreosso-O'Callaghan who discussed the case of a Western country (2004).

3 For example, in Germany and France, this period corresponded to the "Wirtschftswunder" period and to the "trente glorieuses", respectively (30 years of uninterrupted economic growth and development).

4 In the 1950s, the levels of "smog" in large industrialized cities of Germany and the UK compared quite well with the levels of pollution recorded in China at the beginning of this millennium.

5 Some of these problems were already anticipated decades ago by authors from different fields, such as ecologists, botanists and political economists. This is the case of the warnings made in the 19th century by Thomas Malthus in his famous work

Essay on the principle of population. According to Malthus, based on the imbalance between population and resources, the population grows (when there are no obstacles to prevent it) in a geometric progression, while resources do it in an arithmetic progression, as a result humanity is condemned to famine, until the balance is restored by war or catastrophe (Brander, 2007; Thomas, 1798).

6 The Club of Rome was founded in 1968 at the instigation of Dr. Aurelio Peccei (a very well-connected Italian industrialist). The report highlighted the limits to exponential growth in fertilizers, natural resources, population, and demand for food and pollution. It provided several simulations of the world mineral and energy resources which would be depleted over a short time horizon (a few decades only), with respect to the growth in population, industrial output, food production, and pollution. Emphasis is placed not only on population (fertility rates, family size, etc.) but also on the impact of man (human activity) on the environment.

7 In his *Essay on the principle of population* first published in 1798, Thomas Robert Malthus argued that the population grows (when there are no obstacles to prevent it) in a geometric progression, while resources do it in an arithmetic progression; as a result, the population remains "to be repressed by famine or war" (Chapter III, p. 85, 1988 Edition); this is in the context of populations living in distant lands which Malthus calls "Barbarians" (sic!), although in Chapter VII (p. 118, same edition) he calls famines a "most dreadful resource of nature".

8 At the 1972 Stockholm "Only One Earth" Conference, one should note the key role of Maurice Strong, a businessman well connected to the Rockefeller business empire.

9 Gro Harlem Brundtland, the then-prime minister of Norway, member of the Trilateral Commission, chaired the Commission and played an important role in its adoption.

10 Professor Michael Mann's *hockey stick*, used by the Intergovernmental Panel on Climate Change (IPCC) in 2001 to initiate the "climate change" narrative, depicts temperature anomalies since year 1000, from a given base; using undisclosed mathematics and computer techniques, Mann produces a flat curve until the beginning of the 20th century with exponentially rising temperatures since the mid-20th century. Unfortunately for Professor Mann, even a cursory glance at historical manuscripts suffices to prove, beyond any refute, that, for example, during the Middle-Ages, temperatures rose to much higher levels than at the beginning of the third Millenium; see in particular Leroy Ladurie (1967).

References

Ala-Uddin, M. (2019). 'Sustainable' Discourse: A Critical Analysis of the 2030 Agenda for Sustainable Development. *Asia Pacific Media Educator*, *29*(2), 214–224. https://doi.org/10.1177/1326365X19881515

Andreosso-O'Callaghan, B. (2004). 'The role of the Irish state in the catching up process: developmental or growth promoter?', in Linda Low (ed), *Developmental states: Relevancy, redundancy or reconfiguration?*, 219–233, Nova Science Publishers: New York and ISEAS: Singapore.

Andreosso-O'Callaghan, B & Rajmil, D. (2024). *Crises and Globalization: the delineation of a new path.* In *Geopolitical Uncertainty and International Business* (pp. 19–32). Edward Elgar Publishing. DOI: https://doi.org/10.4337/9781035325412.00011.

Atkinson, G., Dietz, S., Neumayer, E., & Agarwala, M. (Eds.). (2014). *Handbook of Sustainable Development* (2nd edition). Edward Elgar Publishing. https://doi.org/10.4337/9781782544708

Bermejo, R. (2014). *Del Desarrollo Sostenible según Brundtland a la sostenibilidad como biomimesis.* Hegoa. http://publicaciones.hegoa.ehu.es/assets/pdfs/315/Sostenibilidad_DHL.pdf?1399365095

Brander, J.A. (2007). Viewpoint: Sustainability: Malthus Revisited? (Durabilité: Malthus revisité?). *The Canadian Journal of Economics/Revue Canadienne d'Economique*, *40*(1), 1–38. http://www.jstor.org/stable/4620595

Bustillo-García, L., & Martínez-Dávila, J.P. (2008). Los enfoques del desarrollo sustentable. *Interciencia*, *33* (5), 389–395. http://ve.scielo.org/scielo.php?script=sci_arttext&pid=S0378-18442008000500014&lng=es&tlng=es

Daly, H.E. (1993). Sustainable Growth: An Impossibility Theorem. In Daly, H. E. & Townsend, K. N. (Eds), *Valuing the Earth: Economics, Ecology, and Ethics*, 267–274, MIT Press.

Dernbach, J. C., & Cheever, F. (2015). Sustainable Development and Its Discontents. *Transnational Environmental Law*, *4*(2), 247–287. Doi: 10.1017/S2047102515000163

Du Pisani, J.A. (2006). Sustainable development – historical roots of the concept. *Environmental Sciences*, *3*(2), 83–96. DOI: 10.1080/15693430600688831

Elizalde, A. (2003). Desde el "Desarrollo Sustentable" hacia sociedades sustentables. *Polis* (4). http://journals.openedition.org/polis/7154

Glyn, A., Hughes, A., Lipietz, A., & Sigh, A. (1988). The rise and fall of the golden age.

Harry, J., & Harry, J. (1974). Causes of contemporary environmentalism. *Humboldt Journal of Social Relations*, *2*(1), 3–7. http://www.jstor.org/stable/23261515

Hickmann, T., Biermann, F., Spinazzola, M., Ballard, C., Bogers, M., Forestier, O., … & Yunita, A. (2023). Success factors of global goal-setting for sustainable development: Learning from the Millennium Development Goals. Sustainable Development, 31(3), 1214–1225.

Hopwood, B., Mellor, M., & O'Brien, G. (2005). Sustainable development: mapping different approaches. *Sustainable Development*, *13*(1), 38–52. https://doi.org/10.1002/sd.244

Hull, Z. (2008). Sustainable development: premises, understanding and prospects. *Sustainable Development*, *16*(2), 73–80. https://doi.org/10.1002/sd.337

Lebada, A.M., & Chasek, P. (June 2021). *Do Mega-Conferences Advance Sustainable Development?*. International Institute for Sustainable Development. https://www.iisd.org/system/files/2021-06/still-one-earth-mega-summits.pdf

Leroy Ladurie Emmanuel (1967). *Histoire du Climat depuis l'an Mille*, Paris: Flammarion.

Malthus Thomas, R., (1798, reprinted 1988). *An Essay on the Principle of Population*, Penguin Classics for the 1988 Edition, London.

Mensah, J. (2019). Sustainable development: Meaning, history, principles, pillars, and implications for human action: Literature review. *Cogent Social Sciences*, *5*(1). https://doi.org/10.1080/23311886.2019.1653531

Montes, C. (2007). Del desarrollo sostenible a los servicios de los ecosistemas. *Ecosistemas*, *16*(3), 1–3. https://www.revistaecosistemas.net/index.php/ecosistemas/article/view/87

National Research Council (NRC). (2011). *Sustainability and the U.S. EPA*. The National Academies Press. https://doi.org/10.17226/13152

Perroux, François (1983). *A New concept of Development*, Croom Helm, London.

Prigogine, I., and Henin F. (1966). On the Entropy of strongly interacting systems, *Physics Letters*, 20, 255–257. DOI: https://doi.org/10.1016/0031-9163(66)90352-0

Raymond, J. (1988). *Robert O. Anderson: Oilman/Environmentalist and his Leading Role in the International Environmentalist Movement*. Aspen Institute of Humanistic Studies, Washington DC. Lanham, MD: University Press of America.

Razak, R.R., & Sanusi, Z.A. (2010). The Concept of Sustainable Development in Human Civilisation: An Introspective View. *KEMANUSIAAN The Asian Journal of Humanities*, (17), 19–36. http://web.usm.my/kajh/KAJH%2017/KAJH%20Art%202%20(19-36).pdf

Redclift, M. (1987). *Sustainable Development: Exploring the Contradictions* (1st ed.). Routledge. https://doi.org/10.4324/9780203408889

Redclift, M. (1991). The Multiple Dimensions of Sustainable Development. *Geography*, *76*(1), 36–42. http://www.jstor.org/stable/40572018

Redclift, M. (2005). Sustainable development (1987–2005): an oxymoron comes of age. *Sustainable Development*, *13*(4), 212–227. https://doi.org/10.1002/sd.281

Kabiru, S.A., and Batsari, L.M. (2020). Assessment of the Millenium Development Goals (MDGs). *KIU Journal of Social Science*, 6(3), 25–31.

United General Assembly (UNGA). (1983). Res. 38/161. *Process of preparation of the Environmental Perspective to the Year 2000 and Beyond*. https://digitallibrary.un.org/record/65594

United Nations (UN). (2015). *The Millennium Development Goals Report 2015*. https://www.un.org/millenniumgoals/2015_MDG_Report/pdf/MDG%202015%20rev%20(July%201).pdf

United Nations Conference on Environment and Development (UNCED). (1992a). *Agenda* 21. https://sustainabledevelopment.un.org/content/documents/Agenda21.pdf

United Nations Conference on Environment and Development (UNCED). (1992b). *Rio Declaration on Environment and Development*. https://www.un.org/en/development/desa/population/migration/generalassembly/docs/globalcompact/A_CONF.151_26_Vol.I_Declaration.pdf

United Nations General Assembly (UNGA). (2015). *Transforming our world: The 2030 agenda for sustainable development*. https://sdgs.un.org/2030agenda

United Nations. (2017). *World Economic and Social Survey 2017: Reflecting on 70 years of development policy analysis*. https://www.un.org/development/desa/dpad/wp-content/uploads/sites/45/publication/WESS_2017-FullReport.pdf

Washington, H. (2015). *Demystifying Sustainability: Towards Real Solutions* (1st ed.). Routledge. https://doi.org/10.4324/9781315748641

Williams, M. (1998). Aid, sustainable development and the environmental crisis. *International Journal of Peace Studies*, *3*(2), 19–33. http://www.jstor.org/stable/41852857

Woodhouse, K. M. (2009). The politics of ecology: environmentalism and liberalism in the 1960s. *Journal for the Study of Radicalism*, *2*(2), 53–84.

World Commission on Environment and Development (WCED). (1987). *Our Common Future*.https://sustainabledevelopment.un.org/content/documents/5987our-common-future.pdf

2 Education for Sustainable Development

A Critical Lens on Economic Progress

Ozéias Rodrigues da Rocha, Lucía Morales and Jon-Hans Coetzer

Introduction

Interweaving the threads of contemporary geoeconomic challenges, such as global interdependence and the unequal distribution of resources, with the principles of economic progress, environmental management and social equity, the fabric of Education for Sustainable Development (ESD) emerges, as advocated by Dodd et al. (2022), Fettes and Blenkinsop (2023) and Zhang et al. (2024). UNESCO (UNESCO, 2012, p.2) defines ESD as education that "*...allows every human being to acquire the knowledge, skills and value necessary to shape a sustainable future.*" ESD integrates sustainable development principles into education, equipping individuals with the skills and knowledge to navigate complex socio-economic landscapes and address environmental challenges. ESD cultivates human capital that drives innovation, entrepreneurship and sustainable economic activities by fostering environmental responsibility and responsible citizenship. This underscores ESD's vital role in fostering inclusive, resilient and sustainable economic progress. This leads to questioning the basic principles of economic growth as understood by the metrics associated with gross domestic product and its dated working context. Education is the foundation for both economic sustainability and peaceful societies. It shapes aspirations and weaves a path towards a harmonious future where people and the planet coexist (Kioupi & Voulvoulis, 2019).

The complex interplay between environmental degradation, social inequality and a multitude of other pressing and multifaceted issues facing our world today reflects the complexity and multidimensional aspects of the challenges of achieving sustainability. However, amidst these challenges, a beacon of hope emerges – education. Žalėnienė and Pereira (2021) argue that education is a pivotal force for driving meaningful change, illuminating paths to sustainability by fostering interconnection between societies, the environment and individuals. Through education, individuals are equipped with the knowledge, critical thinking skills and a sense of global citizenship necessary to navigate the complexities of our world (Danijela Stojanović et al., 2023). Education serves as a catalyst for social transformation, acting as a powerful tool to

DOI: 10.4324/9781032655857-4

break down barriers of ignorance and prejudice while fostering inclusivity and diversity (Nikolaidis, 2023). Furthermore, education fosters equality by providing access to marginalised communities. Empowering individuals with knowledge and skills can help break poverty cycles, foster the development of more just and peaceful societies, and provide the foundations for societies that are more critical towards political and economic decisions and their implications (Berkowitz, 2022). Furthermore, education plays a crucial role in addressing emerging geoeconomic and geopolitical challenges, cultivating innovation and entrepreneurship, and stimulating creative thinking and problem-solving skills needed to address the complexities of our time (Lv et al., 2022). Education stands out as a vital variable as global economic and political dynamics become more interconnected. It provides knowledge and skills to address sustainability, technology and policy issues and plays a transformative role in society. Investing in education empowers citizens to contribute to building a more sustainable, equitable and resilient future. Therefore, it is essential to consider the economic dimension of education as it not only shapes individuals but also shapes and reshapes the global geopolitical and geoeconomic trajectory (Fischer et al., 2020).

This chapter brings a novel insight into the geoeconomic and geopolitical debate as it explores the multifaceted relationship between Education for Sustainable Development (ESD) and economic sustainability, recognising that education plays a crucial role in addressing emerging geoeconomic and geopolitical challenges. By analysing the impact of ESD through critical theory and examining its interaction with broader development goals (Cardiff et al., 2024), this chapter provides some insights to help us understand how education can contribute to facing global economic challenges. In this sense, the opportunities and challenges presented by the UN Agenda 2030 (United Nations, 2015) are investigated, highlighting the importance of considering the economic dimension of education to achieve sustainability objectives and promote equitable and resilient development. Furthermore, the chapter explores the disconnection between traditional economic models and sustainability goals, aiming to link these aspects to geoeconomic and geopolitical elements. Drawing on ideas from the Frankfurt School, it critiques dominant ideologies and advocates inclusive, environmentally conscious alternatives. This analysis hinges on the interconnectedness of education, economic sustainability and development goals, offering insights into how these components can be integrated into broader sustainability frameworks. By critically examining the intersection of Education for Sustainable Development (ESD) and economic theories, the chapter seeks to inform policies and practices that contribute to a more equitable and sustainable future. This groundwork is established by exploring ESD and Critical Theory, followed by an analysis of their convergence while offering critical insights into the reality of the Sustainability Agenda.

Education for Sustainable Development

Education for Sustainable Development (ESD) extends beyond traditional education, fostering a holistic understanding of environmental, social and economic issues (Zhang et al., 2020). It challenges dominant economic models and their impact, prompting a revaluation of progress itself. ESD goes beyond knowledge acquisition, nurturing critical thinking, social justice values and environmental stewardship, enabling the development of competencies and skills that equip individuals to navigate the challenges of achieving a sustainable future (Uralovich et al., 2023). From the perspective of the Frankfurt School, ESD emerges as a powerful instrument to decolonise and redefine progress, confronting the global economic model driven by the continued search for profit, shareholders' wealth maximisation, market-driven economic models and instrumental rationality (Carstensen & Emmenegger, 2023). This model has been criticised for promoting ecological exploitation, social alienation and the commodification of knowledge as the educational system has embraced the corporate world dynamics and operating systems (Fu & Gao, 2024). Integrating global economic trends, ESD challenges the idea that economic growth is the only measure of progress, while political agendas play a crucial role in promoting systemic changes towards truly sustainable development by encouraging fairer and more equitable economic practices, as well as environmental protection and social well-being. ESD empowers individuals to question and transform existing economic and social structures by promoting a critical understanding of these issues. As such, this chapter explores specific Frankfurt School critiques through the lens of ESD's transformative potential. It examines the concept of "reification," where abstract notions like "growth" are treated as tangible realities, obscuring the human and environmental costs. Furthermore, we argue on the importance of ESD to encourage critical analysis of such concepts, fostering a revaluation of current models and envisioning alternative pathways towards progress. Some educational challenges emerge as a result of "instrumental rationality," where actions solely evaluated on efficiency and productivity are subject to scrutiny and critical reflection. We further argue on the need to assess the intrinsic value of nature, social justice and cultural diversity, prompting individuals to embrace values conducive to sustainable development and their implications as we take into account global competition and the imperatives associated with intertwined economic and political agendas.

Ultimately, ESD benefits from the theoretical framework proposed by proponents of the Frankfurt School's critique, as it can be considered a powerful tool for nurturing responsible citizens who actively contribute to a just and sustainable future. By dismantling the myth of "progress as economic growth" and challenging dominant narratives, ESD empowers individuals to collectively imagine and build a future where social well-being and environmental stewardship take precedence. This ushers in a new paradigm of progress for the 21st century, promoting ethical consumption and moving away from consumerism and the irrational demands of a growing economic model that is based on consumption. Therefore, an initial insight on how to facilitate the potential transition towards community-based resource management and social entrepreneurship relates to the significance of integrating economic prosperity with environmental sustainability that needs to be supported by cost-benefit analysis that integrates the needs of the Global North and the Global South.

Before delving deeper into analysing the impact of education on Education for Sustainable Development (ESD), it is essential to adopt a broader economic and political perspective. The integration of global economic trends and political agendas further enriches the analysis of the importance of ESD in the contemporary context. When considering global economic trends, it is clear that the current economic system, based on the incessant search for profit and the maximisation of shareholders' wealth through production and consumption, contributes to perpetuating social inequalities, environmental destruction and marginalisation of communities (Lenton & Scheffer, 2024). Economic policies often privilege the interests of large corporations to the detriment of human and environmental well-being, reinforcing the need for a more critical and sustainable approach. On the other hand, political agendas play a crucial role in promoting the systemic changes necessary to achieve sustainable development. Through policies that encourage fairer and more equitable economic practices, as well as the protection of the environment and the promotion of social well-being, it is possible to create an enabling environment for the effective implementation of ESD. Furthermore, policies that value critical and interdisciplinary education, incorporating sustainability principles into school curricula and educational programs, can further strengthen people's ability to question and transform existing economic and social structures. Therefore, by integrating an analysis of global economic trends and political agendas, it is clear that ESD not only offers a critical perspective on the systemic problems facing contemporary society but also empowers individuals to become agents of change in the pursuit of a fairer, more equitable and sustainable future.

This approach underscores the global economic significance of ESD and emphasises the pivotal role of education within the framework of the UN's 2030 Agenda. Moreover, it sheds light on the unique challenges and opportunities inherent in impoverished regions, offering insights into the economic and political dynamics shaping the implementation of sustainable development initiatives in these areas. The relationship between economic development and education is symbiotic, with education serving as a crucial driver of sustainable economic growth (Uralovich et al., 2023). Education enhances labour productivity, promotes innovation and technological advancement, fosters social inclusion and reduces inequalities (Hughes & Loader, 2023). Moreover, education shapes the broader social and institutional context, contributing to democratic values, civic engagement and social cohesion (Carstensen & Emmenegger, 2023). The world economy faces significant challenges to support inclusive and sustainable growth that could be addressed by investing in human capital development, which is vital as the world economies consider the importance of working within a collaborative framework towards a prosperous future

(Fu & Gao, 2024). The points raised about Education for Sustainable Development (ESD) are highly relevant to our ability to address the rising levels of uncertainty stemming from economic, social and environmental systems. By understanding the context in which changes occur and highlighting the role of education in preparing for these challenges, we can adopt a more holistic and integrated approach to sustainable development. This allows us to not only mitigate immediate uncertainties but also promote long-term resilience and sustainability by integrating policies and promoting global cooperation towards a more stable and equitable future.

Environmental awareness has given rise to Education for Sustainable Development (ESD), which aims to bring human well-being in harmony with the planet. This vision finds its roots in the 1987 Brundtland Commission's report, "Our Common Future," which defined sustainable development as "*development that meets the needs of the present without compromising the ability of future generations to meet their own needs*" (Brundtland et al., p. 8, chapter 2, 1987). This fundamental principle is the development of ecologically aware, empowered and responsible citizens. Essentially, ESD empowers individuals to navigate the complexities of sustainability (Hussain et al., 2024). Furthermore, based on the aforementioned Brundtland Commission's definition of sustainable development, ESD integrates environmental, economic and social dimensions, highlighting their interconnectedness (Türkeş, 2024). Additionally, the diverse meanings associated with ESD reflect its complexity and critical role in fostering environmental responsibility, social justice and economic stability – essential tools for building a more sustainable and equitable future amidst today's challenges. Finally, ESD equips individuals with systems thinking, critical inquiry and collaboration, highlighting the need to foster skills and competencies that empower individuals and societies to contribute meaningfully to sustainable development goals and a more just future (Crawford & Jones, 2024).

The UN's 2030 Agenda, with its 17 SDGs, tackles global challenges like poverty (SDG 1), hunger (SDG 2) and climate change (SDG 13), which are critical elements to help less developed economies move forward and escape a vicious cycle of marginalisation and exclusion. However, economic progress and development require the development of human talent, and SDG 4 – Quality Education can be identified as the foundation to initiate a process of transition that highlights quality education for all that emerges as key to achieving all other goals (Subramony & Rosenbaum, 2024).

Early education is vital for sustainable development. It shapes lifelong values and behaviours, making it the prime time to instil a deep appreciation for sustainable practices (Vesterinen & Ratinen, 2024). Furthermore, early education is crucial for sustainable development. It shapes lifelong values for sustainability and fosters the knowledge, skills and work ethic needed for a future-proof workforce, driving innovation and economic growth (Wheeler, 2023). By nurturing sustainability values and fostering a skilled workforce, inclusive early education becomes a bridge to a future where economic prosperity and environmental well-being go hand in hand. It empowers all to be architects of a sustainable future, leaving no one behind (Kitagawa & Vidmar, 2023). As an educational paradigm, ESD transcends the mere transmission of knowledge, embracing a holistic approach that fosters critical thinking, ethical responsibility and practical skills needed to tackle the complex challenges of the 21st century (Sterling, 2011; Hopkins, 2013). ESD acts as a bridge, connecting economic needs with educational approaches. It highlights the multifaceted role of education in building a sustainable future (Kohl et al., 2022). With the aim of deepening our analysis of the ramifications and implications of ESD, the work of some of the main theorists of this current of thought and their respective propositions is examined. Stephen Sterling, a leading figure in ESD, advocates for a paradigm shift in education towards sustainability and argues for prioritising long-term well-being over short-term gains in the transition to a sustainable economy. Sterling critiques traditional economic models for neglecting environmental and social costs, leading to unsustainable practices. He suggests that ESD challenges these paradigms by promoting critical thinking and integrating ecological economics principles into education. Sterling's work provides valuable insights into how education can catalyse sustainable development while underlining the importance of integrating cost analysis that should also be related to the levels of investment that are needed to support an educational system that is accessible to all, and that requires significant levels of international cooperation, collaboration and financial planning (Sterling, 2021; Salonen et al., 2023).

Also a prominent figure in ESD, Paul Vare advocates for integrating sustainability principles into education, with a focus on economic literacy. His research explores innovative teaching methods for incorporating sustainable development concepts into various educational settings. Vare emphasises the importance of equipping learners with the skills to critically analyse economic systems and their sustainability implications, empowering them to make informed decisions. His work enriches the theoretical understanding of ESD and offers practical guidance for implementation, aligning with the aims of this study (Vare et al., 2022). A leading advocate for sustainable education, Charles Hopkins emphasises education's role in transitioning to sustainable economies. He argues that ESD should address systemic barriers within economic systems, advocating for policy reforms, sustainable business practices and stakeholder collaboration. ESD can drive systemic changes towards equitable and environmentally sustainable economies by engaging economic institutions and promoting dialogue on sustainable development. Hopkins' contributions enrich theoretical frameworks and inform policy and practice, aligning with this study's focus on educational strategies for sustainable economic development (Hopkins et al., 2020; Kohl & Hopkins, 2022).

The figure of David Orr emerges as a defender of rethinking economic paradigms for sustainability (Orr, 2020). He critiques measures like GDP growth for ignoring ecological degradation and social inequalities. Orr suggests ESD challenges narrow economic indicators, promoting alternative visions of prosperity centred on environmental stewardship and social equity. Integrating ecological economics into education can deepen understanding of the link between economic systems and sustainability (Wildemeersch et al., 2023). Moreover, organisations like UNESCO (UNESCO, 2018) and the United Nations (United Nations, 2020) play pivotal roles in promoting ESD globally. UNESCO's initiatives aim to integrate sustainable development principles into education policies and practices worldwide, recognising the importance of addressing economic dimensions alongside environmental and social aspects (Duoblienė et al., 2023). The United Nations advocates for sustainable development, highlighting the interconnectedness of economic prosperity, environmental integrity and social equity (United Nations, 2023). Johan Rockström's (Rockström, 2015) work on planetary boundaries further underscores the urgency of integrating sustainability principles into economic systems to avoid crossing critical thresholds for global environmental stability (Rockström et al., 2021). Additional aspects that need attention can be identified, such as how ESD's economic side tackles traditional models, promotes sustainable alternatives and educates for informed decisions. This, along with support from experts, helps build a more sustainable economic future (Colón-Flores et al., 2023). Additionally, ESD bridges the gap between economic needs and education. It teaches facts and instils values, critical thinking and skills for a sustainable future (Tunji-Olayeni et al., 2023).

Recognition of unsustainable economic models drives the need for ESD, a counterpoint advocating an educational framework that prioritises interconnected ecological, social and economic pillars for a sustainable future. This challenges the current paradigm, which separates economic activity from environmental consequences, fostering a disconnect between knowledge and action (UNESCO, 2014; Toniolo et al., 2023). The significance of critical thinking in analysing the systemic roots of sustainability challenges outlined in the UN 2030 Agenda and its 17 SDGs also requires attention. Educational systems should offer mechanisms that empower individuals to question economic narratives and advocate for just development models. By nurturing ethical responsibility, ESD encourages consideration of long-term environmental and social impacts, fostering intergenerational solidarity for a sustainable future (UNESCO, 2018; Kopnina, 2020).

The UN 2030 Agenda and its 17 Sustainable Development Goals (United Nations, 2015) present a comprehensive framework to address pressing global challenges and achieve sustainable development. However, achieving these goals requires increased global cooperation and political will, as progress often hinges on coordinated efforts across countries and sectors (Cheng et al., 2021). Additionally, unequal access to resources and opportunities for marginalised communities hinders sustainable development (Barua, 2020). Environmental degradation, including climate change, biodiversity loss and pollution, poses another critical challenge, threatening ecosystems and undermining efforts to achieve sustainable development goals. Additional elements to be considered relate to the SDGs' interconnectivity that underline the importance of adopting integrated approaches to effectively address complex, systemic issues (Maksymiv et al., 2021). Overall, the UN's 2030 Agenda charts a sustainable future, but achieving it demands ongoing commitment, fresh ideas and teamwork across all levels. Moreover, ESD equips individuals with skills to turn Theory into sustainable solutions, like managing resources, using renewable energy and designing ecologically (Casati et al., 2023; Kite & Park, 2024).

Based on individual analysis of advocates' thinking of a paradigm shift in education towards sustainability, we can argue that they share a common focus on integrating geoeconomic considerations into educational frameworks. They collectively criticise traditional economic models for their oversight of environmental and social costs, calling for a transition to sustainable economies prioritising long-term well-being. By emphasising economic literacy in education and advocating for systemic changes in economic systems, these advocates aim to empower students to critically analyse economic systems and their sustainability implications from a geoeconomic perspective. Furthermore, they promote alternative visions focused on environmental management and social equity, challenging limited economic indicators. Organisations such as UNESCO and the United Nations, in alignment with these objectives, recognise the interconnectedness of economic prosperity, environmental integrity and social equity. As Education for Sustainable Development (ESD) bridges the gap between economic needs and education, it instils values, critical thinking and skills for a sustainable future, promoting intergenerational solidarity and ethical responsibility in addressing complex global challenges from a geoeconomic perspective. Therefore, we argue on the need to integrate the geoeconomic and geopolitical dimensions into educational frameworks that will help to promote a more sustainable economic future and provide a working framework that becomes more realistic, and that works towards enabling a doable and actionable working plan for the UN 2030 Agenda for Sustainable Development.

Critical Theory from the Frankfurt School

Critical Theory, rooted in Marxism and championed by the Frankfurt School, dissects modern society. It exposes hidden ideologies in culture, industry and social norms, revealing their impact on our lives (Held, 2004). At its core lies a resolute interrogation of how capitalism and mass culture weave their tendrils into the fabric of societal beliefs and norms. Adorno's seminal critique, "The Culture Industry" (Adorno & Horkheimer, 2019), lays bare the mechanisms of mass deception, highlighting how cultural production and media manipulate public opinion and perpetuate conformity. This trenchant analysis resonates through society, revealing the invisible chains that bind individual consciousness and dictate social norms (Adorno & Bernstein, 2001; Cluley & Parker, 2023). Adorno's critique of cultural production in "The Culture Industry" aligns with economic models examining how capitalism and neoliberal dogmas shape and dominate culture and social norms anchored on Western models unsuitable to the context of our global socio-economic and environmental systems.

In traditional economic models, there's often an assumption of rationality among consumers and a focus on market dynamics driven by supply and demand (Lordkipanidze, 2023). However, Adorno goes beyond economic models. He argues that the culture industry, driven by profit in capitalism, actively shapes consumer preferences, values and norms, linking them to ideas of market power and consumer behaviour. It suggests that the commodification of culture within capitalist structures can lead to homogenisation, where diverse cultural expressions are subsumed under a standardised, market-driven model (Khandizaji & Caputi, 2021). This has implications for how economic models understand consumer choice, market competition, and the distribution of cultural goods and services (Durey, 2023). Moreover, Adorno's examination of the culture industry can inform discussions within economic Theory about capitalism's social costs and benefits (Lichtenstein, 2023). It raises questions about the extent to which capitalist systems promote genuine cultural expression and individual autonomy versus fostering conformity and manipulation for profit (Frumer, 2023). Therefore, Adorno's critique sheds light on the intersections between capitalism, mass culture and societal norms, enriching traditional economic analyses of consumption, production and market behaviour (Adorno, 2021). However, critical Theory does not merely diagnose; it yearns to heal. Within its embrace lies a profound educational dimension, exemplified by Paulo Freire's seminal work, "Pedagogy of the Oppressed" (Freire, 1970). This clarion call advocates for an education that ignites critical thinking and dismantles oppressive structures. It envisions education as a catalyst for societal transformation, fostering critical consciousness and propelling social change (Bello, 2023).

This symbiotic relationship finds further grounding in the works of Celso Furtado, a prominent Brazilian economist whose insights bear striking parallels with the Frankfurt School's critical lens. Furtado's works, such as "Development and Underdevelopment" (Furtado et al., 1964), deconstruct the simplistic equation of development with economic growth. He illuminates the complex fabric of historical, political and social factors that weave together to perpetuate underdevelopment, a perspective strikingly reminiscent of critical Theory's emphasis on the interconnectedness of societal structures (Araujo, 2022; Rama, 2022). Moreover, Furtado's critique of the linear trajectory of development echoed by mainstream economic theories aligns with the Frankfurt School's concern regarding dominant narratives serving the interests of the powerful, perpetuating inequalities. His emphasis on a historical and context-specific approach to development resonates with critical Theory's call for a nuanced analysis of power dynamics and systemic issues (Doré & Teixeira, 2022). Like a powerful magnifying glass, Furtado's works spotlight the structural constraints and imbalances within Latin American economies. This echoes the Frankfurt School's focus on understanding underlying social and economic structures perpetuating systemic issues. His structuralist approach highlights historical processes and institutional frameworks contributing to the region's development challenges, aligning with critical Theory's emphasis on historical and social analysis (Rama & Hall, 2021; Treacy, 2022). Furtado's works echo the spirit of critical Theory in challenging mainstream economic perspectives and revealing the interconnectedness of economic and social structures. His call for a transdisciplinary approach to understanding underdevelopment aligns with this ethos, and it challenges educational models that are focused on discipline-specific domains and the dominance of specialisation to detriment of a more holistic approach towards education, laying the groundwork for a transformative approach to societal change. This convergence of ideas transcends disciplinary boundaries, fostering a future that is both ecologically sustainable and socially just (Hayden & Dasilva, 2022; Stilwell, 2023).

However, it is vital to acknowledge the limitations of critical Theory. Its complexity and abstract nature can pose challenges to comprehension and implementation, potentially rendering it inaccessible to wider audiences (Bhambra, 2021). Its macro-level critique, while insightful, may overlook the agency and experiences of individuals within these systems (Bilgin, 2023). Additionally, its foundations in Western philosophical traditions might limit its resonance in non-Western contexts (Bohman et al., 2021). Furthermore, the lack of prescriptive solutions within the framework weakens its practical applicability. Finally, its radical critique of the status quo may encounter resistance from those who benefit from it (Bachmann & Moisio, 2020). Recognising these limitations is crucial for a compelling societal critique. Critical Theory must refine its focus and accessibility to realise its transformative potential and address social challenges fully.

We can argue that Critical Theory takes centre stage in dissecting the intricate mechanisms of economic power, culture and progress needed to understand the conflicting nature between economic progress and development within inclusive social models. Adorno and Horkheimer, armed with scathing critiques, illuminate the manipulative tentacles of the "culture industry," highlighting its potential to fabricate consensus and stifle individuality. Their seminal work, "The Culture Industry," peels back the glossy veneer of mass-produced culture to reveal the mechanisms of manipulation that lie beneath. They dissect how cultural production and media serve the interests of capital, commodifying art, music and entertainment to serve as vehicles for ideological indoctrination and social control. Through their incisive analysis, Adorno and Horkheimer paint a bleak portrait of a society where individual autonomy is subsumed by the homogenising forces of capitalism, where mass-produced culture engenders a false consciousness that perpetuates conformity and stifles dissent (Adorno, 1973; Adorno & Horkheimer, 2019; Reeves & Sinnicks, 2023).

While thought-provoking, critics argue that Adorno and Horkheimer's pessimistic outlook offers limited practical solutions. Their focus on the culture industry's oppressiveness leaves little room for optimism or agency, potentially overlooking avenues for resistance. Additionally, their dense writing style may alienate readers, limiting the accessibility of their ideas beyond academic circles (Ibsen, 2023; Brunkhorst, 2024). Despite criticisms, Adorno and Horkheimer's influential work confronts uncomfortable truths about capitalism's impact on culture and society. Their critique calls for vigilance against mass manipulation and resistance to capitalist commodification, making their work indispensable in the ongoing struggle for social justice and emancipation (Reynolds, 2023). Delving deeper into the complexities of "advanced industrial societies," Marcuse exposes the pernicious construction of "false needs" and the systematic suppression of dissent (Ladero, 2020). In "One-Dimensional Man" (Marcuse, 2002), he peels back the layers of consumer culture to reveal a landscape dominated by manufactured desires and superficial gratification. Within this milieu, individuals are ensnared by a web of false needs perpetuated by the relentless machinery of capitalism (Marcuse, 1978). Marcuse's analysis resonates with unsettling relevance, prompting questions about how individual agency can resist predetermined structures. His critique strikes at the heart of contemporary society, laying bare the mechanisms through which capitalism subverts genuine human flourishing (Maley, 2021). In a world saturated with consumer goods and distractions, the quest for material wealth is equated with happiness, overshadowing deeper inquiries into meaning and fulfilment. Marcuse unveils the insidiousness of this ideological dominance, demonstrating its role in perpetuating social inequality and preserving the status quo (Reitz, 2021).

Yet, amidst this bleak landscape, Marcuse discerns glimmers of hope. He argues that despite the pervasive influence of capitalist ideology, there remains a potential for resistance and dissent (Grimwade, 2022). By reclaiming critical consciousness and challenging the dominant narrative, individuals can begin to rupture the one-dimensional reality imposed upon them (Jansen & Engel, 2023). However, Marcuse acknowledges the formidable challenges that lie ahead, cautioning against simplistic notions of emancipation (Višić & others, 2023). Indeed, his analysis prompts profound existential questions about the nature of freedom and agency in a society dominated by capitalist structures (Karalus & others, 2022). Can individuals break free from false consciousness and reclaim their autonomy, or are they condemned to navigate predetermined realities? Marcuse's work provides no easy answers but calls for introspection and collective action against oppressive systems. In his pursuit of truth and justice, Marcuse urges us to resist complacency and challenge capitalist ideology's hegemony (Walker, 2022).

However, it is important to consider that with different focuses and approaches, it would be possible to provide a working framework that integrates elements of Critical Theory through the work of Jürgen Habermas, who is associated with Adorno through their shared commitment to social criticism. Habermas, championing the power of communication, envisions a vibrant public sphere where open dialogue serves as the catalyst for dismantling dominant ideologies (Habermas, 2022). In his seminal work, "The Structural Transformation of the Public Sphere" (Habermas, 1989), he articulates a vision of democratic deliberation and rational-critical discourse as the cornerstone of societal transformation. Habermas' emphasis on communicative action offers a hopeful vision of emancipation, where individuals engage in reasoned debate and challenge prevailing norms and power structures (Seeliger & Sevignani, 2022).

Central to Habermas' vision is the concept of the public sphere, a realm of open discourse and democratic engagement where citizens come together as equals to discuss matters of common concern (Hofmann, 2021). Within this sphere, rational argumentation and the free exchange of ideas serve as the bedrock of democratic governance, providing a counterbalance to the coercive forces of state power and economic interests (O'Mahony, 2021). Habermas contends that through communicative action, individuals can transcend their particular interests and engage in collective decision-making based on shared norms of rationality and morality (Larsen, 2021).

Critics raise concerns about the capacity of communicative action to address entrenched power dynamics and systemic inequalities. They argue that Habermas' vision of the public sphere neglects structural constraints that influence discourse and marginalise voices within society (Verovšek, 2021). Privileged elites and commercial interests often dominate the public sphere, limiting the accessibility and inclusivity of deliberative processes (Brinkmann et al., 2022). Moreover, digital media and social networks have complicated Habermas' model, blurring public and private boundaries and fuelling misinformation and polarisation (Korstenbroek, 2021).

Representing a crucial Global South perspective, Celso Furtado challenges the prevailing development models fostered by capitalism, revealing their inherent tendency to exacerbate global inequalities (Loureiro et al., 2021). In his seminal work, "Development and Underdevelopment" (Furtado et al., 1964), Furtado interrogates the impact of capitalist economic systems on underdeveloped regions, shedding light on the unequal distribution of wealth and power perpetuated by global economic structures. His critique serves as a powerful indictment of the development paradigms imposed by the Global North, which often prioritise profit over human welfare and perpetuate dependency and exploitation (Caldentey & Vernengo, 2022; Chilcote & Vasconcelos, 2022).

Furtado's plea for structural reform resonates urgently as he contends that traditional development models perpetuate cycles of poverty and marginalisation. He advocates for state intervention and strategic planning to foster economic growth and social equity, challenging neoliberal principles of deregulation and market fundamentalism. Furtado underscores the significance of targeted education, healthcare and infrastructure investments as a pathway to inclusive and sustainable development, prioritising marginalised communities' needs (Palestini, 2023; Bresser-Pereira & Oreiro, 2024).

As a unique figure in the pantheon of Latin American thought, Celso Furtado intertwined his trajectory with the Economic Commission for Latin America and the Caribbean (ECLAC - *CEPAL*), creating an intellectual dialogue that challenged the structures of power and domination imposed by the Global North. We also have good examples of ECLAC's independence in economic thought, not restricted to the philosophical debate about material and ideological domination. Without a doubt, the model of Inflationary Inertia stands out in this list, a theory coined by exponents of ECLAC, which stands as a beacon in this debate, illuminating alternatives to traditional economic thinking and unmasking the fallacy of the Global South as a mere supplier of raw materials. Armed with a critical and interdisciplinary vision, Furtado exposed the roots of underdevelopment: external dependence, the exploitation of natural resources and the concentration of income. Inflationary Inertia, in this context, emerges as a poignant portrait of the Latin American reality. According to the Theory, the expectation of future inflation, fuelled by fearful economic agents, generates a vicious cycle: price increases generate even greater expectations of inflation, leading to new increases and, in extreme cases, hyperinflation. This inflationary spiral, far from being a mere economic phenomenon, carries with it nuances of behavioural economics. Expectations, shaped by past experiences and the perception of the future, become a driver of inflation. Inflationary Inertia, therefore, transcends the limits of traditional economic Theory, embracing a holistic and contextualised view of development. The Theory of Inflationary Inertia proposes a new paradigm by questioning the Global South's narrative as a mere supplier of commodities. Development is not limited to economic growth but requires overcoming structural inequalities and building more just and equitable societies. Inflationary Inertia, more than an economic theory, is a manifesto for an autonomous Global South, capable of charting its own destiny. An ode to hope, an invitation to critical reflection and a call to action to build a more prosperous and fair future for all. In short, Inflationary Inertia reminds us of the vital contribution of Celso Furtado and ECLAC and represents a milestone in economic thinking, challenging orthodoxies and paving the way for a more promising future for the Global South.

However, Furtado's proposed solutions' feasibility and potential pitfalls remain open to debate. Critics argue that state-led development strategies can often lead to inefficiencies, corruption and bureaucratic inertia, undermining their effectiveness in addressing systemic inequalities (Borja, 2021; da Motta e Albuquerque, 2023). Moreover, the influence of global economic forces and multinational corporations presents significant challenges to the implementation of Furtado's vision, as they often wield considerable power over national governments and economic policies (Orsolin-Teixeira et al., 2024). Nevertheless, Furtado's insights provide a valuable counterpoint to mainstream development discourse, highlighting the need for a more nuanced understanding of the complexities of underdevelopment. His work underscores the imperative for structural reform and collective action to address the root causes of inequality and injustice on a global scale. While the road to transformative change may be fraught with obstacles, Furtado's legacy serves as a reminder of the ongoing struggle for economic justice and human dignity in an increasingly interconnected world (Mello Filho, 2023; Saith, 2023). Reflecting on Education for Economic Sustainable Development, we shift from critiquing capitalist structures to exploring education's role in fostering sustainable economic development. Drawing from Critical Theory and Global South perspectives, it is important to examine education's potential for transformative change, exploring its intersection with economic sustainability and social justice. It is essential to uncover how educational practices can build equitable and resilient societies, investigating opportunities and challenges in leveraging education for economic sustainability and human flourishing in the 21st century, as economic development, progress and prosperity need to be supported by systems that nurture human talent as a driver of change and enablers of the transition towards sustainable and inclusive development.

Convergence of Critical Theory from the Frankfurt School and ESD

The convergence of Critical Theory from the Frankfurt School and Education for Sustainable Development (ESD) represents a significant paradigm shift in both educational philosophy and socio-economic discourse. Rooted in the Frankfurt School's critique of modernity and capitalist society, Critical Theory provides a robust theoretical framework for understanding the structural injustices and environmental degradation inherent in prevailing economic systems (Biermann & Kalfagianni, 2020; Soon, 2021). Meanwhile, ESD offers a practical approach to addressing these systemic issues through transformative education that promotes sustainability and social responsibility (Klapper & Fayolle, 2023).

At the heart of Critical Theory lies a deep-seated concern with the alienating effects of capitalist production and consumption patterns on individuals and society (Øversveen, 2022). The Frankfurt School scholars illuminated how instrumental rationality and the commodification of all aspects of life have led to a loss of autonomy, creativity and critical consciousness among the populace (Roth, 2023). Moreover, they highlighted the destructive consequences of unchecked economic growth on the natural environment, pointing to the inherent contradictions between capitalism's pursuit of profit and the planet's ecological limits.

On the other hand, ESD seeks to cultivate a holistic understanding of sustainability that encompasses environmental, social and economic dimensions (Hamadi & El-Den, 2024). It aims to empower learners to critically engage with complex sustainability challenges and envision alternative futures that prioritise ecological integrity, social equity and economic well-being (Sarma et al., 2024). By integrating principles of environmental stewardship, social justice and ethical responsibility into educational curricula, ESD seeks to foster a new generation of environmentally literate and socially conscious citizens capable of effecting positive change (Verhelst et al., 2023). The convergence of Critical Theory and ESD is particularly salient in their shared critique of mainstream economic development paradigms. Both perspectives challenge the hegemony of neoliberal capitalism, which prioritises profit maximisation and economic growth at the expense of social justice and environmental sustainability (Hill, 2021). Critical Theory unveils the underlying power structures and ideological mechanisms that perpetuate inequality and exploitation within capitalist societies, while ESD offers practical strategies for transcending these structural barriers through education and collective action (Welsh, 2020).

One key concept that bridges Critical Theory and ESD is the notion of reification, as elucidated by Frankfurt School scholars (O'Kane, 2021). Reification refers to the process by which abstract social relations are transformed into tangible, commodified entities, thereby obscuring the underlying human labour and ecological resources involved (Gunderson, 2021). In economic development, reification occurs as GDP growth and market expansion are fetishised, masking capitalism's social and environmental costs. ESD challenges this by promoting critical examination of dominant economic narratives and advocating for alternative indicators of well-being that prioritise ecological sustainability and social equity (Nevasto, 2024). Moreover, Critical Theory's emphasis on the role of ideology in legitimising and perpetuating social inequality resonates with ESD's focus on the socio-cultural dimensions of sustainability (Weber, 2022). Both perspectives recognise the importance of critically interrogating dominant discourses and power structures that uphold unsustainable and unjust practices (Sultana, 2023). ESD and critical Theory join forces to challenge assumptions about progress. They equip learners to question the status quo and become agents of change (Southworth, 2022; Golden, 2023).

In essence, the convergence of Critical Theory from the Frankfurt School and Education for Sustainable Development represents a potent synthesis of theoretical insight and practical application in the quest for a more just, equitable and sustainable world that challenges the status quo. By drawing upon Critical Theory's critique of capitalist society and ESD's commitment to transformative education, scholars and practitioners can develop holistic approaches to addressing the pressing challenges of our time, from climate change and biodiversity loss to social inequality and economic injustice (Jervis, 2024). This convergence offers a promising framework for reimagining education as a catalyst for social transformation and environmental stewardship in the pursuit of a more sustainable future for all (Baranowski, 2023).

Conclusion

The political, geoeconomic and sustainability implications arising from the critical lens on economic progress and the analysis of capitalist dominance are crucial for building a sustainable future. From this perspective, we recognise that the global power structure, often dominated by capitalist interests from the Global North, has significant impacts on the sustainable development prospects of the Global South (Fukuda-Parr & Muchhala, 2020). This dominance is reflected in exploitative economic practices, which perpetuate social inequalities, environmental degradation and economic dependence. In this context, Education for Sustainable Development emerges as a crucial variable for transforming these realities. ESD plays a fundamental role in building a more equitable and environmentally conscious world by empowering individuals with the knowledge, skills and values needed to question existing power structures and promote fairer and more sustainable alternatives (Opoku et al., 2024). Furthermore, a critical lens on economic progress highlights the need to rethink dominant economic paradigms, which often prioritise quantitative economic growth over human well-being and environmental sustainability. This implies the promotion of more inclusive economic models, which value not only material development but also social justice, economic equality and respect for planetary limits (Edwards, 2021). The political implications of these analyses emphasise the importance of strengthening the economies of the Global South and promoting their autonomy and sustainable development. This requires implementing policies that value economic diversity and promote resilience against external shocks, rather than simply reproducing economic models imposed by the Global North. Another crucial point is the need for a more holistic and inclusive approach to economic development, which takes into account not only GDP growth but also human well-being, social equality and environmental sustainability. This implies the strengthening of democratic institutions and the effective participation of citizens in the formulation of economic policies that directly affect them (Meyerrose, 2024).

Therefore, the political, geoeconomic and sustainability implications highlight the urgency of a systemic shift towards a more holistic and balanced approach to development. This requires not only fairer and more sustainable economic policies, but also a global commitment to promoting education and building societies that are more conscious and engaged in the search for a truly sustainable future for all. In this context, ESD has emerged as a crucial variable for the transformation of these realities, empowering individuals with the knowledge, skills and values necessary to question existing power structures and promote fairer and more sustainable alternatives. Furthermore, a critical lens on economic progress has highlighted the need to rethink dominant economic paradigms, prioritising quantitative economic growth, human well-being, social justice and environmental sustainability.

In this context, it is worth highlighting the synergy between the Frankfurt School's thinking and the challenges of our contemporary era, as its critical social perspective offers valuable insights into the political, geoeconomic and sustainability implications of our days. Faced with global challenges such as growing socio-economic inequality, environmental degradation and humanitarian crises, the urgency for systemic change and a more holistic approach to development becomes increasingly evident. The critical perspective of the Frankfurt School invites us to question dominant economic paradigms, which tend to prioritise quantitative growth to the detriment of human well-being, social justice and environmental sustainability. When analysing the political implications, the Frankfurt School highlights the need to rethink structures of power and governance in order to promote a more equitable distribution of resources and opportunities. In geoeconomic terms, the importance of an approach that takes into account the interconnections between global economic systems and local realities is emphasised, recognising development disparities and their ramifications for global stability. With regard to sustainability, the Frankfurt School highlights the unsustainability of the economic growth model based on the unlimited exploitation of natural resources and the externalisation of environmental and social costs. Instead, it proposes a vision that integrates environmental and social concerns at the core of economic policies, prioritising the quality of life of communities and the preservation of ecosystems. Thus, the critical social perspective of the Frankfurt School is aligned with the pressing need to rethink dominant economic paradigms, promoting a more balanced and sustainable vision of development. This implies a profound transformation in political, economic and social structures, aiming to build a more fair, inclusive and environmentally conscious society.

The political implications revealed through the analysis of the ideas of thinkers from the Global South, such as Celso Furtado, are vast and significant. First, these analyses highlight the urgent need to reshape global power structures, which have historically favoured the Global North over the Global South. These theories provide a solid foundation for more equitable and inclusive policies by challenging dominant narratives and proposing alternatives to traditional economic thinking. Therefore, the findings of this study point to the urgency of systemic change towards a more holistic and balanced approach to development. This requires not only fairer and more sustainable economic policies, but also a global commitment to promoting critical education and building societies that are more conscious and engaged in the search for a genuinely sustainable future for all. By facing the challenges posed by capitalist dominance and promoting a more inclusive and sustainable vision of development, we can create a more fair, equitable and environmentally conscious world for present and future generations.

References

Adorno, T. W. (1973). *Negative dialectics* (Issue 101, p. 368). Continuum.

Adorno, T. W. (2021). Late capitalism or industrial society? In *Modern German Sociology* (pp. 232–247). Routledge.

Adorno, T. W., & Bernstein, J. M. (2001). *The culture industry: Selected essays on mass culture*. Routledge London; WorldCat.

Adorno, T. W., & Horkheimer, M. (2019). The culture industry: Enlightenment as mass deception. In *Philosophers on Film from Bergson to Badiou: A Critical Reader* (pp. 80–96). Columbia University Press.

Araujo, A. L. Z. D. (2022). Celso Furtado's transdisciplinary view on economic development. *Brazilian Journal of Political Economy*, *42*, 345–363.

Bachmann, V., & Moisio, S. (2020). Towards a constructive critical geopolitics–Inspirations from the Frankfurt School of critical Theory. *Environment and Planning C: Politics and Space*, *38*(2), 251–268.

Baranowski, M. (2023). Critical Theory of the energy transformation: Sociology's approach. *Society Register*, *7*(4), 7–20. https://doi.org/10.14746/sr.2023.7.4.01

Barua, S. (2020). Financing sustainable development goals: A review of challenges and mitigation strategies. *Business Strategy & Development*, *3*(3), 277–293. https://doi.org/10.1002/bsd2.94

Bello, M. B. (2023). An Understanding of Paulo Freire's" Pedagogy of the Oppressed". *Canadian Journal of Family and Youth/Le Journal Canadien de Famille et de La Jeunesse*, *15*(1), 225–231.

Berkowitz, R. (2022). School Matters: The Contribution of Positive School Climate to Equal Educational Opportunities among Ethnocultural Minority Students. *Youth & Society*, *54*(3), 372–396. https://doi.org/10.1177/0044118X20970235

Bhambra, G. K. (2021). Decolonizing Critical Theory?: Epistemological Justice, Progress, Reparations. *Critical Times*, *4*(1), 73–89. https://doi.org/10.1215/26410478-8855227

Biermann, F., & Kalfagianni, A. (2020). Planetary justice: A research framework. *Earth System Governance*, *6*, 100049. https://doi.org/10.1016/j.esg.2020.100049

Bilgin, P. (2023). Critical Theory. In *Security Studies* (pp. 67–81). Routledge.

Bohman, J., Flynn, J., & Celikates, R. (2021). Critical Theory. In E. N. Zalta (Ed.), *The Stanford Encyclopedia of Philosophy* (Spring 2021). Metaphysics Research Lab, Stanford University. https://plato.stanford.edu/archives/spr2021/entries/critical-theory/

Borja, B. (2021). *Chapter 3 Controversy on the Economic History of Brazil: Roberto Simonsen, Caio Prado Jr. And Celso Furtado* (pp. 80–110). Brill. https://doi.org/10.1163/9789004500563_005

Bresser-Pereira, L. C., & Oreiro, J. L. (2024). A brief history of development theory. From Schumpeter and Prebisch to new developmentalism. *Brazilian Journal of Political Economy*, *44*(1), 5–28. https://doi.org/10.1590/0101-31572024-3604

Brinkmann, U., Heiland, H., & Seeliger, M. (2022). Corporate Public Spheres between Refeudalization and Revitalization. *Theory, Culture & Society*, *39*(4), 75–90. https://doi.org/10.1177/02632764221104694

Brundtland, G. H., Khalid, M. et al. (1987). *Our common future*. Oxford University Press, Oxford, GB.

Brunkhorst, H. (2024). Cultural industry in the age of post-truth democracy. *Philosophy & Social Criticism*, *50*(1), 28–42. https://doi.org/10.1177/01914537231215676

Caldentey, E. P., & Vernengo, M. (2022). Varieties of peripheral capitalism: On the institutional foundations of economic backwardness. *Review of Keynesian Economics*, *10*(2), 242–263.

Cardiff, P., Polczynska, M., & Brown, T. (2024). Higher education curriculum design for sustainable development: Towards a transformative approach. *International Journal of Sustainability in Higher Education*, *ahead-of-print* (ahead-of-print). https://doi.org/10.1108/IJSHE-06-2023-0255

Carstensen, M. B., & Emmenegger, P. (2023). Education as social policy: New tensions in maturing knowledge economies. *Social Policy & Administration*, *57*(2), 109–121. https://doi.org/10.1111/spol.12888

Casati, P., Moner-Girona, M., Khaleel, S. I., Szabo, S., & Nhamo, G. (2023). Clean energy access as an enabler for social development: A multidimensional analysis for Sub-Saharan Africa. *Energy for Sustainable Development*, *72*, 114–126. https://doi.org/10.1016/j.esd.2022.12.003

Cheng, Y., Liu, H., Wang, S., Cui, X., & Li, Q. (2021). Global Action on SDGs: Policy Review and Outlook in a Post-Pandemic Era. *Sustainability*, *13*(11). https://doi.org/10.3390/su13116461

Chilcote, R. H., & Vasconcelos, J. S. (2022). Introduction: Whither Development Theory? *Latin American Perspectives*, *49*(1), 4–17. https://doi.org/10.1177/0094582X211070020

Cluley, R., & Parker, M. (2023). Critical Theory in use: Organizing the Frankfurt School. *Human Relations*, *76*(11), 1689–1713. https://doi.org/10.1177/00187267221111219

Colón-Flores, N. de J., Vargas-Martínez, M. R., Tavarez-De Henríquez, J. C., & Domínguez Valerio, C. M. (2023). Environmental, Social and Economic Attitudes and Sustainable Knowledge on the Sustainable Behaviour of Engineering Students: An Analysis Based on Attitudes towards Teachers. *Sustainability*, *15*(18). https://doi.org/10.3390/su151813537

Crawford, E. O., & Jones, M. (2024). "It's Not a Challenge, It's an Opportunity": Empowering Children to Create a Sustainable Future. In *Science, Technology, Engineering, Arts, and Mathematics (STEAM) Education in the Early Years* (pp. 239–253). Routledge.

da Motta e Albuquerque, E. (2023). The Interplay Between Expansionary and Assimilatory Forces. In *Technological Revolutions and the Periphery: Understanding Global Development Through Regional Lenses* (pp. 193–214). Springer International Publishing. https://doi.org/10.1007/978-3-031-43436-5_8

Danijela Stojanović, S. M., Bogdanović, Z., Petrović, L., & Labus, A. (2023). Empowering learning process in secondary education using pervasive technologies. *Interactive Learning Environments*, *31*(2), 779–792. https://doi.org/10.1080/10494820.2020.1806886

Dodd, S., Lage-Arias, S., Berglund, K., Jack, S., Hytti, U., & Verduijn, K. (2022). Transforming enterprise education: Sustainable pedagogies of hope and social justice. *Entrepreneurship & Regional Development*, *34*(7–8), 686–700. https://doi.org/10.1080/08985626.2022.2071999

Doré, N. I., & Teixeira, A. A. (2022). Brazil's economic growth and real (div) convergence from a very long-term perspective (1822-2019): An historical appraisal. *Brazilian Journal of Political Economy*, *42*, 934–956.

Duobliené, L., Kaire, S., & Vaitekaitis, J. (2023). Education for the future: Applying concepts from the new materialist discourse to UNESCO and OECD publications. *The Journal of Environmental Education*, *54*(3), 213–224. https://doi.org/10.1080/00958964.2023.2188576

Durey, M. J. (2023). Cultural Work. In *Art Work: Cities, Identities, and Cultural Work* (pp. 61–96). Springer Nature Singapore. https://doi.org/10.1007/978-981-99-5555-8_3

Edwards, M. G. (2021). The growth paradox, sustainable development, and business strategy. *Business Strategy and the Environment*, *30*(7), 3079–3094. https://doi.org/10.1002/bse.2790

Fettes, M., & Blenkinsop, S. (2023). Designing Education for Eco-Social-Cultural Change. In *Education as the Practice of Eco-Social-Cultural Change* (pp. 21–56). Springer Nature Switzerland. https://doi.org/10.1007/978-3-031-45834-7_2

Fischer, G., Lundin, J., & Lindberg, J. O. (2020). Rethinking and reinventing learning, education and collaboration in the digital age—From creating technologies to transforming cultures. *The International Journal of Information and Learning Technology*, *37*(5), 241–252. https://doi.org/10.1108/IJILT-04-2020-0051

Freire, P. (1970). *Pedagogy of the Oppressed* (M. B. Ramos, D. P. Macedo, & I. Shor, Eds.). Bloomsbury Academic.

Frumer, N. (2023). "A False Classless Society": Adorno's social Theory revisited. *Philosophy & Social Criticism*, *49*(10), 1200–1219. https://doi.org/10.1177/01914537221093720

Fu, H., & Gao, Y. (2024). What makes higher education contribute to high-quality economic development—A synergy effect analysis based on scale, structure and quality elements. *Applied Mathematics and Nonlinear Sciences*, *9*(1). https://doi.org/10.2478/amns.2023.2.01370

Fukuda-Parr, S., & Muchhala, B. (2020). The Southern origins of sustainable development goals: Ideas, actors, aspirations. *World Development*, *126*, 104706. https://doi.org/10.1016/j.worlddev.2019.104706

Furtado, C., De Aguiar, R. W., & Drysdale, E. C. (1964). *Development and underdevelopment*. University of California Press Berkeley; WorldCat.

Golden, B. (2023). Enabling critical thinking development in higher education through the use of a structured planning tool. *Irish Educational Studies*, *42*(4), 949–969. https://doi.org/10.1080/03323315.2023.2258497

Grimwade, R. (2022). Plastic eschatology: On the foundations of Marcuse's philosophical anthropology. *Philosophy & Social Criticism*, *48*(8), 1140–1173. https://doi.org/10.1177/0191453721999689

Gunderson, R. (2021). Things Are the Way They Are: A Typology of Reification. *Sociological Perspectives*, *64*(1), 127–150. https://doi.org/10.1177/0731121420921891

Habermas, J. (1989). *The Structural Transformation of the Public Sphere: An Inquiry into a Category of Bourgeois Society*. Polity Press.

Habermas, J. (2022). Reflections and Hypotheses on a Further Structural Transformation of the Political Public Sphere. *Theory, Culture & Society*, *39*(4), 145–171. https://doi.org/10.1177/02632764221112341

Hamadi, M., & El-Den, J. (2024). A conceptual research framework for sustainable digital learning in higher education. *Research and Practice in Technology Enhanced Learning*, *19*, 1–25. https://doi.org/10.58459/rptel.2024.19001

Hayden, A., & Dasilva, C. (2022). The wellbeing economy: Possibilities and limits in bringing sufficiency from the margins into the mainstream. *Frontiers in Sustainability*, *3*, 966876.

Held, D. (2004). *Introduction to Critical Theory Horkheimer to Habermas*. Polity Press. Kindle Edition.

Hill, D. (2021). Neo-liberalism and hegemony revisited. In *Marxism, Neoliberalism, and Intelligent Capitalism* (pp. 77–92). Routledge.

Hofmann, M. (2021). Theoretical and practical influences of Habermas's global academic best seller: Structural transformation of the public sphere in the United States. *Kybernetes*, *50*(4), 955–968. https://doi.org/10.1108/K-10-2020-0646

Hopkins, C. (2013). Educating for Sustainability: An Emerging Purpose of Education. *Kappa Delta Pi Record*, *49*(3), 122–125. https://doi.org/10.1080/00228958.2013.819193

Hopkins, C. A., Michelsen, G., Salīte, I., Siegmund, A., Wagner, D. A., Yokoi, A., & Tilleczek, K. (2020). Sustainability as a purpose on the new path of learning for the future. *Humanistic Futures of Learning: Perspectives from UNESCO Chairs and UNITWIN Networks*, 58–62.

Hughes, J., & Loader, R. (2023). Shared education: A case study in social cohesion. *Research Papers in Education*, *38*(3), 305–327. https://doi.org/10.1080/02671522.2021.1961303

Hussain, K., Aman, N., Noor, N., & Shah, Z. W. (2024). Education for Sustainable Development (ESD): Pedagogical Approaches that Make a Difference. *International Journal of Social Science Archives (IJSSA)*, *7*(1), 106–112.

Ibsen, M. F. (2023). 27Max Horkheimer and the Original Paradigm of Critical Theory. In *A Critical Theory of Global Justice: The Frankfurt School and World Society*. Oxford University Press. https://doi.org/10.1093/oso/9780192864123.003.0002

Jansen, P.-E., & Engel, I. (2023). Leo Löwenthal and Herbert Marcuse: Analysis of the Enemy and Volumes from the Marcuse Archive. In I. Aubert & M. Nobre (Eds.), *The Archives of Critical Theory* (pp. 203–215). Springer International Publishing. https://doi.org/10.1007/978-3-031-36585-0_14

Jervis, R. (2024). Climate change, critical Theory and economic democracy: 'Small is Beautiful' and the challenge to growth. *European Journal of Social Theory*, 13684310241231227. https://doi.org/10.1177/13684310241231227

Karalus, A. et al. (2022). Some accelerationist remarks on Marcuse's drives theory and his dialectics of civilization. *Analiza i Egzystencja: Czasopismo Filozoficzne*, *59*, 29–56.

Khandizaji, A., & Caputi, M. (2021). The Culture Industry: Adorno and the Frankfurt School. In *David Riesman and Critical Theory: Autonomy Instead of Emancipation* (pp. 115–133). Springer International Publishing. https://doi.org/10.1007/978-3-030-78869-8_4

Kioupi, V., & Voulvoulis, N. (2019). Education for Sustainable Development: A Systemic Framework for Connecting the SDGs to Educational Outcomes. *Sustainability*, *11*(21). https://doi.org/10.3390/su11216104

Kitagawa, F., & Vidmar, M. (2023). Strategic intelligence for the future of places: Enabling inclusive economic growth through the Opportunity Areas Analysis Tool. *Regional Studies*, *57*(4), 656–669. https://doi.org/10.1080/00343404.2022.2045267

Kite, V., & Park, S. (2024). Context matters: Secondary science teachers' integration of process-based, unplugged computational thinking into science curriculum. *Journal of Research in Science Teaching*, *61*(1), 203–227. https://doi.org/10.1002/tea.21883

Klapper, R. G., & Fayolle, A. (2023). A transformational learning framework for sustainable entrepreneurship education: The power of Paulo Freire's educational model. *The International Journal of Management Education*, *21*(1), 100729. https://doi.org/10.1016/j.ijme.2022.100729

Kohl, K., & Hopkins, C. (2022). Reflections of Good Practice of Infusing ESD to Improve Education Outcomes for Indigenous Learners in Light of a Global Pandemic. *Journal of Teacher Education for Sustainability*, *24*(2), 99–112.

Kohl, K., Hopkins, C., Barth, M., Michelsen, G., Dlouhá, J., Razak, D. A., Abidin Bin Sanusi, Z., & Toman, I. (2022). A whole-institution approach towards sustainability: A crucial aspect of higher education's individual and collective engagement with the SDGs and beyond. *International Journal of Sustainability in Higher Education*, *23*(2), 218–236. https://doi.org/10.1108/IJSHE-10-2020-0398

Kopnina, H. (2020). Education for the future? Critical evaluation of education for sustainable development goals. *The Journal of Environmental Education*, *51*(4), 280–291. https://doi.org/10.1080/00958964.2019.1710444

Korstenbroek, T. (2021). Rethinking the public sphere in an age of radical-right populism: A case for building an empathetic public sphere. *Communication Theory*, *32*(1), 68–87. https://doi.org/10.1093/ct/qtab005

Ladero, A. C. V. (2020). Marcuse and the Frankfurt School: Understanding the Function of Critique and His Critique of Society. *SABTON: Multidisciplinary Research Journal*, *2*(1), 9–25.

Larsen, H. (2021). The public sphere and Habermas: Reflections on the current state of Theory in public library research. *Journal of Documentation*, *77*(1), 251–258. https://doi.org/10.1108/JD-05-2020-0075

Lenton, T. M., & Scheffer, M. (2024). Spread of the cycles: A feedback perspective on the Anthropocene. *Philosophical Transactions of the Royal Society B: Biological Sciences*, *379*(1893), 20220254. https://doi.org/10.1098/rstb.2022.0254

Lichtenstein, E. B. (2023). Adorno, Marx, and abstract domination. *Philosophy & Social Criticism*, *49*(8), 998–1023. https://doi.org/10.1177/01914537211059508

Lordkipanidze, R. (2023). New understanding of law of supply and demand and perfect economic competition for effective economic growth and political systems. *Theoretical Economics Letters*, *13*(5), 1152–1158.

Loureiro, P., Rugitsky, F., & Saad-Filho, A. (2021). Celso Furtado and the Myth of Economic Development: Rethinking Development from Exile. *Review of Political Economy*, *33*(1), 28–43.

Lv, M., Zhang, H., Georgescu, P., Li, T., & Zhang, B. (2022). Improving Education for Innovation and Entrepreneurship in Chinese Technical Universities: A Quest for Building a Sustainable Framework. *Sustainability*, *14*(2). https://doi.org/10.3390/su14020595

Maksymiv, Y., Yakubiv, V., Pylypiv, N., Hryhoruk, I., Piatnychuk, I., & Popadynets, N. (2021). Strategic Challenges for Sustainable Governance of the Bioeconomy: Preventing Conflict between SDGs. *Sustainability*, *13*(15). https://doi.org/10.3390/su13158308

Maley, T. (2021). The Relevance of Herbert Marcuse's Thought Today: Or the Historical Fate of Bourgeois Democracy in and Beyond the Neoliberal Era. *Theory, Culture & Society*, *38*(7–8), 107–129. https://doi.org/10.1177/02632764211051419

Marcuse, H. (1978). *The aesthetic dimension: Toward a critique of Marxist aesthetics* (Vol. 595). Beacon Press.

Marcuse, H. (2002). *One-dimensional man: Studies in the ideology of advanced industrial society* (New ed). Routledge London; WorldCat.

Mello Filho, M. S. B. de. (2023). Economic Development as a Social Process of Multiple Space-Time Scales. *Organizações & Sociedade*, *30*(106), 428–447. https://doi.org/10.1590/1984-92302023v30n0015EN

Meyerrose, A. M. (2024). Building strong executives and weak institutions: How European integration contributes to democratic backsliding. *The Review of International Organizations*, *19*(2), 307–343. https://doi.org/10.1007/s11558-023-09507-2

Nevasto, J. (2024). Critique and its foundations: On critical realism and the Frankfurt School. *Journal of Critical Realism*, *23*(2), 1–18. https://doi.org/10.1080/14767430.2023.2301276

Nikolaidis, A. C. (2023). Structural white ignorance and education for racial justice. *Theory and Research in Education*, *21*(1), 52–70. https://doi.org/10.1177/14778785231162106

O'Kane, C. (2021). Reification and the Critical Theory of Contemporary Society. *Critical Historical Studies*, *8*(1), 57–86. https://doi.org/10.1086/713522

O'Mahony, P. (2021). Habermas and the public sphere: Rethinking a key theoretical concept. *European Journal of Social Theory*, *24*(4), 485–506. https://doi.org/10.1177/1368431020983224

Opoku, A., Ekung, S., Kugblenu, G., & Mushtaha, E. S. N. (2024). Chapter 10: Education for sustainable development, the built environment, and the sustainable development goals. In *The Elgar Companion to the Built Environment and the Sustainable Development Goals* (pp. 178–194). Edward Elgar Publishing. https://doi.org/10.4337/9781035300037.00019

Orr, D. W. (2020). Democracy and the (missing) politics in environmental education. *The Journal of Environmental Education*, *51*(4), 270–279. https://doi.org/10.1080/00958964.2020.1753004

Orsolin-Teixeira, F., Arruda Coronel, D., & Oreiro, J. L. (2024). Income distribution and development: Celso Furtado's Theory in a context of global economic changes and its proximity to neo(post)-Kaleckian literature. *PSL Quarterly Review*, *76*(307), 337–351. https://doi.org/10.13133/2037-3643/18411

Øversveen, E. (2022). Capitalism and alienation: Towards a Marxist theory of alienation for the 21st century. *European Journal of Social Theory*, *25*(3), 440–457. https://doi.org/10.1177/13684310211021579

Palestini, S. (2023). The Dependency Research Programme: Its Latin American Origins and Global Contemporary Applications. In *Oxford Research Encyclopedia of International Studies*.

Rama, J. (2022). On Celso Furtado and the French influences found in his development economics. *Review of Evolutionary Political Economy*, *3*(2), 293–318. https://doi.org/10.1007/s43253-021-00055-2

Rama, J., & Hall, J. (2021). Raúl Prebisch and the evolving uses of 'centre-periphery' in economic analysis. *Review of Evolutionary Political Economy*, *2*(2), 315–332. https://doi.org/10.1007/s43253-021-00036-5

Reeves, C., & Sinnicks, M. (2023). Needs, creativity and care: Adorno and the future of work. *Organization*, *30*(5), 851–872. https://doi.org/10.1177/13505084221145592

Reitz, C. (2021). Herbert Marcuse Today: On Ecological Destruction, Neofascism, White Supremacy, Hate Speech, Racist Police Killings, and the Radical Goals of Socialism. *Theory, Culture & Society*, *38*(7–8), 87–106. https://doi.org/10.1177/02632764211050673

Reynolds, I. (2023). The critique of social reason in the Popper–Adorno debate. *History of the Human Sciences*, *36*(3–4), 260–282. https://doi.org/10.1177/09526951221146657

Rockström, J. (2015). Bounding the planetary future: Why we need a great transition. *Great Transition Initiative*, *9*, 1–13.

Rockström, J., Gupta, J., Lenton, T. M., Qin, D., Lade, S. J., Abrams, J. F., Jacobson, L., Rocha, J. C., Zimm, C., Bai, X. et al. (2021). Identifying a safe and just corridor for people and the planet. *Earth's Future*, *9*(4), e2020EF001866.

Roth, B. (2023). The welfare state between juridification and commodification: How the Frankfurt School gave up on economic democracy. *European Law Open*, *2*(2), 386–404. https://doi.org/10.1017/elo.2023.39
Saith, A. (2023). Early post-Keynesian journeys from Cambridge into development: Bridges and boundaries. *The Economic and Labour Relations Review*, *34*(2), 212–232. https://doi.org/10.1017/elr.2023.19
Salonen, A. O., Laininen, E., Hämäläinen, J., & Sterling, S. (2023). A Theory of Planetary Social Pedagogy. *Educational Theory*, *73*(4), 615–637. https://doi.org/10.1111/edth.12588
Sarma, S., Attaran, S., & Attaran, M. (2024). Sustainable entrepreneurship: Factors influencing opportunity recognition and exploitation. *The International Journal of Entrepreneurship and Innovation*, *25*(1), 56–69. https://doi.org/10.1177/14657503221093007
Seeliger, M., & Sevignani, S. (2022). A New Structural Transformation of the Public Sphere? An Introduction. *Theory, Culture & Society*, *39*(4), 3–16. https://doi.org/10.1177/02632764221109439
Soon, V. (2021). Social structural explanation. *Philosophy Compass*, *16*(10), e12782. https://doi.org/10.1111/phc3.12782
Southworth, J. (2022). Bridging critical thinking and transformative learning: The role of perspective-taking. *Theory and Research in Education*, *20*(1), 44–63. https://doi.org/10.1177/14778785221090853
Sterling, S. (2011). Transformative learning and sustainability: Sketching the conceptual ground. *Learning and Teaching in Higher Education*, *5*(11), 17–33.
Sterling, S. (2021). Concern, Conception, and Consequence: Re-thinking the Paradigm of Higher Education in Dangerous Times. *Frontiers in Sustainability*, *2*. https://doi.org/10.3389/frsus.2021.743806
Stilwell, F. (2023). The Future for Political Economy: Towards Unity in Diversity? *Review of Political Economy*, *35*(1), 189–210. https://doi.org/10.1080/09538259.2022.2063515
Subramony, M., & Rosenbaum, M. S. (2024). SDG commentary: Economic services for work and growth for all humans. *Journal of Services Marketing*, *38*(2), 190–216. https://doi.org/10.1108/JSM-05-2023-0201
Sultana, F. (2023). Whose growth in whose planetary boundaries? Decolonising planetary justice in the Anthropocene. *Geo: Geography and Environment*, *10*(2), e00128. https://doi.org/10.1002/geo2.128
Toniolo, S., Pieretto, C., & Camana, D. (2023). Improving sustainability in communities: Linking the local scale to the concept of sustainable development. *Environmental Impact Assessment Review*, *101*, 107126. https://doi.org/10.1016/j.eiar.2023.107126
Treacy, M. (2022). Dependency Theory and the Critique of Neodevelopmentalism in Latin America. *Latin American Perspectives*, *49*(1), 218–236. https://doi.org/10.1177/0094582X211066531
Tunji-Olayeni, P. F., Kajimo-Shakantu, K., Ayodele, T. O., & Philips, B. I. (2023). Students' perception of sustainable construction: Accelerating progress towards construction education for sustainable development. *International Journal of Construction Management*, *23*(2), 276–285. https://doi.org/10.1080/15623599.2020.1861500
Türkeş, M. (2024). The role of sustainability and sustainable development in climate change mitigation and adaptation. *Sustainable Social Development*, *2*(1). https://doi.org/10.54517/ssd.v2i1.2407
UNESCO. (2012). *Education for sustainable development: Building a better, fairer world for the 21st century*. https://unesdoc.unesco.org/ark:/48223/pf0000216673
UNESCO. (2014). *Sustainable Development Begins With Education—How Education Can Contribute to the Proposed Post-2015 Goals.*
UNESCO. (2018). *Issues and trends in Education for Sustainable Development*. UNESCO Publishing.

United Nations. (2015). *Transforming our world: The 2030 Agenda for Sustainable Development* [Technical Report]. UN. sustainabledevelopment.un.org

United Nations. (2020). *Education for Sustainable Development A roadmap*. https://www.gcedclearinghouse.org/sites/default/files/resources/200782eng.pdf

United Nations. (2023). *World Social Report 2023—Leaving No One Behind in an Ageing World*. United Nations Department of Economic and Social Affairs. https://social.desa.un.org/sites/default/files/publications/2023-02/WorldSocialReport2023.pdf

Uralovich, K. S., Toshmamatovich, T. U., Kubayevich, K. F., Sapaev, I., Saylaubaevna, S. S., Beknazarova, Z., & Khurramov, A. (2023). A primary factor in sustainable development and environmental sustainability is environmental education. *Caspian Journal of Environmental Sciences*, *21*(4), 965–975.

Vare, P., Lausselet, N., & Rieckmann, M. (2022). Closing Thoughts: The Role of Educator Competences for ESD in Turbulent Times. In P. Vare, N. Lausselet, & M. Rieckmann (Eds.), *Competences in Education for Sustainable Development: Critical Perspectives* (pp. 195–199). Springer International Publishing. https://doi.org/10.1007/978-3-030-91055-6_23

Verhelst, D., Vanhoof, J., & Petegem, P. V. (2023). School effectiveness for education for sustainable development (ESD): What characterizes an ESD-effective school organization? *Educational Management Administration & Leadership*, *51*(2), 502–525. https://doi.org/10.1177/1741143220985196

Verovšek, P. J. (2021). The philosopher as engaged citizen: Habermas on the role of the public intellectual in the modern democratic public sphere. *European Journal of Social Theory*, *24*(4), 526–544. https://doi.org/10.1177/13684310211003192

Vesterinen, M., & Ratinen, I. (2024). Sustainability competences in primary school education – a systematic literature review. *Environmental Education Research*, *30*(1), 56–67. https://doi.org/10.1080/13504622.2023.2170984

Višić, M. et al. (2023). Onwards and Upwards to the Kingdom of Beauty and Love. Herbert Marcuse's Trajectory to Socialism. *Filozofija i Društvo*, *34*(1), 170–194.

Walker, M. A. (2022). Dimensionality Flattened. In *Spatializing Marcuse* (pp. 14–36). Bristol University Press. https://doi.org/10.51952/9781529211115.ch002

Weber, W. (2022). Exploring the Cultural Mechanics of Social Inequality and Global Cultural Interdependence. *Orbis*, *66*(1), 111–127. https://doi.org/10.1016/j.orbis.2021.11.009

Welsh, J. (2020). Struggling beyond the paradigm of Neoliberalism. *Thesis Eleven*, *158*(1), 58–80. https://doi.org/10.1177/0725513619888667

Wheeler, K. (2023). Educating children as sustainable citizen-consumers: A qualitative content analysis of sustainability education resources. *Journal of Moral Education*, *52*(4), 453–473. https://doi.org/10.1080/03057240.2022.2159344

Wildemeersch, D., Håkansson, M., & Læssøe, J. (2023). No time to waste? Dealing with 'urgency' in environmental and sustainability education. *Environmental Education Research*, *29*(10), 1417–1429. https://doi.org/10.1080/13504622.2023.2213412

Žalėnienė, I., & Pereira, P. (2021). Higher education for sustainability: A global perspective. *Geography and Sustainability*, *2*(2), 99–106.

Zhang, C., Waris, U., Qian, L., Irfan, M., & Rehman, M. A. (2024). Unleashing the dynamic linkages among natural resources, economic complexity, and sustainable economic growth: Evidence from G-20 countries. *Sustainable Development*. https://doi.org/10.1002/sd.2845

Zhang, T., Shaikh, Z. A., Yumashev, A. V., & Chłąd, M. (2020). Applied Model of E-Learning in the Framework of Education for Sustainable Development. *Sustainability*, *12*(16). https://doi.org/10.3390/su12166420

3 Geoeconomics

Impact on Sustainable Development Goals and Corporate Social Responsibility

Robert Taylor

Asian and European companies have, under the ostensible behest of government, espoused policies of Corporate Social Responsibility (CSR) and its concomitant, Environmental Social Goals (ESG). Corporate Social Responsibility is a self-regulatory business model practised by both large and, increasingly, small companies. It mandates that business becomes socially accountable to its stakeholders for its impact on the wider community, with a focus on all economic, social and environmental aspects. Successful business is thus to be based on sustainable growth, positively impacting on both the physical and social environments. In its definition and practice Environmental, Social and Governance (ESG) follows similar principles. Such commitment, however, is currently being vitiated, as moves towards a green transition and fulfilment of the wider remit face serious challenges.

The war in Ukraine has put pressure on global food resources, disadvantaging in price terms, especially developing countries, given that the former country is a major grain producer. In addition, the Russian leader, Putin, has leverage on EU countries' gas supplies, and the government of the United Kingdom is being forced to consider the exploitation of fossil fuels. The implications are global. Likewise, the Ukrainian conflict has compelled Asian countries to prioritise energy security over climate goals. South Korea and Japan are undertaking further forays into nuclear energy. Currently, China is the world's biggest producer of greenhouse gas, accounting for 28% of global emissions, compared with about 15% for the United States and 1% for the United Kingdom, coal producing 70% of China's electricity. The Chinese have, however, seen the potential of renewables, by investing heavily in hydroelectric, wind and solar sources. In 2021, they were building major carbon capture and storage plants, a key to a decarbonised future. The aim is to reach zero emissions by 2060. China is thus a forerunner in renewable energy, ultimately seeking to move away from fossil fuel dependence. Despite these ambitious targets, however, the Chinese have been importing more fossil fuels from Russia, and China's government has ordered coal mines to increase production (US-China Business Council News Overview (2022e). The China syndrome, can COP 26 still succeed if Xi stays at home? (Spencer, 2021).

DOI: 10.4324/9781032655857-5

In their wider remit, CSR and ESG state the goal of gender equality but in China's case, erstwhile COVID restrictions appear to have slowed progress. There is a discernible tendency towards fewer women at the top of government, and Xi Jinping has emphasised the role of women in the home (US-China Business Council News Overview, 2022g).

Gender equality is considered an important concern of corporate social responsibility and, significantly, in contrast with China, the Asia Pacific Economic Cooperation (APEC) economies, including ASEAN states, whose contributions accounted for 62% of world GDP and 48% of global trade, have taken steps to enhance the role of women in employment.[1] In fact, women in APEC have become almost on par with men in terms of literacy and educational attainment. APEC is continuing to address health-related barriers faced by women in entering, remaining and advancing in employment. There nevertheless remain environmental challenges which impact women, especially in rural areas in Southeast Asia, and a continuing need to empower female business entrepreneurs in the region by enhancing cross-border e-commerce as well as global access (Geeta Rao Gupta, 2024).

A further challenge is presented by the incidence of political polarisation in Europe and elsewhere. This trend towards authoritarian populism can reduce sustainable development's capacity to alleviate climate change globally; governments' attitudes may influence commitment on the part of corporate leaders.

The achievement of sustainable developments will also be heavily influenced by the actions of the Chinese and United States governments. China's economic success since 1978 has been largely determined by the introduction of technology through American and other Western company investors; in fact, this is a condition imposed by Chinese legislation. While the Trump and Biden administrations have reacted to the perceived threat from China by limiting the export to China of technology, particularly that deemed to have military applications, and thus preventing Chinese companies from engaging in industrial activities which present a security risk to the United States, any decoupling of the two economies is fraught with risk, given closely interlinked trade and investment. Nevertheless, as in many advanced industrial fields, like semiconductors, China has benefited from the input of American technology; trading relations between the two countries have become a security issue in the perception of United States legislators, the Biden administration believing that their country's firms are exporting too many semiconductors (chips) and the equipment for manufacturing them, required by China for surveillance programmes like those used against the Uighurs in Xinjiang in addition to applications for advanced weapons systems (Stelzer, 2022a,c).

The danger is also highlighted by Chinese espionage; in addition to Chinese companies and research institutes beholden to the Chinese Communist Party (CCP) and their cooperation in natural security mandated by law, China's United Front Work Department (UFWD) is a fifth column, employing Chinese research students operating in the United States (Williams, 2022).

If the cross-border movement of researchers demonstrates the global transmission of knowledge, similarly in other fields, supply chains know no national boundaries, an example being semiconductors. Significantly, however, although the current semiconductor supply chain involves components from many countries, almost every chip made has a Silicon Valley connection or is made with tools designed and built in California. Yet the global supply chains are geographically dispersed; while design software comes from the United States, it is then sent to Taiwan where chips are manufactured, accounting for 37% of the world's computing power each year. This could account for the stated desire of the CCP leaders to take over Taiwan, if necessary, by force (Miller, 2022).

While semiconductor supply chains may still be dependent on American expertise, China is advantaged in its endowment of and processing of key materials like nickel, cobalt, graphite and lithium, crucial for the production of batteries in the context of the green revolution. Copper, for instance, is necessary for conductivity and lithium keeps batteries lightweight. Rare earths contribute to the chemistry of batteries. Such sources, however, do exist elsewhere and through its International Development and Finance Corporation (IDFC), the United States government has sought globally for metals that contribute to the national security imperative of supply chains. In February 2022, the Biden administration announced measures to galvanise the production and processing of critical materials in the United States itself (Yeomans, and Harter, 2022).

Observers see the measures by both the United States and other governments as evidence of the decoupling of the Chinese and American economies. In 2022 the Biden administration named a team of senior advisors to oversee US$52.7 billion of government spending to boost semiconductor manufacturing and research. Also approved by Congress was a 25% investment tax credit for chip plants, estimated to be worth US$24 billion (US-China Business Council News Overview, 2022d).

This is to boost competitive strength in competition with China; the CCP (China Communist Party) is resolved to enhance such technologies. Furthermore, the United States administration is limiting Chinese access to sensitive sectors in industry, commerce and finance. In October 2022, for example, the United States government banned the transfer of key microchip technologies to Chinese entities, with both military and economic implications. This is designed to thwart Chinese ambitions to dominate the development and production of high-end computing chips crucial for strategically important industries. This action may well, however, provide a further incentive for the Chinese to throw money at their own research and development, which is directed towards both state and military goals (Armstrong, 2022d).

The United States is likely to introduce further export controls to prevent crucial equipment and technology from falling into the hands of China's state-run entities (US-China Business Council News Overview, 2022f).

China's rise is seen by many countries as a regional and global danger. Accordingly, the Biden administration is forging economic ties with Asian regional actors like Taiwan in areas like trade, supply chains and technology export controls, amid growing tensions with China. Given Taiwan's leading role in the supply of advanced semiconductors, export controls beamed at China are deemed crucial, and underlined in a new pact with Taipei to promote bilateral relations in such areas as digital trade, clean energy and labour rights (US-China Business Council News Overview, 2022a).

This pact is crucial because Taiwanese companies make 94% of the thinnest Chinese high-end semiconductors that operate cars, washing machines, rockets and missiles (Sherwell, 2022).

Likewise, some Western companies have been adopting the so-called 'China plus strategy', expanding their operations to other Asian countries like Vietnam and India, thereby reducing their exposure to China as a production base, even though they still have a presence in the lucrative Chinese consumer market. In addition, the COVID pandemic indicated the vulnerability involved in relying on long-distance supply chains; operations in other Asian countries can function as an alternative. Again, there are governmental as well as corporate initiatives. The American government has invested billions of dollars in the semiconductor sector under the terms of the Creating Helpful Incentives to Produce Semiconductors for America Act, 2021. Similarly, the Indian government has sought a US$19 billion proposal to encourage global companies to move factories to their country in the areas of automobiles, electronics, pharmaceuticals and textiles (Lewis, 2022).

Finally, the issue of Chinese market share in individual countries may be raised. Action against Chinese companies investing in and exporting to the United States and elsewhere may include tariffs. Consumers, however, benefit from Chinese goods imports; tariffs will only increase prices.

While these security and economic concerns on the part of the United States and to a lesser extent other Western countries are paramount, there are, of course, wider factors in China losing favour as a trading and investment partner. The authoritarian rule of Xi Jinping at times appears to stress ideological credentials above economic growth by jailing entrepreneurs, insisting on the primacy of CCP cadres in corporate decision-making and engaging, according to observers, in human rights violations. This could potentially deter foreign investors (Stelzer, 2022b).

In response to measures by the United States and its allies, the Chinese have been adopting, an albeit selective, retaliatory stance. Acknowledging China's vulnerability in certain technological areas, the Chinese leaders have sought to enhance independent innovative research. Evidence of this is demonstrated by the launching in 2015 of the 'Made in China 2025' Plan and the introduction of the Artificial Intelligence (AI) Development Plan 2017 which emphasises self-reliance and global leadership in AI by 2030. In the past, Chinese companies have relied almost entirely on underlying systems from the United States and it is estimated by engineers that China is behind America in generative AI by at least a year. To date, prime movers in new technologies in China have been private companies like Alibaba which have also sought to foster global partnership with Southeast Asian countries. The CCP, however, is now tightening its control of the development of supercomputing and AI innovations. This suggests the emergence of a state sector in AI which could in turn impact corporate social responsibility there which differs from its private sector counterparts. Thus, the CCP's role in steering its vast technology industry will be strengthened. These investment policies are thus designed to develop technologies in, say, semiconductors, in order to free China from American tutelage (Stelzer, 2022b; Miller, 2022; National Bureau of Asian Research, 2024; US-China Business Council News Overview, 2024; US-China Business Council News Overview, 2023a).

Nevertheless, in spite of these policies, which suggest tendencies towards decoupling, the Chinese and American economies are likely to remain interlinked, as indicated by current trade and investment flows. The cost of decoupling would be huge. The Boston Consulting Group has estimated that in 2019 American companies derived 5% of their revenue from China, while EU companies derived 11.2% of their sales from that country (Shah, 2022). In fact, United States trade with China continues to grow; by over US$77 billion or 12% between 2019 and 2021, and from 11.3% to 12.1% as a total of United States trade. American and Japanese companies were major investors during the same period (Armstrong, 2022b).

It is concluded, then, that given interlinking, the costs of decoupling are too high for the two protagonists. In addition, however, the Chinese economy faces domestic challenges. The first is demographic, with China still paying the price of the previous one-child policy, even though recently measures have been taken to encourage larger families. One result has been an ageing population, with serious consequences for pension and health insurance provision. Ironically, China has a surfeit of graduates seeking employment but an upgrading of skills is necessary if China is to improve the rate of productivity. These problems have been exacerbated by further economic events.

The collapse of the property company, Evergrande, has brought indebtedness and the reluctance of purchasers to pay mortgages for properties still being built, in spite of state financial measures to alleviate resulting distress. The borrowing limits previously imposed on developers have led to a steep downturn in the property market (US-China Business Council News Overview, 2022j).

Since the end of 2023, however, housing has become a priority, given its role in stimulating growth in a number of other sectors. In response to the ongoing housing crisis, the CCP leadership plans to provide at least one billion yuan in low-cost financing for urban village renovation and affordable housing programmes. To this end, the People's Bank of China is to inject phased funds designed ultimately to enable households to purchase housing. The sale of housing stock will undoubtedly boost the sale of consumer durables, thus stimulating overall consumption, now an integral part of economic strategy (US-China Business Council News Overview, 2023a; Spencer, 2024). The COVID lockdown, of course, reduced consumer spending and confidence. Government policies inadvertently contributed to an economic downturn, bordering on a recession, which is only, as of 2024, showing signs of easing.

A growing private sector encouraged, even though with limitations, by the CCP during the late twentieth and early twenty-first centuries, has played a major role in stimulating economic growth, with private and foreign invested firms, for example, accounting for a large proportion of China's foreign trade. But Xi Jinping has opted for continuing terms as CCP leader and, in line with China's authoritarian tradition, has sought to enhance the role of the state at the expense of the private sector. This is evidenced by the composition of delegates to the Twentieth CCP Congress in 2022. While only 18 of the 2,294 delegates at the congress held executive positions in private companies, 34 executives were at the congress in 2012 and 27 at the 2017 congress. State control is thus being consolidated. There has been an increase in the reported number of CCP committees at private companies in the last ten years. Many of these committees, formed by employees who are CCP members, have been more active in corporate decision-making. Significantly, the declining role of private firms has been evidenced by the fact that their revenues, as a share of total Chinese company revenues, fell in 2021 from that in 2020 (US-China Business Council News Overview, 2022h; US-China Business Council News Overview, 2022i). Furthermore, there has been an increase in censorship, especially regarding the Internet and a clampdown on the private sector of education. The implications for entrepreneurship are clear. The functioning of authoritarian regimes depends on the flow of critical information to their top leadership. It is ominous that the line-up in the Politburo, the top CCP body, has included recently those with less experience relating to the economy. This, in tandem with Xi Jinping's authoritarian style, suggests that there will not be a mechanism to challenge an economic course, the tendency being for colleagues to say what they think the leader would like to hear (US-China Business Council News Overview (2022j).

Finally, the elevation of the foreign minister, Wang Yi, to the Standing Committee of the Politburo, could presage a hard line in China's relations with the United States and other Western countries.

Certainly, the pre-eminence of China's state sector may be seen as in line with Xi Jinping's advocacy of his Common Prosperity Signature economic policy. This is aimed at distributing more of China's wealth to the poor and correlates to the clampdown on wealthy private technology companies. It pledges measures to facilitate prosperity through personal effort; low earners will increase their income, allowing an expanding middle class. Excessive and illicit income will be denied (US-China Business Council News Overview, 2022k).

But, in conclusion, while such nominally egalitarian policies hark back to the Maoist era, China's continuing economic advance may only be furthered by incentives for wealth creation by individuals and participation in a global economy still led by the United States.

The roles accorded by the CCP to state and private enterprises have implications for the practice of CSR and sustainable development, both regionally in Asia and globally.

This brings into focus China's relations with Asian states, informed by the rivalry with the United States, involving such issues as territorial disputes, growing regional economic integration and sustainable development. China's territorial maritime claims in the South China Sea and beyond are being characterised not by direct annexation but by so-called 'grey zone' activities, lying between war and peace. These are being countered by diplomatic and defensive means by other regional claimants like Vietnam, Indonesia and Malaysia. Facing 'grey zone' tactics by China, typified by such thinly veiled threats via naval incursions, the Vietnamese have adopted a defensive posture because, unlike the Chinese, they have neither the power nor even the ambition to provoke maritime confrontation. Accordingly, the use of the Vietnamese maritime militia can only be a tactical short-term action rather than a long-term response to China's maritime aggression. In a sense, the threat has been put on hold, and the Vietnamese have accelerated negotiations with other countries facing similar threats like Malaysia, Indonesia and the Philippines. What is needed is a more unified regional response, ostensibly through ASEAN, seen as the only way that China can be deterred (Nguyen, Khao Giang, 2022).

Similarly, Indonesia has faced 'grey zone' incursions by China which, during the period from August to October 2021, were designed to disrupt oil exploration activities in Indonesian waters, the areas in contention being the Natura Islands and surrounding seas. Response has been the arrest of Chinese militia but really only the problems of maritime fishing have been addressed by Indonesia. Diplomatically, Indonesia has sought international solidarity through the United Nations Convention on the Law of the Sea (UNCLOS) (Supriyanto, 2022). Similarly, Malaysia's response has been to strengthen bilateral relations with other territorial claimants and engage in multilateral diplomacy through ASEAN, a key platform for mediation regarding conflicts in the South China Sea (Krishnan, 2022).

Thus, the perceived China threat necessarily influences the foreign policies of Asian states. There have been a number of moves towards Southeast Asian economic integration which have implications for the defence of individual states against Chinese maritime aggression. These moves, however, do not preclude China's participation in regional affairs, whether in terms of trade or action against climate change, given growing relations with states of the Indo-Pacific, where Chinese companies have a leading position in solar and wind power as well as high voltage transmission lines (Bowin, 2022b). A Chinese diplomatic offensive together with ongoing investment in the economies of the island states have prompted the United States to counter China's influence, especially in Asia. United States policy-makers undoubtedly see the viability of regional economic arrangements as a key to stability against Chinese influence. A case in point is the Regional Comprehensive Economic Partnership (RCEP), conceived to include the United States, under the instigation of the Biden administration, in contrast with its rejection by President Trump. RCEP is a free trade agreement, locking much of the Asia-Pacific region into a bloc containing about 30% of the world's population and representing 30% of global GDP, wrapping major economies into greater interdependence. RCEP also includes China's membership, balanced by South Korea and Japan (Frankopan, 2022; Armstrong, 2022a).

In a similar vein and largely at United States initiative, in June 2022 the Group of Seven (G7) pledged to raise US$600 billion over five years to counter China's Belt and Road project (BRI), with a projection that additional funds could come from such sources as multilateral development banks, other finance institutions and sovereign wealth funds. To counter the BRI initiative, the G7 leaders launched the Global Infrastructure and Investment Scheme targeted, over a five-year period, to help low- and middle-level income countries, especially in Asia, to combat climate change as well as improve global health, gender equality and digital infrastructure, key factors in CSR and ESG (US-China Business Council News Overview, 2022b).

Under the guise of philanthropy, the Chinese have spent hundreds of millions of dollars, making loans to developing countries, usually as part of the BRI initiative, to finance infrastructural development, leading to indebtedness on the part of recipients, a case in point being Sri Lanka, where funds have been used to pay for new highways and ports. These investments may not in the short term yield an economic return and countries like Sri Lanka may face bankruptcy, with the result that China will retain the assets financed (Chu, 2022).

Furthermore, American policy-makers have devised the Indo-Pacific strategy which shares common principles with ASEAN in promoting an open exclusive regional architecture. It is designed to expand cooperation in maritime security, the extension of a digital economy and commitment to environmental protection. The objectives of the Indo-Pacific Economic Framework (IPEF) are supported by its membership, comprising Australia, Brunei, Fiji, India, Indonesia, Japan, South Korea, Malaysia, New Zealand, the Philippines, Thailand and Vietnam (Murphy, 2022; US-China Business Council News Overview; 2022c).

To date, however, ASEAN has had a wider remit than RCEP, the G7 and IPEF, though its concerns are similar, even if its consensus decision-making has often precluded unanimity. The United States Indo-Pacific strategy may well influence ASEAN towards greater adherence to more stringent labour, tax, data privacy and anti-corruption standards, key factors in CSR (Murphy, 2022).

China's assertive role in Asia is not unchallenged, informed as it is by rivalry with the United States. But although ASEAN is often seen as a counterweight to Chinese power, its members as a group have asserted their neutrality in the burgeoning Sino-American conflict. In the physical environmental context, they feel the impact of measures taken by powers like China, the United States and Japan in the battle against climate change. The United States has been supporting Indo-Pacific clean energy cooperation through participation in the QUAD group (Quadrilateral Security Dialogue group), other members of which are Japan, India and Australia. The Japanese have been dominant in developing the Indo-Pacific hydrogen markets aiding their own energy transition and that of the Indo-Pacific states. A similar regional role is being played by South Korea in hydrogen development (Bowin, 2022a; National Bureau of Asian Research, 2024).

Digitalisation is often seen as having a positive impact on the environment by reducing the need for physical transportation. This, however, remains to be proven. Nevertheless, ASEAN has been active in promoting cross-border digitalisation. The regional E-commerce Agreement signed by ASEAN members in 2019 signified the emergence of a digital common market. ASEAN's Model Contractual Clauses for Cross Border Data Transfers, adopted in 2021, was designed to enable ASEAN markets to trade in sensitive data without abrogating national privacy requirements, the argument being that supply chains would become more resilient with an interoperable digital system. In summary, such regional interoperability will facilitate moves towards a digital single market which will in turn increase productivity and promote economic interdependence (Armstrong, 2022c).

Digitalisation, however, is not without its costs in energy consumption. Manufacture of electronic devices in connection with, for example, AI, demands the extensive use of raw materials like nickel, cobalt and graphite, the extension and transportation of which will incur environmental costs. Only if the AI systems become more efficient in combating climate change will benefits exceed costs (Teeratanboodee, 2022).

By way of conclusion, sustainable development CSR and ESG goals are geoeconomic; they transcend national boundaries. Asian and European companies have, under the ostensible behest of governments, been adopting policies of CSR and ESG, mandating accountability to stakeholders, an objective being sustainable development. Such policies were, however, vitiated initially by the effects of the COVID pandemic and latterly by the war in Ukraine, the latter placing pressure on energy and fuel supplies. Political polarisation and populism have also become factors limiting the practices of CSR and ESG. Moreover, this has resulted in growing ambivalence about reducing carbon emissions on the part of the two greatest polluters, China and the United States.

In spite of their Asian regional and global rivalry, the interconnectedness of trade and investment between the two powers precludes decoupling of their economies, and supply chains in any case know no national boundaries. The Chinese, still depending on American technology, nevertheless now, like the United States, seek to develop and protect their own technological innovation. The United States authorities seek to diversify their sources of supply, highlighting, for instance, Taiwan's current role in semiconductor production. Similarly, other Western companies have been adopting the 'China Plus One' Strategy. The Chinese, in prioritising their own innovative research, face a number of challenges relating to demography, the residual effects of the earlier pandemic lockdowns, the collapse of property companies, the relationship between the state and private sectors as well as low productivity. Furthermore, the common prosperity policy faces challenges in its implementation. Finally, Xi Jinping's authoritarian style could impede effective policy decision-making on the part of China's central leadership. Chinese policies impact Asia, the main arena of Sino-American rivalry, where China's 'grey zone' maritime incursions evoke responses from Asian countries. While United States policy-makers have sought to counter China's BRI through such initiatives as the Indo-Pacific Strategy, ASEAN countries have promoted further regional economic integration as a counterweight to Chinese incursions. Under the rubric of such integration comes cross-border digitalisation, designed to improve supply chains through a digital common market, even though given the resulting increased energy consumption, the costs and benefits for sustainable development remain contentious, necessarily influencing the practices of CSR and ESG.

Note

1 ASEAN is the Association for South-East Asian Nations.

References

Armstrong, S. (2022a). The strategic importance of RCEP in Asia, East Asia Forum Weekly Digest, 3 March.

Armstrong, S. (2022b). Trying to unscramble Asia's economic interdependence with China. East Asia Forum Weekly Digest, 11 April.

Armstrong, S. (2022c). Asia's Digital Future, East Asia Forum Weekly Digest, 20 June.

Armstrong, S. (2022d). All Asia's saying give economic peace a chance, East Asia Forum Weekly Digest, 1 November.

Bowin, J. (2022a). Enhancing clean energy cooperation in the Indo-Pacific, National Bureau of Asian Research, Commentary from Clean EDGE Asia, 23 June.

Bowin, J. (2022b). Existing Indo-Pacific energy relationships are dominated by China, National Bureau of Asian Research, Commentary from Clean EDGE Asia, 23 June.

Chu, B. (2022). Sri Lanka's protesters took the palace but China holds the key, Sunday Times, 17 July.

Frankopan, P. (2022). Ignore the doom-mongers of Davos - Putin hasn't torpedoed globalization, Sunday Times, 29 May.

Geeta Rao Gupta (2024). Empowerment during the US host year, APEC 2023, National Bureau of Asian Research, 18 January.

Krishnan, T. (2022). Malaysia's view and response to grey zone conflict in the South China Sea, Rajaratnam School of International Studies, IDSS Paper, no 42/2022, available at publications-rsis-edu-sg@gr-mail1.com

Lewis, G. (2022). Chinese puzzle: time for Western firms to diversify their risks, Sunday Times, 1 May.

Miller, C. (2022). The chip war the West must win, Sunday Times, 9 October.

Murphy, A. M. (2022). The US-ASEAN summit: a new era in relations? National Bureau of Asian Research, 23 May.

National Bureau of Asian Research (2024). China's AI development, accessed 30 January.

Nguyen, Khao Giang, (2022). The Vietnamese maritime militia: myths and realities, Rajaratnam School of International Studies, IDSS Paper, no 40/2022, available at rsis-edu-sg@gr-mail1.com

Shah, O. (2022). Pulling out of Russia is one thing, but what if China outages the West, Sunday Times, 13 March.

Sherwell, P. (2022). Taiwan defies the dragon with hope, pride and parties, Sunday Times, 23 October.

Spencer, B. (2021). The China syndrome, can COP 26 still succeed if Xi stays at home? Sunday Times, 24 October.

Spencer, B. (2024). The Chinese dragon falls to earth, Sunday Times, 11 February.

Stelzer, I. (2022a). China's plan: give 'em enough rope, Sunday Times, 2 January.
Stelzer, I. (2022b). Chinese ways turn investors away, Sunday Times, 2 October.
Stelzer, I. (2022c). Chips on the table in a new trade war, Sunday Times, 23 October.
Supriyanto, R.A. (2022). Indonesia's response to China's grey zone strategy: diplomacy, defence and law enforcement, Rajaratnam School of International Studies, IDSS Paper, no 38/2022.
Teeratanboodee, W. (2022). The environmental impact of military AI; Rajaratnam School of International Studies, IDSS Paper no 39/2022, 15 July.
US-China Business Council News Overview (2022a). US launches initiatives to boost economic ties with Taiwan, 2 June.
US-China Business Council News Overview (2022b). G7 aims to raise $600 billion to counter China's Belt and Road, 27 June.
US-China Business Council News Overview (2022c). US to host virtual meeting on Tuesday of Indo-Pacific trade, economic ministers, Reuters, 25 July.
US-China Business Council News Overview (2022d). US picks team to oversee $52.7 billion in semiconductor funding, Reuters, 20 September.
US-China Business Council News Overview (2022e). What the war in Ukraine means for Asia's climate goals, 3 October.
US-China Business Council News Overview (2022f). Taiwan vows to safeguard interests amid US led Chip4 talks, Nikkei, 5 October.
US-China Business Council News Overview (2022g). Fewer women at the top of government in China, 18 October.
US-China Business Council News Overview (2022h). Corporate China shut out of Xi Jinping's party congress, 20 October.
US-China Business Council News Overview (2022i). In China, the state sector is in; private sector stutters, 24 October.
US-China Business Council News Overview (2022j). China's new slate of top leaders stirs concern of the economy, WSJ, 24 October.
US-China Business Council News Overview (2022k). Xi Jinping's common prosperity policy makes a return, WSJ, 24 October.
US-China Business Council News Overview (2023a). China targets 50% growth in computing power in race against US, Reuters, 10 October.
US-China Business Council News Overview (2023b). China mulls $137 billion of new funds to aid housing market, Bloomberg, 14 October.
US-China Business Council News Overview (2024). AI comes with a twist, New York Times, 20 February.
Williams, I. (2022). China's new spy army has arrived - and we're not fighting back, Sunday Times, 17 July.
Yeomans, J. and Harter, F. (2022). Who owns the earth? Sunday Times, 1 May.

4 Energy Dynamics, Economic Diplomacy and Geopolitical Rivalries

Daniel Rajmil

Introduction

The international landscape is shifting into a complex scenario whereby the different administrations intend to impose their foreign policy goals with their economic interests. It is within this confluence of interests that the economic diplomacy concept emerges. To understand its current role, there is a first need to find out what could be considered a good definition of economic diplomacy. As with much of the social sciences literature, the International Relations discipline and the definition of economic diplomacy and its derivative approaches have evolved. For example, Lee and Hocking (2018) understand economic diplomacy beyond a purely interstate relations aspect and also understand economic diplomacy on a double level; traditionally, it comes from the study of the economic tools used by the statecraft[1] and second as a combination of the diplomat as an agent of International Relations (IR) and International Political Economy (IPE). Together with other diplomatic agency officials that are beyond the scope of the foreign ministry, it has provided the emergence of "new" diplomatic actors (Lee and Hocking, 2018).

The current geopolitical landscape is evolving, so the number of international actors and the sophistication and diversity of tools they use to achieve geopolitical and geoeconomics goals are increasing. The economic diplomacy field is also exposed to this evolution and is becoming crucial to the new energy geopolitics that the UN 2030 Agenda sustains and the climate change goals that countries need to fulfil. Understanding the need to define economic diplomacy epistemologically is an initial and necessary step to analyse its current role in today's international affairs and explore its current ramifications in energy dynamics and balance of power games. To properly address this topic, the chapter is systemised in the following structure: the first section explores the economic diplomacy concept by offering insights on reviewed literature examining the origin and main features surrounding the idea. The second section explores UN diplomacy and how it is being shaped by the sustainable diplomacy that the 2030 Agenda unveils, as well as energy needs and climate change consequences. The third section understands the intersection of economic diplomacy with geoeconomics and geopolitics and sees the phenomena

DOI: 10.4324/9781032655857-6

as a broader tool of coercive diplomacy. Economic sanctions could also target economic relations, energy supplies and trade among nations. A critical question emerges as part of the global economic and political landscape: How are economic sanctions deployed? In which way? Reviewing the case of the war in Ukraine and the international community's actions to try to influence the war are elements that would be subject to analysis. Lastly, a conclusion and remarks section unveils the main findings and conclusions of the chapter. This chapter opens the door to future research aiming to explore the economic diplomacy impact, understanding its double side: from promoting trade, development and sustainable goals amongst nations to being used to protect and even diminishing spheres of influence of rivals in geopolitical confrontations or as energy and climate bargaining tool.

Foundations, Definitions and Goals of Economic Diplomacy

Before analysing the economic diplomacy roots and interrelated primary goals, it is important to frame it as a diplomatic tool used to achieve mutually beneficial arrangements between two entities. Understanding that the need for diplomacy comes from the fact that they have their own interests, and if those divergences are not adequately solved, it could have spill-over effects into other aspects, resulting in impacting the global foreign policy relations between the two states involved (Chatterjee, 2020, p.1). The goals behind economic diplomacy could be diverse; whilst bilateral diplomacy is built on identifying common interests, international economic diplomacy, at the multilateral level, should aim to achieve something for the entire international community (ibid.). Consequently, it is logical to infer that there is an interrelationship between economic activities and foreign policy aims within the economic diplomacy realm, as one could include and help to achieve the other. For decades, the literature has tried to define this interrelation between diplomacy, economy and political goals. It is important to mention that the triangular diplomacy notion helped to grasp this interrelation. The idea brought the attention that states could negotiate with multinational firms, which implies the role that institutions can play by hosting countries' economic actors and how conflicts between companies and governments, if not properly addressed, could result in negotiations and mediation needs between them (Stopford et al., 1991).

In addition, it should be remarked that economic diplomacy has been present in different nation's foreign relations much longer than the very own institutions running their diplomatic strategy today, and accordingly, they have been accommodated as part and parcel of foreign policy and diplomacy practised by states (Okano-Heijmans, 2011, p.13). The first forms of economic diplomacy missions within foreign embassies date back to the moment when "the British Foreign Office began appointing commercial attachés in 1880, and by 1914 there were eight of them, based in Paris, Constantinople, Tokyo, Peking, Frankfurt-on-Main and three in London (covering Austria-Hungary, Italy and Greece, Russia, and Spain and Portugal)" (Fisher et al., 2017, p. 3).

In today's foreign relations, most countries have designed their economic interests and trade policies around a more organised economic diplomacy, which, coordinated from the different Foreign Ministry Affairs offices, aims to pursue its goals by bringing economic interests to the geopolitical arena. Further, tools of economic diplomacy interrelate with much broader concepts such as "economic statecraft, economic security, trade diplomacy, commercial diplomacy and financial diplomacy" (ibid., p.15). While there is a need to define the concept, it is no less true that the economic diplomacy concept remains attached to other border concepts in the geopolitical and geoeconomic field, making it difficult to understand one without the other. This brings all the previously mentioned concepts to the centre of the international relations stage and the need to review the basic economic diplomacy tools used by states. Accordingly, understanding economic diplomacy as the economic ends of a foreign policy and national security strategy will probably lead to the simplistic association of economic diplomacy with commercial or trade diplomacy, but often neglecting the economic means and tools available to diplomats in order to develop their states foreign policy (Stanzel, 2018, p. 14).

To sum up, current economic diplomacy has different goals and tools; however, it is interconnected with wider diplomacy strategies that states pursue while executing their foreign policy objectives and policy goals. Following this logic, there are situations whereby a country's foreign trade policy could be aimed to achieve political goals, and the other way around; states that will use their power to enforce their economic goals (Ruffini, 2016, p. 4). Thus, Woolcock and Bayne (2013) did extensive work on tracing the seeds and elements of economic diplomacy and studied how states make domestic and international decisions, finding that they often integrate economic policy considerations into their foreign policy and diplomatic practices. It is for that reason that economic diplomacy could be understood as the diplomacy field that is built on the economic and political paths that diplomacy strategies build on the following axes: the tension between politics and economics, tension between international and domestic pressures and the tension between governments and other forces (Chohan, 2021, p.7). With this in mind, this chapter explores the interconnection between economy and politics, aiming to understand how they shape economic diplomacy strategies in an era of globalisation and crises whereby both international and national interests shape energy dynamics and climate change mitigation.

The United Nations, Economic Diplomacy and Climate Change

Contemporary global politics and economic dynamics impact aspects such as migration, energy security, technological advancements and climate change. This increases the need for a comprehensive and multifaceted approach that not only integrates foreign, security, defence or trade policies but also considers broader aspects such as export promotion and development policies. Understanding how economic growth and development are needed, the United

Nations 2030 Agenda serves as a roadmap for shaping international and domestic policies (Brocková, 2019). Consequently, it will also impact states' and multinationals' economic diplomacy strategies. In this context, where current economic growth and environmental degradation are growing, new actors and politics that address different power-sharing scenarios are foreseen in the 2030 Agenda. There is a relationship between environmental diplomacy and economic concerns contributing to environmental deterioration. Various elements push and affect current climate change diplomacy and its ramifications in economic diplomacy strategies. Within this, any mitigation stance must be a global, collaborative endeavour that addresses economic and environmental issues to be effective (Hasan, Nan and Rizwanullah, 2024).

This needs to evolve in terms of how economic policies are envisioned. Economic diplomacy emerges from classic political economy issues such as trade and tariff standards that should reign in the International Private Law or its consecutive regulations that need to be reviewed (Moons and van Bergeijk, 2017). However, it should not be forgotten that while traditional economic diplomacy has promoted trade and commerce, its push for economic growth and development has been and will be one of the main contributing forces to climate change and environmental damage. The very own commercial and economic activity has led to direct environmental degradation while pursuing economic growth and development, urging countries and, nowadays, multinationals to join ongoing diplomatic efforts to tackle current and future climate change consequences (Nakić and Čulina, 2023). The emergence of a multilateral diplomatic scheme within the 2030 Agenda is not exempted from controversies and contradictions, both political, economic and even legal. If the dual nature of development and economic growth is not comprehensively grasped and only a partial understanding of the Sustainable Development Goals (SDGs) exists, it could result in achieving certain SDGs at the expense of others. Embracing such a perception of the SDGs would contradict their interconnected and interdependent essence and undermine the accumulated knowledge on sustainable development (Cardona-Vallès and Bórquez, 2022, p. 158).

The new multifaceted reality that complex international politics discloses requires working alliances based on economic and political interests and creating new cooperative schemes and development opportunities. Clusters, for example, have been instrumental in advancing the environmental dimension of economic diplomacy that the new sustainability paradigms are foreseeing. The collaboration among diplomatic missions from various nations to execute environmental and economic initiatives (known as medial cluster) has facilitated the exchange of insights among diplomats regarding novel approaches to international environmental and economic engagements (known as lateral clusters) (Bokhan and Zalizniuk, 2022). Their association benefits mobilisation from capital to technology, which, on its own hand, would facilitate the achievement of some of the ambitious and ambiguous 2030 Agenda points. However, the sustainability needs and the SDGs are in conjunction with the increasingly worrying state of inequalities that the COVID-19 socioeconomic crisis and current geopolitical crises such as the war in Ukraine or the War in Gaza are unfolding, bringing the two sides of the economic diplomacy to the front. On the one hand, it is acknowledged that the 2030 Agenda requires multilateral economic diplomacy. On the other hand, as the next section presents, economic diplomacy tools can also be used to increase geopolitical alliances, balance of power, and economic interests while neglecting the collective sustainability needs.

Rivalries, Energy Needs and Economic Diplomacy

The use of economic diplomacy to achieve political and economic goals dictated by governments and foreign ministries does not revert the fact that there has been an increase in the use of coercive economic tools as a means to gain concessions on a wide range of geopolitical and geoeconomic issues. Non-state actors have also emerged as an essential part of the economic diplomacy strategies of nations, and alliances between foreign ministries, and transnational and multinational businesses have been developed to achieve energy and sustainability goals. In this, business diplomacy deals with strategies employed by companies to manoeuvre through the current fragile and complex evolving multifaceted geopolitical landscape. Multinational enterprises must collaborate with home and host governments to guarantee the seamless and lucrative execution of their international economic and trade objectives (Xiaotong, 2023). For this reason, companies and multinationals have also been one possible target of economic sanctions and coercive diplomacy instruments that aim to decrease a nation's economic growth and productivity. Several legal and economic tools could be used to inflict economic slowdown, ranging from tariff hikes, trade conflicting policies or trade and regional economic agreements, which, at their own end, have become a significant source of economic uncertainty and stock market volatility.

While deterrence and coercive diplomacy might look alike, they share some commonalities that might present them as similar, but they are not the same. Deterrence prevents an adversary from initiating an action before it begins aiming to avoid an undesired action, whilst coercive diplomacy intends to shift the course of action being taken by another country. Coercive diplomacy should be understood as a political-diplomatic strategy aiming to influence an adversary's will or incentive structure. To achieve this, it combines threats of force and, if necessary, the limited and selective use of force in discrete and controlled increments, but it does include as well positive reinforcements as a bargaining force (Levy 2008, p. 539). For this reason, coercive diplomacy is often interrelated to military or defence strategies, which ultimately intend to curve countries' policies while achieving the country's own interests. Table 4.1 summarises the main coercive diplomacy strategies.

While having different strategies, the goal of coercive diplomacy is intended to the same goal: persuade an opponent to stop their course of action. Economic sanctions have been widely used as the main coercive diplomacy tool to affect

Table 4.1 Coercive Diplomacy Strategies versus Deterrence

Deterrence	*Coercive Diplomacy*		
	Type A	*Type B*	*Type C*
Persuade the opponent not to initiate an action	Persuade the opponent to stop short of the goal	Persuade the opponent to undo the action	Persuade opponents to make changes in government

Source: Author, 2024 based on George et al., 1994.

the economic assets of a country and, at the same time, pursue policy and defence goals. Sanctions could be understood as economic measures that intend to express disapproval for the acts of the target and will inflict some change of actions on the opponents (Lowenfeld, 2003; Carter, 2011). However, as happens with deterrence theory, the empirical evidence of the success of coercive diplomacy whereby economic measures such as sanctions, have been used, is hard to attribute at the empirical level. At this point, it is relevant to consider the following questions: How do we measure coercive diplomacy? How do we know if a strategy that works in one place could be successful in another case scenario? In general, successful coercion is extremely difficult to predict and is highly context-dependent (Crystal, 2015; p. 21).

Acknowledging that sanctions can be measurable through indirect measures, such as trade and commerce, will help understand or measure their effects on the economic stability of the country or the production of economic assets, such as energy supplies from that country. However, while sanctions have evolved into what is considered to be smart and targeted, there are still several legal, ethical or technical issues to be studied around sanctions that seem to be answered. Do sanctions work without being targeted and specific? And if targeted, how are the targeting entities or individuals decided? Overall, it is generally accepted that the economic effects of trade sanctions on the target nation are evident in their terms-of-trade outcomes, which are more pronounced with multilateral sanctions compared to unilateral ones. Investment sanctions initially increase the return on capital in the target nation, but over time, the reduction in new foreign capital inflows hinders the nation's growth (Kaempfer and Lowenberg, 2007). Nonetheless, how do we know how the country would have performed without them? Or how is it expected that the nation will not reiterate its political and economic strategies that were subject to international scrutiny?

In addition, as seen in this chapter, there is a strong relationship between energy needs, current diplomatic efforts to achieve the SDGs, oil dependency, economic and financial sanctions and geopolitical alliances. Understating that there is a potential contribution of every actor in the oil and gas sector to the achievement of the SDGs, ranging from exploration and production to pipelines, refining, transportation and retail (UNDP, 2017), brings attention to the complexity and interconnected responsibility of the energy sector. If energy needs are taken as a source of geoeconomic competition, it is comprehensible or even politically logical that energy resources will become a natural target of economic sanctions while deploying coercive diplomacy strategies. But do energy resources and political economy uncertainty relation have a relation to the main geopolitical crises events? An interesting indicator of this is the Oil Price Uncertainty Index (OPU) developed by Abdul Abiad and Irfan Qureshi (Abiad and Qureshi, 2023) presented in Figure 4.1.

As can be seen, the OPU spikes during important oil-related news events, such as the oil shock of the 1970s and the oil glut of the 1980s and when some uncertainty episodes, such as the Iran-Saudi conflict, where oil was a political card, have been present. As the financial and economic effects on oil-producing countries require further economic and financial research that will be explored in future research, this chapter adds to the literature by exploring the double side of economic diplomacy by examining the Ukraine war case. Since the war started, in 2022, economic diplomacy tools, in this case, sanctions, have been used to target energy assets, which, in the end, affects both global energy and demand-supply. In addition, the negative effects of the war in Ukraine go beyond Europe, Russia, and Ukraine, reaching the global level. The dispute has sent shockwaves throughout the world economy. Commodity prices, including energy, have increased sharply as uncertainty about supply disruptions has grown. This has also precipitated trade restrictions and sanctions have been imposed on Russian individuals, businesses, and banks (Bin-Nashwan et al., 2022; p. 12). This is resulting in problems of price affecting cereals, energy market dynamics, and other goods supply. Martin and Minot (2022) found that price shocks during the COVID-19 pandemic and the Ukraine food price crisis

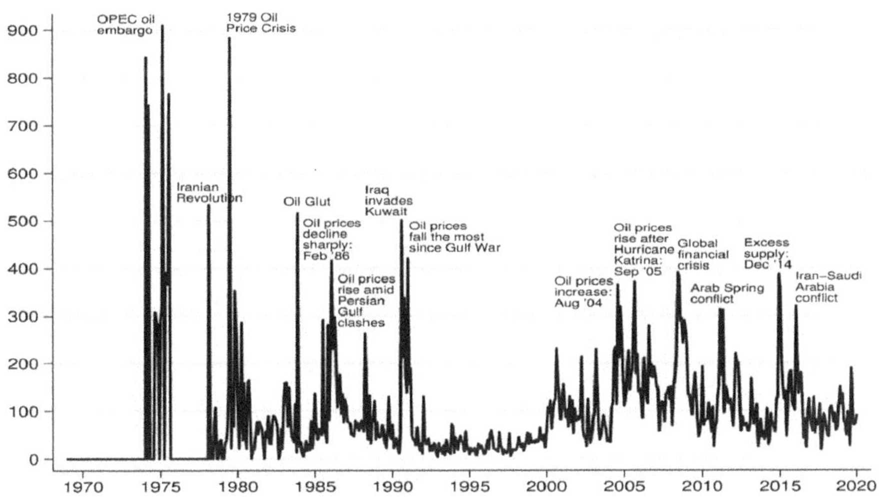

Figure 4.1 OPU-News-based global oil price uncertainty index, January 1969–January 2020 (Abiad and Qureshi, 2023).

finds that price insulation roughly doubled the overall increase in world wheat prices and raised their volatility both during periods of price increase and price decline. Moreover, physical access to food has been affected by disruptions of global supply chains caused, inter alia, by sanctions imposed on Russia, damaging the country's logistics, and exports from Ukraine (El Bilali and Ben Hassen, 2024). Overall, this will have an often neglected effect on the sustainability prospects of the country, the region, and therefore affecting the Agenda 2030 performance indicators.

By the time of this writing, more than two years after the beginning of the war, the sanctions against Russia polarize the international community. The first round of sanctions was imposed in 2014 by US President Barack Obama as the Russian war in Crimea escalated. After a second and third round of sanctions continued, in February 2022, as the Russian war in Ukraine began, countries joined efforts and started targeting Russian individuals, companies, and state officials. A review of the main sanctions imposed on Russia by the European Council and the Council of the European Union are provided in Figure 4.2.

Thus, when examining the main Russian economic indicators as the country's GDP,; it does not show that despite the initial war shock, the country is being particularly affected by the war sanctions, and the GDP growth is recovering from the initial hit (Figure 4.3 below).

Nonetheless, the dilemmas of economic sanctions do appear again. Are macroeconomic indicators such as the GDP a good indicator of unrest produced by the sanctions? Are individuals equally affected by economic sanctions? For example, if we look for alternative indicators, we could

Figure 4.2 European Council and the Council of the European Union Sanctions on Russia imposed on Russia. Based on European Council. Council of the European Union website. Data (Author, 2024).

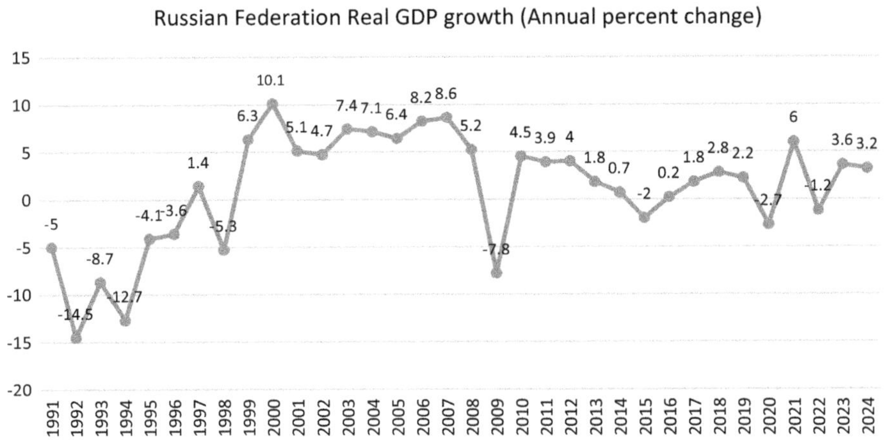

Figure 4.3 Russian Federation GDP growth. Based on International Monetary Fund (IMF). Data (Author, 2024).

Figure 4.4 Russian economic policy uncertainty index. Based on Baker et al. Data set (Author, 2024).

look into the Economic Policy Uncertainty (EPU) index, which uses the same methodology developed by Baker et al. (2016), measures word counts of newspaper articles (in the Russian case the newspaper *Kommersant*) building a measure for the economic policy uncertainty of the country. The index measures, through the newspaper articles counts, how different recent economic and political episodes have affected the state of economic policy uncertainty in the country. The results from data of the years 1994–2024 shown are in Figure 4.4.

As it can be seen, the indicator shows that despite the growth of GDP in different periods, the economic policy uncertainty experienced in the country has not been equally affected. In 1995 there was an index spike due to the First Chechen War (1994–1996), which had a bigger impact than, for example, the following events as the Second Chechen War (1999–2000) and decreasing in May 2000, after Putin was firstly elected and initiating its well carrot and stick policy in Chechnya by using force and repression while seeking a development control in the region. Interestingly, the highest spike observed in the index after the one of 1st Chechnya War comes with the COVID-19 crisis that had, for example, higher effects on uncertainty than, for example, the previous Russia-Ukraine "gas War" back in 2010, which resulted in disputes between the gas companies of the two countries and affecting Europe gas supplies and prices. Lastly, and as expected, the 2022 War in Ukraine and the severing of sanctions had the highest spike in the observed data for the years 1994–2024. Still, the index accommodates uncertainty and returns to normal levels without retaining a high degree of uncertainty since the war started.

Several conclusions can be drawn after exploring the Russian and Ukraine cases. On the one hand, the fact that energy, mainly gas and oil, have been used or been affected by policy uncertainty and economic sanctions in different historical periods shows how different actors can use energy assets as bargaining tools to pursue economic and political goals. The second is understanding that sanctions can affect economic indicators such as the GDP, OPU, or EPU indexes, as they, to a different extent, could be affected directly or indirectly by economic and financial sanctions. However, with the OPU and EPU indexes, can we measure the effects of sanctions by measuring how newspapers portray the situation in the country? Do aggregate variables such as the GDP measure inequality and the suffering of civil populations? And lastly, how do energy resources management policies in the target country perform after sanctions? In Russia's case, despite the country having considerable foreign currency reserves, war machinery, and infrastructure, sanctions imposed a reorientation. They can also affect the country's economic policies and future international energy supplies. In addition, national economic needs will need to be met either by imports or by increasing national manufacturing, affecting labour market features and individuals' professional careers (Vakulenko, 2024). Regardless of the war's length, individuals will undoubtedly bear the brunt of the political decisions made by the ruling elites on both sides, further complicating the economic and political landscape in the aftermath of sanctions.

Conclusions and Final Remarks

This chapter looks into the roots of economic diplomacy, its basics, and its definition. From its inception, economic diplomacy has helped nations achieve their political and economic goals. Since economy and politics are interrelated, economic diplomacy has also evolved into a diverse strategy that goes far beyond the "commercial attaché" role in different embassies. Nowadays, economic diplomacy is, as diplomacy per se, a complex scenario whereby geopolitical and economic interests are shown using the most diverse tools, from social media and communication strategies to trade agreements and investment strategies. It involves different actors, such as multinationals and corporations, that are needed to complete the foreign ministry strategies.

The 2030 Agenda brought international goals that need to be achieved in 15 years, bringing energy needs and climate change mitigation to the front line. In this, energy needs, growth, and economic development must adapt economic diplomacy strategies to implement SDGs and their cooperative schemes. However, due to its geopolitical importance, energy and sustainability needs are also being used as bargaining tools. In this, economic sanctions can serve economic and political diplomacy to achieve a nation goals and increase its geopolitical alliances. Different empirical studies have found a notable agreement among the cross-national studies that economic sanctions cause substantial distress in targeted economies. This distress is evidenced by reduced growth, a higher probability of economic collapse, increased poverty and inequality, worsening health conditions, numerous excess deaths, and declines in human rights and democracy (Rodríguez, 2024). Individual consequences will bear the highest cost of economic sanctions and economic diplomacy decisions.

Finally, the bottom-up question remains open: Are economic diplomacy strategies effective, or are they double-sided and intentionally used to serve complex energy and geopolitical dynamics rather than fulfilling the 2030 Agenda and SDG's needs?

Note

1 Traditionally, statecraft could be defined as the use of instruments at the disposal of central authorities to achieve foreign policy goals. It is typically divided into three categories: diplomatic, military, and economic (Mastanduno, 2012, p. 204).

References

Abiad, A., & Qureshi, I. A. (2023). The macroeconomic effects of oil price uncertainty. *Energy Economics*, *125*, 106839.

Baker, S. R., Bloom, N., & Davis, S. J. (2016). Measuring economic policy uncertainty. *The Quarterly Journal of Economics*, *131*(4), 1593–1636.

Bin-Nashwan, S. A., Hassan, M. K., & Muneeza, A. (2022). Russia–Ukraine conflict: 2030 Agenda for SDGs hangs in the balance. *International Journal of Ethics and Systems*, (ahead-of-print).

Bokhan, A., & Zalizniuk, V. (2022). Economic diplomacy in new projections of activation. *Baltic Journal of Economic Studies*, *8*(4), 19–25.

Brocková, I. (2019). Modern economic diplomacy of small states. *Politické vedy*, *22*(2), 12–25.

Carter, B. E. (2011). Economic sanctions. *Max Planck Encyclopedia of Public International Law*, 3.

Chatterjee, C. (2020). *Economic diplomacy and foreign policy-making* (p. 67). Palgrave Macmillan.

Chohan, U. W. (2021). Economic diplomacy: A review. https://www.academia.edu/download/65736379/EC007UC_Economic_Diplomacy.pdf

Crystal, S.-H. (2015). Coercive diplomacy a theoretical and practical evaluation. *Glendon Journal of International Studies*, *8*(1–2). Available at: https://gjis.journals.yorku.ca/index.php/gjis/article/view/38941 (Accessed: 23 May 2024).

El Bilali, H., & Ben Hassen, T. (2024). Disrupted harvests: how Ukraine–Russia war influences global food systems–a systematic review. *Policy Studies*, 45(3–4), 310–335.

European Council. Council of the European Union website. EU sanctions on Russia. https://www.consilium.europa.eu/en/policies/sanctions-against-russia/

Fisher, J., Pedaliu, E. G., & Smith, R. (Eds.). (2017). *The Foreign Office, commerce and British foreign policy in the twentieth century*. Springer.

George, A. L., Simons, W. E., & Hall, D. K. (1994). *The limits of coercive diplomacy* (2nd ed). Boulder: Westview Press. ISBN 081331786X

Hasan, M. M., Nan, S., & Rizwanullah, M. (2024). The role of environmental diplomacy and economic factors on environmental degradation. *Heliyon*, *10*(2), 1–13.

International Monetary Fund Data Website (n.d.). Russian Federation Data set: https://www.imf.org/external/datamapper/profile/RUS

Kaempfer, W. H., & Lowenberg, A. D. (2007). The political economy of economic sanctions. *Handbook of defense economics*, *2*, 867–911.

Lee, D., & Hocking, B. (2018, January 11). Economic diplomacy. In *Oxford research encyclopedia of international studies*. Retrieved 29 Oct. 2024, from https://oxfordre.com/internationalstudies/view/10.1093/acrefore/9780190846626.001.0001/acrefore-9780190846626-e-384

Levy, J. S. (2008). Deterrence and coercive diplomacy: the contributions of Alexander George. *Political Psychology*, *29*(4), 537–552.

Lowenfeld, A. F. (2003). *International economic law*. Oxford University Press, USA.

Martin, W., & Minot, N. (2022). The impacts of price insulation on world wheat markets during the 2022 food price crisis. *Australian Journal of Agricultural and Resource Economics*, 66(4), 753–774.

Mastanduno, M. (2012). Economic statecraft. Foreign policy: Theories, actors, cases, 204.

Moons, S. J., & van Bergeijk, P. A. (2017). Does economic diplomacy work? A meta-analysis of its impact on trade and investment. *The World Economy*, *40*(2), 336–368.

Nakić, M., & Čulina, V. (2023). Climate Changes, the Role of Economic Diplomacy and the Impact on Global Security. *Strategos*: *Znanstveni časopis Hrvatskog vojnog učilišta" Dr. Franjo Tuđman*", *7*(2), 141–164.

Okano-Heijmans, M. (2011). Conceptualising economic diplomacy: The crossroads of international relations, economics, IPE and diplomatic studies. *The Hague Journal of Diplomacy*, *6*(1–2), 7–36.

Rodríguez, F. (2024). The human consequences of economic sanctions. *Journal of Economic Studies*, *51*(4), 942–963.

Ruffini, P. B. (2016). International trade and foreign affairs–some reflections on economic diplomacy. *Journal of International Logistics and Trade*, *14*(1), 3–28.

Stanzel, Volker (Ed.). (2018). New realities in foreign affairs: Diplomacy in the 21st century, SWP Research Papers 11/2018, Stiftung Wissenschaft und Politik (SWP), German Institute for International and Security Affairs.

Stopford, J. M., Strange, S., & Henley, J. S. (1991). *Rival states, rival firms: Competition for world market shares* (No. 18). Cambridge University Press.

UNDP, I. (2017). Mapping the oil and gas industry to the sustainable development goals: an atlas. Sustainable Development Goals. Available from: https://sdgs.un.org/partnerships/mapping-oil-and-gas-industry-sustainable-development-goals-atlas-sdgs-1-17

Vallès, M. C., & Bórquez, S. P. (2022). The Sustainable Development Goals and the application of International Law: the case of the Grand Ethiopian Renaissance Dam. *Revista iberoamericana de estudios de desarrollo= Iberoamerican journal of development studies*, *11*(2), 144–168.

Vakulenko, S. (2024). Russia has the resources for a long war in Ukraine. Carnegie Endowment for International Peace. Published, on 16th May 2024. Available at https://carnegieendowment.org/research/2024/05/v-usloviyah-voennogo-bremeni-glavnye-voprosy-o-nastoyashem-i-budushem-rossijskoj-ekonomiki?lang=en

Woolcock, S., and Bayne, N. (Eds.). (2013). *The new economic diplomacy: decision-making and negotiation in international economic relations*. Ashgate Publishing, Ltd.

Xiaotong, Z. (2023). Introduction: Now is the Time to Study Economic Diplomacy. *Economic Diplomacy*, *1*(1), 1–6.

5 The Global Economic and Political Landscape through the Lenses of Multiple and Multifaceted Crises

Lucía Morales, Bernadette Andreosso-O'Callaghan, Daniel Rajmil and Suleman Sarwar

5.1 Introduction

Over the past two decades, the world economic and political landscape has been subject to rising levels of uncertainty and to continuous and abrupt changes that are impacting global dynamics. A number of most remarkable events taking place over the past two decades range from political events to economic disruptions, or to a combination of both. The new millennium started with the burst of the dot.com bubble and with the terrorist attacks in the United States of America (USA). September 11, 2001, is identified as an event with deep political implications that has contributed to increasing the world levels of political uncertainty and heightening levels of global insecurity. The ensuing "war on terror" initiated by the USA led to the invasion of Afghanistan, culminating, 20 years later, with a most disorderly exit leaving the country under a new Taliban regime (Rajmil et al., 2022; Council on Foreign Relations, 2022; The 9/11 Commission Report, 2004; Birkland, 2004). Later in the decade, the world economies were shaken by the 2008 Global Economic and Financial Crisis (GEFC). This crisis can be considered as one of the seismic events in geopolitics and geoeconomics history (Rudd, 2009). In the following decade, the affirmation of nationalist tendencies and of retrenchment, with the USA and the UK as central players (Langlois, 2021), initiated a period in the area of geopolitics that questions both the predominant governance structures and the meaning and essence of current democracies. Subsequently, the Global Health Crisis derived from the 2020 COVID-19 outbreak has shown how political and economic interests have a significant impact on how states (or countries) respond to potential crises (IMF, 2022; Transparency International, 2021). For example, political dealers showed a lack of solidarity implying that the response to the outbreak generated negative spillover effects on the countries' economies with some ramifications for their political agendas (Duan et al., 2021). Finally, the world has entered into (yet another) oil market shock derived from the Russia-Saudi Arabia oil price war in early 2020, which was aggravated more recently by the Russia/Ukraine conflict since February 2022; this has once more offered a clear example of states' responses that seek to protect their own political and economic agendas.

DOI: 10.4324/9781032655857-7

When looking more closely at the series of events mentioned earlier, a more precise idea of the relationship between geopolitics and geoeconomics emerges, as these are defined by the mutual impact of one on the other. What is significant about the outlined crises is their tendency to diffuse to every economy of the world and their detrimental impact on social cohesion. By way of an example, the GEFC outburst in 2008 – an economic crisis propagated from the USA subprime market leading to the country's gross domestic product dropping year-on-year by 4.3 percent – evolved into the deepest recession known since World War II (Weinberg, 2013). The crisis uncovered the population's discontent regarding the *status quo*, leading to heightened levels of social unrest, with countries affected by greater degrees of inequality registering higher protest rates (Yagci, 2017). Since the oil shocks of the early 1970s, there has been a continuous decoupling process between wealth and income that has contributed to widening the divide between the world's richest and poorest economies and between rich and poor in different countries (Bogliacino and Maestri, 2016; Rossi, 2012; Reinhart and Rogoff, 2010); this process accelerated dramatically with the GEFC and with the recent COVID-19 related health crisis. Real inequality and its long-term effects have been underestimated, and it can be considered one of the primary triggers of the global rise in nationalism and retrenchment (Cox, 2018, p. 6). For example, as the world economy was somewhat recovering from the effects of the GEFC crisis, the year 2016 witnessed the UK's decision to leave the European Union through the June 23rd Brexit referendum. The world economy seems to be sticking to a pattern of slow growth that affects in particular the world's most developed economies; in turn, this contributes to question: (i) the real benefits of the current globalization process; (ii) the pertinence of the current economic order that emerged from it; (iii) and the relevance of the governance framework inherited from the post-world wars international institutions.

In particular, the year 2020 brought significant levels of uncertainty as it was marked by a dual shock – a global health crisis combined with an oil market shock. After the World Health Organization (WHO) officially declared that COVID-19 was a "deadly" health threat with significant contagion power (WHO, 2020), a period of considerable uncertainty ensued evolving into an officially declared global health crisis. Inadequate policy responses prolonged the health crisis (Andreosso-O'Callaghan, Moon and Sohn, 2022) and, above all, allowed it to evolve into a fully-fledged economic and social crisis, as new waves of social unrest and discontent were reignited. This flagged the need for political reform and social change as inequalities between the rich and the poor continued to widen (The World Bank, 2022; Kammer et al., 2022; IMF, 2021; Cohen and Rappeport, 2022; Hadzi-Vaskov, Pienknagura, and Antonio Ricci, 2021; WHO, 2020). Yet again, as the world economies started to embark upon a new growth path by engaging in the economic reopening process, new geopolitical tensions emerged with the Russian/Ukrainian conflict starting on February 24, 2022. Given the scale of the economic sanctions imposed by Western countries on Russia, and given the weight of Russia in the energy markets (especially in that of Germany), growth rates for 2022 had to be revised downwards (The World Bank, 2022; Kammer et al., 2022; Wolff, 2022). To make matters worse, food shortages, engineered by a series of adverse events over a number of months, as well as the slowdown and sometimes total breakdown of the global value chains system, have contributed largely to fuel inflation at levels reminiscent of those of the "turbulent" 1970s.

Undoubtedly, the last two decades have been marked by growing economic and political uncertainty levels that reveal a very complex international socio-economic and political environment that is heavily interconnected. Recurrent crises have tended to nurture this uncertainty. Therefore, this paper seeks to offer insights into the outlined crises by examining the dynamic causal links between global economic growth and economic policy uncertainty to gain some knowledge into the future implications regarding the economic and political power balance. Section 5.2 summarizes briefly the recurrent phenomenon of crises, be they economic, financial, energy, or as in the case recently, health-related (Kuhn et al., 2018; IMF, 2022). The policy response aspect and the impact on wealth distribution are highlighted in the discussion. In order to portray the connection between economic and political uncertainty and economic performance (between geo-politics and geoeconomics), we use a methodological framework borrowing from econometrics using high-frequency data (Section 5.3). Section 5.4 presents the findings of the dynamic causality testing and it critically discusses the results whereas Section 5.5 concludes.

5.2 Multifaced Crises, Political Imbalances, Conflict, and Growing Economic Uncertainty

Economic and political events continually evolve and their undeniable association can be seen in the fact that they tend to shape societies' history. In this sense, it is logical to understand how the global economy is affected by significant economic imbalances and growing inequality levels associated with globalization, and what role crises play in this process. The long-term available data on wealth and income disparities show that, far from bringing the much-needed solution to a major economic disturbance caused by either an economic or a political crisis, the policy responses to crises tend to exacerbate imbalances, leading to more crises (Andreosso-O'Callaghan, 2022). The financial dimension is key to the understanding of economic imbalances, crises (economic, geo-political or both), and inequality. In other words, the conjunction of different historical episodes of crises has proven that "*inequality, especially extreme inequality, is not just a contextual feature or a downstream outcome issue, but a crucial upstream, causal factor in the pathology of the financial meltdown*" (Saith, 2011, p.70).

On the one hand, the polarization of economic, financial, and business activities and the continuous challenge to the world's educational systems and democratic process are contributing to rising levels of conflict. Education is a significant variable in the context of conflict settings. Still, on its own, it cannot be expected to be a conflict-solving tool as it requires the active role of both governments and non-governmental actors (Bush and Saltarelli, 2000). On the other hand, political and economic instability are likewise threats to national, regional, and global peace. This has enabled global economic inequality and imbalances to accentuate economic and political polarization, combined with the rise of in-between-country income inequality (The World Bank, 2022). The articulation of protectionism, economic and political retrenchment, social unrest, and rising discontent with the political and business classes are significant sources of concern.

Although inequality is visible in the rising gap between the world's most developed and less developed economies, it is also detectable between the most affluent and poorer social groups within countries – developed or less developed; it acts also as a trigger for enhanced levels of conflict at the global and national levels (The World Bank, 2022; IMF, 2021; Cox, 2018). The importance of reducing inequality with the need for increased rates of economic growth intending to eradicate extreme poverty aligns in principle with the proclaimed objectives of the United Nations 2030 Agenda. However, emerging research poses significant doubts as to the governments' real ability to reach such goals that seem unrealistic if current global trends persist, particularly given the paucity of instruments left to the policymakers to act on such objectives (Lakner et al., 2022).

But how do these geopolitical and geoeconomic dynamics between inequality, political uncertainty, and conflict work? The existing literature in conflict studies has found several links between states, scarcity, and civil strife working in two directions: state failure and state exploitation (Kahl, 2006). The first example of this entangled relationship is related to the "war on terror" and the ensuing invasion of Afghanistan and afterwards scenarios. For over 20 years, the country has been suffering from a foreign presence and instability; this resulted in one of the US longest wars culminating in a chaotic withdrawal from the region in the summer of 2021, leaving Afghanistan in the hands of a new Taliban regime (UN, 2022; National Archives, 2022) and unravelling severe socio-economic and political consequences. The Afghan population is now exposed to the systematic violation of human rights and to the collapse of both its economic system and social institutions. This has led the country to experience extreme poverty levels and the failure and destruction of government institutions and services compounded by its over-reliance on foreign aid, condemning it to poverty, exclusion, and discrimination. Flooded with vast amounts of foreign aid, the post-2001 policies fostered corruption and worsened the country's situation (Murtazashvili, (2022). The international community's inability to react to this humanitarian crisis is remarkable, and it has left the country facing severe socio-economic and political challenges (UNHCR, 2021; Rajmil et al., 2022).

As previously stated, inequalities are explained by both political and economic factors. In addition, global events impact political uncertainty, which on its own poses a serious threat to the countries' stability, as government policies and regulatory frameworks are undefined and erratic, contributing eventually to sparking global uncertainty in an interconnected world (Al Thaqeb, 2019). When reviewing and analysing the recent level of political uncertainty and global inequality, it appears that in the case of both the USA and the European Union, the subprime crisis has contributed to enhancing the complexities of the global landscape, as the crisis led to a painful international economic recovery process that unveiled the realities of the growing gap between rich and poor (OECD, 2022; O'Connor, 2017; Piketty, 2017, 2015) The policy responses to that crisis placed a heavy share of the adjustment burden on vulnerable socio-economic groups. As a result, the GEFC acted as the trigger for increasing levels of social unrest and political radicalism, consolidating the rise of nationalism and anti-globalization sentiment across the world (Cox, 2018). As the world economy was somewhat emerging from the legacy of the GEFC and was finding some level of stability, the year 2020 brought a new challenge by the hand of a global health crisis whose origins have allegedly been traced back to the Hubei Province of China. The main medium-term economic response has been a number of fiscal and monetary policy measures which have resulted in the swelling of the Central Banks balance sheets (a multiplication by a factor of more than 8 in the case of the FED).[1] Easy "helicopter money" has raised more than ever the question of the sustainability of the global central banks' centred monetary system (Andreosso-O'Callaghan, 2022). Of specific note is the sustainability of the European single currency and also of the dollar as the key world reference currency. The ensuing ballooning of the public debt in the EU, US, and Japanese economies – to name but a few – which is itself a key cause of current inflationary trends, is likely to contribute to, yet another, financial meltdown. *Ceteris paribus*, and judging by recent experience, the adjustment process is likely to rest disproportionately on the poorer households in these (Western) countries. Although this tends to be neglected by International Institutions, increasing poverty and social exclusion is also a key problem in developed countries; admittedly, the brunt of the current inflationary trends, and of the related food insecurity and rising poverty problems, is undeniably felt first in poorer developing countries, where food riots are in preparation, at the time of writing. In short, the world's developing economies and the poorer households in developed countries have been profoundly neglected, contributing to the growing and acceleration of a two-tier global economic system that differentiates between the wealthy and the poor.

Moreover, energy market dynamics, particularly since March 2020, have exacerbated the complexities of the global economic and financial system, contributing to further imbalances due to increasing prices that are hurting those at lower-income levels. The 2016 agreement between Russia and Saudi Arabia to coordinate production levels (Singh, 2020) was followed in 2020 by an episode of over-supply, due to the closure of most productive sectors, and therefore by erratic prices exacerbating uncertainty. The global economy entered the year 2022 with a "*messy and chaotic*" process of reopening its businesses and re-engaging with social activities. Very few lessons were learned from the previous months of socio-economic hibernation. The opening-up process has been characterized by countries' disconnected actions, lack of cooperation, the dominance of specific national interests, and inadequate uncoordinated policies, all of which epitomize clear cases of retrenchment. The Russia/Ukraine crisis aggravates the ongoing energy crisis, placing an upward pressure on prices. Once more, the international community's response to the conflict has been characterized by its inability to offer a unified response to the unfolding humanitarian crisis. The focus of attention has shifted towards the economic agenda and the need to secure oil and gas resources for the wealthier European economies. Quite remarkably, some countries are taking advantage of the current situation in order to fulfil their economic agendas. For example, despite Western sanctions, India's imports of cheap Russian crude oil have surged since Russia's military operation in Ukraine. The country received more than 14 million barrels of Russian crude oil in May 2022, and it is expected to receive about 28 million of barrels in June 2022 (Reuters, 2022; Financial Times, 2022). Undoubtedly, the world has been immersed in multiple multifaceted crises that impact geoeconomic and geopolitical dynamics, clearly undermining future generations' economic growth prospects and development projections, leaving them with a bleak future in terms of political stability and shared economic growth.

5.3 Data and Methodology

In order to capture the global economic and political dynamics in combination with the world GDP, we use the World Economic and Political Uncertainty Index. The chosen variables for our methodology help us to portray the potential connection between growing levels of economic and political uncertainty and their damaging effects on economic development. The study is also supported by the frequency domain methodology introduced by Breitung and Candelon (2006) that enables the study of dynamic causality. The model is based on a bivariate approach that allows considering the impact of global economic policy uncertainty on rising levels of instability with implications for global economic growth and development. The data was retrieved from Refinitiv-Datastream. The research sample spans from January 15, 1997, to December 15, 2021, as per current data availability. The series frequency is monthly, accounting for a total of 300 observations.

Before proceeding with the estimation of the dynamic causality testing, the series were tested for stationarity properties in compliance with the primary tests used for time series analysis. Both variables were identified to be I(1) processes. The analysis was followed by implementing a VAR(p) model for optimal lag length selection, with the outcome of five lags being identified as being optimal as per the Schwarz Information Criterion. A bivariate causality analysis in the context of the frequency domain brings further evidence to the selected indexes' behaviour over the sample period, as it helps us understand dynamic causal patterns and reveals the existence of unidirectional or bidirectional causal links. The study by Breitung and Candelon (2006) is based on earlier work by Geweke (1982) and Hosoya (1991) that considered the two-dimensional vector containing Y_t and X_t with a finite-order VAR representative of order p; this is expressed as:

$$\Theta(\mathrm{L})\begin{pmatrix} Y_t \\ X_t \end{pmatrix} = \begin{pmatrix} \Theta_{11}(L) & \Theta_{12}(L) \\ \Theta_{21}(\mathrm{L}) & \Theta_{22}(L) \end{pmatrix}\begin{pmatrix} Y_t \\ X_t \end{pmatrix} = \varepsilon_t \tag{5.1}$$

where $\Theta(L) = I - \Theta_1 L - \ldots - \Theta_p L_p$ is a 2 × 2 lag polynomial and $\Theta_1,\ldots,\Theta_p$ are 2 × 2 autoregressive parameter matrices, with $L^k X_t = X_{t-k}$ and $L^k Y_t = Y_{t-k}$. The error vector ε_t represents white noise with zero mean and $E\left(\varepsilon_t \varepsilon_t^t\right) = \Sigma$, where Σ is positive and finite. The matrix expression of the system is:

$$\begin{pmatrix} Y_t \\ X_t \end{pmatrix} = \psi(L)\eta_t = \begin{pmatrix} \psi_{11}(L) & \psi_{12}(L) \\ \psi_{21}(L) & \psi_{22}(L) \end{pmatrix}\begin{pmatrix} \eta_{1t} \\ \eta_{2t} \end{pmatrix} \tag{5.2}$$

with $\psi(L)\eta_t = \Theta(L)^{-1} G^{-1}$ and with G being the lower triangular matrix of the Cholesky decomposition $G'G = \Sigma^{-1}$ such that $E\left(\eta_t \eta_t^{'}\right) = I$ and $\eta_t = G\varepsilon_t$. The causality test developed by Geweke (1982) can then be written as:

$$M_{X \Rightarrow Y}(\Upsilon) = \log\left[1 + \frac{\left|\psi_{12}\left(e^{-i\gamma}\right)\right|^2}{\left|\psi_{11}\left(e^{-i\gamma}\right)\right|^2}\right] \tag{5.3}$$

Within this framework, no Granger causality from X_t to Y_t with a frequency γ corresponds to the condition $\left|\psi_{12}\left(e^{-i\gamma}\right)\right|^2 = 0$. Breitung and Candelon's (2006) main contribution is to show that this condition leads to the relationship below:

$$\left|\Theta_{12}\left(e^{-i\gamma}\right)\right| = \left|\sum_{k=1}^{p} \Theta_{k,12} \cos(k\gamma)\right| - i\sum_{k=1}^{p} \Theta_{k,12} \sin(k\gamma) |= 0 \tag{5.4}$$

where, $\Theta_{k,12}$ is the (1,2) element of Θ_k, such that a sufficient set of conditions for no causality is given by:

$$\sum_{k=1}^{p} \Theta_{k,12} \cos(k\gamma) |= 0 \text{ and } \sum_{k=1}^{p} \Theta_{k,12} \sin(k\gamma) = 0 \tag{5.5}$$

The frequency-domain approach, also known as spectral causality, is a model that tests the null hypothesis of no Granger causality with a frequency γ using a standard *F*-test for the linear restrictions imposed by the VAR representative of order p, which follows an $F(2, T\text{-}2p)$ distribution for every γ between 0 and π (where T is the number of observations in the series; see Breitung and Candelon, 2006). The outcomes of the spectral causality are presented in the section that follows.

5.4 Findings and Critical Discussion

As argued above, the world economies have faced significant levels of disruption due to multiple and multifaceted crises impacting global dynamics, particularly since the 2000s. Figure 5.1 illustrates how the world's emerging and developing economies contribute increasingly to the world's GDP. Since the 2000s, there has been a clear shift in growth patterns from the world's most developed economies towards emerging and developing ones that have shown different levels of resilience in terms of economic recovery. Indeed, the economic recovery process in Western economies such as the EU has further been affected by geopolitical uncertainty derived from the Russia-Ukraine conflict. This conflict has tended to accentuate the trend of emerging and developing countries taking prominence in world GDP growth.

The return to "normal" socio-economic activities in 2021 was accompanied with a severe crisis in global supply chains, which was nevertheless already visible in 2020, with mounting pressures on the energy sector due to rising business activities and to increasing household consumption levels; this drove

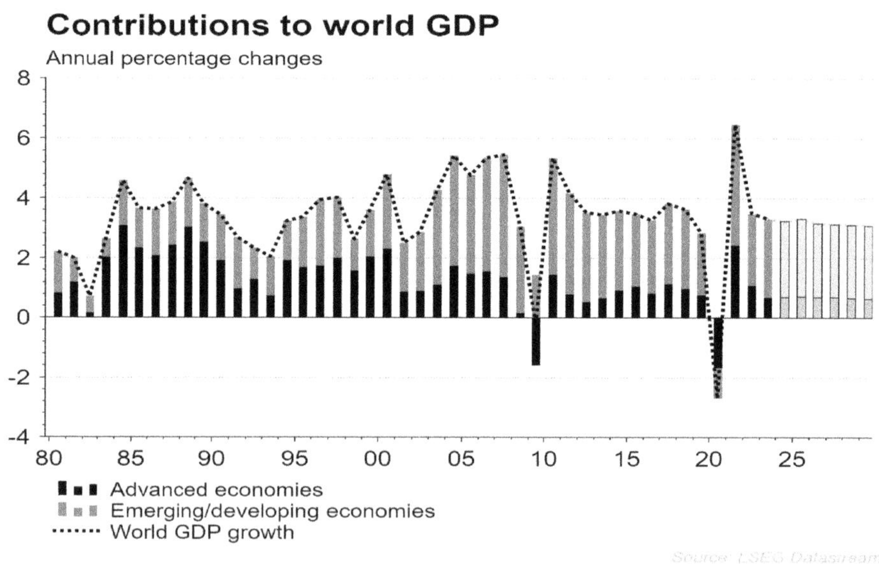

Figure 5.1 World GDP Growth – Annual % Changes by Global Contribution.

Source: Refinitiv DataStream (2022).

inflationary pressures and underlined further the connection between economic growth and political and economic stability.

Over a long period (1998–2020), the World Real GDP and the World Economic Policy Uncertainty Index are positively correlated, as illustrated in Figure 5.2. The indexes registered a positive correlation coefficient of approximately 0.70 over the period under study. As can be seen in Figure 5.2, less political uncertainty (just before 2008 and before 2020) is associated with more growth. This signals the strong connection between economic and political stability and the global economic prospects for economic development. This preliminary statistical analysis shows that over the past two decades, the world economy has been affected by a diverse range of economic and political shocks that have materialised into multiple and multifaceted types of crises that undoubtedly have had a major impact on global economic performance.

Figure 5.3 below outlines the outcomes of the frequency domain test (Breitung and Candelon, 2006) model. The model was implemented to test causality dynamics between changes in the world GDP and changes in the global economic policy uncertainty index. The research findings suggest the existence of significant evidence of a bidirectional dynamic causal relationship. In short, the results indicate the importance of economic and political stability to ensure that the world economy develops and progresses. However, the world economy has been affected by significant disruptions since the 2000s that have contributed to undermining the countries' development with

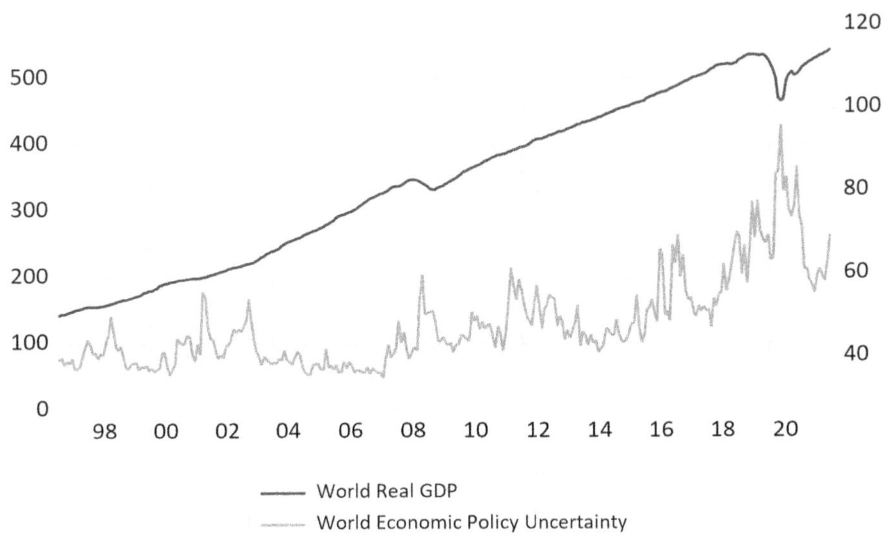

Figure 5.2 World Real GDP and Global Economic Policy Uncertainty.

Source: Refinitiv DataStream (2022).

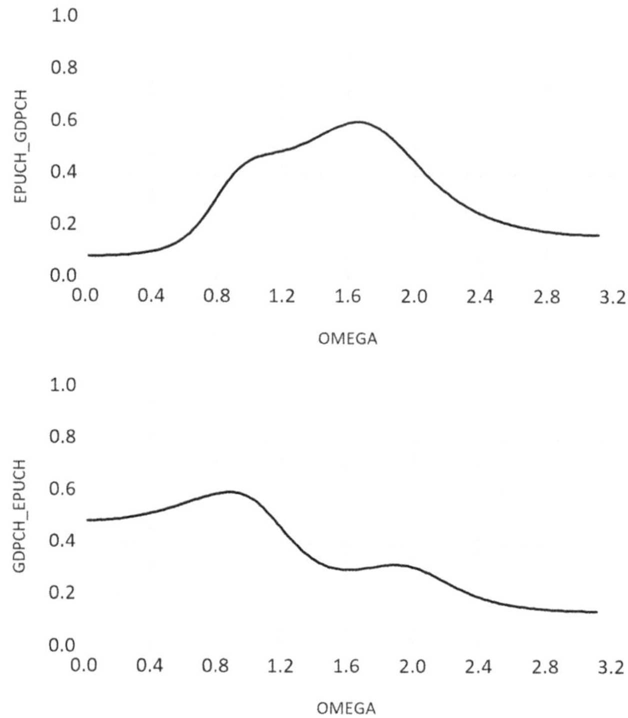

Figure 5.3 Causality in the Frequency Domain – Changes in Global GDP and EPU.
Source: Authors' Calculations (2022).

knock-on effects at the global level, particularly regarding lower-income earners within specific countries.

In order to complete the analysis, final remarks regarding growing levels of within-country inequality can be drawn from the GINI index; Figure 5.4 shows how the USA – the world's most developed economy – is exhibiting inequality levels that align with patterns displayed by some of the world's less-developed economies. Although the Gini coefficient accuracy is significantly affected by the reliability of GDP and income data, thus not capturing, for example, the "shadow" or "informal" economy, the coefficient provides nevertheless a rough idea of income inequality.[2] The positioning of the USA as one of the most unequal countries (Figure 5.4) raises some serious concerns.

Overall, the research findings pose severe concerns regarding the widening gap between the rich and the poor within different countries and the consolidation of countries' domestic problems compounded by rising levels of political uncertainty with powerful implications for global economic stability that are acting as major disruptors for global power balance. The years ahead raise

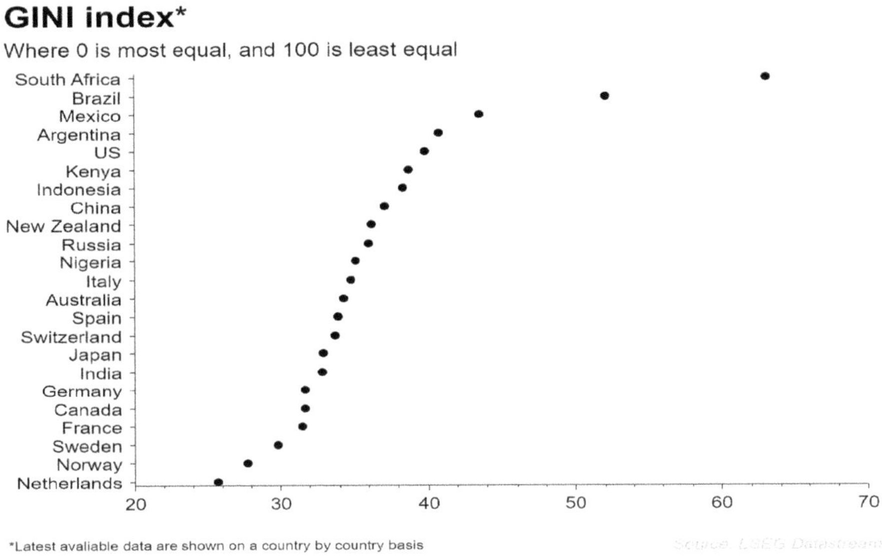

Figure 5.4 Gini Inequality Index.

Source: Refinitiv DataStream (2022).

serious questions regarding the global economic and political leaders' ability to find an appropriate balance between economic and political interests that contributes to sustainable development. Over the past two decades, the world economy has witnessed a variety of events that have shown the inability of the international community to manage the challenges associated with economic and political conflicts. The outcome is the consolidation of wealth in the hands of the few; growing levels of income inequality are bound to lead to increasing levels of social unrest and political discontent.

5.5 Conclusions

By reviewing the recent main geopolitical and geoeconomic events that have shaped the world, as well as their association, this chapter offers a critical assessment of recent international events (e.g. slow growth and crises) and their association with economic and political uncertainty. The primary research finding underlines the strong connection between the political and the economic dimensions, signalling the need for more multidisciplinary studies that help us better understand their association.

Our results also show that, trend-wise and over the long period 1998–2000, World Economic Policy Uncertainty and world's GDP have increased in parallel. This mirrors the increasing share of world GDP represented by the emerging economies. This does not however outweigh the growing inequality problem worldwide, including within the developed countries. Indeed, multiple and multifaceted crises have contributed to enhancing global economic imbalances by allowing wealth to concentrate in the hands of the few and fuelling a myriad of socio-economic and environmental problems. The outcome is that within-country wealth inequality has increased over the last few decades as the world economy has navigated through disparate crises. In particular, the GEFC emerges as an inflection point marked by rising levels of social discontent due to the growing divide between the world's richest and poorest that is no longer limited to developing nations.

As argued in this paper, the responses to crises, particularly in the EU, USA and Japan (all "Western" economies) have tended to exacerbate the economic imbalances and have tended to place a larger share of the adjustment process on lower income groups in different countries.

A key lesson drawn from this study is that although crises do help to reshape the global and political landscape, by giving in particular less economic weight to developed countries, this redistribution of wealth across countries still leaves the problem of income inequality unanswered. Both theory and recent historical episodes prove that there is a relationship between inequalities, prospects of crises and uncertainty, both political and economic. Judging by current policy trends, poor households' incomes will, in the near future, continue to face tighter economic constraints. It will severely be affected by the persistence of economic shocks (future crises) that will contribute to consolidating their marginalization and exclusion from the socio-economic system; this is ultimately a key threat to the world's future sustainable and peaceful development.

Notes

1 The interested reader can refer to the FED Statistical Release (May 5th, 2022) which shows that the FED's total credits amounted to 8,903,65 US million dollars on May the 4th (2022). See: https://www.federalreserve.gov/releases/h41/current/h41.pdf.

2 The Gini Coefficient can be regarded as the salient summary statistic of the Lorenz Curve of the income distribution represented by the following formulae: $G = 1 - 2\int_0^1 L(u)\,du$. The Lorenz curve is denoted by $L(u)$, and it represents the distribution of total income received by different income groups ranked from the lowest (see, for example, Dorfman (1979, p.147)).

References

Andreosso-O'Callaghan, B. (2022) Monetary and Fiscal Response in the euro-area and the EU. In B. Andreosso-O'Callaghan, Woosik Moon and Wook Sohn (Eds), *Economic Policy and the Covid-19 Crisis: The Macroeconomic Response in the US, Europe and East Asia* (Routledge: London).

Andreosso-O'Callaghan, B., Woosik Moon and Wook Sohn (2022) *Economic Policy and the Covid-19 Crisis: The Macroeconomic Response in the US, Europe and East Asia* (Routledge: London).

Al-Thaqeb, S. A., & Algharabali, B. G. (2019) Economic policy uncertainty: A literature review. *The Journal of Economic Asymmetries*, *20*, e00133.
Bogliacino, F., and Maestri, V. (2016) Wealth Inequality and the Great Recession. Itereconomics. *Review of European Economic Policy*, *51*(2), 61–66.
Birkland, T. A. (2004) "The world changed today": Agenda-setting and policy change in the wake of the September 11 terrorist attacks. *Review of Policy Research*, *21*(2), 179–200.
Breitung, J., and B. Candelon (2006) Testing for short-and long-run causality: A frequency-domain approach. *Testing for Short-and Long-Run Causality: A Frequency-Domain Approach*, *132*(2), 363–378.
Bush, K., and D. Saltarelli. (2000) *The Two Faces of Education in Ethnic Conflict: Towards a Peacebuilding Education for Children*. UNICEF.
Cohen, P., and Rappeport, A. (2022) World's Growth Cools and the Rich-Poor Divide Widens. The New York Times. Available at: https://www.nytimes.com/2021/10/12/business/economy/imf-world-economic-outlook.html
Council of Foreign Relations (2022) The US War in Afghanistan 1999–2021. Available at: https://www.cfr.org/timeline/us-war-afghanistan
Cox, M. (2018) Understanding the Global Rise of Populism. LSE Ideas. Strategic Update, February 2018. Available at: https://www.lse.ac.uk/ideas/publications/updates/populism
Dorfman, R. (1979) A Formula for the Gini Coefficient. *The Review of Economics and Statistics*, *61*(1), 146–149. https://doi.org/10.2307/1924845
Duan, Y., Ma, J., Huang, Y., Chen, X., & Zheng, Z. J. (2021) State fragility and the coronavirus disease 2019 (COVID-19) pandemic: an ecologic analysis of data from 146 countries. *Global Health Journal*, *5*(1), 18–23.
Financial Times (2022) Russian oil exports to India surge as Europe shuns cargoes. Available at: https://www.ft.com/content/5efc6338-3f01-4015-aedf-53a4a1944ca8
Geweke, J. (1982) Measurement of Linear Dependence and Feedback between Multiple Time Series. *Journal of the American Statistical Association*, *77*(378), 304–324.
Hadzi-Vaskov, M., Pienknagura, S. and Antonio Ricci, L. (2021). The macroeconomic impact of social unrest. IMF Working Papers, [online] 2021(135), p.1. https://doi.org/10.5089/9781513582573.001
Hosoya, Y. (1991) The Decomposition and Measurement of the Interdependence between Second-Order Stationary Processes. *Probability Theory and Related Fields*, *88*, 429–444.
IMF (2022) Word Economic Outlook Update. Rising Caseloads, a Disrupted Recovery, and Higher Inflation. January, 2022. Available at: https://www.imf.org/en/Publications/WEO/Issues/2022/01/25/world-economic-outlook-update-january-2022
IMF (2021) World Economic Outlook. Recovery During a Pandemic. Health Concerns, Supply Disruptions, and Price pressures, October 2021. Available at: https://www.imf.org/en/Publications/WEO/Issues/2021/10/12/world-economic-outlook-october-2021
Kammer, A., Azour, J., Aemro Selassie, A., Goldfajn, I., and Rhee, C. (2022) How War in Ukraine is Reverberating Across World's Regions. IMF Blog. Available at: https://blogs.imf.org/2022/03/15/how-war-in-ukraine-is-reverberating-across-worlds-regions/
Kahl, C. H. (2006) States, scarcity, and civil strife in the developing world. In *States, Scarcity, and Civil Strife in the Developing World*. Princeton University Press.
Kuhn, M., Schularick, M. and Steins, U. (2018) How the Financial Crisis Drastically Increased Wealth Inequality in the US. Harvard Business Review. Available at: https://hbr.org/2018/09/research-how-the-financial-crisis-drastically-increased-wealth-inequality-in-the-u-s
Langlois, L. (2021) The Brexit Vote and The Trump Vote: A comparative study of the common trends and factors that led to a populist radical right vote in Britain and

the United States. *Revue LISA/LISA e-Journal* [Online], 19(51)|2021, document 3, Online since July 20 2021. https://doi.org/10.4000/lisa.13054
Lakner, C., Mahler, D. G., Negre, M., & Prydz, E. B. (2022) How much does reducing inequality matter for global poverty?. *The Journal of Economic Inequality*, 20, 1–27.
Murtazashvili, J. "The Collapse of Afghanistan". *Journal of Democracy*, 33(1), Jan. 2022, 40–54.
National Archives (2022) George W. Bush Presidential Library Museum. Material at the George W. Bush Presidential Library Pertaining to the Global War on Terror. 2943 SMU Boulevard, Dallas. Available at: file:///I:/UNITAR%20Partnership/Russia-Ukraine/Literature/DRAFT_ResearchGuide_GWOT_Jan2022%20(1).pdf
O'Connor, N. (2017) Three connections between rising economic inequality and the rise of populism. *Irish Studies in International Affairs*, *28*(1), 29–43.
OECD (2022) OECD Policy Responses to Coronavirus (COVID-19). First Lessons from Government Evaluations of COVID-19 responses: A synthesis. Available at: https://www.oecd.org/coronavirus/policy-responses/first-lessons-from-government-evaluations-of-covid-19-responses-a-synthesis-483507d6/
Rajmil, D., Morales, L., Aira, T., and Cardona Valles, M. (2022) Afghanistan: A Multidimensional Crisis. *Peace Review: A Journal of Social Justice*, 1–10. https://doi.org/10.1080/10402659.2022.2023428
Reinhart, C., and Rogoff, K. (2010) *This Time is Different. Eight Centuries of Financial Folly*, Princeton NJ, Princeton University Press.
Reuters (2022) India's imports of cheap Russian Crude surge since Ukraine invasion. Available at: https://www.reuters.com/business/energy/indias-imports-cheap-russian-crude-surge-since-ukraine-invasion-2022-05-30/
Rossi, U. (2012) There's no hope: The global economic crisis and the politics of resistance in Southern Europe. *Belgian Journal of Geography, Inaugural Issue*, 1–2. https://doi.org/10.4000/belgeo.7071
Rudd, K. (2009) The global financial crisis. *The Monthly*, (Feb 2009), 20–29.
Piketty, T. (2017) *Capital in the 21st Century*. Cambridge Massachusetts. The Belknap Press of Havard University Press.
Piketty, T. (2015) *The Economics of Inequality*. Cambridge Massachusetts. The Belknap Press of Harvard University Press.
Saith, A. (2011) Inequality, imbalance, instability: Reflections on a structural crisis. *Development and Change*, *42*(1), 70–86.
Singh, A. K. (2020) The "Oil War" of 2020 Between Saudi Arabia and Russia. *Indian Journal of Asian Affairs*, *33*(1/2), 24–42.
The 9/11 Commission Report (2004): *Final Report of the National Commission on Terrorist Attacks upon the United States*. New York: Norton, 2004
Transparency International (2021) Is Covid-19 Nationalism Corruption? Transparency International Global Health. Available at: https://ti-health.org/content/is-covid-19-vaccine-nationalism-corruption/
UN(2022) To Avert "Irreversible" Damage in Afghanistan, International Community Must Engage with Country's De Facto Authorities, Mission Head Tells Security Council. Available at: https://www.un.org/press/en/2022/sc14815.doc.htm
UNHCR (2021) UNHCR warns Afghanistan's conflict taking the heaviest toll on displaced women and children. Available at: https://www.unhcr.org/en-ie/news/briefing/2021/8/611617c55/unhcr-warns-afghanistans-conflict-taking-heaviest-toll-displaced-women.html
Weinberg, J. (2013) The Great Recession and Its Aftermath. Federal Reserve History. Available at: https://www.federalreservehistory.org/essays/great-recession-and-its-aftermath

WHO (2020) WHO Director-General's Opening Remarks at the Media Briefing on COVID-19 – March 11 2020. Available at: https://www.who.int/director-general/speeches/detail/who-director-general-s-opening-remarks-at-the-media-briefing-on-covid-19---11-march-2020

Wolff, G. (2022) The EU Without Russian Oil and Gas. *Intereconomics*, *57*(2), 66–67.

World Bank Group (2022) Economic Monitoring. Global Monthly NEwletter – March Issue. Available at: https://www.worldbank.org/en/research/brief/economic-monitoring

Yagci, A.H. (2017) The Great Recession, Inequality and Occupy Protests around the World. *Government and Opposition*, 52(4), 640–670.

Part 2

Energy Dilemma

6 China's Ambition for Energy Sustainability

The Challenges Ahead

Intesar Madi, Lucía Morales, Bernadette Andreosso-O'Callaghan and Suleman Sarwar

6.1 Introduction

Ahead of the 28th Conference of Parties (COP28), the USA and China, the world's leading carbon-emitting countries, issued a Sunnyland Agreement that announced a new phase to "*accelerate the substitution for coal, oil, and gas generations*" instead of "*phasing out*" fossil fuels. The USA and China have agreed to further their commitment to implementing both the April 2021 US-China Joint Statement on Tackling the Climate Crisis, and the COP26 US-China Joint Commitment of the Glasgow Declaration to strengthen Climate Action in the 2020s. The Glasgow Agreement aimed to accelerate the reduction of "*Greenhouse gas emissions*" in line with the targets set in the 2015 Paris Agreement. However, for both nations, the effective execution of the Paris Agreement and related decisions, such as the COP27 Sharm el-Sheikh Implementation Plan and the COP26 Glasgow Climate Pact, remains a top priority. The significance of COP28 in addressing environmental degradation during this decade and beyond was highlighted, with a need to engage in discussions that seek to put forward a working agenda with actionable goals supported by policies that enable progress (China Energy Transformation Outlook (CETO) report, 2023).

Over the past decades, coal has been the dominant energy source used to fuel China's rapid economic development, soaring from 114 Million tons (in 1965) to nearly 1,958 Mtoe of Coal extracted in 2019 (Guilhot, 2022). Energy supply in China's economy heavily depends on coal power, making up nearly 80 percent. However, coal's negative effects on the environment and human health have been singled it out as being associated with carbon emissions in China (Dong et al., 2017; Guilhot, 2022). Therefore, the country's coal emissions demonstrate its level of responsibility and the reason why other nations require China's cooperation in monitoring coal production and use (Dong et al., 2018). The country has recently transitioned from double-digit growth rates to a new growth ambition guided by high-quality growth, which will inevitably increase the demand for energy infrastructure that is expected to have an impact on the environment more than its previous high-speed

DOI: 10.4324/9781032655857-9

development (Hu et al., 2021). As China's economy moves into a new growth stage known as the *new normal*, it shifts its focus towards higher quality, greater energy efficiency, improved fairness, and enhanced sustainability (Heng, 2018). In reality, China has been actively implementing various major policies in the past few years to foster a shift from rapid economic growth to a focus on top-notch development. To achieve a comprehensive and integrated growth level encompassing all aspects of its political, socioeconomic, cultural, and ecological dimensions, China must place a significant emphasis on its economic structure (at both the production and consumption levels) by embracing the five pillars of development based on innovation, coordination, sustainable growth, international engagement, and collaboration and by considering the needs of an evolving economy (Wan et al., 2023; Guilhot, 2022; Wang et al., 2022a; Heng, 2018).

In response to the urgent need to confront the global challenges caused by environmental degradation, China has prioritised the goal of reaching peak carbon emissions by 2030 and of striving for complete "*carbon neutrality*" by 2060. Unfortunately, with the current energy crisis that started in 2022 and with the dual shock that took place in March 2020 caused by the COVID-19 health crisis and the oil price war between Russia and Saudi Arabia the world economic system suffered a significant disruption (Ma et al., 2021). The implications of the current situation in terms of energy uncertainty enhanced by the demands of *Industry 4.0*, and combined with the exponential growth of industrialisation and urbanisation, imply that China's energy demands will continue to overgrow, making carbon emission targets more difficult to achieve compared to other countries (Li et al., 2022; Chang et al., 2019).

As an emerging economy – a status that has been questioned by academics, researchers, and experts – China continues to face various obstacles; one of the biggest challenges is that the planned transition period between its carbon peak and "*zero emissions*[1]" targets is relatively short. In developed countries, the peak of carbon emissions typically occurs after the completion of industrial and urban developments (Dong et al., 2021). Energy transition and its demands seem to be following some of the theoretical fundamentals associated with the well-known Kuznets curve.[2] An environmental connection can be identified, as economic growth and development lead towards increasing emissions of pollutants that are closely connected to the use of energy (Stern, 2004). The economic miracle associated with China's fast economic development can also be connected to the ideas underlying the environmental Kuznets curve which provides a working framework connecting energy use, economic growth and the environment when considered from the (negative) externalities dimension and from its implications in terms of environmental erosion and degradation. China is still at an early stage of economic development with a very large population, profound economic imbalances, and inadequacy in its regional development patterns. Moreover, the expansion of industrial and urban areas will result in a continuous rise in energy demands, but the dominance of coal in the energy mix is unlikely to change in the near future as coal remains the cheapest energy resource (Wan et al., 2023; Madi et al., 2022; Zheng et al., 2019).

President Xi Jinping has announced that the world's second-largest economy will aim to achieve its carbon "*net zero*" targets by 2060 and will effectively strive to cap the levels of CO_2 emissions by 2030. Although China has shown an intention to achieve a "*zero-carbon*" economy by 2060, the fact that President Xi Jinping has not specified the country's carbon emission levels raises doubts about the achievability of this ambition. China's target of reaching its "*carbon neutrality*" is only six years behind major developed economies. However, the transition towards carbon net zero emissions takes approximately 30 years (2030–2060), and this is significantly shorter than the EU's targets (Dong et al., 2021). In short, China has put itself under much strain to keep its economic growth on target while conducting social transformations faster (Liang et al., 2021).

Therefore, this research chapter offers critical insights by examining whether China's 2060 carbon-neutral footprint schedule is realistic while offering insights on the challenges and opportunities that emerge from the reviewed literature. Although several studies have been conducted to assess China's carbon emissions and track its progress in meeting emission reduction targets, offering valuable insights for future decarbonisation strategies, the majority of these studies have suggested that it is crucial to conduct well-structured energy-modelling studies in shedding light on the connection between China's 2060 carbon neutrality targets and its ambition, capability, and realisation (Liu et al., 2021b; Sun et al., 2022; Zhang et al., 2021). To accomplish the paper's goal, a systemic and critical literature review was developed to understand China's ambitions and the feasibility of reaching its net-zero targets. The remainder of the chapter is thus organised as follows. Section 2 presents the literature review and discusses the related research on China's energy model and the feasibility of "*net zero*" targets. Section 3 describes China's energy transition pathways. Section 4 presents policy implications, and Section 5 concludes the paper by offering general thoughts for further research.

6.2 China's Energy Model

In light of rising environmental concerns and significantly slowing economic growth, the country has been forced to change its energy model to a more environmentally friendly one that meets its energy needs. The reviewed literature provides updated insights into the country's energy transition as several studies have begun to examine China's carbon neutrality agenda to accomplish its 2060 goals. Globally, China has made tremendous progress in lowering its coal consumption. China's dependence on coal, oil and natural gas accounted for 54.3 percent, 15.7 percent, and 8.6 percent of the total energy

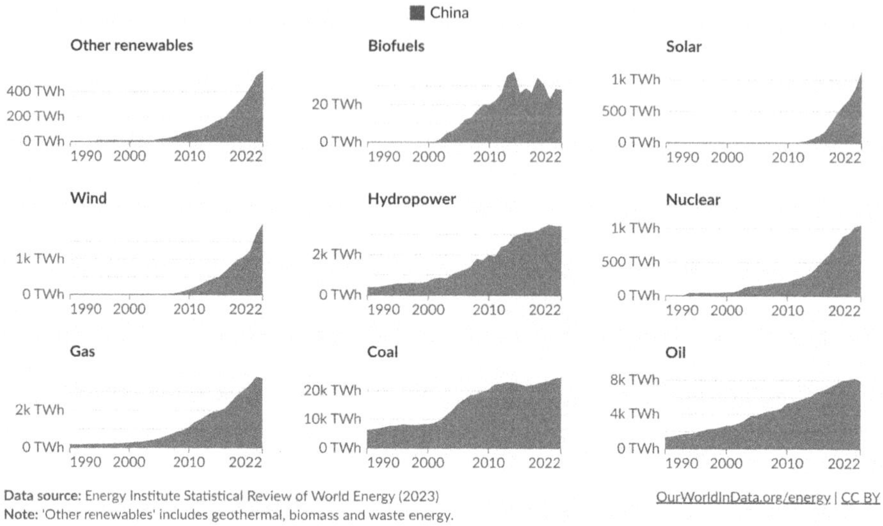

Figure 6.1 Total Energy Consumption, China (1990–2021).

Source: Our World in Data based on BP Statistical Review of World Energy (2023).

Key: TWh is tetra watt per hour.

consumption in 2020, respectively (Xu et al., 2023). China has been a net oil importer since the 1990s, and the energy mix reflects the country's overreliance on fossil fuels (Figure 6.1). As the Asian economy seeks to identify an energy model that complies with international sustainability demands, a major dilemma emerges regarding renewable energy availability and affordability; this is closely linked to required infrastructure patterns that support the country's energy sustainability demands. China's new orientation towards oil generates concerns about its energy security interests and its long-term economic growth aspirations. To address this threat, and in an effort to promote a strong and sustainable economy and reduce pollution, China has started diversifying its energy sources by decreasing its reliance on energy imports. However, despite attempts to reduce its dominance, coal remains the primary energy source, while clean energy usage has risen to 24.3 percent, with non-fossil fuel energy contributing 15.8 percent to the total energy consumption (NBS, 2021). The Center for International Knowledge on Development (CIKD, 2023) recently released a report on China's progress towards the 2030 sustainable development agenda. The report demonstrates that the energy production mix saw an increase in non-fossil fuel energy from 14.5 percent to more than 20 percent in the period of 2015–2021, while the share of unrefined coal decreased to 66.7 percent. However, there was a noticeable shift in the mix in terms of energy consumption as the share of non-fossil fuel energy increased from 12 percent to more than 16 percent, while the share of coal declined from 63.8 percent to 55.9 percent. During the same period, China emerged as a global leader in renewable energy in 2022, with its national capacity surpassing 1.2 billion kilowatts and creating a paradoxical situation where China is identified as the world's biggest emitter of carbon dioxide and the world's leading power in the development of renewable energies. Furthermore, the utilisation of renewable energy sources has reached 47.3 percent of the total installed productive capacity. It is projected that by the year 2030, non-fossil consumption will make up approximately 25 percent of the total energy consumption (CIKD Report, 2023). China's position towards leading investment in renewable energy is consolidating at a time when the country faces a dilemma on how to become less dependent on coal as a primary energy source (Zhang & Chen, 2022; Liu et al., 2022; Dong et al., 2021; Hepbum et al., 2021; Change et al., 2019).

Unlike many emerging countries, China's energy sources have remained relatively unchanged over the last few decades. According to the China Energy Transformation Outlook report (2023), coal has remained China's leading energy source for the past 20 years, accounting for more than 72 percent of total energy consumption in 2005 and constituting 56.2 percent of energy consumption in 2022 (CETO, 2023). Although the country appears to be shifting from coal to oil and natural gas, coal still dominates China's energy mix, and the dependency on fossil fuels provides evidence of the challenges associated with green energy transformation. With such high coal consumption, China has been facing numerous environmental issues – such as rising CO_2 emissions and worsening air quality, as well as significant overcapacity in the energy sector, natural resource constraints, and increased reliance on foreign energy sources, which have harmed China's economic performance. Coal consumption was responsible for over 70 percent of total CO_2 emissions in China in 2019. The combustion of fossil fuels in China contributed to the gradual and slow increase in CO_2 emissions between 1980 and 2001. Throughout this time, there was an annual increase of 8 percent in China's emission rate, rising from 1,467 to 3,694 million tons. The rise in emission rates can be attributed to the country's development and the demands posed by manufacturing activities, which expanded formidably after China joined the World Trade Organization (WTO) in 2001.

Consequently, China's greenhouse gas emissions increased dramatically, with an annual average of 13 percent from 2002 to 2007. However, human-caused CO_2 emissions in China account for over half of the worldwide yearly CO_2 emissions, propelling China to be identified as the world's leading energy consumer and CO_2 emitter. On the other hand, China's investment in renewable energies contributes to reducing global emissions and addressing environmental degradation (CETO, 2023; Shan et al., 2018; Khan & Chang, 2018; Guan et al., 2009). Even though coal has contributed significantly to the country's rapid economic expansion, it is indisputably linked to many environmental challenges resulting from rising extraction and consumption patterns.

While adjusting to its "*new normal model*" and achieving "*carbon neutrality*" targets by 2026, China's government faces many environmental difficulties, including improving energy use, reducing emissions, and transitioning to more sustainable energy sources. Thus, a zero-tolerance policy[3] was adopted to successfully address ecological difficulties and obstacles in balancing industrial or public emissions and long-term economic growth (Khan & Chang, 2018). During his speech at the 75th session of the United Nations General Assembly's General Debate, President Xi Jinping emphatically declared China's unwavering commitment to ardently pursue the ambitious goal of attaining "*carbon neutrality*" by the year 2060 while simultaneously endeavouring to achieve CO_2 emissions peak no later than 2030 (Zhao, 2022). However, China's target for cutting CO_2 emissions by 2030 is being questioned as it could lead to rising power shortages. A recent report published by China's Energy Foundation (2022) stated that China's energy system has been dramatically influenced by the recent conflict between Russia and Ukraine, resulting in significant effects that will be felt both in the present and the future.

Nonetheless, the current energy crisis has affected China's energy imports, with energy price hikes. The ongoing energy crisis has also been compounded by a scarcity of coal and rising demand due to global COVID-19 lockdowns and the unresolved Russian-Ukraine crisis that caused significant uncertainty and increasing volatility levels in the global energy market. The impact of sanctions and potential supply cuts from Russia has caused oil and gas prices to skyrocket and exhibit erratic market behaviour. This has resulted in China's government enacting measures to enhance domestic coal production and protect supplies, for energy security reasons (China's Energy Foundation, 2022). China's dependency on Russian commodity exports and global markets leaves the country vulnerable. However, the Russia-Ukraine conflict greatly affected China's immediate energy supplies, influencing its policy priorities for the upcoming year and shaping its long-term energy strategies. In the short term, China is likely to encounter increased energy costs and commodity prices, much like other energy-importing countries (Meidan, 2023).

According to its initial Nationally Determined Contribution (NDC) for the Paris Agreement, China has set a target to reach its peak CO_2 emissions by 2030, in addition to three other objectives (Table 6.1): (i) achieving a 40–45 percent drop in carbon emissions per unit of GDP by 2020, relative to 2005 levels (Xu et al., 2023); (ii) By 2030, the goal is to raise the proportion of non-fossil fuels in primary energy usage to approximately 20 percent; (iii) the amount of forest stock is expected to have increased by approximately 6 billion cubic meters based on 2005 levels, and by 2030, the total capacity of wind and solar energy installed in the country is expected to rise (Ritchie and Roser, 2022; Yang et al., 2017). The enhanced NDC objectives offer significant additions to global climate regulations and establish more substantial expectations for China's climate efforts (UNFCCC, 2020).

Table 6.1 Summary of China's NDC Strategies for Carbon Neutrality

Scenario	*Original NDC to Carbon Neutrality*	*Updated NDC to Carbon Neutrality*
Net-Zero GHG Year	2060	2060
Net CO_2 Emissions Peak Year	2030	Before 2030
Alignment with Near-Term Policies	Aligns with first NDC submission up to 2030	Aligns with updated NDC up to 2030
Goals	• To integrate energy efficiency in essential energy-consuming sectors with international guidelines. • To significantly decrease the energy intensity of economic activity. • To achieve a decrease of more than 65% in CO_2 per unit of GDP, relative to the 2005 level. • To enhance the adoption of renewable energy to a level of 25%. • To exceed 1,200 GW in total installed capacity for wind and solar power. • To raise the forest coverage to 19 billion m^3. • To hit the peak and reach the plateau of carbon emissions.	• To create a foundational structure for an environmentally friendly, sustainable, and cyclical economy. • It is strengthening the energy efficiency of essential industries. • To reduce energy consumption per unit of GDP by 13.5% compared to the 2020 level. • To achieve an 18% reduction in carbon dioxide emissions per unit of GDP from the 2020 level. • To enhance the percentage of non-fossil power consumption to about 20% • To achieve a 24.1% forest coverage and a total of 18 billion m^3 of forest stock.

Source: Adapted from Energy Foundation China (November, 2022).

Key: GHG: greenhouse gas.

6.3 China Energy Transition Pathways

6.3.1 Paris Agreement Targets vs COPs

In adherence to the Paris Agreement (COP21), 196 nations committed to decreasing their greenhouse gas (GHG) emissions and were required to submit a Nationally Determined Contribution (NDC) outlining their approaches to reducing CO_2 emissions (Carlson et al., 2021). The implementation of these NDCs was put into effect in November 2016, highlighting the determination of countries to mitigate emissions and cope with the consequences of environmental degradation. In the negotiation process leading to the Paris Agreement, and in an effort to reduce carbon emissions, the Chinese government has established a target to reach its peak and boost the utilisation of non-fossil fuels in its energy combination to 20 percent by 2030 (Zhao et al., 2022). Thus, in its first NDC plan, China has set a goal to cap CO_2 emissions around 2030 and endeavours to reach this peak sooner. In addition, the strategy sets a target of decreasing CO_2 emissions per unit of GDP by 60–65 percent from the 2005 level, increasing the use of renewable energy sources to approximately 20 percent of primary energy consumption, and enhancing the total volume of forests by approximately 4.5 billion cubic meters compared to the 2005 levels. On October 28, 2021, China announced its NDC update and set a goal for achieving carbon neutrality. China's latest NDC objectives are centred on: achieving a peak in CO_2 emissions prior to 2030 and reaching "*carbon neutrality*" before 2060 while also lowering CO_2 emissions levels per unit of GDP by over 65 percent compared to the 2005 level; to achieve a notable growth of approximately 25 percent in the integration of non-fossil fuels into the primary energy consumption, and to reach a total installed capacity of over 1.2 billion Kilowatts in total installed wind and solar power capacity by 2030, and to raise forest stock by 6 billion cubic meters from its 2005 level (UNFCCC, 2022). The amended NDC targets constitute a significant contribution to global climate governance,[4] and they have established heightened expectations for China's commitment to addressing environmental degradation. China's CO_2 emission per unit of GDP in 2019 was only 51.9 percent of what it was in 2005. It surpasses the 2020 objective of decreasing CO_2 emissions per unit of GDP by 40–45 percent from the 2005 level, resulting in a cumulative reduction of around 5.7 billion tonnes in CO_2 emissions (Qi et al., 2023; Liu et al., 2021a; Zheng et al., 2019).

The Paris Agreement has not established a defined objective for achieving "*carbon neutrality*[5]", which poses significant challenges regarding countries' commitment towards the 1.5^{0}C target. According to the World Bank's most updated report, China is well positioned to transition towards a greener economy while meeting its developmental goals (World Bank, 2022). However, this is a debatable issue, as the country still shows a high dependency on coal (CAT, 2023). To successfully achieve carbon neutrality, China must adopt a strategic mindset encompassing sustainable economic development, social progress, and environmental preservation (Dong et al., 2021; Hepburn et al., 2021). The "Climate Pact", which was adopted by almost 200 countries at COP26, is an essential part of the Paris Agreement rulebook and provides a way to preserve the aims of the treaty and spur the decarbonisation of the global economy (Zhao, 2022). In light of the Glasgow summit, various measures were introduced to decrease emissions further by 2030, including plans to reduce emissions, a commitment to promoting zero-emission vehicles for more environmentally friendly transportation, and acknowledging the problem of deforestation. However, despite the conference's efforts, the evaluation shows that the objectives were not met and that the roadmap remains unclear (Arora & Mishra, 2021). To effectively implement the objectives of COP26, a crucial step was to phase out coal and for all countries to discontinue financing or subsidising the construction of new coal-fired power stations (Guilhot, 2022).

However, in contrast to the 26th Conference of Parties that took place in Glasgow, the COP27 stood out for its remarkable China Pavilion, which was the epicentre of a plethora of enriching events focusing on crucial topics such as climate finance, the adoption of sustainable practices, and the effective implementation of the Chinese Emissions Trading Scheme (ETS) that accelerates actions to reach "*net-zero*" before 2050 (Climate Cooperation China, 2022). The ETS can potentially be a vital tool in China's efforts to meet its Nationally Determined Contribution and long-term low-carbon strategy as outlined in the Paris Agreement for climate change. In addition, at the 28th Conference of Parties (COP28), China made notable progress in multiple aspects, including the global stocktake, climate financing, the Loss and Damage Fund, the food security and agriculture fund, tripling renewable energy capacity by 2030, and addressing methane emissions, which may be a highly potent greenhouse gas according to Xu (2023) (Table 6.2).

Table 6.2 COPs' Core Outcomes Agreed upon at the UN Climate Talks and China's Position

2015 Paris Agreement (COP21)		
Topic	*Issue*	*Position*
Recognising the emergency	Aim to cap the temperature rise at 1.5°C above pre-industrial levels.	Oppose
Moving away from fossil fuels	Peak CO_2 emissions by 2030. Increase non-fossil fuel share to 20% by 2030.	Priority
Delivering on climate finance	Delivery of $100bn from 2020 onwards	Priority
COP26		
Topic	Issue	Position
Recognising the emergency	Proceeds under Article 6.2	Priority
Moving away from fossil fuels	Coal phase-down	Priority
Accelerating action	No Action	No Action
Delivering on climate finance	Delivery of $100bn	Priority
Stepping up support for adaptation	No Action	No Action
Completing the Paris rulebook		Priority
Focusing on loss & damage	Loss and damage finance	Priority
COP27		
Topic	Issue	Position
Recognising the emergency	No Action	No Action
Moving away from fossil fuels	No Action	No Action
Accelerating action	Developed nations reach net-zero before 2050	Priority
Delivering on climate finance	Delivery of $100bn	Priority

(*Continued*)

Table 6.2 (Continued)

COP27		
Topic	*Issue*	*Position*
Stepping up support for adaptation	No Action	No Action
Completing the Paris rulebook	Language on *"major emitters"*	Red line
	Runs until 2030	Oppose
	New rules for specific industries, sectors or greenhouse gases	Oppose
Focusing on loss & damage	Establish loss and damage finance facility	Priority
COP28		
Topic	Issue	Position
Recognising the emergency	No Action	No Action
Moving away from fossil fuels	Phase out all fossil fuels	Oppose
	Phase out unabated fossil fuels	Do not support
	Triple renewable energy capacity	Support
	Use of CCS	Support
Accelerating action	Peaking global emissions by 2030	Priority
Delivering on climate finance	No Action	No Action
Stepping up support for adaptation	GST to set up CMA mechanism to implement GGA goals	Priority
	Recognise adaptation finance gap	High Priority
Completing the Paris rulebook	No Action	No Action
Focusing on loss & damage	Hosted by the World Bank	Oppose
	Only/mainly developed countries contribute	Priority

Source: author's elaborations (2023).

6.3.2 The Reality of **"Net-Zero"** *Targets*

The growth of the world's second-largest economy goes in tandem with its energy consumption and its need for power (Xu et al., 2023). However, as the new energy model shifts towards other types of fossil fuels, serious concerns emerge regarding the fight against environmental degradation or achieving its "*zero carbon*" targets. During COP 26, China was praised for reducing its coal emissions, yet in order to meet the targets for carbon neutralities, China must overcome a considerable challenge in reconciling its ambitions in terms of decarbonisation with the need to maintain a compelling economic growth rate (Reuters, 2021). Table 6.3 below highlights the need to implement a strategic plan that enables energy efficiency. China might consider different approaches that help to consolidate the country's position as a lead on renewable energies. To help address sustainability challenges and to face growing levels of uncertainty, the government needs to engage in a phase-out decarbonisation plan. Furthermore, it is vital to take into consideration the global landscape defined by "permacrisis[6]" and "polycrises[7]", which bring additional risks and uncertainties with direct implications for the

Table 6.3 Summary of China's 2030–2060 Carbon Neutrality Opportunities and Challenges

China's 2030–2060 Carbon Neutrality	
Opportunities	*Challenges*
• Energy efficiency improvement. • Implement a strategic plan to phase-out of fossil fuels, especially coal. • Enhancing the share of renewable energy in the overall energy mix from 18% to 77%–85%, in 30 years will be a difficult challenge. • Geoeconomics and Geopolitics uncertainties and energy security.	• Low-carbon cities • Green technology markets • Leading Renewable Energy • Leading position in solar and wind energy • Diversifying energy model • Addressing environmental degradation • Shift to local and regional economies • Growing Levels of development in the Asian Regions

Source: Authors' elaborations (2023).

economic agenda and countries' ability and capabilities to support the required investments associated with energy transition (World Economic Forum, 2023, 2024). For many years, China has been regarded as the world's factory, with a global manufacturing share of 27 percent of GDP in 2021, much higher than any developed economy such as Germany or Japan (World Bank 2023). Manufacturing is concentrated heavily in sectors characterised by high CO_2 emissions such as energy production; the country's CO_2 emissions alone equal 2.2 times the total emissions of Europe (WEF, 2022). Nevertheless, the carbon-intensive foundation of the Chinese economy necessitates a significant reallocation of resources, creativity, advancements in technology, and investments to improve energy efficiency and achieve net zero emissions (World Bank, 2023).

By intending to reach carbon peak objectives by the year 2030 and ultimately to achieve complete decarbonisation by 2060, China has set itself a challenging 30-year timeline that is bound to present numerous difficulties and hurdles (Tan et al., 2022; Jiang et al., 2019). However, the transition to "*zero carbon*" has only begun, and for China to achieve the peak of its CO_2 emissions before 2030 is dependent on progress in three key fields: energy efficiency, renewable energy and reduction of coal use (IEA, 2021). The energy sector accounts for nearly 90 percent of China's greenhouse gas emissions. Despite economic projections, the initial stage of this roadmap – the Announced Pledges Scenario (APS) – predicts slower growth in China's primary energy demand until 2030. Additionally, by 2060, coal demand will decrease by over 80 percent, oil by approximately 60 percent, and natural gas by more than 45 percent, with solar energy emerging as the leading primary energy source by 2045 (IEA, 2021; Yang et al., 2018). The Chinese government has tried to reduce its energy consumption and had made efforts to change the energy system (Madi et al., 2022). In order to achieve this goal, China's government revised its renewable energy law in 2005. A few years later, in 2009, the government launched a pilot program to explore the potential of utilising the golden sun for solar thermal purposes. The share of renewable energy sources like hydro-, nuclear-, wind-, and solar-power experienced significant growth in the 12th Five-Year Plan (2011–2015), rapidly increasing by 20.8 percent by 2017 (Yang et al., 2019).

Investing in low-carbon and resilient city development is the key to reducing city emissions and addressing climate change issues. According to a report from the World Bank (2023), China's manufacturing in large concentrated areas contributes more than 70 percent of global emissions of CO2, the majority of which comes from industries using massive amounts of fossil fuels (World Bank, 2023). Furthermore, in 2016, policymakers were greatly concerned by including 10 Chinese cities on the World Health Organisation's list of the world's most polluted cities (Ethan et al., 2021). Figure 6.2 identifies most of China's polluted provinces in 2022, showing that more than 75 percent of China's coal-fired, wind-powered, solar-powered and Hydropower reserves are in China's western region. The five provinces of the East Coast, namely Fujian, and Guangdong, account for almost two-fifths of China's total energy consumption. The emission trajectory for most countries has been slower than expected in the modelling, leading to a considerable gap between the actual reductions in emissions of greenhouse gases (GHG) and those required to meet the Paris Agreement (Luderer et al., 2018; UNEP, 2019). The same situation could be happening in China, as policymakers have yet to find a solution to this problem.

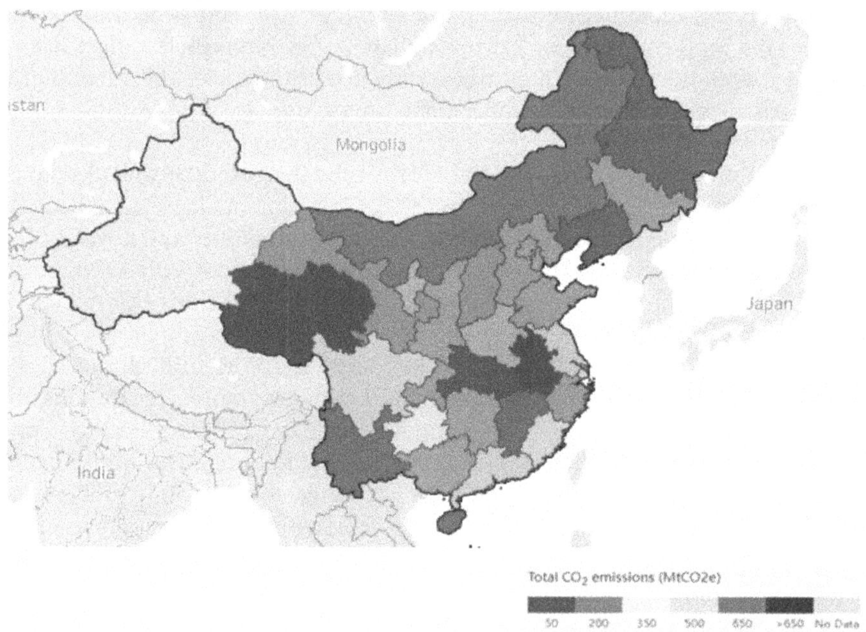

Figure 6.2 CO_2 Emissions Levels in China's Provinces.

Table 6.4 Summary of China's Top Provinces with CO_2 Emission Value

Rank	*Province*	*Total value of CO_2 Emissions ($MtCO_2e$)*
1	Shandong	1000.86
2	Inner Mongolia	921.31
3	Hubei	794.18
4	Jiangsu	778.45
5	Guangdong	617.97
6	Shanxi	544.39
7	Liaoning	527.75
8	Xinjiang	502.77
9	Henan	491.68
10	Zhejiang	441.23

Source: China City Greenhouse Gas Working Group (CCG, 2020) & author's elaboration (2023).

6.3.3 China's 2030–2060 Carbon Neutrality Pledges

In September 2020, Chinese President Xi Jinping committed to reach peak carbon emissions by 2030 and achieve carbon neutrality by 2060. Within 40 years, China must alter its energy productive system to reach carbon neutrality on schedule (Zhao, 2022). The energy system's dependence on coal makes achieving a zero-carbon target by 2060 a major undertaking with many implications. China needs to prioritise expanding its use of renewable energy and investing in energy-related advancements to drive economic growth. This unilateral commitment has a crucial impact on the global stage by catalysing efforts towards more ambitious climate goals and policies. It also solidifies China's position as the leader in climate diplomacy (Meidan, 2020). In 2007, China showed its dedication to the world by setting up the National Leading Group on Climate Change, Energy Conservation, and Emission Reduction. This group was tasked with creating effective strategies and addressing urgent issues related to climate change, energy conservation, and emission reduction (Zhao et al., 2022). China first declared its plans for carbon reduction and control in 2009, aiming to achieve a 40–45 percent decrease in CO_2 emission per unit of GDP by 2020 relative to 2005 (Xu et al., 2023). In 2011, China introduced a plan to develop a carbon trading policy for CO_2 in key cities, including Beijing, Shanghai, and Guangdong, to reduce GHG emissions levels, particularly carbon dioxide, from energy usage. As the top carbon polluter in the world expands its pilot program, Shenzhen launched its inaugural carbon emission exchange in 2013 as illustrated in Figure 6.3 below, with Shanghai and Beijing joining later to curb emissions. Furthermore, China acted in 2017 by implementing a national emissions trading scheme (ETS) to

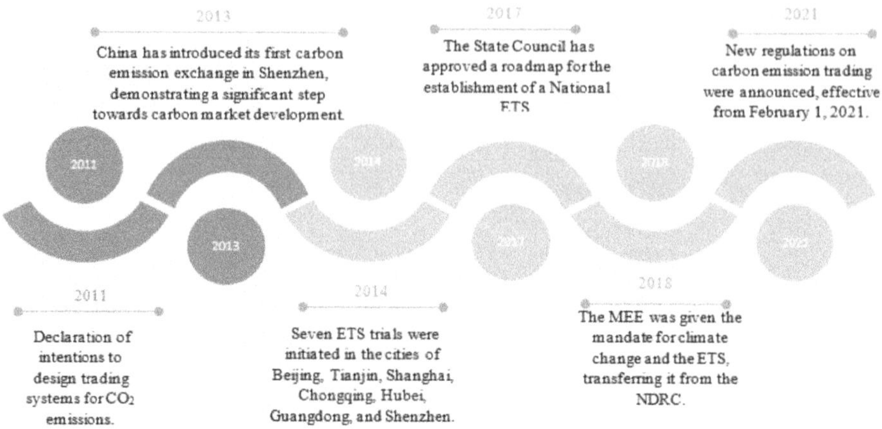

Figure 6.3 Key Dates in the Development of China's National ETS.

Source: Author elaboration adopted from Karplus (2021).

effectively control and decrease CO2 emissions. The ETS has the potential to be a vital tool in China's efforts to meet its Nationally Determined Contribution and long-term low-carbon strategy as outlined in the Paris Agreement for climate change. Therefore, China's emissions trading system (ETS), which is set to encompass seven additional sectors, will become the largest in the world by a significant margin, accounting for approximately one-seventh of global CO_2 emissions from burning fossil fuels as reported by the International Energy Agency (IEA, 2020). In addition, China has outlined a new objective in 2020 to attain peak carbon emissions prior to 2030 and attain complete carbon neutrality by 206**0**.

6.4 Conclusion and Policy Implications

The main outcomes of this study hold significant policy implications for the Chinese government and provide insights into the challenging situation faced in the design of efficient policies and the complex issues for decision-makers. Meeting the 2060 net-zero goal in China will require strategic policy-making and interventions that align with their carbon neutrality pledges from 2030 to 2060. Despite China's commitments to achieving a zero-carbon economy by 2060, the lack of specific targets for total energy use and carbon emissions raises doubts about this plan's feasibility, as President Xi Jinping outlined. Since the 1990s, China has consistently increased its carbon emissions, making it one of the top countries in terms of carbon emission levels. Carbon capture and storage processes, technologies and policies to effectively reduce carbon emissions and achieve the 2060 agenda are challenging. However, the country's Carbon capture, utilisation, and storage (CCUS) strategies are not directly applicable. Although CCUS technology has gained international recognition as a highly efficient and promising solution for reducing carbon emissions,

China has yet to implement a widespread and comprehensive long-term strategy for advancing CCUS technology, which would help lower the expenses associated with carbon capture and storage.

Securing energy resources is identified as one of the main priorities for the Chinese government. However, the transition towards an eco-friendly economic development strategy poses significant difficulties for China. Unlike many emerging countries, China's energy sources have remained relatively unchanged over the last few decades. According to the China Energy Transformation Outlook report (CETO, 2023), coal has remained China's leading energy source for the past 20 years, accounting for more than 72 percent of total energy consumption in 2005 and constituting 56.2 percent of energy consumption in 2022. Although the country appears to be shifting from coal towards oil and natural gas, coal still dominates China's energy mix (Madi et al., 2022). The world economy is facing significant challenges as a result of geopolitical conflicts in the Middle East & North Africa (MENA) region, the ongoing war between Russia and Ukraine, the energy crisis and mismanaged economic policy decisions regarding the COVID-19 crisis that led to significant disruption of the global energy supply chains (Morales et al., 2023). Fossil fuel consumption is significant in China, making it one of the leading consumers. However, the ongoing global events are creating new challenges for China's progression with its green energy model and the pressures associated with economic development. The ongoing Russia-Ukraine conflict has disrupted global energy markets, increasing oil and gas prices (Morales et al., 2023). As a net energy importer, China's ambition for energy sustainability and the reality of its net-zero targets will be subject to the availability of energy supply and energy security. As a result of the current global turmoil, China has been facing increased energy costs and rising commodity prices. Domestically, in 2021 and 2022, China faced numerous power shortages, leading to a primary focus on ensuring a consistent and dependable energy supply. The shift towards "*carbon neutrality*" poses a dilemma for China as it must balance decarbonisation ambitions and the need for robust economic growth. However, meeting China's climate pledges of carbon neutrality and sustainable economic growth will require a significant transition in the energy system; therefore, the country's effort to ensure energy security remains a top priority during this transition, underlining the significance of further research studies in this field.

Notes

1 Zero carbon means that no carbon emissions are being emitted through the production of a product or service.
2 Simon Kuznets hypothesised the idea that income inequality experiences an initial rise and decreases as the economic development process evolves.
3 The Zero Tolerance policy for Carbon-Dioxide Emissions states that coal plants must capture and sequester their carbon dioxide.
4 Global climate governance (negotiations) are the processes developed to create agreements between countries to promote and ensure ambitious action against "climate change" and its effects.

5 Carbon neutrality means having a balance between emitting carbon and absorbing carbon from the atmosphere in carbon sinks.
6 Permacrisis: "an extended period of instability and insecurity".
7 Polycrisis: "The simultaneous occurrence of several catastrophic events".

References

Arora, N. K., & Mishra, I. (2021). COP26: more challenges than achievements. In *Environmental Sustainability* (Vol. 4, Issue 4, pp. 585–588). Springer Science and Business Media LLC. https://doi.org/10.1007/s42398-021-00212-7

Carlson, D., Robinson, S., Blair, C., & McDonough, M. (2021). China's climate ambition: Revisiting its First Nationally Determined Contribution and centering a just transition to clean energy. In *Energy Policy* (Vol. 155, p. 112350). Elsevier BV. https://doi.org/10.1016/j.enpol.2021.112350

Centre for International Knowledge on Development (CIKD), (2023). China's Progress Report on Implementation of the 2030 Agenda for Sustainable Development.

CETO. (2023). China energy Transformation Outlook 2023 (p.301). Energy Research Institute of Chinese Academy of Macroeconomic research. https://www.cet.energy/2023/12/14/china-energy-transformation-outlook-2023/

China City Greenhouse Gas Working Group (CCG). (2020). Cityghg.com. https://www.cityghg.com/

Chang, C.-P., Dong, M., Sui, B., & Chu, Y. (2019). Driving forces of global carbon emissions: From time- and spatial-dynamic perspectives. In *Economic Modelling* (Vol. 77, pp. 70–80). Elsevier BV. https://doi.org/10.1016/j.econmod.2019.01.021

China's Progress Report. (2023). https://www.mfa.gov.cn/web/ziliao_674904/zt_674979/dnzt_674981/qtzt/2030kcxfzyc_686343/yw/202310/P020231018367257234614.pdf

Climate Action Tracker (CAT), (2023). Pulling the plug on fossils in power. https://climateactiontracker.org/documents/1158/CAT_2023-09-19_Briefing_PullingThePlug.pdf

Climate Cooperation China. (2022). China at COP27. https://climatecooperation.cn/climate/china-at-cop27/

Dong, F., Hua, Y., & Yu, B. (2018). Peak Carbon Emissions in China: Status, Key Factors and Countermeasures—A Literature Review. In *Sustainability* (Vol. 10, Issue 8, p. 2895). MDPI AG. https://doi.org/10.3390/su10082895

Dong, H., Dai, H., Geng, Y., Fujita, T., Liu, Z., Xie, Y., Wu, R., Fujii, M., Masui, T., & Tang, L. (2017). Exploring impact of carbon tax on China's CO2 reductions and provincial disparities. In *Renewable and Sustainable Energy Reviews* (Vol. 77, pp. 596–603). Elsevier BV. https://doi.org/10.1016/j.rser.2017.04.044

Dong, H., Xue, M., Xiao, Y., & Liu, Y. (2021). Do carbon emissions impact the health of residents? Considering China's industrialisation and urbanisation. In *Science of The Total Environment* (Vol. 758, p. 143688). Elsevier BV. https://doi.org/10.1016/j.scitotenv.2020.143688

Energy Foundation China (2022). "Synthesis Report 2022 on China's Carbon Neutrality: Electrification in China's Carbon Neutrality Pathways." Energy Foundation China, Beijing, China. Available at: https://www.efchina.org/Attachments/Report/report-lceg-20221104/Synthesis-Report-2022-on-Chinas-Carbon-Neutrality-Electrification-in-Chinas-Carbon-Neutrality-Pathways.pdf

Ethan, C. J., Mokoena, K. K., & Yu, Y. (2021). Air Pollution Status in 10 Mega-Cities in China during the Initial Phase of the COVID-19 Outbreak. *International Journal of Environmental Research and Public Health, 18*(6), 3172. https://doi.org/10.3390/ijerph18063172

Guan, D., Peters, G. P., Weber, C. L., & Hubacek, K. (2009). Journey to world top emitter: An analysis of the driving forces of China's recent CO_2 emissions surge.

Geophysical Research Letters, *36*(4), 2008GL036540. https://doi.org/10.1029/2008GL036540
Guilhot, L. (2022). An analysis of China's energy policy from 1981 to 2020: Transitioning towards to a diversified and low-carbon energy system. In Energy Policy (Vol. 162, p. 112806). Elsevier BV. https://doi.org/10.1016/j.enpol.2022.112806
Heng, Q. (2018). Navigating China's Economic Development in the New Era: From High-Speed to High-Quality Growth. In *China Quarterly of International Strategic Studies* (Vol. 04, Issue 02, pp. 177–192). World Scientific Pub Co Pte Lt. https://doi.org/10.1142/s2377740018500161
Hepburn, C., Qi, Y., Stern, N., Ward, B., Xie, C., & Zenghelis, D. (2021). Towards carbon neutrality and China's 14th Five-Year Plan: Clean energy transition, sustainable urban development, and investment priorities. In *Environmental Science and Ecotechnology* (Vol. 8, p. 100130). Elsevier BV. https://doi.org/10.1016/j.ese.2021.100130
Hu, W., Tian, J., & Chen, L. (2021). An industrial structure adjustment model to facilitate high-quality development of an eco-industrial park. *Science of The Total Environment*, *766*, 142502. https://doi.org/10.1016/j.scitotenv.2020.142502
IEA (2020), *Global Energy Review 2020*, IEA, Paris https://www.iea.org/reports/global-energy-review-2020, Licence: CC BY 4.0
International Energy Agency (IEA), (2021). An energy sector roadmap to carbon neutrality in China, https://www.iea.org/reports/an-energy-sector-roadmap-to-carbon-neutrality-in-china
Jiang, T., Huang, S., & Yang, J. (2019). Structural carbon emissions from industry and energy systems in China: An input-output analysis. *Journal of Cleaner Production*, *240*, 118116. https://doi.org/10.1016/j.jclepro.2019.118116
Karplus, V. (2021). China's CO2 Emissions Trading System: History, Status, and Outlook 1. https://heep.hks.harvard.edu/files/heep/files/karplus_china_national_ets_june_2021_english.pdf
Khan, M., & Chang, Y.-C. (2018). Environmental Challenges and Current Practices in China—A Thorough Analysis. *Sustainability*, *10*(7), 2547. https://doi.org/10.3390/su10072547
Li, W., Zhang, S., & Lu, C. (2022). Exploration of China's net CO2 emissions evolutionary pathways by 2060 in the context of carbon neutrality. In *Science of The Total Environment* (Vol. 831, p. 154909). Elsevier BV. https://doi.org/10.1016/j.scitotenv.2022.154909
Liang, G., Yu, D., & Ke, L. (2021). An Empirical Study on Dynamic Evolution of Industrial Structure and Green Economic Growth—Based on Data from China's Underdeveloped Areas. *Sustainability*, *13*(15), 8154. https://doi.org/10.3390/su13158154
Liu, H., Ren, Y., & Wang, N. (2021a). Energy efficiency rebound effect research of China's coal industry. *Energy Reports*, *7*, 5475–5482. https://doi.org/10.1016/j.egyr.2021.08.131
Liu, Z., Deng, Z., He, G., Wang, H., Zhang, X., Lin, J., Qi, Y., & Liang, X. (2021b). Challenges and opportunities for carbon neutrality in China. In *Nature Reviews Earth & Environment* (Vol. 3, Issue 2, pp. 141–155). Springer Science and Business Media LLC. https://doi.org/10.1038/s43017-021-00244-x
Liu, X., Li, Y., Chen, X., & Liu, J. (2022). Evaluation of low carbon city pilot policy effect on carbon abatement in China: An empirical evidence based on time-varying DID model. *Cities*, *123*, 103582. https://doi.org/10.1016/j.cities.2022.103582
Luderer, G., Vrontisi, Z., Bertram, C., Edelenbosch, O. Y., Pietzcker, R. C., Rogelj, J., De Boer, H. S., Drouet, L., Emmerling, J., Fricko, O., Fujimori, S., Havlík, P., Iyer, G., Keramidas, K., Kitous, A., Pehl, M., Krey, V., Riahi, K., Saveyn, B., … Kriegler, E. (2018). Residual fossil CO2 emissions in 1.5–2 °C pathways. *Nature Climate Change*, *8*(7), 626–633. https://doi.org/10.1038/s41558-018-0198-6

Ma, R. R., Xiong, T., & Bao, Y. (2021). The Russia-Saudi Arabia oil price war during the COVID-19 pandemic. *Energy Economics*, *102*, 105517. https://doi.org/10.1016/j.eneco.2021.105517

Madi, I., Morales, L., & Andreosso-O'Callaghan, B. (2022). China's Rise in the Middle East: Fuelling a Tired Dragon? In *Sustainable Development in Asia* (pp. 75–98). Springer International Publishing. https://doi.org/10.1007/978-3-030-94679-1_5

Meidan, M. (2020 January 24). *China: Key Themes for 2020 - Oxford Institute for Energy Studies*. Oxford Institute for Energy Studies. https://www.oxfordenergy.org/publications/china-key-themes-for-2020/

Meidan, M. (2023). *The outlook for China's fossil fuel consumption under the energy transition and its geopolitical implications*. Oxford Institute for Energy Studies. www.oxfordenergy.org

Mi, Z., Zheng, J., Meng, J., Shan, Y., Zheng, H., Ou, J., Guan, D., & Wei, Y. (2018). China's Energy Consumption in the New Normal. In *Earth's Future* (Vol. 6, Issue 7, pp. 1007–1016). American Geophysical Union (AGU). https://doi.org/10.1029/2018ef000840

Morales, L., Rajmil, D., & Andreosso-O'Callaghan, B. (2023). Navigating the Ukraine War: Unraveling the Interplay of Geoeconomics, Geopolitics and Deterrence. In *Peace Review* (Vol. 35, Issue 4, pp. 663–671). Informa UK Limited. https://doi.org/10.1080/10402659.2023.2262408

National Bureau of Statistics of China (NBS), (2021). China Statistical Yearbook 2021. Beijing, China.

Qi, Y., Liu, T., & Jing, L. (2023). China's energy transition towards carbon neutrality with minimum cost. *Journal of Cleaner Production*, *388*, 135904. https://doi.org/10.1016/j.jclepro.2023.135904

Reuters, (2021). China, India, other big coal users missing from COP26 phase-out deal. https://www.reuters.com/business/cop/cop26-coal-deals-take-aim-dirtiest-fossil-fuel-2021-11-03/

Ritchie, H. and Roser, M. (2022) CO_2 Emissions. https://ourworldindata.org/co2-emissions

Shan, Y., Guan, D., Zheng, H., Ou, J., Li, Y., Meng, J., Mi, Z., Liu, Z., & Zhang, Q. (2018). China CO2 emission accounts 1997–2015. In *Scientific Data* (Vol. 5, Issue 1). Springer Science and Business Media LLC. https://doi.org/10.1038/sdata.2017.201

Stern, D. I. (2004). Economic Growth and Energy. In *Encyclopedia of Energy* (pp. 35–51). Elsevier. https://doi.org/10.1016/B0-12-176480-X/00147-9

Sun, L.-L., Cui, H.-J., & Ge, Q.-S. (2022). Will China achieve its 2060 carbon neutral commitment from the provincial perspective? In *Advances in Climate Change Research* (Vol. 13, Issue 2, pp. 169–178). Elsevier BV. https://doi.org/10.1016/j.accre.2022.02.002

Tan, X.-C., Kong, L.-S., Gu, B.-H., Zeng, A., & Niu, M.-M. (2022). Research on the carbon neutrality governance under a polycentric approach. *Advances in Climate Change Research*, *13*(2), 159–168. https://doi.org/10.1016/j.accre.2022.01.005

UNFCCC. (2022). Nationally Determined Contributions Registry. Unfccc.int. https://unfccc.int/NDCREG

United Nation Framework Convention on Climate Change (unfccc). (2020). China's Achievements, New Goals and New Measures for Nationally Determined Contributions. https://unfccc.int/gcse?q=China%E2%80%99s%20Achievements,%20New%20Goals%20and%20New%20Measures%20for%20Nationally%20Determined%20Contributions

United Nations Environment Programme (2019). Emissions Gap Report 2019. UNEP, Nairobi.

Wan, J., Wang, Z., Ma, C., Su, Y., Zhou, T., Wang, T., Zhao, Y., Sun, H., Li, Z., Wang, Y., Li, J., Ding, Y., & Tang, X. (2023). Spatial-temporal differentiation pattern and

influencing factors of high-quality development in counties: A case of Sichuan, China. In *Ecological Indicators* (Vol. 148, p. 110132). Elsevier BV. https://doi.org/10.1016/j.ecolind.2023.110132
Wang, D., Hou, Y., Li, X., & Xu, Y. (2022a). Developing a functional index to dynamically examine the spatio-temporal disparities of China's inclusive green growth. In *Ecological Indicators* (Vol. 139, p. 108861). Elsevier BV. https://doi.org/10.1016/j.ecolind.2022.108861
Wang, W., Kao, X., Lin, Z., & Zhang, Y. (2022b). Has China's coal consumption really peaked?—Prediction and scenario analysis of China's coal consumption peak under the double-carbon target. In *Frontiers in Environmental Science* (Vol. 10). Frontiers Media SA. https://doi.org/10.3389/fenvs.2022.974763
World Bank. (2022). China Country Climate and Development Report.
World Bank. (2023). *Sustaining Growth through the Recovery and Beyond* [Review of *Sustaining Growth through the Recovery and Beyond*]. World Bank Group. https://thedocs.worldbank.org/en/doc/a9fcfb131b5dc335abe8d283998fd9f6-0070012023/original/CEU-June-2023-EN.pdf
World Economic Forum. (2023, January 11). Global Risks Report 2023. World Economic Forum. https://www.weforum.org/publications/global-risks-report-2023/
World Economic Forum. (2024, January 10). Global Risks Report 2024. World Economic Forum. https://www.weforum.org/publications/global-risks-report-2024/
World Economic Forum in Collaboration with Oliver Wyman, (2022). China's Climate Challenge: Financing the Transition to Net Zero. https://www.weforum.org/publications/china-s-climate-challenge-financing-the-transition-to-net-zero/
Xu, G., Zang, L., Schwarz, P., & Yang, H. (2023). Achieving China's carbon neutrality goal by economic growth rate adjustment and low-carbon energy structure. In *Energy Policy* (Vol. 183, p. 113817). Elsevier BV. https://doi.org/10.1016/j.enpol.2023.113817
Xu, Y.-C. (2023). COP28: Why China's Clean Energy Boom Matters for Global Climate Action.
Yang, F., Cheng, Y., & Yao, X. (2019). Influencing factors of energy technical innovation in China: Evidence from fossil energy and renewable energy. *Journal of Cleaner Production*, *232*, 57–66. https://doi.org/10.1016/j.jclepro.2019.05.270
Yang, T., Pan, Y., Yang, Y., Lin, M., Qin, B., Xu, P., & Huang, Z. (2017). CO 2 emissions in China's building sector through 2050: A scenario analysis based on a bottom-up model. In *Energy* (Vol. 128, pp. 208–223). Elsevier BV. https://doi.org/10.1016/j.energy.2017.03.098
Yang, Z., Shao, S., Yang, L., & Miao, Z. (2018). Improvement pathway of energy consumption structure in China's industrial sector: From the perspective of directed technical change. *Energy Economics*, *72*, 166–176. https://doi.org/10.1016/j.eneco.2018.04.003
Zhang, S., & Chen, W. (2022). Assessing the energy transition in China towards carbon neutrality with a probabilistic framework. In *Nature Communications* (Vol. 13, Issue 1). Springer Science and Business Media LLC. https://doi.org/10.1038/s41467-021-27671-0
Zhang, Y., Zhang, X., & Feng, S. (2021). Power to gas: an option for 2060 high penetration rate of renewable energy scenario of China. In *Environmental Science and Pollution Research* (Vol. 29, Issue 5, pp. 6857–6870). Springer Science and Business Media LLC. https://doi.org/10.1007/s11356-021-16137-x
Zhao, W. (2022). China's goal of achieving carbon neutrality before 2060: experts explain how. In *National Science Review* (Vol. 9, Issue 8). Oxford University Press (OUP). https://doi.org/10.1093/nsr/nwac115
Zheng, J., Mi, Z., Coffman, D., Milcheva, S., Shan, Y., Guan, D., & Wang, S. (2019). Regional development and carbon emissions in China. *In Energy Economics* (Vol. 81, pp. 25–36). Elsevier BV. https://doi.org/10.1016/j.eneco.2019.03.003

7 Kuwait at the Crossroads

The Interplay of Climate, Migration and Water Scarcity Dynamics

Abrar Alzankawi, Lucía Morales, Bernadette Andreosso-O'Callaghan, Daniel Rajmil and Suleman Sarwar

Introduction

Recent studies suggest that significant water scarcity will impact the global population in the coming years, with an estimated 60% of individuals facing difficulty accessing fresh water. The availability and accessibility of freshwater resources have emerged as a pressing concern, posing considerable challenges to the global economy (Boulange et al., 2023; El-Dessouky & Ettouney, 2002; Esen et al., 2020; Mishra, 2023; Sun et al., 2021; Tzanakakis et al., 2020; Wada et al., 2016). The global apprehension regarding water scarcity arises from its fundamental importance in sustaining human life and as a result of increasing environmental deterioration that impacts the quality and availability of potable water (Hassan Rashid et al., 2018; Irfeey et al., 2023; Mishra, 2023; Mkubwa, 2023). Worldwide, the availability of fresh water is vital for ecological harmony, societal well-being, and survival. It also confronts escalating hurdles amidst increasing demands for water resources and raises concerns due to its fluctuating availability. Such imbalances in distribution frequently ignite tensions among nations. Natural resources have the potential to pose a threat to national and international security and they have been a significant source of historical conflict. Lack of control and scarcity of natural resources, such as freshwater, can lead to conditions that cause social violence and rising levels of instability.

The Iraqi-Kuwaiti war in 1990 serves as an example of how resources can trigger conflicts and war. As an example of violent confrontation, we can cite the Gulf Region conflict when Saddam Hussein targeted Kuwait's resources, including water, energy, and oil production infrastructure, leading the country into a very complex situation. At the time, strategic actions were intended to deny Kuwaiti citizens access to water and power, as part of the strategy was to weaponise environmental resources. Different actions led to the intentional spilt of oil into the Arabian Gulf, paralysing Kuwait's ability to use desalination plants, causing international outrage and prompting calls for intervention. This act of intentional use of natural resources as a political weapon led to what could be considered as a significant environmental terrorism act in history, and it caused significant environmental and economic losses to Kuwait

DOI: 10.4324/9781032655857-10

(Gleick, 2019; Gleick & Shimabuku, 2023; Kaplan et al., 2022; Westing, 2003). This war shows that nations are willing to confront to secure natural resources when facing a situation that directly affects their interests, and in the context of environmental deterioration, and the pressures posed by climate change it is expected that competition for natural resources can lead to higher levels of international conflict. In this case, Kuwait lost its most valuable resources, oil and water, and had to fight to regain its power. Restoring the country's economic and natural resources took a long time.

Kuwait invested in desalination plants and diversified water sources beyond oil to secure an adequate fresh water supply. However, political constraints prevented it from succeeding in this regard. Today, Kuwait is working with its neighbour, Iraq, to establish a water deal in the area and overcome previous conflicts (Allan, 1998; Al-Qallaf et al., 2020; Alzankawi et al., 2023; Amery, 2012; Freedman & Karsh, 1991; Gleick & Shimabuku, 2023; Hamoda, 2001; Salberg, 2023). Moreover, as policy practices show, unsustainable management policies intensify conflicts as countries and communities compete to safeguard their water reservoirs, potentially leading to violent escalations. Growing levels of environmental deterioration due to economic activities and human exploitation of natural resources are a significant source of concern due to their negative impact on water resources. In the context of the Arabian Gulf region's economic prosperity, it has long relied on the availability of abundant oil and natural gas reserves as economic development and growth sources. However, this dependency has also exposed these nations to the combined threats posed by climate change and political cleavages that originated from management policies. Recognising the looming spectre of severe water scarcity within the region, it is vital to help develop strategies that ensure adequate water preservation (Gleick, 1998; United Nations, 2021c; Odhiambo, 2017), as the United Nations on Climate Change has issued stark warnings. Reports underscore the need to improve water resource management, as demand outstrips the sustainable supply of fresh water. The 2024 United Nations World Water Development Report, presented by UNESCO on behalf of UN-Water, emphasises the exacerbation of global conflicts related to water resources. The report recommends the need to increase international and transboundary collaboration to ensure sustainable management of water resources, which could help in spreading global peace. It also reveals that the lack of access to safe drinking water in some countries worldwide hinders the achievement of the UN's 2030 goals and further intensifies inequalities (Sherif, Baig et al., 2023; UNESCO, 2023; United Nations, 2024). The IPCC report on climate change and land highlights the connection between land degradation and food–water availability and security and its direct linkage to climate change, stressing the need for sustainable land management. It calls for the integration of land use strategies in climate action plans to mitigate adverse impacts and ensure socio-economic stability (Alzankawi et al., 2023; IPCC, 2019, 2022; Moyer & Hedden, 2020; Sherif, Baig et al., 2023). This precarious situation presents a significant hurdle to the region's future. Water security strategy raises concerns regarding increasing levels of conflict at the world level as countries' competition to secure natural resources intensifies.

The significance of water to human survival and the need to preserve water resources is highlighted by the United Nations Sustainable Development Goals (SDG). Water has been placed as SDG 6 for Clean Water and Sanitation, with several targets to help achieve universal sustainable water for all by the year 2030, looking in particular into SDG 6.4 and 6.5, which state that by the year 2030, there should be a significant improvement in water-use efficiency across various sectors, alongside sustainable management of freshwater resources to combat water scarcity and notably reduce the number of individuals affected (United Nations, 2022, 2023b).

Furthermore, comprehensive water resources management should be implemented at all levels, including cooperation across borders when necessary. While SDG 13 is about climate action and climate change and its implications on nations with targets established directly from climate change hazards, targets 13.1 and 13.2 enhance the ability to withstand and adapt to climate-induced risks and natural calamities globally. The guidelines highlight the importance of embedding climate change initiatives into national policies, strategies, and planning frameworks. There is also a need to evaluate the combined effect of climate change-related hazards and water scarcity due to their long-term implications for the management of resources to ensure their sustainability (Fraisl et al., 2020; Gomez-Echeverri, 2018; Hwang et al., 2021; Mulligan et al., 2020).

The research methodology in this paper is based on a systematic literature review to evaluate the impact of water and climate research on advancing SDGs 6 and 13, particularly within Gulf Cooperation Council (GCC) countries. This analysis employed text mining, and a systematic analysis was conducted to investigate publications about climate and water sectors, encompassing various areas such as management of water resources, scarcity, climate change, migration, promotion of awareness, oil dependency and measures for mitigation and adaptation to climate change (Al-Saidi, 2021a; UNESCO, 2023; United Nations, 2022, 2023a, 2023b). The chapter structure provides a comprehensive overview of the multifaceted relationship between Kuwait, its regional context within the Gulf Cooperative Council (GCC), and the critical issues surrounding water resources management, population dynamics, oil reliance, climate change, and migration.

Kuwait in Context

Kuwait is located northwest of the Arabian Gulf Peninsula, with a total area of 17,818 km^2. The weather is characterised by long, hot summer days and temperate winters, mainly dry with little rain. Kuwait lies within an arid and semiarid region in the Middle East and North Africa (MENA), with temperatures falling below 0°C in winter and maximum exceeding 50°C in summer.

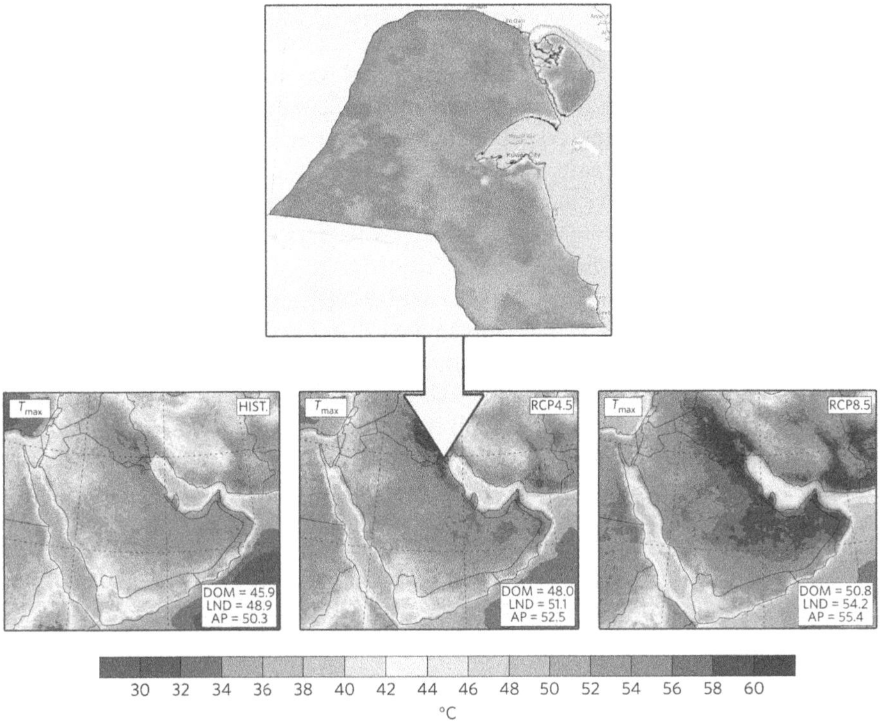

Figure 7.1 Kuwait and GCC region temperature atlas (United Nations, 2021; Sedaghat et al., 2021).

Figure 7.1 was adapted from a study carried out by the United Nations and shows the high temperatures recorded within the summer period, where temperatures will reach very high levels ranging from 49°C to 50°C (United Nations, 2021a; Sedaghat et al., 2021). Furthermore, the increased populations and migration into the Gulf parallel to increasing temperatures have heightened the need to manage water scarcity and address climate change-related issues. This underscores the significance of developing research studies that comprehensively assess water pressures and efficient policy implementation. Hence, this chapter offers insights to help enhance strategy and policy formulation and address the pressing challenges of water scarcity and climate change in the GCC region amidst increasing population and migration pressures.

The connection between climate change migration and freshwater scarcity in Kuwait is outlined in the following research question: How do change migration patterns contribute to Kuwait? The outlined research question encompasses the multifaceted nature of climate-induced migration, focusing specifically on the Middle East region and Gulf countries like Kuwait. The discussions explore the relationship between climate change, migration trends and freshwater stress in Kuwait.

According to the World Meteorological Organisation (WMO, 2016), Kuwait City was recorded in 2016 to be one of the hottest cities in the world by reaching a temperature of 54°C breaking the national records by a couple of degrees higher (Alahmad et al., 2022; Merlone et al., 2019; Samenow, 2016). While high-temperature patterns continue to rise, a temperature of 50.88°C was recorded in AlJahra, Kuwait, in June 2021 (MEE, 2021). These scorching high temperatures continue to increase, causing significant health, infrastructure and habitability issues. High temperatures soften asphalt, impacting take-off distance for aeroplanes and even being recorded to cause health-related issues that lead to fatality (Vicedo-Cabrera et al., 2021). Exposure to high atmospheric temperatures can cause various health-related issues that can significantly impact public health. High temperatures and air pollution can worsen respiratory health problems. In Kuwait, where high temperatures, frequent sandstorms, and air pollution from oil refineries are commonplace, the impact on public health and the environment is significant. Episodes of high temperature are linked to an increase in mortality from respiratory and cardiopulmonary conditions, as well as a rise in hospital admissions for chronic obstructive pulmonary disease, emergency hospital transports for asthma, and cases of acute and chronic bronchitis leading to an increase in deaths caused by respiratory diseases. Furthermore, the elderly and young children are more vulnerable to these health hazards, making them more susceptible to the adverse effects of such conditions (Alahmad et al., 2021, 2022; Al-Hemoud et al., 2021; Alshemmari, 2021; Ebi et al., 2021; Raymond et al., 2020). Moreover, weather-related issues have a significant impact on workers. More specifically, the health and well-being of migrant workers in Kuwait are significantly impacted by the country's extreme temperatures, frequent sandstorms, and air pollution from industrial activities, including oil refineries. Regrettably, the factors above have contributed to an increase in the rates of heat-related fatalities among workers. It is thus imperative to devise effective measures to prevent the occurrence of such tragedies, especially given the critical role played by migrant workers in the country's economy. Therefore, policymakers and industry leaders should prioritise developing and implementing appropriate health and safety regulations to safeguard the health of these workers (Alahmad et al., 2020, 2022, 2023; Ebi et al., 2021). Furthermore, regional climate and the aggravating problems derived from climate change contribute to enhancing issues related to water scarcity due to the country's limited access to freshwater resources.

This problem is exacerbated by the lack of rainfall, with a low annual rainfall between 25 mm and 200 mm (Sedaghat et al., 2021). The country's demographics also need to be considered in the context of water pressures. Kuwait has experienced significant changes in its economic model, which is defined by an increasing representation of migrant workers and their contribution to the economy. The population of Kuwait is estimated at a total of 4,420,110, with Kuwaiti nationals making up 30% of the total population while the other 70% accounts mainly for migrant workers (United Nations, 2021b). The country's economic model and its dependency on fossil fuels are other significant aspects to be considered, as well as its connection to the usage and exploitation of water. The United Nations 2030 Sustainability Agenda requires an international shift towards renewable energy models (IEA, 2020; Ottesen et al., 2023; Ritchie et al., 2024; Salim & Alsyouf, 2020; United Nations, 2023b). Kuwait's oil reserves are quite substantial, and oil revenue is the primary driver of the country's economic model (Al-Ahmad et al., n.d.; Lasrado, 2022; Salem et al., 2023). Oil secures the population's water needs and supports business activities. However, water scarcity aggravates the country's ability to pursue an economically sustainable agenda, as there is a high dependence on oil to guarantee the desalination process of seawater to obtain needed fresh water for Kuwait. International concerns regarding environmental sustainability and the need to minimise fossil fuel consumption pose significant threats to oil-rich economies' quest for economic development and environmental sustainability (Alotaibi, 2011; Alrukaibi & AlSalem, 2022; Alsayegh, 2021). Furthermore, the Kuwaiti economy, heavily reliant on fossil fuels, confronts significant challenges in global efforts towards sustainability and environmental preservation. The economic model, dependent on oil revenue, is at odds with the United Nations 2030 Sustainability Agenda (Abbasi et al., 2024), which underscores the need for economies to minimise fossil fuel consumption and enhance environmental sustainability. Kuwait's oil reserves, a primary source of national wealth and a means to secure water through desalination processes highlight the country's vulnerability to shifts towards the international requirements demanding global energy markets that transition towards renewable energy and in alignment with sustainability policies as the world energy needs keep increasing (Al-Hemoud et al., 2019; Alzubair, 2021; MacDonald, 2022).

Socio-Economic Challenges

The relationship between sustainability, migration, and rising temperatures in Kuwait is a complex interplay that influences the country's socio-economic systems and development perspectives. The increasing occurrences of sand and dust storms, aggravated by climate change, have considerable economic impacts on Kuwait's oil and gas industry, resulting in substantial economic losses and operational disruptions. These challenges underscore the pressing need for a sustainable system to counteract the effects of environmental degradation and economic losses. The transition towards a more sustainable and diversified economy less reliant on fossil fuels is crucial for Kuwait. It necessitates addressing the interconnected challenges of climate change, environmental degradation, and economic dependence on oil. This transition is critical not only for Kuwait's environmental sustainability but also for its long-term economic resilience and the well-being of its populace. Environmental deterioration and the aggravation of water scarcity outline the need to explore and implement strategies that align economic development with environmental sustainability goals, ensuring Kuwait's adherence to the global sustainability agenda while safeguarding its economic interests (Abdelbaki, 2010; Alhajeri et al., 2020;

Alkasasbeh et al., 2023; Alzankawi et al., 2023; Bader & Ganguli, 2019; Salahuddin & Gow, 2014). According to Hofste et al. (2019), Kuwait is one of the 17th countries facing extremely high levels of water stress. Kuwait's growing population and urbanisation pushed freshwater sources scarcity into more extreme stress due to drought and high temperatures. As a result, water stress is growing and posing severe threats to human lives, livelihoods, and business stability. In contrast, there has been rapid growth and evolution in socioeconomics and environmental aspects, creating further pressure on water accessibility. In comparison, in the GCC region, there is a 2% increase in population growth and urbanisation (World Bank, 2018), while Kuwait's annual change in population is recorded at 1.5% (The World Bank, 2021). This population change prompted a new wave of water scarcity that emerged as more challenging and different than a decade ago, posing new challenges and threats to the country's ability to secure access to fresh water resources.

Overview of Kuwait's Freshwater Pressures

Freshwater scarcity has long been a pressing issue in the Arabian Gulf countries, particularly in the case of Kuwait, where it has remained a persistent concern. The onset of freshwater scarcity became increasingly severe in the 1970s, coinciding with Kuwait's rapid economic and social transformation fueled by its oil wealth. Until the early 20th century, Kuwait relied primarily on rainwater and wells to fulfil its water requirements (Alazmi et al., 2024; Alfalah, 2021; Alzankawi et al., 2023). The country has the highest per capita daily freshwater consumption among the Gulf Cooperation Council (GCC) nations and globally (Alawadhi et al., 2021; Ben Hassen & El Bilali, 2022; Sherif, Liaqat et al., 2023; Statista Research Department, 2020). The United Nations Water Stress Index is a global standardised indicator that is crucial for monitoring water stress levels, measuring the proportion of freshwater withdrawals to the available resources, highlighting unsustainable water usage and guiding policy intervention, with 6.4.2 Level of Water Stress, revealing that Kuwait already faces severe water scarcity (United Nations, 2023b). The country has been ranked as the world's top country in terms of high consumption per capita due to the nation's arid climate, limited freshwater sources, and increasing population growth (Statista Research Department, 2020; MEW, 2022; Alazmi et al., 2024; Zubari et al., 2017).

Higher per capita consumption further exacerbates the strain on these resources, leading to increased depletion and unsustainable usage rates. This, in turn, necessitates greater energy demand, particularly for desalination, the country's primary method for obtaining fresh water (Al Rashed et al., 2023; Mabrok et al., 2022). Such an approach requires significant energy inputs, resulting in increased energy demand, associated costs, and environmental concerns related to carbon emissions. Further areas of concern emerge from the financial dimension, as meeting the demand for higher water consumption requires substantial investment in desalination infrastructure, water treatment facilities, and distribution networks (Alazmi et al., 2024; Alfalah, 2021; Al-Zuhair & Al-Bazali, 2022). This significantly burdens the government and consumers, potentially resulting in higher water tariffs and utility bills (AlAnzi et al., 2024; Alazmi et al., 2024). Recent data from the Ministry of Electricity and Water (MEW, 2022) indicates that Kuwait's Maximum freshwater consumption averages around 475.9 litres per day, surpassing that of its regional counterparts in the GCC with an increase of 2.5 in the percentage of freshwater customers in 2022. With nearly 2.9 billion people worldwide projected to grapple with water scarcity in the next decade, the strain on freshwater resources is exacerbated by factors such as population growth, elevated standards of living, and the ensuing demand for increased agricultural output; all of these problems are compounded by the effects of climate change and environmental challenges such as rising atmospheric temperatures, droughts, and decreased rainfall. As Kuwait is located in an arid desert environment, this increase in temperature intensifies the effects of climate change in the area (Alkandari, 2023; Al-Qallaf et al., 2020; Radha et al., 2022; Shariff Sharp et al., 2021). Addressing this issue will require significant investment and innovative solutions to ensure that Kuwait can continue to meet its water needs sustainably and financially (Ismail et al., 2021; Mohammadi et al., 2019a; Moossa et al., 2022).

One promising approach is seawater desalination, particularly favoured by arid regions like those in the Gulf Region, to meet their freshwater needs; despite such efforts, the GCC region remains highly stressed regarding securing freshwater resources, underscoring the urgency for sustainable solutions. Population growth and declining groundwater have dramatically dropped renewable freshwater per capita, as illustrated in Figure 7.2 (Alazmi et al., 2024; Alzubair, 2021). This led Kuwait to construct desalination plants and

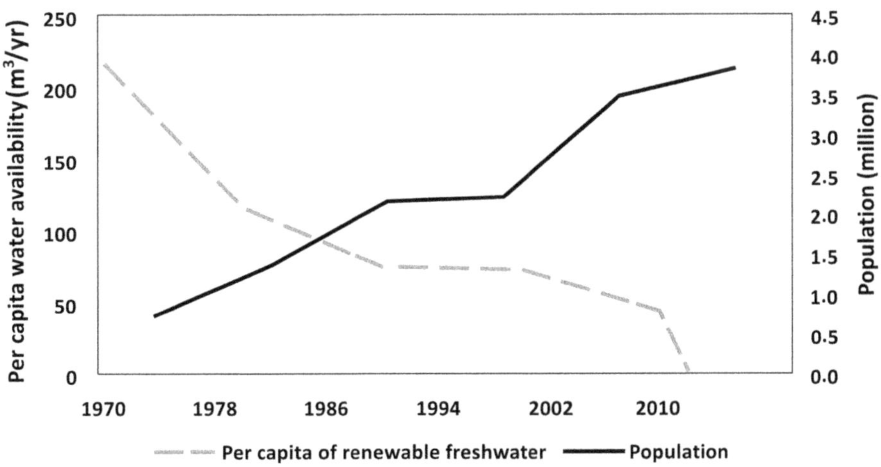

Figure 7.2 Kuwait's population and renewable freshwater per capita availability since 1970 (Alazmi et al., 2024; Zubari et al., 2017).

draw down fossil groundwater. Unconstrained by supply, water demand increased sharply. While some conservation measures were introduced to protect the strategic fossil aquifers, the demand for water resources and water stress have increased unsustainably. Due to the high water demand, Kuwait has significantly invested in desalination technology to address water scarcity issues. With the rapidly growing population and high consumption rates, Kuwait is heavily dependent on desalination as its primary source of water, which currently satisfies approximately 90% of its water needs. However, the desalination plants are predominantly powered by fossil fuels, which raises significant sustainability concerns (Al-Shayji & Aleisa, 2018; Ayaz et al., 2022).

In addition, with the entire population living in urban areas, the potential increase in population due to climate change migrations in Kuwait will pose significant challenges, particularly regarding water consumption (Knoema, 2021; Hussain et al., 2019; Qureshi, 2020). The influx of people would further strain these resources, as more individuals would require access to clean water for drinking, sanitation, and other daily needs. Therefore, the country needs to consider and assess the design and development of effective strategies to address the challenge of water scarcity in Kuwait (Alazmi et al., 2024; Aldababseh, 2019; Omar Asem, 2020; Tariq et al., 2022).

In countries with limited agriculture or industry, such as Kuwait, most water is used in households (Alqallaf et al., 2020). While demand for water in all sectors has increased rapidly, it is increasing most quickly domestically. Population growth is another relevant factor as it typically drives demand for water across all sectors of the economy: agricultural, industrial, and domestic (Akber & Mukhopadhyay, 2021; Alfalah, 2021; Al-Humoud & Al-Ghusain, 2003).

Another aspect that requires assessment relates to the necessity of implementing a comprehensive monitoring system in the Gulf countries to examine and evaluate the impact of migration on their economies and societies. Such a system would enable the identification of the effects of migration on various sectors, including labour markets, public services, and social cohesion, among others. By analysing the data generated by the monitoring system, policymakers and stakeholders would be better equipped to make informed decisions that promote sustainable economic growth and social development (Ayaz et al., 2022; Borgomeo et al., 2020; Dinbabo & Badewa, 2020; Fragaszy et al., 2020; Le Quesne et al., 2021; Valenta et al., 2020; Zekri, 2020). Therefore, it is essential to prioritise the development of such a system to ensure that the Gulf countries continue to thrive in the face of migration challenges. Therefore, it is vital to recognise the impact of climate change on migrant dislocation and the associated effects on water accessibility and availability.

Population and Water Demand

Kuwait's daily consumption of freshwater per capita grew significantly over the last decade, marking it as one of the highest among other countries in the world relative to its total size area (Netherlands Enterprise Agency, 2019), with

Kuwait's water consumption per capita averaging around 457.6 Liters/Day (MEW, 2021). However, according to Crumpler (2022) and the Food and Agricultural Organisation (Aliewi & Alomirah, 2020; Suleiman & Shahid, 2023a, 2023b), Kuwait and the GCC countries are the most water-stressed regions globally. While there has been a significant increase in freshwater demands and a decline in freshwater renewable resources in the past decade, the future holds a dire state of freshwater availability within the next fifty years (Crumpler, 2022). Predictably, almost 2.9 billion people worldwide will face water scarcity in the next decade, with a large proportion of that population being based in or around the GCC area. At the same time, it is projected that the population of the GCC region will reach 65 million by 2030, stressing water usage, food security and energy demands (Qureshi, 2020). In addition, the increased population growth rate and enhanced living conditions and costs in the GCC region placed more stress on agricultural growth, which is already highly impacted by climate change, global warming and other environmental problems (Mohammadi et al., 2019b). As a result, the world is expected to face significant water scarcity within the coming years, leaving about 53% of the global population facing rising problems in securing freshwater resources (He et al., 2021; Boretti & Rosa, 2019; El-Dessouky & Ettouney, 2002).

The population in Kuwait exceeded 4 million in the year 2021 (CSB, 2023; United Nations, 2021a) 100% of the population lives in urban areas around Kuwait City and aggregates in the coastal area, with a population growing at an average annual rate of 0.91% (Knoema, 2021; World Bank, 2023; World Population Review, 2024). Due to the urbanisation of lands and increased industrialisation, the water demand has increased. The increasing population and growth in Kuwait and the GCC region and the projected impacts of climate change on the primary causes of increased freshwater usage with an annual increase of 20–30%, threatening food security and rising agricultural demand for fresh water for irrigation purposes, pressuring the countries to find an alternative water source to reduce the agriculture share of fresh water. Eighty per cent of freshwater usage in the GCC goes toward irrigation. The annual freshwater use per capita in the GCC countries is 560 L/day, compared to the global average of 180 L/day (Hussain et al., 2019; Qureshi, 2020).

The Arabian Gulf, especially Kuwait, has long faced freshwater scarcity, shaping its relations with its neighbours. This scarcity poses significant security risks, exacerbated by population growth and climate change. Historical ties link water scarcity to migration, influenced by economic downturns and extreme environmental conditions (Alzankawi et al., 2023; Borgomeo et al., 2021; Wrathall et al., 2018). Moreover, the recurring drought is a natural hazard severely impacting freshwater availability in the GCC. Therefore, the GCC countries are moving toward securing the future of their growing generations by being sufficient in providing agricultural products locally rather than relying on imports, which also raises concerns in terms of water needs and economic efficiencies and the sustainability dimension associated with developing agricultural activities in arid regions. In order to achieve this goal, the GCC countries are heavily investing in non-conventional water resources, such as desalination and recycling wastewater. However, only 39% of wastewater is being reused in industries, construction, landscaping, gardens, and road ornamentals, while the remaining is discharged into the sea. Moreover, treated wastewater is not used for food crop irrigation due to health, social and environmental concerns. The gap between the agricultural need for fresh water and water supply is met by the extensive uncontrolled exploitation of groundwater, threatening non-renewable and unsustainable water resources (Qureshi, 2020). While the collective treatment and reuse of wastewater is a multistage and costly process, the GCC region could benefit significantly from investing in new technologies and ways to achieve a high-efficiency process to treat wastewater, enabling reusing it for irrigation purposes, making it potable drinking water, and raising awareness to overcome the social, environmental and economic challenges. While only 19.1% of land in the GCC is agricultural land or arable land, the main concern in the GCC's agricultural sector is water availability. Food and water are closely linked. Water security directly impacts food security in any given country. Table 1 (OECD/FAO, 2018) shows the percentage of arable land and freshwater sources each GCC country holds, indicating the stress these countries face in securing the growth of their population and food security. Table 2 shows the impact of climate change on the GCC region, indicating that the region's climate is worsening and is combined with population growth (Bucchignani et al., 2018). The region will face real challenges shortly in securing water and food resources, underlining the importance of addressing water stress through a regional approach (Ben Hassen & El Bilali, 2019).

Another aspect that emerges as critical for the development of Kuwait relates to socio-economic drought: the availability of freshwater resources for the population. It examines the dynamics of human activities and water availability, especially when demand significantly exceeds supply, leading to an imbalance. This concept also explores how human actions influence communities' long-term and sustainable development (Hameed et al., 2020; IPCC, 2021; Karami, 2019). Drought is a complex natural hazard with many definitions and types (McSweeney, 2021). Given the arid climate and high reliance on desalination, the discussion of socio-economic drought and freshwater resource availability is of paramount importance for ensuring water security and sustainable development in the GCC region. Understanding and addressing issues related to water availability, accessibility and sustainability may be instrumental in achieving the region's sustainable development goals. It is still one of the GCC region's leading complex climate change concerns. Climatic drivers of drought are physical climate systems, main events or conditions that directly affect human or ecological systems (IPCC, 2021), such as decreased precipitation, increased temperatures, and radiation, impacting soil evaporation, water, and soil moisture storage. Long periods of drought slowly deplete water reserves, adding to other factors like a substantial decrease in precipitation for an extended period, population, and urbanisation growth vastly contributed to increased freshwater demands (McSweeney, 2021). Although there is a spare in the literature of direct research studies examining the effects of socio-economic drought in Kuwait and the GCC, broader research on the impact of drought and fresh water resources management in arid regions can be of help in offering insights into policies and strategies that could help mitigate this issue. However, the global shift toward more sustainable living and minimising the reliance on oil by switching to renewable energy sources highlight the importance of addressing water scarcity and its socio-economic implications more directly. Climate change adds to this stress and accelerates the impact on economies of climate-related freshwater scarcity issues, which the World Bank estimates to cause about a 14% reduction in the Middle East country's GDP to make up for the losses of climate change-related freshwater scarcity. Moreover, climate change not only impacts the availability of fresh water in the hottest and driest countries like Kuwait but also impacts variability in rainfall that significantly affects agriculture and intensifies the drought situation faced by Kuwait (World Bank, 2018).

The degree of economic development of a given country constitutes a fundamental determinant in quantifying the proportion of migration into the country. This aligns with the notion that more work opportunities within a particular state tend to attract more migration expats. In Kuwait's specific case, a country with a high GDP per capita and a substantial proportion of foreign expats, the relationship between migration and employment is relatively complex. This is further compounded by a significant expatriate population contributing significantly to the overall population growth rate. The economic model of Kuwait, which relies heavily on oil, attracts an increasing influx of expatriate workers and their families, contributing primarily to population growth. The ability to reach a sense of balance between freshwater resourcing and rapid population growth is prioritised by countries worldwide, developing methods to help balance the demands and the need to provide fresh water to all populations.

Conversely, in Kuwait, the absence of rivers and permanent freshwater sources preserves Kuwait on the seventh rank of the World Resources Institute (WRI) of most countries at risk from water scarcity, scoring 4.43 out of 5, which is stated as extremely high for a country that depends on 90% on seawater desalination to cover its national water demand (Dormido, 2019). In Kuwait, most of the population is concentrated in and around the capital city. The country faces many challenges, including climate change, water scarcity, high temperatures, and migration. These challenges are further intensified by the country's economic policies that facilitate water and electricity subsidies. Although this may benefit consumers, it also contributes to increased water consumption and waste, exacerbating the problem of water scarcity. Furthermore, the heavy reliance on oil for desalination and power generation not only carries a significant financial burden on the state but also has environmental implications, contributing to climate change (Aljamal et al., 2020, 2022; Alotaibi, 2011; Al-Rashed & Aliewi, 2018; Zaveri et al., 2020).

Climate Migration

The current state of the climate has prompted migration as people seek safer and more stable living conditions in response to harsh climatic conditions. Adaptive responses to evolving environmental and climatic conditions have often driven population mobility throughout history. However, modern migration is influenced by many complex factors, including globalisation, technological advancements in travel and communication, socio-economic inequalities, demographic shifts, and geopolitical conflicts. Climate change exacerbates many migration drivers, intensifying pressures that compel individuals, families, and communities to relocate (Burroughs, 2005; Khan & Arokkiaraj, 2021; Rajan & Oommen, 2020). In 2020, climate-related conditions led to the migration of over 30 million individuals, which indicates a direct correlation between worsening weather patterns and global migration rates (Nabong et al., 2023). Many factors may contribute to an individual's decision to migrate, such as unemployment, political uncertainties, famines, economic instability, and environmental changes resulting from climate change (Giovanis & Abdeldjalil, 2023). Understanding the relationship between population growth, migration trends, and the political landscape is crucial for ensuring national stability. Mismanagement of the migration process and related policies and failure to address resource allocation challenges could fuel anti-migrant sentiments, leading to a possible deterioration of the traditional welcoming long-standing Kuwaiti community's social cohesion. Therefore, it is important to understand these dynamics to help the country on the development of efficient policies that address migration challenges appropriately (Alharbi & Csala, 2021; Blaydes & Gengler, 2023; Scartozzi, 2021).

The Middle East significantly feels the impact and influence of global trends in politics and economics, which is experiencing an overall increase in migration due to climate change and its attached political-economic instability effects. This trend is expected to exacerbate over time, making it necessary for many people to seek more favourable living conditions (Abou Dagher & Nassar, 2023; Nabong et al., 2023). Since the 1970s, refined migration programs have operated within the Gulf states, resulting in over 35 million migrated workers. These figures are rising with the increasing urbanisation of the Gulf states (Babar, 2020b; Rahman et al., 2023; Rajan & Oommen, 2020). Gulf countries rely heavily on expats, which could pose significant challenges in the event of reverse migration of professional migrants out of the region due to climate-related challenges, poor living conditions, and increasing geopolitical risk levels. As a result, it is essential to evaluate the potential consequences of this reverse migration. Therefore, policymakers and governments must prioritise a comprehensive assessment of the impact of climate change on Gulf countries' expat populations (Rahman et al., 2023; Puaschunder, 2020; Khan & Arokkiaraj, 2021; Nisrane et al., 2020).

The Triple Nexux: Oil Reliance, Climate Change, and Migration

Kuwait's oil production has continued since 1974; oil and petroleum exports drive the country's high GDP, and it holds the fifth largest oil reserves globally (Al-Naffakh et al., 2021; Hilmi et al., 2020; OPEC, 2019) that combined with a relatively small population makes it a wealthy country. This wealth allowed Kuwait to expand its growth as a small desert country and made it possible to secure water and food using oil-powered desalination plants. At the same time, Kuwait is quite vulnerable because of its high dependence on oil to maintain its access to fresh water. The stress from the fluctuation of oil prices and rapid population growth, with over 4 million people living in urban areas within Kuwait City, is inextricably linked to energy and water consumption increases. The increase in the need for natural resources, population growth, and climate change challenge Kuwait's ability to withstand this growth, with the scarcest freshwater resources affecting the country (Netherlands Enterprise Agency, 2019).

This fluctuation of temperature and drought severely affects Kuwait's habitability, which, in parallel with increased temperatures, can cause mental and physical stress to people and the ecosystem in Kuwait (Abdulmajeed, 2023; Alharbi, 2022; Arnout, 2023; El Kenawy et al., 2024). A study by Alahmad et al. (2020) shows that extreme temperatures in Kuwait possibly double the mortality risk for a particular subgroup. Impacting the health and economy of the state. Rising temperature also increases the need for indoor cooling systems and sheltered transportation, thus adding additional pressures to pollution and environmental deterioration. In contrast, the increased use of energy results in more CO_2 emissions, giving the country's reliance on oil and gas to generate electricity; the climate impact intensifies as a result of heat generated from the running cooling system, which is released into the air creating a looped cycle of negative impact (Alsaad, 2021). The transformation after the discovery of oil led Kuwait's life from boat building and sailing to a significant oil-producing and exporting economy, changing the socio-economic and environmental aspects of living. At the same time, these developments were halted in 1990 due to the Iraqi invasion of Kuwait during the Gulf War. After the stalled growth, Kuwait increased oil production and exportation to recuperate the war losses (Netherlands Enterprise Agency, 2019).

The Gulf countries face many environmental threats, such as desertification, marine and coastal area pollution, and water scarcity. While these environmental threats have been happening for a long time, the emerging climate change has made these threats more severe. Traditional and emerging environmental threats are increasingly interconnected. In addition, desertification is defined as land degradation due to natural reasons and human activities like over-exploitation of non-renewable natural resources (Zhang & Xie, 2019). Therefore, desertification leads to a loss in biodiversity and increased livestock, as well as increased methane gasses and desertification, which adds to global warming that increases desertification, enhancing water scarcity problems.

Natural resources are the crucial real wealth of all nations as they play a significant role in countries' development, with almost 90% of developed countries depending on natural resources (Lebdioui, 2021). While seawater desalination is proven to help decrease water scarcity by providing a more reliable and strategic freshwater source, conventional desalination techniques create a pronounced environmental toll through the extensive extraction and utilisation of energy. The considerable energy demand, predominantly reliant on fossil fuels, poses a formidable obstacle to the Gulf Cooperation Council (GCC) region's pursuit of more sustainable avenues for securing freshwater resources (Mahmoudi et al., 2023).

Desalination is Kuwait's primary source of freshwater. At the same time, there was a rapid population growth of almost a 1200% increase in the GCC region between 1950 and 2015. This remarkably increased demographics was enabled by making life possible in a highly arid region like the GCC region. For example, when the first desalination plant in 1953 was built in Kuwait and Qatar (Le Quesne et al., 2021), despite being in an arid region, Kuwait's population's access to fresh, clean water was above average (World Bank, 2018). Although this might look promising for the coming years, future demand forecasts that desalination plants will continue to be in higher demand with population growth. As of 2030, Ashfaq et al. (2019), the estimated population of the GCC region is thought to reach 56 million, and the water resources capacities will reach half of its current capacity, thus making it difficult to maintain the high standard of living and quality and availability of fresh water and this will flag the region as a water-stressed region. Moreover, as desalination will continue to be the primary freshwater source for the GCC region and one of the leading social and economic development tools, the impact of using desalination does not come without a cost; the direct economic and environmental cost of using desalination is high, and the cost in generating freshwater versus CO_2 emissions (Moossa et al., 2022).

Finding a solution to the problem of securing freshwater is a great challenge for many countries, especially those affected by arid and desert conditions. Seawater desalination is one of the encouraging techniques mainly dryland countries use to secure their freshwater needs (Mohammadi et al., 2019b). However, the GCC was recorded to be the region with the most stress regarding securing freshwater resources compared to the availability of sustainable resources. Most importantly, Kuwait has the highest dependency rate on seawater desalination (Statista Research Department, 2020). Also, it faces an acute lack of fresh groundwater resources. In contrast, groundwater is brackish and primarily exploited for agricultural purposes, and the national demands for freshwater are mainly met by seawater desalination and wastewater management (Mukhopadhyay & Akber, 2018). Climate change rapidly affects living conditions in Kuwait, and the environment is significantly impacted and degraded. As the option of economic diversification remains very limited for Kuwait and its position as a country with a community-dependent economy, transitioning to a more sustainable economy is not easy. Notwithstanding the importance of diversification and acknowledging the impact of oil extraction and burning on the environment, the international mitigation and policies have made the GCC oil-rich countries aware of the need to prioritise a movement toward a more sustainable future (Burt & Bartholomew, 2019).

This shift is crucial to the country in light of Kuwait's escalating issues with water scarcity and growing challenges concerning oil resource depletion, which have been integral to its economy since the first oil export shipment in 1946 (Alzubair, 2021). While this reliance on petrodollars transformed Kuwait's aspects of life, taking Kuwaiti society into a new welfare system with high living standards providing social benefits and social protection to all Kuwaiti citizens (Al-Ramadan, 2018), it has also led to significant climate impacts due to fuel consumption and emissions from energy-generating plants (AlKheder, 2021). Meanwhile, alike in most of modern societies, the population's high consumption of electricity and water, in the Kuwaiti case, the government subsidises, impacts the environment. Whereas cutting and reducing these subsidies will generate political issues, the public views the government's subsidies as their fundamental civil right, which the government is obliged to provide (Aljamal et al., 2022). In comparison, reducing or smoothing water and electricity subsidies for migrant residents in Kuwait could have significant political implications and impact rising conflicts. Given the magnitude of these subsidies in residents' daily lives, this could result in increasing internal levels of discontent and political cleavages leading to rising levels of tension Any such action could result in diplomatic, economic, and social consequences, such as social unrest due to increased living expenses resulting would impact a high proportion of the population This might also cause a demand for wage increases to cover the upcoming living expenses, leading to labour market disruption and expatriates leaving the country. With Kuwait highly reliant on expatriates for its workforce, this could strain public services and cause an imbalance in the workforce if expatriates decide to leave the country due to the high cost of living. Another significant aspect to consider is the political pressure the Kuwaiti government could face domestically and internationally to maintain or reinstate subsidies for migrant workers. On the other hand, this might strain Kuwait with international criticism, especially from countries that are major sources of migrant labour. These countries might view the reduction or removal of subsidies as unfair treatment of their citizens, leading to diplomatic tensions (Desmond, 2020; Girgis et al., 2022; Shehabi, 2020). For Kuwait to meet the 2030 UN agenda and protect human rights, there would be a need to protect migrants' living standards, viewing the subsidy cuts as a violation of migrants' rights to decent living conditions (Abulibdeh et al., 2019; Al-Ansari & AlKhaled, 2023; Al-Saidi, 2021b; Babar, 2020a; Desmond, 2020). In a detailed study conducted by Naderi Beni et al. (2021), the research discussed the impact of fossil fuels on the economies of the Gulf region. Unlike non-oil economies, the economic models of the GCC region are influenced by various factors. The study highlighted potential conflicts arising from the rich oil economies and the complexities of addressing climate change and environmental

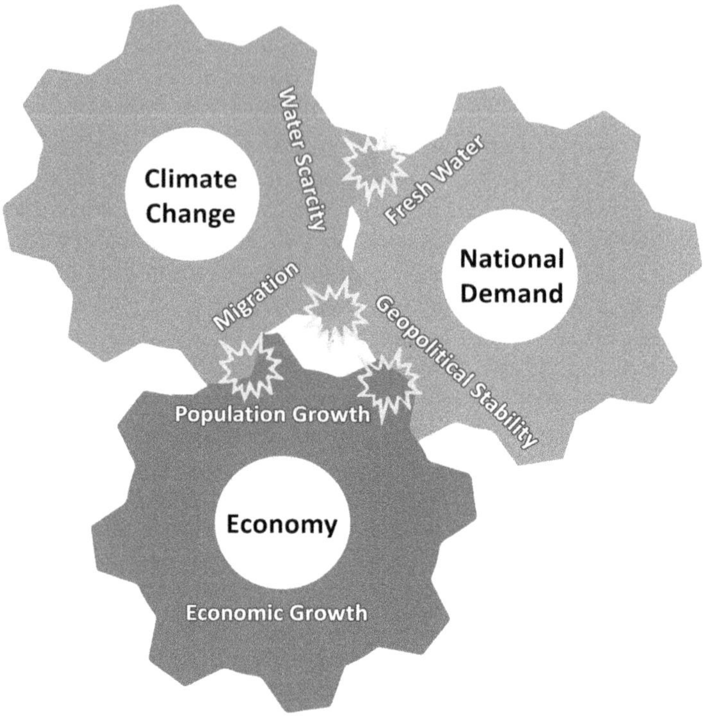

Figure 7.3 Conflict areas model in oil-rich economies.

Source: Authors (2024).

concerns, especially concerning government subsidies on electricity and water. Moreover, the study highlighted that population growth, migration, and water scarcity pose significant challenges to transitioning towards a more sustainable future, potentially leading to conflicts in the context of climate change. As depicted in Figure 7.3, the economy and population demands delineate the potential conflict that may arise in affluent oil economies. This passage contributes to the ongoing discourse within this chapter regarding the impact and implications of climate change in exacerbating existing conflicts or instigating new ones, particularly in regions with migrant populations. It also addresses the importance of meeting affected populations' energy demands and living conditions, emphasising the imperative for stringent measures to mitigate the impact of climate-related challenges and to pave the way for a more sustainable, environmentally friendly future in the nation.

Conclusion

The global awareness of the immediate direct impact of climate change on our lives and the environment is becoming more visible, and it is creating significant socio-economic pressures that are seeking more sustainable economic models. Securing the economic development of countries such as the GCC and changing and moving away from fossil fuels are the main economic drivers as the world economies assess their needs within the demands of the international sustainability agenda. In contrast, the long-term future goal of the global economies depends on moving away from the fossil fuels vulnerability of the Gulf states to the extreme of climate change-related conditions such as drought and increased temperature-related evaporation tied significantly to human-induced CO_2 emissions linked to fossil fuel combustion. In contrast, the economic growth of the Gulf countries, especially Kuwait, continues to rely on the discovery of fossil fuels, which has made CO_2 emissions increase dramatically. The fossil fuel combustion impacts on the Gulf's environment could link to the need for economic diversification and movement to more sustainable resources of income, hampering a long-term movement to a post-oil era (Naderi Beni et al., 2021). However, with an urgent need for Kuwait to start reducing emissions to minimise the impact of global warming, the country needs to orientate towards reaching the required conditions for a country that will ensure to be liveable in the future, understanding and foreseeing it will be affected by climate change increasing adversities. In there, one of the key aspects will be enhancing a population's educational tools and knowledge on global warming and climate change effects (MacDonald, 2022). New challenges and environmental threats require a gradual shift towards a multidimensional policy resources management approach that considers the current natural resources distress as the key to succeed in a sustainable future.

References

Abbasi, K. R., Zhang, Q., Ozturk, I., Alvarado, R., & Musa, M. (2024). Energy transition, fossil fuels, and green innovations: Paving the way to achieving sustainable development goals in the United States. *Gondwana Research*, *130*, 326–341. https://doi.org/10.1016/j.gr.2024.02.005

Abdelbaki, H. H. (2010). Assessing The Impact Of The Global Financial Crisis On GCC Countries. *Journal of Business & Economics Research (JBER)*, *8*(2). https://doi.org/10.19030/jber.v8i2.682

Abdulmajeed, S. M. A. (2023). A Qualitative Assessment of Biomimetic and Vernacular Approaches to Design for Extremely Hot Environments of the GCC Countries [Ph.D., Texas A&M University]. In *ProQuest Dissertations and Theses*. https://www.proquest.com/docview/2890179288/abstract/500924BFA4040A4PQ/1

Abou Dagher, M., & Nassar, S. (2023). Policy Brief on Climate Change and Internal Human Mobility. *The European Institute of the Mediterranean*. https://south.euneighbours.eu/wp-content/uploads/2023/06/Policy-Study29_compressed-1.pdf#page=55

Abulibdeh, A., Zaidan, E., & Al-Saidi, M. (2019). Development drivers of the water-energy-food nexus in the Gulf Cooperation Council region. *Development in Practice*, *29*(5), 582–593. https://doi.org/10.1080/09614524.2019.1602109

Akber, A., & Mukhopadhyay, A. (2021). An overview of Kuwait's water resources and a proposed plan to prevent the spread of the Novel Corona Virus (COVID-19) pandemic through Kuwait's water supply facilities and groundwater system. In A. L. Ramanathan, C. Sabarathinam, F. Arriola, M. V. Prasanna, P. Kumar, & M. P. Jonathan (Eds.), *Environmental Resilience and Transformation in Times of COVID-19* (pp. 79–88). Elsevier. https://doi.org/10.1016/B978-0-323-85512-9.00005-X

Alahmad, B., Al-Hemoud, A., Al-Bouwarthan, M., Khraishah, H., Kamel, M., Akrouf, Q., Wegman, D. H., Bernstein, A. S., & Koutrakis, P. (2023). Extreme heat and work injuries in Kuwait's hot summers. *Occupational and Environmental Medicine*, *80*(6), 347–352. https://doi.org/10.1136/oemed-2022-108697

Alahmad, B., Al-Hemoud, A., Kang, C.-M., Almarri, F., Kommula, V., Wolfson, J. M., Bernstein, A. S., Garshick, E., Schwartz, J., & Koutrakis, P. (2021). A two-year assessment of particulate air pollution and sources in Kuwait. *Environmental Pollution*, *282*, 117016. https://doi.org/10.1016/j.envpol.2021.117016

Alahmad, B., Shakarchi, A. F., Khraishah, H., Alseaidan, M., Gasana, J., Al-Hemoud, A., Koutrakis, P., & Fox, M. A. (2020). Extreme temperatures and mortality in Kuwait: Who is vulnerable? *Science of The Total Environment*, *732*, 139289. https://doi.org/10.1016/j.scitotenv.2020.139289

Alahmad, B., Vicedo-Cabrera, A. M., Chen, K., Garshick, E., Bernstein, A. S., Schwartz, J., & Koutrakis, P. (2022). Climate change and health in Kuwait: Temperature and mortality projections under different climatic scenarios. *Environmental Research Letters*, *17*(7), 074001. https://doi.org/10.1088/1748-9326/ac7601

Al-Ahmad, D. M., Dimashki, D. M., Al-Duaij, S., & Roundell, T. (n.d.). *Harnessing the Potential for Green Growth in Kuwait*. 4.

Al-Ansari, M., & AlKhaled, S. (2023). Sustainable urban forms in the Arabian Gulf: An evidence-based analysis of Kuwaiti social housing neighborhoods at Jaber Al-Ahmed City. *Frontiers in Built Environment*, 9. https://doi.org/10.3389/fbuil.2023.1154523

AlAnzi, A. A., Bourisli, R. I., & AlKhaled, S. R. (2024). Guidance on subsidy strategies for optimum life cycle cost in government-owned and -operated assembly occupancy buildings in Kuwait. *Sustainable Energy Technologies and Assessments*, *63*, 103668. https://doi.org/10.1016/j.seta.2024.103668

Alawadhi, A., Burney, N., & Gelan, A. (2021). *The Effect of Conservation on Residential Fresh Water Consumption: Evidence From Kuwait*.

Alazmi, H. J., Mitchell, G., & Trigg, M. A. (2024). Kuwait household water demand in 2050: Spatial microsimulation and impact appraisal. *Water and Environment Journal*, *38*(1), 139–152. https://doi.org/10.1111/wej.12906

Aldababseh, A. (2019). *Kuwait National Adaptation Plan 2019-2030*. 174.

Alfalah, O. (2021). *Estimating Residential Demand for Water in Kuwait: A Cointegration Analysis - ProQuest*. https://www.proquest.com/docview/2610031145?pq-origsite=gscholar&fromopenview=true

Alhajeri, H. M., Almutairi, A., Alenezi, A., & Alshammari, F. (2020). Energy Demand in the State of Kuwait During the Covid-19 Pandemic: Technical, Economic, and Environmental Perspectives. *Energies*, *13*(17), Article 17. https://doi.org/10.3390/en13174370

Alharbi, A. (2022). PERCEIVED NEW RISKS TO CONSTRUCTION WORKERS IN KUWAIT DUE TO RISING TEMPERATURES. *Research Papers*. https://opensiuc.lib.siu.edu/gs_rp/1058

Alharbi, F. R., & Csala, D. (2021). Gulf Cooperation Council Countries' Climate Change Mitigation Challenges and Exploration of Solar and Wind Energy Resource Potential. *Applied Sciences*, *11*(6), Article 6. https://doi.org/10.3390/app11062648

Al-Hemoud, A., Al-Dousari, A., Misak, R., Al-Sudairawi, M., Naseeb, A., Al-Dashti, H., & Al-Dousari, N. (2019). Economic Impact and Risk Assessment of Sand and Dust Storms (SDS) on the Oil and Gas Industry in Kuwait. *Sustainability*, *11*(1), Article 1. https://doi.org/10.3390/su11010200

Al-Hemoud, A., Gasana, J., Alajeel, A., Alhamoud, E., Al-Shatti, A., & Al-Khayat, A. (2021). Ambient exposure of O3 and NO2 and associated health risk in Kuwait. *Environmental Science and Pollution Research International*, *28*(12), 14917–14926. https://doi.org/10.1007/s11356-020-11481-w

Al-Humoud, J. M., & Al-Ghusain, I. (2003). Household demand for water: A case study in Kuwait. *Kuwait Journal of Science & Engineering*, *30*, 197–211.

Aliewi, A., & Alomirah, H. (2020). Assessment of the Significance of Water-Energy-Food Nexus for Kuwait. In M. Kumar, F. Munoz-Arriola, H. Furumai, & T. Chaminda (Eds.), *Resilience, Response, and Risk in Water Systems: Shifting Management and Natural Forcings Paradigms* (pp. 357–367). Springer. https://doi.org/10.1007/978-981-15-4668-6_19

Aljamal, A., Speece, M., & Bagnied, M. (2020). Sustainable Policy for Water Pricing in Kuwait. *Sustainability*, *12*(8), Article 8. https://doi.org/10.3390/su12083257

Aljamal, A., Speece, M., & Bagnied, M. (2022). Understanding resistance to reductions in water subsidies in Kuwait. *Local Environment*, *27*(1), 97–111. Scopus. https://doi.org/10.1080/13549839.2021.2002287

Alkandari, A. J. (2023). Climate and Climate Change Aspects of Kuwait. In M. K. Suleiman & S. A. Shahid (Eds.), *Terrestrial Environment and Ecosystems of Kuwait: Assessment and Restoration* (pp. 57–91). Springer Nature Switzerland. https://doi.org/10.1007/978-3-031-46262-7_3

Alkasasbeh, O. M., Alassuli, A., & Alzghoul, A. (2023). Energy Consumption, Economic Growth and CO2 Emissions in Middle East. *International Journal of Energy Economics and Policy*, *13*(1), Article 1. https://doi.org/10.32479/ijeep.13904

AlKheder, S. (2021). Promoting public transport as a strategy to reduce GHG emissions from private vehicles in Kuwait. *Environmental Challenges*, *3*, 100075. https://doi.org/10.1016/j.envc.2021.100075

Allan, T. (1998). *Avoiding war over natural resources—ICRC*. https://www.icrc.org/en/doc/resources/documents/misc/57jpl4.htm

Al-Naffakh, J., Al-Qassab, M., & Al-Makhzoomi, Z. (2021). *Share of CO2 emissions in Iraq, Saudi Arabia and Kuwait from the combustion of fossil fuels: A statistical study*. *2*, 114–120.

Alotaibi, S. (2011). Energy consumption in Kuwait: Prospects and future approaches. *Energy Policy*, *39*(2), 637–643. https://doi.org/10.1016/j.enpol.2010.10.036

Alqallaf, A., Al-Anzi, B., & Alabdullah, M. (2020). Assessing the effectiveness of supplemental irrigation to improve soil moisture in an arid ecosystem with an emphasis on climate change: A case study from the state of kuwait. *Sustainability (Switzerland)*, *12*(21), 1–17. Scopus. https://doi.org/10.3390/su12219104

Al-Qallaf, H., Aliewi, A., & Abdulhadi, A. (2020). Assessment of the effect of extreme rainfall events on temporal rainfall variability in Kuwait. *Arabian Journal of Geosciences*, *13*(21), 1129. https://doi.org/10.1007/s12517-020-06086-z

Al-Ramadan, M. (2018). *Modeling Life Expectancy Improvement among Kuwaiti Population*. http://www.iei1946.it/en/rivista-articolo.php?id=117

Al-Rashed, M., & Aliewi, A. (2018). Water resources sustainability in Kuwait against United Nations Sustainable Development Goals. In *Sustainability in the Gulf*. Routledge.

Al Rashed, M., Sefelnasr, A., Sherif, M., Murad, A., Alshamsi, D., Aliewi, A., & Ebraheem, A. A. (2023). Novel concept for water scarcity quantification considering nonconventional and virtual water resources in arid countries: Application in Gulf Cooperation Council countries. *Science of The Total Environment*, *882*, 163473. https://doi.org/10.1016/j.scitotenv.2023.163473

Alrukaibi, D., & AlSalem, A. (2022). A comparative analysis of the carbon dioxide emissions-energy profile in Kuwait: Status quo versus 2030. *Journal of Engineering Research*, *10*(3B), Article 3B. https://doi.org/10.36909/jer.14403

Alsaad, M. (2021). Climate Adaptation and Kuwait's Built Environment. *Middle East Centre*. https://blogs.lse.ac.uk/mec/2021/03/31/climate-adaptation-and-kuwaits-built-environment/

Al-Saidi, M. (2021a). Cooperation or competition? State environmental relations and the SDGs agenda in the Gulf Cooperation Council (GCC) region. *Environmental Development*, *37*, 100581. https://doi.org/10.1016/j.envdev.2020.100581

Al-Saidi, M. (2021b). Cooperation or competition? State environmental relations and the SDGs agenda in the Gulf Cooperation Council (GCC) region. *Environmental Development*, *37*, 100581. https://doi.org/10.1016/j.envdev.2020.100581

Alsayegh, O. A. (2021). Barriers facing the transition toward sustainable energy system in Kuwait. *Energy Strategy Reviews*, *38*, 100779. https://doi.org/10.1016/j.esr.2021.100779

Al-Shayji, K., & Aleisa, E. (2018). Characterizing the fossil fuel impacts in water desalination plants in Kuwait: A Life Cycle Assessment approach. *Energy*, *158*, 681–692. https://doi.org/10.1016/j.energy.2018.06.077

Al-Zuhair, M., & Al-Bazali, T. (2022). Causality between energy consumption and economic growth: The case of Kuwait. *International Journal of Energy Economics and Policy*, *12*(6), 22–29.

Alshemmari, H. (2021). An overview of persistent organic pollutants along the coastal environment of Kuwait. *Open Chemistry*, *19*(1), 149–156. https://doi.org/10.1515/chem-2021-0198

Alzankawi, A., Morales, L., Andreosso-O'Callaghan, B., & Rajmil, D. (2023). Geoeconomic and Geopolitical Dynamics of Water Scarcity in Oil-Rich Economies: The Case of Kuwait. *Peace Review*, *35*(4), 683–694. https://doi.org/10.1080/10402659.2023.2272615

Alzubair, A. (2021). *The Need for Economic Diversification in the Oil-Dependent Nations of Saudi Arabia, UAE, and Nigeria: Possible Pathways and Outcomes*. 46.

Amery, H. (2012). Water security for Kuwait: Assessing the feasibility of water imports from Iran. *Int. J. of Hydrology Science and Technology*, *2*, 292–305. https://doi.org/10.1504/IJHST.2012.049165

Arnout, B. A. (2023). An epidemiological study of mental health problems related to climate change: A procedural framework for mental health system workers. *Work*, *75*(3), 813–835. https://doi.org/10.3233/WOR-220040

Ashfaq, M. Y., Al-Ghouti, M. A., Qiblawey, H., Zouari, N., Rodrigues, D. F., & Hu, Y. (2019). Use of DPSIR Framework to Analyse Water Resources in Qatar and Overview of Reverse Osmosis as an Environment Friendly Technology. *Environmental Progress & Sustainable Energy*, *38*(4), 13081. https://doi.org/10.1002/ep.13081

Ayaz, M., Namazi, M. A., Din, M. A ud, Ershath, M. I. M., Mansour, A, & Aggoune, el-H. M. (2022). Sustainable seawater desalination: Current status, environmental implications and future expectations. *Desalination*, *540*, 116022. https://doi.org/10.1016/j.desal.2022.116022

Babar, Z. (2020a). Migrant labor and human rights in the Gulf Cooperation Council (GCC) countries. In *Why Human Rights Still Matter in Contemporary Global Affairs*. Routledge.

Babar, Z. R. (2020b). Understanding Labour Migration Policies in the Gulf Cooperation Council Countries. *Asianization of Migrant Workers in the Gulf Countries*, 37–53.

Bader, Y., & Ganguli, S. (2019). Analysis of the association between economic growth, environmental quality and health standards in the Gulf Cooperation Council during 1980-2012. *Management of Environmental Quality: An International Journal*. https://doi.org/10.1108/MEQ-03-2018-0061

Ben Hassen, T., & El Bilali, H. (2019). Food Security in the Gulf Cooperation Council Countries: Challenges and Prospects. *Journal of Food Security*, *7*, 159–169. https://doi.org/10.12691/jfs-7-5-2

Ben Hassen, T., & El Bilali, H. (2022). Chapter 26 - Water management in the Gulf Cooperation Council: Challenges and prospects. In A. K. Tiwari, A. Kumar, A. K. Singh, T. N. Singh, E. Suozzi, G. Matta, & S. Lo Russo (Eds.), *Current Directions in*

Water Scarcity Research (Vol. 5, pp. 525–540). Elsevier. https://doi.org/10.1016/B978-0-323-85378-1.00026-X

Blaydes, L., & Gengler, J. (2023). Arab identity and attitudes toward migration in Kuwait and Qatar. *Research & Politics*, *10*(4), 20531680231223289. https://doi.org/10.1177/20531680231223289

Boretti, A., & Rosa, L. (2019). Reassessing the projections of the World Water Development Report. *Npj Clean Water*, *2*(1), 1–6. https://doi.org/10.1038/s41545-019-0039-9

Borgomeo, E., Fawzi, N. A.-M., Hall, J. W., Jägerskog, A., Nicol, A., Sadoff, C. W., Salman, M., Santos, N., & Talhami, M. (2020). Tackling the Trickle: Ensuring Sustainable Water Management in the Arab Region. *Earth's Future*, *8*(5), e2020EF001495. https://doi.org/10.1029/2020EF001495

Borgomeo, E., Jägerskog, A., Zaveri, E., Russ, J., Khan, A., & Damania, R. (2021). *Ebb and Flow, Volume 2: Water in the Shadow of Conflict in the Middle East and North Africa*. World Bank. https://doi.org/10.1596/978-1-4648-1746-5

Boulange, J., Yoshida, T., Nishina, K., Okada, M., & Hanasaki, N. (2023). Delivering the latest global water resource simulation results to the public. *Climate Services*, *30*, 100386. https://doi.org/10.1016/j.cliser.2023.100386

Bucchignani, E., Mercogliano, P., Panitz, H.-J., & Montesarchio, M. (2018). Climate change projections for the Middle East–North Africa domain with COSMO-CLM at different spatial resolutions. *Advances in Climate Change Research*, *9*(1), 66–80. https://doi.org/10.1016/j.accre.2018.01.004

Burroughs, W. J. (2005). *Climate Change in Prehistory: The End of the Reign of Chaos*. Cambridge University Press.

Burt, J. A., & Bartholomew, A. (2019). Towards more sustainable coastal development in the Arabian Gulf: Opportunities for ecological engineering in an urbanized seascape. *Marine Pollution Bulletin*, *142*, 93–102. https://doi.org/10.1016/j.marpolbul.2019.03.024

Crumpler, K. (2022). *Regional analysis of the nationally determined contributions in the Near East and North Africa: Opportunities and gaps in the agriculture, water and land use sectors*. FAO. https://doi.org/10.4060/cb8662en

CSB. (2023). *Population Estimates in Kuwait by Age, Nationality and Sex at 2023*. Central Statistical Bureau. https://www.csb.gov.kw/Pages/Statistics_en?ID=67&ParentCatID=1

Desmond, A. (2020). Migrants' rights finally front and centre of the international agenda? Exploring the perils and possibilities of the SDGs and the GCM. *International Journal of Law in Context*, *16*(3), 217–221. https://doi.org/10.1017/S1744552320000348

Dinbabo, M. F., & Badewa, A. S. (2020). Monitoring migration policy frameworks, treaties and conventions for development in Africa. *Journal of African Union Studies*, *9*(1), 23–49. https://doi.org/10.10520/EJC-1d58d96abb

Dormido, H. (2019). These Countries Are the Most at Risk From a Water Crisis. *Bloomberg.Com*. https://www.bloomberg.com/graphics/2019-countries-facing-water-crisis/

Ebi, K. L., Capon, A., Berry, P., Broderick, C., Dear, R. de, Havenith, G., Honda, Y., Kovats, R. S., Ma, W., Malik, A., Morris, N. B., Nybo, L., Seneviratne, S. I., Vanos, J., & Jay, O. (2021). Hot weather and heat extremes: Health risks. *The Lancet*, *398*(10301), 698–708. https://doi.org/10.1016/S0140-6736(21)01208-3

El Kenawy, A. M., Aboelkhair, H., Mohamed, E. K., Gaber, I. M., Fernández-Duque, B., Peña-Angulo, D., & Abdelaal, M. M. (2024). Modes of summertime thermal urban stress over major cities in the Middle East: A comprehensive assessment of heat exposure risks. *Sustainable Cities and Society*, *102*, 105236. https://doi.org/10.1016/j.scs.2024.105236

El-Dessouky, H., & Ettouney, H. (2002). *Fundamentals of Salt Water Desalination* (1st Edition). Elsevier Science. https://www.elsevier.com/books/fundamentals-of-salt-water-desalination/el-dessouky/978-0-444-50810-2

Esen, Ö., Yıldırım, D. Ç., & Yıldırım, S. (2020). Threshold effects of economic growth on water stress in the Eurozone. *Environmental Science and Pollution Research*, *27*(25), 31427–31438. https://doi.org/10.1007/s11356-020-09383-y

Fragaszy, S. R., Jedd, T., Wall, N., Knutson, C., Fraj, M. B., Bergaoui, K., Svoboda, M., Hayes, M., & McDonnell, R. (2020). Drought Monitoring in the Middle East and North Africa (MENA) Region: Participatory Engagement to Inform Early Warning Systems. *Bulletin of the American Meteorological Society*, *101*(7), E1148–E1173. https://doi.org/10.1175/BAMS-D-18-0084.1

Fraisl, D., Campbell, J., See, L., Wehn, U., Wardlaw, J., Gold, M., Moorthy, I., Arias, R., Piera, J., Oliver, J. L., Masó, J., Penker, M., & Fritz, S. (2020). Mapping citizen science contributions to the UN sustainable development goals. *Sustainability Science*, *15*(6), 1735–1751. https://doi.org/10.1007/s11625-020-00833-7

Freedman, L., & Karsh, E. (1991). How Kuwait Was Won: Strategy in the Gulf War. *International Security*, *16*(2), 5–41. https://doi.org/10.2307/2539059

Giovanis, E., & Abdeldjalil, A. (2023). The Impact of Climate Change-Induced Migration on Well-being. *The European Institute of the Mediterranean*, 15.

Girgis, M., Hanna, R., & Al-Fulaij, S. (2022). Do Wage Subsidies to Nationals Enhance Their Employability? New Evidence from Kuwait. *Asian Social Science*, *18*(11), Article 11. https://doi.org/10.5539/ass.v18n11p17

Gleick, P. H. (1998). Water in Crisis: Paths to Sustainable Water Use. *Ecological Applications*, *8*(3), 571–579. https://doi.org/10.2307/2641249

Gleick, P. H. (2019). Water as a weapon and casualty of armed conflict: A review of recent water-related violence in Iraq, Syria, and Yemen. *WIREs Water*, *6*(4), e1351. https://doi.org/10.1002/wat2.1351

Gleick, P. H., & Shimabuku, M. (2023). Water-related conflicts: Definitions, data, and trends from the water conflict chronology. *Environmental Research Letters*, *18*(3), 034022. https://doi.org/10.1088/1748-9326/acbb8f

Gomez-Echeverri, L. (2018). Climate and development: Enhancing impact through stronger linkages in the implementation of the Paris Agreement and the Sustainable Development Goals (SDGs). *Philosophical Transactions of the Royal Society A: Mathematical, Physical and Engineering Sciences*, *376*(2119), 20160444. https://doi.org/10.1098/rsta.2016.0444

Hameed, M., Ahmadalipour, A., & Moradkhani, H. (2020). Drought and food security in the middle east: An analytical framework. *Agricultural and Forest Meteorology*, *281*, 107816. https://doi.org/10.1016/j.agrformet.2019.107816

Hamoda, M. F. (2001). Desalination and water resource management in Kuwait. *Desalination*, *138*(1), 385–393. https://doi.org/10.1016/S0011-9164(01)00288-0

Hassan Rashid, M. A., Manzoor, M. M., & Mukhtar, S. (2018). Urbanisation and Its Effects on Water Resources: An Exploratory Analysis. *Asian Journal of Water, Environment and Pollution*, *15*(1), 67–74. https://doi.org/10.3233/AJW-180007

He, C., Liu, Z., Wu, J., Pan, X., Fang, Z., Li, J., & Bryan, B. A. (2021). Future global urban water scarcity and potential solutions. *Nature Communications*, *12*(1), 4667. https://doi.org/10.1038/s41467-021-25026-3

Hilmi, N., Farahmand, S., & Shehabi, M. (2020). Climate Agreements' Implementation Through Energy Transition and Economic Diversification in Kuwait. In H. Miniaoui (Ed.), *Economic Development in the Gulf Cooperation Council Countries: From Rentier States to Diversified Economies* (pp. 19–42). Springer. https://doi.org/10.1007/978-981-15-6058-3_2

Hofste, R. W., Reig, P., & Schleifer, L. (2019). *17 Countries, Home to One-Quarter of the World's Population, Face Extremely High Water Stress*. https://www.wri.org/insights/17-countries-home-one-quarter-worlds-population-face-extremely-high-water-stress

Hussain, M. I., Muscolo, A., Farooq, M., & Ahmad, W. (2019). Sustainable use and management of non-conventional water resources for rehabilitation of marginal lands in arid and semiarid environments. *Agricultural Water Management*, *221*, 462–476. https://doi.org/10.1016/j.agwat.2019.04.014

Hwang, H., An, S., Lee, E., Han, S., & Lee, C. (2021). Cross-Societal Analysis of Climate Change Awareness and Its Relation to SDG 13: A Knowledge Synthesis from Text Mining. *Sustainability*, *13*(10), Article 10. https://doi.org/10.3390/su13105596

IEA. (2020, April 21). *Global Energy Review 2019 – Analysis*. IEA. https://www.iea.org/reports/global-energy-review-2019

IPCC. (2019). *Special Report on Climate Change and Land*. https://www.ipcc.ch/srccl/

IPCC. (2021). *Climate Change 2021: The Physical Science Basis*. Cambridge University Press. https://www.ipcc.ch/report/ar6/wg1/downloads/report/IPCC_AR6_WGI_Full_Report.pdf

IPCC. (2022). *Climate change: A threat to human wellbeing and health of the planet. Taking action now can secure our future — IPCC*. https://www.ipcc.ch/2022/02/28/pr-wgii-ar6/

Irfeey, A. M. M., Alotaibi, B. A., Najim, M. M. M., & Shah, A. A. (2023). Water Valuation in Urban Settings for Sustainable Water Management. *Water*, *15*(17), Article 17. https://doi.org/10.3390/w15173105

Ismail, I., El Desoki, F., & AlAnzi, A. (2021). EVALUATING THE ECONOMIC RETURN OF THE WATER DESALINATION AND SANITATION PROJECT IN THE STATE OF KUWAIT. *Journal of Productivity and Development*, *26*(1), 19–39. https://doi.org/10.21608/jpd.2021.140279

Kaplan, G., Rashid, T., Gasparovic, M., Pietrelli, A., & Ferrara, V. (2022). Monitoring war-generated environmental security using remote sensing: A review. *Land Degradation & Development*, *33*(10), 1513–1526. https://doi.org/10.1002/ldr.4249

Karami, N. (2019). The Modality of Climate Change in the Middle East: Drought or Drying up? *The Journal of Interrupted Studies*, *2*(1), 118–140. https://doi.org/10.1163/25430149-00201003

Khan, A., & Arokkiaraj, H. (2021). Challenges of reverse migration in India: A comparative study of internal and international migrant workers in the post-COVID economy. *Comparative Migration Studies*, *9*(1), 49. https://doi.org/10.1186/s40878-021-00260-2

Knoema. (2021). *Kuwait Urban population 1960-2021*. Knoema. https://knoema.com//atlas/Kuwait/Urban-population

Lasrado, J. (2022). GCC Population Will Be Lesser and Older by the End of this Century | Marmore MENA Intelligence. *Marmore MENA Intelligence (MMI) -Economy*. https://www.marmoremena.com/en/insights/gcc-population-will-be-lesser-and-older-by-the-end-of-this-century/

Le Quesne, W. J. F., Fernand, L., Ali, T. S., Andres, O., Antonpoulou, M., Burt, J. A., Dougherty, W. W., Edson, P. J., El Kharraz, J., Glavan, J., Mamiit, R. J., Reid, K. D., Sajwani, A., & Sheahan, D. (2021). Is the development of desalination compatible with sustainable development of the Arabian Gulf? *Marine Pollution Bulletin*, *173*, 112940. https://doi.org/10.1016/j.marpolbul.2021.112940

Lebdioui, A. (2021). The Multidimensional Indicator of Extractives-based Development (MINDEX): A new approach to measuring resource wealth and dependence. *World Development*, *147*, 105633. https://doi.org/10.1016/j.worlddev.2021.105633

Mabrok, M.A., Saad, A., Ahmed, T., & Alsayab, H. (2022). Modeling and simulations of Water Network Distribution to Assess Water Quality: Kuwait as a case study. *Alexandria Engineering Journal*, *61*(12), 11859–11877. https://doi.org/10.1016/j.aej.2022.05.038

MacDonald, F. (2022). One of the World's Wealthiest Oil Exporters Is Becoming Unlivable. *Bloomberg.Com*. https://www.bloomberg.com/news/articles/2022-01-16/kuwait-a-wealthy-oil-exporter-is-becoming-unlivable

Mahmoudi, A., Bostani, M., Rashidi, S., & Valipour, M. S. (2023). Challenges and opportunities of desalination with renewable energy resources in Middle East countries. *Renewable and Sustainable Energy Reviews*, *184*, 113543. https://doi.org/10.1016/j.rser.2023.113543

McSweeney, R. (2021, August 10). Explainer: What the new IPCC report says about extreme weather and climate change. *Carbon Brief*. https://www.carbonbrief.org/explainer-what-the-new-ipcc-report-says-about-extreme-weather-and-climate-change

MEE. (2021). *Middle East heatwave: Temperatures top 50C in several countries*. Middle East Eye. http://www.middleeasteye.net/news/middle-east-heatwave-oman-uae-kuwait-iran-temperatures-top

Merlone, A., Al-Dashti, H., Faisal, N., Cerveny, R. S., AlSarmi, S., Bessemoulin, P., Brunet, M., Driouech, F., Khalatyan, Y., Peterson, T. C., Rahimzadeh, F., Trewin, B., Wahab, M. M. A., Yagan, S., Coppa, G., Smorgon, D., Musacchio, C., & Krahenbuhl, D. (2019). Temperature extreme records: World Meteorological Organization metrological and meteorological evaluation of the 54.0°C observations in Mitribah, Kuwait and Turbat, Pakistan in 2016/2017. *International Journal of Climatology*, *39*(13), 5154–5169. https://doi.org/10.1002/joc.6132

MEW. (2021). *Statistical Year Book (Water) of 2020*. Ministry of Electricity & Water. https://www.mew.gov.kw/media/rckpzmm4/%D9%83%D8%AA%D8%A7%D8%A8-%D8%A7%D9%84%D8%A7%D8%AD%D8%B5%D8%A7%D8%A1-%D8%A7%D9%84%D8%B3%D9%86%D9%88%D9%8A-%D8%A7%D9%84%D9%85%D9%8A%D8%A7%D9%87-compressed.pdf

MEW. (2022). *State of Kuwait Water Statistical Year Book*. Ministry of Electricity & Water & Renewable Energy. chrome-extension://oemmndcbldboiebfnladdacbdfmadadm/ https://www.mew.gov.kw/media/xsjdbhjx/water-annual-report-2022-for-qr.pdf

Mishra, R. K. (2023). Fresh Water availability and Its Global challenge. *British Journal of Multidisciplinary and Advanced Studies*, *4*(3), Article 3. https://doi.org/10.37745/bjmas.2022.0208

Mkubwa, I. G. (2023). *Impact of Social- Economic Activities on Water Scarcity in Tanzania* [Thesis, Institute of Accountancy Arusha (IAA)]. http://dspace.iaa.ac.tz:8080/xmlui/handle/123456789/2206

Mohammadi, F., Sahraei-Ardakani, M., Al-Abdullah, Y., & Heydt, G. T. (2019a). Can Desalination be an Economically Viable Solution for Water Scarcity? *2019 IEEE Global Humanitarian Technology Conference (GHTC)*, 1–4. https://doi.org/10.1109/GHTC46095.2019.9033050

Mohammadi, F., Sahraei-Ardakani, M., Al-Abdullah, Y., & Heydt, G. T. (2019b). Can Desalination be an Economically Viable Solution for Water Scarcity? *2019 IEEE Global Humanitarian Technology Conference (GHTC)*, 1–4. https://doi.org/10.1109/GHTC46095.2019.9033050

Moossa, B., Trivedi, P., Saleem, H., & Zaidi, S. J. (2022). Desalination in the GCC countries- a review. *Journal of Cleaner Production*, *357*, 131717. https://doi.org/10.1016/j.jclepro.2022.131717

Moyer, J. D., & Hedden, S. (2020). Are we on the right path to achieve the sustainable development goals? *World Development*, *127*, 104749. https://doi.org/10.1016/j.worlddev.2019.104749

Mukhopadhyay, A., & Akber, A. (2018). Sustainable water management in Kuwait: Current situation and possible correctional measures. *International Journal of Sustainable Development and Planning*, *13*(03), 425–435. https://doi.org/10.2495/SDP-V13-N3-425-435

Mulligan, M., van Soesbergen, A., Hole, D. G., Brooks, T. M., Burke, S., & Hutton, J. (2020). Mapping nature's contribution to SDG 6 and implications for other SDGs at policy relevant scales. *Remote Sensing of Environment*, *239*, 111671. https://doi.org/10.1016/j.rse.2020.111671

Nabong, E. C., Hocking, L., Opdyke, A., & Walters, J. P. (2023). Decision-making factor interactions influencing climate migration: A systems-based systematic review. *WIREs Climate Change*, *14*(4), e828. https://doi.org/10.1002/wcc.828

Naderi Beni, A., Marriner, N., Sharifi, A., Azizpour, J., Kabiri, K., Djamali, M., & Kirman, A. (2021). Climate change: A driver of future conflicts in the Persian Gulf Region? *Heliyon*, *7*(2), e06288. https://doi.org/10.1016/j.heliyon.2021.e06288

Netherlands Enterprise Agency. (2019). *Nexus in Kuwait OPPORTUNITIES FOR DUTCH COOPERATION*. Ministry of Foreign Affairs Netherlands. https://www.rvo.nl/sites/default/files/2019/07/Kuwait-Nexus-Report.pdf

Nisrane, B. L., Ossewaarde, R., & Need, A. (2020). The exploitation narratives and coping strategies of Ethiopian women return migrants from the Arabian Gulf. *Gender, Place & Culture*, *27*(4), 568–586. https://doi.org/10.1080/0966369X.2019.1611545

Odhiambo, G. O. (2017). Water scarcity in the Arabian Peninsula and socio-economic implications. *Applied Water Science*, *7*(5), 2479–2492. https://doi.org/10.1007/s13201-016-0440-1

OECD/FAO. (2018). *OECD-FAO Agricultural Outlook 2018–2027—Special focus: Middle East and North Africa | FAO* [Agricultural outlook]. OECD Publishing, Paris/Food and Agriculture Organization of the United Nations, Rome. https://www.fao.org/family-farming/detail/en/c/1145263/

Omar Asem, S. A. S. (2020). Reserch and Development Challenges and Opportunities in the Arab World: Case Study on Kuwait Institute for Scientific Research (KISR). In A. Badran, E. Baydoun, & J. R. Hillman (Eds.), *Higher Education in the Arab World: Building a Culture of Innovation and Entrepreneurship* (pp. 357–369). Springer International Publishing. https://doi.org/10.1007/978-3-030-37834-9_16

OPEC. (2019). *OPEC: OPEC Share of World Crude Oil Reserves*. https://www.opec.org/opec_web/en/data_graphs/330.htm

Ottesen, A., Thom, D., Bhagat, R., & Mourdaa, R. (2023). Learning from the Future of Kuwait: Scenarios as a Learning Tool to Build Consensus for Actions Needed to Realise Vision 2035. *Sustainability*, *15*(9), Article 9. https://doi.org/10.3390/su15097054

Puaschunder, J. (2020). Global Climate Change-Induced Migration and Financial Flows. In J. Puaschunder (Ed.), *Governance & Climate Justice: Global South & Developing Nations* (pp. 111–143). Springer International Publishing. https://doi.org/10.1007/978-3-319-63281-0_7

Qureshi, A. S. (2020). Challenges and Prospects of Using Treated Wastewater to Manage Water Scarcity Crises in the Gulf Cooperation Council (GCC) Countries. *Water*, *12*(7), Article 7. https://doi.org/10.3390/w12071971

Radha, S. V. V. D., Sabarathinam, C., Al Otaibi, F., & Al-Sabti, B. T. (2022). Variation of centennial precipitation patterns in Kuwait and their relation to climate change. *Environmental Monitoring and Assessment*, *195*(1), 20. https://doi.org/10.1007/s10661-022-10587-7

Rahman, M. M., Luna, S. S., & Raj, P. (2023). Disgraceful return: Gulf migration and shifting national narratives amid COVID-19. *Journal of Ethnic and Migration Studies*, *49*(20), 5238–5258. https://doi.org/10.1080/1369183X.2024.2268987

Rajan, S. I., & Oommen, G. Z. (2020). *Asianization of migrant workers in the Gulf countries*. Springer.

Raymond, C., Matthews, T., & Horton, R. M. (2020). The emergence of heat and humidity too severe for human tolerance. *Science Advances*, *6*(19), eaaw1838. https://doi.org/10.1126/sciadv.aaw1838

Ritchie, H., Roser, M., & Rosado, P. (2024). Renewable Energy. *Our World in Data*. https://ourworldindata.org/renewable-energy

Salahuddin, M., & Gow, J. (2014). Economic growth, energy consumption and CO2 emissions in Gulf Cooperation Council countries. *Energy*, *73*, 44–58. https://doi.org/10.1016/j.energy.2014.05.054

Salberg, F. (2023). *Turning Oil Into Water: Water security in the Middle East and North Africa*. https://urn.kb.se/resolve?urn=urn:nbn:se:uu:diva-503309

Salem, H. S., Pudza, M. Y., & Yihdego, Y. (2023). Harnessing the energy transition from total dependence on fossil to renewable energy in the Arabian Gulf region, considering population, climate change impacts, ecological and carbon footprints, and United Nations' Sustainable Development Goals. *Sustainable Earth Reviews*, *6*(1), 10. https://doi.org/10.1186/s42055-023-00057-4

Salim, A. M., & Alsyouf, I. (2020). Development of renewable energy in the GCC region: Status and challenges. *International Journal of Energy Sector Management*, *14*(6), 1049–1071. https://doi.org/10.1108/IJESM-07-2019-0012

Samenow, J. (2016). Two Middle East locations hit 129 degrees, hottest ever in Eastern Hemisphere, maybe the world. *Washington Post*. https://www.washingtonpost.com/news/capital-weather-gang/wp/2016/07/22/two-middle-east-locations-hit-129-degrees-hottest-ever-in-eastern-hemisphere-maybe-the-world/

Scartozzi, C. M. (2021). Reframing Climate-Induced Socio-Environmental Conflicts: A Systematic Review. *International Studies Review*, *23*(3), 696–725. https://doi.org/10.1093/isr/viaa064

Sedaghat, A., Sabati, M., Alkhatib, F., Amir Abbas Oloomi, S., Sabri, F., Salem, H., Jan Zafar, W., & Ashtian Malayer, M. (2021). Climate change and thermo-solar patterns of office buildings with/without window films in extreme hot-arid climate of Kuwait. *Solar Energy*, *217*, 354–374. https://doi.org/10.1016/j.solener.2021.02.051

Shariff Sharp, D., Alshammari, A., & Hameed, K. (2021, October). *The quiet emergency: Experiences and understandings of climate change in Kuwait* (Monograph 13). LSE Middle East Centre, Kuwait Programme. https://www.lse.ac.uk/middle-east-centre/publications

Shehabi, M. (2020). Diversification effects of energy subsidy reform in oil exporters: Illustrations from Kuwait. *Energy Policy*, *138*, 110966. https://doi.org/10.1016/j.enpol.2019.110966

Sherif, M., Baig, F., & Kabeer, S. (2023). Gulf Cooperation Council countries' water and climate research to strengthen UN's SDGs 6 and 13. *Heliyon*, *9*, e14584. https://doi.org/10.1016/j.heliyon.2023.e14584

Sherif, M., Liaqat, M. U., Baig, F., & Al-Rashed, M. (2023). Water resources availability, sustainability and challenges in the GCC countries: An overview. *Heliyon*, *9*(10), e20543. https://doi.org/10.1016/j.heliyon.2023.e20543

Statista Research Department. (2020). *Water management in the GCC*. Statista. https://www.statista.com/topics/4851/water-management-in-gcc/

Suleiman, M. K., & Shahid, S. A. (2023a). Agricultural Water Footprint of Major Crops Grown in Kuwait Compared to the World Average: A Review. In M. K. Suleiman & S. A. Shahid (Eds.), *Terrestrial Environment and Ecosystems of Kuwait: Assessment and Restoration* (pp. 393–414). Springer Nature Switzerland. https://doi.org/10.1007/978-3-031-46262-7_16

Suleiman, M. K., & Shahid, S. A. (2023b). Prospective of Agricultural Farming in Kuwait and Energy-Food-Water-Climate Nexus. In M. K. Suleiman & S. A. Shahid (Eds.), *Terrestrial Environment and Ecosystems of Kuwait: Assessment and Restoration* (pp. 363–391). Springer Nature Switzerland. https://doi.org/10.1007/978-3-031-46262-7_15

Sun, D., Addae, E. A., Jemmali, H., Mensah, I. A., Musah, M., Mensah, C. N., & Appiah-Twum, F. (2021). Examining the determinants of water resources availability in sub-Sahara Africa: A panel-based econometrics analysis. *Environmental Science and Pollution Research*, *28*(17), 21212–21230. https://doi.org/10.1007/s11356-020-12256-z

Tariq, M. A. U. R., Alotaibi, R., Weththasinghe, K. K., & Rajabi, Z. (2022). A detailed perspective of water resource management in a dry and water scarce country: The case in Kuwait. *Frontiers in Environmental Science*, *10*, 20.

The World Bank. (2021). *Population growth (annual %)—Kuwait | Data* (Population Growth (Annual %) - Kuwait) [Data Page]. https://data.worldbank.org/indicator/SP.POP.GROW?locations=KW

Tzanakakis, V. A., Paranychianakis, N. V., & Angelakis, A. N. (2020). Water Supply and Water Scarcity. *Water*, *12*(9), Article 9. https://doi.org/10.3390/w12092347

UNESCO. (2023). *The United Nations World Water Development Report 2023: Partnerships and cooperation for water*. UN-Water. https://unesdoc.unesco.org/ark:/48223/pf0000384655

United Nations. (2021a). Kuwait: Common core document. https://docstore.ohchr.org/SelfServices/FilesHandler.ashx?enc=FhOD6sgqgzAhFXD9F%2feKaFMm83LbFY75RhkIFGrig%2b66CppE44IJXNE88VRH9RobNWN8Neh9ytsolqi4YnNvLXp%2bu1Heu3%2fMV3AxS39Fy6OOx%2ftghUP%2fWiqz%2brCUQRPe

United Nations. (2021b). Migrant workers bear the brunt of extreme heat in Kuwait. https://www.who.int/news-room/feature-stories/detail/migrant-workers-bear-brunt-extreme-heat-kuwait

United Nations. (2021c). Water scarcity. https://www.unwater.org/water-facts/scarcity/

United Nations. (2022). *THE 17 GOALS | Sustainable Development*. https://sdgs.un.org/goals

United Nations. (2023a). Goal 13: Climate action|Sustainable Development Goals|United Nations Development Programme. UNDP. https://www.undp.org/sustainable-development-goals/climate-action

United Nations. (2023b). *State of Kuwait—2nd Voluntary National Review Report 2023 | United Nations in Kuwait*. https://kuwait.un.org/en/245739-state-kuwait-2nd-voluntary-national-review-report-2023

United Nations U, (2023c). Goal 6: Clean water and sanitation|Sustainable Development Goals|United Nations Development Programme. UNDP. https://www.undp.org/sustainable-development-goals/clean-water-and-sanitation

United Nations. (2024). *UN World Water Development Report 2024*. https://unesdoc.unesco.org/ark:/48223/pf0000388948

Valenta, M., Knowlton, K. E., Jakobsen, J., Al Awad, M., & Strabac, Z. (2020). Temporary Labour–Migration System and Long–term Residence Strategies in the United Arab Emirates. *International Migration*, *58*(1), 182–197. https://doi.org/10.1111/imig.12551

Vicedo-Cabrera, A. M., Scovronick, N., Sera, F., Royé, D., Schneider, R., Tobias, A., Astrom, C., Guo, Y., Honda, Y., Hondula, D. M., Abrutzky, R., Tong, S., Coelho, M. de S. Z. S., Saldiva, P. H. N., Lavigne, E., Correa, P. M., Ortega, N. V., Kan, H., Osorio, S., … Gasparrini, A. (2021). The burden of heat-related mortality attributable to recent human-induced climate change. *Nature Climate Change*, *11*(6), Article 6. https://doi.org/10.1038/s41558-021-01058-x

Wada, Y., Flörke, M., Hanasaki, N., Eisner, S., Fischer, G., Tramberend, S., Satoh, Y., van Vliet, M. T. H., Yillia, P., Ringler, C., Burek, P., & Wiberg, D. (2016). Modeling global water use for the 21st century: The Water Futures and Solutions (WFaS) initiative and its approaches. *Geoscientific Model Development*, *9*(1), 175–222. https://doi.org/10.5194/gmd-9-175-2016

Westing, A. H. (2003). Environmental Dimension of the Gulf War of 1991. In H. G. Brauch, P. H. Liotta, A. Marquina, P. F. Rogers, & M. E.-S. Selim (Eds.), *Security and Environment in the Mediterranean: Conceptualising Security and Environmental Conflicts* (pp. 523–534). Springer. https://doi.org/10.1007/978-3-642-55854-2_33

WMO. (2016). *WMO examines reported record temperature of 54°C in Kuwait*. World Meteorological Organization. https://public.wmo.int/en/media/news/wmo-examines-reported-record-temperature-of-54%C2%B0c-kuwait

World Bank. (2018). *Beyond Scarcity: Water Security in the Middle East and North Africa*. World Bank. https://doi.org/10.1596/978-1-4648-1144-9

World Bank. (2023). *World Bank Open Data: Kuwait population*. World Bank Open Data. https://data.worldbank.org

World Population Review. (2024). *Kuwait Population* 2024. https://worldpopulationreview.com/countries/kuwait-population

Wrathall, D. J., Van Den Hoek, J., Walters, A., & Devenish, A. (2018). Water stress and human migration: A global, georeferenced review of empirical research. *FAO Land and Water Discussion Paper (FAO) Eng No. 11*. http://www.fao.org/3/I8867EN/i8867en.pdf

Zaveri, E. D., Wrenn, D. H., & Fisher-Vanden, K. (2020). The impact of water access on short-term migration in rural India. *Australian Journal of Agricultural and Resource Economics*, *64*(2), 505–532. https://doi.org/10.1111/1467-8489.12364

Zekri, S. (2020). Oman Water Policy. In S. Zekri (Ed.), *Water Policies in MENA Countries* (pp. 113–134). Springer International Publishing. https://doi.org/10.1007/978-3-030-29274-4_6

Zhang, H., & Xie, Y. (2019). Alleviating freshwater shortages with combined desert-based large-scale renewable energy and coastal desalination plants supported by Global Energy Interconnection. *Global Energy Interconnection*, *2*(3), 205–213. https://doi.org/10.1016/j.gloei.2019.07.013

Zubari, W., Al-Turbak, A., Zahid, W., Al-Ruwis, K., Al-Tkhais, A., Al-Mutaz, I., Abdelwahab, A., Murad, A., Al-Harbi, M., & Al-Sulaymani, Z. (2017). An overview of the GCC Unified Water Strategy (2016-2035). *Desalination and Water Treatment*, *81*, 1–18. https://doi.org/10.5004/dwt.2017.20864

8 Africa's Geopolitical Landscape

Assessing China and Russia's Engagement and Motivations

Maria (Mary) Papageorgiou

Introduction

Over the past decade, there has been a notable surge in geopolitical competition among major global powers. While considerable attention has been devoted to the Indo-Pacific region, countries such as Russia and China have also shifted their attention towards Africa. The continent has emerged as a prominent geopolitical arena, providing these nations with significant advantages, including access to abundant energy resources, raw materials, new markets, and a shared worldview with many political regimes in the region against liberal values and American hegemony. Additionally, Africa presents them with opportunities to extend their influence beyond their borders and position themselves within regional hierarchies (Mousavi Shafaee & Golmohammad, 2022).

China and Russia's relationship has expanded and strengthened in the post-Cold War period, raising concerns about the implications for the international system and security, and their joint initiatives and the dynamics of their relationship have been extensively documented (Papageorgiou & Vieira, 2022); however, their joint initiatives in other regions remain relatively unexplored.

This chapter aims to bridge this research gap by investigating the engagement of the two states in Africa over the past decade, analysing their geoeconomic and geopolitical activities, exploring their motivations, evaluating existing joint initiatives, and assessing the implications of their involvement on African development and the attainment of the United Nations Sustainable Development Goals (SDGs). This aspect is particularly pertinent, as the geopolitical risks of competition in Africa involving various external powers significantly affect the progress towards achieving the SDGs (Nguyen et al., 2023).

The findings suggest that Russia and China have pursued distinct approaches to enhance their influence and establish themselves as prominent external powers in Africa. Russia's economic presence in Africa, while not as prominent as powers like the US, UK, or China, has allowed it to engage in economic collaborations based on an 'anti-Western ideology' with lenient standards regarding transparency, accountability, corruption, and democratic governance (Kachur, 2020). Russia's economic engagement in Africa appears to be transactional, driven by practical concerns, and relatively limited in scope, particularly

DOI: 10.4324/9781032655857-11

focused on arms transfers and political or security assurances, reflecting an opportunistic, profit-oriented, and disruptive approach (Murphy, 2023).

On the other hand, China's approach to Africa is grounded in its shared developing country status and non-colonial involvement, setting it apart from Western nations while it champions the 'Beijing Consensus' model of economic success in the region (Naidu et al., 2009). China's engagement in Africa is comprehensive, covering various domains of cooperation, including economy, culture, security, and technology. Furthermore, China's extensive economic involvement in Africa since the early 2000s has had a profound impact, reshaping the continent's economic landscape (Alden, 2017).

When it comes to joint approaches, it is evident that the two states have not engaged in collaborative efforts, but rather, they have focused on political coordination to achieve common objectives; these objectives include strengthening authoritarian regimes and diminishing the influence of the United States and Europe on the continent (Kim, 2023). The conflict in Ukraine also underscored the significance of gaining support from the Global South for both states, as they are frequently portrayed as threats by the West (Kroenig & Starling, 2023). In conclusion, this research highlights the central role of geopolitics in shaping the foreign policies of both Russia and China, contributing to the existing body of literature on great power politics and the Sino-Russian engagement in various regions.

China's Engagement in Africa

Deeply rooted in history, Sino-African relations date back to the Han dynasty and have recently experienced a significant intensification (Power et al., 2012; Jinyuan, 1984). Following the introduction of its "Going Out Strategy" in 2001, China aimed to enhance relations with developing countries and access their abundant resources and markets to sustain its economic growth by promoting trade and investment opportunities (Lei & Sui, 2023). Over the past two decades, Beijing's economic involvement in Africa encompasses a diverse range of activities, including foreign aid, loans, foreign direct investments (FDI), imports and exports of products and services (Chen et al., 2018).

Sino-African ties have been significantly bolstered by initiatives like the Forum on China–Africa Cooperation (FOCAC), established in 2000; playing a crucial role in fostering economic and trade relations while also cultivating the concept of a shared community based on mutually beneficial cooperation (Carrozza, 2021). Additionally, the Belt and Road Initiative (BRI) and its various infrastructure projects, coupled with the forging of strategic partnerships with different states in the region, have solidified and enhanced Beijing's presence in Africa (Papageorgiou & Cardoso, 2021). Besides, most countries in the continent trade with China or are recipients of foreign direct investments or have signed a Memorandum of Understanding (MOU) for the BRI.[1] Moreover, several African countries have supported China's most recent initiatives, such as the Global Development Initiative and Global Security Initiative, thereby allowing China to strengthen both its economic and security presence in the region (Kuo, 2023).

In the economic dimension, China's exports to Africa have exhibited a noteworthy upward trajectory over the last decade, as illustrated in Graph 1, despite a few intermittent declines, notably in 2015 and 2016. Of particular interest are the years 2021 and 2022, which demonstrate a substantial surge in exports. In 2022, this trend culminated with China's exports to Africa surpassing a remarkable milestone, exceeding $160 billion. This data underscores the growing economic ties between China and African nations, highlighting the continent's importance as a trading partner for China's goods and services.

Africa has become an increasingly significant market for China's exports, a trend clearly depicted in Graph 2, where the annual growth in exports to Africa has often outpaced that of the global market. Notably, in 2020 and 2021, despite the overall slowdown in China's global exports caused by the COVID-19 pandemic, trade with African countries continued to thrive, growing by approximately 30% in 2021, on par with global growth rates. In 2022, exports to Africa continued to expand, albeit at a slightly lower rate of around 13%, surpassing those to the rest of the world. This increase can be attributed to several factors, including the expansion of China's Belt and Road Initiative (BRI) in the region, substantial Chinese investments, and the presence of burgeoning markets in these African countries, particularly for Chinese manufactured products which are cheaper and better suited to the needs of African market making China the preferred choice (Calabrese & Tang, 2023).

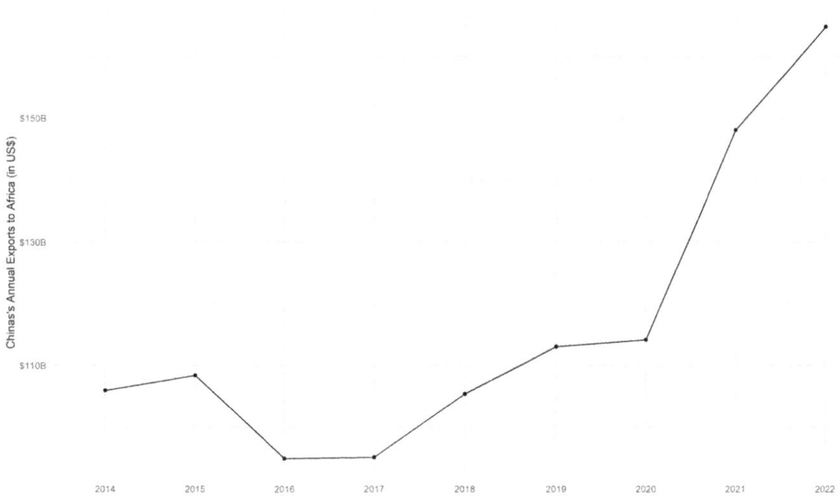

Figure 8.1 Annual Chinese exports to Africa.

Source: Author's calculation with data from IMF (n.d.).

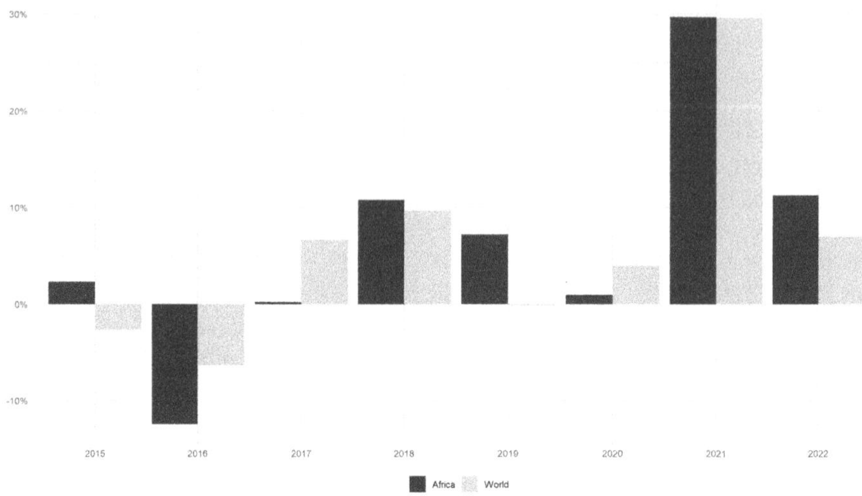

Figure 8.2 Annual growth of Chinese exports to Africa/World.

Source: Author's calculations with data from IMF (n.d.).

A specific aspect of China's trade relations in Africa revolves around the arms trade. While China is a notable arms exporter in the region, it lags behind its two primary competitors, the United States and Russia. As depicted in Graph 3, Chinese arms exports to Africa have exhibited a declining trend, despite a peak in 2016. Subsequently, there was a continued downward trajectory until 2019, followed by a slight upturn peaking in 2021, only to resume a declining trend in 2022. These findings suggest that China has not yet firmly established itself as a dominant arms exporter to the African market, a pattern that is also evident in other regions beyond Asia.

Regarding the annual growth rates depicted in Graph 5, it is noteworthy that only in two years, 2016 and 2020, did China's exports to Africa outpace its global export growth. However, in 2022, there was a negative growth rate compared to the global trend. This data indicates the volatility in China's export performance in the African market in different years, with occasional surges in growth but also periods of decline which further indicates that China has not been up to parity with its two competitors.

Another important indication of China's engagement in Africa is its foreign direct investments, which have significantly increased since the early 2000s, with Beijing surpassing the US since 2013; however, Africa as a region lags behind other regions in terms of the amount received in Chinese FDI.[2] The main recipients of the FDIs are countries such as South Africa, DR Congo, Zambia, Ethiopia, Angola, Nigeria, Kenya, Zimbabwe, Algeria, Ghana, Tanzania, and Mozambique, which collectively accounted for nearly three-quarters of China's FDI by stock in 2020, indicating a preference for investing in resource-rich countries; nevertheless, China tends to invest more in smaller

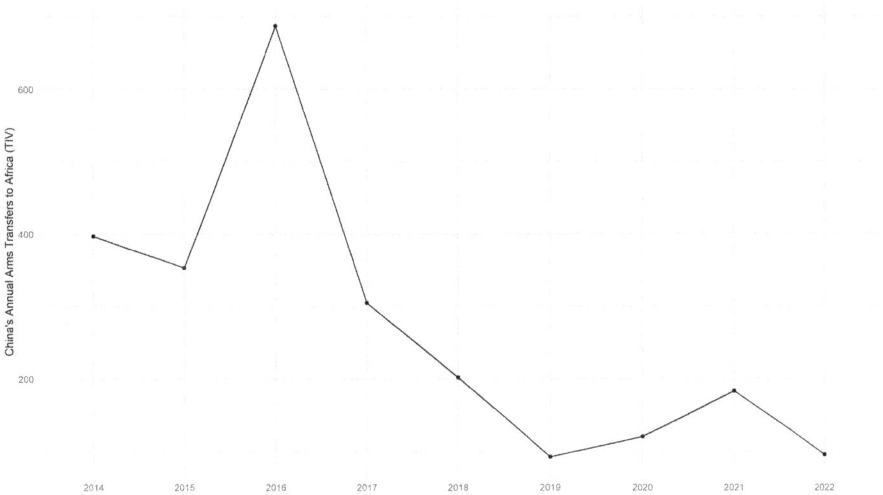

Figure 8.3 China's annual arms transfers to Africa.

Source: Author's calculations with data from SIPRI (n.d.).

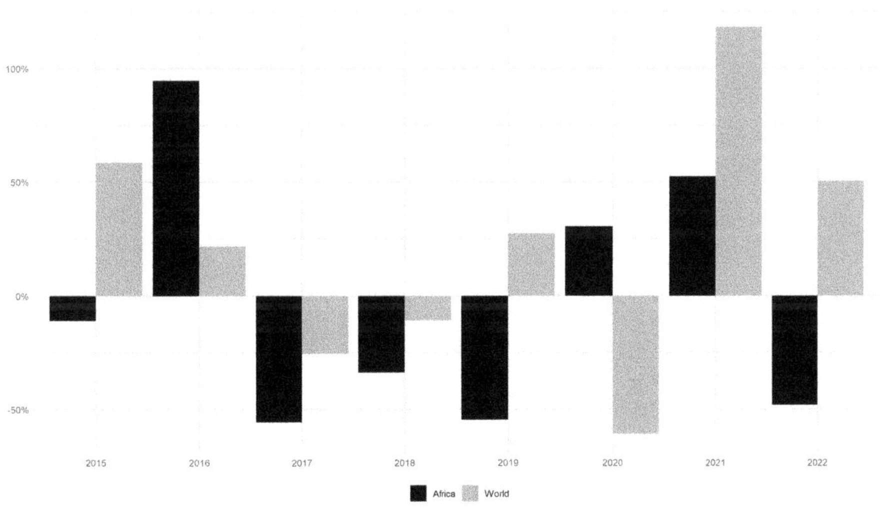

Figure 8.4 Annual Growth of Chinese arms transfers to Africa/World.

Source: Author's calculation with data from SIPRI (n.d.).

African economies, which receive a higher share of Chinese FDI relative to their GDP share compared to larger economies (Yu, 2022).

The primary sectors in which China is investing, as indicated in Table 8.1, are primarily construction and mining, followed by manufacturing, scientific, and leasing. Construction, in particular, has experienced a continuous upward trend, while financial services have shown a decreasing trend.

Table 8.1 Main sectors of Chinese FDI in Africa

Year	*Construction*		*Mining*		*Manufacturing*		*Financial*		*Scientific*		*Leasing*		*Other*		*Total, US$*
2013	68.38	26.1%	69.17	26.4%	35.11	13.4%	36.68	14.0%	13.36	5.1%			39.30	0.15	262.00
2014	79.90	24.7%	79.26	24.5%	44.00	13.6%	53.05	16.4%	13.59	4.2%			53.70	16.6%	323.50
2015	95.10	27.4%	95.40	27.5%	46.30	13.3%	34.20	9.9%	14.60	4.2%			61.42	17.7%	347.02
2016	113	28.3%	104.1	26.1%	50.9	12.8%	45.6	11.4%	19.1	4.8%			66.22	16.6%	398.92
2017	128.8	29.8%	97.6	22.5%	60.8	14.0%	57.1	13.2%			23.1	5.3%	65.85	15.2%	433.25
2018	147.6	32.0%	104.8	22.7%	59.7	13.0%	50.7	11.0%			29.7	6.4%	68.72	14.9%	461.22
2019	135.9	30.6%	110.2	24.8%	55.9	12.6%	52.4	11.8%			24.9	5.6%	64.85	14.6%	444.15
2020	151.5	34.9%	89.4	20.6%	61.3	14.1%	41.4	9.6%			23.5	5.4%	66.82	15.4%	433.92
2021	163.4	37.0%	99.9	22.6%	59.3	13.4%	42.0	9.5%			20.4	4.6%	57.0	12.9%	442.02

Source: Author's elaboration with data from Johns Hopkins University China-Africa Research Initiative (CARI https://www.sais-cari.org/chinese-investment-in-africa) (represented in $100 million)

China has also substantial investments in technology projects in the region which they have predated the Digital Silk Road (DSR), particularly in the telecommunications sector companies like Huawei Technologies, ZTE, and China Telecom play a pivotal role in building and upgrading cost-effective telecom infrastructure, from internet backbone networks to last-mile solutions, making technology products and services more accessible and appealing to African countries (Agbebi, 2022). Under the DSR, various initiatives have been launched, including the development of "smart cities in African nations like Mozambique, Angola, and Ghana other include Huawei's contributions to Africa's 4G infrastructure, support for the African Union's Agenda 2063 digital transformation strategy, the establishment of the China-Africa Internet Development and Cooperation Forum with training centres and R&D programs, partnerships between e-commerce platforms and Alibaba to enhance the promotion of African agricultural products (Eguegu, 2022).

Nevertheless, China has also leveraged loans and development aid as policy instruments to enhance its soft power (Fijałkowski, 2014). These loans aim to support the development goals of recipient countries and according to data from the CLA Database spanning from 2000 to 2022, 39 Chinese lenders[3] entered into 1,243 loan agreements with a total value of $170.08 billion, with 49 African governments and seven regional institutions.[4] More specifically, as shown in Table 8.2, China has provided loans to various countries to support different sectors, with Angola having received the most loans across multiple sectors.

Table 8.2 Chinese loans to African countries per sector

Sector	*Total number of Loans*	*Amount*	*Country with most Loans*	*Total number of Loans/country*
Energy	188	59.9b	Angola	34
Transport	308	49.1b	Angola	42
ICT	152	13.9b	Cameroon & Angola	40
Financial services	52	9.1b	South Africa	8
Industry, trade, services	81	8.8b	Angola	30
Other	192	8.6b	Angola	39
Water, sanitation, waste	93	7.1b	Angola	21
Public Administration	30	4.2b	Zambia	15
Defence and military	27	3.0b	Zambia	8
Agriculture	41	2.3b	Angola	8
Education	35	2.0b	Angola	15
Health	31	1.3b	Angola	12
Environment	2	503.m	Senegal & Angola	2
Non-energy mining	7	144.7m	Zimbabwe	6
Social Protection	2	26.5m	Angola	1

Source: Author's elaboration from Chinese Loans to Africa Database https://www.bu.edu/gdp/chinese-loans-to-africa-database/ numbers in US$.

In its efforts to promote soft power, China has not overlooked cultural and educational initiatives in the region. While Hu Jintao emphasised the importance of soft power for China's rise, under Xi Jinping's leadership, China has continued to invest in such initiatives in Africa, including promoting diplomatic and cultural events, establishing Confucius Institutes, and engaging in educational exchanges with various African states (Cha et al. 2023; Papageorgiou & Cardoso, 2021). Confucius Institutes, established by the Chinese government, play a crucial role in promoting Chinese language and culture in Africa through teaching, cultural exchange, vocational training, scholarships for African students, and on-the-ground education and training by Chinese teachers and technicians (Lam, 2019). As shown in Table 8.3, several African countries host at least one institute in their universities. Studies suggest that these institutes are recognised as the most proactive and effective foreign institutions in African countries (Li, 2023), promoting positive reporting on China-related events and fostering a favourable Chinese image among the African public (Brazys & Dukalskis, 2020).

Table 8.3 Confucius institutes in African countries

Country	*Host Institute*
Angola	Agostinho Neto University
Benin	University of Abomey-Calavi
Botswana	University of Botswana
Burkina Faso	Bobo-Dioulasso Polytechnic University
Burundi	University of Burundi
Cabo Verde	University of Cabo Verde
Cameroon	University of Yaounde II
Central African Republic	University of Bangui
Chad	University of N' Djamena
Comoros	University of the Comoros
Democratic Republic of Congo	University of Marien Ngouabi
Cote d' Ivoire	Université Félix Houphouët-Boigny
Egypt	Cairo University
	Suez Canal University
Equatorial Guinea	National University of Equatorial Guinea
Eritrea	National Board for Higher Education
Ethiopia	Technical & Vocational Education and Training Institute at the University of Adis Ababa
Gabon	Omar Bongo University
Gambia	University of Gambia
Ghana	University of Ghana
	University of Cape Coast
Guinea	Gamal Abdel Nasser University of Conakry
Kenya	University of Nairobi
	Kenyatta University
	Egerton University
	Moi University

(*Continued*)

Table 8.3 (Continued)

Country	*Host Institute*
Liberia	University of Liberia
Madagascar	Antananarivo University
	Toamasina University
Malawi	University of Malawi
Mali	University of Letters and Human Science of Bamako
Mauritania	University of Nouakchott
Mauritius	University of Mauritius
Morocco	Mohammed V University
	Hasan II University
	Abdelmalek Essaadi University
Mozambique	Eduardo Mondlane University
Namibia	University of Namibia
Nigeria	University of Lagos
	Nnamdi Azikiwe University
Rwanda	University of Rwanda
Sao Tome and Principe	Sao Tome and Principe University
Senegal	University of Dakar
Seychelles	University of Seychelles
Sierra Leone	University of Sierra Leone
South Africa	Stellenbosch University
	University of Cape Town
	Rhodes University
	Durban University of Technology
	University of Johannesburg
	University of Western Cape
Sudan	University of Khartoum
Tanzania	University of Dodoma
	University of Dar Es Salaam
Togo	University of Lome
Tunisia	University of Carthage
Uganda	Makerere University
Zambia	University of Zambia
Zimbabwe	University of Zimbabwe

Source: Author's compilation with data from STATISTA, https://www.statista.com/statistics/879192/china-confucius-institutes-in-african-countries/; Xinhua, 61 Confucius Institutes, 48 Confucius Classrooms established in Africa: white paper – Xinhua (news.cn) and Confucius Institutes Around the World – 2023 (digmandarin.com).

Motivations

China's extensive involvement in Africa encompasses geopolitical, geoeconomic, and status considerations. Its economic activities in the region have targeted the import of raw materials, minerals and agricultural products to China's growing economy which requires a stable and consistent supply of these resources (Zhang et al., 2013). These imports however not only have economic significance to the supply and demand of China's economy but also constitute a political leverage for the CCP Chinese Communist Party to remain in power and strengthen its position, acting as a form of legitimacy of the party's economic delivery (Shinn & Brown, 2012). Apart from securing new markets, China, through its investments, particularly in infrastructure, can ensure long-term access to these markets while also enhancing connectivity and trade routes between China and other parts of the world through the Belt and Road Initiative (BRI) (Githaiga et al., 2019). When it comes to exports to Africa, China is pursuing markets for its industrialised products and as various studies have examined its foreign direct investment in the region, promote these processed goods to the continent (Zhang et al., 2022), and at the same time boosting its own manufacturing prowess and securing its competitive advantage (Wuttke, 2017).

Other motivations of China include its attempts to marginalise Taiwan's engagement and establish adherence to the One Country principle (Alden, 2017). Furthermore, China's engagement in the arms trade is driven by its aspiration to establish itself as a prominent player in arms transfers (Papageorgiou, 2023). Its strategic collaborations with African nations and its participation in UN multilateral peacekeeping operations are primarily driven by politico-military competition among major powers, notably the United States (Boutin, 2018), as well as its commitment to advancing a multipolar world (Tull, 2006). Simultaneously, China's geopolitical motivations encompass efforts to ensure security and stability in the region, especially in countries where Beijing has made substantial investments or that are critical for the Belt and Road Initiative (BRI) trade routes (Johnston, 2019).

Moreover, China's non-interference in political affairs and flexible strategic partnerships, resonates with African elites, strengthening bilateral relations, enhancing China's positive image, and fostering alignment and mutual support (Struver, 2016). Particularly within a competitive geopolitical landscape, China seeks to mitigate emerging perceptions of itself as a threat (Røren & Beaumont, 2019) and cultivate a more favourable political image. This was evident during the COVID-19 pandemic when China donated medical equipment, provided aid to African countries, and offered debt relief, portraying itself as a responsible global power (Papageorgiou & Melo, 2022). Besides, the embrace of China's development model by African nations serves to bolster its international standing and global influence (Hodzi, 2020) while its emphasis on non-interference and its avoidance of publicly criticising other states for human rights violations have further solidified its position as a valuable partner for African countries, positioning itself as a mediator rather than a rules enforcer such as the US and European countries (Sultan & Degang, 2020). As such, China has rejected claims of unequal resource extraction, trade imbalances, and debt traps in Africa (Martuscelli, 2020), as Western propaganda and interference, emphasising its careful and restrained approach to lending (Monyae & Chapotera, 2023).

Overall, when it comes to Africa, China's key strategies include boosting its economic power, actively supporting the causes of developing states, positioning itself as a leader of the developing world, safeguarding its citizens and business interests abroad, maintaining regional stability and using primarily soft power initiatives to countering the American influence and presence in the region (Sharma, 2023; Alden, 2017).

Russia's Engagement in Africa

Diplomatic ties between Africa and the Russian Federation trace back to the continent's decolonisation and independence struggle, with Russia being positively regarded for its historical support against colonialism and in African states' efforts for independence (Balytnikov et al., 2019). However, the African continent was largely neglected in Russian foreign policy in the aftermath of the Cold War, with severe limitations throughout the 1990s due to both policy choices and economic constraints (Pham, 2010). It was only under President Vladimir Putin's leadership in the 2000s that Russia began to express more interest in Africa. During this period, Russia's involvement in the region remained limited compared to the United States and European states, primarily centred on raw material and military exports (Marten, 2019; Babić, 2022).

In the mid to late 2000s, high-level visits by Presidents Putin and Medvedev to African states facilitated the entry of Russian state-owned companies into selected African states and laid the foundation for Russia's presence on the continent (Olivier & Suchkov, 2015). Additionally, the adoption of the "Long-term Concept of Social-Economic Development of the Russian Federation until 2020 in 2008 recognised Africa's potential for Russian companies, and the establishment of AFROCOM in 2009 addressed political obstacles and facilitated Russian companies' economic activities in the region (Svoboda, 2024). The activities were primarily centred on securing significant arms contracts (Egypt and Sudan), cooperation in gas and oil extraction (Nigeria and Angola), telecommunications (Angola) and space exploration (Angola and Nigeria) (Matusevich, 2019). Moreover, South Africa's accession to BRICS in 2010 marked a turning point, leading to a more systematic interaction between the Russian Federation and African countries (Daniel & Virk, 2014). This interaction gained momentum, particularly after Western sanctions were imposed on Russia following the annexation of Crimea in 2014, further accelerating Russia's involvement in the continent (Marten, 2019). Accordingly, since the war against Ukraine in 2022 and its aftermath with the highly anti-Russian sentiment in the West and the sanctions imposed revealed the growing importance of Africa in Russian foreign policy is seen in the sequence of regional priorities to its latest 2023 Foreign Policy concept with Africa coming fifth ahead of Latin America, EU and US as shown in Table 8.4.

In the economic domain, Africa represents only 2.5% of Russia's overall trade, mostly with Egypt and Algeria Russia and focuses on a limited range of fields such as arms transfers, machinery exports, mineral resources, and nuclear energy equipment (Jurčák & Marek 2020). As illustrated in Graph 5, Russian exports to Africa have exhibited a volatile trend, reaching their lowest point in 2015, which can be attributed to Russia's overall decline in exports following Western sanctions imposed in 2014. Subsequently, there was an

Table 8.4 Africa in Russia's foreign policy regional priorities

Year	*Position*
2023	6 out of 10
2016	10 out of 10
2013	10 out of 10
2008	9 out of 10
2000	10 out of 10

Sources: Author's compilation with data from THE FOREIGN POLICY CONCEPT OF THE RUSSIAN FEDERATION (fas.org), The Foreign Policy Concept of the Russian Federation 2013 (voltairenet.org), The Foreign Policy Concept of the Russian Federation 2016 (voltairenet.org), The Concept of the Foreign Policy of the Russian Federation - The Ministry of Foreign Affairs of the Russian Federation (mid.ru), THE FOREIGN POLICY CONCEPT OF THE RUSSIAN FEDERATION • President of Russia (kremlin.ru). The Concept of the Foreign Policy of the Russian Federation – The Ministry of Foreign Affairs of the Russian Federation (mid.ru), The Foreign Policy Concept of the Russian Federation 2016 (voltairenet.org), https://www.voltairenet.org/article202037.html, THE FOREIGN POLICY CONCEPT OF THE RUSSIAN FEDERATION (russiaeu.ru), https://nuke.fas.org/guide/russia/doctrine/econcept.htm

upward trend, peaking in 2018, followed by declines in 2019 and 2020 which can also be attributed to the COVID-19 pandemic. However, exports increased in 2021 and experienced a more significant surge in 2022, reaching approximately 25 billion US dollars.

Examining this trend in a comparative context with global exports, as depicted in Graph 6, it becomes evident that in 2016 and 2017, Africa emerged

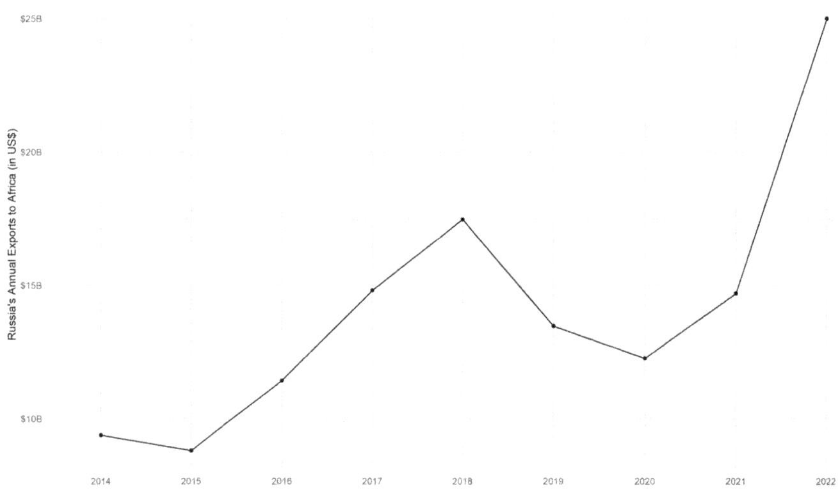

Figure 8.5 Russia's annual exports to Africa.

Source: Author's calculation with data from IMF (n.d.).

as a crucial market for Russia, surpassing its exports to the rest of the world, albeit with fluctuating trends since then. The substantial increase in 2022, showing double-digit growth compared to its global exports, suggests that Russia sought alternative markets to compensate for trade gaps resulting from its strained relations with the EU after the conflict in Ukraine.

A critical component of Russia's exports, closely tied to its identity as a military power and carrying both security and political implications, is its arms transfers. As illustrated in Graph 7, there was a substantial increase in arms exports to the continent, peaking in 2018, followed by significant declines. These fluctuations can be attributed to factors such as the COVID-19 pandemic and Russia's mobilisation of infantry during the conflict in Ukraine. It is noteworthy that Russia's arms transfers encompass small weapons, and as a non-signatory to the UN International Arms Trade Treaty (ATT) of 2014, they hold particular appeal for many African militaries due to their familiarity with Soviet-era weaponry (Neethling, 2020).

As Africa represents the largest market for Russia's arms exports, the annual growth in Graph 8 shows that in several years (2015, 2016, 2017, 2020), exports to Africa grew at a higher rate compared to the global average. However, there was a significant decline in both 2021 and 2022, largely attributable to COVID-19 Russia's war in Ukraine.

Russia's investments in Africa make up less than 1% of its total foreign direct investment, primarily directed towards nuclear energy and mining.[5] The 2019 Russia-Africa summit, being the first summit of its kind, was attended by 43 African heads of state and resulted in the signing of numerous treaties and joint projects valued at approximately USD 10 billion, but still less than other

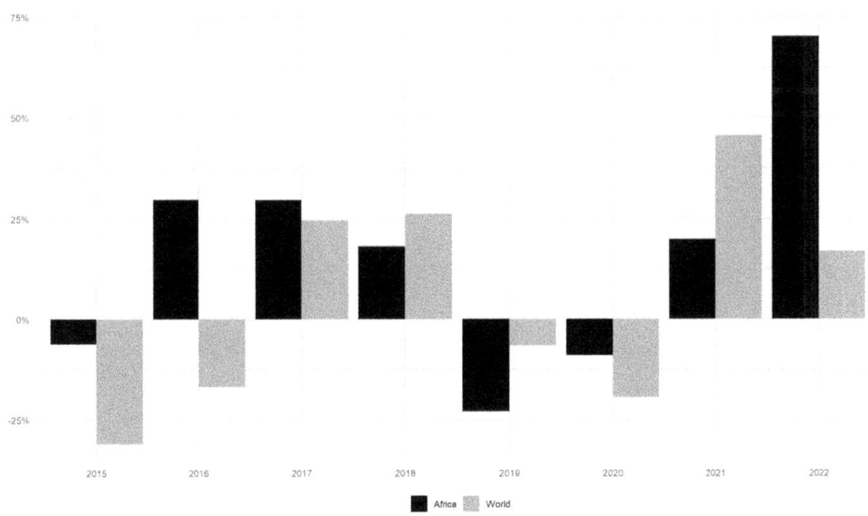

Figure 8.6 Annual growth of Russia's exports to Africa.

Source: Author's calculation with data from IMF (n.d.).

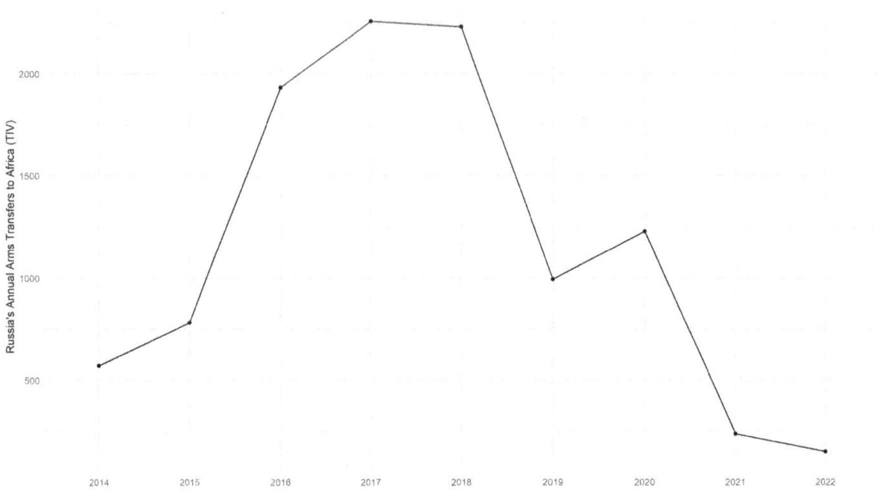

Figure 8.7 Russia's annual arms transfers to Africa.
Source: Author's calculation with data from SIPRI (n.d.).

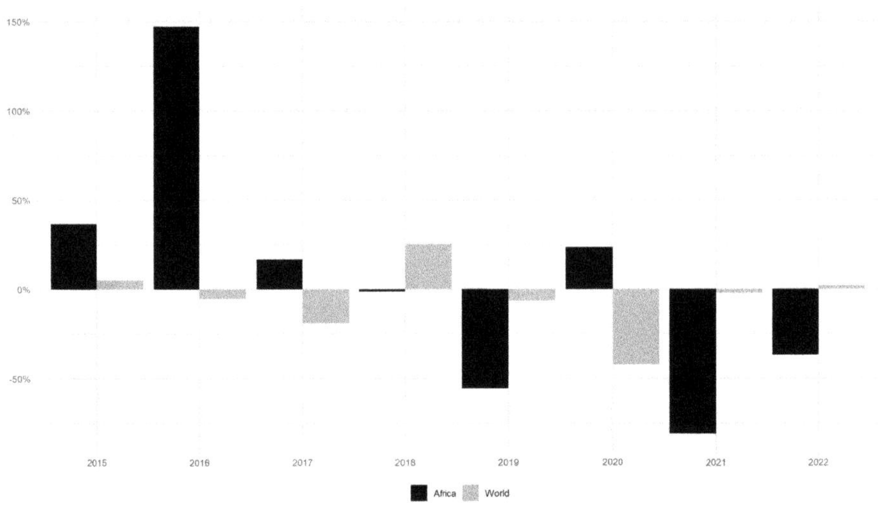

Figure 8.8 Annual growth of Russian arms transfers to Africa/World.
Source: Author's calculation with data from SIPRI (n.d.).

states such as the United States and China's USD 60 billion packages (Clifford, 2021; Svoboda, 2024).

Russia's approach to development assistance comes with strings attached. Being a newcomer to providing loans to foreign governments, Russia and its affiliated corporate entities strategically target countries where Western competitors have a limited presence (ibid). Despite its international isolation and sanctions since 2014, the Russian government has expanded its ODA allocations since 2015, which total to about $1 billion annually (Zaytsev, 2021). Russian development assistance mainly covers food security, global health, debt relief, bilateral aid, trade preferences and educational support (Makarychev & Simão, 2014). Furthermore, as a means to mitigate criticism in the aftermath of the Ukraine war and to appease international voices against its invasion, Russia has forgiven the debts of African nations amounting to more than $20 billion, as confirmed by President Putin (Tass, 2023). Moscow was inclined to offer support to governments with reduced credibility, providing both political and economic assistance as part of their strategy. This calculated approach enables Russia to leverage the political dynamics within the recipient country to advance its own economic interests, consequently leading to the deepening of political ties exhibiting a mutually reinforcing and complementary relationship.

Russia's engagement in the security domain in Africa includes anti-piracy efforts, military cooperation, arms trade facilitation, and nuclear energy promotion (Mathew & Moolakkattu, 2022). Russia has strategically positioned itself to offer security-oriented services, where its positions appear notably competitive compared to its trade and economic endeavours (Issaev et al., 2023). One notable aspect of Russia's security engagement is its utilisation of private military companies such as Wagner Group that have expanded their activities in countries such as the Central African Republic, Chad, Sudan, Madagascar, and Zimbabwe involved in various activities aimed at advancing the Kremlin's interests. These activities include engagement in extrajudicial violence, meddling in local elections, conducting influence campaigns, suppressing pro-democracy demonstrations, advising politicians, and undermining constitutional protections in democratic processes offering Kremlin a plausible deniability (Pokalova, 2023; Svoboda, 2024).

In addition, Russia's presence in Africa has also been facilitated by extensive disinformation campaigns and by employing mercenary interventions in support of isolated leaders or proxies (Siegle, 2021). By employing a three-faced through state media such as Russia Today and Sputnik; parastatal company Internet Research Agency (IRA), managed by Yevgeny Prigozhin; and diaspora organisations Russia has maintained a positive image in various regions, including Africa (Olivier & Suchkov, 2015). Even amidst the conflict in Ukraine, most parts of Africa continue to hold a positive view of Russia. Notably, the Africa-Francophone region exhibits the highest level of positivity at 68%, followed by the Africa-Arabic-speaking region at 58% (Foa et al., 2022).

Of course, Russia has also adopted soft power initiatives, primarily focused on culture and education. This includes the establishment of Russkiy Mir centres and Rossotrudnichestvo offices in various countries (Table 8.5). However, unlike the Confucius institutes, Russia tends to focus on hospitable political systems (Popovic et al., 2020). Additionally, amidst the COVID-19 crisis, Russia implemented extensive public policies to promote its Sputnik vaccine to third-world countries (Papageorgiou & Vieira, 2022). However, its failure in its

Table 8.5 Russian educational centres in Africa

Rossotrudnichestvo	*Russkiy Mir*
Democratic Republic of Congo	Democratic Republic of Congo Kinshasa Diplomatic Academy
Egypt (Alexandria & Cairo)	Egypt, Russian University in Cairo and Hurghada Rodnik Educational Centre
Ethiopia (Addis Ababa)	Kenya, Nairobi East African Education Network
Morocco (Rabat)	Madagascar, University of Antananarivo
Nigeria (Abuja)	Nigeria, University of Nigeria in Nsukka and University of Lagos
South Africa (Pretoria)	Senegal, Cheikh Anta Diop University in Dakar
Tanzania (Dar es Salaam)	South Africa, University of Pretoria, and Johannesburg Parish of St Sergius of Radonezh
Tunisia (Tunisia)	Republic of Cote d' Ivoire, University of Abidjan
Zambia (Lusaka)	Tanzania, University of Dodoma, and University of Dar es Salaam Uganda, Kampala Zambia, Lusaka University of Zambia

Source: Author's elaboration with data from: Cabinets of the Russian World (russkiymir.ru) and Russian Houses abroad Россотрудничество (rs.gov.ru).

"vaccine diplomacy" and delivery of Sputnik V indicated its limited economic engagement in the region (Stronski, 2021). Additionally, Russia's soft power initiatives have produced mixed results, as seen in the diverse responses of African states to the resolutions presented in the UN General Assembly in 2022 and 2023 concerning the Ukraine conflict and Russia's suspension from the Human Rights Council; some countries abstained from voting, others supported the resolutions, and very few opposed them (Repnikova, 2023).

Motivations

Russia's involvement with African nations encompasses various dimensions, including political and economic. Nevertheless, its overarching motivation lies in creating a favourable international environment to advance its foreign policy objectives and reestablish Russia as a global power (Nkuna & Shai, 2021). In line with these objectives, Russia's engagement in Africa can be categorised into three main pillars: securing new markets and imports, establishing itself as a reliable security provider, and upholding its great power status. To realise these goals, Russia has leveraged its non-interventionist history and anti-colonial policy to garner support from African nations at the United Nations General Assembly and has actively discouraged African governments from relying solely on the Bretton Woods institutions as the sole model for economic development while promoting alternative institutions such as BRICS (Nkuna & Shai, 2021).

Facing Western sanctions in both 2014 and 2022, Russia has actively sought to circumvent economic restrictions by exploring new markets and trade routes for its products. Africa, with its promising prospects, becomes a key focus for Russian enterprises, especially in sectors such as energy, arms trade, infrastructure development, and tourism. This economic diversification aims to underscore Russia's global significance, showcase its reduced reliance on the West, indicate that it is not isolated, and solidify its position as a prominent player in the evolving global power dynamics (Diesen, 2023). Even the provision of development assistance falls under its grand strategy to promote a multipolar world order but primarily legitimises its own great power status by undertaking global responsibilities (Makarychev & Simão, 2014). Moreover, engaging with African countries provides Russia with valuable diplomatic leverage, enabling it to shape regional dynamics and influence conflicts, especially through the Wagner group activities by providing military and security assistance (Titeca, 2023).

Overall, Russia's engagement in Africa, seen through its strategic partnerships with Algeria, Morrocco, Egypt, and South Africa, engagement with regional organisations, and involvement in institutions like BRICS, reflects Primakov's multivector approach, aimed at diversifying diplomatic ties, pursuing issue-based cooperation, and strengthening its global standing (Locoman & Papa, 2022).

Joint Initiatives and Points of Friction

While the Soviet Union and China were asymmetric rivals from the 1960s to the early 1980s, the current Sino-Russian relationship is notably more cordial, primarily driven by their shared goal of countering US influence and safeguarding their respective global interests in the post-Cold War era (Papageorgiou & Vieira, 2022). Nevertheless, despite the strengthening and deepening of their cooperation in various areas, the two states have exhibited limited joint initiatives when it comes to promoting common interests in regions beyond their individual spheres of influence (Ramani, 2021). Africa has gained prominence in the foreign policies of both states since the 2000s and has reinforced the rhetoric of a multipolar world where the Global South has a stronger voice and more opportunities. In their engagements in Africa, both states have adopted either a bilateral approach in pursuing their interests in international affairs through state consent and direct collaboration with recipient governments, allowing Russia and China to tailor their approaches to align with the specific interests and priorities of the countries they are engaging with or most of their collaborations taking place in multilateral forms one such initiative is BRICS or their association with the African Union. The appeal of participating in BRICS is evident by the acceptance of Egypt and Ethiopia in BRICS in 2023 while a number of other African countries have expressed their interest to join (including Algeria, Democratic Republic of Congo, Comoros, Gabon). Their expressed shared vision for global governance and the growing influence that the two states exert in multilateral forums that focus on the Global South are evidenced by UN voting, where Sino-Russian positions garner broader global support compared to the United States, especially from states that belong to the Group of 77 (G-77) and institutions such as the BRICS which are more likely to align with China and Russia's stances on various issues (Nurullayev & Papa, 2023).

At the diplomatic level, both states have jointly vetoed resolutions, as seen in the 2008 veto[6] against imposing sanctions on Zimbabwe's President Mugabe. They have also supported African causes and expressed support for South Africa's inclusion as a permanent UN Security Council member, although they have been hesitant to grant Pretoria veto power (Maseng & Mothibinyane, 2023). However, their positions do not consistently align concerning security crises on the continent, as evidenced by their differing stances on issues like Libya and the Central African Republic (Ramani, 2021).

In the security domain, both states have shown a joint commitment to fight terrorism, piracy and extremism and have conducted numerous bilateral and multilateral military exercises for these causes. In Africa the only country that has participated in trilateral naval exercise is South Africa with Operation Mosi taking place in 2019 and Exercise Mosi-2 in the Indian Ocean off the port of Durban which coincided with the one-year anniversary of Russia's invasion of Ukraine in February 2023 (Kim, 2023). However, while these trilateral naval exercises hold limited warfighting significance, they greatly serve the diplomatic interests of each country. They allow Russia to emphasise its ongoing ties with Global South nations and enable China to showcase the expanding global presence of its navy, emphasising both nations' endeavours to project naval power in African waters (Atlantic Council, 2023).

In the information domain, Russia and China share narratives highlighting their contrasting approaches to the West and their dedication to building equal partnerships with African nations, with their state-owned media services, like RIA Novosti and the Chinese Global Times, reciprocally supporting each other's positions on various issues (Ramani, 2021).

Overall, the engagement of the two states in Africa indicates that they tend to pursue " "parallel rather than coordinated policies" (Kaczmarski, 2024, p. 105) Furthermore, the conflict in Ukraine has underscored the strategic autonomy of China and Russia, as their interests and policies may align on some matters, yet they maintain independent actions, exemplifying a conventional great power dynamic rooted in realpolitik (Lo, 2023).

A potential area of contention arises from Russia losing its share in the regional arms market, with China emerging as a formidable competitor equipped with advanced weapon systems. China is increasingly capable of forming defence-industrial export relationships with customer countries and selling more sophisticated weaponry, which could pose a threat to Russia's arms export interests in the Middle East and Africa where Russia's biggest markets are (Papageorgiou, 2023). Simultaneously, Russia's military prowess has come under scrutiny due to its unsuccessful operations in Ukraine, causing some nations to question the effectiveness of its arms and resulting in significant declines in its military exports and its status as a major military power (Šćepanović, 2024). However, thus far, the two countries have managed not only to coexist in certain countries but also to offer different types of weaponry, for instance, in Sudan, both Russia and China have been among its top arms suppliers since 2008, with China providing UAVs and missiles, while Russia supplied tanks, helicopters, and aircraft (Peter & Plichta, 2023).

At the economic level, China's proven capabilities in infrastructure development and its robust economic power position it as a leader in large-scale reconstruction projects, potentially straining relations with Russia, which may not be able to match such projects (Liu, 2023). Also, the civilian nuclear technology exports and project development present a source of contention between China and Russia, given their economic asymmetry and capacity, potentially hindering their ability to secure contracts and markets (Siddi & Kaczmarski, 2019). While both states engage in selective competition for commercial deals in Africa, they have not hesitated to highlight each other's shortcomings. For instance, Chinese nuclear energy companies have capitalised on the high costs associated with Rosatom's projects, as observed in their dealings with Libya on infrastructure (Ramani, 2021). Moreover, the differing approaches of Russia, which offers loans as an accessible funding source, and China, which emphasises International Monetary Fund conditions for its loans, can lead to competition for markets and projects (Svoboda, 2024). All in all, and despite the absence of joint initiatives in Africa and the missed opportunity to collectively address COVID-19 with joint efforts and even developing a vaccine, China and Russia share the common objective of diminishing the influence of other regional actors and exerting greater influence over African nations. While pursuing independent strategies, their shared interest remains the expansion of their presence in Africa and promoting their own separate national interests.

Implications for African countries' SDGs adoption

The engagement of two states in the African continent has multifaceted implications for recipient countries, but an area that remains understudied is the impact of such initiatives on the African states' progress towards achieving the United Nations Sustainable Development Goals (SDGs).

China, in particular, has placed significant emphasis on the SDGs within its Belt and Road Initiative (BRI).[7] This commitment is evident in its multilateral interactions with African nations through platforms like the Forum on China-Africa Cooperation (FOCAC), its engagement with the African Union and its strategic partners in the region (Alden, 2017). Accordingly, it has actively promoted infrastructure projects that align with specific SDGs and has advocated for eco-designed products and services, green international trade, and green finance instruments to support SDG-related objectives (Lewis et al., 2021). Also, the GDI indicates China's commitment to actively contributing to the achievement of these goals and Agenda 2063, aligning with the FOCAC Action Plan and directly promoting initiatives within African economies (Alden, 2017).

Certain studies suggest that China's Foreign Direct Investment (FDI) in Africa has had a generally positive impact on specific SDGs related to economic and environmental aspects but has shown limited influence on achieving SDGs related to social dimensions, such as Affordable and Clean Energy, Decent Work and Economic Growth, Industry, Innovation, and Infrastructure, Sustainable Consumption and Production, Climate Action, and Life on Land (Fang, 2021). Chinese companies pay particular emphasis on the goal "Decent Work and Economic Growth" (19%); however, the main priority is focus on "Industry Innovation and Infrastructure (20%) (Ali et al., 2018)

Moreover, China's imports in Africa have been associated with reduced carbon emissions, especially in non-resource-rich countries, suggesting potential long-term environmental benefits from China's investments in cleaner energy infrastructure (Tawiah et al., 2021). In the healthcare sector, China's aid projects in Africa, often short-term and decentralised, are considered less effective in addressing the health-related aspects of the SDGs due to their scattered and unsustainable nature, particularly in the case of "turn-key projects" like hospital construction in Africa (Wang et al., 2017).

When it comes to SGD, Russia has supported these initiatives; however, given that it has not yet enacted a specific national law regarding compliance with Sustainable Development Goal (SDG) commitments, some of the SDGs align with the country's national priorities outlined in the 2018 Presidential May Decree (Zaytsev, 2021). As such, although Russian ODA Official Development Assistance (ODA) has increased in Africa there is still a lack of evidence to help judge the "systemic change of Russia's current efforts and results in the field of international development or whether they directly align with the core targets of the SDGs. Rossotrudnichestvo, the government agency responsible for Russia's foreign aid policy presents Russian assistance efforts as part of Russia's global efforts to achieve the sustainable development goals approved by the United Nations (Ignatov et al., 2019).

Russian companies' strategic vision and mission statements seem to prioritise certain of the SDG goals with " Decent Work and Economic Growth" (18%) being the priority something that is also reflected in how they conduct their economic operations abroad as well as in countries they are investing (Ali et al., 2018). Some Russian companies have already integrated the SDGs into their activities, with approximately 200 companies implementing over 500 projects aimed at addressing social and environmental challenges aligning with the SDGs (Zaytsev, 2021).

Despite some Russian companies' cooperation with African partners on energy projects to enhance technological sovereignty and global value chain integration, others have faced accusations of violating human rights, fuelling conflicts, and undermining governance and transparency through the involvement of the private military company Wagner Group, suggesting limited Russian commitment and capacity to foster sustainable development in Africa beyond military-security engagement (Droin & Dolbaia, 2023).

Moreover, the recent conflict between Russia and Ukraine and the sanctions against Russia have significant implications for the Sustainable Development

Goals (SDGs) in Africa leading to food and energy shortages, surging inflation, and commodity price spikes in Africa, further endangering poverty and food insecurity in the region (Mhlanga & Ndhlovu, 2023). As highlighted by the United Nations Development Programme (UNDP) in 2022,[8] the conflict exacerbates Africa's debt crisis, as nations struggle to fulfil their obligations amid surging fuel and food prices, further deepening wealth inequality, and affecting poverty rates, food security, stability, peace, security risks, and prosperity, as presented more specifically under SDGs 1, 2, 4, 7, 8, 9, and 13, potentially amplifying disparities between resource-rich and other African nations.

Overall, the engagement of both China and Russia in Africa signifies a burgeoning form of South-South cooperation characterised by bilateralism, flexibility, and a unique approach to economic development that includes geopolitical and geoeconomic considerations. This approach often deviates from established international norms and is shaped in opposition to Western influence. As these changing dynamics continue to evolve, there is an increasing need to thoroughly assess how the engagement of various actors, such as China and Russia, either supports or obstructs African countries in their pursuit of the Sustainable Development Goals due to conflicting interests. Equally important is for African nations to contemplate unified frameworks for the utilisation of development assistance and funding they receive, empowering them to assert greater agency in shaping their domestic policies and goals and harness the full potential of their newfound sources of funding.

Conclusion

This chapter concludes that Russia and China have engaged in Africa with distinctive strategies and objectives, primarily seeking to expand their geopolitical influence and economic presence. While Russia's engagement has been characterised by limited economic projects, albeit with a significant presence on mining and nuclear power; and focused primarily on arms exports on the other hand China has pursued a more comprehensive approach across various sectors, especially in infrastructure and technology as part of its BRI. The objectives of the two states differ as well with Russia seeking to uphold its great power status whereas China focuses on access to markets and natural resources which are essential for its economic rise. Both countries have often positioned themselves in contrast to Western influence in the region and adopted soft power tools to bolster a positive image. However, their activities show limited coordination or promotion of extensive joint projects and reflect parallel, rather than collaborative, initiatives in the region. This engagement of Russia and China in Africa has also significant implications for the attainment of the United Nations Sustainable Development Goals by African nations. Although framed under South-South cooperation, both countries prioritise bilateralism and economic strategies that diverge significantly from international norms with the objective of countering Western influence rather than boosting regional resilience and sustainability. While some initiatives, particularly from China, align with and support specific SDGs, overall progress is hindered by geopolitical interests and the competitive dynamics between these two powers and the West. It is evident that with the increasing presence of these countries in the region and heightened competition with the West, African countries operate in a complex environment and need to evaluate whether the benefits of foreign engagement support or hinder sustainable development across the continent.

Notes

1 See more https://greenfdc.org/countries-of-the-belt-and-road-initiative-bri/?cookie-state-change=1706721020657.
2 China Power Team. "Does China Dominate Global Investment?" China Power. September 26, 2016. Updated January 28, 2021. Accessed January 15, 2024. https://chinapower.csis.org/china-foreign-direct-investment.
3 Includes: commitments from Chinese development finance institutions (DFIs), commercial banks, government entities and companies to African governments, state-owned enterprises and regional multilateral institutions.
4 https://www.bu.edu/gdp/chinese-loans-to-africa-database/.
5 https://www.csis.org/analysis/russia-still-progressing-africa-whats-limit.
6 See more Security Council fails to adopt sanctions against Zimbabwe leadership as two permanent members cast negative votes | UN press.
7 As exemplified by the recent overt inclusion of BRI within the UN's 2030 Agenda.
8 United Nations Development Programme (UNDP) (2022), "The impact of the war in Ukraine on sustainable development in Africa", available at: www.undp.org/africa/publications/impact.

References

Agbebi, M. (2022). China's Digital Silk Road and Africa's Technological Future. https://www.cfr.org/sites/default/files/pdf/Chinas%20Digital%20Silk%20Road%20and%20Africas%20Technological%20Future_FINAL.pdf
Alden, C. (2017). New Actors, New Models, New Outcomes? African countries' engagement with China and other development partners in achieving the SDGs and Agenda 2063.
Ali, S., Hussain, T., Zhang, G., Nurunnabi, M., & Li, B. (2018). The implementation of sustainable development goals in "BRICS" countries. *Sustainability*, *10*(7), 2513.
Atlantic Council. (February 28, 2023). What we learned from the Russia-China-South Africa military drills - Atlantic Council.
Babić, D. (2022). Russia's new role in Africa–Reach and limits of Russia's re-emergence. *The Review of International Affairs*, *73*(1184), 49–70.
Balytnikov, V., Barabanov, O., Yemelyanov, A., Poletaev, D., Sid, I., & Zaiser, N. (2019). Russia's Return to Africa: Strategy and Prospects. *Valdai Discussion Club Reports*.
Boutin, K. (2018) Feeding the Lion: China and defence development in African states, *Defense & Security Analysis*, *34*(3), 232–248.
Brazys, S., & Dukalskis, A. (2020). China's message machine. *J. Democracy*, *31*, 59.
Calabrese, L., & Tang, X. (2023). Economic transformation in Africa: What is the role of Chinese firms? *Journal of International Development*, *35*(1), 43–64.
Carrozza, I. (2021). Legitimizing China's Growing Engagement in African Security: Change within Continuity of Official Discourse. *The China Quarterly*, *248*(1), 1174–1199.
Cha, S., Ryoo, Y., & Kim, S.E. (2023). Losing hearts and minds? Unpacking the effects of Chinese soft power initiatives in Africa. *Asian Survey*, *63*(1), 1–30.
Chen, W., Dollar, D., & Tang, H. (2018). Why is China investing in Africa? Evidence from the firm level. *The World Bank Economic Review*, *32*(3), 610–632.

Clifford, C. (8 Jul 2021). The Bear is back: Russian re-engagement with Africa is picking up with Putin in the driving seat. Johannesburg: South African Institute of International Affairs, University of the Witwatersrand.

Daniel, R., & Virk, K. (2014). South Africa and the BRICS: Progress, problems and prospects. A. Adebajo & J. Cook, (Eds.). Centre for Conflict Resolution. http://www.jstor.org/stable/resrep05118

Diesen, G. (2023). *The Think Tank Racket: Managing the Information War with Russia*. Atlanta, GA: Clarity Press.

Droin, M., & Dolbaia, T. (15 August, 2023). Russia Is Still Progressing in Africa. What's the Limit. *Center for Strategic and International Studies*.

Eguegu, O. (2022). The Digital Silk Road: Connecting Africa with New Norms of Digital Development. *Asia Policy*, *29*(3), 30–39.

Fang, Y. (2021). Influence of foreign direct investment from China on achieving the 2030 Sustainable Development Goals in African countries. *Chinese Journal of Population, Resources and Environment*, *19*(3), 213–220.

Fijałkowski, Ł. (2014). China's 'soft power'in Africa? In *China's Rise in Africa* (pp. 95–104). Routledge.

Foa, R.S., Mollat, M., Isha, H., Romero-Vidal, X., Evans, D., & Klassen, A. J. (2022). A world divided: Russia, China and the West. https://www.bennettinstitute.cam.ac.uk/publications/a-world-divided/

Githaiga, N.M., Burimaso, A., Wang, B., & Ahmed, S.M. (2019). The belt and road initiative: Opportunities and risks for Africa's connectivity. *China Quarterly of International Strategic Studies*, *5*(01), 117–141.

Hodzi, O. (2020). African political elites and the making (s) of the China model in Africa. *Politics & Policy*, *48*(5), 887–907.

International Monetary Fund (n.d.). Direction of Trade Statistics dataset. Direction of Trade Statistics - DOTS Home - IMF Data

Ignatov, A., Mikhnevich, S., Popova, I., Safonkina, E., Sakharov, A., & Shelepov, A. (2019). leading Donors' Approaches to SDGs Implementation1. *International Organisations Research Journal (IORJ)*, *14*(1), 164–187.

Issaev, L.M., Shishkina, A.R., & Liokumovich, Y.B. (2023). Russian Policy of Securitization in Africa: Features of Perception. *Vestnik RUDN. International Relations*, *23*(2), 322–338.

Jinyuan, G. (1984). China and Africa: The Development of Relations over Many Centuries. *African Affairs*, *83*(331), 241–250. http://www.jstor.org/stable/721561

Johnston, L.A. (2019). The Belt and Road Initiative: what is in it for China?. *Asia & the Pacific Policy Studies*, *6*(1), 40–58.

Jurčák, V., & Marek, J. (2020). The Russian Geopolitical Interests In Africa1. *Politické Vedy*, (4), 196–212.

Kachur, D., (2020). Russia's Resurgence in Africa: Zimbabwe and Mozambique, South African Institute of International Affairs (SAIIA). https://policycommons.net/artifacts/1451418/russias-resurgence-in-africa/2083229/

Kaczmarski, M. (2024). The Russia–China entente: Implications for the transatlantic community. In *The Transatlantic Community and China in the Age of Disruption* (pp. 105–119). Routledge.

Kim, P. (2023). The Limits of the No-Limits Partnership China and Russia Can't Be Split, but hey Can Be thwarted. *Foreign Aff.*, *102*, 94.

Kroenig, M., & Starling, C.G. (2023). US Lessons from Russia's War on Ukraine. *Asia Policy*, *30*(2), 64–74.

Kuo, M. (2023). China-Russia Cooperation in Africa and the Middle East. The Diplomat, https://thediplomat.com/2023/04/china-russia-cooperation-in-africa-and-the-middle-east/#:~:text=Russia%20and%20China%20are%20pursuing%20different%20strategies%20toward,in%20Africa%20from%20the%20West%20to%20the%20East

Lam, K. (2019). The Chinese dream: China-Africa educational exchanges. *COOPEDU IV — Cooperação E Educação De Qualidade*, édité par Clara Carvalho et al., Centro de Estudos Internacionais, https://books.openedition.org/cei/798, 133–144.
Lei, Y., & Sui, S. (2023). China–Russia strategic partnership and the oil and gas collaboration. *Innovation: The European Journal of Social Science Research*, 1–20. https://doi.org/10.1080/13511610.2023.2289827
Lewis, D.J., Yang, X., Moise, D., & Roddy, S.J. (2021). Dynamic synergies between China's belt and road initiative and the UN's sustainable development goals. *Journal of International Business Policy*, *4*, 58–79.
Li, S. (2023). China's Confucius Institute and its European counterparts in Africa: A six-dimensional comparative study. *Research in Comparative and International Education*, *18*(3), 419–440.
Liu, Y. (2023). A comparative study on the involvement of China and Russia in Syria's crisis: from a realist-constructivist perspective. *International Journal of Russian Studies*, *12*(1), 45–60.
Lo, B. (2023). The Sino-Russian Partnership: Assumptions, Myths and Realities, IFRI: Institut Français des Relations Internationales. Russie. NEI Reports.
Locoman, E., & Papa, M. (2022). Transformation of alliances: Mapping Russia's close relationships in the era of multivectorism. Contemporary Security Policy, *43*(2), 274–307.
Makarychev, A., & Simão, L. (July 2014). Russia's Development Assistance with a Focus on Africa. *NOREF Policy Brief*. Oslo: Norwegian Peace Building Resource Centre (NOREF).
Marten, K. (2019). Russia's back in Africa: is the cold war returning? *The Washington Quarterly*, *42*(4), 155–170.
Martuscelli, A. (2020). The economics of China's engagement with Africa: What is the empirical evidence? *Development Policy Review*, *38*(3), 285–302.
Maseng, J.O., & Mothibinyane, P. (2023). An Analysis of Chinese and Russian Positions on South Africa's Inclusion as a Permanent Member of the UNSC. *Journal of African Foreign Affairs*, *10*(1), 89.
Mathew, J., & Moolakkattu, J.S. (2022). Russia in the Horn of Africa: Re-engagement in a new strategic environment. *South African Journal of International Affairs*, *29*(4), 535–548.
Matusevich, M. (2019). Russia in Africa. *Insight Turkey*, *21*(1), 25–40.
Mhlanga, D., Ndhlovu, E. (2023). The Implications of the Russia–Ukraine War on Sustainable Development Goals in Africa. *Fudan J. Hum. Soc. Sci. 16*, 435–454.
Monyae, D., Chapotera, K. (2023). China's Africa Debt Trap Question: Ethiopia and Kenya Infrastructure Case Studies. In: Ndzendze, B., Monyae, D. (eds) *Perspectives on Africa-China Infrastructural and Industrial Cooperation*. Africa-East Asia International Relations. Springer.
Mousavi Shafaee, S.M., & Golmohammadi, V. (2022). The Regional-Supremacy Trap: Disorder in the Middle East. *Middle East Policy*, *29*(1), 61–73.
Murphy, D.C. (2023). *Strategic Competition for Overseas Basing in Sub-Saharan Africa*. Brookings Institution.
Naidu, S., Corkin, L., & Herman, H. (2009). China's (re)-emerging relations with Africa: Forging a new consensus? *Politikon*, *36*(1), 87–115.
Neethling, T. (2020). Assessing Russia's New Interaction with Africa: Energy Diplomacy, Arms Exports and Mineral Resource Markets. *The Strategic Review for Southern Africa*, *42*(2), 15–42.
Nguyen, D.T., Le, T.H., Do, D.D., & Nguyen, H.N. (2023). Does geopolitical risk hinder sustainable development goals? Evidence from a panel analysis. *Journal of Environmental Management*, *347*, 119204. https://doi.org/10.1016/j.jenvman.2023.119204

Nkuna, V.M., & Shai, K.B. (2021). What drives Russia's involvement in Africa? [An Afrocentric review of Russia–South Africa relations, 2000–2018]. *Journal of Public Affairs*, *21*(2), e2176.

Nurullayev, D., & Papa, M. (2023). Bloc Politics at the UN: How Other States Behave When the United States and China–Russia Disagree. *Global Studies Quarterly*, 146–167.

Olivier, G., & Suchkov, D. (2015). Russia is back in Africa. *The Strategic Review for Southern Africa*, *37*(2).

Papageorgiou, M., & de Melo, D.D.S.N. (2022). China as a responsible power amid the COVID-19 crisis: Perceptions of partners and adversaries on twitter. *Fudan Journal of the Humanities and Social Sciences*, *15*(2), 159–188.

Papageorgiou, M., & dos Santos Cardoso, F. (2021). Chinese diplomacy, strategic partnerships and global economic supremacy. In *The New Chinese Dream: Industrial Transition in the Post-Pandemic Era* (pp. 51–68). Springer International Publishing.

Papageorgiou, M.M., & Vieira, A. (2022). Mapping the literature on China and Russia in IR and area studies: A bibliometric analysis (1990–2019). *Journal of Chinese Political Science*, *27*, 155–181. https://doi.org/10.1007/s11366-021-09768-x

Papageorgiou, M.M. (2023). China's Growing Presence in the Middle East's Arms Race and Security Dynamics. In *The Arms Race in the Middle East: Contemporary Security Dynamics* (pp. 257–272). Cham: Springer International Publishing.

Peter, M., & Plichta, M. (2023). China and Russia in Sudan: Surveying Data on Economic and Military Engagement. 1–35.

Pham, J. P. (2010). Back to Africa: Russia's New African Engagement. In *Africa and the New World Era: From Humanitarianism to a Strategic View* (pp. 71–83). New York: Palgrave Macmillan.

Pokalova, E. (2023). The Wagner group in Africa: Russia's quasi-state agent of influence. *Studies in Conflict & Terrorism*, 1–23. https://doi.org/10.1080/1057610X.2023.2231642

Popovic, M., Jenne, E.K., & Medzihorsky, J. (2020). Charm offensive or offensive charm? An analysis of Russian and Chinese cultural institutes abroad. *Europe-Asia Studies*, *72*(9), 1445–1467.

Power, M., Mohan, G., & Tan-Mullins, M. (2012). *China's resource diplomacy in Africa: Powering development?* Springer.

Ramani, S. (2021). Russia and China in Africa: Prospective partners or asymmetric rivals. *Johannesburg: South African Institute of International Affairs, University of the Witwatersrand, SAIIA Policy Insights*, (120). https://saiia.org.za/wp-content/uploads/2021/12/Policy-Insights-120-ramani.pdf

Repnikova, M. (2023). Russia's war in Ukraine and the fractures in western soft power. Place Branding and Public Diplomacy, *19*(2), 190–194.

Røren, P., & Beaumont, P. (2019). Grading greatness: evaluating the status performance of the BRICS. *Third World Quarterly*, *40*(3), 429–450.

Šćepanović, J. (2024). Still a great power? Russia's status dilemmas post-Ukraine war. *Journal of Contemporary European Studies*, *32*(1), 80–95.

Sharma, A. (2023). China's Soft Power in the Middle East. In: Kim, YC. (eds) *China's Engagement with the Islamic Nations*. Understanding China. Springer.

Shinn, D, & Brown, K. (2012). *China and Africa: A Century of Engagement*. Chatham House. https://www.chathamhouse.org/sites/default/files/public/Research/Africa/290612summary.pdf

Siddi, M., & Kaczmarski, M. (2019). Russia and China in the Middle East: Playing their best cards. FIIA Briefing Papers 175.

Siegle, J. (2021). *Russia's strategic goals in Africa*. African Center for Strategic Studies.

Stockholm International Peace Research Institute (SIPRI) (n.d.). Arms Transfers Database. SIPRI Arms Transfers Database | SIPRI

Stronski, P., 2021. *Russia's Response to Its Spiraling COVID-19 Crisis Is Too Little*, Too Late, CEIP: Carnegie Endowment for International Peace.
Strüver, G. (2016). What friends are made of: Bilateral linkages and domestic drivers of foreign policy alignment with China. *Foreign Policy Analysis*, *12*(2), 170–191.
Svoboda, K. (2024). Russia's Loans as a Means of Geoeconomic Competition in Africa and Latin America. *Problems of Post-Communism*, *71*(2), 156–166.
Sultan, H. E. M., & Degang, S. U. N. (2020). China's Participation in the Conflict Resolution in Sudan and South Sudan: A Case of "Creative Mediation". *Belt & Road Initiative Quarterly*, *1*(2), 6–23.
Tass (2023). Russia wrote off $20 bln of African nations' debts, Putin says - Business & Economy - TASS.
Tawiah, V.K., Zakari, A., & Khan, I. (2021). The environmental footprint of China-Africa engagement: an analysis of the effect of China–Africa partnership on carbon emissions. *Science of the Total Environment*, *756*, 143603.
Titeca, K. (2023). Russian influence, anti-Western sentiments and African agency: The struggle for influence in the Democratic Republic of Congo. *Strategic Review for Southern Africa*, *45*(1), 49–68.
Tull, D.M. (2006). China's engagement in Africa: scope, significance and consequences. *The Journal of Modern African Studies*, *44*(3), 459–479.
Wang, Y.P., Fan, X.D., Jin, N., (2017). History, current situation and trend of China's overseas health facilities aid. *Chinese Journal of Health Policy*, *10*, 60–67.
Wuttke, J. (2017). The dark side of China's economic rise. *Global Policy*, *8*, 62–70.
Yu, S.Z. (2022, November 4). What is China's investment end game in Africa? | Africa at LSE.
Zaytsev, Y.K. (2021). Russia's Approach to Official Development Assistance and Its Contribution to the SDGs. In: Chaturvedi, S., et al. *The Palgrave Handbook of Development Cooperation for Achieving the 2030 Agenda*. Palgrave Macmillan.
Zhang Q, Wang Z, Okafor G. (2022). Understanding China's Economic Engagement in Africa: An Exploration of the FDI-Trade Nexus. *Sustainability*. *14*(23), 15632.
Zhang, J., Wei, W.X., & Liu, Z. (2013). Strategic entry and determinants of Chinese private enterprises into Africa. *Journal of African Business*, *14*(2), 96–105.

9 Charting Nigeria's Economic Curse and the Sustainability Agenda through Education

Olubunmi Oludipe, Lucía Morales and Jon-Hans Coetzer

Introduction

Economic Development has been described as the series of changes that lead to the improvement of the welfare of the citizens (Onuchuku & Felix, 2023; Obidike et al., 2022; Onyekwere, 2016). It focuses on the qualitative and quantitative growth of the country's economy. It addresses matters that relate to education, wealth, health, employment, environmental conservation, and quality living conditions of the population (Onuchuku & Felix, 2023; Obidike et al., 2022; Belshaw & Livingstone, 2002) and invariably the economic, social and technical progress of nations (Onuchuku & Felix, 2023, Haller 2012; Adelman, 2000).

For economic development to occur, there must be economic growth (Haller, 2012; Dragoi, 2020, Malizia 1990), as economic development implies that there is qualitative and quantitative growth in all aspects (Dragoi, 2020). Economic growth is understood as the increase in a country's output per capital overtime, which is the process of increasing the size of a nation's economy and is measured by the increase of the nation's Gross Domestic Product (GDP) as discussed by Obidike et al. (2022), David, Noah & Agbalajobi (2016), and Haller (2012). It is a continuous expansion of different production possibilities, and it is measured by the increase in GDP over a certain period (Parkin, 2011; Susilo, Hayati & Pujiati, 2023). In differentiating between Economic Growth and Economic Development, Flammang (1979) and Malizia (1990) noted that growth is seen as an increase while development is often associated with change. The authors suggested that economic growth should be seen as a process of increase overtime while economic development should be noted as a process of structural change because economic development usually leads to structural change (David, Noah & Agbalajobi, 2016; Adelman, 2000; Haller, 2012; Malizia, 1990). Furthermore, growth contributes to expanding the economy while development leads to a better distribution of income and wealth, as discussed by Malizia and Fesser (2000) and David, Noah and Agbalajobi (2016).

In creating quality economic growth, education has been found to be the basic capital, and it is considered to have an important role to play in the process of improving human well-being and in determining human quality (Arifin,

DOI: 10.4324/9781032655857-12

2019; Arman, Purwandaya, Saefuddin, 2020). The development of human resources emerges as the topmost basis for the wealth of nations (Harbison, 1973), and the development of human resources is identified as a necessary condition for development and the only way that leads nations to economic progress and prosperity (Todaro & Smith, 2012). A critical aspect to be considered is that economic development without essential investment in education and training becomes an illusion, and it can be identified as the source of significant problems as countries engage with sustainable development programmes and policies that might not be efficient (Emediegwu & Monye-Emina, 2016). The educational dimension becomes quite evident in countries rich in natural resources, as they require knowledge and skills that help the country manage the wealth associated with natural resources.

The availability and access to natural resources characterise several countries at the global level, with a need for policy frameworks that help to promote nations' wealth management and distribution efficiently (Saidu, Aliyu & Zubair, 2016). The African continent has abundant natural resources and oil reserves (Global Citizen, 2012). However, the exploitation of these natural resources, such as fossil deposits, minerals and agriculture, results in the generation of foreign exchanges and revenues, creates employment opportunities and provides raw materials that can be used in the production of goods and services (Saidu, Aliyu & Zubair, 2016). There has been an accelerated Gross Domestic Product (GDP) growth rate in several African economies. The development of the country's oil industry has played an important role; however, to some countries, oil discovery has enabled them to unlock growth and secure development, while to some, oil has become a "*resource curse*" due to countries' inability to manage the wealth associated with the availability of natural resources (Global Citizen, 2012). Prof. Richard Auty first coined the term "*resource course*" in 1994 to explain the ineffectiveness of nations to their windfall wealth in improving the lot of the population and boosting the economy of such nations (Mohammed, 2021). The major proponents of the Resource Curse Theory are Harford and Klein (2005), Sachs and Warner (2001), and Auty (1993), and their assumption of this theory is that developing countries will likely have negative economic growth and development from the substantial proportion of the revenue from their nation's natural resources (Jack et al. 2016). In Africa, five countries, Nigeria, Libya, Algeria, Egypt, and Angola, dominate the upstream oil production, accounting for 85 percent of the continent's oil reserves (Adeola et al., 2021). Despite the natural resources of developing countries like Gambia, Angola, Ghana, and Nigeria, these countries are still under-developed, as compared to other African countries like Botswana and Kuwait that managed their resources efficiently and used their wealth to support the development of their countries (The World Bank, 1989; Mohammed, 2021). This chapter aims to examine the significance of education in supporting the development of professionals and the business sector while considering the importance of sustainability in Nigeria's geoeconomic and geopolitical context. The chapter considers the opportunities and challenges associated with e-learning in Nigeria by building on the research findings of studies by Yusuf (2006); Ajadi et al. (2008), Nneka (2010); Bugi (2012); Ifijeh et al. (2015); and Olugbeko and Izu's (2013) that point to major challenges faced by the nation and that are still prevalent in the country at present.

The Nigerian Economy in Context

Nigeria is the most populous African nation (Onuoha, 2009, Fasanya, Onakoya & Adabanija, 2013; Akinyetun 2016; Paul, 2014), and is usually referred to as the Giant of Africa due to its large population and economy (NPC,2021). The nation will likely soon be the third most populous country in the world as per 2050 forecasts (Peterson, 2012; Rice, 2011) (UNFPA, 2023), and the most prominent black nation market (Fasanya, Onakoya & Adabanija, 2013). According to the Worldometer's elaboration of the 2024 Revision of the United Nations World Population Prospects, Nigeria's population is 234,796,129 as at December 9, 2024 (WPP, 2024), although the Nigerian Population Commission (NPC) as of August 2013 admitted that it does not have accurate data on the population of Nigeria (IOM, 2024). The last National Population and Housing Census conducted in 2006 revealed that Nigeria has a population of 140,431,790 persons, and there was a projection that it will grow at 3.2 percent per annum (NPC, 2021). In the absence of a census, the veritable sources of population data have been sample surveys like the Nigeria Demographic and Health Surveys (NDHS), the National Sentinel Surveys (NSS), and the Multiple Indicator Cluster Surveys (MICS) to mention a few. The National Population Commission (NPC) released a population projection for the years 2006–2022 (NPC, 2022; NBS 2023) as illustrated in Figure 9.1.

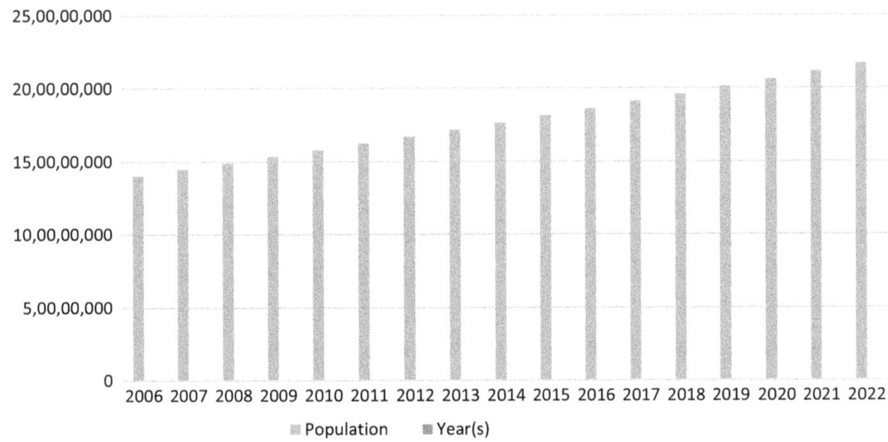

Figure 9.1 Nigeria's Total Projected Population (2006–2022).

Source: National Bureau of Statistics (NBS), 2023; National Population Commission, 2022.

If the annual growth rate persists, Nigeria's population is projected to reach 400 million by the year 2050 (UNFPA, 2023; Federal Ministry of Finance & Budget & Planning, 2023). Nigeria is endowed with natural resources like gold, coal, oil, gas, (Akinyetun 2016), coal, lime-stones, bitumen, gold crude oil, iron-ore, tin and ignite, to mention but a few that makes the country very attractive in the context of growing competition to secure natural resources (Sani, Nasir & Bakare, 2019). In terms of geographical land mass, Nigeria is blessed with 923,773 km (Fasanya, Onakoya & Adabanija, 2013; Paul, 2014). Before the discovery of oil in Nigeria in 1956, Nigeria was an agrarian society (Fasanya, Onakoya & Adabanija, 2013, Sani, Nasir & Bakare, 2019). From the creation of Nigeria in 1914 to mark the end of the era of colonialism, Nigeria's chief source of revenue was agriculture. The country was well known for its products, mainly cocoa from the West, Groundnut and cotton from the North, and Palm Oil from the East (Bello & Nwaeke, 2023). Nigeria exploited its agricultural potential before 1975 to earn an international leader position in the production and exportation of agricultural products, like groundnut, cocoa, palm produce, rubber, cotton, timber, and hide and skin (Fasanya, Onakoya & Adabanija, 2013). Nigeria became the largest exporter of groundnut, the second largest exporter of cocoa and palm produce, and a significant exporter of rubber, cotton, hides, and skin in the 1960s (Fasanya, Onakoya & Adabanija, 2013). Prior to the 1970s, the agricultural sector made up 50 percent of the Gross Domestic Product (GDP), the food grains for the country's growing population were supplied by it, and the raw materials to both agro-allied and non-agro allied, including several advantages that made it the Nigerian economy's main stay (CBN, 2000, Fasanya, Onakoya & Adabanija, 2013). Oil revenue in the early 1960s was less than 10 percent of Nigeria's oil revenue base (Bello & Nwaeke, 2023). The Nigerian economy grew at a steady rate when it operated as an agrarian-based economy, a trend that continued into the 1960s, and with the agricultural sector playing a vibrant role in the economy, which added value to the GDP and foreign exchange earnings (Ogundipe & Oluwatobi, 2011, Sani, Nasir & Bakare, 2019). The country enjoyed the benefits of a continuous sustainable economy for growth and development before discovering oil resources (Sani, Nasir & Bakare, 2019). The three main regions in Nigeria – the Western, Eastern and Northern regions produced agricultural products that have a comparative advantage, thus creating healthy rivalry among them, and this led to an economically vibrant economy with a high level of employment (Chidi, Mbah & Ogunyomi, 2018).

Discovery of Oil and its Effects on the Nigerian Economy

In 1956, oil was discovered in commercial quantity in a remote town in the present-day Bayelsa State called Oloibiri in Nigeria (Chidi, Mbah & Ogunyomi, 2018; Onuoha, 2009; Sani, Nasir & Bakare, 2019; Paul, 2014; Akinyetun 2016; Jack et al., 2016; Agbaeze & Ukoha, 2018; Adeola et al., 2021, Chukwuma, 2015, Ishioro, 2022; Saidu, Aliyu & Zubair, 2016. Oil exploration and exploitation originated in Nigeria in 1859 at Oloibiri, argued Tamuno & Felix (2006),

However, it was when Shell Darcy Petroleum Company, which later became Shell BP Petroleum Development Company of Nigeria Limited, commenced operations in 1956 that they drilled in commercial quantity, which led to a joint venture by two major oil companies Shell and British Petroleum, to form a 50/50 joint venture refining company in Nigeria. There were subsequent crude oil discoveries at Afam in 1957, Ebubu and Bomu in 1958, which boosted the production of oil between 1958 and 1964 and transformed the Nigerian economy to a crude-petroleum-led and dominated economy from an agriculture-led economy (Ishioro, 2022). The discovery of oil paved the way for wealth in Nigeria. It increased the country's value in the area of Organisation of Petroleum Exporting Countries (OPEC) with a consistent increase in oil revenue (Agbaeze & Ukoha, 2018; Sani, Nasir & Bakare, 2019). Nigeria became a cynosure among a comity of nations because of the need and demand for and the wealth from oil (Akinyetun 2016). After this discovery, oil became an integral part of the economy (Abu & Chidi, 2012; Chidi, Mbah & Ogunyomi, 2018), and the economy became a mono-product as other sources of revenue were neglected over the years with reliance on the revenue of the crude oil that led to a conflict situation as a result of the deterioration of the country's economic system in terms of a healthy diversified economy followed by the erosion of its environment (Akinyetun 2016).

The government began to invest the generated wealth from the exploitation of oil resources in socio-economic infrastructure in the country (Sani, Nasir & Bakare, 2019), which made the urban centres attractive and able-bodied Nigerians began to migrate from the rural areas, which means an abandonment of farmlands to partake in the oil-driven urban economy, and invariably led to the agricultural sector been abandoned, a sector that had sustained the economy (Uzonwanne, 2015, Sani, Nasir & Bakare, 2019), thus making the Nigerian economy monolithic (Sani, Nasir & Bakare, 2019). Eighty percent of Nigeria's wealth comes from the oil industry, and with the huge earnings, only 1% of the population benefits from the proceeds (Amnesty International, 2009; Sani, Nasir & Bakare, 2019). The Nigerian economy and its evolution since the discovery of oil aligns with the principles of the Dutch Disease Theory that links to research studies that were carried out in the 1980s by Corden (1984), Corden and Neary (1982), Wijnbergen (1984), Edwards and Aoki (1983) and Harberger (1983), Corden and Neary (1982), whose core model comprises of the spending effect and the resource movement effect to describe the mechanism where what seems like an economic boom for a nation began to materialise in adverse consequences (Sani, Nasir & Bakare, 2019, Agbaeze & Ukoha, 2018). This refers to situations in which a country is endowed with abundant resources. However, its economy is under-developed, and the manufacturing sector is defined by its decline (Ross, 2004; Agbaeze & Ukoha, 2018; Sani, Nasir & Bakare, 2019). The discovery of oil in Nigeria can be seen as a blessing because of increased exports and the generation of revenue that has developed the nation, according to Sani, Nasir & Bakare (2019). This can, however, also be seen as a curse since it has led to the neglect of other sectors like agriculture and manufacturing, which could have positively impacted the economy by enabling diversification and benefiting from its prosperous agrarian sector, but instead the country was led to weaker economic development (Agbaeze & Ukoha, 2018).

On the other hand, Elwerfelli and Benhin (2018) argued that the discovery of oil in Nigeria has been a curse rather than a blessing because the vast oil revenue has not shown any positive impact on the economy nor for the people's benefit. Nigeria's oil boom brought a turnaround in revenue. It pushed Nigeria to the international limelight as a major oil production country in Africa and the world, but it also brought about the desecration of the environment and loss of occupation in the host communities, corrupt practices and search of white collar jobs leading to migration from rural to urban areas (Agbaeze & Ukoha, 2018). In the same opinion, oil revenue and booms have resulted in wasteful spending, corruption, and a resource curse, preventing the country from reaching its full potential (Ijere, 2015; Mohammed, 2021). Buttressing their opinion, Agbaeze & Ukoha (2018) found out that Nigerian citizens have not benefitted from the oil revenues as 70 percent of the population still live below the poverty line, despite Nigeria being the world's seventh largest exporter of crude oil (Adeola et al., 2021, Onuoha, 2009; Amnesty International, 2006, Donwa et al. 2015; Akinyetun, 2016; Paul, 2014). The foreign earnings brought into several African countries as a result of the exploration of crude oil, if properly harnessed and managed, were meant to improve the population's living conditions. However, the cost of managing these natural resources is high which is due to corruption, poor education, lack of infrastructure, overdependence on foreign experts, and managerial incompetence, which has hindered the economic growth and development of the country, highlighting the importance of developing a functional education system that provides the needed and required support to the country's development strategies (Kalu & Ott, 2019; Adeola et al., 2021). This has largely been attributed to the inability of the government to diversify the economy and channel the resources to the education sector and other sectors, which has been a critical menace to the development of the country's industrial sector (Okpanachi & Andrews, 2012). The significant of education to a country's development strategy cannot be over-emphasised as education has been found to also positively relate to employment rate increase, as the rate of employment increases with the increase in the level of education and the same vein, the rate of unemployment has been found out to negatively relate to the level of education (Ziberi et al., 2022; Mojsoska-Blazevski, 2009). High levels of unemployment are another issue prevalent in Nigeria and have become an unending problem that the administrations of successive governments have tried to solve to no avail (The Nigerian Economic Summit Group, 2022).

Nigeria's Unemployment Rate – Year 2011–2023

The multidimensional poverty rate recorded at 63 percent and unemployment levels at 33.3 percent in Nigeria is a major source of concern as the country confronts the reality of an economy that requires solutions (Afdb, 2023).

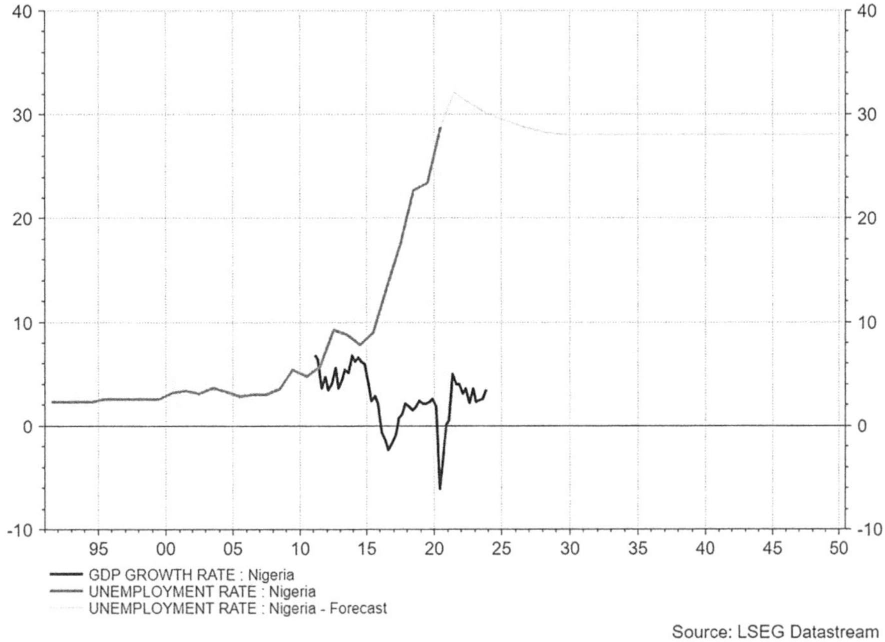

Figure 9.2 Nigeria Unemployment Rate (2011–2023).

Source: London Stock Exchange Group (LSEG) Datastream. Data retrieved on May 13, 2024.

Nigeria ranks second on the global unemployment list of countries (The Nigerian Economic Summit Group, 2022; Olurounbi, 2021). The issue of unemployment in Nigeria has slowed down the development of the nation and led to unrest, brain drain, lower standard of living, and distrust between the populace and the government (The Nigerian Economic Group Summit, 2022). In this regard, we argue that the government should consider the importance of outlining a plan of action that is supported by a strong foundation that creates wealth by investing in education (Berger and Fisher, 2013).

According to Todaro and Smith (2009) and Edet & Beyin (2018), for poor countries to become rich, they would need to invest in education, as education plays an essential role in a developing country to engage with modern technology and develop the ability for self-sustaining growth and development. Education has been found to be the catalyst that can accelerate economic development rates (Onuchuku & Felix, 2023) and unlock the potential of a country towards national transformation and sustainable national development (Ilechukwu et al., 2014).

In the year 2013, Olugbeko and Izu studied the "*Reality and Challenges of e-Learning Education in Africa: The Nigeria Experience*." The research findings revealed the importance of education, particularly e-learning, to support Africa's economic development. The importance of education, flexibility, and various alternatives to the continent is critical due to its population explosion and the need to facilitate as many people as possible. In some parts of the world, e-learning is not new in promoting education (Egolum, 2021). In Nigeria, the global challenge to ensure that education was available and affordable to everyone who would like to take advantage of education led to the emergence of e-learning in parallel to general dissatisfaction resulting from a "*traditional*" educational sector that is identified as being dysfunctional (Olugbeko & Izu, 2013). Some of the advantages of on-line learning include the freedom to choose the needed teaching materials, accessibility from anywhere and anytime, the universality of the programme, low cost and the opportunity to follow the latest developments (Hamid et al., 2020). The challenges of e-learning in Nigeria, however, are geographical location because living in an area where there is no basic infrastructure will make e-learning impossible or very complex (Olugbeko & Izu, 2013). Some other challenges as investigated by them were lack of required skills, lack of access to Information and Telecommunications, the problem of generalisation where the e-learning designer assumed that all students had access to the latest accessories related to the computer, cost of purchasing the computer and the high cost of subscribing to the internet that is above the reach of the average Nigerian. Disastra and Wahyuningtyas (2019) studied the significant factors that added to the satisfaction and interest in and the use of e-learning systems as part of corporate training and development programmes. They affirmed that organisations that have adopted e-learning have increased, however, some failures in the continued use of the system and neglect of the system have been noticed. They found out that there was no known reason why professionals suddenly stopped using the e-learning platform, and there were also no known ways that professionals could be encouraged to use the e-learning programmes voluntarily. To examine how users' satisfaction can be increased and the future intention to adopt e-learning systems, factors such as perceived usefulness and perceived ease of use on user satisfaction and the effect of user satisfaction on the intention to adopt e-learning were examined. The prospects and challenges of e-learning and the availability of the equipment were studied by Olugbenga and Qiu (2020). The authors' findings indicated that equipment is used to enhance its operation in ten northern parts of Nigeria. It was revealed that challenges like instability and shortage of power supply, low internet coverage/bandwidth, inadequate computer laboratories, and the issue of trust are some of the challenges of e-learning in Nigeria and that if these can be improved upon, there will be a greater acceptance of e-learning by the Nigerian secondary students.

Abdulmajeed et al. (2020) studied the challenges to embrace e-learning in Nigeria categorising their findings into IT Infrastructure, Socioeconomic, and Sociocultural. They stated that due to these challenges, the advantages of online learning and the opportunity it creates to scale education are not always realised. The survey was to rank these challenges by how severe they are and to propose solutions to the challenges. The survey samples were university undergraduates, and half of the respondents participated in e-learning programmes. The main challenges are identified in Table 9.1.

Table 9.1 Challenges of E-learning

Challenges	*Factors*
IT Infrastructure	• Accessibility/Availability of Internet Service • Affordability • Power Supply • Quality of IT Device/Service • Nature of IT Device/Service
	Individual Level: IT know-how, access to appropriate digital devices and technical support **National Level**: government policies, internet coverage or Nigeria's communication infrastructure
Socioeconomic	Social and economic interactions impact purchasing power to obtain supporting materials and resources. This includes: • cost of living • the ability to pay for on-line courses. • monthly income and expenditure • family status • geopolitical zone, and • academic competence
Sociocultural	• Cultural beliefs • Race • Gender • Language and Communication • Religion and • The use of technology

Source: Data taken from Abdulmajeed, K. & Joyner, D. & McManus, C. (2020). https://doi.org/10.1145/3386527.3405953.

Costs and structural factors are constraints to internet infrastructure in African, as found out by Oyelaran-Oyeyinka and Adeya (2004); and thin bandwidth and electricity supply problems are constraints to digital services and on-line learning in Nigeria (Ofuyatan, Opaluwa, & Adeola, 2014)). High employment rates (Innocent, 2014) and low-income wages (Aderemi & Fidelis, 2017) affect lifestyles adversely, strain living costs, and limit the purchase of internet subscriptions. Socio-Cultural issues can often be a challenge in Nigeria as some cultures still do not believe in training the girl child. This gender discrimination was found by Cooray and Potrafke (2011) as emanating from religious and cultural influences. This leads to early marriage, religious misunderstanding, and male domination. The issue of Boko-Haram, a sect that ravaged the northern part of Nigeria from Year 2009 is notorious for killings because they frown at Western education and civilisation (Onuoha, 2012; Peters, 2014). Furthermore, Abdulmajeed et al. (2020) argued that the socio-economic challenge is ranked as the most severe challenge, followed by the IT infrastructural challenge, and the socio-cultural factors are ranked last. They believe these challenges can be overcome and suggested that the government can solve them.

The Nexus between Education and Economic Growth

The significance of education to support economic development and progress has been subject to study to help gain a better understanding of countries' economic development and the impact of education. Oba-Adenuga and Adeleke (2019) and Adegbesan (2011) have described education as the bedrock of development in the world's nations. Education affects economic growth through different channels depending on the country's level of development (Ziberi et al., 2022). Economic Growth is the increase in a country's output per capita over time, which is the process of increasing the size of a nation's economy and is measured by the increase of the nation's Gross Domestic Product (GDP) (Obidike et al., 2022; David, Noah & Agbalajobi, 2016; Haller, 2012).

In describing Education, Topcu (2023) and Odit et al. (2010) referred to it as an investment in human capital because an educated individual enjoys the benefits of a lifetime of activities, and it is a causal factor of economic well-being that leads to human capital increase in a country's employment, being essential for an economy to flourish (Temple, 2000; Khan, Sarwar & Niazi 2023). Education is a fundamental tool for sustainable economic development, and without investing in human capital, any nation cannot achieve economic development, as Abanyam, David & Ibrahim (2020) argued. Investing in education has several benefits to the state and society (Ziberi et al., 2022). When a country invests in education, it means investing in human resources or creating a skilled workforce that can influence innovations, accumulation of tax by the increment of the state budget, increase productivity and wages, and improvement in living standards, which will eventually lead to having a positive impact on the economic growth of the country by the country's economy growing and developing (Ziberi et al., 2022). A country develops faster when, among other things, at the level of consciousness, the degree of education and civilisation rises to record a leap forward (Haller, 2012). An increase in education leads to a positive effect on GDP growth (Ziberi et al., 2022). There is no country that is able to achieve sustainable economic development when there is no substantial investment in human capital (Ozturk, 2008). This impact is more visible in underdeveloped nations (Khan, Sarwar & Niazi, 2023) like Nigeria. According to Osunyikanmi (2018) and Ogunode (2020), the educational sector is the key to the social, political and economic development of any country, which was corroborated by Omojimite (2011) that human capital development through education is a major contributor to economic development as it imparts the general attitudes, specific skills and the improvement of living standards. Moreover, education affects a country's productivity by increasing the collective ability of the labour force to enable it to complete any existing tasks at faster and more efficient performance rates. Knowledge transfer about new information, products and technologies created by others is facilitated, leading to the knowledge exchange process that contributes to enhancing economic growth and development (Barro & Lee, 2010, Ziberi et al., 2022). A country's capacity for the creation of new knowledge, products and technologies is enhanced (Grant, 2017; Ziberi et al., 2022), and this is important because it leads to the growing of the country's economy and invariable a positive effect on the GDP growth (Ziberi et al., 2022, Marquez-Ramos and Mourelle 2019). The case of the United Arab Emirates can be used as an example. Part of the country's success story is the government's continuous commitment to economic diversification and its decision to prioritise education, innovation, and the creation of a knowledge economy. The government distributed large oil revenues in terms of infrastructure, health, education, and high salaries, which raised the living standards of the country's citizens (Elwerfelli & Benhin, 2018). The Dubai government considered that investing in education and innovation would play a significant role in increasing productivity and competitiveness, and therefore, they identified the development of the knowledge economy as a priority which was intended to become the "*backbone*" of the economy (Elwerfelli & Benhin, 2018).

Education develops people's skills and capabilities and makes them more productive and environmentally conscious (Onuchuku & Felix, 2023). Investing in human capital development also assists in closing any developmental gap between developing and developed countries (Barro, 1991; Omojimite, 2010). The quality of a country's manpower depends on the quality of its educational systems, and according to Onuchuku and Felix (2023) and Adetula et al. (2017), there cannot be any progress in a country without quality education. E-learning, however, according to Garrison (2017), is a disruptive technology that is beginning to transform how learning should be approached in an educational context, especially due to the outbreak of coronavirus disease (COVID-19), which led to a global shutdown of most countries and causing several sectors of the economy to begin to work on-line (Oba-Adenuga, 2019). It can be said that the COVID-19 pandemic revolutionised digital and on-line education in several nations, including Nigeria. For the first time in Nigeria, educationalists and teachers have started to embrace on-line education. Online learning has several benefits for students, society and the nation. However, several factors contribute to its limitation in Nigeria, that is, unstable electricity, poor internet connectivity, insufficient computers and accessories, shortage of ICT personnel in schools, teachers' unpreparedness and poor attitudes (Oba-Adenuga, 2019). These factors limit effective on-line learning in Nigeria and developing economies, invariably contributing to low economic growth in such economies. Although, education is recognised globally as an important venture that every nation requires for economic transformation (Adetula et al., 2017), and with the tremendous change taking place in developed economies through higher education quality with technology and innovations, some developing countries like Nigeria have not been able to adapt to this level of change, and this has led to them struggling to increase their GDP and been unable to provide for several sectors of their societies (Abanyam, David & Ibrahim, 2020).

A well-educated labour force has a positive and vital impact on the economic growth of a country and its communities and business sector (Babatunde & Adefabi, 2005; Loening, 2005; Omojimite, 2010). This is because education develops individuals' personality and creativity, enabling them to assist in promoting a healthy society (Sapru, 2021). It also is a process that develops the total man/woman and develops their cognitive, affective and psychomotor domains so that they can effectively function in society to take mastery of the physical, social, economic and political environment to improve their general well-being (Onuchuku & Felix, 2023). The benefit of education is that when organisations have employees that are educated, which is when organisations have more skilled manpower, the companies are able to take advantage of new economic opportunities, which would invariably lead to improved performance and the improved performance (economic development) is more likely to lead to greater wealth that increases educational opportunities and the availability of resources (Lu, 2018; Earle, 2010, Onuchuku & Felix, 2023).

Education to Support Economic Development

Education is a crucial factor for sustainable economic growth and an important pillar that affects society in various dimensions (Ziberi et al., 2022). On-line education, often referred to as e-learning, is where most or all of the content is delivered on-line (Allen & Seaman, 2011). It is an alternative to face-to-face classroom education and is studied within the context of distance learning. It was established that it is able to act as a complementary approach (Peimani & Kamalipour, 2021) and serves as an alternate/complement to face-to-face education (Al-Karaki et al., 2021). It as a form of distance education that is based on technology training and encompasses computer-assisted and web-based training (Hentea et al. (2003), in the same vein, e-learning was described as learning that moves network technologies and computers to the task of education (Horton, 2011). Several authors describe on-line learning as learning which is the transfer of knowledge and skills through some technological/electronic device in a well-designed course content in contrast to traditional face-to-face learning (Benson, 2002; Conrad, 2002; Carliner, 1999; Fayomi, Adepoju & Ayo, 2015; Choudhury & Pattnaik, 2020).

On-line education is an educational process where teachers and learners are separated by distance (Simonova, Faltynkova & Kostolanyova, 2023). The method embraced by e-learning is to deliver learning using computers, which is a learner-centred, well-designed, and interactive learning environment to utilise the internet and digital technologies with instructional design principles (Hedge and Hayward, 2004; Peslak et al., 2020). E-learning and the face-to-face type of education both have the same goal but are delivered by different methods. Explaining the goals of e-learning, Clark and Mayer (2016) affirmed that the "*why*" of e-learning is to assist organisations in building the skills they require to improve job performance and assist employees in achieving their educational goals. The demand for higher education is growing rapidly and has led to an increase in student enrolment, a decrease in funding, and a reduction in the brain drain of people who travel abroad to study (Wright, Dhanarajan & Reju,

2009). The provision of school-based education and the preparation of students to be able to get involved in a global information society at an economic rate has also led to an increase in the demand for e-learning (Nwagwu, 2020). On the other hand, Kpolovie et al. (2014) affirmed that the advantage of open and flexible learning that e-learning provides, which encourages older students and working individuals to have access to education, also contributed to the increase in the demand for e-learning. Other factors like convenience (Poole, 2000) of completing a degree with a busy schedule, that is, for non-traditional students who work on a full-time basis and who have family responsibilities and flexibility (as argued by Chizmar & Walbert, 1999) of accommodating different individual's lifestyle are also factors that contributed to the increase in demand of e-learning.

In the context of the global economy and the need to support collaboration, cooperation, participation, knowledge exchange, inclusion and diversity, among many other skills, e-learning provides an inclusive instructional platform that caters to anyone who desires a good education and can have a global context due to its flexibility. There then became a paradigm shift to learner-centred from learning to teacher-centred due to the changes experienced in education (Kasse & Blunywa, 2013). There are constraining factors like distance, time, and occupation when attending face-to-face university education, but e-learning plays a significant role in narrowing the gap (Ikegulu & Oranusi, 2014). Students from different backgrounds, environments, and geographical settings access education without requiring the use of scarce and on-site space with e-learning, enabling developing countries to respond to the increased demands of education (Paygar, 2014). Despite the poor government support e-learning has continued to grow in almost all developing countries (Paygar, 2014). Adults whose parents could not send them to school due to harsh economic conditions in developing countries now have access to education to build their capacity while earning their income, contributing to the development of communities and providing the foundations to access quality education. Nwagwu (2020) corroborates this by stating that with the promise of empowering the marginalised sectors of society to enable them to become lifelong learners and acquire the capacity that they require to function in this knowledge and information age, e-learning has become the wave of the future at the start of the twenty-first century. Capacity building is the process of developing the competencies and the capabilities of individuals and different groups that are expected to lead to sustained and improved performance (AusAID, 2004). E-learning has provided opportunities for citizens to acquire certain and specific skills to build the individual's capacity, as stated by Bolger (2000). E-learning is of great significance in the professional development of adults in the workplace, and it is being recognised more and more as a vital means of meeting the challenges of growing education (Daniel, 2009). Organisations now leverage e-learning to train their employees either for professional development programs or degree programs (Caruth & Caruth, 2013).

Organisations can also leverage the opportunity that e-learning provides to enhance the skills of their employees (Zaheer, Jabeen & Qadri, 2015), thereby developing their capacity and, invariably, the organisation's capability, indicating the need to assess educational needs and how they can be supported in the context of changing global economic dynamics.

Challenges of e-Learning and Impact on the Business Sector

Developed countries consider the challenges of e-learning to be issues like communication delays and technical difficulties; however, some challenges apply to all nations, irrespective of whether they are developed or developing (Song et al., 2004). These challenges that apply to every country are presented in Table 9.2.

Table 9.2 E-learning Challenges Related to Developed and Developing Nations

Challenges	*Researched Sources*
Computer anxiety/ Technophobia	Compeau & Higgins (1995); Ali et al. (2018); Picolli et al. (2001); Graham & Jones (2011); Wang (2014); Yoo & Huang (2016); Choudhury & Pattnaik (2020)
Bandwidth issues	De Rouin et al. (2005); Tai (2005); Choudhury & Pattnaik (2020)
Technology & Technical disruptions	Ali et al. (2018); Kaushik (2012); DeSanctis et al. (2003); Choudhury & Pattnaik (2020)
Lack of learner familiarity	Alavi & Leidner (2001); Tai (2005); Choudhury & Pattnaik (2020)
Improper structuring	Bondarouk & Ruel (2010); Blount (2016); Kimiloglu & Ozturan (2017); Ali et al. (2018); Choudhury & Pattnaik (2020)
Learner low self-efficacy	Kim et al. (2011); Choudhury & Pattnaik (2020)
Lack of Management support	Welsh et al. (2003); Choudhury & Pattnaik (2020)
Inequality in access to technology and internet	Graham & Jones (2011); Ali et al. (2018); Choudhury & Pattnaik (2020)
Lack of sense of community	Rabe-Hemp et al. (2009)
Delay in communication	Song et al. (2004)

Source: Reviewed Literature.

Furthermore, developing countries are faced with infrastructural problems that hinder or reduce access to e-learning facilities, as discovered by Nneka (2010) and Ahlan et al. (2014). They further discovered that other parts of the world suffer less than African nations from lacking these infrastructures. These challenges are either those that can be influenced by the students or those that cannot but need the government's intervention before any change can be made. In the context of Nigeria, some of the significant challenges associated with e-learning in developing countries are presented in Table 9.3.

Table 9.3 E-learning Challenges that are prevalent in Developing countries, using Nigeria as a Case Study

Challenges	*Researched Sources*
Leadership challenge	Nwabufo et al. (2013), Somayeh et al. (2016); Olupona (2001)
Poor policy implementation	Yusuf (2006); Olutola & Olatoye (2015)
Low educational budget	Olutola & Olatoye (2015); Bugi (2012)
Lack of good infrastructure i.e. unstable power supply	Ajadi (2008); Nneka (2010); Ahlan et al. (2014); Ikegulu & Oranusi (2014) and Bugi (2012)
High cost of internet bandwidth and equipment that hampers internet accessibility	Ikegulu & Oranusi (2014); and Ajadi et al. (2008)

Source: Reviewed Literature.

Many developed nations have applied electronic technology in the delivery of learning, but tertiary institutions in Nigeria are still behind in adapting these technologies due to inadequate educational frameworks, financial policies, and deficiency in the area of engineering and technological development (Salawudeen, 2010; Ayodele, 2010; Egolum, 2021). Despite these challenges, learners' demand for on-line education continues to increase. According to Peters (2002), there will be a considerable worldwide increase in the number of people seeking higher education via on-line learning. This claim was made because the overcrowded lecture theatres and seminar halls affected the country's educational institutions. Unfortunately, the research findings remain unchanged for more than two decades. With a growing number of students seeking to gain admission into Nigerian universities, the face-to-face mode of delivering lectures can no longer address this growing demand. Most countries, including Nigeria, lack the resources to build universities to accommodate these students. As such, education is identified as one of the most significant investments towards the growth and development of a nation (Denison, 1966; Bowman, 1980; Barro, 2013; Emediegwu & Clement, 2016), and as the development of nations can actually be traceable to the level of its human capital, usually education and health (Umo, 2007; Dauda, 2010; Kakar, Khiljiand & Khan, 2011), several countries in the world have been investing in this critical sector. When a country invests in education, the population becomes a skilled workforce and could be geared to accelerating economic development or improving the quality of society (Yogish, 2006; Eregha, Irughe & Edafe, 2018). Education is a means of increasing output because it can improve productivity and health and can help to enable an escape route from poverty, social marginalisation and economic detachment. (Eregha, Irughe & Edafe, 2018). Through education, transformation occurs as the population is equipped with the requisite knowledge, competencies, skills, and techniques that make them more functional and productive and contribute to the advancement of society (Emediegwu & Clement, 2016).

Researchers have recommended that the government should intervene in infrastructural development and e-learning. The reviewed literature underlines that some nations have been able to transition from underdeveloped societies to modern industrial states through education and training and that if Nigeria seeks to transform its economy to meet the challenges of global demand (Abdulmajeed et al., 2020; Disastra & Wahyuningtyas, 2019; Ogeh & Chiemeka, 2015), the country needs to reconsider investment in human resources to spur them for nation-building and enable her to assert her status among the nations of the world. The country's authorities and relevant stakeholders might consider assessing how education and training can support developmental goals if they aim to significantly seize the opportunity that e-learning provides so more people can access education and training programmes at national and international levels.

Critical Discussion and Policy Implications

A monolithic oil and gas economy has replaced Nigeria's agrarian economy, and the government relies on this for foreign exchange earnings, which is the country's GDP from the exportation of oil (Akinyetun, 2016). To some people, the discovery of oil in Nigeria is a blessing due to its gains, like increased exports and improved infrastructure and state creation. To some, it is a curse because of the problems that come with it, such as corruption, poverty, environmental pollution, mono-cultural economy (Paul, 2014). The reviewed literature points out that oil discovery in Nigeria came with positive and adverse elements (Agbaeze & Ukoha, 2018; Akinyetun, 2016; Paul, 2014). The country's reliance on oil resources has led to the retardation of the economy as regards neglect and under-development of other sectors, especially agriculture and manufacturing. In the past few years, the economy of Nigeria has fallen in and out of recession (Tijani, 2020), and the debt profile is on the rise consistently, with very high inflation rates at an average of 16 percent as of the first quarter of Year 2022 (NBS, 2023). To improve Nigeria's economic growth, Nigeria needs to reposition its monolithic economy to multiple revenue sources and keep economic empowerment and diversification at the front burner (Sani, Nasir & Bakare, 2019). There is a need to adopt a policy that will promote large-scale agricultural sector mechanisation and curtail the importation of food items (Ajayi, 2020). It is also vital that there should be prudency at all levels of government to reduce financial profligacy and the need to prune down the bloated government size to enable Nigeria to achieve sustainable economic development (Chidi, Mbah & Ogunyomi, 2018).

It is essential to develop the people's political rights and consciousness to enable them to elect good leaders with sound economic management skills and knowledge, as recommended by Ajayi (2020). To do this, education can play a critical role in enabling the development of competencies and skills that the country requires to move forward within growing levels of uncertainty, global

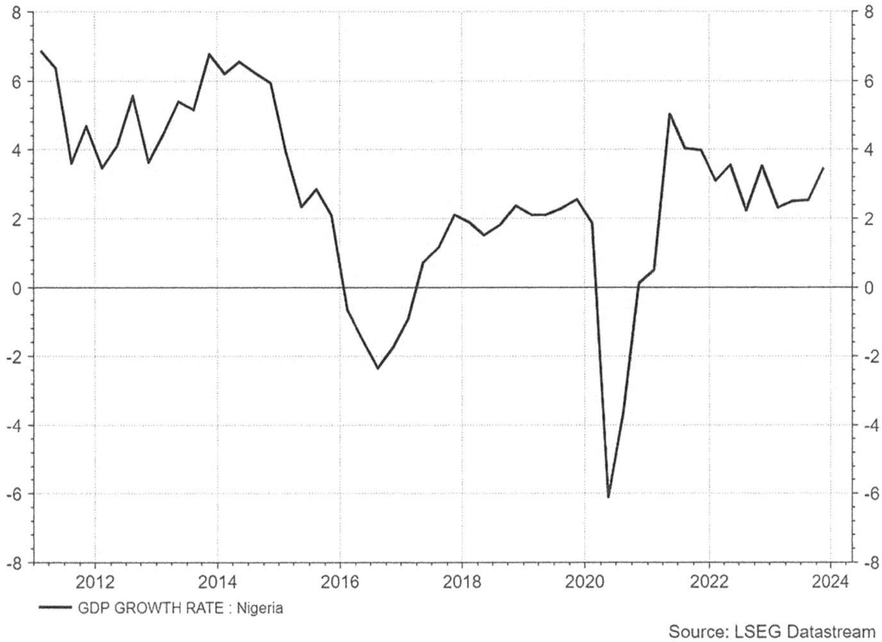

Figure 9.3 Nigeria's Gross Domestic Product (GDP) Rate (2012–2024).

Source: London Stock Exchange Group (LSEG) Datastream. Data retrieved on May 13, 2024.

economic and political systems and rising levels of competition and technological change. According to Onwioduokit (2020), education can facilitate and drive the emergence of a political structure that enables the development of leadership skills that help the country move forward.

Conclusion

Education emerges as a critical variable that could help increase participation in the economic growth process, reduce unemployment and make growth more inclusive; therefore, Nigeria should improve the quality of its education curriculum to increase participation in the growth process, increase benefit sharing and promote inclusive growth. Education is a key contributing factor that can encourage the growth of any economy (Glewwe et al., 2014; Benos and Zotou, 2014; Mariana, 2015; Megasan & Dauda, 2016). It is the most productive investment a country can make towards its economic development and a pathway that sustainable development could be secured and maintained (Onwioduokit, 2020). Education is highly rated for all countries' development plans as it is the most significant instrument for change (Boyi, 2013). The reviewed literature indicates that education is required for the development of a country, along with physical infrastructure (Onwioduokit, 2020). Having an education is essential, however, individuals participating actively in the productive sectors of the economy is much more critical, and this is how education can be transmitted to the economic system by enabling economic growth (Campbell, 2017). The importance of understanding economic growth and the need to examine how other concepts like inclusive growth (IG) can help to ensure the integration of all segments of society (including the poor) can benefit from growth, prosperity and development (Campbell 2017). IG is the sole means to rectify severely entrenched regional imbalances and inequities and consolidate economic gains, according to the World Bank (2006), while the United Nations Development Programme (UNDP) describes it as "*equity with growth or as broadly shared prosperity resulting from economic growth*" (UNDP, 2017). The Organisation for Economic Cooperation and Development (OECD) defines inclusive growth as "*economic growth that is distributed fairly across society and one that creates opportunities for all*" (OECD, 2024). This chapter concludes with a need for a critical reflection on the meaning of economic growth and how it can be articulated within our global economic system that demands sustainability. For growth to be sustainable, all the sectors of the economy have to be involved. Within the context of inclusive growth, will entail the achievement of sustainable growth to create and expand economic opportunities, to ensure broader access to the opportunities and to enable the members of the society to participate in and benefit from economic growth, and also the provision and facilitation of access to quality education and training that is relevant and better, among others (Campbell, 2017). With the aim of giving some initial steps towards improving and reconducting Nigeria's socio-economic and environmental systems, it is essential that the Nigerian Government adheres to the United Nations Educational, Scientific, and Cultural Organisation (UNESCO) statutory requirements "*of a minimum of 26% of developing country's total annual budget to be devoted to education*" (Egolum, 2021; Osunyikanmi, 2018; Adetula et al., 2017; Olupona, 2001). School enrolment has an important role in promoting inclusive growth in Nigeria, as tertiary enrolment impacts GDP per capita positively and significantly if the country seeks to reconduct its economic model (Megasan & Dauda, 2016).

References

Abanyam, N. L., David, F., & Ibrahim, Y. D. 'The Role of Higher Education in Sustainable Economic Development in Nigeria: A Functionalist Theoretical Perspective Analysis. *Sapientia Global Journal of Arts, Humanities and Development Studies (SGOJAHDS)*, Vol.3 No.2 pp. 276–284, 2020 https://www.sgojahds.com/index.php/SGOJAHDS/article/view/80#:~:text=The%20study%20concludes%20that%20higher,poverty%20and%20provides%20the%20skills

Abdulmajeed, K. & Joyner, D. & McManus, C. 'Challenges of On-line Learning in Nigeria' *Computer Science, Psychology, Proceedings of the Seventh ACM Conference on Learning @ Scale* pp. 417–420, 2020. https://doi.org/10.1145/3386527.3405953

Abu, I.N., & Chidi, O.C. 'Deregulation and privatisation of the upstream and downstream oil and gas industry in Nigeria: Curse or blessing?' *International Journal of Business Administration, 3* (1), 16–20, 2012.

Adegbesan, S. O. 'Establishing Quality Assurance In Nigerian Education System: Implication for Educational Managers'. *Educational Research and Reviews* 6(2), 147–155, 2011.

Adelman, I. Editorial: Development history and its implications for development theory, *World Development*, 25(6). 1997.

Adelman, I. 'Fifty Years of Economic Development: What Have we Learned?' World Bank ABCDE – Paris, 2000.

Adeola, A.O., Akingboye, A.S., Ore, O.T., Oluwajana, O. A., Adewole, A. H., Olawade, D.B., & Ogunleye, A. C. 'Crude oil exploration in Africa: socio-economic implications, environmental impacts, and mitigation strategies'. *Environ Syst Decis*, *42*, 26–50, 2021. https://doi.org/10.1007/s10669-021-09827

Aderemi, T., & Fidelis, O. 'Welfare implications of minimum wage increase in Nigeria Structured'. *International Journal of Social Economics*, 2017. https://doi.org/10.1108/IJSE-07-2016-0198

Adetula, Dorcas, Adesina, Kehinde, Owolabi, Folashade, & Stephen, O. 'Investment in Education for The Nigerian Economic Development'. *The Journal of Internet Banking and Commerce*, *22*, 1–15, 2017.

(African Development Bank), 'Africa Economic Outlook 2023 - Mobilizing Private Sector Financing for Climate and Green Growth in Africa' 2023. https://www.afdb.org/en/documents/african-economic-outlook-2023

Agbaeze, E. K. & Ukoha, K. 'Oil a blessing or a curse: The Nigerian experience'. *European Journal of Social Sciences*, *56*(3), 262–270, 2018.

Ahlan, A.R., Atanda, B.N., Yahaya, I.S., and Shehu, Y. 'Information Technology Enhances Students' Academic Performance: A case Of University of Ilorin. *The Online Journal of Distance Education and e-Learning* 2(2) pp. 15–20, 2014.

Ajadi, T. O., Salawu, I. O., & Adeoye, F. A. 'E-Learning and Distance Education in Nigeria', *The Turkish On-line Journal of Educational Technology*, *7*(4), 2008.

Ajayi, T.A. (2020). Did diversification impact economic growth in Nigeria in the last 20 years of democratic government (1999–2019)? A vector error correction model. *Journal of Economics and Sustainable Development*.

Akinyetun, Tope. 'Nigeria and Oil Production: Lessons for Future'. *International Journal of Multidisciplinary Research and Development*. *3*, 19–24, 2016.

Alavi, M., & Leidner, D. E. 'Research commentary: Technology-Mediated learning-A call for greater depth and breadth of research'. *Information Systems Research*, *12*(1), 1–10, 2001.

Ali, S., Uppal, M. A., and Gulliver, S. 2018. A conceptual framework highlighting e-learning implementation barriers. *Information Technology & People*, 31 (1). pp. 156–180. doi: https://doi.org/10.1108/ITP-10-2016-0246 Available at https://centaur.reading.ac.uk/70274/

Al-Karaki JN, Ababneh N, Hamid Y, Gawanmeh A. Evaluating the Effectiveness of Distance Learning in Higher Education during COVID-19 Global Crisis: UAE Educators' Perspectives. *CONT ED Technology*, 13(3), ep311, 2021. https://doi.org/10.30935/cedtech/10945

Allen, I.E., and Seaman, J. (2011) Going the Distance: Online Education in the United States, 2011. Babson Survey Research Group and Quahog Research Group. https://www.onlinelearningsurvey.com/reports/goingthedistance.pdf

Amnesty International. 'Nigeria: oil, poverty and violence'. AI Index: AFR 44/017/2006, Public. 2006 https://www.amnesty.org/en/documents/afr44/017/2006/en/

Amnesty International, 'Petroleum, Pollution and Poverty in the Niger Delta.', 2009. https://www.amnestyusa.org/wp-content/uploads/2017/04/afr440172009en.pdf

Arifin. 'The Effect of Education on Economic Growth in Riau Province'. *Turast: Journal of Research and Community Services*, *7*(2), 1–9, 2019.

Arman, A., Purwandaya, B., & Saefuddin, A. 'The Impact of Quality of Education and Higher Education on Economic Growth' *Journal of Economic Education*, *9*, 64–70, 2020.

AusAID' Volunteers and Australian Development Cooperation'. Australian Aid Program Volunteer Policy, 2004.
Auty R. '*Sustaining Development in Mineral Economies: The Resource Curse', Thesis*, Routledge, London, 1993.
Ayodele, A. 'Taking Advantage of On-line Learning', *Punch Newspaper*, 1st Dec., 2007, 2010.
Babatunde, M. A. and Adefabi, R. A., 'Long-Run relationship between Education and Economic growth in Nigeria: Evidence from Johannes's cointegration Approach'. Paper presented at *the Regional conference on education in West Africa: constraints and opportunities*. Dakar Senegal Nov. 1st – 2nd 2006, 2005.
Barro, R. L. 'Economic Growth in a Cross Section of Countries'. *Quarterly Journal of Economics*, 106; p. 407–443, 1991.
Barro, R. J. 'Education and Economic Growth. *Annals of Economics and Finance'*, 14 (2), 301–328, 2013.
Barro, R.J. and J-W. Lee. 'A new data set of educational attainment in the world, 1950–2010'. NBER Working Paper No. 15902. National Bureau of Economic Research, Cambridge, Massachusetts, April, 2010.
Bello, A. T., & Nwaeke, T. 'Impacts of Oil Exploration (Oil and Gas Conflicts; Niger Delta as a Case Study)'. Journal of Geoscience and Environment Protection, 11, 189–200, 2023. https://doi.org/10.4236/gep.2023.113013
Belshaw, D. & Livingstone, I. '*Reviewing Development in Sub-Saharan Africa: Policy, Performance and Prospects'*. London: Routledge, 2002.
Benos, N., Zotou, S. 'Education and Economic Growth: A Meta-Regression Analysis'. *World Development*, 64: p. 669–689, 2014.
Benson, A. Using on-line learning to meet workforce demand: A case study of stakeholder influence. *Quarterly Review of Distance Education*, 3(4), 443–452, 2002.
Berger, Noah, and Peter Fisher. 'A well-educated workforce is key to state prosperity'. *Economic Policy Institute* 22: 1–14, 2013.
Blount, E. V. '*A qualitative phenomenological study exploring lived experiences of employees and managers and their engagement with E-learning courses*', Dissertations. ProQuest, 2016.
Bolger, J. 'Capacity development: why, what and how. *Capacity Development' Occasional Paper Series, No. 1*, CIDA Policy Branch, 2000.
Bondarouk, T., & Ruel, H. 'Dynamics of e-learning: Theoretical and practical perspectives'. *International Journal of Training and Development*, *14*(3), 149–154, 2010.
Bowman, M. J. 'Education and economic growth: an overview'. Central Bank of Nigeria (2008). *Statistical Bulletin (Golden Jubilee Edition)*. Abuja: CBN, 1980.
Boyi, A. A. 'Education and Sustainable National Development in Nigeria: Challenges and Way Forward', *Mediterranean Journal of Social Sciences MCSER Publishing, Rome-Italy*, *4*(8), 147–152, 2013.
Bugi, S. Z. 'Challenges of Attending E-learning Studies in Nigeria', Turkish On-line Journal of Distance Education-TOJDE 13(3) Article 11, 2012.
Campbell, O. A. Inclusive Growth and Sustainable Human Development in Nigeria. Advances in Social Sciences Research Journal, 4(7) 79–95, 2017.
Carliner, S. 'Overview of on-line learning'. Amherst, MA: Human Resource Development Press, 1999.
Caruth, G. D. & Caruth, D. L. 'Distance Education in the United States: From Correspondence Courses to the internet' *Journal of Distance Education*, *14*(2), 2013.
Central Bank of Nigeria (CBN). 'The Changing Structure of the Nigerian Economy and Implications for Development", Research Department, August, Lagos. 2000.
Chidi, C. O., Mbah, S. E. & Ogunyomi, P. O. 'Dwindling Global Oil Prices: Curse or Blessing in Disguise for the Nigerian State?', Nigerian Journal of Management Studies. Vol. 18, No. 1, 142–149, 2018.

Chizmar, J. F., & Walbert, M. S. 'Web-based learning. Environments guided by principles of good teaching practice', *Journal of Economic Education* 30(3). P. 248–264, 1999.

Choudhury S. and Pattnaik, S. 'Emerging themes in e-learning: a review from the stakeholders' perspective'. Computers and Education. 144 pp. 1–20, 2020. https://doi.org/10.1016/j.compedu.2019.103657

Chukwuma, I. T. 'The resource curse in Nigeria: Lessons and policy option'. *International Journal of Research in Humanities and Social Studies*, *2* (8), 38–48, 2015.

Clark, R.C. & Mayer, R. E. 'e-Learning and the Science of Instruction: Proven Guidelines for Consumers and Designers of Multimedia Learning', 4th Edition, 2016. https://onlinelibrary.wiley.com/doi/book/10.1002/9781119239086

Compeau, D. R., & Higgins, C. A. 'Computer self-efficacy: Development of a measure and initial test'. *MIS Quarterly*, 189–211. 1995.

Cooray, A., & Potrafke, N. 'Gender inequality in education: Political institutions or culture and religion?' *European Journal of Political Economy*, *27*(2), 268–280, 2011.

Corden, W. M. 'Booming Sector and Dutch Disease Economics: Survey and Consolidation', *Oxford Economic Papers*, Vol. 36, No. 3, pp. 359–380, 1984.

Corden W M and Neary J. P. 'Booming Sector and De-Industrialization in a Small Open Economy', *Economic Journal*, Vol. 92, No. 368, pp. 825–848, 1982.

Conrad, D. '*Deep in the hearts of learners: Insights into the nature of on-line community*'. Journal of Distance Education, 17(1), 1–19, 2002.

Daniel, J. 'E-learning for Development: Using Information and Communications Technologies to Bridge the Digital Divide', *Common Wealth Ministers Reference*. Henley Media Group, 2009.

Dauda, R.O.S. 'Investment in education and economic growth in Nigeria: An empirical evidence'. International Research Journal of Finance and Economics, 55: 158–159, 2010.

David, O.O., Noah, O.A., & Agbalajobi, S.A. 'An Empirical Analysis of the Contribution of Mining Sector to Economic Development in Nigeria'. *Journal of Humanities and Social Sciences*, *19*, 88–106Parkin, 2016.

Denison, E.F. 'Measuring the contribution of education to economic growth' In *The Economics of Education* (pp. 202–260). Basingstoke: Palgrave Macmillan UK, 1966.

DeSanctis, G., Fayard, A. L., Roach, M., & Jiang, L. 'Learning in online forums'. *European Management Journal*, *21*(5), 565–577, 2003.

Derouin, R.E., Fritzsche, B.A. and Salas, E. 'Elearning in organisations', *Journal of Management*, 31(6), pp. 920–940, 2005.

Disastra, G. & Wahyuningtyas, R. 'User Satisfaction of E-Learning System Implementation for Training and Development Program in Organization'. 2019. https://doi.org/10.2991/aebmr.k.200410.038

Donwa, P. A., Mgbame, C. O., Ogbeide, O. L. 'Corruption in the Nigerian oil and gas industry and implication for economic growth'. Int J African Asian Stud 14:29–41, 2015.

Dragoi, Doina. 'Economic growth versus economic development', Atlantic Review of Economics (ARoEc), ISSN 2174-3835, Colegio de Economistas de A Coruña, A Coruña, Vol. 4, Iss. 1, pp. 1–11, 2020.

Earle, D. 'How can tertiary education deliver value to the economy?' Tertiary education occasional paper, 2010. http://thebub.seperu.govt.nz/site/defaultfiles/41943.value-of-tertiary-education.o.pdf

Edwards, Sebastian & Aoki, Masanao, 'Oil export boom and Dutch-disease: A dynamic analysis,' *Resources and Energy*, Elsevier, Vol. 5(3), pages 219–242, 1983.

Egolum, P. U. 'E-Learning in Nigeria Tertiary Institutions: A Panacea to Quality Education for National Development'. 3. 47–59, 2021. https://www.researchgate.net/publication/354534799

Elwerfelli, A. and Benhin, J. 'Oil a Blessing or Curse: A Comparative Assessment of Nigeria, Norway and the United Arab Emirates'. *Theoretical Economics Letters*, 8, 1136–1160, 2018. https://doi.org/10.4236/tel.2018.85076

Emediegwu, Lotanna Ernest and Clement, Ighodaro (2016) "The Connection between Education and Sustainable Economic Growth in Nigeria," *Zambia Social Science Journal*: Vol. 6: No. 1, Article 6, 2016. https://scholarship.law.cornell.edu/zssj/vol6/iss1/6

Emediegwu, L. E. and Monye-Emina, A. (2016), 'Attainment of the Millennium Development Goal of Poverty Reduction in Nigeria – An Appraisal'. *Ghana Social Science Journal*, *13*(1), 94–118, 2016.

Eregha, P.B., Irughe, R. I., and Edafe, J. 2018. "Education and Economic Growth: Empirical Evidence from Nigeria," *Managing Global Transitions*, University of Primorska, Faculty of Management Koper, vol. 16(1 (Spring), 59–77.Available at: https://doi.org/10.26493/1854-6935.16.59-77

Fasanya, Ismail & Onakoya, Adegbemi & Adabanija, Misbaudeen. (2013). Oil Discovery and Sectoral Performance in Nigeria: An Appraisal of the Dutch Disease, 2013.

Fayomi, O. O., Adepoju, O. and Ayo, C. K. '*The Impacts of On-line Education on the Educational Advancement in Nigeria: A Study of National Open University of Nigeria (NOUN)*'. In: *INTED 2015 International Conference*, 2–4 March 2015, Madrid, Spain, 2015.

Federal Ministry of Finance & Budget & Planning. Technical Reports and Documents – United Nations Population Fund Country Programme Document for Nigeria. 12 p. 2023. Available at: https://nigeria.unfpa.org/en/publications/united-nations-population-fund-country-programme-document-nigeria

Flammang, Robert A. 'Economic Growth and Economic Development: Counterparts or Competitors?" EDCC, 28 47–61, 1979.

Garrison, D. R. '*E-learning in the 21st Century: A Community of Inquiry Framework for Research and Practice*', 3rd ed.; Routledge: New York, NY, USA, 2017.

Graham, M. C., & Jones, N. 'Improving business performance with web 2.0 technologies'. *Journal of Business Excellence*, *2*(1), 12–17, 2011.

Grant, Catherine. 'The Contribution of Education to Economic Growth'. Brighton: Institute of Development Studies, 2017.

Glewwe, P., Maiga, E., Zheng, H. (2014). 'The Contribution of Education to Economic Growth: A Review of the Evidence, with Special Attention and an Application to Sub-Saharan Africa'. *World Development*. 59: p. 379–393, 2014.

Global Citizen. Is Oil In Nigeria A Growth Cure Or a 'Resource Curs e'? And At What Cost will Oil Shape the Future of Africa? Available at: https://www.globalcitizen.org/en/content/oil-in-nigeria-a-cure-or-curse/. 2012.

Haller, A. 'Concepts of Economic Growth and Development. *Challenges of Crisis and of Knowledge*', 2012. https://www.researchgate.net/publication/309577823

Hamid, Y., Al-Karaki, J. N., Nseobot, I. R., Effiong, A. I., Dinnoo, V. & Edet, A. U. 'A simple and predictive model for COVID-19 evolution in large scale infected countries'. *Journal of Theoretical and Applied Information Technology*, *98*(24), 3961–3971, 2020.

Harberger, A. 'Dutch Disease - How Much Sickness, How Much Boom?' Resources and Energy 5, 1–20, North-Holland, 1983.

Harbison, F. H. '*Human Resources as the Wealth of Nations*'. New York: Oxford University Press, 1973.

Harford, T. and M. Klein. Aid and the Resource Curse. The World Bank Group, Private Sector Development Vice Presidency, Note # 291, Washington D.C, 2005.

Hedge, N. & Hayward, L. 'Redefining roles. University e-learning contributing to Life-long learning in a networked world'. E-learning, 1:128, 2004.

Hentea, M., Shea, M. J., and Pennington, L. 'A perspective on fulfilling the expectation of distance education'. Paper presented at the proceeding of the 4th conference on *Information technology curriculum*, New York, USA. Published in CITC4 2003 *Proceedings of the 4th conference on information technology curriculum*, pp. 160–167, 2003.

Horton, W. '*E-Learning by Design*' (2nd Edition). San Francisco: John Wiley & Sons, 2011. http://dx.doi.org/10.1002/9781118256039

Ifijeh, G., Osinulu, I., Esse, U., Adewole-Odeshi, E. and Fagbohun, M. 'Assessing E-Learning Tools in an Academic Environment: A Study of Availability and Use among Undergraduate Students in a Nigeria University', 2015. *International Journal of Progressive Education*. 11(2). P.76–87.

Ijere, T. C. (2015). The resource curse in Nigeria: Lessons and policy option. *International Journal of Research in Humanities and Social Studies*, 2(8), 38–42.

Ikegulu, B. & Oranusi, S. 'Distance and Open Learning in Nigeria: Progress, Concerns & Prospects'. *Journal of Education & Practice*, 5(35), 2014.

Ilechukwu, L. C., Njoku, C. C. & Ugwuozor, F. O. 'Education and Development Disconnect in Nigeria: Education for Sustainable Development (ESD) as the 21st Century Imperative for Nigeria's National Transformation, Sustainable Development and Global Competitiveness'. *Journal of Economics and Sustainable Development*, 5(23), 44–56., 2014.

Innocent, E. O. 'Unemployment Rate in Nigeria: Agenda for Government'. *Academic Journal of Interdisciplinary Studies*, *3*(4), 103–114, 2014.

IOM (International Organization for Migration) Nigeria. News: Local National Population Commission (NPC). Available at: https://nigeria.iom.int/news/npc-we-lack-accurate-figures-nigeriaspopulation#:~:text=The%20National%20Population%20Commission%20(NPC,have%20been%20mired%20in%20controversy. Retrieved February 2024.

Ishioro, Bernhard Ozofere. 'Crude Oil & Economic Growth in Nigeria: A Simplified Pairwise Causality Test'. Journal of Academic Research in Economic. 12(2) p. 224, 2022. https://www.jare-sh.com/downloads/jul_2020/ishioro.pdf

Itari, E. P. & Beyin, U. T. 'Education for Sustainable Development in Nigeria and Other Developing Nations', British Journal of Education, Published by European Centre for Research, Training and Development, UK. Vol. 6 No.5. pp. 41–51. 2018. https://www.eajournals.org/wp-content/uploads/Education-for-Sustainable-Development-in-Nigeria-and-Other-Developing-Nations.pdf

Jack, J.T., Uchechukwu, D.A., Azubuike, B.O., & Akujobi, C. 'Crude Oil Exploration and Underdevelopment in Nigeria: A Resource Curse Analysis'. 2016. https://www.academia.edu/32980740/CRUDE_OIL_EXPLORATION_AND_UNDERDEVELOPMENT_IN_NIGERIA_A_RESOURCE_CURSE_ANALYSIS

Kakar, Z.K., B.A. Khiljiand and M.J. Khan. "Relationship between education and economic growth in Pakistan: A time series analysis". *Journal of International Academic Research*, 11(1): 27–32, 2011.

Kalu, K.I., & Ott, K. 'Ethical Issues in Environmental Pollution: Multinational Corporations (MNCs) and Oil Industries in Tropical Regions—The Nigerian Niger-Delta Case'. *The International Library of Environmental, Agricultural and Food Ethics*. 2019. DOI:10.1007/978-3-030-18807-8_18

Kasse J.P. and Blunywa, W. 'An Assessment of E-learning Utilization by a Section of Ugandan Universities Challenges, Success Factors and Way Forward'. *International Conference of ICT for Africa*; Harare, Zimbabwe, 2013.

Kaushik, S. 'Training and Development: Emerging ways towards manpower development'. *Journal of Strategic Human Resource Management*, *1*(1), 23–27, 2012.

Khan, M., Sarwar, K. and Niazi, G.R., 'The Impact of Education System on Economic Growth: An Empirical Evidence from Developing Economy'. *Administrative and Management Sciences Journal, 1*(2), pp.94–102, 2023.

Kim, J. S., Erdem, M., Byun, J. W., & Jeong, H. 'Training soft skills via e-learning: International chain hotels'. *International Journal of Contemporary Hospitality Management, 23*(No. 6), 739–763, 2011.

Kimiloglu, H., & Ozturan, M. 'Perceptions about the attitude towards e learning in Corporate Training'. *Computers in Human Behavior, 72*, 339–349, 2017.

Kpolovie, P. J., Iderima, E. C. and Ololube, N. P. 'Computer literacy and candidate performance on computer based test'. In N.P. Ololube (Ed). Advancing technology and educational development through blended learning in emerging economies'. USA: *Information Science References*, 2014. http://www.igiglobal.com

Loening, J.L. 'Effects of Primary, Secondary and Tertiary Education: Evidence from Guatemala Policy' Research Working Paper (3610), 2005.

Lu, C. 'Social status, compulsory education and economic growth' *Economic modelling, 68*, 425–434, 2018.

Megasan, Ekundayo P. & Dauda, R. O. S. 'Does Education matter for inclusive Growth? The Nigerian Case', Journal of Economics and Business Research, ISSN: 2068 - 3537, E – ISSN (on-line) 2069 – 9476, ISSN – L = 2068 – 3537 Year XXII, No. 1, pp. 168–189, 2016.

Malizia, E. 'Economic Growth and Economic Development: Concepts and Measures'. *The Review of Regional Studies, 20*, 30–36, 1990.

Malizia, E. E. & Fesser, E. J. '*Understanding Economic Development'*. London: Rutgers. Martin, X.S. and A. Subramanian (2003); *Addressing the Natural Resource Curse: An illustration from Nigeria*. NBER Working Paper No. 9804', 2000.

Mariana, D. R. 'Education as a Determinant of the Economic Growth: The Case of Romania'. *Procedia-Social and Behavioural Sciences*. 197: p. 404–412, 2015.

Marquez-Ramos, L., and Estefanía, M. 2019. Education and economic growth: An empirical analysis of nonlinearities. *Applied Economic Analysis* 27 21–45.

Mohammed, K. 'A wealth of sorrow: Why Nigeria's abundant oil reserves are really a curse' *The Guardian Online Newspaper*. Available at: https://www.theguardian.com/global-development/2021/nov/09/a-wealth-of-sorrow-why-nigerias-abundant-oil-reserves-are-really-a-curse#img-1 2021.

Mojsoska-Blazevski, Nikica. '*Labour Market in the Former Yugoslav Republic of Macedonia a Study for the European Commission Employment', Social Affairs and Equal Opportunities DG*. Skopje: Euro-Balkan Institute, 2009.

National Bureau of Statistics 'Demographic Statistics Bulleting 2022' 2023. https://www.nigerianstat.gov.ng/pdfuploads/DEMOGRAPHIC_BULLETIN_2022_FINAL.pdf

National Population Commission. 'Federal Government of Nigeria - National Policy on Population for Sustainable Development' 1st Edition. 2021.

National Population Commission. 'Federal Government of Nigeria - National Policy on Population for Sustainable Development' 2022.

Nneka, E.H. 'The perspective of e-learning and libraries in Africa: challenges and opportunities', *Library Review*, Vol. 59 No. 4, pp. 274–290, 2010.

Nwabufo, B. N., Umoru, T. A. and Olukotun, J.O., (2013). 'The challenges of e-learning in tertiary institutions in Nigeria' *International Conference the Future of Education Florence*, June.

Nwagwu, W. E. 'E-learning Readiness of Universities in Nigeria- What Are The Opinions of The Academic Staff of Nigeria's Premier University?' *Education and Information Technologies*; New York 25(2), 1343–1370, 2020.

Oba-Adenuga, O. A. "Implementation of On-line Learning in Nigeria: Significance of Teachers' Preparedness". *West African Journal of Open and Flexible Learning*, 7(2) pp. 127–142, 2019. https://wajofel.org/index.php/wajofel/article/view/39

Obidike, J., Onyeka, M. and Nduka, A. 'Effect of selected macroeconomic variables on the Nigerian economy'Z 1987-2020. *International Journal of Business & Law Research*, *10*(3), pp.84–96, 2022.

Odit, M. P., Dookhan, K. and Fauzel, S. 'The impact of education on economic growth: the case of Mauritius'. *International Business & Economics Research Journal (IBER)* 9(8), 141–152, 2010.

Ogeh, O.W. & Chiemeka, N. 'Creativity and Innovation in Open and Distance Education: A Paradigm for Human Development in the 21st Century for Nation-Building in Nigeria'. *Journal of Education and Practice*. 6, 143–147, 2015.

Ogunode, Niyi Jacob, Nigerian Universities and their Sustainability: Challenges and Way Forward 2020. https://ssrn.com/abstract=3695789 or http://dx.doi.org/10.2139/ssrn.3695789

Ofuyatan O., Opaluwa, E. and Adeola, A. Challenges and effects of e-learning in the development of architecture and engineering in Nigeria's private tertiary institution. *Developing Country Studies* 4 (23), 130–134, 2014. www.iiste.org

Okpanachi, E., & Andrews, N. 'Preventing the Oil "Resource Curse In Ghana: Lessons From Nigeria"'. *World Futures*, *68*(6), 430–450, 2012. https://doi.org/10.1080/02604027.2012.693854

Olugbenga, Michael & Qiu, Allison. 'Prospects and Challenges of On-line Education in Secondary Schools in Northern Nigeria', *Journal of American Academic Research*. 2020. https://www.researchgate.net/publication/342003559

Olugbeko, S. O., and Izu, G. O., 'The reality and challenges of E-Learning education in Africa: The Nigerian Experience'. *International Journal of Humanities and Management Sciences (IJHMS)* Vol. 1, No: 3, pp.205–209, 2013.

Olupona, A. M. 'Students Characteristics and Willingness to Pay Fees at University of Ibadan'. *Topical Issues in Education*. Ibadan: University of Ibadan, 2001.

Olurounbi, R. 'Nigeria Unemployment Rate Rises to 33%, Second Highest on Global List', 2021. https://www.bloomberg.com/news/articles/

Olutola, A.T. & Olatoye, O.O. (2015). Challenges of E-Learning Technologies in the Nigerian University Education; *Journal of Education and Social Research*. 5(1), 301.

Omojimite, B.U. 'Education and Economic Growth in Nigeria: A Granger Causality Analysis'. *African Research Review*, *4*(3), 2010. DOI: 10.4314/afrrev.v4i3.60158

Omojimite, B.U. (2011). Building human capital for sustainable economic development in Nigeria. *Journal of Sustainable Development*, 4 (4), 21–36.

Onuchuku, O. and Felix, J.M., 'Education and Economic Development in Nigeria'. *Journal of Education in Developing Areas*, *31*(3), pp.26–36, 2023.

Onuoha, F. C. 'The audacity of the Boko Haram: Background, analysis and emerging trend'. *Security Journal*, *25*(2), 134–151, 2012.

Onuoha, Freedom Chukwudi. 'Why the poor pay with their lives: oil pipeline vandalisation, fires and human security in Nigeria.' *Disasters* 33 3, 369–389, 2009.

Onwioduokit, E. 'Education, inclusive growth and development in Nigeria: empirical examination', Bullion, 44(2), 3–30, 2020.

Onyekwere, B.A. 'Economic Growth and Development in Nigeria'. *Kuwait chapter of Arabian Journal of Business & Management Review*, *6*, 32–39, 2016.

Organisation for Economic Cooperation and Development (OECD) website, Inclusive Growth Home Page, 2024.

Osunyikanmi, A.F., 'Prioritising Quality Education in Nigeria: a Commitment to Sustainable Development Goals'. *International Journal of Advanced Studies in Economics and Public Sector Management*, *6*(2), pp.221–224, 2018. https://internationalpolicybrief.org/wp-content/uploads/2023/10/ARTICLE16-11.pdf

Oyelaran-Oyeyinka, B., & Adeya, C. N. 'Internet access in Africa: Empirical evidence from Kenya and Nigeria.' *Telematics and Informatics*, *21*(1), 67–81, 2004.

Ozturk, I. The Role of Education in Economic Development: A Theoretical Perspective. ERPN: Economic Development & Technological Change (Topic). 2008 Available at SSRN: https://ssrn.com/abstract=1137541 or http://dx.doi.org/10.2139/ssrn.1137541

Parkin, M. (2011). '*Macroeconomics (Pearson Series in Economics)*', 10th ed., Addison-Wesley (Pearson Education Inc.): Boston, 396 p.

Paul, I. A. (2014). Petroleum and Nigeria's economy: A paradox of global reality since 1956. *Research and Human Society Science*, *4*, 94–101.

Paygar, A. 'Challenges and Opportunity of On-line Learning In Developing Countries with Specific Focus on Liberia' (Senior Thesis), 2014.

Peslak, A., Kovalchick, L., Wang, W., & Kovacs, P. 'Effectiveness of Educational Delivery Modes: A Study in Computer Information Systems.' *Journal of Information Systems Education*, 32(4), 253–261, 2020.

Peters, M. A. 'Western education is sinful: Boko haram and the abduction of chibok schoolgirls'. *Policy Futures in Education*, *12*(2), 186–190, 2014.

Peters, O. 'Distance Education In Transition, New Trends and Challenges'. Oldenburg: Carl von Ossietzky University Centre for distance education, 2002.

Peterson, Jakob. 'The Resource Curse in Nigeria A Story of Oil and Corruption', 2012.

Piccoli, G., Ahmad, R., & Ives, B. 'Web-based virtual learning environments: A research framework and a preliminary assessment of effectiveness in basic it skills training'. *MIS Quarterly*, 401–426, 2001.

Peimani, N.; Kamalipour, H. On-line Education and the COVID-19 Outbreak: A Case Study of On-line Teaching during Lockdown. *Education Sciences* 2021, 11, 72. https://doi.org/10.3390/educsci11020072

Poole, D. M. 'Student participation in a discussion-oriented on-line course: A case study'. *Journal of Research on Computing in Education*. 33(2), 162–177, 2000.

Rabe-Hemp, C., Woollen, S., & Humiston, G. S. 'A comparative analysis of student engagement, learning, and satisfaction in lecture hall and on-line learning settings'. *The Quarterly Review of Distance Education*, 10(2), 207–218, 2009.

Rice, X. 'Youth could be source of wealth, or conflict', *Financial Times, Special Report*, p. 13. 2011.

Ross, M. L. 'Does Taxation Lead to Representation?', *British Journal of Political Science*. 34(2):229–249,2004. DOI: https://doi.org/10.1017/S0007123404000031

Sachs J D and Warner A M 'The Curse of Natural Resources', *European Economic Review*, Vol. 45, pp. s827–838, 2001.

Saidu, S. A., Aliyu, B. S., Zubair, A. U. 'Is the discovery of oil a curse or a blessing to Nigeria?' *CBN Bullion*, 40(1), 21–32, 2016.

Salawudeen, O.S. 'E-learning Technology. The Nigerian Experience', Roger Printing and Publishing limited, Abuja, 2010.

Sani, A.B., Nasir, A.K. & Bakare, T.O., 'Financial Implication of Crude Oil Discovery in Nigeria: A Blessing or A Curse?' *AE-Funai Journal of Accounting, Business & Finance (FJABAF)*, 2019. WWW.FUJABF.ORG

Sapru, 2021, cited in Onuchuku, O. and Felix, J.M., Education and economic development in Nigeria. *Journal of Education in Developing Areas*, *31*(3), pp.26–36, 2023.

Simonova, I.; Faltynkova, L.; Kostolanyova, K. 'New Blended Learning Enriched after the COVID-19 Experience? Students' Opinions. *Sustainability* 15, 5093, 2023. https://doi.org/10.3390/su15065093

Somayeh, M., Dehghani, M., Mozaffari, F., Ghasemnegad, S.M., Hakimi, H., and Samaneh, B. 'The effectiveness of E-learning in learning: A review of the literature'. *International Journal of Medical Research & Health Sciences*. 2016 5(2): pp. 86–91.

Song, L., Singleton, E. S., Hill, J. R., and Koh, M. H. 'Improving on-line learning: Student perceptions of useful and challenging characteristics'. *The Internet and Higher Education*, 7(1), 59–70, 2004.

Susilo S. A. K., Hayati B., Pujiati A. 'The Linkage Among Economic Growth, Education and Health: Empirical Study in Java Island', *Jurnal Ekonomi Pembangunan: Kajian Masalah Ekonomi dan Pembangunan*, 24(1), 24–39, 2023. doi:https://doi.org/10.23917/jep.v24i1.20194

Tai, L. '*Corporate e–learning: How E-learning is created in three large corporations*', Dissertations. ProQuest, AAI3168048, 2005.

Tamuno, S., and Felix, J. M. (2006). Crude oil resource: A blessing or curse to Nigeria–The case of the Niger Delta. *Journal of Research in National Development*, *4*(2), 53–58.

Temple, J. (2000), Education and Economic Growth. Seminar on Economic Growth and Government Policy, 12 October 2000.

The Nigerian Economic Summit Group, *Economic and Policy Review Journal*. Vol. 20 (1). 2022.

The World Bank. 1989. World Development Report. Oxford University Press.

The World Bank (2006). India: Inclusive Growth and Service Delivery: Building on India's Success. *Development Policy Review*, Report No 34580-1N, Washington DC.

Tijani M. 'It's Official: Nigeria slides into worst recession in 33 years'. The Cable, 2020. https://www.thecable.ng/

Todaro, M. P. and Smith, S. L. 'Economic Development' (11th Ed). Boston: Pearson Education, 2012.

Todaro, M. P. and Smith, S. C. 'Economic Development' Tenth Edition. Essex: Pearson Education Limited, 2009.

Topçu, E. 'Education and Economic Growth: Evidence from the EUROMED Countries'. *European Review*, *31*, 632–646, 2023.

Umo, J. 'Moving Nigeria into the new economy: A human capital perspective'. Presidential address at the 48th Annual Conference of The Nigeria Economic Society (NES), Abuja. 23rd–25th October, 2007.

UNFPA (United Nations Population Fund). Country programmes and related matters, Country programme document for Nigeria, Item 10 of the provisional agenda, 30 January to 3 February 2023, New York, 2023.

United Nations Development Programme. 'UNDP's Strategy for Inclusive and Sustainable Growth' 2017. https://www.undp.org/publications/undps-strategy-inclusive-and-sustainable-growth

United Nations DP/FPA/CPD/NGA/9 Executive Board of the United Nations Development Programme, the United Nations Population Fund and the United Nations Office for Project Services Distr.: 2022.

Uzonwanne, Maria Chinecherem. 'Economic Diversification in Nigeria in the Face of Dwindling Oil Revenue.' *Journal of economics and sustainable development* 6(4) 61–67, 2015. https://core.ac.uk/download/pdf/234646874.pdf

Van Wijnbergen, S. 'The Dutch disease: A disease after all?' *Economic Journal*, Vol.94, 1984.

Wang, R. 'Push – pull factors of E learning in the hotel Industry'. *Industrial Management and Data Systems*, *114*(8), 1169–1185, 2014.

Welsh, E. T., Wanberg, C. R., Brown, K. G., & Simmering, M. J. 'E-learning: Emerging uses, empirical results and future directions'. *International Journal of Training and Development*, *7*(4), 245–258, 2003.

World Bank. 1989. *World development report*. Oxford University Press.

World Bank (2006). India: Inclusive Growth and Service Delivery: Building on India's Success. *Development Policy Review*, Report No 34580-1N, Washington DC.

WPP (World Population Prospects). The 2024 Revision. U.N. Dept. of Economic and Social Affairs - Population Division. World Population Prospects: The 2024 Revision. (Medium-fertility variant). Retrieved on December 9, 2024.

Wright, C. R., Dhanarajan, G., & Reju, S. A. 'Recurring Issues Encountered by Distance Educators in Developing and Emerging Nations', *International Review of Research in Open & Distance Learning* 10(1), 2009.

Yogish, S.N. 'Education and economic development'. *Indian Journal of Social Development*, 6(2): 255–270, 2006.

Yoo, S. J., & Huang, W. D. 'Can e-learning system enhance learning culture in the workplace? A comparison among companies in South Korea'. *British Journal of Educational Technology*, *4*(47), 575–591, 2016.

Yusuf, M.O. 'Problems and Prospects of Open and Distance Education in Nigeria'. *The Turkish On-line Journal of Distance Education*, *7*, 22–29, 2006.

Zaheer, M., Jabeen, S. & Qadri, M. 'Role of e-learning in capacity building: An Alumni View. *Open Praxis'*, *7*(1), 71–81. International Council for Open and Distance Education, 2015. https://www.learntechlib.org/p/150756/

Ziberi, Besime Fekri, Donat Rexha, Xhemazie Ibraimi, and Besnik Avdiaj. 'Empirical Analysis of the Impact of Education on Economic Growth'. *Economies* 10: 89. 2022. https://doi.org/10.3390/economies10040089

10 Geoeconomic and Geopolitical Challenges and the Future of Education

Lucía Morales, Wael Rashwan, Intesar Madi, Anna Zherdeva, Ozéias Rodrigues da Rocha, Daniel Kamphambale, Abrar Alzankawi, Lia Pop, Jon-Hans Coetzer, Ivaylo Peev and Murat Gulmez

Introduction

The world's socioeconomic systems are facing significant challenges, and current educational models are often criticised for their inability to provide interactive and immersive learning environments that engage students effectively. Traditional methods fall short in addressing the diverse needs of learners and fail to leverage modern technological advancements. As we move towards a more interconnected and technologically driven world, it is imperative to integrate Artificial Intelligence (AI) and data analytics into educational frameworks to enhance learner engagement and improve educational outcomes. Educational models are failing to provide more interactive, immersive, and experienced-based learning environments and contexts that connect learners with the reality of our global society. Almost two decades ago, the OECD (2007) "*No More Failures*" Report challenged the assumption of student retention and increasing dropout rates, underlining the need for initiatives that can help reduce the economic and social costs as a result of an adult population that lack basic skills to function on our evolving socio-economic systems (Field, Kuczera and Pont, 2007). Technology and innovation can bring value to educational contexts as they can facilitate and foster learners' engagement, where a closer connection with real problems and decision-making processes supported by economic and financial literacy skills are needed. However, at the same time, technology and innovation can accentuate economic inequalities and imbalance as lack of access to the internet, digital tools, and technologies remind us of the need to look at digital inclusion and implications for the digital divide (World Economic Forum, 2022). Transferable and transversal skills emerge as fundamental as critical thinking and analytical skills are vital to navigating the digital age and the knowledge-based economy, where discipline-specific and specialisation-focused education requires a paradigm shift that supports and enables the integration of a holistic approach towards learning, teaching and research atmospheres within multidisciplinary, interdisciplinary and transdisciplinary working environments. Discipline-specific skills are

DOI: 10.4324/9781032655857-13

critical to support decision-making processes but are limited if not considered in a broader context that facilitates working environments that can ponder problems and challenges from multifaceted and multidimensional angles. Discipline-specific knowledge does not contradict the need for an educational portfolio that is complemented with a training and educational approach that takes a broader view and understanding of our complex working contexts that require a more holistic understanding of our global society, the economic, political, and environmental systems and their challenges. The development of critical thinking, forward-thinking, data skills, digital skills, creative thinking, culture integration, and knowledge sharing are highlighted by the United Nations (2023a) *"Our Common Agenda Policy Brief 11"*, outlining the UN 2.0 Quintet of change. Co-creation, co-design, and analytical skills within collaborative, participatory and proactive training, learning and research spaces can contribute to nurturing knowledge exchange and co-creation (Brandsen et al., 2018; Leicht et al., 2018; Rădulescu et al., 2023).

We are witnessing the continuous deterioration of the environment, rising levels of detachment and isolation, and the consolidation of individualism and competitive behaviour due to increasing societal pressures and the economic and political systems' needs and demands (Napolitano, 2012). The world economy demands sustained economic growth, prosperity and progress supported by economic models that have not been updated and that are not taking into consideration a required shift from consumption-leading and wealth maximisation metrics towards models that foster higher quality, durability, reusable and minimalist elements that integrate, evaluate, and assess cost-derived externalities from human intervention in the environment because of businesses and economic activities. The environmental costs and their spillover effects towards the economy and society remain neglected, with a dominance of the world governments' myopic insight and inefficient policies towards public spending that support inclusive economic development and progress. Sustainability demands are leading some experts to propose decelerating economic growth rates, seeking to transition towards a zero-growth phase that does not compromise societies' well-being (World Economic Forum, 2022). Degrowth is an idea that poses severe challenges as the world's economic, political, and business leaders are not finding alternatives to existing practices, with a lack of clarity on how emerging and less developed countries' economic and financial needs need to be contextualised according to their level of development and economic integration (Bornstein et al., 2022; Barbier, 1999). The argument revolves around the idea of finite resources and accessibility in a context where wealthy economies are looking to secure access to natural resources to keep raising the living-quality standards of their population. In contrast, less developed economies do not meet their basic economic, social, and environmental needs (Lasenby, 2022; Mastini, 2017; UN, 2019).

The idea of a zero-growth or degrowth phase requires questioning, careful consideration, and debate among experts, as economic growth is fundamental to support society's development and prosperity. Moreover, the needs and demands of the wealthier Global North, compared to the progress made by the poorest Global South when discussing economic growth, prosperity, well-being, and the way forward, cannot be overlooked. According to the 2024 Financing for Sustainable Development Report (DESA, 2024), the world is at a crossroads with its financial plan, as financing gaps for sustainable development are rising. The financial divide has not been bridged, and less developed economies face a lack of access to affordable finance. The critical issue relates to our understanding of economic growth, which is currently defined by models that value Gross Domestic Product, where growth is defined, understood, and represented by dated GDP metrics (GDP = C + I + G + X − M).[1] From the economic perspective, we might need to reflect on Schumpeter's idea of "*creative destruction*", which has been considered by generations of economists when trying to understand the free-market dynamics (Schumpeter, 1934). There is a need to rethink and redesign alternative models supported by economic, political, financial, and social thinking that provide a roadmap to understanding the role of economic activities and businesses within the United Nations Sustainability Agenda (UN, 2015) and the UN 2.0 Agenda (UN, 2023a, 2023b). The role that education, technology and innovation can play in bringing alternatives to existing development models and how they are presented as part of the long-run economic growth guided by knowledge, education and the development of human talent can help us understand the importance of education as part of countries' ability to grow and develop. An initial question to be considered is: to what extent should growth be understood as a model based on consumption, wealth accumulation, and competition guided by the capitalist system and the market-driven economy? This chapter offers critical insights that consider the geoeconomic and geopolitical landscape, by integrating insights on the challenges faced by the business sector, and the future of education to drive change for sustainable and inclusive development. The chapter reflects and questions current economic growth that supports the needs of the world's most advanced economies while overlooking and neglecting the growth and developmental needs of emerging and less developed economies and the so-called Third World (OECD, 2016; UN, 2023b; World Bank, 2023).

Global North and Global South Conflicting Agendas

The wealthiest Global North's economic, social, and environmental working agenda is directly in confrontation with the needs of the Global South to progress and develop. The idea of wealth distribution and redistribution has been introduced within economic debates, but the reality is that growth models remain static and anchored on the principles that guide classical or orthodox economic thinking. We are immersed in socio-economic systems that are defined by high levels of individualism, fierce competition, economic polarisation, and wealth concentration, enhanced by a shift towards inward-looking economic models that have become prevalent as a result of the 2008 Global

Economic and Financial Crisis (GEFC). Some of the world's most advanced economies have shifted towards protectionism and bilateralism, posing significant challenges when trying to bring a more social dimension to a market-driven economic and financial system. We are facing a significant dilemma as existing economic and social systems supported by dated economic and energy models heavily dependent on consumption and the intensive over-exploitation of natural resources do not align with the United Nations 2030 Sustainability Agenda (UN, 2015), and the rapid deterioration of the environment (IPCC, 2023; Goldberg & Reed, 2023; WEF, 2024).

International working frameworks defined by bilateralism and protectionism must closely examine present economic models focusing on consumption and resource extraction and their associated externalities. When these models are shown to not work with the UN's 2030 Sustainability Agenda, they call into question the foundations of our global economy and discussions underlining the significance of inclusion and integration. Either how sustainability is used and built into market-based economies or its basic ideas are at the heart of the problem. On the other hand, by ignoring consumption-based models from the discussions, we engage in what becomes an oversimplistic exercise as we confront our global economy and its foundations. The need to have a more in-depth conversation is critical to help us better understand what parts can be changed or improved to fit with sustainable ideas and the urgent need for change. The Agenda for Sustainable Development has been identified as over-ambitious, making it hard to measure and keep track of progress and adding complexities when defining specific plans that drive actions that contribute to meaningful change. At this point, it is vital to take advantage of emerging opportunities that can help to reconsider how technology, innovation, and human talent can contribute to the development of a socio-economic and environmental model that works for all (Naidu & Sanchez, 2021; Weiland et al., 2021; Issever Grochová & Litzman, 2021).

The differences between the world's most advanced economies and how they engage with their industrial transformation is another aspect that needs to be carefully considered. Some researchers and economic experts are engaged in debates that support the idea of degrowth, wealth distribution, and economic models that slow down and become more inclusive. To some extent, the sustainability agenda and the environmental pressures seeking to preserve the environment do not align with countries' economic needs. We argue on the necessity of moving away from wishful thinking and taking a more pragmatic approach that integrates an economic assessment of the feasibility of the UN Sustainability Agenda due to its potential disconnection from the reality of our contemporary society. Degrowth, wealth sharing, redistribution of natural resources, equity, equality, inclusion, integration, and diversity represent a significant challenge due to their economic, political, and financial unfeasibility as we reflect on existing and alternative economic models and what is being proposed where the economic and financial costs are neglected (Raworth, 2017). The global financial architecture is dysfunctional, and the financing of the development agenda emerges as an insurmountable task (DESA, 2024). The United Nations 2030 Agenda and its 17 Sustainable Development Goals (UN, 2015) were presented in 2015 as the continuation of the 8 Millennium Development Goals (MDGs), which aimed to address issues related to 1) extreme poverty rates, 2) achieve universal primary education, 3) promote gender equality and empower women, 4) reduce child mortality, 5) improve maternal health, 6) combat the spread of HIV/AIDS, Malaria and other diseases, 7) ensure environmental sustainability, and 8) promote global partnership for development with a target date 2015. The 17 Sustainable Development Goals were presented as a plan of action that seeks "*to leave no one behind*" that supports people, the planet, and prosperity. Unfortunately, we are confronted with a stark reality: the world did not manage to commit to the MDGs, and the 17 SDGs are materialising as a very ambitious and unfeasible agenda as financial sources, inadequate policies to drive change, and the assessment of the economic costs associated with the agenda where overlooked. According to the United Nations 2023 report on progress, we are failing in most of the identified objectives and targets. This is an expected outcome due to the significant economic and financial challenges presented by a very ambitious agenda that requires the world economies' collaboration and a joint action plan. However, global economic development is defined by slow progress and a lack of collaboration and cooperation at the global level, which are compounded by economic and financial limitations that are creating growing imbalances and exacerbating growing levels of conflict, violence, and isolation. The financing agenda is not in alignment with the promise of the Addis Ababa Action Agenda (UN, 2015) that was endorsed in July 2015. Debt levels affecting less developed economies prevent economic progress, which, combined with a significant failure of the 2030 Sustainability Agenda and the SDGs, jeopardise the prospects for sustainable and inclusive global economic development. Undoubtedly, the architecture of existing global economic, political, and financial systems needs to be reconsidered to enable progress (WBG, 2019; UN, 2021; OECD, 2023).

Similarly, the global financial system looks like a picture full of possibilities and problems when seen through the eyes of developing economies. Limits on international finance, reliance on foreign aid, and high levels of public debt add significant complexity and present a bleak picture that is hard to overcome and the world's less developed economies need to become economically independent and grow over the long run if we seek to make a realistic contribution to the global sustainable economic model. Also, the poorest economies depend on informal parts of the economy that might not work well with formal ways of managing economic and financial resources. To create a financial system that works for everyone, we need to carefully look at the rules that guide foreign currency and make sure that they consider the problems that developing countries face. For example, mobile money and other digital financial services have made it much easier for people all over Africa to use official financial services. However, the risks associated with the development of the

FinTech sector also need to be considered as they can lead to additional challenges due to the current vacuum of regulations (Kaponda & Tembo, 2018). Furthermore, poor economies are very diverse and different, significantly questioning the idea that a global economic and financial system designed as a one-size-fits-all method will work. The international reality is defined by countries' different levels of growth, government structures, and economic needs across countries, regions, and continents. As such, it is essential to push for more nuanced and situation-specific socio-economic, financial, and environmental policies that are cognisant of the international landscape complexities. The global financial infrastructure needs to be changed if it seeks to support economic goals and long-term plans better. To reach this goal, global organisations need to help build regional economic communities and encourage investments in businesses and facilities that are accountable and that operate within working frameworks that respect the three Sustainability Pillars: Economic, Social and Environmental. Therefore, there is a need to explore the value of developing and integrating more regional and customised solutions and to re-evaluate the link between different countries and existing global financial institutions (Balasubramanian et al., 2021; Palmieri et al., 2022)

Dated Global Economic and Financial Systems

Global economic and financial systems are dated, and the Global South remains isolated and marginalised. According to the Finance for Sustainable Development Report (DESA, 2024), estimates by international organisations and others are coalescing around $4 trillion in additional investment needed annually for developing countries. Less developed economies' access to financial resources and their management needs to be subject to scrutiny as countries are facing different challenges, including the lack of fair access to international funding sources or the global market driven by higher levels of risk associated with countries affected by high levels of corruption, weak institutions and quite frequently growing levels of political uncertainty, social unrest, and heightened conflict. Risk elements The world's less developed economies face major challenges to be able to the funds needed for sustainable development projects, and alternatives are needed (Atkinson, 2020; Quiroga-Garza et al., 2022). The 2030 Sustainability Agenda is defined by its lack of progress, the worsening of existing problems, and the rise of new challenges. Unfortunately, the agenda for sustainable development has emerged as a very complex and overambitious agenda that is being defined by nations' inability to cooperate and coordinate a feasible plan of action, as by 2023, progress is defined as being "*weak and insufficient*" (United Nations, 2023a). Worldwide, the economic and political landscape presents a bleak picture as the 2020 decade is being defined by a convoluted economic and political landscape that started with the Global Health Crisis due to the COVID-19 pandemic. Global instability is on the rise as a result of the war in Ukraine, Israel's war against Hamas, increasing levels of polarisation and radicalisation, hate speech, rise in populism, undermining of democracy and its pillars, discrimination and marginalisation, which are identified as critical threats, to name just a few. The consolidation of existing conflicts and emerging new ones are signalling the steady deterioration of the global economic and social outlook due to rising levels of uncertainty and conflict that put forward systemic risks and weaknesses that question the implementation of the 17 Goals and its 169 targets. The available data and estimates present a sobering picture, as approximately 140 targets are affected by deviation from the desired trajectory. Over 30% of the targets have experienced no progress or regression below the 2015 baseline (United Nations, 2023a). Furthermore, the United Nations Secretary-General Antonio Guterres has said:

> "Halfway to the deadline for the 2030 Agenda, we are leaving more than half the world behind. We have stalled or gone into reverse on more than 30 percent of the SDGs"[.....] "Unless we act now, the 2030 Agenda will become an epitaph for a world that might have been".
>
> (UN, Press Release, 2023)

The world economy, guided by global leaders, is not progressing as expected. Countries need help finding a way to collaborate and identify models that enable sustainable development. Economic and financial principles dominate discussions while the planet's ecosystems continue their unstoppable erosion, paving the way for a potential human-self-inflicted destruction. We argue about the importance of education and the role that it can play in helping us understand the urgent need for change and the importance of supporting businesses and society through the sustainability transition. Our understanding of education and research activity and how they are integrated into learning environments are aspects that require questioning and active debate. At present, the educational system separates elements of learning processes where it is quite common to face a differentiation between learning, teaching, and research. Within the context of this chapter, we are challenging the idea of research being separated from the learning process. We argue for the need to consider education from a holistic perspective that considers the humanistic dimension carefully. As such, education emerges as an umbrella that integrates learners, where learners' roles are interchangeable as they engage in the process of remembering, understanding, applying, analysing, creating, and evaluating, as understood by Blooms' taxonomy and later reviewed in 2003 by Anderson (Bloom & Krathwohl, 1956; Anderson & Krathwohl, 2001). The learning process is being redefined by the concept of Circular Pedagogy introduced by Morales et al. (2022), which supports a continuous and evolving learning process that does not separate learning, teaching, and research activity. Through education, we can start a discussion that provides an alternative to existing economic models, and that enables a transition towards a knowledge economy that can support economic growth and development by shifting from existing dominant trends that are exhausting the planet's natural resources and increasing imbalances as a result of differentiation between the world most advanced economies and those that are understood to be emerging or less developed, what has led to a differentiation between the wealthiest Global North and the poorest Global South (Braun-Munzinger & Zuell, 2023; IE University, 2020, UNESCO, 2021). As we reflect further on the required changes, we consider that initial steps need to assess and evaluate existing educational models and the potential need for a new educational model or alternatives that promote the interchangeable roles of the educator, researcher, and learner (Morales et al., 2022; Pop et al., 2022). The role of the teacher and the student needs to be reconsidered, and to which extent an educator and learner dimension can contribute to a deeper understanding of learning complexities that require the integration and redefinition of the meaning of research activity and how it becomes part of the learning process. At this point, Jacques Delors's report is identified as significant and more relevant than when it was introduced in 1996. Almost forgotten, the report highlights the need and the importance of education for a "*global village*" based on four pillars of fundamental personal and social development: learning to be, learning to know, learning to do, and learning to live together in order to make the stringent transition from highly inequitable economic growth to human development in a common and shared future beyond all the tensions that emerge as a result of the dominance of economic and political agendas cemented on the principles of the market-driven economy and that need to be overcome as the sustainability agenda is considered (Delors et al., 1996; UN, 2015; UNESCO, 2016; UNESCO, 2023).

The Challenges of Sustainable and Inclusive Development

Solving the challenges highlighted in the Sustainable Development Goals (SDGs) requires embracing inclusive and sustainable economic growth. As we strive for the SDGs wealthier nations find themselves at having competitive advantages in harnessing the necessary capital for sustainable development, despite the challenges posed by geopolitical contention and economic volatility. We cannot ignore that rich countries usually have the required resources to keep investing in growth-oriented programmes or even increase them during times of global conflict while still ensuring they have enough funds for defence and security. Even if there are government problems in a country, investors may still risk their capital as they perceive the political and economic stability of the country as being solid and offering perspective for long-term gains. Furthermore, when faced with global economic outlooks that are unstable, wealthy countries are better able to navigate problems and recover at faster rates than less developed economies as they often get access to needed resources and required support as they are perceived as having lower levels of risk (Lashitew et al., 2020, Al-Roubaie et al., 2020). On the other hand, poor countries have a high level of dependency on foreign aid to help grow their economies. Wealthier nations' ability to address the impact of diverse shocks and crises underscores the uneven playing field in achieving the SDGs and highlights the crucial need for international support and cooperation to ensure equitable progress for all countries (Kondratenko, 2020; Fedirko & Gamkrelidze, 2023).

Nevertheless, the current development model has led to increased inequalities and placed more strain on natural resources, worsening biodiversity loss, climate change, and social conflicts (Herrmann, 2024). Therefore, it is suggested that sustainable development can only be achieved through sector integration, centering on people; inclusive economic growth, equity, and social development are also deemed critical for the preservation of ecosystem goods and services, but they are quite questionable within a global economic system that is defined, designed and directed by the world's most affluent economies located in the Global North in detriment of those that are less developed and that are located in the poorest Global South (United Nations 2012). The world economy is defined by persistent poverty levels and increasing inequalities. As a result, to accomplish the 2030 Agenda for Sustainable Development and the goals of SDG 1 (No Poverty) and SDG 10 (Reduced Inequalities), it is essential to address the ongoing poverty and inequality issues at both national and international levels worldwide, while being mindful of domestic imbalances affecting nations. According to the World Bank's recent report (World Bank, 2024), nearly half of the world's population is still suffering from extreme poverty, as the global number of individuals living in extreme poverty reached 712 million in 2022, marking an increase of 23 million people since 2019 (World Bank, 2024). The widespread inequality, political instability, recent conflicts, the climate crisis, the COVID-19 pandemic, a series of major shocks during 2020–2022, and the rising cost of living hindered the global poverty reduction process, has reversed decades of progress and threatens less developed economies ability to provide their populations with basic needs of food, shelter, sanitation, and education (Global Multidimensional Poverty Index Report, 2023; Yu and Huang, 2021).

Achieving poverty eradication involves addressing its various dimensions, including promoting more equitable access to healthcare, education, essential infrastructure and services, and digital technology. Crespo Cuaresma et al. (2018) examined the connection between the SDGs and the upcoming poverty trends in 188 countries and territories, representing 99.7% of the global population. Their research findings indicate that achieving the first goal of the SDGs – No Poverty – will be challenging without the additional development of policy measures. The authors highlight the need to invest in education in Eastern African countries such as the Democratic Republic of Congo, Kenya, Mozambique, and Tanzania as examples of countries with serious needs to grow and develop and where education is expected to play a crucial role in their ability to be able to progress. In contrast to poverty, inequality is concerned with differences in economics or social status among individuals or groups. The inability to address extreme inequalities across economic, social, political, and environmental aspects will consistently hinder the attainment of sustainable development and social cohesion (World Bank, 2024). The United Nations Sustainable Development Goals (SDG 10) emphasise the importance of addressing inequality within countries and globally and is intricately intertwined with the broader

2030 Agenda, particularly the targets aimed at eliminating poverty (SDG 1), achieving good health and well-being (SDG 3), ensuring quality education (SDG 4), supporting gender equality (SDG 5), securing clean water and sanitation (SDG 6), and ensuring affordable and clean energy (SDG 7), supporting the growth of decent work and economy (SDG 8), building resilient infrastructures and promoting inclusive industrialisation (SDG 9), enhancing inclusivity in cities (SDG 11), and ensuring the sustainability of ecosystems (SDG 15) (United Nations, 2024; European Commission, 2024; Gharleghi & Jahanshahi, 2020). Although there has been a reduction in inequalities among countries over the past decades, the 2020 Global Health Crisis contributed to reversing achieved progress and revealing new trends highlighting domestic imbalances, particularly in emerging economies where income inequality has increased by 11%, and the situation is deteriorating in the Middle East, as reported by the United Nations (Li et al., 2023; United Nations, 2023). Reducing income and gender inequality is identified as an important step towards a sustainable future and Inclusive Development (Madi et al., 2023; Azcona & Bhatt, 2020).

We identify the global socio-economic transition and its connection to educational systems as vital if we seek to contribute to developing a global society capable of navigating and addressing growing levels of conflict and lack of caring and support towards more vulnerable societies (Pop et al., 2022). The relationship between educational systems and socioeconomic transformations emerges as crucial but becomes much more complex in the Global South that cannot secure resources to cover its population's basic needs. What may be disregarded is the fact that educational changes, although vital to address long-standing social inequalities, cannot be solved by education alone, and the economic and financial elements need to be carefully integrated as part of the discussion. Unequal investment flows and commercial linkages impact education in many regions of the world's poorest countries. In light of the often-limited governmental capacity and resources that define the socio-political landscapes of these countries, an objective perspective should also challenge the ability of educational institutions to address and ultimately eradicate these pervasive inequities (Gnangnon, 2020). According to Salamatov et al. (2019), poverty levels are increasing, hunger is becoming more widespread, and the population in developing countries, which are already densely populated, is growing. Numerous studies indicate that families with higher socioeconomic resources tend to create more favourable learning environments for their children through superior material and social support, in contrast to families with lower socioeconomic status, and that provides the foundation to keep enhancing a divided global society between the most developed and affluent economies and the poorest ones (Burger, 2023; Amgalan et al., 2021; Fergusson et al., 2008). Poverty levels and social detachment are closely linked to fragile societies that are affected by violent and persistent conflicts. Sustainability and security are often connected through the framework of human security, which plays a significant role in the Sustainable Development Goals (SDG 16). However, the links between human security and violent conflict have become increasingly evident among researchers as they feature prominently in the

SDGs. The concept of human security, as defined by the United Nations Development Program (2006), means protecting individuals from all forms of threats, whether violent or non-violent, ensuring their rights to safety, which food, water, and environmental and human security. Nguyen et al. (2023) analysed the impact of geopolitical conflicts on SDGs, their study found that rising geopolitical risks may hinder the advancement of sustainable development goals. Korotayev et al. (2019) studied the impact of wars and conflicts on economic growth and education, and they found that the rise of economic inequality and unemployment, combined with the resistance of traditional groups to societal shifts, may trigger a rise in terrorist violence within developed countries. The Arab Spring revolution is identified as an example where the rise in terrorist attacks and protests in Arab nations, along with the spread of social populism, separatist movements, and unexplained outbreaks of mass violence, led to an increase in poverty, inequalities, corruption, and negatively affected the health and education system (Madi et al., 2023; Korotayev et al., 2019). Finally, some studies look particularly at the impacts of conflict on education. Lai and Thyne (2007) studied the influence of conflict on education, examining two distinct pathways: the first being that a country's education system can be destroyed by civil conflict by causing the loss of personnel and infrastructure; the second issue involves shifting resources from education to support military spending, while they found strong evidence on the first claim only by showing a decrease in both spending and student enrolment during times of conflict. In light of the poorest developing nations, the aforementioned effects of civil conflicts are more complicated in the global south because of its unique culture and society. It is crucial that research studies not only look at the loss of infrastructure and people resources but also the effect on students' culture and mental health. The suggested educational models need to be carefully examined to see how well they take into account and integrate different teachings and language practices from the Global South. How these plans are supposed to include and protect local knowledge while also meeting the needs of globalisation (Cindi, 2021). On the other hand, Pop & Morales (2023) investigate the relationships among global crises, geoeconomic factors, and geopolitical elements, and the requirement for a revised educational framework, suggesting that education is the fundamental building block for fostering inclusive, fair, and resilient societies, empowering individuals with the necessary skills to address conflicts and power disparities through a collaborative and proactive approach to promote inclusivity. Therefore, the assessment of the reviewed literature and consideration of economic and political agendas point out towards educational systems as being essential to support economic, political, and business leaders as they seek to integrate innovation, social inclusion, and environmental respect and accountability as part of their decision-making processes, which will lead to improved health, well-being, and economic development opportunities (Coetzer et al., 2023).

Therefore, education is essential to help address the causes of war, such as resource scarcity and foreign geopolitical interests, and advance national economic and political agendas and human security. This begs the question of how much weight people from the world's most advanced economies give to each other's perspectives in particular to which extent the contributions made by the Global South are taken into consideration and that are not primarily based and dominated on Western notions of growth and security. Since disputes in developing nations are typically sparked by competing demands for control over other nations' geopolitical interests and a shortage of resources, it is essential to exercise caution while discussing human security and sustainable development during times of war. We contend that these connections necessitate more examination to guarantee that they incorporate the perspectives and realities of individuals residing in the Global South. Investigating local value systems and alternative approaches to peace and security that do not include Western ideas is in keeping with this principle. Another element that requires further reflection and insights is whether or not the solutions proposed by Western diplomats adequately incorporate local methods of conflict resolution and development promotion or if they are mostly based on Western assumptions about security. As a result, methods of conflict resolution must evolve to bring opposing viewpoints into a more balanced dialogue that does not disregard local knowledge and practices (Van, 2019; Chaggu, 2023).

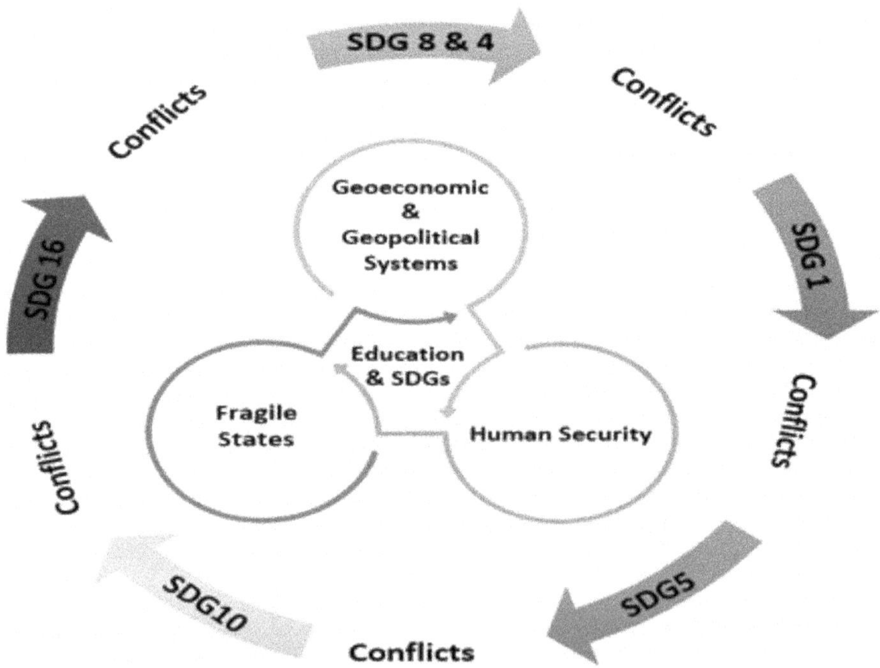

Figure 10.1 Geoeconomic and Geopolitical Systems and the SDGs.

Source: Authors (2024; Adapted from Pop & Morales; 2023; and Coetzer et al., 2023).

The future of our global society requires careful consideration of the sustainability agenda and the challenges associated with growing levels of uncertainty within the geopolitical and geoeconomic systems that connect to fragile states and affect human security, as illustrated in Figure 10.2. Global socio-economic systems face paramount challenges, and among them, we identify the gap between existing educational models and the need to provide more dynamic learning environments connected to the realities of contemporary society where economic growth and education represented by SDG 8 and SDG 4 become foundational pillars to drive change. In this context, technology and innovation emerge as catalysts for a significant transformation in education, capable of creating more engaging and immersive experiences essential for the development of critical and analytical skills necessary to thrive in the digital era and the knowledge economy (Abuhassna et al., 2020). In this scenario of urgent changes, developing critical, analytical, and forward-thinking skills to support a vision of the future through sharing knowledge aided by co-creation becomes crucial in collaborative educational environments that encourage the active and proactive participation of students/learners (Atenas et al., 2020). It is essential to rethink conventional notions of growth and development to move towards a more sustainable and inclusive economic model. This requires a review of the metrics used to assess economic progress

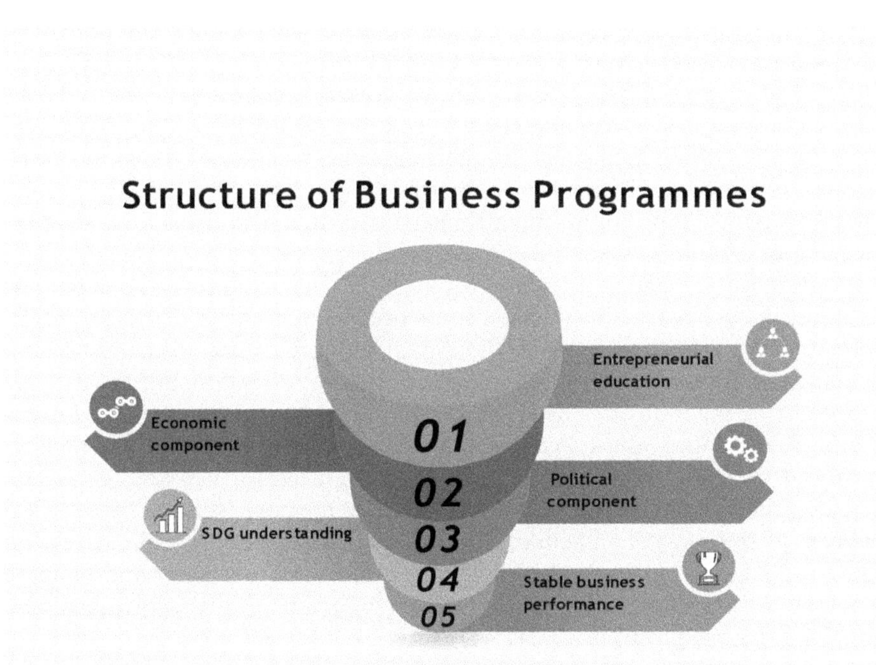

Figure 10.2 Business Education in the Global Political Economy.

Source: Authors (2024).

and a redefinition of the role of education, technology, and innovation in promoting viable alternatives. However, the challenges are not restricted to the field of education. Increasing environmental degradation, increasing social isolation, and the prevalence of individualism and competition reflect the failures of economic and political systems to address the complexities of modern society. Furthermore, it is necessary to consider how educational policies can be reshaped to promote a more holistic understanding of development, incorporating sustainability principles and social responsibility (Ruggerio, 2021).

Business Education and the International Political Economy

Sustainability challenges outlined in the 2030 Agenda demand a high level of knowledge and understanding of the complexities associated with businesses working agendas, as well as the maximisation of wealth and profit generation goals. The alignment of business aims and goals and the conflicting nature of the sustainable goals and their implementation directly impact the functioning of businesses. When comparing small and medium enterprises, microbusinesses and start-ups with large corporations, there is a clear differentiation as, in most cases, small businesses are unable to access the required financial resources to support their activities and have significant limitations in accessing the required human talent and to provide training programmes seeking to skill and upskill workers. Due to their representation and employment capacity, SMEs are essential to every economy as growth and development drivers. They are critical of transitioning to a more sustainable economic model (OECD, 2023). However, SMEs are immersed in complex dynamics as they experience difficulties accessing finance due to their high-risk profiles. At the global level, reports from the OECD throughout their SME and Entrepreneurship Outlook (2023) recognise innovation, management, and digital skills as a catalyst for sustainable economic development, as well as knowledge, data, networks and understanding of foreign markets. However, the financial needs and economic pressures associated with the green transition, digitalisation of working contexts and the transition towards the digital economy through the needs and demands of Industry 4.0 and 5.0 require different policy frameworks that are cognisant of the industry's needs and required competencies, skills and capabilities to drive and adjust to change. For example, the use of AI in manufacturing processes automates tasks and raises the need for workers to be data literate. Small business owners may not have had formal education, so a critical analysis of the support and educational systems required to help them develop these skills could clarify how policy can lessen these obstacles and increase the long-term sustainability of these companies in the fast-evolving digital economy (Dogan & Birant, 2021).

It is essential to consider that most small business owners are "self-made" individuals; they do not enrol in university programmes, benefiting instead from high contextual experience and learning by doing within changing and continuously evolving working systems as they confront the reality of the market economy (Olson et al., 2008; Storey, 2011; Kindström et al., 2022). Entrepreneurs need a basic understanding of complex economic processes and unpredictable political systems to navigate an ever-changing global business environment. However, business education seems to be detached from the global economic reality and its complexity as most educational programmes seem to be focused on finding innovative ideas, writing business plans, and venture starts, creating a critical disconnection between college studies and required skills by real business that is attuned with a myriad of challenges, which leads to a high level of small companies' fail rates, especially at the early stages of their life cycles (Fatoki, 2010; Katundu & Gabagambi, 2016; Iwu et al., 2021). Entrepreneurs, policymakers, and higher institutions poorly recognise the complexity of the problem, as the main concern focuses on leadership or management training and how to write funding applications that become more complex when looking at the global economy and the interconnection between the economic and political systems that contribute to creating uncertainty and risks that affect the operations of businesses and their survival. To constructively address this gap, we need to examine how well experiential learning prepares future business owners for the actual world. The integration of real-world experience into the academic curriculum might be accelerated by collaborations between academic institutions and businesses. Additionally, to better align educational programmes with the real-world demands of companies, decrease educational disconnection, and enhance the effectiveness of entrepreneurial endeavours, it would be helpful to conduct a critical review of the present status of academic research in entrepreneurship and determine whether it adequately represents the ever-changing nature of the market (Norris, 2021; Andriole, 2023).

The importance of understanding the international political economy and its effects on businesses cannot be underestimated, as in order to enable a transformation and transition from existing economic and business practices, there is a need to understand the associated dimension of the global economy and its spillover effects towards industry (Mopelola et al., 2024). Education and its connection to economic development put forward the need to connect industry with an understanding of required analytical skills, critical thinking abilities and problem-solving competencies. Businesses operational context is connected to the proposed idea of a more holistic approach towards training and educational programmes that facilitate the development of working environments that are more diverse and that integrate a multidimensional and multifaceted approach towards discipline-specific and expert knowledge. Businesses need to be able to assess and evaluate their operations within a forward and future-thinking strategic plan, which allows for evaluating the consequences of decision-making processes in uncertain, evolving, and unpredictable environments. Moreover, businesses need to understand the political landscape and its impact on their operations to be able to make more accurate decisions and predict trends (Hmieleski and Lerner, 2016; Sun, 2020; Yang, 2020; Zhao & Zhang, 2021). A more realistic approach towards business education that is connected to geoeconomic and geopolitical dynamics is becoming increasingly essential due to the impact of wars, rising levels of conflict and uncertainty, and the complexities associated with international capital markets and capital flows. Growing levels of conflict and uncertainty from their multidimensional levels directly impact global value chains. The efficient management of supply chains provokes delays for importing and exporting companies, and their spill-over effects affect consumers due to price increases and shortages of needed goods and services. Thus, we argue for the need to rethink business education, which requires the integration of economic and political studies that should become integrated layers in business studies, as represented in Figure 10.1. The transition towards a more sustainable economic model requires a change in business education and training aiming to provide a pipeline of qualified and equipped business leaders and entrepreneurs capable of navigating the complexities and challenges posed by the global economy while providing a leadership role within their communities.

By embedding economic and political components in business education, it would be possible to guide business leaders and entrepreneurs in the best, most optimal, and efficient practices to navigate the SDG agenda, giving them a comprehensive understanding of what needs to be done and providing realistic cost-gain guidelines and projections on needed changes that can help on the implementation of required changes while acknowledging the need for investment and allocation of financial resources which are identified as scarce. We argue that business education should be reassessed from economic and political dimensions, as existing educational models are not attuned to societal, environmental, political, and economic demands. Additionally, prioritising which sustainable development goals entrepreneurs should address might appear to be an outstanding challenge (Kuhlmann and Rip, 2018; Ciarli and Ràfols, 2019; Confraria et al., 2024) due to the lack of clear guidelines, policies, and procedures. However, any SDG implementation demands enormous financial resources, unintentionally putting economic growth (goal 8) as a top priority. Therefore, the focus on economic growth might have contradicting results, encouraging entrepreneurs to sacrifice all other intentions to maximise their profits and wealth creation. Thus, education and its critical role in addressing potential misunderstandings regarding the role played by businesses as part of the sustainability transition requires further thinking.

AI Perspectives on Geoeconomic and Geopolitical Challenges in Education

Integrating AI and data analytics into educational frameworks is crucial for addressing many of the shortcomings of current educational models. AI technologies offer unprecedented opportunities to personalise learning experiences, catering to individual student needs and learning paces. Adaptive learning systems powered by AI analyse real-time performance data to adjust content delivery dynamically. This personalisation can significantly enhance student engagement and learning outcomes, as seen in the work of Chin et al. (2010)

and Matsuda et al. (2020), who found that teachable agents (TAs) effectively promoted learning among elementary students. However, these systems also pose significant challenges, including ensuring data privacy, mitigating biases in AI algorithms, and integrating these technologies across diverse educational contexts without exacerbating existing inequalities (Kabudi et al., 2021). The practical implementation of AI in education often needs to catch up to its theoretical potential, highlighting the need for more empirical studies focusing on AI technologies in authentic teaching and learning settings (Kabudi et al., 2021).

Integrating AI in education holds promise for addressing the digital divide, a significant challenge in our educational landscape. AI can play a crucial role in bridging this gap by identifying regions most affected by digital exclusion and developing targeted interventions to promote digital inclusion and accessibility. However, it is essential to acknowledge that disparities in access to technology and the internet remain significant barriers (Zhang & Aslan, 2021). In order to overcome these barriers, AI technologies should be developed to create low-bandwidth solutions and affordable technologies to ensure equitable access. Studies by Gomede et al. (2020) and Fryer et al. (2017) emphasise the importance of inclusivity in AI applications, suggesting that AI could potentially bridge the existing educational disparities with careful implementation. This potential of AI to level the playing field in education should instil hope in our audience about the future of education, particularly in terms of promoting social equity. Further aspects that can be considered related to the ability of AI to process vast amounts of data that can revolutionise data-driven decision-making in education. Predictive analytics can help educational institutions identify at-risk students and tailor interventions to support their success, improving retention rates and educational outcomes. However, implementing robust data analytics frameworks requires significant investment in infrastructure and training for educators to interpret and act on data insights effectively. Educators must develop new skills, including data and digital literacy and the ability to interpret AI-generated insights, to fully harness AI's potential in education. Moreover, interdisciplinary and transdisciplinary collaborations are essential to bridge the gap between AI technological innovations and their practical educational applications.

AI can support the development of critical thinking, forward-thinking, and analytical skills essential for navigating the digital age and in alignment with the UN 2.0 Quintet for Change (UN, 2023a; 2023b). Educational models should integrate these skills into the curriculum to prepare students for the knowledge-based economy (Gulz et al., 2020). Encouraging interdisciplinary and transdisciplinary learning environments can foster a broader understanding of complex global challenges and support the development of innovative solutions (Flogie & Abersek, 2015). Research by Chin et al. (2010) and Tarning et al. (2019) indicates that intelligent tutoring systems and teachable agents can enhance students' critical thinking and problem-solving skills. Furthermore, AI can play a crucial role in environmental education by providing real-time data on ecological impacts and helping students understand the importance of sustainability, where educational programmes could emphasise the role of AI in addressing environmental challenges (Hwang et al., 2020). Additionally, AI can facilitate social cohesion by promoting inclusive and equitable education. We argue for the need for efforts that focus on using AI to enhance access to education for marginalised groups and foster a more inclusive learning environment (Keshav et al., 2017). The integration of AI in educational settings must be managed carefully to ensure that it aligns with broader geoeconomic and geopolitical goals, promoting sustainability and social equity. Learning and development opportunities emerge as a result of recent advancements in AI, particularly with large language models (LLMs) like ChatGPT, Explainable AI (XAI), and Generative AI (GenAI), heralding a new era in education. LLMs are AI models trained on large amounts of text data and can generate human-like responses. With their ability to provide personalised tutoring, real-time feedback, and comprehensive support, these technologies are poised to revolutionise educational outcomes. For instance, ChatGPT can serve as a personal tutor, offering explanations and guiding students through complex topics at their own pace, thus bridging gaps in understanding and catering to diverse learning needs. By facilitating interactive and engaging learning experiences, LLMs can make education more enjoyable and effective, simulating conversations with historical figures, providing immersive language learning experiences, and creating interactive problem-solving scenarios.

Moreover, these models provide round-the-clock support, enabling students to access help whenever needed, which is particularly beneficial for remote or self-paced learners. Additionally, XAI makes AI decision-making processes transparent, increasing trust and adoption among educators and students by making AI systems' decisions understandable and mitigating biases. Students can benefit from understanding the reasoning behind AI-generated feedback or recommendations, which can enhance their critical thinking and analytical skills. GenAI supports education by generating customised learning materials, creating realistic simulations, and fostering creativity through gamified learning environments and creative projects. These advancements in AIEd promise a future where education is more accessible, personalised, and effective than ever before.

Integrating AI into educational frameworks offers significant potential to address current educational challenges and enhance learning outcomes. However, it is crucial to underscore that careful management must accompany this integration to ensure equity, ethical use, and alignment with broader geoeconomic and geopolitical goals. Ethical considerations, including data privacy, consent, and transparency, are not just important; they are paramount. This necessitates the establishment of robust frameworks and policies to protect students' rights and data (Reiss, 2021). Educators need comprehensive training to effectively integrate AI tools into their teaching practices, understand AI systems, and address ethical and practical issues that may arise (Zawacki-Richter et al., 2019). Continuous research and development, involving longitudinal studies and interdisciplinary collaborations, are essential to refine AI technologies and maximise their benefits in educational settings.

By addressing these challenges and leveraging AI's capabilities, educational systems can better prepare students to navigate and thrive in an increasingly complex and interconnected world. The advancement of AI in education (AIEd) necessitates critical initiatives to address AI ethics and privacy concerns. It requires interdisciplinary and transdisciplinary collaborations in large-scale, longitudinal research and development efforts (Zhang & Aslan, 2021). This emphasis on ethics and responsible use of AI in education should reassure our audience about the commitment to their student's well-being and privacy, fostering confidence in the responsible use of AI in education.

Conclusion

The challenges of sustainable and inclusive development require a broad and heterogeneous approach that addresses economic, social, and environmental issues in an integrated way, as observed by Dörffel and Schuhmann (2022). The current scenario of tragedies sponsored by human action can only be reversed through a collective commitment to innovation, collaboration, and a global compromise to support the needed economic paradigm shift. This radical turnaround in thoughts and attitudes could allow us to aspire to a future where economic growth is in harmony with human well-being and environmental preservation (Rockström et al., 2024). Such a bleak picture has been fostered and sustained by the relentless pursuit of economic growth as a predominant feature of global policies, often at the expense of the environment and the social well-being of vulnerable communities. It is observed that traditional growth metrics, such as Gross Domestic Product (GDP), do not take into account associated environmental and social costs, highlighting the urgent need to rethink the predominant economic models (Rose, 2020). Furthermore, the disparity between the Global North and Global South in terms of access to financial resources and economic progress highlights the need for more equitable approaches to sustainable and inclusive economic development (Müller, 2018). In this context, bold proposals emerge, such as the idea of transitioning to a phase of zero growth or even economic degrowth. However, such proposals raise complex issues and require careful debate. While economic growth is widely considered to be a driver of progress, development, and prosperity, it is critical to question the extent to which the current growth paradigm based on consumption and competition is sustainable in the long term (Priewe, 2022). Alternatively, within the history of economic thought itself, we have more promising models to face this reality of chaos that have been created by ourselves. For example, the concept of "*creative destruction*" proposed by Schumpeter and Swedberg (2013) can provide a starting point for rethinking economic and business models that prioritise sustainability over growth at any cost (Mavi, 2024). Schumpeter's "*creative destruction*" can be associated with a logic of "*adaptive resilience*" by redefining the traditional economic models, which seek profit and wealth maximisation, to incorporate urgent environmental and social considerations within a complex and ever-evolving geoeconomic and geopolitical landscape that requires a paradigm shift that facilitates the discussions and debate on how to advance and design alternative growth models (McClure et al., 2023). The future of the global economy is associated with our ability to redesign and redefine the educational sector and its systems. There is a need to engage in a comprehensive understanding and assessment of economic and political challenges to help us identify the required skills and capabilities that our global society needs to navigate growing levels of uncertainty and risk within proactive, collaborative, and knowledge exchange driving learning environments.

Note

1 *GDP=Gross Domestic Product; C= Consumption, I=Investment; G=Government Expenditure; X=Exports; M=Imports.

Bibliography

Abuhassna, H., Al-Rahmi, W. M., Yahya, N., Zakaria, M. A. Z. M., Kosnin, A. Bt. M., & Darwish, M. (2020). Development of a new model on utilising online learning platforms to improve students' academic achievements and satisfaction. *International Journal of Educational Technology in Higher Education*, *17*(1), 38. https://doi.org/10.1186/s41239-020-00216-z

Al-Roubaie, A., Hamdan, A., & Sarea, A. (2020). Economic Diversification in a Digital Economy, 665–671. https://doi.org/10.1007/978-3-030-44289-7_62

Amgalan, N., Shin, J.-S., Lee, S.-H., Badamdorj, O., Ravjir, O. and Yoon, H.B. (2021). The socio-economic transition and health professions education in Mongolia: a qualitative study. *Cost Effectiveness and Resource Allocation*, *19*(1). https://doi.org/10.1186/s12962-021-00269-5

Anderson, L.W., & Krathwohl, D.R. (2001). *A taxonomy for learning, teaching, and assessing, abridged edition*. Boston: Allyn & Bacon

Andriole, S. J. (2023). Case-based experiential/immersive learning for business problem-solving: a plan in progress. *Informing Science and IT Education Conference, 14*. https://doi.org/10.28945/5119

Arpaci, I. (2019). A hybrid modeling approach for predicting the educational use of mobile cloud computing services in higher education. *Computers in Human Behavior*, *90*, 181–187.

Atenas, J., Havemann, L., Neumann, J. and Stefanelli, C. (2020). *Open Education Policies: Guidelines for co-creation*. [online] oro.open.ac.uk. London: Open Education Policy Lab. Available at: https://oro.open.ac.uk/73769/ [Accessed 26 Feb. 2024].

Atkinson, C. (2020). Theme-based Book Review: The Global South and Complexity. *International Journal of Public Administration*, *44*, 699–704. https://doi.org/10.1080/01900692.2020.1744646

Azcona, G. and Bhatt, A. (2020). Inequality, gender, and sustainable development: measuring feminist progress. *Gender & Development*, *28*(2), 337–355. https://doi.org/10.1080/13552074.2020.1753390

Balasubramanian, S., Bounader, L., Bricco, M. J., & Vasilyev, D. (2021). *Is there a one-size-fits-all approach to inclusive growth? A case study analysis*. International Monetary Fund.

Barbier, E.B. (1999). Endogenous Growth and Natural Resource Scarcity. *Environmental and Resource Economics*, *14*(1), 51–74. https://doi.org/10.1023/a:1008389422019

Bhatia, V. & World Economic Forum (2023). *How to bridge Europe's digital divide*. [online] World Economic Forum. Available at: https://www.weforum.org/agenda/

2023/08/how-to-bridge-the-digital-divide-in-the-eu/#:~:text=In%202022%2C%20about%202.4%25%20of [Accessed 6 May 2024].

Bin-Nashwan, S., Hassan, M., & Muneeza, A. (2022). Russia–Ukraine conflict: 2030 Agenda for SDGs hangs in the balance. *International Journal of Ethics and Systems*. https://doi.org/10.1108/ijoes-06-2022-0136

Bloom, B.S. and Krathwohl, D. R. (1956). *Taxonomy of Educational Objectives: The Classification of Educational Goals, by a committee of college and university examiners*. Handbook I: Cognitive Domain. NY, NY: Longmans, Green

Bornstein, G., Krusell, P., & Rebelo, S. (2022). A World Equilibrium Model of the Oil Market. *The Review of Economic Studies*. https://doi.org/10.1093/restud/rdac019

Bozkurt, A. (2023). Generative artificial intelligence (AI) powered conversational educational agents: The inevitable paradigm shift. *Asian Journal of Distance Education*, *18*(1), 198–204.

Brandsen, T., Steen, T., & Verschuere, B. (2018). *Co-production and co-creation: engaging citizens in public services*. Abingdon, Oxon: Routledge.

Braun-Munzinger, Corinna, & Zuell, Patrick. (2023). *Beyond Growth? Alternative Models for Economic Development*. [online] Available at: https://www.giz.de/expertise/downloads/giz2023-en-BGR-7-chapter.pdf [Accessed 11 May 2024].

Burger, K. (2023). Revisiting the power of future expectations and educational path dependencies. *Current Perspectives on Aging and the Life Cycle*, *58*(58), 100581–100581. https://doi.org/10.1016/j.alcr.2023.100581

Calvin, K., Dasgupta, D., Gerhard Krinner, Mukherji, A., Thorne, P., Trisos, C.H., Romero, J., Aldunce, P., Barret, K., Blanco, G., William, Connors S., Denton, F., Diongue-Niang, A., Dodman, D., Matthias Garschagen, Geden, O., Hayward, B., Jones, C.D., & Jotzo, F. (2023). *IPCC, 2023: Climate Change 2023: Synthesis Report, Summary for Policymakers. Contribution of Working Groups I, II and III to the Sixth Assessment Report of the Intergovernmental Panel on Climate Change* [Core Writing Team, H. Lee and J. Romero (eds.)]. IPCC, Geneva, Switzerland. IPCC, 1–34(34), 1–34. https://doi.org/10.59327/ipcc/ar6-9789291691647.001

Can Askan Mavi (2024). Creative destruction vs destructive destruction: A Schumpeterian approach for adaptation and mitigation. *Mathematical Social Sciences*, *127*(127), 36–53. https://doi.org/10.1016/j.mathsocsci.2023.12.002

Chaggu, B. (2023). Comparison of the Western and Traditional African Methods of Conflict Resolution on the Example of International Criminal Tribunal of Rwanda (ICTR) and Gacaca Method in the Context of the 1994 Rwanda Genocide. *Historia i Polityka*, *51*(44), 73–85.

Chin, D. B., Dohmen, I. M., Cheng, B. H., Oppezzo, M. A., Chase, C. C., & Schwartz, D. L. (2010). Preparing students for future learning with teachable agents. *Educational Technology Research & Development*, *58*(6), 649–669.

Chui, K. T., Fung, D. C. L., Lytras, M. D., & Lam, T. M. (2020). Predicting at-risk university students in a virtual learning environment via a machine learning algorithm. *Computers in Human Behavior*, *107*, 105584.

Ciarli, T., & Ràfols, I. (2019). The relation between research priorities and societal demands: The case of rice. *Research Policy*, *48*(4), 949–967. https://doi.org/10.1016/j.respol.2018.10.027

Cindi, L. (2021). Incorporating African Indigenous Knowledge Systems into the Basic Education curriculum: Experiences from two schools in the Gauteng and KwaZulu-Natal Provinces, South Africa.

Coetzer, J.-H., Morales, L., Flynn, P., Pop, L., Barkoczi, N., Munteanu, S., et al. (2023). Enhancing Human Security by Transforming Education Through Science, Technology, and Innovations. *Cadmus Journal*, *5* (1). Available at: http://cadmusjournal.org/node/973

Confraria, H., Ciarli, T., & Noyons, E. (2024). Countries' research priorities in relation to the Sustainable Development Goals. *Research Policy*, *53*(3), 104950–104950. https://doi.org/10.1016/j.respol.2023.104950

Crespo Cuaresma, J., Fengler, W., Kharas, H., Bekhtiar, K., Brottrager, M., & Hofer, M. (2018). *Will the Sustainable Development Goals Be fulfilled? Assessing Present and Future Global Poverty*. Palgrave Communications, [online] *4*(1). https://doi.org/10.1057/s41599-018-0083-y

de Paulo Gewehr, L.L., & de Andrade Guerra, J.B.S.O. (2022). Geopolitics of hunger: Geopolitics, human security and fragile states. *Geoforum*, *137*(137), 88–93. https://doi.org/10.1016/j.geoforum.2022.10.015

DESA. (2024, April 9). *Financing for Sustainable Development Report 2024* | DESA Publications. Desapublications.un.org. https://desapublications.un.org/publications/financing-sustainable-development-report-2024

Delors et al. (1996). *Learning: the treasure within; report to UNESCO of the International Commission on Education for the Twenty-first Century (highlights)*. Available at: https://unesdoc.unesco.org/ark:/48223/pf0000109590

Dogan, A., & Birant, D. (2021). Machine learning and data mining in manufacturing. *Expert Systems With Applications*, *166*, 114060. https://doi.org/10.1016/J.ESWA.2020.114060

Dörffel, C., & Schuhmann, S. (2022). What is Inclusive Development? Introducing the Multidimensional Inclusiveness Index. *Social Indicators Research*, *163*(3). https://doi.org/10.1007/s11205-021-02860-y

EC (n.d.). *Reducing inequalities*. [online] international-partnerships.ec.europa.eu. Available at: https://international-partnerships.ec.europa.eu/policies/human-development/reducing-inequalities_en

European Commission. (2024). *Commission report shows how social investments and reforms can support competitiveness, economic growth and inclusion*. [online] Available at: https://ec.europa.eu/commission/presscorner/detail/en/ip_24_4744

Fatoki, O. O. (2010). Graduate entrepreneurial intention in South Africa: Motivations and obstacles. *International Journal of Business and Management*, *5*(9), 87–98.

Fedirko, N. & Gamkrelidze, K. (2023). The financial-economic mechanism of resolving the Russian-Ukrainian conflict. *Business Inform*, 2. 46–55. 10.32983/2222-4459-2023-2-46-55. *(PDF) Original Article Vol 5 |Issue 1 | 2024 Conflict*. Available from: https://www.researchgate.net/publication/385188537_Original_Article_Vol_5_Issue_1_2024_Conflict [accessed Nov 27 2024].

Fergusson, D.M., Horwood, L.J., & Boden, J.M. (2008). The transmission of social inequality: Examination of the linkages between family socio-economic status in childhood and educational achievement in young adulthood. *Research in Social Stratification and Mobility*, *26*(3), 277–295. https://doi.org/10.1016/j.rssm.2008.05.001

Field, S., Kuczera, M., & Pont, B. (2007). *No More Failures. Education and Training Policy*. OECD. https://doi.org/10.1787/9789264032606-en

Flogie, A., & Abersek, B. (2015). Transdisciplinary approach of science, technology, engineering and mathematics education. *Journal of Baltic Science Education*, *14*(6), 779–790.

Foster, J. B. (2023). Planned Degrowth: Ecosocialism and Sustainable Human Development. [online] *Monthly Review*, *75* (3), 1–29. Available at: https://monthlyreview.org/2023/07/01/planned-degrowth/

Fryer, L. K., Ainley, M., Thompson, A., Gibson, A., & Sherlock, Z. (2017). Stimulating and sustaining interest in a language course: An experimental comparison of chatbot and human task partners. Computers in Human Behavior, *75*, 461–468.

Gharleghi, B., & Jahanshahi, A. A. (2020). The shadow economy and sustainable development: The role of financial development. *Journal of Public Affairs*, *20*(3), e2099. https://doi.org/10.1002/pa.2099

Gnangnon, S. (2020). Does poverty deter foreign direct investment flows to developing countries?. *International Journal of Economic Policy Studies*, *16*, 297–330. https://doi.org/10.20944/preprints202011.0230.v1

Goldberg, P. and Reed, T. (2023). *Growing Threats to Global Trade*. [online] IMF. Available at: https://www.imf.org/en/Publications/fandd/issues/2023/06/growing-threats-to-global-trade-goldberg-reed

Gomede, E., Miranda de Barros, R., & de Souza Mendes, L. (2020). Use of deep multi-target prediction to identify learning styles. *Applied Sciences*, *10*(5), 1756.

Grochová, L., & Litzman, M. (2021). The efficiency in meeting measurable sustainable development goals. *International Journal of Sustainable Development & World Ecology*, *28*, 709–719. https://doi.org/10.1080/13504509.2021.1882606

Gulz, A., Londos, L., & Haake, M. (2020). Preschoolers' understanding of a teachable agent-based game in early mathematics as reflected in their gaze behaviors–an experimental study. *International Journal of Artificial Intelligence in Education*, *30*, 1–36.

Hassler, J., Krusell, P. and Olovsson, C. (2022). Finite resources and the world economy. *Journal of International Economics*, *136*(136), 103592. https://doi.org/10.1016/j.jinteco.2022.103592

Herrmann, S. D., Willis, E. A., Ainsworth, B. E., Barreira, T. V., Hastert, M., Kracht, C. L., Schuna, J. M., Cai, Z., Quan, M., Tudor-Locke, C., Whitt-Glover, M. C., & Jacobs, D. R. (2024). 2024 Adult Compendium of Physical Activities: A third update of the energy costs of human activities. *Journal of Sport and Health Science*, [online] *13*(1), 6–12. https://doi.org/10.1016/j.jshs.2023.10.010

Hmieleski, K. M., & Lerner, D. (2016). The Dark Triad and Nascent Entrepreneurship: An Examination of Unproductive versus Productive Entrepreneurial Motives. *Journal of Small Business Management*, *54*, 7–32. https://doi.org/10.1111/jsbm.12296

Hogeforster, M., & Wildt, M. (2023). Leveraging digital learning and work-based learning to enhance employee skills in small and medium enterprises. *International Scientific Conference, Business and Management*. https://doi.org/10.3846/bm.2023.1001

Holland, C., Hughes, J., & Leitch, R. (2016). Neoliberalism and education: Spotlight on Ireland. *Policy Futures in Education*, *14*(8), 1041–1045. https://doi.org/10.1177/1478210316664264

Hwang, G., Sung, H., Chang, S., & Huang, X. (2020). A fuzzy expert system-based adaptive learning approach to improving students' learning performances by considering affective and cognitive factors. Computers and Education: Artificial Intelligence, *1*(1), 100003.

IE University (2020). *The dynamic knowledge economy: Shifting industries and technologies*. [online] IE Driving Innovation. Available at: https://drivinginnovation.ie.edu/the-dynamic-knowledge-economy-shifting-industries-and-technologies/

International Monetary Fund. (2023). Global financial stability report, October 2023: Financial and climate policies for a high-interest-rate era. Retrieved from https://www.imf.org/en/Publications/GFSR/Issues/2023/10/10/global-financial-stability-report-october-2023

IPCC (2023). *AR6 Synthesis Report: Climate Change 2023*. [online] www.ipcc.ch. Available at: https://www.ipcc.ch/report/ar6/syr/

Iwu, C.G., Opute, P.A., Nchu, R., Eresia-Eke, C., Tengeh, R.K., Jaiyeoba, O., & Aliyu, O.A. (2019). Entrepreneurship education, curriculum and lecturer-competency as antecedents of student entrepreneurial intention. *The International Journal of Management Education*, *19*(1), p.100295. https://doi.org/10.1016/j.ijme.2019.03.007

Iwu, C. G., Opute, P. A., Nchu, R., Eresia-Eke, C., Tengeh, R. K., Jaiyeoba, O., and Aliyu, O. A. (2021). Entrepreneurship education, curriculum, and lecturer-competency as an-tecedents of student entrepreneurial intention. *The International Journal of Management Education*, 19(1): 100295. *(PDF) Entrepreneurship education challenges in the African setting*. Available from: https://www.researchgate.net/publication/358358868_Entrepreneurship_education_challenges_in_the_African_setting [accessed Nov 27 2024].

Jolly, R., & Ray, D. (n.d.). United Nations Development Programme Human Development Report Office National Human Development Report Series NHDR Occasional Paper 5 *The Human Security Framework and National Human Development Reports* 5. [online] Available at: https://hdr.undp.org/system/files/documents/human-security.human-security#:~:text=report%2C%20%E2%80%9Chuman%20security%20means%20safety
Kabudi, T., Pappas, I., & Olsen, D. H. (2021). AI-enabled adaptive learning systems: A systematic mapping of the literature. Computers and Education: Artificial Intelligence, *2*, 100025.
Kaponda, K., & Tembo, S. (2018). An investigation into the Policy and Regulatory Challenges of Digital Financial Services ICT infrastructure in Zambia. *International Journal of Innovative Science, Engineering & Technology*, *5*(9), 211–214.
Kasneci, E., Seßler, K., Küchemann, S., Bannert, M., Dementieva, D., Fischer, F., ... & Kasneci, G. (2023). ChatGPT for good? On opportunities and challenges of large language models for education. *Learning and individual differences*, *103*, 102274.
Katundu, M. A., & Gabagambi, D. M. (2016). Barriers to business start-up among Tanzanian university graduates: Evidence from the university of dar-es-salaam. *Global Business Review*, *17*(1), 16–37.
Keshav, N. U., Salisbury, J. P., Vahabzadeh, A., & Sahin, N. T. (2017). Social communication coaching smartglasses: Well tolerated in a diverse sample of children and adults with autism. *JMIR MHealth and UHealth*, *5*(9), e8534.
Khosravi, H., Shum, S. B., Chen, G., Conati, C., Tsai, Y. S., Kay, J., ... & Gašević, D. (2022). Explainable artificial intelligence in education. *Computers and Education: Artificial Intelligence*, *3*, 100074.
Kindström, D., Carlborg, P., & Nord, T. (2022). Challenges for Growing SMEs: a Managerial Perspective. *Journal of Small Business Management*, *17*(1), 1–24.
Kondratenko, O. (2020). US Policy Towards Ukraine in Conditions of the New World Order. https://doi.org/10.17721/2521-1706.2020.09.3
Korotayev, A., Vaskin, I., & Tsirel, S. (2019). Economic Growth, Education, and Terrorism: A Re-Analysis. *Terrorism and Political Violence*, *33*(3), 572–595. https://doi.org/10.1080/09546553.2018.1559835
Kuhlmann, S., & Rip, A. (2018). Next-Generation Innovation Policy and Grand Challenges. *Science and Public Policy*, *45*(4), 448–454. https://doi.org/10.1093/scipol/scy011
Lai, B., & Thyne, C. (2007). The Effect of Civil War on Education, 1980—97. In Journal of Peace Research (Vol. *44*, Issue 3, pp. 277–292). SAGE Publications. https://doi.org/10.1177/0022343307076631
Lasenby, A. (2022). *Degrowth: A Socially and Ecologically Just Economic Alternative*? [online] Earth.org. Available at: https://earth.org/degrowth/
Lashitew, A., Ross, M., & Werker, E. (2020). What Drives Successful Economic Diversification in Resource-Rich Countries?. *ERN: Other Development Economics: Agriculture*. https://doi.org/10.2139/ssrn.3661533
Leicht, A., Heiss, J., & Byun, W.J. (2018). *Issues and trends in education for sustainable development*. UNESCO Publishing.
Li, Q., Chen, W., Zhang, S., & Shi, H. (2023). Achieving sustainable development by reducing income inequality: The differential impact of industrial land expansion in urban agglomerations. *Sustainable Development*, *31*(4), 2770–2783. https://doi.org/10.1002/sd.2546
Li, Y., Wu, W., & Wang, Y. (2021). Global poverty dynamics and resilience building for sustainable poverty reduction. *Journal of Geographical Sciences*, *31*(8), 1159–1170. https://doi.org/10.1007/s11442-021-1890-4
Madi, I., Morales, L., Yosef, F., & Andreosso, B. (2023). Women Inequality in the MENA Region: Insights from the Arab Spring Revolution. *Peace Review*, *35*(4), 695–707. https://doi.org/10.1080/10402659.2023.2269124

Masterson, V. (2022). Degrowth: what's behind this economic theory and why it matters today. [online] *World Economic Forum*. Available at: https://www.weforum.org/agenda/2022/06/what-is-degrowth-economics-climate-change/

Mastini, R. (2017). *Degrowth: the case for a new economic paradigm*. [online] openDemocracy. Available at: https://www.opendemocracy.net/en/degrowth-case-for-constructing-new-economic-paradigm/

Matsuda, N., Weng, W., & Wall, T. (2020). Metacognitive scaffolding by teaching a teachable agent: Effects on students' learning and transfer. Computers & Education, *144*, 103705.

McClure, J., Snow, N., & Thomas, D. (2023). A struggle of incomplete visions: Creative destruction vs. The economy of knowledge. *The Review of Austrian Economics*. https://doi.org/10.1007/s11138-023-00629-9

Meyer, J. G., Urbanowicz, R. J., Martin, P. C., O'Connor, K., Li, R., Peng, P. C., ... & Moore, J. H. (2023). ChatGPT and large language models in academia: opportunities and challenges. *BioData Mining*, *16*(1), 20.

Mopelola, A.-S., Abidat, O. &, & Mohammed, O. (2024). Role of Entrepreneurship Education in Shaping the Entrepreneurial Intentions and Self-Efficacy of Economics Education Students in Public Universities in Lagos State, Nigeria. *Educational Perspectives*, *12*(3), 62–68.

Morales, L., Coetzer, J.H., Barkoczi, N., Pop, L., Marian, C., & Flynn, P. (2022). *A Circular Pedagogy for Higher Education*.

Müller, M. (2018). In Search of the Global East: Thinking between North and South. *Geopolitics*, *25*(3), 1–22. https://doi.org/10.1080/14650045.2018.1477757

Naidu, J. P., & Sanchez, G. (2021). Special Issue on Innovations in Technology, Management & Design for Achieving Sustainable Development Goals (SDGs): ICSDG 2020. *IETE Journal of Research*, *67*(5), 585–586.

Napolitano, J. (2012). Development, Sustainability and International Politics. *Transgovernance*, [online] *163*(211), 163–211. https://doi.org/10.1007/978-3-642-28009-2_4

Nguyen D. T., Thai Hong Le, Dinh, D., & Hai Nam Nguyen (2023). Does geopolitical risk hinder sustainable development goals? Evidence from a panel analysis. *Journal of Environmental Management*, *347*(374), 119204–119204. https://doi.org/10.1016/j.jenvman.2023.119204

Norris, S. E. (2021). The development of the entrepreneurial mindset, critical thinking skills, and critical reflective practices through experiential learning activities in graduate business school. In *Research Anthology on Developing Critical Thinking Skills in Students* (pp. 210–231). IGI Global.

OECD. (2007). No More Failures. In *Education and Training Policy*. OECD. https://doi.org/10.1787/9789264032606-en

OECD (2016). Innovating Education and Educating for Innovation. [online] *Educational Research and Innovation*. OECD. https://doi.org/10.1787/9789264265097-en

OECD (2020). Developing countries and development cooperation: What is at stake? Retrieved from: https://www.oecd.org/coronavirus/policy-responses/developing-countries-and-development-co-operation-what-is-at-stake-50e97915/

OECD (2023). *Bottlenecks to Access Sustainable Development Goals Finance for Developing Countries*, OECD, Paris, www.oecd.org/g20/oecd-g20-bottlenecks-sdg-finance-developing-countries.pdf

Olson, M. S., van Bever, D., & Verry, S. (2008). "When growth stalls". *Harvard Business Review*, *86*(3), 50.

Palmieri, E., Geretto, E., & Polato, M. (2022). European banks' business models as a driver of strategic planning: one size fits all. *Journal of Financial Regulation and Compliance*. https://doi.org/10.1108/jfrc-08-2021-0068

Pop, L., & Morales, L. (2023). Education to Navigate Global Power Dynamics and Conflict through the Lens of Caring. *Peace Review*, *35*(4), 724–735. https://doi.org/10.1080/10402659.2023.2263389

Pop, L., Barkoczi, N., Morales, L., Jon-Hans Coetzer, Marian, C., & Flynn, P. (2022). *Circular Pedagogy for Smart, Inclusive and Sustainable Education*. https://doi.org/10.13140/RG.2.2.36078.69449

Priewe, J. (2022). Growth in the ecological transition: Green, zero or degrowth? *European Journal of Economics and Economic Policies Intervention*, *19*(1), 19–40. https://doi.org/10.4337/ejeep.2022.01.04

Quiroga-Garza, A., Garza-Cisneros, A. N., Elizondo-Omaña, R. E., Vilchez-Cavazos, J. F., de-Oca-Luna, R. M., Villarreal-Silva, E., … & Gonzalez-Gonzalez, J. G. (2022). Research barriers in the global south: Mexico. *Journal of Global Health*, *12*, 1–6.

Rădulescu, M. A., Wim Leendertse and Arts, J. (2023). How Can Co-Creation Support Capacity Building for Adaptive Spatial Planning? Exploring Evidence from a Co-Creative Planning Process in The Netherlands. *Planning theory & practice*, *24*(5), 639–662. https://doi.org/10.1080/14649357.2023.2288203

Raworth, K. (2017). A Doughnut for the Anthropocene: humanity's compass in the 21st century. *The Lancet Planetary Health*, [online] *1*(2), 48–49. https://doi.org/10.1016/s2542-5196(17)30028-1

Reiss, M. J. (2021). The Use of Al in Education: Practicalities and Ethical Considerations. *London Review of Education*, *19*(1), n1.

Rockström, J., Kotzé, L., Milutinović, S., Biermann, F., Brovkin, V., Donges, J., Ebbesson, J., French, D., Gupta, J., Kim, R., Lenton, T., Lenzi, D., Nakicenovic, N., Neumann, B., Schuppert, F., Winkelmann, R., Bosselmann, K., Folke, C., Lucht, W., … Steffen, W. (2024). The planetary commons: A new paradigm for safeguarding Earth-regulating systems in the Anthropocene. *Proceedings of the National Academy of Sciences*, *121*(5), e2301531121. https://doi.org/10.1073/pnas.2301531121

Rose, J. L. (2020). On the value of economic growth. *Politics, Philosophy & Economics*, *19*(2), 128–153. https://doi.org/10.1177/1470594X19889123

Ruggerio, C. A. (2021). Sustainability and sustainable development: A review of principles and definitions. *Science of the Total Environment*, *786*, 147481.

Salamatov, A. A., Gnatyshina, E. A., & Gordeeva, D.S. (2019). The concept of sustainable environmental and economic development in the transition to the digital economy. [online] https://doi.org/10.2991/iscde-19.2019.170. Article published by Atlantis Press.

Schumpeter, J.A. (1934). *The Theory of Economic Development: An Inquiry into Profits, Capital, Credit, Interest, and the Business Cycle*. New Brunswick (U.S.A.) London (U.K.) Transaction Publishers.

Schumpeter, J. A., & Swedberg, R. (2013). *Capitalism, socialism and democracy*. Routledge. https://doi.org/10.4324/9780203202050

Storey, D.J. (2011). Optimism and chance: The elephants in the entrepreneurship room. *International Small Business Journal: Researching Entrepreneurship*, *29*(4), 303–321. https://doi.org/10.1177/0266242611403871

Sun, X. (2020). Exploration and practice of "Internet + Maker Education" University Innovative Entrepreneurship Education Model from the perspective of Positive psychology. *Frontiers in Psychology*, *11*. https://doi.org/10.3389/fpsyg.2020.00891

Tarning, B., Silvervarg, A., Gulz, A., & Haake, M. (2019). Instructing a teachable agent with low or high self-efficacy–does similarity attract?. *International Journal of Artificial Intelligence in Education*, *29*, 89–121.

UN (2012). *United Nations Millennium Development Goals*. [online] www.un.org. Available at: https://www.un.org/millenniumgoals/#:~:text=The%20eight%20Millennium%20Development%20Goals

UN (2023a). A/78/XX-E/2023/XX General Assembly Economic and Social Council ADVANCE UNEDITED VERSION *Progress towards the Sustainable Development Goals: Towards a Rescue Plan for People and Planet Report of the Secretary-General*

(Special Edition) Summary. [online] Available at: https://hlpf.un.org/sites/default/files/2023-04/SDG%20Progress%20Report%20Special%20Edition.pdf
UN (2023b). *Our Common Agenda.* [online] unfoundation.org. Available at: https://unfoundation.org/our-common-agenda/?gad_source=1&gclid=Cj0KCQjw6PGxBhCVARIsAIumnWbacdRcy0K-mYgbDSA18yTugW2dMq1yjz0XAbmjKs13TSNrpMd0IcMaAjXEEALw_wcB [Accessed 10 May 2024].
UN (2024). *Bridging Gender Gaps with a Sustainable Care Economy: Investment Opportunities and Challenges*. [online] UNDP. Available at: https://www.undp.org/publications/dfs-bridging-gender-gaps-sustainable-care-economy-investment-opportunities-and-challenges [Accessed 29 Apr. 2024].
UNDP. (2006). *United Nations Development Programme Human Development Report Office National Human Development Report Series NHDR Occasional Paper 5 The Human Security Framework and National Human Development Reports 5*. https://hdr.undp.org/system/files/documents/human-security.human-security
UNESCO (2016). UNESCO *Institute for Lifelong Learning Technical Note Lifelong Learning*. [online] Available at: https://uil.unesco.org/fileadmin/keydocuments/LifelongLearning/en/UNESCOTechNotesLLL.pdf
UNESCO (2021). *Reimagining our futures together: a new social contract for education.* UNESCO. https://doi.org/10.54675/asrb4722
UNESCO (2023). *Reworking Four Pillars of Education to Sustain the Commons* | UNESCO. [online] www.unesco.org. Available at: https://www.unesco.org/en/articles/reworking-four-pillars-education-sustain-commons
United Nations (2015). *Transforming Our World: the 2030 Agenda for Sustainable* Development. [online] United Nations. Available at: https://sdgs.un.org/2030agenda
United Nations (2019). *The future is now science for achieving sustainable development. Global sustainable development report 2 19*. [online] Available at: https://sustainabledevelopment.un.org/content/documents/24797GSDR_report_2019.pdf
United Nations (2021). *Debt as an Obstacle to the Sustainable Development Goals* | Nações Unidas. [online] United Nations. Available at: https://www.un.org/pt/desa/debt-obstacle-sustainable-development-goals
United Nations (2023a). *Press Release | UN Chief calls for fundamental shift to put world back on track to achieving the Sustainable Development Goals*. [online] United Nations Sustainable Development. Available at: https://www.un.org/sustainabledevelopment/blog/2023/04/press-release-un-chief-calls-for-fundamental-shift-to-put-world-back-on-track-to-achieving-the-sustainable-development-goals/
United Nations (2023b). *The Sustainable Development Goals Report 2023*: Special Edition. [online] unstats.un.org. Available at: https://unstats.un.org/sdgs/report/2023/
United Nations (2023c). *World risks big misses across the Sustainable Development Goals unless measures to accelerate implementation are taken, UN warns*. [online] United Nations. Available at: https://www.un.org/en/desa/world-risks-big-misses-across-sustainable-development-goals-unless-measures-accelerate [Accessed 15 Dec. 2023].
Van Stam, G. (2019). Why do foreign solutions not work in Africa? Recognising alternate epistemologies. *Roaming Africa: Migration, Resilience and Social Protection*, 55–82. https://doi.org/10.2307/j.ctvvh85q7.9
Vincent-Lancrin, S., & Van der Vlies, R. (2020). Trustworthy artificial intelligence (AI) in education: Promises and challenges. *OECD Education Working Papers*, No. 218, OECD Publishing, Paris, https://doi.org/10.1787/a6c90fa9-en
WEF (2024). *The Global Risks Report 2024. 19th Edition. Insight Report*. Available at: https://www3.weforum.org/docs/WEF_The_Global_Risks_Report_2024.pdf
Wei, H., Yang, X., Chen, G., & Hu, F. (2018). Application of machine learning in the assessment of ESL/EFL learners' learning styles. *Educational Technology Research and Development*, *66*(6), 1619–1638.

Weiland, S., Hickmann, T., Lederer, M., Marquardt, J., & Schwindenhammer, S. (2021). The 2030 agenda for sustainable development: transformative change through the sustainable development goals?. *Politics and Governance*, *9*(1), 90–95.

WFE (2022). *World Economic Forum Annual Meeting 2022*, Davos. [online] World Economic Forum. Available at: https://www.weforum.org/events/world-economic-forum-annual-meeting-2022/

World Bank (2023). *Why is education more important today than ever? Innovation*. [online] World Bank Blogs. Available at: https://blogs.worldbank.org/en/education/why-education-more-important-today-ever-innovation

World Bank. (2024). *A World Bank Group Flagship Report Global Economic Prospects*. https://openknowledge.worldbank.org/server/api/core/bitstreams/d644659c-2e22-410e-98a5-b8a40dc6c183/content

World Bank Group (2019). *The 2030 Sustainable Development Agenda and the World Bank Group: Closing the SDGs Financing Gap*. [online] Available at: https://pubdocs.worldbank.org/en/259801562965232326/2030Agenda-2019-final-web.pdf

Yang, Y. (2020). Exploration and practice of maker education mode in IEE. *Frontiers in Psychology*, *11*. https://doi.org/10.3389/fpsyg.2020.01626

Yu, Y., & Huang, J. (2021). Poverty Reduction of Sustainable Development Goals in the 21st Century: A Bibliometric Analysis. *Frontiers in Communication*, *6*(6). https://doi.org/10.3389/fcomm.2021.754181

Zawacki-Richter, O., Marin, V. I., Bond, M., & Gouverneur, F. (2019). Systematic review of research on artificial intelligence applications in higher education – where are the educators? *International Journal of Educational Technology in Higher Education*, *16*(1), 39.

Zhang, K., & Aslan, A. B. (2021). AI technologies for education: Recent research & future directions. *Computers and Education: Artificial Intelligence*, *2*, 100025.

Zhao, X., & Zhang, J. (2021). The Analysis of Integration of Ideological Political Education With Innovation Entrepreneurship Education for College Students. *Frontiers in Psychology*, *12*(12). https://doi.org/10.3389/fpsyg.2021.610409

Part 3

Policy Implications

11 Driving Impactful Change

Entrepreneurial Insights for Social Responsibility in the Irish Context

Anna Zherdeva, Deirdre McQuillan and Lucía Morales

11.1 Introduction

The United Nations 2030 Agenda identified a very ambitious working outline supported by the 17 Sustainable Development Goals (SDGs) and its 169 targets (UN, 2015). The Agenda offers countries possibilities and insights on addressing the rising global tensions and challenges economies and governments face (UN, 2015). The international landscape is affected by significant uncertainty, growing levels of conflict and violence. At the time of writing this chapter, we are witnessing a very volatile situation at the global level defined by a significant increase in Economic and Political Uncertainty, as countries are trying to manage the climate change crisis, armed conflicts, the rising cost of living, a growing divide between the more prosperous Global North and the poorest Global South that are reflected on the emergence of multifaceted, multiple and long-lasting crises (McGinnity and Kingston, 2017a; Alesina Marco Tabellini et al., 2022; Santoire, 2023). The European economy is facing significant challenges as a result of the ongoing Russia-Ukraine war that has completed a two-year period without envisioning a potential diplomatic solution. The Israel war on Hamas is proving to be challenging international laws with economic implications due to disruptions in supply chains provoked by the Red Sea crisis and an increase in inflation and overall cost of living (European Commission, 2024). Re-rooting vessels via the Cape of Good Hope in South Africa pushes shipping rates and results in enabling sustained growth that affects global trade. At the same time, Figure 11.1 demonstrates that the US showed robust GDP growth mainly in terms of private consumption, which revealed better outcomes than expected (World Bank, 2024). In contrast, China demonstrates a slight slowdown in economic growth due to weak domestic demand and the continuing real estate crisis. On the other hand, the European economy has to catch up, as consumption and investments barely moved, and imports were falling dramatically, worsening the 2024 economic prognosis (European Commission, 2024).

During periods of heightened instability and economic uncertainty, businesses struggle to build trusting relationships with stakeholders as they seek to reduce costs (Kim, 2019a; Vural-Yavaş, 2020; Alandejani & Al-Shaer, 2023).

DOI: 10.4324/9781032655857-15

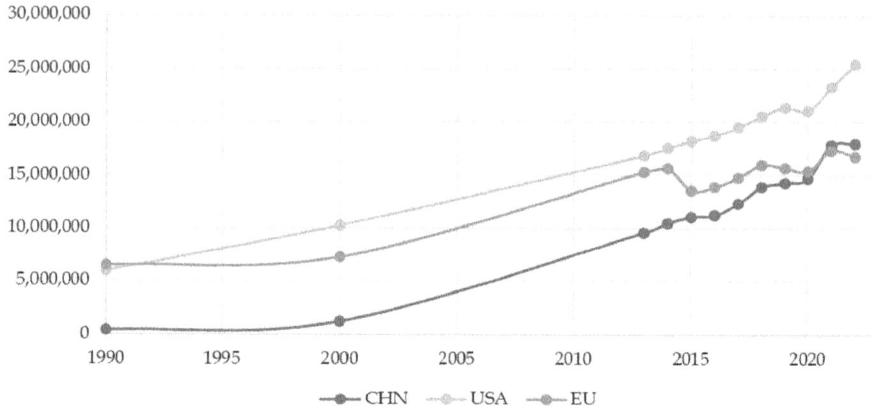

Figure 11.1 US, China and EU GDP (1990–2023).

Source: Adapted from World Bank (2024).

Additionally, companies seek deep engagement as they confront the costs associated with the sustainability challenges and try to alleviate economic uncertainty (Vural-Yavaş et al., 2021; Alandejani & Al-Shaer, 2023). Thus, the role of SMEs is critical as they directly influence economies by determining their stable growth, having important spillover effects on the country's GDP, revenue generation, and employment creation. In Ireland, the latest research findings highlight SMEs' high growth potential, positive attitudes, and relevance to economic development (Azadnia et al., 2022; Kren et al., 2021; OECD, 2019). As such, the global economic and political outlook is critical when trying to understand existing and emerging challenges faced by small enterprises as they are severely exposed to national, regional, and international instability within a global interconnected and integrated economic and political system (Kren et al., 2021; Azadnia et al., 2022; Alesina Marco Tabellini et al., 2022; Santoire, 2023; Finnegan et al., 2023; European Commission, 2024; World Bank, 2024).

As we turn our attention to the Irish case, the research findings show some level of resilience to the geoeconomic challenges due to stable consumer spending, supported by a strong labour market capable of decelerating inflation and providing further consumption growth (European Commission, 2024; CSO, 2024). To guarantee the resilience of Irish businesses and high competitiveness in the global market, small companies need to cope with investment attraction, technology implementation, management skills improvement, and direct access to finance (McGeever et al., 2020; OECD, 2019). However, access to funding has remained an obstacle to small businesses (OECD, 2022a, 2022b) due to a possible lack of credit history, insufficient savings, and constraints in reaching direct funding through the bank system. High levels of competition to access resources also increase competition between companies in the labour market, enhancing the importance of managerial skills development. Moreover, improving management development standards has become a priority for the Irish government, which is highlighted in Project Ireland 2040, which presents the country's overarching long-term strategy for economic and social development (Boeske & Murray, 2022; Kindström et al., 2022; McQuillan et al., 2020), as the existing competency level in Irish SMEs is insufficient.

The major dilemma today is recognising the necessity of improving the personal managerial skills of owners as they invest more in their teams' training than in themselves. We argue about the significant role of quality education in alignment with SDG 4

> By 2030, ensure that all learners acquire the knowledge and skills needed to promote sustainable development, including, among others, through education for sustainable development and sustainable lifestyles, human rights, gender equality, promotion of a culture of peace and non-violence, global citizenship and appreciation of cultural diversity and of culture's contribution to sustainable development.
>
> (UN, the 2030 Agenda for Sustainable Development, 2015, p. 21)

which can foster SMEs' sustainable development in conditions of the shift to the Industry 5.0 paradigm. As the focus shifts from technical skills to human-centred, the most required competencies for the owner and whole team become the ability to work with the demands and pressures that emerge from the knowledge-based economy, the digital age, leadership skills, and the significance of entrepreneurial mindset within increasing levels of uncertainty due to geoeconomic and geopolitical shifts (Ortiz-Martínez et al., 2023; Smith et al., 2022; Reporting Lab, 2021). The latter includes expanded communication competencies, a diversity-driven approach, and an intercultural vision for integrating international staff into the company's culture.

For these purposes, government and academia should consider the importance of engaging in the co-design and co-creation of programmes directed towards executive education that nurtures a comprehensive understanding of global dynamics from the economic and political angle (Zhong et al. 2017; Machado et al. 2020; Oztemel and Gursev 2020; Zheng et al. 2021). The role of education in driving change needs to be considered due to its global implications. The needs and demands of Industry 4.0 and 5.0 pose important global challenges with core implications as countries try to secure the required resources to position their industries' competitive positions (Borch and Madsen, 2007; Gherhes et al., 2016; Owalla et al., 2022; Economic and Financial Affairs, 2024). Within a context where technology, innovation, digital skills development, and the sustainability paradigm provide a critical thinking context that nurtures proactive thinking and collaborative working environments framed in an active and realistic problem-solving context that addresses socio-economic and environmental challenges (Santos et al., 2012; Ng and Kee, 2018; Tam & Gray, 2021). Developing executives' leadership skills and entrepreneurial mindset are essential as part of an educational offer that prepares and makes executive education more aware of the importance of SDGs and the fierce competition for natural resources, and the better integration of highly qualified employees with intercultural backgrounds that can contribute to a better understanding of the complexities of an evolving and changing socio-economic and environmental international context with ramifications and direct implications to working businesses environments (Vanhanen et al., 2023; Lawless et al., 2000, 2019).

This research paper aims to provide a comprehensive analysis of the existing literature to identify if Irish SME executives are trained to lead the country's economic growth agenda in the context of sustainable development. The conducted literature review assists in determining the core challenges faced by SMEs and provides an appropriate conceptual and theoretical framework to address the following question: What are the critical competencies for SME executives in the context of Industry 5.0 and increasing geoeconomic challenges and uncertainty? The question gained significant importance due to small companies' need to navigate economic uncertainty, disrupted supply chains, and an ever-changing political context. The role of small companies has completely changed, converting them from local entities into full-fledged market players (Rozuli, 2021; Irawan et al., 2023; Yuniarti, 2023). The conducted literature review allowed us to identify the main constraints SMEs face on their way to sustainable development in questions of social responsibility and job creation. As these questions are of significant importance to the Irish economy, existing programmes in the leadership field and their effectiveness demand that requires additional analysis.

11.2 Development of Entrepreneurship in Ireland

For many years of the 20th century, Ireland has been a poor and primarily agricultural country. Everything started to change at the beginning of the 1960s with the Irish government's attempts to increase the local market's attractiveness to multinational corporations (MNCs). At the time, MNCs began their massive investment policy that benefited Ireland by gradually transforming the Irish economy and expanding the manufacturing and export operations sectors. Fast transformation and economic growth have determined the boom of entrepreneurial opportunities and their attractiveness to the vast majority of the population as an obvious career choice (Birdthistle, 2019). These measures have transformed the Irish economic sector's landscape, leaving agriculture at 1.08%, as illustrated by Figure 11.2. The sector is still vital. However, according to industry classification, the principal sectors are manufacturing and services, which account for 40% and 55% of all Irish businesses. The importance of these sectors explains their capacity for employment possibilities and entrepreneurial opportunities that need to take into consideration the Irish economy model and its exposure to global dynamics (FAME, 2023).

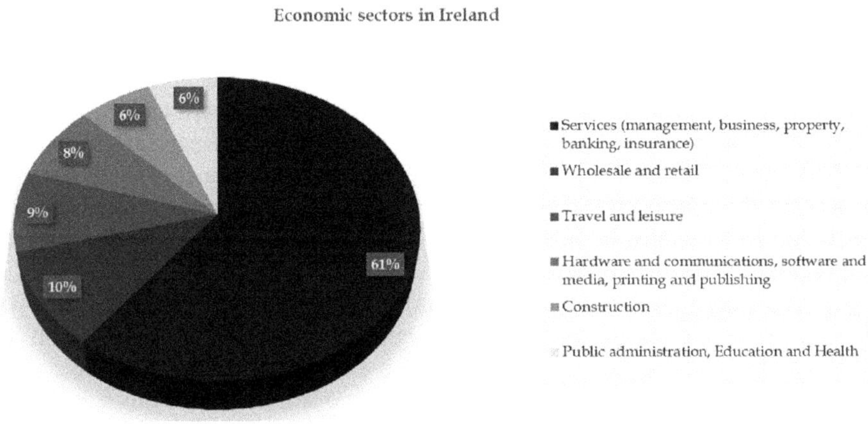

Figure 11.2 2023 Structure of Irish economy across economic sectors.

Source: Adapted from FAME (2023).

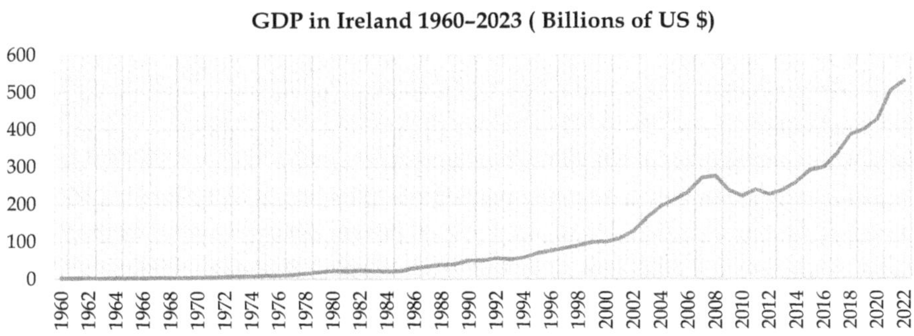

Figure 11.3 GDP in Ireland (1960–2023).

Source: Adapted from CSO (2023).

The entrepreneurial spirit in Ireland has emerged as an answer to challenges in navigating situations of continuous and enhanced uncertainty and instability (Birdthistle, 2019; Fitzsimons & O'Gorman, 2021). The growth that started at the beginning of 1990 was disrupted by the global economic and financial crisis (GEFC) in 2008, which is illustrated in Figure 11.3. As a result, the government's budget experienced a deficit for a limited time, a drop in household revenue, and a massive outflow of the qualified workforce. However, the economy turned to a recovery trend in 2014, pulling up the budget, population prosperity, and growth of employment needs (Birdthistle, 2019; van Aarle et al., 2015). The attitude towards migrants has also changed, shifting to encouraging employers and policymakers to reconsider their attitudes towards migrants and the necessity of attracting them due to skills shortages and a lack of qualified staff.

Even though the Irish economy managed to recover relatedly fast from the 2008 Global Economic and Financial Crisis (GEFC), the fragile balance reached after the economic recovery remains complex for small companies, forced to seek extra support as they can significantly contribute to the Irish economy, putting it to a new level within the global landscape (Finnegan & Kapoor, 2023; Irawan et al., 2023; Yuniarti, 2023). Empowering SMEs to contribute to the economy can appear to be a complicated process as entrepreneurs have to operate in circumstances of economic instability and political unpredictability (Rozuli, 2021; Irawan et al., 2023; Yuniarti, 2023). Being a significant player in the economy forming, small businesses still struggle with finance attraction, as access to finance remains a considerable constraint to SMEs as they heavily rely on banks, which experience difficulties due to the country's debt crisis and prefer to invest in corporations (Finnegan & Kapoor, 2023). It is worth mentioning that SMEs are more vulnerable than corporations, as the constraints they face while operating significantly vary, as illustrated in Figure 11.4. Despite the changing economic and political environment, SMEs experience high pressure as they struggle with resources, finance, and human capital attraction. Without these essential components, small companies cannot quickly adapt to changing industry demand and properly apply advanced technologies, such as the advance of artificial intelligence (AI), as a part of knowledge management within knowledge-intensive ecosystems (Finnegan & Kapoor, 2023; Irawan et al., 2023). Among the most important factors for companies in the manufacturing and service sectors are the lack of resources and competencies and organisational, technical, economic, and legal (Jamwal et al., 2023). Moreover, as economies become more knowledge-intensive and actively transition to digital practices with high demand to operate sustainably, the level of digital competencies and skills is becoming more and more vital.

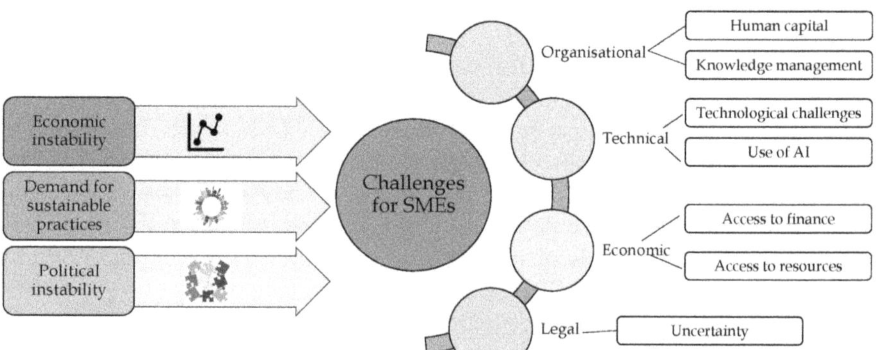

Figure 11.4 Challenges faced by SMEs in transition from Industry 4.0 to Industry 5.0.

Source: Adapted from Jamwal (2023).

Additionally, a lack of digital and management skills was identified as a gap in the transition process to the concept of Industry 4.0 and extensively raised the question of the role of humans in human-machine and machine-machine interaction in digitalised businesses (Zhong et al. 2017; Machado et al. 2020; Oztemel and Gursev 2020; Zheng et al. 2021). Corporations lead the process of automation and digitalisation, while small companies have to attract the relevant workforce or invest in the upskilling of current staff. Acquiring the necessary knowledge and skills can reduce the gap in talent attraction between corporations and small companies, which is a need to rethink international collaboration and knowledge exchange processes amidst enhanced competitive working environments.

Investments in the Irish economy and significant educational reform have decreased the level of workforce outflow from the country and significantly determined the country's further development. On its way to success, the Irish economy had to increase human capital, open up the economy to imports and foreign capital, and improve the fiscal policies and regulatory mechanisms for local companies (Birdthistle, 2019; van Aarle et al., 2015; Ó Gráda & O'Rourke, 2021). As a result, driven by the huge second wave of FDI flows directed by tech giants that started in the 1990s and the implementation of an attractive corporate tax regime, the Irish economy was characterised as an economic miracle named as "*Celtic Tiger*" (Birdthistle, 2019, van Aarle et al., 2015, Ó Gráda & O'Rourke, 2021). Rapid economic development and significant investments have changed Irish immigration policy, making the country an attractive place to relocate for work or start a business (see Figure 11.5). This trend started in the middle of the 1990s by attracting employees mainly from Europe, and it is becoming increasingly diverse nowadays (CSO, 2024). Migration's increase was slowed during the 2020 Global Health Crisis; however, it has demonstrated a stable rise in the last two years. This shift has a significant meaning for the Irish

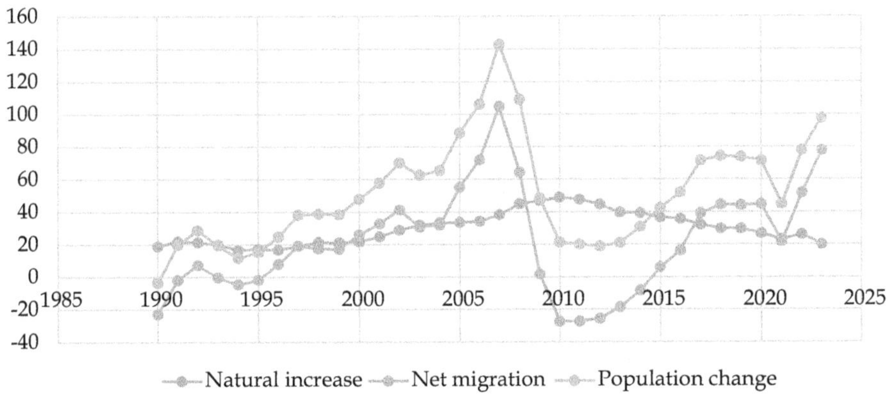

Figure 11.5 Migration in Ireland.

Source: Adapted from CSO (2024).

economy, as historically, Ireland was a country of emigration with very low numbers of a non-Irish population (Hughes et al., 2007; McGinnity and Kingston, 2017a). Expanding the number of immigrants can simultaneously provoke positive and negative effects, as natives perceive migrants as a threat to their prosperity and stable economic growth. Corporations and governments recognise the need to support foreign nationals in accessing the job market, as they help reduce the skills shortages and support the Irish economy by providing educated and skilled employees. However, efforts are still needed to explain to natives that migrants do not threaten their well-being and prosperity (McGinnity and Kingston, 2017a; Deloitte, 2022; DETE, 2023). Ireland is still struggling with the overcoming of the idea that immigrants can be seen as a threat to economic stability, and this perception will highly rely on economic conditions and results (McGinnity and Kingston, 2017a). The qualified workforce helped to rapidly transform the Irish economy into a growing and stable economy and catapulted the country into one of the world's most advanced economies (Brownlow et al., 2020; Barry et al., 2019; Lawless et al., 2019).

Today, the Irish entrepreneurial rate is equivalent to that of the US and is much higher than that of the rest of Europe (OECD, 2023; Fitzsimons and O'Gorman, 2017). However, to provide a high level of entrepreneurial development in the country, the educational system must match high education and professional training standards. Consequently, the government is considering the importance of a reform strategy in the education system, embedding lifelong learning and putting digital literacy skills as a top priority (Breznitz & Feldman, 2010; Breznitz, 2012; Government of Ireland, 2023; UN, 2024) has become the primary benchmark of government policy, represent in the government strategy "The Digital Ireland Framework" (Government of Ireland, 2023). In the middle of the 1960s, Ireland had one of the poorest levels of education among its employees. To guarantee its competitiveness in the European market, Ireland needed to reform its current educational system, as providing high-quality education allows the country to reach the United Nations Goal 4.7, Quality Education, and, as a result, Goal 8, Decent Work and Economic Growth to reach the goals of transition to Industry 5.0 paradigm (UN, 2015; UN, 2024). Quality education includes targets that build the framework of the consistent educational process, starting from primary and secondary school, growing to higher educational institutions, and lifelong learning during working life. Therefore, quality education provides the economy with a qualified and skilled labour force and simultaneously allows for enhanced productivity, consequently acting as a catalyst for economic growth, prosperity, and sustainable development (Owalla et al., 2022). Ireland reacted accordingly to these challenges and made secondary education accessible to everyone, where higher education became fully public and affordable. All these measures allowed Ireland to shift its educational level to one of the highest in the world.

However, the 21st century demands from employees not only the quality of education but also a high level of professional skills, which is essential for entrepreneurs to provide a company with constant growth and development. Moreover, companies need to equip workers with the required competencies and skills to help them navigate uncertain working environments that are more exposed to global dynamics and rising levels of uncertainty. Companies operate now in a situation where they need to address the demands of Industry 4.0 and 5.0 and emerging pressures from high levels of engagement with the fast pace of innovation and technological progress. As manufacturing shifts to the social side of things and becomes more people-oriented (European Commission, 2023), personal skills, perceptions, forward-thinking skills, transferable and transversal skills, and attitudes are identified as critical to navigate current and emerging socio-economic, environmental, and political challenges, which are represented in Figure 11.6 (OECD, 2023; UNESCO, 2023; UN, 2023). Skills for Industry 5.0 are based on the Industry 4.0 demand, including personal, methodological, technical, and social, with significant emphasis on the ability to work with knowledge, leadership skills, and entrepreneurial mindset. Focus on learning as an ability to work with knowledge has become a solid trend and supports a lifelong learning concept, defined as learning during an entire lifetime (Håkansson Lindqvist et al., 2023). Learning develops people and raises awareness about effective knowledge sharing, communications, and environmental impact. Companies and employees face the urgent demand for constant learning and obligatory knowledge sharing and interpretation to ease the amount of necessary information. Leadership skills today play an essential role not only for managers inclusively but for line employees as well, as problem-solving, creativity, and decision-making have come into everyday

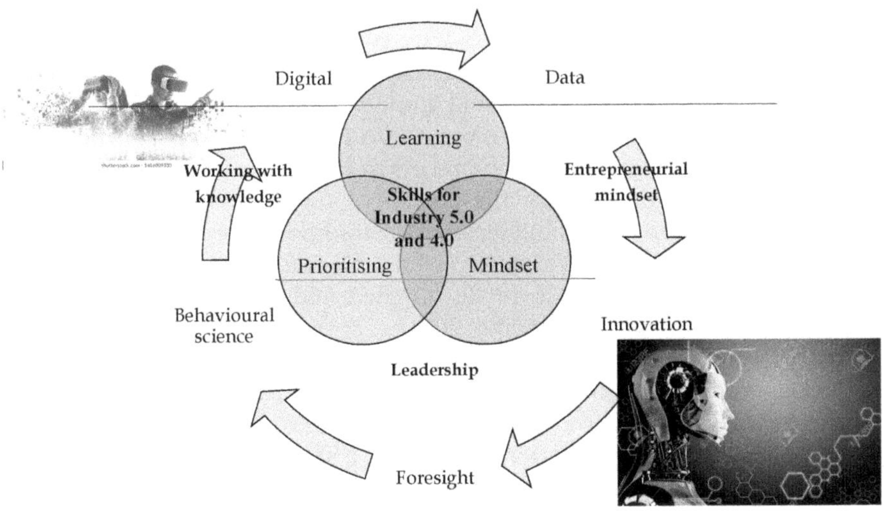

Figure 11.6 Necessary skills in industry 4.0 and 5.0.

Source: Adapted from European Commission (2023), World Manufacturing Foundation report, (2019), UN 2.0 Quintet for Change (2023).

performance. Separately stands the entrepreneurial mindset, covering communications questions in the diverse and intercultural environments caused by changed immigration policy and growing numbers of working internationals (EC, 2023; Håkansson Lindqvist et al., 2023; DETE, 2023). Entrepreneurs are vital for the Irish, European, and global economies as they represent a considerable cohort of business people with extensive employment possibilities and demand investments in their development. Thus, entrepreneurial vision should be based on the innovation, foresight, behavioural science, data and digital framework defined by the United Nations in the UN 2.0 Quintet for Change as a significant accelerator for systemic shifts and sustainable goals achievement (OECD, 2023; UNESCO, 2023; UN, 2023).

Companies' dilemma of attracting qualified employees, training, and retaining them is pivotal to further sustainable development and business operations. According to Ireland's Global Citizens 2030 Ireland's Talent and Innovation Strategy, Ireland intends to invest in improving leadership and management development standards in Irish SMEs and attract international learners, researchers, and innovators, which have become a priority for the Irish government. In addition, a wider uptake of programmes to develop management capabilities in leading growth for sustainable development through the prism of an entrepreneurial mindset in Irish SMEs can address fundamental weaknesses in the sector. The emphasis on recognising the reality of a diverse and multicultural working environment will benefit SMEs' engagement in upskilling and developing a better understanding and implementation of responsible practices.

Additionally, at the level of management skills, Irish policy regulators determine socially responsible behaviour as another critical challenge SMEs face. Most businesses across entire sectors were completely closed for a significant period (Bank of Ireland, 2022), and even now, their survival is still threatened by the lack of qualified employees and liquidity. Thus, SMEs need to consider carefully integrating digital technologies into their operations and fastening the online learning implementation process to close the existing skill gap. The employees' demand has shown the necessity of changes in getting specific learning quickly instead of going through the traditional long-term curriculum (Nachmias & Hubschmid-Vierheilig, 2021). Digital learning might be very effective for SMEs if it is correctly targeted and based on specific goals (Nachmias & Hubschmid-Vierheilig, 2021).

The level of technological literacy has begun to play a crucial role. According to the Digital Economy and Society Index (DESI), Ireland ranks third among 27 EU members, with 70% of people having basic digital skills (European Commission, 2022). Digitalisation has become a new reality, helping to provide significant changes in organisational structures (Penco et al., 2022) and decision-making processes. Thus, the question of professional training for SME owners on how to develop their entrepreneurial mindset considering social responsibility and achieving sustainable growth remains open. Additionally, learning and developing an entrepreneurial mindset are expected to help entrepreneurs survive, improve their business processes for effective growth, and, as a result, create new employment capacity and benefit the economy.

11.3 The Dilemma of Social Responsibility

Business management was seen as a source of maximising profits for shareholders; therefore, corporate social responsibility (CSR) was perceived as a potential threat to financial performance (Lee & Isa, 2024). Later, the idea of shareholders was transformed into stakeholders, including customers, employees, and communities, who might benefit from the company's performance and sustained levels of growth (Freeman, 1984). Therefore, for entrepreneurs, delivering social and environmental benefits to the stakeholders has become vital in supporting sustainable development (Adomako et al., 2023). The United Nations 2030 agenda supports the shift of SDGs from the global economy to the private sector. The important factor is that sustainable development is not economic exclusively but should address ecological and social demand (Tiep Le et al., 2023). To ensure the necessary balance between these factors, firms should reassess their social values and their impact on the sustainable development of business (Tiep Le et al., 2023; Abdelhalim and Amani, 2019; Youn et al., 2018). The vast majority of corporations have embedded socially responsible practices into their performance. However, small companies experience a lack of these practices. SMEs usually have to survive, putting financial performance as a leading priority and ignoring the implementation of environmental practices and community involvement. Compared to multinational corporations, SMEs are rarely involved in sustainable development issues due to various constraints, such as a lack of resources, power, and awareness of how they can influence sustainable development (Smith et al., 2022; Lewis et al., 2015; Djupdal & Westhead, 2015). Thus, the sustainability agenda is failing due to the costs, and its targets are not achieved yet. Entrepreneurs find implementing sustainability challenges costly and complex and prefer to ignore them until the government forces them (Sundström et al., 2020). However, this situation has started to change gradually in recent years, especially in internationally operating SMEs that will be significantly exposed to geoeconomic and geopolitical dynamics (Torkkeli & Durst, 2022a).

Experiencing heavy dependence on foreign investors, the Irish government aims to increase the number of entrepreneurs and fast-growing start-ups to diversify its economy and receive more independence from multinational corporations (Enterprise Ireland, 2022). Considering their quantity and employment capacity, these intentions should extensively support "*domestic*" businesses. Additionally, they are crucial for the economy, being a critical link between global–macro-level, meso, and individual–micro-level economies (Smith et al., 2022), and they deserve strong attention from global and local partners. However, support for companies should not explicitly focus on financial resources; entrepreneurs should also be aware of how to operate socially responsibly, stay financially successful and keep society and the environment in mind.

Additionally, companies constantly develop, do not stand in the same place, and pass different life cycle stages: start-up, growth, maturity, and recession. Start-ups are newly registered young companies in the process of their business model exploration and transforming their idea into a consolidated business for further successful operation. Operational activity in start-ups might be unstable during their exploration and development. Thus, government support for them becomes crucial to provide conditions for the companies to consolidate their positions and progress to the next stage as SMEs (OECD, 2023; Smith et al., 2022; Torkkeli & Durst, 2022a; OECD, 2022a). Additionally, the government should ensure that they offer an appropriate policy framework that emerges as vital in supporting SMEs to consolidate their operations and avoid potentially high levels of failure associated with this sector.

The smooth transition from start-up to growth company requires substantial operating finance, receiving management experience for the owner, and a successful track record. For further growth and development in a long-term perspective, the small company's owner has to expand managerial skills, build an effective team, and move from short-term planning to strategic one. Reaching the maturity stage will ease pressure on the owner by having an established team, reputation, and strong partner connections (Smith et al., 2022; Torkkeli & Durst, 2022a; OECD, 2022a). At every stage of a company's development, entrepreneurs need to decide how to perform with regard to the economy, society, and environment to be socially responsible and environmentally friendly, as illustrated in Figure 11.7. To guarantee the company's successful

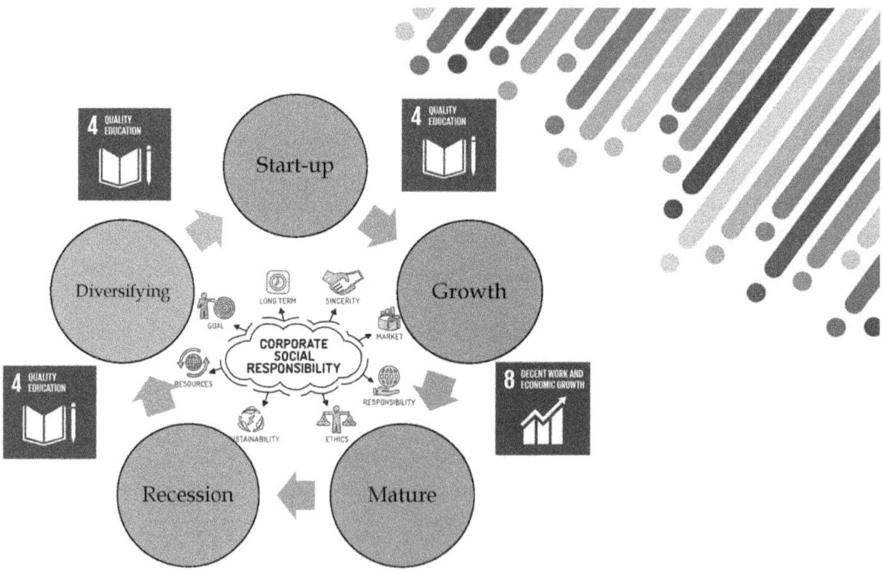

Figure 11.7 SMEs development stages.

Source: Adapted from UN (2015), Smith (2022), Tiep Le, (2023).

transition from one stage to another, company executives can address through the implementation of SDG 4 – Quality Education, which will benefit SDG 8 – Decent Work and Economic Growth, considering not only profits but also raising own awareness on how to perform responsibly about society and the environment. Quality Education stands for reaching this goal. If SMEs perform successfully, they contribute to Economic Growth and create workplaces for employees.

This framework, applied in small companies, will help to attract qualified staff, customers, and investors, decrease operational costs, build a strong relationship between different stakeholders, and ease the pressure of economic uncertainty where SMEs should operate (Tiep Le et al., 2023; Abdelhalim and Amani, 2019; Youn et al., 2018). Irish Small Advanced Economic model, characterised by strong international orientation and foreign investment attraction, puts pressure on SMEs to compete with corporations in resource and talent attraction (Government of Ireland, 2023; OECD, 2022a). Thus, offering opportunities to learn and develop with a personalised approach can become a competitive advantage for small companies compared with the pressure of corporations.

Although the determination of instruments and resources necessary for SMEs to include SDGs in their everyday activity might be unclear, SDG 4 education can manage the challenges such as a quickly changing business landscape driven by fast-evolving technologies, innovation, and economic uncertainties (Ortiz-Martínez et al., 2023; Smith et al., 2022; Reporting Lab, 2021). Therefore, defining these instruments and SME executives' training on understanding and implementing SDG practices can become an important competitive advantage (Torkkeli & Durst, 2022a) in the future of Irish SMEs and their national, regional, and global position. Companies' sustainable development is interconnected with corporate social responsibility (CSR), and CSR is viewed as a part of the sustainability goals from the stakeholders' perspective (Ortiz-Martínez et al., 2023). Economic intention promoted by the United Nations in SDG 8 in the aspect of entrepreneurship support, SME growth, and protecting labour rights, specifically women's rights, should positively impact economic growth (UN, 2015); however, all initiatives demand money, leaving business owners in front of the choice between profits and costly socially responsible way of performing.

Despite SMEs' small size, they significantly impact the community, government, and environment. However, there is a gap in research on how senior executives might be trained to perform in a CSR frame. According to Torkkeli and Durst (2022b), learning might become a starting point for exploring CSR in SMEs, and there is a direct link between the concept of SDGs learning, responsible operating in small companies, and developing an entrepreneurial mindset. Small and medium-sized businesses might consider creating their learning strategies and networks as sources of knowledge (internal or external) for effective collaboration. These conclusions have been supported by the latest reports from the World Bank (2021) and OECD (2023). While operating in the

SME context, the organisational learning theory might become a frame of the company's educational system and corporate social responsibility. Recent empirical studies (Valdez-Juárez et al., 2019) state that owners are trying to focus on new forms of studying to achieve socially responsible behaviour, which includes social, economic, and environmental responsibility. Furthermore, empowerment and continuous training are crucial for building competitive advantage (Torkkeli & Durst, 2022a); thus, the next section will delve into the importance of executives' education and their teams' development, as they cannot succeed alone.

11.4 The Importance of Executives' Training and Team Development in SMEs

Human talent is an essential part of any company, which forms the competitive advantage and determines the effectiveness of firm performance (Shela et al., 2023). Employees help the company reach the goals of productive performance by applying their knowledge, skills, and competencies. In the context of the transition to the green economy and the challenges posed by dominant economic models require major changes that enable an industrial shift to a more human-centric approach, such skills as collaboration and the ability to perform as a team are becoming critical aspects of the future company and its integration within the notion of economies that support sustainable development (Bendickson and Chandler, 2019; Kengatharan, 2021; Ployhart, 2021).

Education in small and medium-sized companies remains a relatively new field of science that demands reflections on its further integration, cohesion, and development. As mentioned, working with knowledge, leadership, and an entrepreneurial mindset are the skills needed for responsible and successful performance in Industry 5.0 conditions. However, in the circumstances of constant economic and political challenges, acquiring valuable information and converting it into a knowledge management strategy becomes a priority. The question is how busy entrepreneurs can engage with vast volumes of information so that they can extract all necessary economic and political information if their background relies on knowledge received in school, college, and experience and the global economic landscape is defined by its high levels of uncertainty and fast pace of change (St-Pierre et al., 2023). Here, the team starts to play a crucial role as a critical information holder and a source of invaluable insights. The importance of team learning could be hardly compared to any other initiative as it determines companies' ability to reach success, productivity growth, and efficacy (Lazarević & Lukić, 2018a) while developing teams is a necessary skill for every entrepreneur focus on the company's growth (Borch and Madsen, 2007; Gherhes et al., 2016; Owalla et al., 2022).

Global economic challenges highlight the significance of collaboration, cooperation, knowledge sharing, and teamwork. As such, learning in teams has become a subject of significant exploration since the beginning of the 21st century (Van der Haar et al. 2013; Guchait et al., 2014; Hedlund & Österberg,

2013; Matić, 2022). Meanwhile, large enterprises have more possibilities to broaden the exploration of learning issues (Matić, 2022). However, these questions are mostly neglected in small and medium-sized businesses, resulting in a negative effect when taking into consideration businesses' competitive dimensions. Large corporations and SMEs employ different approaches to design learning strategies. According to Jones et al. (2010), learning in SMEs occurs mainly as a reaction to some crisis and seeks immediate solutions rather than implementing a consistent learning strategy. Besides, SMEs' executives are critical in the decision-making process and play a significant role in the company's performance. Conversely, they might become the main barrier to building a learning environment (Man et al., 2008; Santos et al., 2012; Ng and Kee, 2018; Tam & Gray, 2021). Owners' sceptical perceptions and unawareness of learning necessities can negatively impact firm performance and effectiveness, as in most cases, owners positively perceive employees training and quite negatively their own (Mohammad, 2019). Besides, sources of knowledge for SMEs might be limited compared to large corporations due to the lack of internal resources, budgets, and expertise (Audretsch & Belitski, 2021), and the return on knowledge investment can significantly vary (Usman et al., 2018).

Although skills in working with knowledge are becoming a priority for entrepreneurs, the learning possibilities can be modest, using only learning from peers, competitors, and the market (Puthusserry et al., 2020) without any strategic approach to designing knowledge creation mechanisms and knowledge sharing within the team what poses important challenges when working in complex and interrelated economic systems (Audretsch & Belitski, 2021). The executives' loose direction in collecting knowledge for SMEs remains strategic, managerial, and organisational components (Brunswicker and Vanhaverbeke, 2014). Most SMEs do not have a clear vision of knowledge system building and tend to do it operationally and irregularly (Mohammad, 2019; Audretsch & Belitski, 2021; St-Pierre et al., 2023). Moreover, difficulties appear in recognising the necessary skills for learning in teams due to a lack of knowledge sharing and communication, which could fasten the acquisition of the required leadership and entrepreneurial skills, as team members might already have this knowledge and simple sharing would be more effective than entering into the learning process. The problem can be solved according to the mechanism of converting team learning inputs into team learning outputs (Kérivel et al., 2022; McKeown, 2012). While working together, team members can learn from one another (Woerkom & Croon, 2009) as team members have more expertise, experience, skills, and knowledge than individuals (Tannenbaum et al., 2012). Knowledge in teams, which consolidates collective knowledge, helps companies to compete and innovate as teams bring together individual knowledge, skills, and expertise to achieve shared goals (Manohar Singh and Gupta, 2014; Chen et al., 2018; Berraies & Chouiref, 2023). Teams can compensate for any individual member's lack of skills or knowledge by replacing them with other team members' capabilities.

Effective team learning is a complex process and may be affected by different factors, including team psychological safety, team development, team learning dynamics, team structure, and organisational strategy (Decuyper et al., 2010; Edmondson, 1999). Figure 11.8 represents connections between factors influencing team learning, which can be mitigated by team members' experience and expertise and correct roles defining and building a picture of an entrepreneurial mindset (Lazarević & Lukić, 2018a). To build effective team learning in the firm, SME senior managers should understand business strategy and leadership practices as well as deal with their employees' diverse backgrounds and intercultural features (Tam & Gray, 2021). Since any team learning starts from building the team, entrepreneurs need to consider employees' experience, education, and level of skills to identify appropriate programmes that can help compensate for missing learning pods and contribute to SDG 4 (Journeault et al., 2021). However, owners sometimes struggle with hiring the right people in a highly competitive labour market, offering different positions to the non-nationals equally as to nationals. Understanding that results will lead to company success, economic growth, and reaching business strategy goals, contributing to SDG 8 is as essential as recognising the diversity of employees and their intercultural backgrounds in a global context.

To operate successfully in an uncertain and dynamic environment while taking into consideration the growing impact of geoeconomic and geopolitical systems within integrated economies (UN, 2015; Ashauer & Macan, 2013), SME owners need to understand how to build a diverse learning team which aims to receive knowledge, expand leadership skills and techniques, and deepen entrepreneurial mindset, while enabling quality education and continuous

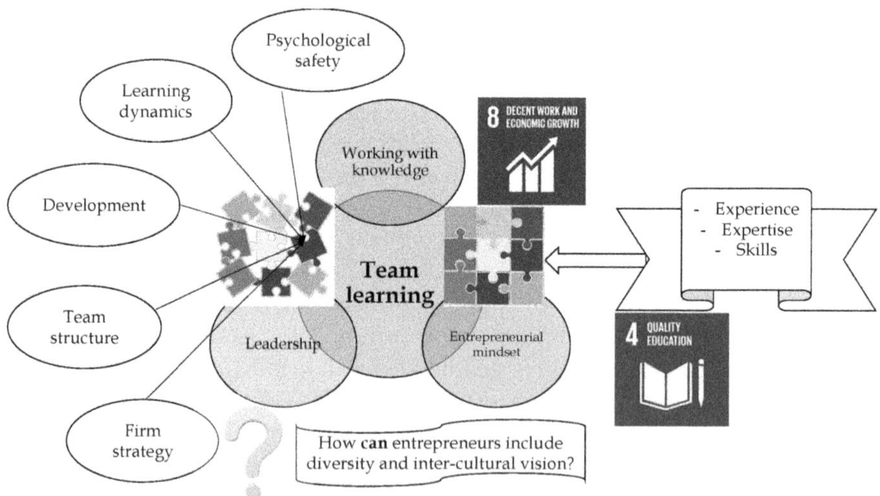

Figure 11.8 Challenges and solutions in team learning.

Source: Adapted from Lazarević and Lukić (2018b), Decuyper (2010).

training to their workforce. Developing leadership skills and working with knowledge should not appear to be challenging to address, as the offer of training programmes from educational and professional companies is exhaustive. However, the question of improving the entrepreneurial mindset of their staff in the framework of diversity and intercultural backgrounds might be quite challenging to address. The following section explores these programmes offers/possible demands and the varieties of government support provided to entrepreneurs.

11.5 Educational Offer and Government Support

Small businesses operate in a highly unpredictable economic environment, and their success is not guaranteed. At the same time, the possibility of failure remains high; approximately 50% of SMEs may survive longer than 6 years, and 30% may last less than 18 months (OECD, 2019; Bureau of Labour Statistics, 2021). Such a short life span makes it hard for this group to get government and educational support. Developing managerial skills is much more challenging than developing any other skills as they require more complicated knowledge (Whetten et al., 2011). While SMEs are growing from small to larger firms, the managerial challenges are growing progressively (Kindström et al., 2022). According to Parker (2010), Lee (2014), Littumen and Tohmo (2003), and Cavallo (2019), the most challenging factors for executives may become human resources development, as the complexity of resolving these issues relates to owners' experience and background (Lee et al., 2014). Considering that most entrepreneurs are mostly 'self-made' individuals, they lack fundamental knowledge and managerial training and can benefit from high contextual experience and ambitions (Olson et al., 2008; Storey, 2011; Kindström et al., 2022). Experience, education, and cultural background, as well as the ability to use them in company performance, are vital competencies in the framework of economic transition to the 5.0 model. However, entrepreneurs need to understand complex economic processes and the changing political landscape, which requires additional skills. This urgent demand was identified in the concept of Industry 5.0 and the United Nations 2.0 framework (European Commission, 2023; UN, 2023), arguing that an entrepreneurial mindset and work with knowledge should be embedded through digital, data, innovation, behavioural, and foresight skills. Companies that successfully implement this set will benefit in the future despite geoeconomic and geopolitical challenges.

SMEs in Ireland are the main employment entity, as in 2023, they employed approximately 1.2 million people, compared to MNCs, with four times less. Thus, the Irish government provides various supportive programs to SMEs, including financial assistance, mentoring, networking, and leadership training (IDA Ireland, 2023; Enterprise Ireland, 2023). However, the interest in this offer from small companies might be unstable; business owners recognise the necessity of managerial training for their executives (McQuillan et al., 2020) but do not address themselves. SME owners' unwillingness to learn can cause challenges to the Irish economy with the rising trend of workforce migration. Being historically a country of emigration, Ireland experienced a rise in the number of non-Irish people, some of whom are more qualified and experienced and can benefit from specific sectors, rising unemployment rate and provoking tensions (Hughes et al., 2007; McGinnity and Kingston, 2017b). In 2023, a 31% increase in migration numbers in Ireland was stated compared to 2022, which equals almost 142 thousand (CSO, 2023). Despite the attraction and integration of international workers, it is vital for Irish economic development. Migration is a critical factor for the economic development of the recipient country as it creates added value for the entire economic sector and stimulates country cooperation, which is crucial for small open economies like Ireland (Savin et al., 2023; Kozlovskyi et al., 2024). The ICT sector is a leading recipient of internationals, with 33% of employment, compared to 18% across all sectors (Central Bank, 2023).

The rising migration trend can provide the Irish economy with a pipeline of qualified and experienced professionals and ease the problem of population ageing and the need for a diverse workforce. To identify and embed highly skilled workers into the working environment, companies need to recognise the professional background of these employees, and in case candidates are successful, companies need to apply for a work permit. All permits are issued through the Department of Enterprise, Trade and Employment (DETE). The permit application process is not straightforward, and a timeline of receiving a final decision prevents owners from hiring non-nationals. In 2023, DETE issued 30,981 permits (Table 11.1), a 29% decline compared to 2022. The main recipient of migrant workers has become the health sector, moving from second place in 2022 and leaving the IT sector far behind, while manufacturing and service sectors occupy third and fourth places. Thus, the primary attention of government and private educational bodies might consider the need to focus on those sectors.

Companies' executives hiring international workers should be aware of the main challenges in integrating such employees as cultural identity processes in everyday interaction, work-related language skills and nationality (Vanhanen et al., 2023; Kindström et al., 2022; Suni et al., 2022). DETE report permits issued to companies in 2023 were used to explore what nationalities usually apply for work permits. Figure 11.9 shows that applicants from 133 countries were granted work permits in 2023, predominating India, the Philippines, and Brazil, equal to 55% of all applications. Asian, African, and North American applicants represent the top 10 countries' donors. The distribution of nationalities has changed slightly since 2022; the only change in the list represents moving Russian nationality from the top ten to the 21st place.

The integration of international workers is vital for economic development, and Ireland is not an exception. Integrating internationals into a company's culture is a complex and lengthy process; while SME owners focus on their company's survival, they ignore this issue, not recognising the necessity (Vanhanen

Table 11.1 Permits number through economic sectors

Economic Sector	
Q - Health & Social Work Activities	10,037
J - Information & Communication Activities	5,009
C - Manufacturing	3,037
I - Accommodation & Food Services activities	2,606
S - Other Service activities	3,994
A - Agriculture, Forestry & Fishing	1,385
F - Construction	1,349
M - All other Professional, Scientific & Technical	1,293
H - Transport & Storage	907
D - Electricity & Gas & Air Conditioning Supply	371
R - Arts, Entertainment and Recreation	336
G - Wholesale & Retail Trade	294
P - Education	246
E - Water Supply - Sewerage Waste Management & Rem	87
B - Mining & Quarrying	30
Grand Total	**30,981**

Source: Adapted from DETE (2023).

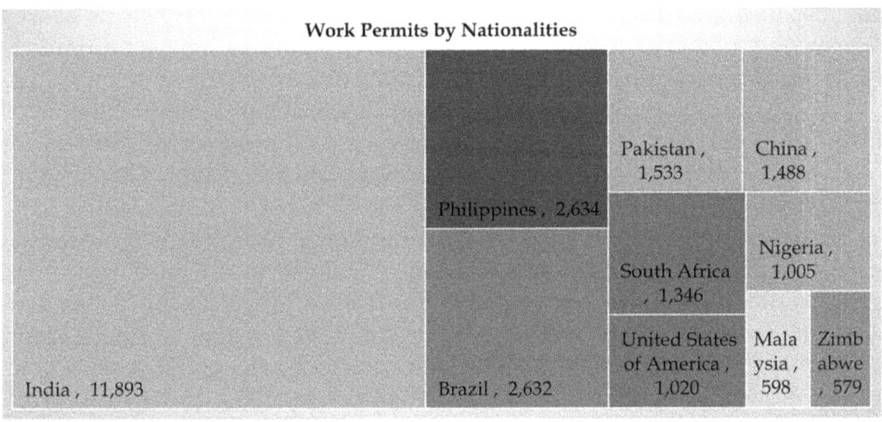

Figure 11.9 Permits according to the nationalities.

Source: Adapted from DETE (2023).

et al., 2023; Lawless et al., 2022). However, the company's ability to build a productive learning environment will guarantee achieving all the necessary skills to operate effectively and responsively (Asher & Popper, 2021) and dealing with intercultural employees is becoming essential. Building a learning organisation is a lengthy process which requires the owner's awareness and deep involvement. SMEs have an advantaged position as they have more flexibility, agility, and openness to new ideas (Matić, 2022).

In geoeconomic and geopolitical uncertainty conditions, SMEs face numerous challenges and disruptions. Understanding economic challenges and political changes requires new essential skills, new approaches to learning, and entrepreneurial thinking in a global context. Leadership and management competencies need to be reconsidered. New demands urgently require entrepreneurs' involvement in working with knowledge, leadership, and innovatively operating data with the help of digital skills to expand foresight and change their behaviour. Integrating qualified employees with intercultural backgrounds will expand companies' possibilities for acquiring knowledge and skills through team learning and knowledge sharing. Implementing this framework into the company learning strategy will help benefit from the perspective of quality education SDG 4, improve economic development with the growing rate of employment possibilities for SDG 8, and strengthen the Irish economy.

11.6 Critical Discussion and Policy Implications

To operate successfully, businesses have to consider the level of economic uncertainty and be able to foresee the political challenges, adjusting their performance and expenditures accordingly (Kim, 2019b; Vural-Yava, 2020; Alandejani & Al-Shaer, 2023). As a small open economy, Ireland is heavily dependent on foreign investors, represented by multinational corporations (Enterprise Ireland, 2022). It needs to balance investment attraction and support of "domestic" businesses. This support should focus on a combination of financial resources and providing entrepreneurs with upgraded skill sets for receiving profits without damaging the environment and society (Tiep Le et al., 2023; Abdelhalim and Amani, 2019; Youn et al., 2018).

The research findings suggest that organisational, technical, economic, and legal competencies, crucial for companies to succeed in the green transition, stay insufficient to remain successful and provide a prognosis for further economic and political challenges (Jamwal et al., 2023). Digital and management skills always represent a gap in small companies' entrepreneurial skills (Zhong et al. 2017; Machado et al. 2020; Oztemel and Gursev 2020; Zheng et al. 2021). Thus, working with knowledge is becoming a pillar to addressing geoeconomic challenges and embedding it as an integral part of a lifelong learning concept (Håkansson Lindqvist et al., 2023). The concept of Industry 5.0 and the United Nations 2.0 framework (European Commission, 2023; UN, 2023) demands are new skillset further to embed an entrepreneurial mindset and work with knowledge through digital, data, innovation, behavioural, and foresight skills. Companies that successfully implement this set will benefit despite geoeconomic and geopolitical challenges. However, regarding employee attraction, small companies face the dilemma of hiring the relevant workforce or increasing expenditures in upskilling. Policymakers should consider that addressing training possibilities for improving leadership skills and deepening team learning should not cause difficulties.

For small open economies like Ireland, significant GDP increase and empowering country cooperation become benefits brought by migration as a critical factor for the economic development of the recipient country (Savin et al., 2023; Kozlovskyi et al., 2024). Ireland fully experiences the rising migration trend, which can provide it with qualified and experienced professionals and ease the problem of population ageing. Companies need to apply for a work permit to hire highly skilled employees. Due to the unstraightforward permit application process and a long waiting time to receive a final decision, owners prefer not to hire non-nationals. Therefore, another practical implication for policymakers is recognising the necessity to reassess the application process and raise the awareness of SME owners on the benefits of migrant hiring (Vanhanen et al., 2023; Lawless et al., 2022). Quite a similar situation appears when internationals intend to start their own company and face the need to address the eligibility criteria and afford the complicated bureaucratic process. Policymakers should also reassess the approach of starting the business for non-Irish people as they can bring new skills to the labour market and add substantial value to the economy, raising GDP and creating employment opportunities (CSO, 2023).

11.7 Conclusion

As a significant player in the economy, small businesses are sensitive to economic and political responses to circumstances of uncertainty in an open economy model with high demand for investments (Finnegan & Kapoor, 2023). Small businesses should carefully prioritise their financial performance and shareholders' interests (Lee & Isa, 2024). Therefore, entrepreneurs should be aware of the major global trends in the economy, politics, and environmental response to navigate uncertain and ever-changing circumstances.

Despite their size, SMEs have a powerful impact on society (Smith et al., 2022), producing around 68% of employment in Ireland and benefiting the Sustainable Agenda and SDG 8 by providing job opportunities for employees. For entrepreneurs, further training for upskilling and obtaining the required managerial skills in working with knowledge, creating a knowledge management strategy in line with the entrepreneurial mindset is vital in the economic transition to Industry 5.0, creating an entrepreneurial-friendly environment that nurtures and encourages innovative initiatives to provide Ireland with a stable position in the highly competitive European and Global economy and ease heavy dependence from transnational corporations. Knowledge management has become so important in companies as it helps SME owners to foresight and address geoeconomic and geopolitical challenges. To design an adequate knowledge strategy, executives can use the power of team learning and knowledge sharing and embedding skilled and qualified migrants who can share their unique experiences, which natives might not have.

Due to executives' impact on the company's learning environment (Asher & Popper, 2021), additional research is required to offer insights into how SME owners can expand their entrepreneurial mindset and better integrate staff with intercultural backgrounds. SMEs have more chances to succeed in reacting to challenges as they meet less inertial forces and are more flexible, having less bureaucracy through the decision-making process (Bratianu et al., 2020). Managers may lack understanding of the necessity of learning and its impact on company performance; therefore, developing managerial competencies in conditions of manufacturing paradigm shift and rising employee roles is significant. Quality education, as SDG 4, supports SME executives in achieving competencies of the new technological era and providing decent work and economic growth.

The research has identified limitations that can be considered part of future research. An initial aspect to be considered relates to how managers need to re-examine and interpret their role in management practices and organisational context and the evolution of their perception and behaviour during operational and learning activities (Rostron, 2021). Moreover, the research interest broadens to include learning approaches and executives' abilities to facilitate team learning according to the latest requirements to influence development in SMEs. Entrepreneurial teams need to be adequately trained and evaluated based on multiple criteria and aligned with sustainable development indicators of Quality Education and Economic Growth applicable to SMEs. This further research would encourage small businesses to assess themselves through the lens of knowledge management strategy to address geoeconomic and political challenges. Furthermore, entrepreneurs need to reconsider the question of employees' better integration with various backgrounds, cultures, and languages.

References

Abdelhalim, K., & Amani, G.E. (2019). Can CSR help achieve sustainable development? Applying a new assessment model to CSR cases from Egypt. *The International Journal of Sociology and Social Policy*, 39(9), 773–795.

Adomako, S., Abdelgawad, S. G., Ahsan, M., Amankwah-Amoah, J., & Azaaviele Liedong, T. (2023). Nonmarket strategy in emerging markets: The link between SMEs' corporate political activity, corporate social responsibility, and firm competitiveness. *Journal of Business Research*, 160. https://doi.org/10.1016/j.jbusres.2023.113767

Alandejani, M., & Al-Shaer, H. (2023). Macro Uncertainty Impacts on ESG Performance and Carbon Emission Reduction Targets. *Sustainability (Switzerland)*, 15(5). https://doi.org/10.3390/su15054249

Alesina Marco Tabellini, A., Boustan, L., Enke, B., Farina, S., Fouka, V., Gennaioli, N., Giavazzi, F., Giuliano, P., Nagler, M., & Tabellini, M. (2022). The political effects of immigration: culture or economics? http://www.nber.org/papers/w30079

Ashauer, S. A., & Macan, T. (2013). How can leaders foster team learning? Effects of leader-assigned mastery and performance goals and psychological safety. *Journal of Psychology: Interdisciplinary and Applied*, 147(6), 541–561. https://doi.org/10.1080/00223980.2012.719940

Azadnia, A. H., Stephens, S., Ghadimi, P., and Onofrei, G. (2022). A comprehensive performance measurement framework for business incubation centres: Empirical evidence in an Irish context. *Business Strategy and the Environment*. https://doi.org/10.1002/bse.3036

Bank of Ireland (2022). No.2 SME liquidity needs during the COVID-19 shock (McGeever, McQuinn and Myers). https://ec.europa.eu/growth/smes/business-friendly-environment/sme-definition_en

Barry, F., & Bergin, A., (2019). 'Export structure, FDI and the rapidity of Ireland's recovery from crisis', *Economic and Social Review*, 50, 707–724.

Bendickson, J.S., & Chandler, T.D. (2019), "Operational performance: the mediator between human capital developmental programs and financial performance", *Journal of Business Research*, 94, 162–171, 10.1016/j.jbusres.2017.10.049

Berraies, S., & Chouiref, A. (2023). Exploring the effect of team climate on knowledge management in teams through team work engagement: evidence from knowledge-intensive firms. *Journal of Knowledge Management*, 27(3), 842–869. https://doi.org/10.1108/JKM-09-2021-0720

Birdthistle, N. (2019). Under the microscope – an examination of the supports for ethnic entrepreneurs in Ireland. *Education and Training*, 61(6), 666–683. https://doi.org/10.1108/ET-07-2018-0157

Borch, O. J., & Madsen, E. L. (2007). Dynamic capabilities facilitating innovative strategies in SMEs. *International Journal of Techno entrepreneurship*. 1 (1), 109–125. https://doi.org/10.1504/IJTE.2007.014731

Breznitz, D. (2012). Ideas, structure, state action and economic growth: Rethinking the Irish miracle. *Review of International Political Economy*, 19(1), 87–113. https://doi.org/10.1080/09692290.2010.514260

Brownlow, G., (2020). 'Industrial policy in Northern Ireland: past, present and future', *Economic and Social Review*, 51, pp. 407–424.

Central Bank, (2023). The Role of the ICT Services Sector in the Irish Economy. https://www.centralbank.ie/docs/default-source/publications/quarterly-bulletins/quarterly-bulletin-signed-articles/the-role-of-ict-services-sector-irish-economy.pdf

Central Statistics Office. (2023). Population and Migration Estimates. https://www.cso.ie/en/releasesandpublications/ep/p-pme/populationandmigrationestimatesapril2023/keyfindings/

Chen, H., Baptista Nunes, M., Ragsdell, G., & An, X. (2018), "Extrinsic and intrinsic motivation for experience grounded tacit knowledge sharing in Chinese software organisations", *Journal of Knowledge Management*, 22(2), pp. 478–498

Decuyper, S., Dochy, F., & Van den Bossche, P. (2010). Grasping the dynamic complexity of team learning: an integrative model for effective team learning in organisations. *Educational Research Review*, 5(2), 111–133. https://doi.org/10.1016/j.edurev.2010.02.002

Department of Enterprise, Trade and Enterprise. (2023). Employment Permits Statistivs. https://enterprise.gov.ie/en/publications/employment-permit-statistics-2023.html

Deloitte (2022). The benefits of encouraging an international workforce to come to Ireland. https://www2.deloitte.com/ie/en/pages/tax/articles/the-benefits-of-encouraging-an-international-workforce-to-come-here.html

Djupdal, K., & Westhead, P. (2015). Environmental certification as a buffer against the liabilities of newness and smallness: Firm performance benefits. *International Small Business Journal*, 33(2), 148–168.

Economic and Financial Affairs European Economic Forecast, European Economy. (2024). https://doi.org/10.2765/01964

Edmondson, A. (1999). Psychological safety and learning behaviour in work teams. *Administrative Science Quarterly*, 44 (2), 350–383.

Enterprise Ireland. (2022). Annual Report and Accounts 2022. https://www.enterprise-ireland.com/resource/blob/129110/527ce35e01b558f59131e842d065d4f0/2022-annual-report-and-accounts-new-data.pdf

Enterprise Ireland. (2023). Learn about Enterprise Ireland. https://www.enterprise-ireland.com/en/About-Us/

European Commission. (2022). EU Research and Innovation in Ireland. https://ireland.representation.ec.europa.eu/strategy-and-priorities/key-eu-policies-ireland/eu-research-and-innovation-ireland_en

Finnegan, M., & Kapoor, S. (2023). ECB unconventional monetary policy and SME access to finance. *Small Business Economics*, 61(3), 1253–1288. https://doi.org/10.1007/s11187-023-00730-0

Fitzsimons, P., & O'Gorman, C. (2021). A Survey of entrepreneurship in Ireland. Global Entrepreneurship Monitoring (GEM).

Freeman, R. E. (1984). *Strategic management: A stakeholder perspective*. Pitman Publishing Inc.

Gherbes, C., Williams, N., Vorley, T., & Vasconcelos, A. C. (2016). Distinguishing micro-businesses from SMEs: a systematic review of growth constraints. *Journal of Small Business and Enterprise Development*, 23(4), 939–963. https://doi.org/10.1108/JSBED-05-2016-0075

Håkansson Lindqvist, M., Mozelius, P., Jaldemark, J., & Cleveland Innes, M. (2023). Higher education transformation towards lifelong learning in a digital era–a scoping literature review. *International Journal of Lifelong Education*. https://doi.org/10.1080/02601370.2023.2279047

Hughes, G., F. McGinnity, P. O'Connell and E. Quinn, 2007. The Impact of Migration. In T. Fahey, H. Russell and C. Whelan, *Best of Times? The Social Impact of the Celtic Tiger*, Dublin: Institute of Public Administration.

IDA Ireland. (2023). Scale with IDA. https://www.idaireland.com/explore-your-sector/business-sectors/business-services

Irawan, B., Rofiah, C., & Hasan, W. (2023). Empowering Micro Small and Medium Enterprises (MSMEs) to Improve. *Global Economic Welfare*. 1(2). https://edujavare.com/index.php/IARE/

Jamwal, A., Agrawal, R., & Sharma, M. (2023). Challenges and opportunities for manufacturing SMEs in adopting industry 4.0 technologies for achieving sustainability: Empirical evidence from an emerging economy. *Operations Management Research*. https://doi.org/10.1007/s12063-023-00428-2

Jones, O., Macpherson, A., and Thorpe, R. (2010), Learning in owner-managed small firms: mediating artefacts and strategic space', *Entrepreneurship and Regional Development*, 22, 649–673.

Kengatharan, N. (2021), "A jack of all trades is a master of none: the nexus of firm-specific Human capital, ambidexterity, productivity and firm performance", *South Asian Journal of Human Resources Management*, 8(1), 79–102.

Kérivel, T., Bossard, C., & Kermarrec, G. (2022). Team learning process: a longitudinal study in dynamic situation. *Learning Organization*, 29(1), 52–68. https://doi.org/10.1108/TLO-09-2020-0177

Kim, O.S. (2019a). Does Political Uncertainty Increase External Financing Costs? Measuring the Electoral Premium in Syndicated Lending. *The Journal of Financial and Quantitative Analysis*. 54, 2141–2178.

Kindström, D., Carlborg, P., & Nord, T. (2022). Challenges for growing SMEs: A managerial perspective. *Journal of Small Business Management*, 1(24). https://doi.org/10.1080/00472778.2022.2082456

Kozlovskyi, S., Kulinich, T., Vechirko, I., Lavrov, R., Zayukov, I., & Mazur, H. (2024). "Relationship between net migration and economic development of European countries: Empirical conclusions." *Problems and Perspectives in Management*, 22(1), 605–618. https://doi.org/10.21511/ppm.22(1).2024.48

Kren, J., Lawless, M., O'Toole, C., Mccann, F., and Mcquinn, J. (2021). New survey evidence on COVID-19 and Irish SMEs: Measuring the impact and policy response. https://www.cso.ie/en/releasesandpublications/ep/p-covid19/covid-

Lawless, M., Neary, J. P., & Studnicka, Z., (2019). 'South-North trade in Ireland: gravity and firms from the Good Friday Agreement to Brexit', *Economic and Social Review*, 50, 751–766.
Lazarević, S., & Lukić, J. (2018a). Team Learning Processes And Activities In Organisation: A Case Study, 56(3). http://www.economic-themes.com/
Lee, S. P., & Isa, M. (2024). Corporate sustainability practices and financial performance: The moderating role of corporate controversies and Shariah screening. *Corporate Social Responsibility and Environmental Management*. https://doi.org/10.1002/csr.2763
Lewis, K. V., Cassells, S., & Roxas, H. (2015). SMEs and the potential for a collaborative path to environmental responsibility. *Business Strategy and the Environment*, 24(8), 750–764
Machado, C.G., Winroth, M.P., Ribeiro da Silva, E. H. D. (2020). Sustainable manufacturing in industry 4.0: an emerging research agenda. *International Journal of Production Research*, 58(5), 1462–1484.
Man, T.W.Y., Lau, T., & Snape, E. (2008), "Entrepreneurial competencies and the performance of small and medium enterprises: an investigation through a framework of competitiveness", *Journal of Small Business and Entrepreneurship*, 21(3), 257–276.
Manohar Singh, R., & Gupta, M. (2014), "Knowledge management in teams: empirical integration and development of a scale", *Journal of Knowledge Management*, 18(4), 777–794.
McGeever, N., Sarchi, C., & Woods, M. (2020). Irish company births and insolvent liquidations during the COVID-19 shock, *Economic Letters*, 13: 544–560. www.centralbank.ie
McKeown, I. (2012). Team Learning in SMEs: Learning the Lessons. *Industry and Higher Education*, 26(6), 491–503. https://doi.org/10.5367/ihe.2012.0123
McGinnity, F., Kingston, G., (2017a). An Irish Welcome? Changing Irish Attitudes to Immigrants and Immigration: the Role of Recession and Immigration. *The Economic and Social Review*. 48(3), 253–279.
Mcquillan, D., Nolan, T., Osaghae, C., Sweeney, O., & Rashwan, L. (2020). Leading the Way: Investing in Management Development for SME Leading the Way: Investing in Management Development for SME Productivity and Growth: Report by the Expert Group on Future Productivity and Growth: Report by the Expert Group on Future Skills Needs Skills Needs Expert Group on Future Skill Needs. https://doi.org/10.21427/fdje-0016
Mohammad, H.I. (2019). Mediating effect of organisational learning and moderating role of environmental dynamism on the relationship between strategic change and firm performance. *Journal of Strategy and Management*, 12(2), 275–297.
Ng, H.S., & Kee, D.M.H. (2018), "The core competence of successful owner-managed SMEs", *Management Decision*, 56(1), pp. 252–272.
OECD. (2022a). OECD Recommendation on SME and Entrepreneurship Policy. https://www.oecd.org/cfe/smes/oecdrecommendationonsmeandentrepreneurshippolicy/
OECD. (2022b). OECD Recommendation on SME and Entrepreneurship Policy. https://www.oecd.org/cfe/smes/oecdrecommendationonsmeandentrepreneurshippolicy
OECD. (2019). The Future of Work: OECD Employment Outlook. Retrieved from http://www.oecd.org/employment/Employment-Outlook-2019-Highlight-EN.pdf
OECD (2023). OECD SME and Entrepreneurship Outlook 2023. https://www.oecd.org/en/publications/2023/06/oecd-sme-and-entrepreneurship-outlook-2023_c5ac21d0.html
Olson, M. S., van Bever, D., & Verry, S. (2008). When growth stalls. *Harvard Business Review*, 86(3), 50
Ortiz-Martínez, E., Marín-Hernández, S., & Santos-Jaén, J. M. (2023). Sustainability, corporate social responsibility, non-financial reporting and company performance:

Relationships and mediating effects in Spanish small and medium sized enterprises. *In Sustainable Production and Consumption* 35, 349–364). https://doi.org/10.1016/j.spc.2022.11.015

Owalla, B., Gherhes, C., Vorley, T., & Brooks, C. (2022). Mapping SME productivity research: a systematic review of empirical evidence and future research agenda. *Small Business Economics*, 58(3), 1285–1307. https://doi.org/10.1007/s11187-021-00450-3

Oztemel, E., & Gursev, S. (2020). Literature review of industry 4.0 and related technologies. *Journal of Intelligent Manufacturing*, 31(1), 127–182. https://doi.org/10.1007/s10845-018-1433-8

Ployhart, R.E. (2021). "Resources for what? Understanding performance in the resource-based view and strategic human capital resource literatures", *Journal of Management*, 01492063211003137.

Rostron, A. (2021). How to be a hero: How managers determine what makes a good manager through narrative identity work. *Management Learning*. https://doi.org/10.1177/13505076211007275

Santoire, B. (2023). Neither the Global North nor the Global South: locating the post-Soviet space in/out of the Women, Peace and Security agenda. *International Feminist Journal of Politics*, 25(5), 819–842. https://doi.org/10.1080/14616742.2023.2195412

Santos, F.J., Romero, I., & Fernandez-Serrano, J. (2012). "SMEs and entrepreneurial quality from a macroeconomic perspective", *Management Decision*, 50(8), pp. 1382–1395.

Savin, V., Yin, L., Chernobay, L., Konokhov, S., Vasiltsova, N., & Mosliuk, S. (2023). Analysis of the Impact of International Migration on the Financial and Economic Cooperation of Countries. *International Jornal of Professional Business Review*, 8(5), https://doi.org/10.26668/business-review/2023.v8i5.1591

Shela, V., Ramayah, T., & Noor Hazlina, A. (2023). Human capital and organisational resilience in the context of manufacturing: a systematic literature review. *Journal of Intellectual Capital*, 24(2), 535–559. https://doi.org/10.1108/JIC-09-2021-0234

Smith, H., Discetti, R., Bellucci, M., & Acuti, D. (2022). SMEs engagement with the Sustainable Development Goals: A power perspective. *Journal of Business Research*, 149, 112–122. https://doi.org/10.1016/j.jbusres.2022.05.021

Storey, D. J. (2011). Optimism and chance: The elephants in the entrepreneurship room. *International Small Business Journal: Researching Entrepreneurship*, 29(4), 303–321. https://doi.org/10.1177/0266242611403871

St-Pierre, J., Julien, P. A., & Fadil, N. (2023). How do entrepreneurial firms behave in the face of environmental turbulence and uncertainty? Evidence from the manufacturing sector. *Journal of Small Business and Enterprise Development*, 30(5), 880–901. https://doi.org/10.1108/JSBED-11-2022-0459

Tam, S., & Gray, D. E. (2021). Is there a decision to make, boss? From understanding SME growth to managing employees' learning preferences. *Journal of Strategy and Management*, 14(4), 511–528. https://doi.org/10.1108/JSMA-07-2020-0184

Tannenbaum, S. I., Mathieu, J. E., Salas, E. & Cohen, D. (2012). Teams Are Changing: Are Research and Practice Evolving Fast Enough? *Industrial and Organizational Psychology*, 5, 2–24.

The United Nations. (2015). Transforming our world: the 2030 Agenda for Sustainable Development.

Tiep Le, T., Ngo, H. Q., & Aureliano-Silva, L. (2023). Contribution of corporate social responsibility on SMEs' performance in an emerging market – the mediating roles of brand trust and brand loyalty. *International Journal of Emerging Markets*, 18(8), 1868–1891. https://doi.org/10.1108/IJOEM-12-2020-1516

Torkkeli, L., and Durst, S. (2022a). Corporate Social Responsibility of SMEs: Learning Orientation and Performance Outcomes. *Sustainability (Switzerland)*, 14(11). https://doi.org/10.3390/su14116387

U.S. Bureau of Labour Statistics. (2021). Entrepreneurship and U.S. Economy https://www.bls.gov/bdm/entrepreneurship/entrepreneurship.htm

van Aarle, B., Tielens, J., & van Hove, J. (2015). The financial crisis and its aftermath: the case of Ireland. *International Economics and Economic Policy*, 12(3), 393–410. https://doi.org/10.1007/s10368-014-0305-8

Vanhanen, S., Raunio, M., Heikkilä, E., & Olegário, G. (2023). How Diversity Matters in Working Life: A Literature Review in a Finnish Context. *Migration Letters*, 4, 76–87. www.migrationletters.com

Vural-Yavaş, Ç. (2021). Economic Policy Uncertainty, Stakeholder Engagement, and Environmental, Social, and Governance Practices: The Moderating Effect of Competition. *Corporate Social Responsibility and Environmental Management*, 28, 82–102.

Vural-Yavaş, Ç. (2020). Corporate Risk-Taking in Developed Countries: The Influence of Economic Policy Uncertainty and Macroeconomic Conditions. *Journal of Multinational Financial Management*, 54, 100616.

World Bank. (2021). Confronting the Learning Crisis Lessons from World Bank Support for Basic Education, 2012–22. https://ieg.worldbankgroup.org/evaluations/confronting-learning-crisis

Woerkom, M. & Croon, M. (2009). The relationships between team learning activities and team performance. *Personnel Review*, 38(5), 560–577

Youn, H., Lee, K., & Lee, S. (2018), "Effects of corporate social responsibility on employees in the casino industry", *Tourism Management*, 68, 328–335.

Zhong, R.Y., Xu, X., Klotz, E., & Newman, S.T. (2017). Intelligent manufacturing in the context of industry 4.0: A review. *Engineering*, 3(5), 616–630

Asher, D., & Popper, M. (2021). Eliciting tacit knowledge in professions based on interpersonal interactions. *The Learning Organization*, *28*(6), 523–537. https://doi.org/10.1108/tlo-03-2021-0035

Fitzsimons, P., and O'Gorman, C. (2017). A Survey entrepreneurship in Ireland 2016. Project Report. Global Entrepreneurship Monitor. (GEM). https://doras.dcu.ie/22208/1/GEM_2016_Report_for_Ireland_Complete.pdf

Audretsch, D. B., & Belitski, M. (2021). Knowledge complexity and firm performance: evidence from the European SMEs. *Journal of Knowledge Management*, 25(4), 693–713. https://doi.org/10.1108/jkm-03-2020-0178

Boeske, J., & Murray, P. A. (2022). The intellectual domains of sustainability leadership in SMEs. *Sustainability*, 14(4), 1978. https://doi.org/10.3390/su14041978

Bratianu, C., Prelipcean, G., & Bejinaru, R. (2020). Exploring the latent variables which support SMEs to become learning organizations. *Management & Marketing*, 15(2), 154–171. https://doi.org/10.2478/mmcks-2020-0010

Breznitz, S. M., & Feldman, M. P. (2010). The larger role of the university in economic development: introduction to the special issue. *The Journal of Technology Transfer*, *37*(2), 135–138. https://doi.org/10.1007/s10961-010-9184-5

Brunswicker, S., & Vanhaverbeke, W. (2014). Open Innovation in Small and Medium-Sized Enterprises (SMEs): external knowledge sourcing strategies and internal organizational facilitators. *Journal of Small Business Management*, *53*(4), 1241–1263. https://doi.org/10.1111/jsbm.12120

Cavallo, A., Ghezzi, A., Dell'Era, C., & Pellizzoni, E. (2019). Fostering digital entrepreneurship from startup to scaleup: The role of venture capital funds and angel groups. *Technological Forecasting and Social Change*, 145(August), 24–35. https://doi.org/10.1016/j.techfore.2019.04.022

CSO. (April 2024). Population and Migration Estimates, https://www.cso.ie/en/releasesandpublications/ep/p-pme/populationandmigrationestimatesapril2024/keyfindings/#:~:text=Immigration,86%2C800%20other%20citizens%20including%20Ukrainians

CSO. (2023). Annual National Accounts 2023. https://www.cso.ie/en/releasesandpublications/ep/p-ana/annualnationalaccounts2023/gdpandgrowthrates/

European Commission. (2023). Annual Report on European SMEs 2022/2023. https://single-market-economy.ec.europa.eu/smes/sme-strategy/sme-performance-review_en

European Commission. (2024). Winter 2024 Economic Forecast: A delayed rebound in growth amid faster easing of inflation. https://ec.europa.eu/commission/presscorner/detail/en/ip_24_730

FAME. (2023). https://fame-r1-bvdinfo-com.tudublin.idm.oclc.org/version-20240617-1-8/fame/1/Companies/Search

Government of Ireland. (2023). Harnessing Digital the Digital Ireland Framework 2023 Progress Report. file:///C:/Users/anna.zherdeva/Downloads/280518_e7f7f7c5-2af8-4209-849a-8c75caf5ceab.pdf

Guchait, P., Hamilton, K., & Hua, N. (2014). Personality predictors of team taskwork understanding and transactive memory systems in service management teams. *International Journal of Contemporary Hospitality Management*, 26(3), 401–425. https://doi.org/10.1108/IJCHM-05-2013-0197

Hedlund, E., & Österberg, J. (2013). Team Training, Team Learning, Leadership and Psychology Safety: A Study of Team Training and Team Learning Behavior during a Swedish Military Staff Exercise. *Sociology Mind*, *03*(01), 89–98. https://doi.org/10.4236/sm.2013.31014

Journeault, M., Perron, A., & Vallières, L. (2021). The collaborative roles of stakeholders in supporting the adoption of sustainability in SMEs. *Journal of Environmental Management*, *287*, 112349. https://doi.org/10.1016/j.jenvman.2021.112349

Kim, H. (2019b). The Perception of Teachers and Learners towards an Exploratory Corpus-based Grammar Instruction in a Korean EFL Primary School Context. *The Korea Association of Primary English Education*, 25(1), 123–152. https://doi.org/10.25231/pee.2019.25.1.123

Lawless, N., Allan, J., & O'Dwyer, M. (2000). Face-to-face or distance training: two different approaches to motivate SMEs to learn. *Education + Training*, *42*(4/5), 308–317. https://doi.org/10.1108/00400910010347777

Lawless, S., Cohen, P. J., McDougall, C., Mangubhai, S., Song, A. M., & Morrison, T. H. (2022). Tinker, tailor or transform: Gender equality amidst social-ecological change. *Global Environmental Change*, *72*, 102434. https://doi.org/10.1016/j.gloenvcha.2021.102434

Lazarević, S., & Lukić, J. (2018b). Team Learning Processes and Activities in Organization: a case study. *Economic Themes*, *56*(3), 301–319. https://doi.org/10.2478/ethemes-2018-0018

Lee, C., Lee, H., Lee, J., & Park, J. (2014). A multiple group analysis of the training transfer model: exploring the differences between high and low performers in a Korean insurance company. *The International Journal of Human Resource Management*, *25*(20), 2837–2857. https://doi.org/10.1080/09585192.2014.934887

Littumen, H., & Tohmo, T. (2003). The high growth firm in new metal-based manufacturing and business services in Finland. *Small Business Economics*, 21(2), 187–200. https://doi.org/10.1023/A:1025014427294

Matić, I. (2022). Managerial Interpersonal Competencies - Benefiting from Learning Organization Characteristics in SMEs. *Management Dynamics in the Knowledge Economy*, 10(1), 19–36. https://doi.org/10.2478/mdke-2022-0002

McGinnity, F., Kingston, G., (2017b). An Irish Welcome? Changing Irish Attitudes to Immigrants and Immigration: the Role of Recession and Immigration. *The Economic and Social Review*. 48(3), 253–279.

Nachmias, S., & Hubschmid-Vierheilig, E. (2021). "We need to learn how to love digital learning 'again': European SMEs response to COVID-19 digital learning needs". *Human Resource Development International*, *24*(2), 123–132). Routledge. https://doi.org/10.1080/13678868.2021.1893503

Ó Gráda, C., & O'Rourke, K. H. (2021). The Irish economy during the century after partition. *The Economic History Review*, *75*(2), 336–370. https://doi.org/10.1111/ehr.13106

Parker, S. K., Bindl, U. K., & Strauss, K. (2010). Making Things Happen: a model of proactive motivation. *Journal of Management*, *36*(4), 827–856. https://doi.org/10.1177/0149206310363732

Penco, L., Profumo, G., Serravalle, F., & Viassone, M. (2022). Has COVID-19 pushed digitalisation in SMEs? The role of entrepreneurial orientation. *Journal of Small Business and Enterprise Development*, *30*(2), 311–341. https://doi.org/10.1108/jsbed-10-2021-0423

Puthusserry, P., Khan, Z., Knight, G., & Miller, K. (2020). How Do Rapidly Internationalizing SMEs Learn? Exploring the Link Between Network Relationships, Learning Approaches and Post-entry Growth of Rapidly Internationalizing SMEs from Emerging Markets. *Management International Review*, *60*(4), 515–542. https://doi.org/10.1007/s11575-020-00424-9

Reporting Lab. (2021). Sustainability Reporting Standards Roadmap. https://www.efrag.org/en/about-us/about-efrag/the-european-corporate-reporting-lab

Rozuli, A. I. (2021). Praktik Akumulasi Lebenswelt Sebagai Basis Strategi BUMDes Yang Berkelanjutan. Jurnal Transformative, 7(2), 201–225.

Sundström, A., Adolfsson, A. N., Nordin, M., & Adolfsson, R. (2020). Loneliness increases the risk of All-Cause dementia and Alzheimer's disease. *The Journals of Gerontology Series B*, 75(5), 919–926. https://doi.org/10.1093/geronb/gbz139

Suni, S., Hall, E., Bahu, E., & Hayes, H. (2022). Urbanization increases floral specialization of pollinators. *Ecology and Evolution*, *12*(3). https://doi.org/10.1002/ece3.8619

Torkkeli, L., & Durst, S. (2022b). Corporate Social Responsibility of SMES: learning orientation and performance Outcomes. *Sustainability*, *14*(11), 6387. https://doi.org/10.3390/su14116387

UN 2.0 Quintet for Change. (2023). Evolving for Impact: Skills and Culture for Tomorrow. https://www.un.org/two-zero/en

UN (2023). *Our Common Agenda*. [online] unfoundation.org. Available at: https://unfoundation.org/our-common-agenda/?gad_source=1&gclid=Cj0KCQjw6PGxBhCVARIsAIumnWbacdRcy0K-mYgbDSA18yTugW2dMq1yjz0XAbmjKs13TSNrpMd0IcMaAjXEEALw_wcB [Accessed 10 May 2024].

UN (2024). *Bridging Gender Gaps with a Sustainable Care Economy: Investment Opportunities and Challenges*. [online] UNDP. Available at: https://www.undp.org/publications/dfs-bridging-gender-gaps-sustainable-care-economy-investment-opportunities-and-challenges [Accessed 29 Apr. 2024].

UNESCO (2023). *Reworking Four Pillars of Education to Sustain the Commons* | UNESCO. [online] www.unesco.org. Available at: https://www.unesco.org/en/articles/reworking-four-pillars-education-sustain-commons

Usman, M., Roijakkers, N., Vanhaverbeke, W., & Frattini, F. (2018). A Systematic Review of the literature on open Innovation in SMEs. *WORLD SCIENTIFIC eBooks*, 3–35. https://doi.org/10.1142/9789813230972_0001

Valdez-Juárez, L. E., Gallardo-Vázquez, D., & Ramos-Escobar, E. A. (2019). Organizational learning and corporate social responsibility drivers of performance in SMEs in north-western Mexico. *Sustainability*, *11*(20), 5655. https://doi.org/10.3390/su11205655

Van der Haar, S., Segers, M. & Jehn, K. A. (2013). "Towards a contextualised model of team learning processes and outcomes". *Educational Research Review*, 10, pp. 1–12

Whetten, K., Ostermann, J., Whetten, R. A., Pence, B. W., O'Donnell, K., Messer, L. C., & Thielman, N. M. (2011). A comparison of the wellbeing of orphans and abandoned children ages 6–12 in institutional and Community-Based care settings in 5 less wealthy nations. *PLoS ONE*, *4*(12), e8169. https://doi.org/10.1371/journal.pone.0008169

World Bank. (2024). GDP. Data from database: World Development Indicators. https://data.worldbank.org/indicator/NY.GDP.MKTP.CD

World Manufacturing Foundation Report. (2019). Skills for Future Manufacturing. https://worldmanufacturing.org/report/report-2019/#:~:text=The%202019%20World%20Manufacturing%20Forum,skills%20assessments%20and%20development%2C%20and

Yuniarti, A. (2023). Pemberdayaan UMKM tentang Pentingnya Adaptasi Digital dan Legalitas Usaha di Limpomajang Kec. Majauleng Kab. Wajo. Jurnal Pengabdian Masyarakat Dan Riset Pendidikan, 2(1), 299–306.

Zheng, Y., Zhang, W., Lopez, D. M. B., & Ahmad, R. (2021). Scientometric analysis and systematic review of Multi-Material Additive Manufacturing of polymers. *Polymers*, *13*(12), 1957. https://doi.org/10.3390/polym13121957

12 Japan's Demographic Decline and its Geoeconomic Implications in the Long Run

Sophie Nivoix and Serge Rey

Introduction

The phenomenon of demographic transition and falling birth rates has affected not only all industrialized countries for many years but also most emerging countries. However, Japan is undoubtedly the one in which the consequences are already and will be the most extensive. Demography has recently been pointed out as Japan's main problem by Luttwak (2020).

In 2022, for the first time since records began in 1899, the number of births in Japan has fallen below 800,000 after already 6 years of decline.[1] In the same way, the total fertility rate, defined as the number of children a child-bearing age woman has in her lifetime, dropped to only 1.26, far from the 2.1 level which stabilizes the population level. The decrease has been fast, with the number of births dropping to under 1 million in 2016 and then falling below 900,000 in 2019. Moreover, in 2022 the marriages reached only 504,878, which is close to the lowest level since World War II. It is also worth mentioning that births out of marriage represent only 2% of the total in Japan, contrary to most industrialized countries where this ratio is between 20% and 50%. Since 2008, declining dynamics have strengthened as the number of deaths overtook the number of births, while the number of marriages has continued to decrease. Considering the active population, the decline already began in 2006 and was only partly compensated by automation in the services and manufacturing sectors (Ministry of Economy, Trade and Industry, Japan industrial production, METI, 2022). The first macroeconomic consequence was that the Japanese GDP never reached again its all times high of 6203 billion USD in 2012 (World bank, https://databank.worldbank.org/reports.aspx?source=2&series=NY.GDP.MKTP.CD&country=JPN).

Indeed, weakening domestic demand cannot be balanced with exportations (METI, Japan exports, 2022) because they are directed toward countries that are also facing a demographic slowdown.

A prospective analysis of demographic changes in Japan and in its Chinese and Korean neighbors leads to several scenarios for 2050 and beyond; this is what this chapter will explore. Indeed, Fettweis (2015) mentioned that some geopolitical mistakes have been made in the past because of overweighting

DOI: 10.4324/9781032655857-16

geography, and he thus suggested to integrate more demographic data into geopolitical analyses. This is what this chapter presents, with a focus on the demographic weight of China and its geopolitical influence. Indeed, China possesses nuclear weapons, alongside the other four permanent members of the United Nations Security Council (Falk and Krieger, 2020), contrary to Japan. The coming decades in Japan will thus be determined not only by the demographic trends, but also by their economic and strategic consequences, and by the geopolitical strategy of China and the United States. Our prospective analysis will also integrate items based on historical trends but also the apophatic dimension they may contain (Zajec, 2016).

This chapter is structured as follows. Section 1 presents the demographic characteristics of Japan; Section 2 describes the main economic consequences; Section 3 discusses the geopolitical implications; and Section 4 describes the potential geoeconomic future in the long run, before the conclusion in Section 5.

The demographic characteristics of Japan

It is possible to describe the growth of a population by making some generalizations and by using simple differential equations: for a year *t+1*, the size n_{t+1} of a population depends upon: the number of individuals during the previous year n_t, the number of births b_t, the number of deaths d_t, the number of immigrants im_t and the number of emigrants em_t. This gives the following equation: $n_{t+1} = n_t + b_t - d_t + im_t - em_t$. When a country is closed, as one can consider Japan to be, the dynamics of population depend only on births and deaths. Clearly, the Japanese population decreases since $b_t < d_t$.

Often cited as an example of the country with the highest life expectancy in the world, Japan is a demographic singularity in several respects. Its very low fertility rate (less than 1.4 children per child-bearing age woman[2]) is close to that of South Korea (close to 1.2) or Italy, and the proportion of the population over 65 (30 % in 2022) is equivalent to either that of Germany or Italy. What differentiates Japan from other countries lies more in its particularly low immigration rate. Indeed, in 2019 only 2% of the population was born abroad (OECD, 2019) while the countries mentioned above see the regular arrival of foreign populations as a means of compensating for the decline in their active population and the demographic as a whole. In Japan, almost a quarter of immigrants are Chinese, 20% are Filipino, followed by Koreans and Vietnamese. Note that "in December 2018, Japan passed amendments to the Immigration Control and Refugee Recognition Act which took effect in April 2019. The amendments introduced two new grounds for temporary labor migration" (OECD, 2019, p.1) labeled as "Specified Skilled Worker", that is, with a high knowledge or expertise in 14 specific fields, along with a ceiling for admission for the period 2019–2023 of 345,000 people. These specific fields include the care industry (60,000 people), the food services industry

(53,000), the construction industry (40,000) and agriculture (36,500). A so-called Specified Skilled Worker may renew his/her stay and work for up to five years and may bring his spouse or children under several legal requirements.

As shown in Figure 12.1, Japan's population boom accompanied its economic development from the Meiji era (1868–1912) until the beginning of the 21st century. The decline in the number of inhabitants since 2008 will be more noticeable over the next 100 years, to the point of perhaps seeing the country's population halved by 2120.

This demography can be compared to that of its two neighbors, China and Korea (Figure 12.2). The relative weight of the population of each country compared to its neighbor is fascinating when the values are rebased to 100 in

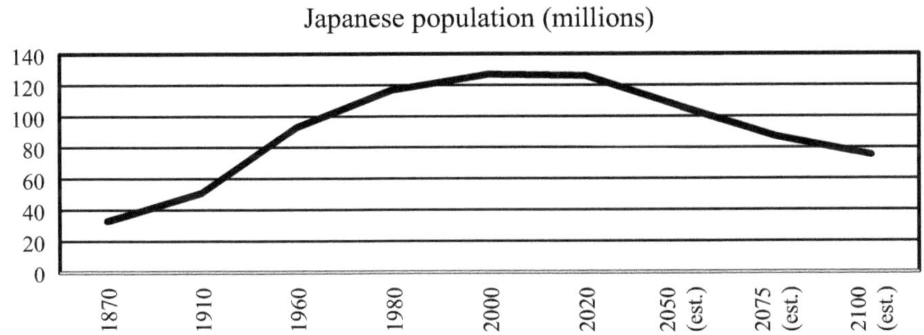

Figure 12.1 Long-term demographic evolution of Japan.

Source: United Nations, 2019 and authors' calculations.

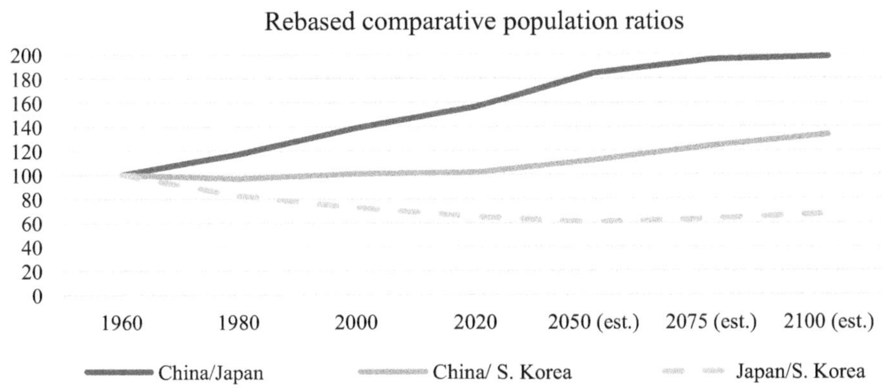

Figure 12.2 Comparative population ratios between Japan, China, and South Korea

Source: United Nations, 2019 and authors' calculations.

Note: The following ratios were calculated and rebased at 100 in 1960 for a better trend comparison: Chinese population/Japanese population, Chinese population/South Korean population, Japanese population/South Korean population.

Table 12.1 Old age dependency ratio in Japan, China, and South Korea

Old age dependency ratio	1980	2000	2020	2050 (est.)	2075 (est.)
China	10.5	11.4	18.5	47.5	58.8
Japan	15.0	27.3	52.0	80.7	75.3
S. Korea	7.6	11.2	23.6	78.8	79.0

Source: OECD, 2023.

1960. Japan will thus have lost by 2050 nearly 40% of its demographic weight compared to South Korea, which would no longer weigh a third of Japan as in 1990 but half. As for China, it will have multiplied its demographic weight by almost 2 compared to Japan by 2050, but only by 1.1 compared to Korea, then by 1.3 in 2100.

The Japanese working population, which represented 79 million people in 1980 according to the National Institute of Population and Social Security Research (IPSS), has fallen to 68 million in 2020 and could drop to 54 million in 2050, which represents a decrease of one-third in 70 years.

Regarding the age structure of the population, it is worth mentioning that the old-age dependency ratio, defined as the ratio between the number of people aged 65 and over and the number of people in the 20–64 age group, is changing dramatically (Table 12.1).

This ratio more than tripled in Japan between 1980 and 2020, reaching 52%, and it should be around 80% in 2050, to then decline slightly according to the OECD, or stabilize at this level until the end of the century (Kato, 2022). As a consequence, South Korea could catch up with Japan with a rate close to 80%, but only in 2050, and China would experience a proportionally slower aging process. Indeed, in the latter country, the one-child policy (1979–2015) is over, and currently, Chinese households have the right to have two children, which will make it possible to mitigate the financial shock of aging until the end of this century, while maintaining a satisfactory domestic demand.

Economic and social consequences

The impact of demographic changes on economic growth can be detected directly in the total labor inputs in the short and the long term. This modifies both future savings and investments at the macroeconomic level, which affects Gross Domestic Product (GDP). The positive effect of an increase in birth rates can be detected through an increasing future demand, a larger labor force, and larger consumption. On the opposite, population aging decreases the production potential of the country, reduces the potential productivity gains, and increases the social and care funding requirements (Lindblad and Sellin, 2003). Lindh and Malmberg (1999) indicated that an increase in the proportion of middle-aged people (50–64 years) has a positive impact on investment and savings, while a higher old-age dependency ratio reduces savings and investment. Nevertheless, as stated by Bloom and Williamson (1998), population aging sometimes increases public investment in elderly care but overall the impacts on economic growth are mostly negative. This concerns all industries, that is, not only the production of goods. Thus, Daniele et al. (2020, p.1), analyzing OECD countries conclude:

> In principle, the negative impact of ageing on the growth of per capita gross domestic product (GDP) could be offset by increases in productivity. However, for many regions, the actual growth rates recorded have been lower than productivity growth required to maintain per capita GDP levels in recent years". They add (2020, p.1) that aging "has a direct negative impact on productivity growth, with the effect being concentrated in urban areas". It can be explained partly by the specialization of some cities "in sectors such as tradable services, where the content of tasks makes it difficult to automate the production process, and where business dynamism – negatively affected by demographic change – is a key driver of productivity growth

On a social level, the demographic imbalance between age groups raises the problem of financing pensions by a decreasing active population, while in 2021 the public debt exceeded 250% of GDP; some 43% of this debt was held by the Bank of Japan, 18% by insurance companies, 16% by banks and 23% by foreign investors.[3]

Considering past long-run trends, Figure 12.3 presents the evolution of the active population and the GDP per capita in Japan, China, and South Korea.

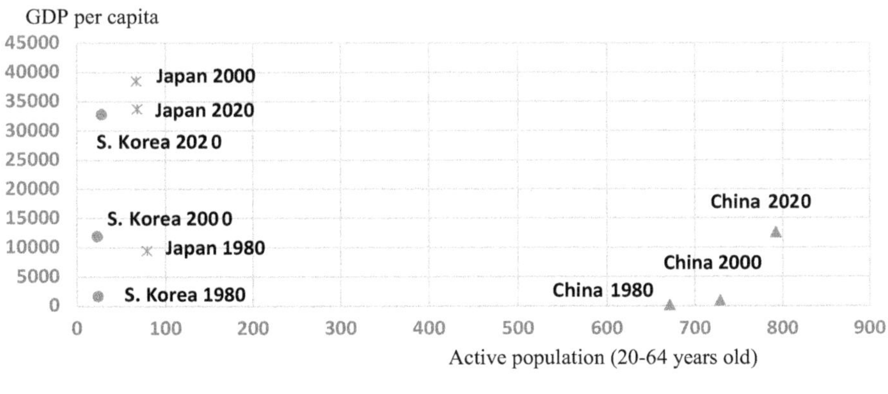

Figure 12.3 Active population and GDP per capita in purchasing power parity, in Japan, China, and South Korea.

Source: World Bank (2023) and authors' calculation.

The economic consequences of population aging can be seen clearly: Japan's GDP per capita declined between 2000 and 2020, while despite a bad recent demographic trend, South Korea's GDP per capita continued to increase between 2000 and 2020. According to very recent data on GDP per capita (see Figure 12.3) South Korea has now overtaken Japan, for the first time in history. As for China, both the active population and the GDP per capita have increased continuously since 1980, at the beginning of the economic reforms. The consequences of the beginning of population aging have thus not had really an impact yet on this indicator for this country.

Considering future trends and without including the inflationary effects of the rise in the price of energy and agricultural raw materials following the war in Ukraine, Kato (2022) estimated that the Japanese GDP could grow until 2036, with an increase in GDP per capita of almost 2% per year. Unfortunately, according to the Statistical Handbook Japan 2022,[4] Japanese GDP has already begun to decrease in 2022 for the very first time, even if it was not the case for the GDP per capita in purchasing power parity according to the International Monetary Fund. The rather optimistic forecast of Kato (2022) included an increase in demand in the pharmaceutical, insurance, elderly care, and medical care sectors in particular. Indeed, he estimated that the long-term care sector will create several million jobs in the decades to come.

The elderly dependency ratio is all the more worrying as people over 65 already represent almost a third of the population, knowing that in 2021 the country experienced its strongest population decline ever recorded.[5] Investigating this increasingly difficult problem, Lunga and Sobane (2019) advocate government decisions integrating both internal parameters, such as the length of working life or the employment rate of women (52% in 2020[6]), as well as external factors such as an increased recourse to immigration. This last possibility, as previously indicated, remains considered with reluctance by the Japanese authorities despite a slight opening since 2019 as mentioned above.

If one considers the economic attractiveness of the two close neighbors and competitors, i.e. China and South Korea, it appears that in the 2021 Doing Business[7] ranking of the World Bank, South Korea was better evaluated than Japan or China for 7 out of 10 major economic criteria, including, for example, obtaining building permits, access to electricity, access to credit, tax pressure or international transactions. It should also be noted that natural or climatic risks (typhoons, earthquakes), very present in Japan, affect China less and Korea very little.

Population decline has various impacts on the economy, such as a decline in the active population, a shrinking of the domestic market, but also a threat to many industries because of a lack of workers. From a geopolitical and military viewpoint, fewer people means fewer soldiers in the military forces and a potential weakening of the geostrategic influence of the country. Geoeconomics show the relationships between international competition in the military area and economic competition (Luttwak, 1990) and they include both a discourse on the world and a method of action (Gomart, 2020). As a consequence, geoeconomics does have an impact on countries, strategic industries, multinational and domestic firms, whether they are private or public.

Geopolitical implications

The major global geoeconomic and geopolitical balances identified by Brzezinski (1997) still remain valid today around the main actors he had identified. Indeed, it is worth noticing that at the forefront facing the United States still stand the European Union, China (the new Heartland and Eurasian center of gravity), as well as Russia and India. At a lower level, in addition to the United Kingdom, there are Japan and Indonesia, and among the countries that can be seen as geopolitical pivots, it is important to mention Korea, Ukraine, Turkey, and Iran. This explains why the United States needs to make alliances with countries such as Japan, South Korea, or Taiwan, in order to implement a containment strategy against China, as the USA did previously against the Soviet Union (MacKinder, 1943). The coastal or island location is thus a key strategic factor in containing large coastal powers (rimlands) such as China or Europe.

Such a viewpoint was presented during World War II by Spykman (1942) and it is still useful considering the increase in the defense budgets of many Asian countries in 2023 and 2024 like Taiwan,[8] and China's desire for maritime projection. Japan is also incentivized to strengthen its self-defense forces,[9] with an annual increase of more than $30 billion in the budget allocated to it since 2014 (Ministry of Defense of Japan, 2021).

Considering a geopolitical reading of Japan and China through the prism of alternate history (Zajec, 2016), it is possible to suggest three viewpoints.

The first is that of "panism", which aims to bring together a large human group according to a unifying criterion, such as language, ethnicity, religion, or geography for example. Following this logic, any Chinese speaker in the world could be considered as inhabiting a piece of Chinese territory, or any Shintoist believer as occupying a space belonging to Japan. The weight of the diasporas is a major factor here, but apart from Hong Kong, Macao, or Taiwan, China hardly uses this argument and neither does Japan. Indeed, as Japan has no long-run colonial history, it may not consider panism as a way to maintain or expand its influence or even to balance its lack of birth and population aging.

The second perspective is referred to as the "golden age myth", namely that of a State referring to a glorious period of its past in order to set it up as an objective of expansion. As borders are shifting over the long term, the confrontation of strategies linked to the myth of the golden age between two neighboring countries quickly creates incompatible territorial claims and can lead to a latent or open conflict. The choice of the historical period corresponding to the largest territorial extent would refer, for Japan, to 1941, with a presence in Korea, Manchuria, Taiwan, and Hong Kong, but also in Malaysia, the Philippines, Indonesia, and many islands from Southeast Asia. Such conquests represent a considerable geographic, economic, and demographic weight, which could be a possible immediate remedy for a decline in the Japanese population, but the painful memory of 1945 and its defeated status are enough to dismiss these aims. The same reasoning applies to the Japanese presence in Korea and Manchuria during the Russo-Japanese War in 1904–1905. As a consequence, the demographic parameter cannot help Japan in such a perspective, as the population is already decreasing in the country. On the Chinese side, the period of maximum expansion is much more distant historically since it can be located between the 6th and 9th centuries. The Chinese empire included Korea, Mongolia, southeastern Siberia, but, significantly, not Japan, which was never invaded by anyone. Nor does China seem to be guided by a desire to return to a glorious past period, as it is more focused on development based on globalization: it is interesting to mention for instance the Belt and Road Initiative, the trade shipping with the rest of Asia and Africa, and massive exports to the United States.

The third way of approaching geopolitics through alternate history is "grandism", the objective of which is to allow a State to regain control of all the territories that once belonged to it, even briefly. If it is clear that Japan does not harbor such ambitions, it is different for China. The very expression of "Great China" as opposed to "Mainland China" perfectly illustrates the desire of the country to extend its influence, its presence, even its territory beyond its current limits. Thus, in addition to the control of Taiwan, another issue is that of China's control of maritime routes that are economically vital for Japan to South Asia, India, and the Middle East. Indeed, Chinese maritime claims follow the "nine-dash line" which includes the Senkaku Islands (in Japanese) or Diaoyu Islands (in Chinese), the Paracel Islands (claimed by Taiwan and Vietnam), the Spratly Islands (claimed by Vietnam, Taiwan, the Philippines, Brunei and Malaysia) and Scarborough Atoll (claimed by Taiwan and the Philippines). The economic stakes here do not only relate to trade routes but also to access to raw materials such as oil around the Senkaku/Diaoyu, to fishery resources off the coast of Vietnam and Thailand, and to guano, a natural fertilizer present on the emerged reefs and the numerous islets of the South China Sea. Here again, the Chinese economic and strategic ambitions cannot be balanced by Japan's poor economic growth and demographic decline.

Finally, the apophatic dimension of the geostrategic perspective consists in defining it in the negative. In other words, the strategy of a country includes the will to avoid the repetition of a trauma or a painful event of the past. This may correspond to the Japanese military defeat in 1945, to the "unequal treaties" imposed on China in the 19th century by Western powers, or to the occupation of Manchuria by Japan twice during the 20th century. The revival of military spending in Japan since 2014 and the growing economic and military weight of China seem in line with the desire not to relive situations of weakness or past defeat, but here again, demographics can represent a favorable or penalizing factor. Clearly, for both economic and military aspects, population aging impairs any long-term growth and enhances the potential need for resources to implement a strategy.

As a consequence, Japan may not use any of these readings in order to revive its demography, whereas China might justify the potential inclusion of Taiwan within its borders with the "grandism" or the "Golden age" viewpoints. Such an enlargement would not modify its total population much but would give the country a strategic economic influence on South Asian shores, and a control position on the intense maritime trade in this area.

The potential geoeconomic consequences

The Asian and the world geoeconomic balances depend mostly on the development strategy of China. Some illustrative examples are the Belt and Road Initiative (BRI), linking China to Europe through Central Asia; the BRI illustrates the global reach of China and the Chinese increasing economic influence in Africa. As a matter of fact, as China is now the second largest economic power in the world it needs tremendous supplies of raw materials and commodities for its industry. This explains why the control of Asian maritime straits and Taiwan are crucial issues, and as mentioned by Xu (1998) economic integration does not always imply peaceful development.

From the Japanese viewpoint, strategic autonomy requires economic, food, energy, and strategic security despite the strained relations between the United States and China. In the same way, whereas Japan did rely mainly on the US since World War II, it must progressively manage a larger part of its defense alone (Fatton, 2018) with its Self-Defense Forces. Moreover, the ban on Japanese weapon exports enforced in 1976 was relaxed in 2014 by authorization under some conditions (Ministry of Foreign Affairs, 2014).

All of the above elements lead us to propose three scenarios within the framework of a twenty or thirty-year projection of the geoeconomic consequences of Japan's demographic development.

As presented by Nivoix and Rey (2023), three main scenarios could be forecasted considering the answers of Japan to its demographic issues.

The first one is a status quo strategy, implying a continuous slowdown of the economy, along with the demographic decline down to its 1950 population level. The major difference with the situation 70 years ago is that the population was much younger and that the working-age population was larger. In this way, Japan could be overtaken by India around 2040 considering the global GDP.

In this scenario, a major issue is the Chinese geopolitical strategy, with or without the integration of Taiwan in the long run. Another threatening country is North Korea, and as mentioned by Yoshida (2019) Japan is directly concerned by any agreement on freezing strategic nuclear forces that could reach the United States, even if Pyongyang keeps some non-strategic nuclear forces that keep Japan within range.

Another geoeconomic issue is also related to the mutual trade dependence between the US and China, which could lead the US to make some concessions to its main partner, such as not being so committed in the future to the defense of Japan.

Moreover, as Japan already has a long experience with civilian nuclear power and possesses the technical knowledge related to military nuclear power, the development of nuclear weapons is a more political than a scientific question. This pending issue refers partly to scenario 2 of the CIA report (National Intelligence Council, 2021), and seems less unthinkable as the awful memory of the earthquake that hit the Fukushima power plant in 2011 fades. Indeed, the continuation of civil nuclear power was quickly decided after the accident, given Japan's total external energy dependence on fossil fuels.

As described in Figure 12.4, the inclusion of Japan in the Chinese economic area (CHN+JPN) could help China to become quicker the first economic power in the world, despite the economic slowdown of Japan. Fueling the long-term growth of the country and overtaking the US are major goals for China, as key technological issues are already to be addressed at the worldwide level, such as the control of artificial intelligence, rare earth elements supply, and all new technological standards related to renewable energies. The demographic problem is thus also a technological one, as well as an energy or security challenge.

In the second scenario presented by Nivoix and Rey (2023), Japan eases its migration policy, as initiated in 2019. Indeed, if current trends go on for many years Japan cannot expect any bounce back of its fertility rate, seeing that the average age of mothers at the birth of their first child reached 31 in 2023, the number of babies born in Japan reached an all-time low in 2022, and the proportion of single women in the population is still increasing; the

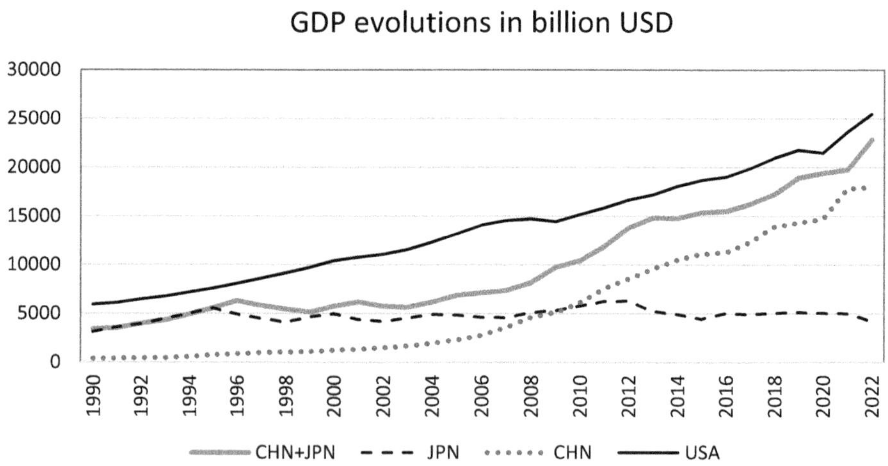

Figure 12.4 Comparative GDP evolutions in billion USD.

Source: World Bank (2024a) and authors' calculation, https://databank.worldbank.org/indicator/NY.GDP.PCAP.CD/1ff4a498/Popular-Indicators.

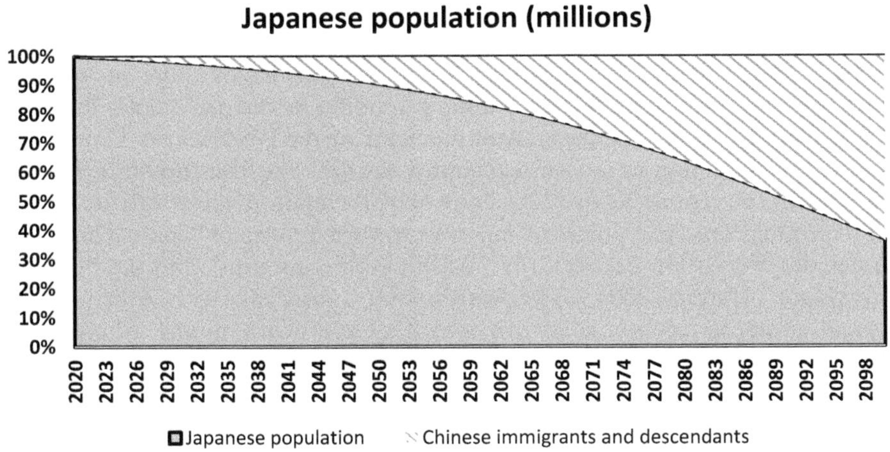

Figure 12.5 Long-term Japanese population simulation with Chinese immigration.

Source: World Bank (2024b) and authors' calculation.

latter represents now represent 39% among the 30–35 years old, 26% among the 35–40 and 21% among the 40–45.[10]

As the Chinese represent the first group of immigrant population in Japan (apart from the descendants of Koreans who arrived during the last century), and given the demographic concentration experienced by China on its entire Eastern facade, Figure 12.5 shows a simulation of the weight of a long-term regular Chinese immigration. The analysis presented here is based on the assumption of a Japanese fertility rate of 1.25, which was the 2023 value. The simulation includes the arrival of 200,000 immigrants per year until the year 2100, with a fertility rate of 2, which is fairly high but possible for a young population. A lower rate, to which the possibility of family reunification could be added, would lead to results quite similar to those in Figure 12.5.

This simulation shows that the combination of the Japanese demographic decline and the arrival of immigrants strongly modifies the structure of the population in the long run. Such a perspective, whether based on the arrival of Chinese, Korean, Filipino, or Vietnamese populations, raises the question of the integration of these people into the Japanese population, which has never been accustomed to mixity in its long insular history. It is thus highly improbable that Japan would prefer "dilution" in order to avoid "reduction".

For the sake of simplicity, the simulation did not include possible intermarriage or possible migratory pressure from Asian countries exposed to the harmful consequences of climate change on the coasts, the ravages of the monsoon or floods.

Such a scenario, which could be adapted with other immigrants, could mitigate the demographic and economic decrease of the country, at least maybe until China faces a similar demographic situation.

In the third scenario of Nivoix and Rey (2023), Japan faces a much more geoeconomically and geopolitically strained perspective, whatever the immigration decisions of the archipelago. China can put Japan under pressure in various ways, even without any military action. On the diplomatic level, as China belongs to the five permanent members of the UN Security Council, it can receive the support of Russia against the US, and thus possibly against Japan. On the economic level, the control of the main Asian straits by China in its strategy creates a power of nuisance toward Taiwan or Japan. This illustrates the opposition between the "Washington consensus" and the "Beijing consensus" (Ramo, 2004). The Washington consensus, with which Japan agrees, promotes economic growth according to a liberal model, whereas the Beijing consensus involves first structural development, non-interference in the internal business of economic partners, and secondarily economic and social reforms. This means that so-called "friendly" relations with an economic partner imply non-interference in its internal politics, and in this way, China increasingly tends to point out that Taiwan and the South China Sea are part of its domestic affairs. According to this viewpoint, China implemented its "9-dash line" strategy in order to control a maritime zone in the Southern Asian Sea. The country progressively implements a "cabbage tactics", which is a military strategy that aims to take control of an island by surrounding it with several layers of ships, not only military ones, while isolating the island from any outside support (Konishi, 2018). This highly strategic area for China is located in the eastern extension of the Strait of Malacca, located between Malaysia and Indonesia, and through which 80% of China's energy imports transited in 2020.

In a global strategy aiming at the extension of the Chinese maritime influence, Japan could be seen as one more pearl to be added to the Chinese "string of pearls" theorized by Hamilton (2004, cited by Pehrson, 2006), which in addition to the Senkaku/Daoyu claimed islands, relies on several harbors such as Hambantota in Sri Lanka, Gwadar in Pakistan, and even Piraeus in Greece, which was partly bought in 2016 by the Chinese company COSCO. The latter is in the geographical extension, on land this time, of the Belt and Road Initiative.

Finally, considering a possible invasion of Taiwan by China, Luttwak (2020, p. 2) is pessimistic about Japan and mentioned that "if Japan does not have a way to help Taiwan in case of an invasion, then the Chinese might take Taiwan. But if the Chinese took Taiwan, Japan would suffer a catastrophic security loss". Meanwhile, China launched in June 2022 the Fujian, its third aircraft carrier, which was made in China, and a fourth one is under construction. In order to illustrate the economic gains that China could benefit from the takeover of Taiwan, Figure 12.6 shows that the perspective of GDP per capita growth in the coming years is very favorable for Taiwan, and far better than the forecasts for China, Japan, and even South Korea.

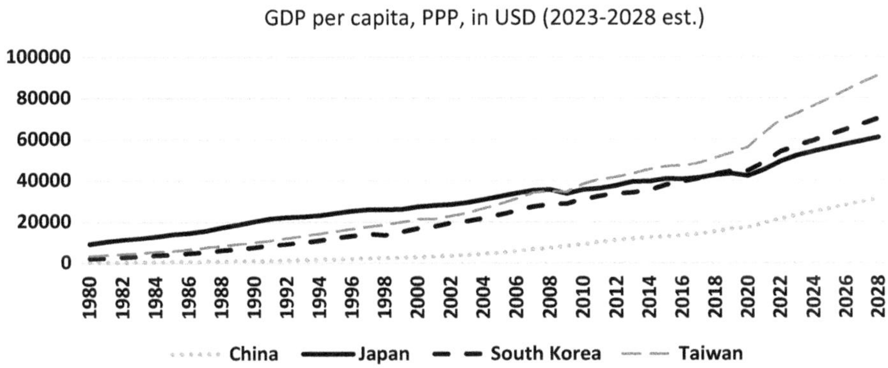

Figure 12.6 Comparative GDP per capita in purchasing power parity.

Source: IMF (2023) and authors' calculation.

Conclusion

The declining demography of Japan is an increasingly worrying issue for the country in the long run, as the population drop has never been so large than in 2023. As the fertility rate is not about to increase, the country will continue to face major problems in the coming decades. The first more urgent one is an ever-climbing old-age dependency ratio and a lack of working-age population. This has immediate implications for many economic sectors and this slows down economic growth as well as the evolution of the country's GDP per capita. The second major question is the shrinking geopolitical influence of the archipelago in Asia and, at the worldwide level, compared to the expanding China. Chinese designs on Taiwan and their desire to weigh more in international diplomacy in general and in Asia in particular may impair the Japanese influence, even if it is backed by the United States. The third issue is a geoeconomic one: to what extent can Japan afford such a shrinking process? Among the possible future scenarios, we focused on three possible hypotheses: first, the status quo in the demographic policy would not ease at all the present situation, as the declining population in Japan is a long-term trend that is not so strong in the neighboring Asian countries like South Korea or China; second, a progressively larger opening to immigration could be part of a solution with new skilled workers in Japan, contributing to ongoing economic development, but it raises the issues of integration of immigrants; third, a weak Japan, on both demographic and economic sides, facing a military and economically more powerful China could lead to high diplomatic tensions and larger threats for Japan. The relationship between China and Taiwan in the near future will help to anticipate the situation of Japan in the coming decades.

Notes

1 https://www.nippon.com/en/japan-data/h01699/.
2 http://data.worldbank.org/indicator/SP.DYN.TFRT.IN/countries.
3 Ministry of Finance of Japan, https://www.mof.go.jp/english/policy/jgbs/reference/Others/holdings01.pdf.
4 https://www.stat.go.jp/english/data/handbook/pdf/2022all.pdf#page=23.
5 "Shrinking Japan: even Tokyo sees first population decline in 26 years", https://www.nippon.com/en/japan-data/h01310/, April 28, 2022.
6 https://data.worldbank.org/indicator/SL.TLF.ACTI.1524.FE.NE.ZS?locations=JP.
7 https://www.worldbank.org/en/programs/business-enabling-environment/doing-business-legacy.
8 https://globaltaiwan.org/2023/09/taiwan-announces-an-increased-defense-budget-for-2024/.
9 https://www.sipri.org/commentary/topical-backgrounder/2023/proposed-hike-japans-military-expenditure.
10 https://www.nippon.com/en/japan-data/h01363/.

References

Bloom, David E. and Jeffrey G. Williamson, (1998). "Demographic transitions and economic miracles in emerging Asia", *The World Bank Economic Review*, 12(3), 419–455.

Brzezinski, Zbigniew, (1997). *The grand chessboard – American primacy and its geostrategic imperatives*, Basic books, New York.

Daniele, Federica, Honiden, Taku and Alexander C. Lembcke (2020). "Ageing and productivity growth in OECD regions: Combatting the economic impact of ageing through productivity growth", in Kim, J. and S. Dougherty (eds.) *Ageing and Fiscal Challenges across Levels of Government*, chapter 2, OECD, Paris, https://doi.org/10.1787/dc2ae16d-en

Falk, Richard, and David Krieger, (2020). "The nuclear age persists after 75 years", *Peace Review: A Journal of Social Justice*, 32:3, 313–324, DOI: 10.1080/10402659.2020.1867348

Fatton, Lionel Pierre, (2018). "Japan is back: Autonomy and balancing amidst an unstable China-USA-Japan triangle", *Asia Pacific Policy Studies*, 5, 264–278. (https://doi.org/10.1002/app5.240)

Fettweis, Christopher J., (2015). "On Heartlnds and Chessboards: Classical Geopolitics, Then and Now", Orbis, 59 (2), 233–248, https://doi.org/10.1016/j.orbis.2015.02.005

Gomart, Thomas, 2020. *L'affolement du monde*, Tallandier, Paris.

IMF (2023). GDP per capita open data, https://www.imf.org/external/datamapper/PPPPC@WEO/OEMDC/ADVEC/WEOWORLD

Kato, Ryuta Ray, 2022. "Population aging and Labor Mobility in Japan", *Japan and the world economy*, 62, 1–23.

Konishi, Weston S., (2018). "China's Maritime Challenge in the South China Sea: Options for US Responses", Chicago Council on Global Affairs.

Lindblad, Hans and Peter Sellin, (2003). "The Equilibrium Rate of Unemployment and the Real Exchange Rate: An Unobserved Components System Approach", *Sveriges Riksbank Working Paper Series*, n°152.

Lindh, Thomas and Bo Malmberg, (1999). "Age Structure Effects and Growth in the OECD 1950-1990", *Journal of Population Economics*, 12, 431–449.

Lunga, Wilfred and Konosoang Sobane, (2019). "Investment in Social Capital and Migrant Labour as a Solution for Population Aging", G20-2019 Japan, Aging population and its economic impact + immigration, https://t20japan.org/category/task-forces/aging-population-and-its-economic-impact-immigration/

Luttwak, Edward N., (1990). "From Geopolitics to Geo-Economics: Logic of Conflict, Grammar of Commerce", *The National Interest*, 20 (Summer 1990), 17–23.
Luttwak, Edward N., (2020). "Edward Luttwak Predicts that 'Technological Acceleration' Will Drive Forward 2021", https://japan-forward.com/edward-luttwak-predicts-that-technological-acceleration-will-drive-forward-2021/
MacKinder, John Halford, (1943). "The Round World and the Winning of the Peace", *Foreign affairs*, 21, 595–605.
METI, Japan industrial production (2022) https://tradingeconomics.com/japan/industrial-production (last accessed on 14 June 2022).
METI, Japan exports (2022) https://tradingeconomics.com/japan/industrial-production (last accessed on 15 June 2022).
Ministry of Defence of Japan, (2021). Defence Programs and Budget of Japan – Defence strengthening acceleration package, overview of fiscal year 2022 budget, https://mod.go.jp/en/d_act/d_budget/pdf/20220420.pdf
Ministry of Foreign Affairs of Japan, (2014), The three principles on transfer of defence equipment and technology, https://www.mofa.go.jp/press/release/press22e_000010.html (last accessed on 14 June 2022).
National Intelligence Council, (2021). Global trends: a more contested world, https://www.dni.gov/files/ODNI/documents/assessments/GlobalTrends_2040.pdf
OECD, (2019). International migration outlook 2019, https://www.oecd-ilibrary.org/sites/e025d47d-en/index.html?itemId=/content/component/e025d47d-en
OECD, (2023). https://data.oecd.org/pop/old-age-dependency-ratio.htm#indicator-chart
Nivoix, Sophie and Rey, Serge, (2023). "What Are the Geo-Economic Consequences of Japanese Demography?", *Peace Review*, ISSN: 1040-2659 print / 1469-9982 online. DOI: 10.1080/10402659.2023.2255549
Pehrson, Christopher J., (2006). "*String of pearls: meeting the challenge of China's rising power across the Asian littoral*", Strategic Studies Institute, US Army War College, http://www.jstor.com/stable/resrep11277
Ramo, Joshua Cooper, (2004). The Beijing Consensus. The Foreign Policy Centre, Spring, http://fpc.org.uk/publications/TheBeijingConsensus
Spykman, Nicholas John, (1942). *America's strategy in world politics: The United States and the balance of power*, Reprinted by Routledge in 2017, New York.
United Nations, (2019). World Population Prospects, The 2019 Revision, Middle variant scenario, https://population.un.org/wpp/Publications/Files/WPP2019_Highlights.pdf
Xu, Yi-Chong, (1998). "Maintaining peace and prosperity in the Asia-pacific rim", *Peace Review: A Journal of Social Justice*, 10:1, 49–56, DOI: 10.1080/10402659808426121
Yoshida, Shingo, (2019). "Nuclear Deterrence: Mixed Messages for Japan", *The diplomat*, 17th October 2019, https://thediplomat.com/2019/10/nuclear-deterrence-mixed-messages-for-japan/
World Bank (2023). Active population open data, https://data.worldbank.org/indicator/SP.POP.TOTL?locations=1W
World Bank (2024a). World development indicators open data, https://databank.worldbank.org/indicator/NY.GDP.PCAP.CD/1ff4a498/Popular-Indicators
World Bank (2024b). Net immigration open data, https://data.worldbank.org/indicator/SM.POP.NETM
Zajec, Olivier, (2016). *Introduction à la géopolitique*, Editions du Rocher, Paris.

13 Global Disruptions in Seafood Trade during COVID-19

The Effects of Mobility Restrictions on Crustacean Exports from Indonesia, Thailand, and Vietnam

Ayu Pratiwi, Guenwoo Lee, Heli Marjanen and Erja Kettunen

Introduction

Aquaculture and fisheries have been among the fastest-growing food sectors in Indonesia, Thailand and Vietnam, providing livelihoods to millions of people and contributing to global food security. The long-term liberalization of global trade until the 2000s facilitated the expansion of export opportunities in the Asia-Pacific countries (e.g., Baldwin & Kawai, 2013; Kawai & Wignaraja, 2011; Mölders & Volz, 2011). However, the trends reversed post-2008 global financial crisis (Evenett, 2019), with protectionism rising amidst geopolitical tensions and trade disputes (e.g., Baldwin & Evenett, 2020; Cuervo-Cazurra et al., 2020; Evenett et al., 2022). The COVID-19 pandemic further exacerbated these challenges, introducing disruptive measures such as border closures and transport restrictions, which raised trade costs and delayed border clearance (Maliszewska et al., 2020; Banga et al., 2020). The tense geopolitical situation changed the global dynamics of geoeconomics and geopolitics, thus affecting trade partnerships and even leading to trade 'wars' between economic powers. All this had profound impacts on export-oriented Southeast Asian economies, such as Indonesia, Thailand and Vietnam, especially in the food sector affected by COVID-19-related food safety concerns (Thammachote & Trochim, 2021). A case in point is the global exports of crustaceans.

On the supply side, transport restrictions and physical distancing measures hit the crustacean sector (Baldwin & Tomiura, 2020; FAO, 2020; FAO, 2021a). Specifically, the sector faced supply chain disruptions, including shortages in imported feeds and broodstock, and scarcity of labour that had the most substantial impact on small-scale producers who dominate the shrimp aquaculture industry (WorldFish, 2020; Alam et al., 2022; Van Duijn et al., 2012; Kumaran et al., 2021; Pazir et al., 2022). The rise in maritime freight rates (UNCTAD, 2022: 63) further exacerbated these challenges. Furthermore, the sector is highly vulnerable to biosecurity and disease (Bondad-Reantaso et al., 2012).

DOI: 10.4324/9781032655857-17

On the demand side, lockdowns and business closures led to reduced consumer spending on durable goods (Verma & Gustafsson, 2020; Kassa, 2020), whereas the food sector encountered concerns about food safety that drew attention to preventing coronavirus transmission among producers, retailers, and consumers (Aday & Aday, 2020; Samadi et al., 2022). Consumer behaviour also changed, marked by panic buying, stockpiling, and altered purchasing patterns (Kassa, 2020; Banga et al., 2020). Consequently, the seafood export sector, crucial to several Southeast Asian nations, saw a decline due to weakened domestic and global demand, port access restrictions, and disruptions in processing business (Waiho et al., 2020; Azra et al., 2021). Many producing nations experienced cancellations of shipments as the epidemic resulted in closures and significant layoffs at the fish processing businesses (Waiho et al., 2020). Manufacturing processes and other labour-intensive jobs were thus severely impacted (Dingel & Neiman, 2020). In addition to reduced demand and supply, several countries also imposed import restrictions on seafood products.

In this study, we assess the effects of mobility restrictions in importing and exporting countries on crustacean export performance in three Southeast Asian countries that are among the leading crustacean exporters in the world: Indonesia, Thailand, and Vietnam. The effects of strict lockdown (SLD) policies on people's livelihood in lower and middle-income countries have been a subject of extensive debate (e.g., Aday & Aday, 2020; Alam et al., 2022; Azra et al., 2021; Kaewnuratchadasorn et al., 2020), and whether the economic disruptions stemmed more from the virus threat itself or the government-imposed mobility restrictions remains unclear. Therefore, drawing from data on stringency indices that record the number and strictness of government policies, we discuss the restrictions imposed by the exporting and importing countries, respectively. Stringency indices are composite scores based on a set of indicators that are comparable across countries. However, as the government's domestic responses to the pandemic may or may not correlate with the stringency indices, the indices should not be interpreted as 'scoring' the appropriateness or effectiveness of a country's response.

Our research questions are as follows: (1) How did the first strict lockdowns (hereafter, SLDs) implemented in Indonesia, Thailand, and Vietnam influence their export dynamics? (2) How did the restrictions in importing countries affect the exports from Indonesia, Thailand, and Vietnam? Employing a three-way fixed effects estimation and event study regression, we examine the export volume and value trends during the twelve months preceding and following the SLDs implemented in each country. This approach allows us to isolate the distinct influences of importing and exporting countries' restrictions on the crustacean export sector.

The paper proceeds as follows. We begin by providing an overview of the significance of the aquaculture sector and crustacean exports in Indonesia, Thailand, and Vietnam, as well as the concurrent lockdown policies affecting global trade in this sector. Then, the methodology of the study is described, including the primary data sources and the empirical methodology used. We then continue by presenting the estimation results. Finally, the findings are discussed, highlighting the main contributions to existing literature.

The aquaculture sector, crustacean trade, and lockdown policies

The seafood industry in general, and especially aquaculture, are a significant part of many Southeast Asian economies. In Vietnam, the seafood sector accounted for 3.18% of its Gross Domestic Product (GDP) in 2021 (SEAFDEC, 2021a), and in Indonesia, fisheries and aquaculture contributed 2.78% of the GDP (SEAFDEC, 2021b). In Thailand, the aquaculture sector accounted for 1.2 % of the total GDP in 2020 (FAO, 2022). Aquaculture is a more significant contributor to the national economy in all three countries than captured fisheries. While the COVID-19 pandemic was generally found to have little or no effects on food exports (Lashitew & Socrates, 2021), the cases on fisheries and aquaculture products are more complex. The deepening of the global economic recession and prolonged periods of disruption in the global and local supply chains assumedly considerably impacted the production and availability of food, including fish and other seafood (see, e.g. FAO 2020).

Indonesia, Thailand, and Vietnam as crustacean exporters

Although most seafood is consumed domestically in producing countries, it is one of the world's most traded goods (Nisar et al., 2023). Figure 13.1 illustrates the export trends of crustaceans by the leading global exporters from 2017 to 2021. In volume and value each year, India and Ecuador have been among the top five countries. Notably, Ecuador's crustacean export volume quadrupled within five years from 2017 to 2021, mainly because of the more intensive farming that enabled bigger harvests per hectare. By 2020, Ecuador had replaced India as the top-exporting country in volume. India experienced a period of substantial growth between 2012 and 2019. However, issues with the spread of crustacean diseases, high production costs, and low prices recently translated into a decline in production (Fletcher, 2023).

In contrast to India and Ecuador, the export growth in Vietnam and Indonesia has been marginal. Environmental and political issues partially explain Thailand's poor performance as the country faced a devastating flood in 2011, followed by a spread of Early Mortality Syndrome (EMS) in shrimp farms. The EMS spread all over Asia, starting in China and then spreading to Vietnam, Malaysia, Thailand, and the Philippines, causing a drastic decrease in crustacean exports. In 2014, when shrimp production in Asia started to recover, Thailand was downgraded by the United States' policy to Tier 3 (the lowest grade for countries that do not eliminate human trafficking), thus facing sanctions because of the human trafficking issues. The following year, the Thai fishery industry was further hit by receiving the EU's "yellow card", the EU's official warning to trade partners for illegal, unreported, and unregulated

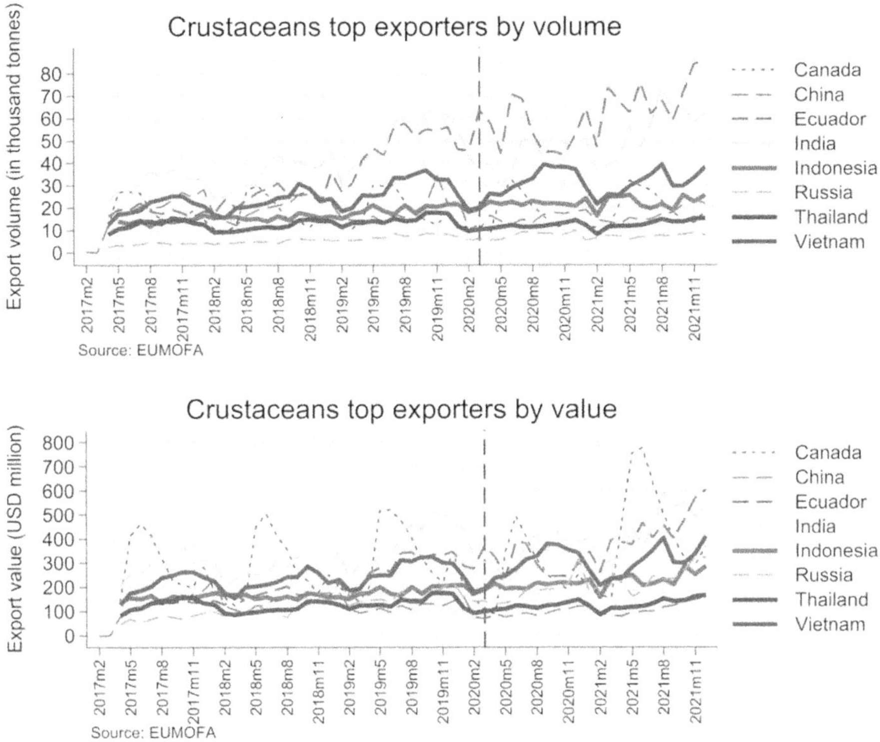

Figure 13.1 Crustacean top exporting countries by export volume and value, monthly, 2017–2021.

fishing practices. Although the Tier 3 status was upgraded in 2016 and the yellow card was removed in 2019, by that time, Thai exporters had already lost their market share to other countries (Thammachote & Trochim, 2023). The same occurred in Vietnam in 2017 when the European Commission posed the EU yellow card due to accusations of illegal, unreported, and unregulated fishing. With the yellow card, all exports to the EU are subject to pre-check, resulting in the increased cost of seafood exports and decreased volume due to extended delivery times (Nam & Le, 2021).

Figure 13.2 presents the export volumes and values of Indonesia, Thailand, and Vietnam by region in 2017–2021. The three countries exhibit distinct profiles as to their main trading partners. The most important export market for Indonesia has been Northern America, followed by Eastern Asia since early 2019. In contrast, the shares of the EU and the rest of the world have remained low. For Vietnam, since early 2019, the Eastern Asian countries have been the most important trading partners, followed and sometimes taken over by Northern American countries. Compared to Indonesia, Vietnam has a more diversified and balanced exporting profile as exports to the EU and the rest of

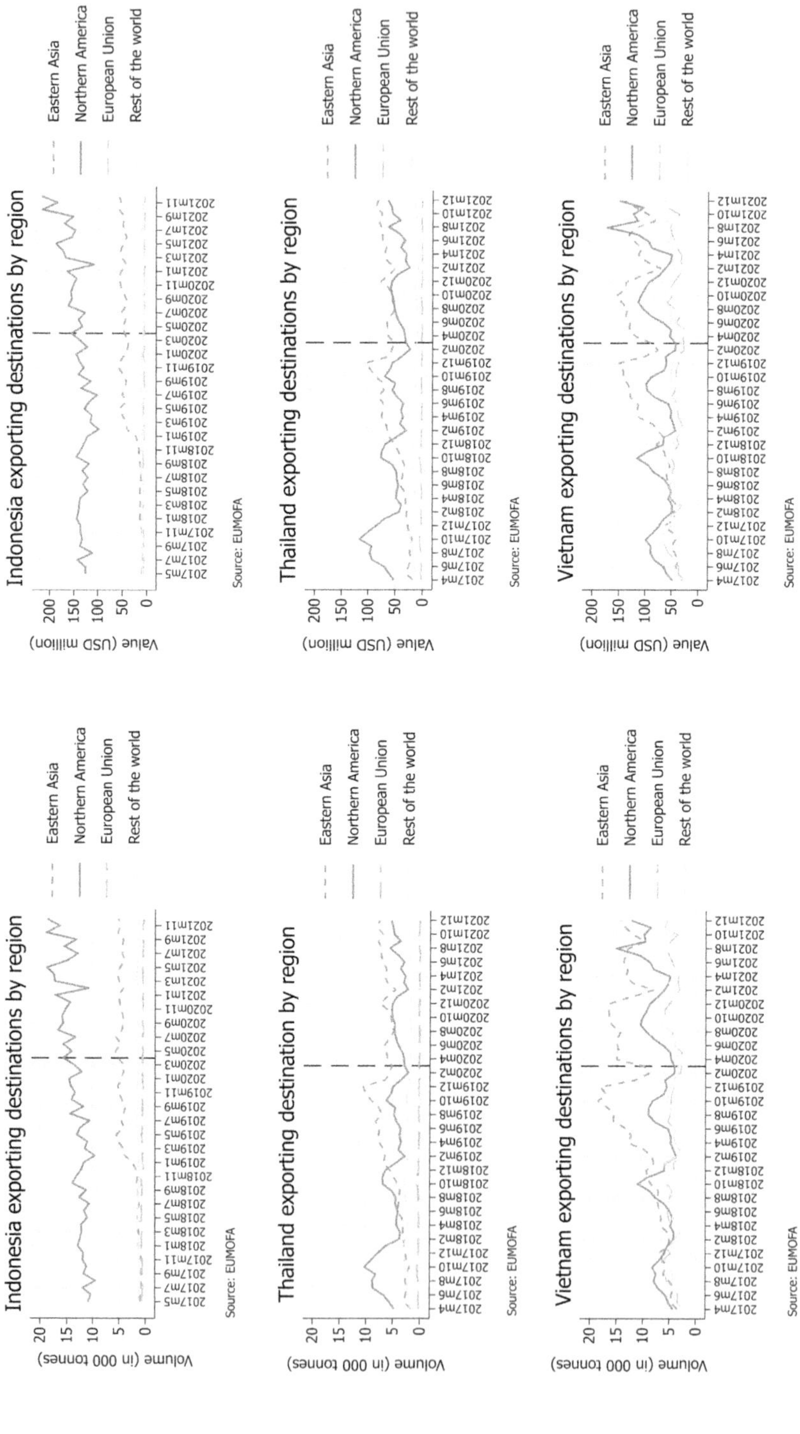

Figure 13.2 Crustacean exports of Indonesia, Thailand, and Vietnam by region, 2017–2021.

the world also play a significant role, although there has been a substantial increase in both values and volumes within 2017–2021 to Eastern Asia and Northern America. For Thailand, exports to the prior primary market, Northern America, declined sharply in 2017, presumably because of the Tier 3 status. Since then, exports have been increasingly targeted to Eastern Asian countries, whereas exports to the EU region and the rest of the world have remained modest.

Trade policies affecting crustacean exports vary across countries. Indonesia's main export destination is the United States, which has a very low average MFN[1] import tariff for crustaceans at 0.43%. The second and third biggest export destinations, Japan and China, impose somewhat higher average tariffs at 2.08% and 6.19%, respectively. As these three countries buy almost 90% of all Indonesian crustacean exports, the tariff burden has been relatively moderate.

The leading countries that import Vietnamese crustaceans are China, Japan, South Korea, and the United States, the share of these four countries being ca. 60%. Thus, Vietnam's crustacean exports face somewhat higher tariff protection, especially in South Korea, where the tariff is as high as 19.80%.

The most significant markets for Thailand are China, the United States, and Japan, which absorb almost 70% of the total. Therefore, the average tariff burden for Thailand's crustacean exports is between Indonesia and Vietnam.

All food exports are also subject to sanitary and phytosanitary requirements (SPS) to ensure that food is safe and to prevent the spread of pests or diseases among animals and plants (GATT, 1994; WTO, n.d.). These require the products "to come from a disease-free area, [as well as an] inspection of products, specific treatment or processing of products, and setting of allowable maximum levels of pesticide residues or permitted use of only certain additives in food" (ibid.).

Lockdown policies in Indonesia, Thailand, and Vietnam

The three countries applied dissimilar policies for lockdowns. In a global comparison as well, there were differences in the restrictive measures of all exporting and importing countries, which affected the operations of industries, transportation, and the mobility of workers and consumers. Figure 13.3 displays the stringency indices for the leading crustacean-exporting countries, the average stringency indices of their importing countries, and the average stringency indices by main importing regions. The restrictions include workplace closures, stay-at-home requirements, public transportation closures, restrictions on internal movements, and travel controls, with higher scores indicating stricter measures (Hale et al., 2020). During the initial months of the pandemic, Vietnam and Indonesia implemented more stringent restrictions than Thailand. However, Thailand's pattern was notably volatile, with drastic fluctuations in the index starting in 2021.

As Figure 13.3 shows, the average stringency indices of the importing countries followed similar patterns, except that Ecuador recorded the highest

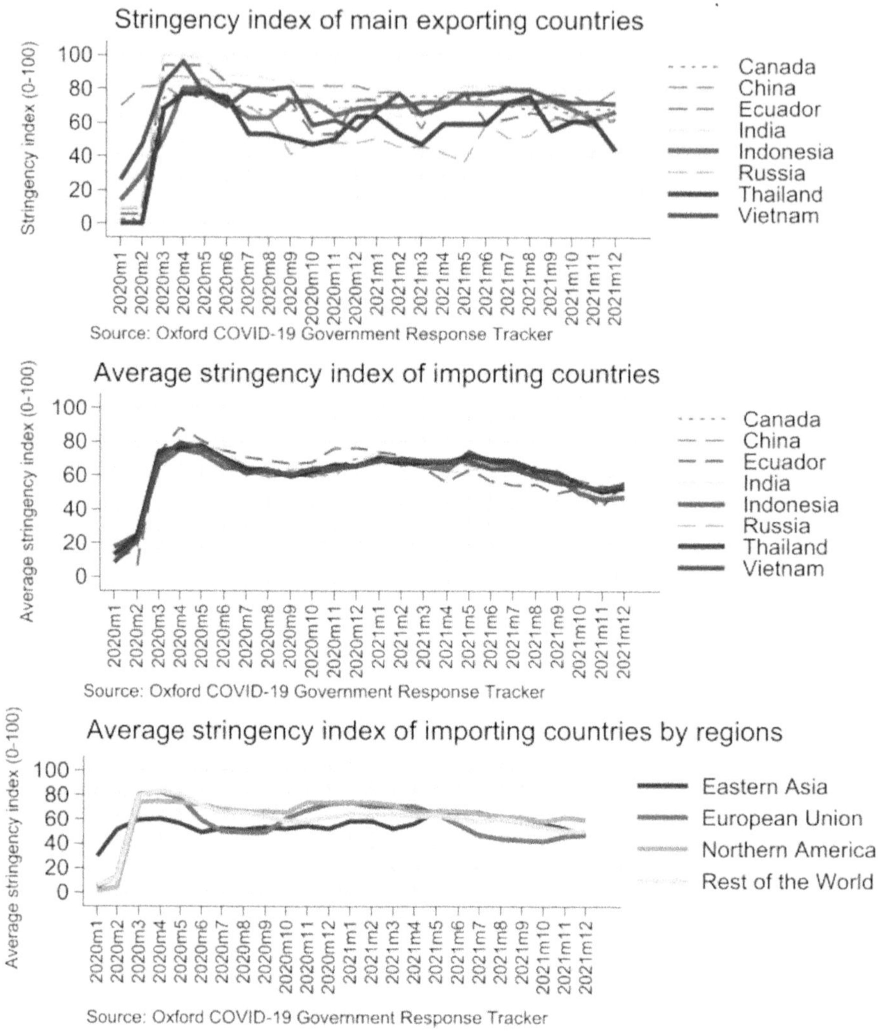

Figure 13.3 Stringency indices of the leading crustacean exporters and the average indices of their importing countries, 2020–2021.

stringency index at the onset of the pandemic but turned to less stringent restrictions before the others. Regarding the main importing regions, East Asia was the first to implement restrictions, as the pandemic's epicentre was in this region. However, their stringency index was at a lower level compared to other regions until May 2021. Most importantly, strict restrictions (lockdowns) were imposed almost simultaneously worldwide starting in March 2020.

Indonesia's lockdown approach was decentralized and gradual. On March 15th, 2020, Indonesia's President advised working from home whenever possible, leaving lockdown decisions to provincial and district governments (The Jakarta Post, 2020). That led to the initiation of "large-scale social restrictions" (Pembatasan Sosial Berskala Besar) in various provinces, formalized on March 31st (Gaduh et al., 2020). From April 2nd, Indonesia closed its international borders and barred foreigners from entering the country. Shortly after, the district and municipal governments implemented individual measures, established coordinated contact tracing and bolstered social support systems supported by community mobilizations (Meckelburg, 2021).

In contrast, Vietnam's response to COVID-19 was more centralized and influenced by its experience with the SARS epidemic. Vietnam's stringency indices are consistent with this, being the highest among the three countries. The country's responses were swift, including establishing a national steering committee after the first COVID case was identified in January 2020. National committees comprise representatives across different ministries, sectors, media, and information technology companies to coordinate and oversee the country's strategy to curb the pandemic (Pollack et al., 2020). After detecting the second wave of cases on March 6th, the government rapidly implemented mass quarantines, with the international borders fully closed on March 22nd. Vietnam's proactive measures included early implementation of closures, mask mandates, and restrictions on domestic and international travel (Hoang, 2022), with the Ministry of Health communicating threats and strategies clearly and effectively from January 9th.

Thailand's stringency indices are the lowest among the three countries. Its strategy for handling the COVID-19 pandemic combined aspects of Indonesia's decentralized approach and Vietnam's centralized strategy. The Thai government began closing the international borders on March 23rd. The government's COVID response included rigorous contact tracing, extensive testing, and early social distancing. An extensive public awareness campaign was initiated to inform citizens about the virus and the necessary preventative measures (Virakul et al., 2022). However, Thailand faced challenges balancing virus containment and economic impacts, especially given its dependence on tourism. Financial aid programmes were introduced to support affected workers and businesses (Pongsakornrungsilp et al., 2021), but the pandemic's economic strain, particularly on the tourism sector, remained significant.

Methodology

Data sources

We utilize several data sources for our analysis. We start with the **European Market Observatory for Fisheries and Aquaculture Products** (EUMOFA, 2022) data on monthly imports and exports on fishery and aquaculture. In this paper, we focus on "crustacean" commodity groups, which are listed in Table 13.2, notes. The **Oxford COVID-19 Government Response Tracker**, compiled by the University of Oxford, contains international, daily time series data for the days the lockdown measures were effective (Hale et al., 2020). We specifically apply the stringency index, which measures the degree of restrictions that limit people's mobility. The World Health Organization reported COVID-19 cases and deaths, in turn, include the number of COVID-19 cases and monthly mortality data (WHO, 2023).

Melchior (2015) found that ascension to WTO membership has contributed to lower tariffs for seafood trade. Therefore, we use the **World Trade Organization membership** information as of 2020 to proxy for tariffs, thus capturing the trade preferences of the partners. The **Overall Trade Restriction Indices** (OTRI) developed by Looi Kee et al. (2009) calculates the weighted average tariff of a given country, with the weights reflecting the composition of import volume and import demand elasticities of each imported product and is thus used to account for the trade policy stance of the importing countries. Furthermore, we use the **CEPII distance measures dataset** to consider bilateral distances (in kilometres) between paired capital cities of exporting and importing countries (Mayer & Zignago, 2011). Additional data include the yearly GDP of both exporting and importing countries obtained from the **World Bank World Development Indicator** and the monthly export value of exporting countries obtained from **IMF's International Financial Statistics database**. In addition, we use the **Trade Map** database and **Market Access Map** of the International Trade Center for data on import tariffs of the main crustacean importing countries.

Estimation strategy

In the **Oxford COVID-19 Government Response Tracker**, the 'stringency index' variable is an aggregate score ranging from 0 to 100, measuring containment and closure policy indicators and public information campaigns. Based on this information and following the methodology of Lashitew and Socrates (2021) and Arenas et al. (2022), we identify an event of 'strict lockdown' (SLD) in the first month when a country's stringency index surpasses the global median for the respective year. Thus in 2020, an SLD was indicated by a score of over 64.35 and in 2021, over 58.8. The first SLDs in our study occurred in April 2020 for Indonesia and March 2020 for Thailand and Vietnam. In this period, each country implemented international border closures. As countries adjusted over time, restrictions were relaxed and reimposed as case numbers changed. For instance, Thailand's first SLD period lasted from March to June 2020, and the second from January to March 2021. For Vietnam, the first SLD extended from March to September 2020, and the second from January to March 2021. Indonesia's first SLD period spanned from April to June 2020, the second from September to October 2020, and the third from December 2020 to April 2021. Given these variations in timing and extent, we set our reference point to the month when each studied country implemented their first SLD.

In our empirical analysis, we first utilize a three-way fixed effects (TWFE) model (cf. Wooldridge, 2021) to estimate the effects of mobility restrictions on export volumes and values in Indonesia, Thailand, and Vietnam, as follows:

$$Y_{igt} = \alpha_g + \lambda_t + \delta_i + \tau W_{gt} + \beta_1 PostSLD_{gt} + \beta_2 X'_{gt} + \epsilon_{igt} \quad (1)$$

Here, Y_{igt} represents the monthly crustacean trade volume and value for importing country g in period t for product type and complexity i. α_g, λt, and δ_i are the fixed effects for importing countries, time (month), product-type and complexity, respectively. These country-fixed effects will account for time-invariant heterogeneity features that may affect the outcomes, such as geography, infrastructure, the efficacy of the public health system, and demographic characteristics (Chen et al., 2020). W_{gt} is the mobility restriction indicator, denoted by the stringency index for exporting and importing countries. $PostSLD_{gt}$ accounts for the post-SLD period equals to 1, 0 otherwise. X'_{gt} includes control variables like WTO membership, distance to exporting countries, and GDP. Considering the potential endogeneity of lockdowns and their representation of pandemic severity, we include monthly COVID-19 deaths and new cases in importing countries to represent factors related to demand shocks (Berthou & Stumpner, 2022). The key parameter of interest is τ, the effects of mobility restrictions as reflected by the stringency indices. We examine a 24-month window period, divided into 12 months of pre- and 13 post-first SLD implementation in each exporting country, with one month in post-first SLD subject to an omission in the model.

Secondly, we apply the event-study analysis to explore the time-varying effects of mobility restrictions on export trade volume over time. In this estimation, the regressors of interest are a set of non-parametric event indicators defined relative to the event (Schmidheiny & Siegloch, 2023). Following Lashitew and Socrates (2021) and Arenas et al. (2022), the event-study design is estimated as follows:

$$\begin{aligned} Y_{ipgt} = {} & \alpha_t + \alpha_{it} + \alpha_{ig} + \sum_{j=-12}^{-2} \beta_j 1\{tdiff_p = j\} + \sum_{j=0}^{11} \beta_j 1\{tdiff_p = j\} \\ & + \eta_{igt} + \gamma_{ipt} + \delta_{igt} + \epsilon_{ipgt} \end{aligned} \quad (2)$$

Y_{ipgt} is the bilateral export trade volume and value between the exporting countries p and importing countries g, across product type and complexity i and month t. α_t, α_{it}, and α_{ig} control for month-time, product type, and importing country characteristics, respectively, to consider the seasonal patterns. β_j is our coefficient of interest, indicating the implementation of the first SLD effects on export volume and value. The indicator function $1\{tdiff_p = j\}$ equals 1 if the time t in the data for exporting country p corresponds exactly to j months relative to the lockdown. Otherwise, it equals 0. Following Schmidheiny and Siegloch (2023), the baseline period is one month before the first lockdown (j = -1); where periods j < -1 are "leads" (anticipatory effects), and j >1 are "lags" (post-implementation effects). As the lag in month 12 will be omitted from the model, our time period will be 24 months, allowing for 12 lead and 11 lag months at maximum. η_{igt} represents the stringency indices of importing countries g, γ_{ipt} stands for stringency indices of exporting countries p, and δ_{igt} is the vector of country-level variables.

Results

Descriptive analysis

Here, we present the results of the analyses and estimations based on the models; the interpretations and explanations will follow in the Discussion section. Below in Table 13.1, column 1 presents the descriptive statistics for Indonesia, Thailand, and Vietnam, showcasing the mean values and standard deviations (sd) of export-related variables for each country. It also presents our set of control variables for each respective country. Columns 2 and 3 describe the key variables before and after the first SLDs were implemented in respective countries. Although Vietnam and Indonesia were able to increase their monthly crustacean exports during the post-SLD period and Thailand experienced a decline, none of these differences (column 4) is statistically significant in our models. However, in terms of the general economic trends, a statistically significant post-SLD decline in total exports and annual GDP was detected for Thailand. In contrast, the findings concerning Indonesia and Vietnam show the opposite.

Estimation results

In Table 13.2, we first present the results of the TWFE estimations at the global level. Our analysis revealed varying trends after controlling for the country, product type and complexity, and seasonal trends in both importing and exporting countries. For Indonesia, no statistically significant correlations were detected. Thailand experienced a decrease of 6.6 thousand tonnes and 61 million USD during the post-SLD period, while Vietnam saw a 0.3 thousand tonnes increase in volume. Further examination of the relationships between the stringency indices of exporting countries and their trade performance revealed that a one-point increase in the domestic stringency index resulted in 0.085 thousand tonnes and a 0.78 million USD increase in exports for Thailand. Vietnam's export volume slightly declined by 0.004 thousand tonnes for each one-point increase in the domestic stringency index. The stringency indices of importing countries were also positively correlated with export value and volume for Thailand, but no such effects were found for Indonesia and Vietnam.

Next, we conducted TWFE estimations by region to evaluate the performance of each exporting country across its primary export destinations. During the post-SLD period, Vietnam's crustacean export volume to the

Table 13.1 Summary statistics before and after the implementation of the first strict lockdown measures (SLD) in exporting countries (24 months window)

Variables	*(1)*		*(2)*		*(3)*		*(4)*
	24 month period		*Pre SLD*		*Post SLD*		*Differences*
	mean	*sd*	*mean*	*sd*	*mean*	*sd*	*=(3)-(2)*
Exporting country: Indonesia (first strict lockdown 2020/4)							
Net weight of crustacean trade volume (in 000 tonnes)	0.120	0.771	0.108	0.699	0.132	0.836	0.024
Crustacean export value in USD million	1.145	6.943	1.037	6.296	1.252	7.535	0.215
Total exports USD million	14399.886	1738.568	14054.074	837.225	14746.333	2260.531	**692.259*****
Annual GDP (in 100 million USD)	11025.899	462.946	11038.341	261.515	11013.434	600.253	**24.907***
Stringency index	39.064	33.343	7.773	15.355	70.414	5.027	**62.641*****
Monthly cumulative cases	88904519	1.46e+07	959.978	3242.486	17796259.790	16435175.411	**17795299.811*****
Importing countries							
Stringency index	57.328	23.736	8.805	21.773	63.044	17.295	**54.239*****
Monthly cumulative cases	22086508.799	82997537.027	26065.440	194504.100	27748916.360	92238509.030	**27722850.920*****
Monthly new deaths	3037.470	8773.483	78.841	621.825	3733.029	9698.018	**3654.187*****
Distance to exporting countries (km)	8116.675	4857.651	8161.642	4933.197	8071.893	4782.087	-89.749
Annual GDP (in 100 million USD)	898833.695	4005186.469	699826.600	3605447	1098206	4360880	**398379.600*****
WTO member (1 = yes)	0.988	0.107	0.894	0.307	0.900	0.300	0.005
Market Access Overall Trade Restrictiveness Index (MAOTRI) in %	8.894	4.369	9.172	4.767	8.613	3.908	**-0.559*****
Observations	4362		2183		2179		4362
Time period	2019m4-2021m4		2019m4-2020m3		2020m4-2021m4		

(Continued)

Table 13.1 (Continued)

Variables	*(1)*		*(2)*		*(3)*		*(4)*
	24 month period		*Pre SLD*		*Post SLD*		*Differences*
	mean	*sd*	*mean*	*sd*	*mean*	*sd*	*=(3)-(2)*
Exporting country: Thailand (first strict lockdown 2020/3)							
Net weight of crustacea trade volume (in 000 tonnes)	0.090	0.330	0.095	0.349	0.086	0.309	-0.009
Crustacean export values in USD million	0.889	3.461	0.907	3.590	0.870	3.322	-0.038
Total export values USD million	20104.971	1620.737	20495.989	991.454	19700.386	2001.772	**-795.603*****
Annual GDP (in 100 million USD)	5194.867	210.748	5367.514	161.982	5016.230	21.451	**-351.283*****
Stringency index	50.479	23.191	0.00	0.00	59.150	10.820	**59.150*****
Monthly cumulative cases	189486.117	243004.076	93.499	270.055	221940.458	249022.328	**221846.960*****
Importing countries variables							
Stringency index	56.849	23.294	3.512	11.437	62.988	17.544	**59.476*****
Monthly cumulative cases	25377354.384	95509500.703	8361.068	113470.587	29749278.070	1.28e+08	**29691945,03*****
Monthly new deaths	3883.504	11106.917	14.493	186.975	4536.896	11905.346	**4522.403*****
Distance to exporting countries (km)	6738.107	4263.146	6714.477	4263.082	6762.695	4264.404	48.218
Annual GDP (in 100 million USD)	1423643.770	5072892.978	1135686.408	4650041.143	1721434.622	5461337.587	**585748.215*****
WTO member (1 = yes)	0.997	0.052	0.921	0.270	0.918	0.275	0.003
Market Access Overall Trade Restrictiveness Index (MAOTRI) in %	9.081	4.117	9.119	4.195	9.040	4.034	-0.079
Observations	3577		1819		1758		3577
Time period	2019m3-2021m3		2019m3-2020m2		2020m3-2021m3		

Vietnam (first strict lockdown starts 2020/3)							
Net weight of crustacean trade volume (in 000 tonnes)	0.169	0.504	0.162	0.498	0.175	0.509	0.013
Crustacean export values in USD million	1.585	4.850	1.506	4.605	1.660	5.070	0.155
Total export values USD million	23654.471	3178.992	22291.813	1844.943	24942.803	3609.715	**2650.990*****
Annual GDP (in 100 million USD)	3440.727	100.738	3364.118	45.700	3513.166	83.488	**149.057*****
Stringency index	67.506	16.733	5.967	14.020	72.521	11.040	**66.554*****
Monthly cumulative cases	27995.763	23354.973	31.799	105.525	32385.429	22140.708	**32353.630*****
Importing countries							
Stringency index	56.751	23.573	2.930	10.070	62.941	17.529	**60.011*****
Monthly cumulative cases	21092162.849	88188878.779	190.44	191.18	32385.43	22140.71	**32194.99*****
Monthly new deaths	3235.198	10218.858	8.253	140.974	3730.530	10902.173	**3722.277*****
Distance to exporting countries (km)	6788.491	4024.694	6768.062	3985.891	6807.826	4061.946	39.764
Annual GDP (in 100 million USD)	1099874.747	4531740.010	906412.200	4204825	1282785	4814267	**376372.600*****
WTO observer (1 = yes)	0.990	0.100	0.935	0.247	0.933	0.251	0.002
Market Access Overall Trade Restrictiveness Index (MAOTRI) in %	9.396	4.581	9.494	4.641	9.305	4.523	0.189
Observations	4387		2132		2255		4387
Time period	2019m3-2021m3		2019m3-2020m2		2020m3-2021m3		

* $p < 0.10$, ** $p < 0.05$, *** $p < 0.01$

Table 13.2 Effects of strict lockdowns (SLDs) on crustacean export volume (thousand tonnes) and value (million USD)

Exporting countries:	*Indonesia*		*Thailand*		*Vietnam*	
Variables	*Export volume (1)*	*Export value (2)*	*Export volume (3)*	*Export value (4)*	*Export volume (5)*	*Export value (6)*
Importing regions: Global						
Post-SLD period, exporting country	-2.290	-16.533	**-6.614****	**-61.031****	**0.317****	2.361
	(2.008)	(19.479)	(2.824)	(28.742)	(0.161)	(1.621)
Stringency index, **exporting** country	0.033	0.229	**0.085****	**0.784****	**-0.004***	-0.028
	(0.031)	(0.300)	(0.037)	(0.374)	(0.002)	(0.020)
Stringency index, **importing** countries	-0.000	-0.001	**0.001*****	**0.009*****	0.000	0.004
	(0.000)	(0.002)	(0.000)	(0.003)	(0.000)	(0.004)
Observations	3720	3720	3072	3072	3853	3853
R-squared	0.082	0.086	0.048	0.045	0.045	0.045
Importing regions: East Asia						
Post-SLD period, exporting country	-3.248	-39.998	-18.540	-169.697	**1.327***	10.903
	(5.056)	(42.331)	(11.596)	(107.431)	(0.756)	(7.075)
Stringency index, **exporting** country	0.045	0.561	0.237	2.167	**-0.017***	-0.112
	(0.077)	(0.649)	(0.151)	(1.395)	(0.009)	(0.085)
Stringency index, **importing** countries	**0.002****	**0.022*****	0.002	**0.023****	-0.001	-0.017
	(0.001)	(0.006)	(0.001)	(0.013)	(0.002)	(0.022)
Observations	600	600	639	639	637	637
R-squared	0.051	0.084	0.096	0.095	0.104	0.102
Importing regions: European Union						
Post-SLD period, exporting country	-0.134	0.131	-0.383	-3.316	**0.160***	1.327
	(0.324)	(3.654)	(0.302)	(3.389)	(0.093)	(0.816)
Stringency index, **exporting** country	0.002	-0.005	0.005	0.043	-0.002	-0.015
	(0.005)	(0.056)	(0.004)	(0.044)	(0.001)	(0.010)
Stringency index, **importing** countries	-0.000	-0.001	-0.000	-0.000	0.000	0.001
	(0.000)	(0.001)	(0.000)	(0.001)	(0.000)	(0.003)
Observations	1316	1316	819	819	1127	1127
R-squared	0.022	0.019	0.067	0.061	0.145	0.136

Importing regions: North America						
Post-SLD period, exporting country	-25.853	-218.072	-17.188	-189.217	-1.910	-20.194
	(17.826)	(176.894)	(11.898)	(144.067)	(2.240)	(24.818)
Stringency index, **exporting** country	0.439	3.792	0.209	2.275	-0.004	-0.023
	(0.280)	(2.780)	(0.151)	(1.828)	(0.012)	(0.138)
Stringency index, **importing** countries	**-0.046*****	**-0.465*****	0.016	0.204	0.036	0.362
	(0.017)	(0.168)	(0.013)	(0.157)	(0.027)	(0.304)
Observations	334	334	366	366	337	337
R-squared	0.231	0.234	0.150	0.144	0.179	0.168
Importing regions: Rest of the world						
Post-SLD period, exporting country	**-1.593****	**-8.903*****	-2.454	-16.126	0.099	0.881
	(0.756)	(3.391)	(1.667)	(10.818)	(0.096)	(0.990)
Stringency index, **exporting** country	**0.024****	**0.135****	0.032	0.210	-0.001	-0.013
	(0.012)	(0.052)	(0.022)	(0.141)	(0.001)	(0.012)
Stringency index, **importing** countries	**-0.000****	**0.001***	-0.000	0.001	**0.001*****	**0.007*****
	(0.000)	(0.000)	(0.000)	(0.001)	(0.000)	(0.002)
Observations	1470	1470	1248	1248	1752	1752
R-squared	0.031	0.050	0.034	0.042	0.057	0.054
Month FE	Yes	Yes	Yes	Yes	Yes	Yes
Country FE	Yes	Yes	Yes	Yes	Yes	Yes
Product FE	Yes	Yes	Yes	Yes	Yes	Yes
Monthly COVID death	Yes	Yes	Yes	Yes	Yes	Yes
Country-level variables	Yes	Yes	Yes	Yes	Yes	Yes

Standard errors in parentheses * $p < 0.10$, ** $p < 0.05$, *** $p < 0.01$

Note: Product type and complexity FE includes the following main commercial types and code: Crab (063), Shrimp Crangon spp (089), Shrimp, (064), Coldwater (065), Freshwater crayfish (065), Lobster Homarus spp (066), Lobster, Norway (067), Rock lobster and sea crawfish (068); the variation of preservation types: Live/Fresh (PS1), Frozen (PS2), Smoked (PS3), Prepared/Preserved (PS4), Unspecified (PS5), Salted (PS7) and Dried (PS8); as well as the following presentation types: Whole/Gutted (PR1), Other cuts (PR2), Others (PR4). Country-level variables include GDP (in hundred million USD) of both exporting and importing countries, paired-distances to capital cities between exporting and importing countries, WTO membership of both exporting and importing countries, and Market Access Trade Restrictiveness Index of exporting countries. COVID death include variables for importing and exporting countries' monthly new deaths and cumulative new cases.

East Asian and European regions increased by 1.3 and 0.16 thousand tonnes, respectively. For Indonesia and Thailand, no statistically significant changes were detected regarding these regions. In turn, Indonesia saw a decline of 1.6 thousand tonnes and 8.9 million USD in its exports to the rest of the world.

Upon examining the stringency indices of the importing regions, we found that for each one-point increase in the average stringency index of the importing East Asian countries, Indonesia's trade increased by 0.002 thousand tonnes and 0.022 million USD, respectively. For Thailand, a one-point increase in the stringency indices of East Asian countries resulted in a 0.023 million USD increase in exports to these countries but did not affect volume. For Vietnam, no statistically significant effects were found regarding this region. The restrictions imposed by North American importing countries reduced Indonesia's exports by 0.046 thousand tonnes and 0.465 million USD, respectively, but no such effects were detected for Thailand or Vietnam. For trade with the rest of the world, the average stringency index of importing countries is positively associated with export volume and value from Vietnam, showing an increase of 0.001 thousand tonnes and 0.007 million USD, respectively.

Regarding the domestic stringency indices of exporting countries, we found that an increase by one point decreased Vietnam's exports to East Asia by 0.017 thousand tonnes during the post-SLD period of 12 months. In turn, for Indonesia, a one-point increase in the domestic stringency index resulted in an increase of 0.024 thousand tonnes and 0.135 million USD in exports to the rest of the world, respectively. No significant effects are found for Thailand's domestic stringency index.

Figure 13.4 and Table 13.3 display the outcomes of the event-study estimations for Indonesia, Thailand, and Vietnam. The coefficients for lag variables are given in Table 13.3, with lag 0 reflecting the month when the first SLD in each country occurred: March 2020 for Thailand and Vietnam and April 2020 for Indonesia. Even though there was a contraction of 0.026 thousand tonnes for Vietnam in March 2020 (lag 0), both export volume and value started to grow in June (lag 3) and remained higher compared to the baseline (lag -1) until December 2020 (lag 9). Also, Thailand experienced an increase both in export volume and value of 0.04 thousand tonnes and 0.4 million, respectively, until December 2020 (lag 9), followed by a decrease of 0.03 million in February 2021 (lag 11). Indonesia's performance appeared relatively stable, without any statistically significant differences, except for a decrease of 0.012 thousand tonnes in volume in November 2020 (lag 7). The analysis extends to the ramifications of the first SLDs on crustacean exports from these countries across various import regions, with Appendix A specifying the countries within each region. Appendices B through C offer a thorough examination, presenting detailed results and statistical data that shed light on regional disparities in export trends due to SLD.

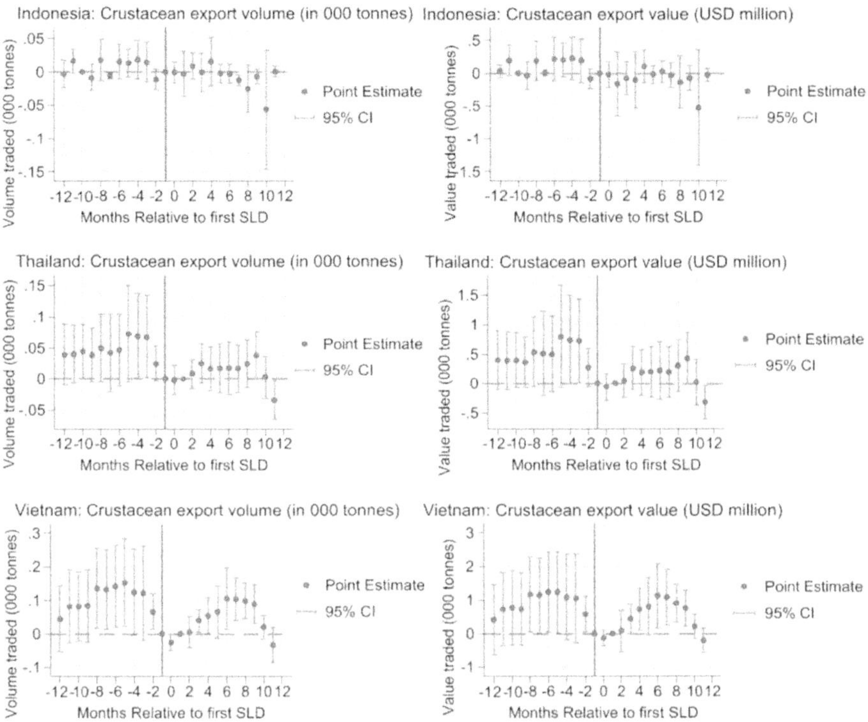

Figure 13.4 Crustacean export trade volume and value.

Table 13.3 Effects of the first SLDs on crustacean exports

Event dummies	*(1)*	*(2)*	*(3)*	*(4)*	*(5)*	*(6)*
	Indonesia	*Thailand*	*Vietnam*	*Indonesia*	*Thailand*	*Vietnam*
	Export volume (thousand tonnes)			*Export value (USD million)*		
lag0	-0.000	-0.002	**-0.026***	-0.022	-0.058	-0.127
	(0.008)	(0.012)	(0.013)	(0.099)	(0.113)	(0.119)
lag1	-0.003	0.000	0.000	-0.163	0.000	0.000
	(0.017)	(.)	(.)	(0.246)	(.)	(.)
lag2	0.009	0.008	0.005	-0.081	0.046	0.090
	(0.009)	(0.012)	(0.023)	(0.125)	(0.139)	(0.309)
lag3	-0.000	0.025	**0.040****	-0.105	0.254	**0.438****
	(0.014)	(0.016)	(0.017)	(0.218)	(0.183)	(0.219)
lag4	0.015	0.016	**0.054****	0.103	0.187	**0.723****
	(0.018)	(0.018)	(0.027)	(0.126)	(0.198)	(0.308)
lag5	-0.002	0.017	**0.066***	-0.017	0.197	**0.804***
	(0.007)	(0.020)	(0.039)	(0.069)	(0.218)	(0.427)

(Continued)

Table 13.3 (Continued)

Event dummies	*(1)*	*(2)*	*(3)*	*(4)*	*(5)*	*(6)*
	Indonesia	*Thailand*	*Vietnam*	*Indonesia*	*Thailand*	*Vietnam*
	Export volume (thousand tonnes)			*Export value (USD million)*		
lag6	-0.002	0.017	**0.105****	0.024	0.217	**1.122****
	(0.007)	(0.021)	(0.045)	(0.085)	(0.245)	(0.482)
lag7	**-0.012*****	0.017	**0.104*****	-0.032	0.194	**1.080****
	(0.004)	(0.019)	(0.031)	(0.096)	(0.220)	(0.408)
lag8	-0.025	0.024	**0.098*****	-0.141	0.300	**0.904*****
	(0.018)	(0.019)	(0.026)	(0.200)	(0.221)	(0.276)
lag9	-0.007	**0.038****	**0.088*****	-0.075	**0.429***	**0.757*****
	(0.006)	(0.019)	(0.029)	(0.096)	(0.217)	(0.263)
lag10	-0.056	0.003	0.020	-0.527	0.020	0.216
	(0.045)	(0.017)	(0.018)	(0.442)	(0.198)	(0.183)
lag11	0.001	**-0.034****	-0.034	-0.028	**-0.320****	-0.201
	(0.004)	(0.015)	(0.026)	(0.050)	(0.143)	(0.191)
Observations	3720	3072	3853	3720	3072	3853
R-squared	0.076	0.039	0.038	0.079	0.036	0.038

Estimation was conducted on the monthly trade data using a fixed effects estimator that accounts for the heterogeneity of cross-country product type and complexity. Standard errors are clustered by importing countries and reported in parentheses. Asterisk indicate the level of significance, *** $p < 0.01$, ** $p < 0.05$, * $p < 0.1$. Only coefficients for lags are displayed due to space constraint. Lag 0 represents the month the SLD began in each country: March 2020 for Thailand and Vietnam, and April 2020 for Indonesia. Lag1…k denotes the addition of one-month increments to the base month Lag0.

Discussion

In this paper, we have examined the effects of mobility restrictions on the crustacean export performance of Indonesia, Thailand, and Vietnam, all of which represent not only prominent crustacean exporters in the region but also export-oriented economies on a global scale. Our study makes a novel contribution by examining the effects of mobility restrictions in exporting and importing countries simultaneously. Moreover, while previous literature on the subject area tends to be descriptive (see, e.g. Patunru & Amanta, 2021; Dang, 2022; Chanrachkij et al., 2020), our study employs three-way fixed effects (TWFE) and event-study designs, which enabled us to address the anticipatory effects of the SLDs at a monthly level. We also performed a heterogeneity analysis by region to understand the varying effects of restrictions in different regions.

Interestingly, we found no significant differences in export performance in any studied countries when comparing the pre-SLD and post-SLD periods. However, regarding general economic performance, Indonesia and Vietnam experienced significant increases in annual GDP and total export value, while Thailand suffered declines in both. These findings align with IMF reports highlighting Vietnam's economic resilience with a 2.9% growth in GDP in 2020 despite COVID-19, due to rapid containment measures and strong exports, especially in electronics which constituted 38% of its 2019 exports (IMF, 2021; Thorbecke & Atsuyuki, 2022). In Thailand, despite the importance of exports in high-value machinery and spare parts, along with traditional items like natural rubber and rice, the contraction of the global value chain and a severe downturn in service sectors, such as tourism, led to a decline in total exports (Thammachote & Trochim, 2021; World Bank, 2020). Conversely, Indonesia's export composition, characterized by agriculture (23%) and minerals (18.7%), contracted due to the US-China trade war and the pandemic until mid-2020; however, exports of oil and non-oil products have seen a steady recovery since then (Thorbecke & Atsuyuki, 2022).

Our estimation results, considering timing, product complexity, seasonality, and country-level effects, revealed variations of crustacean exports from Thailand and Vietnam within the post-SLD period, albeit with a modest effect. The findings reveal a significant decrease in Thailand's crustacean export volume and value during the post-SLD period, which may be attributed to the intensifying global competition and consumers' confidence, as Thammachote and Trochim (2021) noted. A COVID-19 cluster in a prominent Thai fish market led to stringent food safety regulations and the closure of the main distribution centres, further compounded by increased labour costs, shrimp disease, and a decline in catches, which resulted in diminished export volumes to major importing countries, except for Taiwan, in 2020 (Thammachote & Trochim, 2021). At the same time, the period is remarked by the strong baht that made the export less competitive due to higher costs (ibid, 33). Vietnam encountered complex trade dynamics during the pandemic, with main export products like white leg shrimp, marine shrimp, variable fish, crabs and bivalve molluscs experiencing positive market trends while some other seafood products, e.g. pangasius, were declining (Nam & Le, 2021). The positive development is partly due to increasing investor confidence in Vietnam, credited to the government's successful policy management of the pandemic while maintaining social security and economic development (cf. Hoang, 2022). Meanwhile, some of its main competitors, like India and Ecuador, saw significant reductions in production and export due to blockades and quarantine in the first half of 2020. Additionally, the end of 2020 marked a production shift from China to Vietnam due to demand from the US, influenced by the US-China trade war (Nam & Le, 2021).

The impact of mobility restrictions on crustacean trade varied significantly across the studied countries, depending on their export destinations. Generally, the high scores on stringency indices of importing countries positively affected Thailand's trade volume and value, even though the effects were small. These effects were significantly contributed by the East Asia regions, with China, Japan, and Taiwan being its primary trading partners. A similar trend was observed for Indonesia regarding East Asia and for Vietnam with the rest of the world. The phenomenon may be partly due to the reduced tariffs on agricultural goods in various importing countries during SLD periods, with many countries facilitating more food imports whilst some others banned exports to meet domestic demand (Evenett et al., 2022). Furthermore, with East Asia as the epicentre of COVID-19, governments likely increased imports to meet domestic food demands amidst the crisis, supported by relatively mature infrastructure and food supply channels. Our findings are consistent with those of Hayakawa and Mukunoki (2020), who noted that restrictions may limit people's mobility but do not affect their food consumption and essential supplies. As food industries were considered critical, production was generally allowed to operate normally despite the restrictions, particularly in many Asian regions (ibid., p. 10). Additionally, anticipating a grim future may have prompted consumer hoarding behaviour, leading to an immediate and short-term increase in demand.

For Indonesia, in turn, exports to North America presented a different case; the higher stringency index in these importing countries affected Indonesian crustacean export volumes and values negatively. This might be attributed to rising competition, e.g. from Vietnam and Ecuador, and negative impacts from airfreight and seaport closure in North America (cf. Lashitew & Socrates, 2021; Karam et al., 2022). During April-September 2020, export prices of Ecuadorean vannamei shrimp were at the lowest, and Ecuador suffered a loss of market share in China due to COVID-19 restrictions (FAO, 2021b). These supplies and favourable prices from Ecuador may have caused an increase in trade with North American regions. Furthermore, the high intensity of the pandemic in the region caused consumers to prefer processed/canned shrimp products as opposed to fresh products, which sectors are dominated by Vietnam and Thailand (FAO, 2021b).

While Vietnam's export performance was negatively associated with its domestic stringency index, highlighting the complex interplay between national health policies and international trade dynamics, Thailand's domestic index positively correlated with its trade volume and value. The rapid changes in Thailand's restriction policy enabled domestic production to quickly adapt to shifting global demands, like from fresh to canned/processed crustaceans, with Thailand and Vietnam emerging as industry leaders (Thammachote & Trochim, 2021). A positive correlation was also observed for Indonesia, where their decentralized restrictions policy may have allowed production to resume quickly, particularly in the localities where they occurred, filling market gaps in the rest of the world where competitors faced challenges.

We also found that the fluctuations happened temporarily during the study period, with our event study analysis observing an upsurge in Vietnam's export volume and value from the third to ninth month after the first SLD before stabilizing. That may reflect the decline in competition in the global market during the period. Over time, as businesses and individuals adjust to new circumstances, the effects of the pandemic on consumption and trade are likely to evolve (Berthou & Stumpner, 2022).

Conclusion and policy implications

Despite our efforts to control for time-invariant country-level heterogeneities, our study has two limitations. First, we acknowledge the challenge of distinguishing direct policy impacts on trade outcomes from a myriad of "intervening" factors such as price fluctuations, exchange rate variations, delayed customs declarations, and the difficulty of separating restriction effects from other market dynamics. Second, while policymakers globally have introduced stimulus packages exceeding 10% of global GDP (UNDESA, 2020), our analyses do not explicitly consider the impact of government fiscal and trade support, which could have played a significant role in sustaining the export volume and value in the study period.

The pandemic resulted in many types of restrictions and lockdowns worldwide for purely health and safety reasons. The already tense geopolitical situation, particularly between the United States and China, had led to trade wars and increased protectionism. The spread of COVID-19 then led to extensive disruptions across industries, transport, and the general mobility of people. Whereas it is clear that the pandemic also disrupted the exports of seafood in many ways, the direct impacts of mobility restrictions are hard to identify. The simultaneous effects of numerous other factors resulting from stringent food safety regulations to the closure of production and distribution sites further complicate the picture. The COVID-19-related stimulus packages and the widely applied fisheries subsidies may have spurred seafood exports. Of the three studied countries, Vietnam seemed to manage the pandemic effectively by imposing a centralized policy while simultaneously succeeding in balancing and even increasing crustacean exports in the long term despite the disruptions. Indonesia's export performance developed positively, but Thailand faced a decrease in crustacean exports.

These developments had three main geoeconomic impacts. First, there were changes in the geography of trade after the restrictions, as the importance of East Asia and Europe as export destinations appeared to have increased at the cost of North America and the rest of the world. This was shown in the increased crustacean exports, particularly from Vietnam to East Asian and European regions, and the concurrent decrease in exports from Indonesia to Northern America and the rest of the world. Second, the restrictions of importing countries were variably associated with the trends in crustacean exports from the three countries. When mobility restrictions increased in importing East Asian countries, crustacean exports were growing, in particular from Indonesia and Thailand to these countries. However, the opposite was observed for the North American region, where the increase in restrictions correlated with a decrease in Indonesian crustacean exports to this region. Third, more recent trade data shows that Vietnam's global exports of crustaceans continue to grow. The country is the world's fifth biggest exporter of this commodity, while Indonesia is the sixth and shows mainly a growing export trend. In contrast, Thailand's crustacean exports have not reverted to the pre-COVID level but have declined.

The post-pandemic time is subject to fast-changing global geopolitics, where both trade policies and trade flows in seafood may be affected by challenges in the international political economy, such as superpower rivalry and environmental issues. In light of the post-pandemic and Russia's invasion of

Ukraine, countries appeared to reevaluate their trading partners, influenced not only by economic and foreign policy interests but also by the ramifications of their COVID-19 experiences. Moreover, amidst the US-China trade war, investment and trade flows have been re-channelled through third-party countries to circumvent the direct economic links between the US and China, with countries like Vietnam emerging as connectors, cushioning the global economic impact (Gopinath, 2024). All in all, the future of global seafood trade will be influenced by many factors, including the recently adopted WTO Agreement on Fisheries Subsidies. This agreement, which targets the Sustainable Development Goals, aims to prevent subsidies promoting unsustainable fishing practices, which will take effect once two-thirds of the 164 WTO members ratify it.

Acknowledgements

Financial support from Maj and Tor Nessling Foundation (grant number: 202000186), Scandinavia-Japan Sasakawa Foundation (GA24-FIN-0167), JSPS KAKENHI (21K14923) and Toshiba International Foundation are gratefully acknowledged.

Appendix A

Table A.1 List of regions and importing countries recorded for the studied countries (EUMOFA classification)

Regions	*Importing countries*
Eastern Asia	China, Hong Kong, Japan, Macao, South Korea, Taiwan
European Union	Austria, Belgium, Bulgaria, Croatia, Cyprus, Czech Republic, Denmark, Estonia, Finland, France, Germany, Greece, Hungary, Ireland, Italy, Latvia, Lithuania, Luxembourg, Malta, Netherlands, Poland, Portugal, Romania, Slovakia, Slovenia, Spain, Sweden
Northern America	Canada, United States of America
Rest of world	Albania, Algeria, Argentina, Australia, Bahrain, Belarus, Belize, Bolivia, Bosnia & Herzegovina, Botswana, Brazil, Brunei Darussalam, Chile, Colombia, Costa Rica, Cote d'Ivoire, Ecuador, Egypt, El Salvador, Ethiopia, Georgia, Ghana, Guatemala, Honduras, Iceland, India, Indonesia, Iran, Kazakhstan, Kenya, Kosovo, Malaysia, Mauritius, Mexico, Montenegro, Morocco, Mozambique, New Zealand, Nicaragua, North Macedonia, Norway, Pakistan, Panama, Paraguay, Peru, Philippines, Qatar, Russia, Senegal, Serbia, Singapore, South Africa, Sri Lanka, Switzerland, Thailand, Turkey, Ukraine, United Kingdom, Uruguay, Venezuela

Appendix B Crustacean export trade volume (by region)

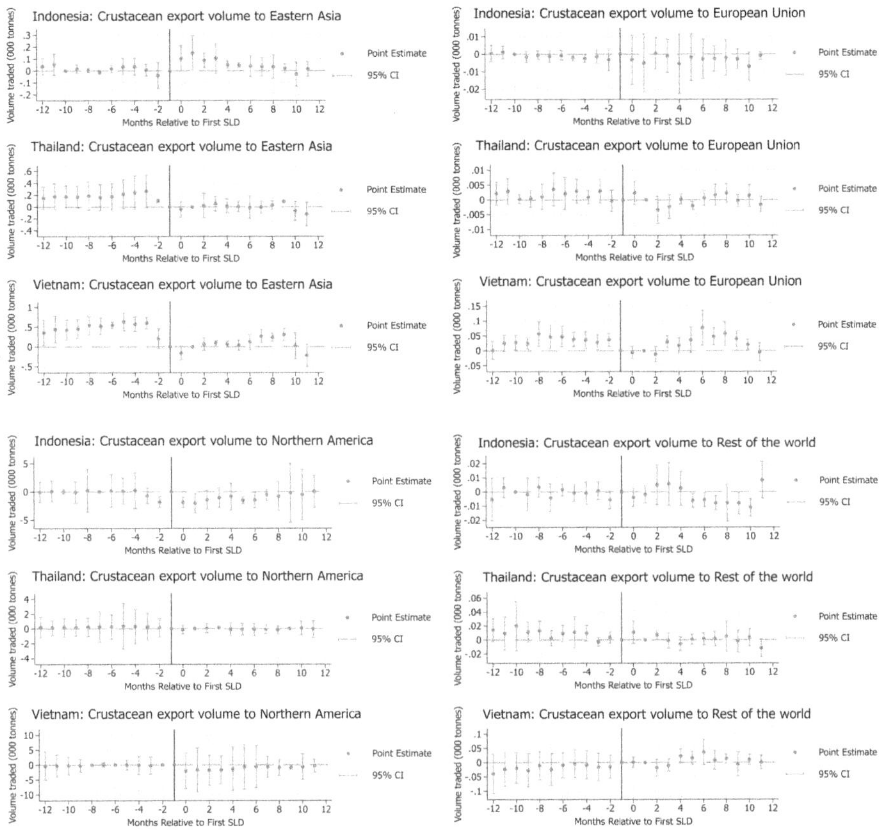

Table B.1 Effects of SLD on net weight of trade volume (in 000 tonnes) by regions

	(1)	*(2)*	*(3)*	*(4)*	*(5)*	*(6)*	*(7)*	*(8)*	*(9)*	*(10)*	*(11)*	*(12)*
	Net weight of trade volume (in 000 tonnes)											
Importing regions:	*Eastern Asia*			*European Union*			*Northern America*			*Rest of World*		
Exporting countries:	*Indonesia*	*Thailand*	*Vietnam*	*Indonesia*	*Thailand*	*Vietnam*	*Indonesia*	*Thailand*	*Vietnam*	*Indonesia*	*Thailand*	*Vietnam*
lag0	**0.104***	-0.043	**-0.159***	-0.003	0.002	-0.007	**-1.893****	-0.126	-1.990	-0.004	0.011	0.001
	(0.038)	(0.047)	(0.061)	(0.007)	(0.002)	(0.010)	(0.071)	(0.045)	(0.472)	(0.003)	(0.008)	(0.009)
lag1	**0.150****	0.000	0.000	-0.005	0.000	0.000	**-2.039****	0.000	-1.667	-0.002	0.000	0.000
	(0.052)	(.)	(.)	(0.008)	(.)	(.)	(0.135)	(.)	(0.584)	(0.003)	(.)	(.)
lag2	**0.089****	0.020	0.064	0.000	-0.003	-0.011	**-1.423***	0.061	-1.805	0.005	**0.007****	-0.018
	(0.022)	(0.073)	(0.055)	(0.004)	(0.002)	(0.012)	(0.128)	(0.049)	(0.399)	(0.007)	(0.003)	(0.014)
lag3	**0.105***	0.052	**0.093****	-0.001	-0.002	**0.030*****	**-1.040***	**0.121****	-1.697	0.005	-0.001	-0.010
	(0.046)	(0.044)	(0.020)	(0.005)	(0.002)	(0.010)	(0.135)	(0.003)	(0.368)	(0.007)	(0.005)	(0.011)
lag4	**0.051*****	0.010	0.060	-0.006	0.000	0.018	-0.852	-0.114	-1.313	0.003	-0.006	**0.022***
	(0.011)	(0.043)	(0.029)	(0.008)	(0.001)	(0.012)	(0.185)	(0.069)	(0.579)	(0.006)	(0.005)	(0.012)
lag5	**0.048*****	0.005	0.036	-0.002	**-0.002*****	**0.036***	**-1.541****	-0.082	-0.709	**-0.006****	0.001	0.016
	(0.007)	(0.033)	(0.048)	(0.006)	(0.001)	(0.021)	(0.049)	(0.062)	(0.591)	(0.002)	(0.004)	(0.011)
lag6	0.039	-0.011	0.118	-0.003	0.001	**0.077****	**-1.473****	-0.119	-0.536	**-0.006****	0.001	0.036
	(0.032)	(0.068)	(0.067)	(0.005)	(0.001)	(0.028)	(0.107)	(0.066)	(0.554)	(0.002)	(0.004)	(0.021)
lag7	0.033	-0.004	**0.264****	-0.003	0.002	**0.048*****	**-0.542***	-0.109	-0.657	**-0.008*****	0.002	0.008
	(0.028)	(0.038)	(0.058)	(0.004)	(0.002)	(0.014)	(0.079)	(0.048)	(0.277)	(0.002)	(0.005)	(0.016)
lag8	0.034	0.028	**0.238*****	-0.002	0.002	**0.057*****	-0.798	-0.182	-0.920	-0.008	0.005	0.013
	(0.036)	(0.026)	(0.036)	(0.005)	(0.002)	(0.019)	(0.201)	(0.040)	(0.209)	(0.006)	(0.011)	(0.008)
lag9	0.019	**0.091*****	**0.303*****	-0.003	-0.000	**0.040*****	-0.166	-0.003	**-0.931****	**-0.008****	-0.002	-0.005
	(0.014)	(0.002)	(0.054)	(0.003)	(0.001)	(0.013)	(0.416)	(0.002)	(0.051)	(0.004)	(0.008)	(0.020)
lag10	-0.030	-0.073	0.023	**-0.007***	0.001	**0.020****	-0.496	0.082	-0.667	**-0.011*****	0.003	0.010
	(0.037)	(0.057)	(0.119)	(0.004)	(0.002)	(0.008)	(0.351)	(0.075)	(0.340)	(0.003)	(0.006)	(0.009)
lag11	0.015	-0.125	**-0.223***	-0.001	-0.002	-0.004	0.048	-0.063	-0.299	0.008	**-0.012***	0.001
	(0.022)	(0.073)	(0.102)	(0.001)	(0.001)	(0.015)	(0.222)	(0.091)	(0.175)	(0.006)	(0.006)	(0.012)
Observations	600	639	637	1316	819	1127	334	366	337	1470	1248	1752
R-squared	0.005	0.054	0.062	0.000	0.034	0.123	0.160	0.079	0.104	0.013	0.012	0.042

Estimation was conducted on the monthly trade data using a fixed effects estimator that accounts for cross-country product heterogeneities. Standard errors are reported in parentheses. Asterisk indicate the level of significance, *** $p < 0.01$, ** $p < 0.05$, * $p < 0.1$. Only coefficients for lags are displayed due to space constraint.
Note: the reference period when t = -1 post SLD is March 2020 for Vietnam and Thailand, and April 2020 for Indonesia.

Appendix C Crustacean export trade value (by region)

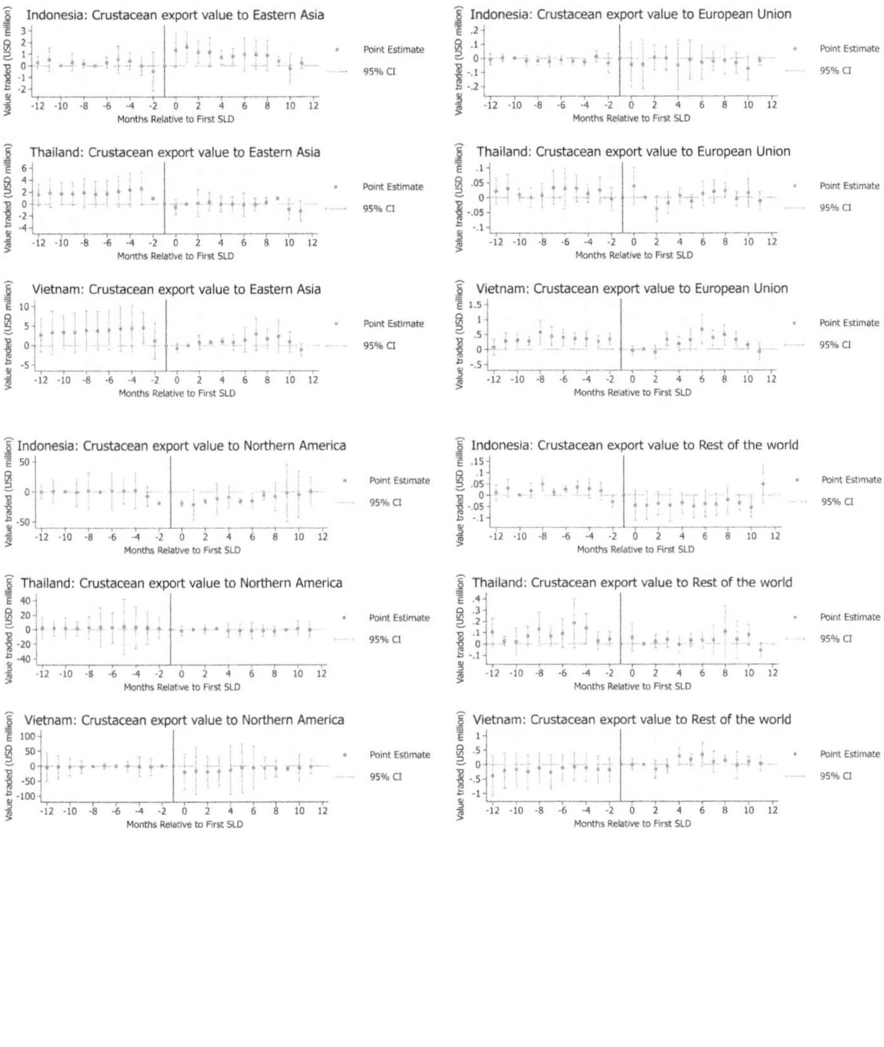

Table C.1 Effects of SLD on value in USD million by regions

	(1)	*(2)*	*(3)*	*(4)*	*(5)*	*(6)*	*(7)*	*(8)*	*(9)*	*(10)*	*(11)*	*(12)*
	Crustacean export value in USD million											
Importing regions:	*Eastern Asia*			*European Union*			*Northern America*			*Rest of World*		
Exporting countries:	*Indonesia*	*Thailand*	*Vietnam*	*Indonesia*	*Thailand*	*Vietnam*	*Indonesia*	*Thailand*	*Vietnam*	*Indonesia*	*Thailand*	*Vietnam*
lag0	**1.326***	-0.496	-0.779	-0.045	0.038	-0.036	**-19.229****	-1.733	-20.016	-0.046	0.054	-0.002
	(0.523)	(0.452)	(0.433)	(0.078)	(0.030)	(0.071)	(0.370)	(0.533)	(4.736)	(0.033)	(0.061)	(0.094)
lag1	1.605**	0.000	0.000	-0.045	0.000	0.000	**-21.490***	0.000	-16.405	-0.045	0.000	0.000
	(0.464)	(.)	(.)	(0.084)	(.)	(.)	(1.976)	(.)	(6.122)	(0.031)	(.)	(.)
lag2	**1.152****	0.141	0.786	0.005	**-0.038***	-0.097	**-15.792****	0.575	-18.212	-0.037	0.020	-0.159
	(0.346)	(0.809)	(0.650)	(0.044)	(0.021)	(0.107)	(0.256)	(0.480)	(4.086)	(0.025)	(0.027)	(0.151)
lag3	**1.184***	0.368	**0.792****	-0.000	-0.017	**0.346*****	-11.189	**1.303*****	-17.010	-0.046	0.038	-0.062
	(0.456)	(0.581)	(0.182)	(0.041)	(0.018)	(0.105)	(2.014)	(0.003)	(3.847)	(0.035)	(0.033)	(0.121)
lag4	**0.725****	-0.019	**1.033****	-0.050	0.007	0.187	-9.140	-1.698	-12.817	-0.034	-0.004	**0.286***
	(0.220)	(0.481)	(0.296)	(0.086)	(0.013)	(0.115)	(1.483)	(0.733)	(6.374)	(0.023)	(0.035)	(0.145)
lag5	1.817**	-0.026	0.814	-0.010	-0.013	**0.321***	**-16.023****	-1.309	-6.705	**-0.050***	0.032	0.167
	(0.230)	(0.440)	(0.732)	(0.067)	(0.011)	(0.184)	(0.374)	(0.627)	(6.384)	(0.025)	(0.028)	(0.103)
lag6	0.977	-0.122	1.407	-0.030	0.013	**0.666****	**-15.276****	-1.639	-5.077	-0.038	0.032	**0.344***
	(0.518)	(0.702)	(1.115)	(0.059)	(0.020)	(0.235)	(0.988)	(0.842)	(5.746)	(0.030)	(0.034)	(0.203)
lag7	0.935	-0.120	2.880	-0.022	0.021	**0.390*****	**-5.709***	-1.637	-6.397	**-0.041***	0.032	0.094
	(0.448)	(0.397)	(1.496)	(0.032)	(0.019)	(0.122)	(0.626)	(0.626)	(2.849)	(0.024)	(0.062)	(0.180)
lag8	0.878	0.287	1.668	-0.015	**0.023***	**0.488*****	-8.088	-2.569	-8.966	-0.022	0.108	0.135
	(0.467)	(0.277)	(0.937)	(0.049)	(0.012)	(0.167)	(1.851)	(0.544)	(2.230)	(0.031)	(0.111)	(0.092)
lag9	**0.399****	**0.916*****	2.286	-0.035	-0.005	**0.335*****	-2.020	**-0.308***	**-9.233****	**-0.035****	0.037	-0.039
	(0.136)	(0.089)	(1.509)	(0.035)	(0.011)	(0.110)	(3.771)	(0.030)	(0.482)	(0.017)	(0.080)	(0.232)
lag10	-0.260	-0.880	0.910	**-0.073***	0.016	**0.144****	-4.742	0.862	-6.626	**-0.055****	**0.080***	0.106
	(0.451)	(0.635)	(0.951)	(0.041)	(0.023)	(0.062)	(3.042)	(0.890)	(3.503)	(0.021)	(0.045)	(0.082)
lag11	0.211	-1.213	-1.125	-0.021	-0.012	-0.070	0.246	-0.708	-2.796	0.048	**-0.058***	0.027
	(0.171)	(0.621)	(0.559)	(0.014)	(0.015)	(0.137)	(1.869)	(0.939)	(1.938)	(0.043)	(0.032)	(0.128)
Observations	600	639	637	1316	819	1127	334	366	337	1470	1248	1752
R-squared	0.039	0.054	0.061	-0.002	0.028	0.114	0.163	0.073	0.092	0.032	0.020	0.039

Estimation was conducted on the monthly trade data using a fixed effects estimator that accounts for cross-country product heterogeneities. Standard errors are reported in parentheses. Asterisk indicate the level of significance, *** $p < 0.01$, ** $p < 0.05$, * $p < 0.1$. Only coefficients for lags are displayed due to space constraint. Note: the reference period when $t = -1$ post SLD is March 2020 for Vietnam and Thailand, and April 2020 for Indonesia.

Note

1 The so-called most-favoured-nation (MFN) tariff is the simple average of all national tariff line (NTL) rates under the specified product category applied by the importing country. Tariff data sources used here: Trade Map and Market Access Map.

References

Aday, Serpil, and Mehmet Seckin Aday. (2020). "Impact of COVID-19 on the Food Supply Chain." *Food Quality and Safety* 4 (4): 167–180. https://doi.org/10.1093/fqsafe/fyaa024

Alam, G. M., Sarker, M. N. I., Gatto, M., Bhandari, H., & Naziri, D. (2022). Impacts of COVID-19 on the fisheries and aquaculture sector in developing countries and ways forward. *Sustainability*, *14*(3), 1071. https://doi.org/10.3390/su14031071

Arenas, G. C., Majune, S., & Montfaucon, A. F. (2022). The impacts of lockdown policies on international trade in the Philippines. Policy Research Working Paper No 9911. World Bank Group, Washington DC. URL: https://openknowledge.worldbank.org/bitstream/handle/10986/36882/The-Impacts-of-Lockdown-Policies-on-International-Trade-in-the-Philippines.pdf

Azra, M. N., Kasan, N. A., Othman, R., Noor, G. A. G. R., Mazelan, S., Jamari, Z. B., … & Ikhwanuddin, M. (2021). Impact of COVID-19 on aquaculture sector in Malaysia: Findings from the first national survey. *Aquaculture Reports*, *19*, 100568. URL: https://doi.org/10.1016/j.aqrep.2020.100568

Baldwin, R. and S. J. Evenett (2020). Introduction. In *COVID-19 and Trade Policy: Why Turning Inward Won't Work*, edited by R. Baldwin and S.J. Evenett, 1–19. VoxEU.org. CEPR Press. URL: https://cepr.org/system/files/publication-files/60044-covid_19_and_trade_policy_why_turning_inward_won_t_work.pdf

Baldwin, R. and M. Kawai (2013). Multilateralizing Asian Regionalism. ADBI Working Paper 431. Tokyo: Asian Development Bank Institute. URL: https://www.adb.org/sites/default/files/publication/156286/adbi-wp431.pdf

Baldwin, R. and Tomiura, E. (2020). 'Thinking ahead about the trade impact of COVID-19', in Baldwin, R. and di Mauro, B. W., *Economics in the Time of COVID-19*. London, UK: Centre for Economic Policy Research (CEPR), pp. 59–72.

Banga, K., Keane, J., Mendez-Parra, M., Pettinotti, L. and Sommer, L. (2020). Africa trade and Covid 19: The supply chain dimension (Working paper 586). Addis Ababa, Ethiopia: African Trade Policy Centre.

Berthou, A., & Stumpner, S. (2022). Trade under lockdown. Working Paper #867. Banque de France, Paris. URL: https://publications.banque-france.fr/sites/default/files/medias/documents/wp867.pdf

Bondad-Reantaso, M. G., Subasinghe, R. P., Josupeit, H., Cai, J., & Zhou, X. (2012). The role of crustacean fisheries and aquaculture in global food security: past, present and future. *Journal of invertebrate pathology*, *110*(2), 158–165. https://doi.org/10.1016/j.jip.2012.03.010

Chanrachkij, I., Laongmanee, P., Lanmeen, J., Suasi, T., Sornkliang, J., Tiaye, R., Yasook, N., Putsa, S., & Chumchuen, S. V. (2020). Severity of the Impacts of COVID-19 Pandemic on Smallscale Fisheries of Thailand: A Preliminary Assessment. *Fish for the People*, *18*(2), 43–47. http://hdl.handle.net/20.500.12066/6563

Chen, L., Raitzer, D., Hasan, R., Lavado, R., & Velarde, O. (2020). What works to control COVID-19? Econometric analysis of a cross-country panel. *Asian Development Bank Economics Working Paper Series*, (625). URL: http://dx.doi.org/10.22617/WPS200354-2

Cuervo-Cazurra, A., Y. Doz, and A. Gaur (2020). Skepticism of globalization and global strategy: Increasing regulations and countervailing strategies. *Global Strategy Journal* 10 (1): 3–31. https://doi.org/10.1002/gsj.1374

Dang, D. A. (2022). COVID-19 in Viet Nam. in Ing YL, Basri MC (eds) *COVID-19 in Indonesia: Impacts on the Economy and Ways to Recovery*. Routledge, New York. https://doi.org/10.4324/9781003243670-10

Dingel, J. I., & Neiman, B. (2020). How many jobs can be done at home?. *Journal of Public Economics*, *189*, 104235. https://doi.org/10.1016/j.jpubeco.2020.104235

European Market Observatory for Fisheries and Aquaculture Products (2022) – Monthly Import-Export fisheries and aquaculture products. URL: https://www.eumofa.eu/sources-of-data

Evenett, S. (2019). "Protectionism, state discrimination, and international business since the onset of the Global Financial Crisis." *Journal of International Business Policy* 2: 9–36. https://doi.org/10.1057/s42214-019-00021-0

Evenett, S., M. Fiorini, J. Fritz, B. Hoekman, P. Lukaszuk, N. Rocha, M. Ruta, F. Santi, and A. Shingal (2022). Trade Policy Responses to the COVID-19 Pandemic Crisis: Evidence from a New Data Set. *The World Economy* 45 (2):342–364. https://doi.org/10.1111/twec.13119

FAO (2020). *The impact of COVID-19 on fisheries and aquaculture – a global assessment from the perspective of regional fishery bodies*. Rome: Food and Agriculture Organization of the United Nations. https://doi.org/10.4060/ca9279en

FAO (2021a). *The impact of COVID-19 on fisheries and aquaculture food systems: possible responses*. Rome: Food and Agriculture Organization of the United Nations. https://doi.org/10.4060/cb2537en

FAO (2022). *The State of World Fisheries and Aquaculture 2022. Towards Blue Transformation*. Rome: Food and Agriculture Organization of the United Nations. https://doi.org/10.4060/cc0461en

FAO (2021b). Shrimp demand may be dampened by recurrence of COVID-19. URL: https://www.fao.org/in-action/globefish/market-reports/resource-detail/en/c/1379259/ accessed 12.5.2024.

Fletcher, R. (2023). Ecuador set to hit 1.5 million tonnes of shrimp exports. The Fish Site, Ireland. URL: https://thefishsite.com/articles/ecuador-set-to-hit-1-5-million-tonnes-of-shrimp-exports accessed 30.1.2024.

Gaduh, A., Hanna, R., Kreindler, G., & Olken, B. (2020). Lockdown and Mobility in Indonesia. Retrieved from Center for History and Economics Harvard University. URL: https://histecon.fas.harvard.edu/climate-loss/indonesia/index.html

GATT (1994) Annex 1A. Multilateral Agreements on Trade in Goods. Sanitary and Phytosanitary Measures. URL: https://www.wto.org/english/docs_e/legal_e/15-sps.pdf

Gopinath, G (2024). Geopolitics and its Impact on Global Trade and the Dollar. Series on the Future of the International Monetary System (IMS). Stanford Institute for Economic Policy Research, California. URL: https://www.imf.org/en/News/Articles/2024/05/07/sp-geopolitics-impact-global-trade-and-dollar-gita-gopinath accessed 13.5.2024.

Hale, T., Webster, S., Petherick, A., Phillips, T., and Kira, B. (2020). Oxford covid-19 government response tracker. Blavatnik School of Government.

Hayakawa, K., and Mukunoki, H. 2020. Impacts of COVID-19 on International Trade: Evidence from the First Quarter of 2020. IDE Discussion Paper No. 791. Chiba: Institute of Developing Economies. URL: https://doi.org/10.20561/00051734

Hoang V. (2022). The COVID-19 pandemic in Vietnam - success, crisis, and endemic: Key thresholds and lessons. *Journal of Global Health*, 12: 03065. https://doi.org/10.7189/jogh.12.03065. URL: https://www.ncbi.nlm.nih.gov/pmc/articles/PMC9676043/

IMF (2021). IMF Country Focus: Vietnam: Successfully Navigating the Pandemic. URL:https://www.imf.org/en/News/Articles/2021/03/09/na031021-vietnam-successfully-navigating-the-pandemic accessed 6.2.2024.

Kaewnuratchadasorn, P., Smithrithee, M., Sato, A., Wanchana, W., Tongdee, N., & Sulit, V. T. (2020). Capturing the Impacts of COVID-19 on the Fisheries Value Chain of Southeast Asia. *Fish for the People*, *18*(2), 2–8.

Karam, A., Eltoukhy, A. E., Shaban, I. A., & Attia, E. A. (2022). A review of COVID-19-related literature on freight transport: impacts, mitigation strategies, recovery measures, and future research directions. *International Journal of Environmental Research and Public Health*, *19*(19), 12287. https://doi.org/10.3390/ijerph191912287

Kassa, W. (2020). COVID-19 and Trade in SSA: Impacts and Policy Response (Issue 1, No.1). Washington D.C., United States: World Bank.

Kawai, M., & Wignaraja, G. (2011). Asian FTAs: Trends, prospects and challenges. *Journal of Asian Economics*, 22(1), 1–22. https://doi.org/10.1016/j.asieco.2010.10.002

Kumaran, M., Geetha, R., Antony, J., Vasagam, K. K., Anand, P. R., Ravisankar, T., ... & Vijayan, K. K. (2021). Prospective impact of Corona virus disease (COVID-19) related lockdown on shrimp aquaculture sector in India–a sectoral assessment. *Aquaculture*, *531*, 735922. https://doi.org/10.1016/j.aquaculture.2020.735922

Lashitew, A. and Socrates, M. (2021). The effects of lockdown policies in Kenya. Global Economy and Development at Brookings. Global Working Paper #148. URL: https://www.brookings.edu/wp-content/uploads/2021/03/The-effects-of-Lockdown-Policies-Kenya.pdf

Looi Kee, H., Nicita, A., & Olarreaga, M. (2009). Estimating trade restrictiveness indices. *The Economic Journal*, *119*(534), 172–199. https://doi.org/10.1111/j.1468-0297.2008.02209.x

Maliszewska, M., Mattoo, A. and Van Der Mensbrugghe, D. (2020). The potential impact of COVID-19 on GDP and trade: A preliminary assessment. Washington D.C., United States: World Bank.

Mayer, T. & Zignago, S. (2011), Notes on CEPII's distances measures: the GeoDist Database, CEPII Working Paper 2011-25.

Meckelburg, R. (2021). Indonesia's COVID-19 emergency: Where the local is central. *Contemporary Southeast Asia*, *43*(1), 31–37. https://www.jstor.org/stable/27035521

Melchior, A. (2015). The World Trade Organization enlargement, tariffs and global seafood trade. *FAO Fisheries and Aquaculture Circular*, (C1100), I.

Mölders, F. and U. Volz (2011). Trade creation and the status of FTAs: Empirical evidence from East Asia. *Review of World Economics* 147 (3): 429–456. https://doi.org/10.1007/s10290-011-0095-9

Nam, N. H. T., & Le, N. T. H. (2021). A Trade-Based Analysis of the Economic Impact of Non-Compliance with Illegal, Unreported and Unregulated Fishing: The Case of Vietnam. World Bank. URL: https://doi.org/10.1596/36132

Nisar, U., Zhang, Z., Cui, Z., Mu, Y., & Hongzhi, Z. (2023). Impact of Covid-19 on Fish and Crustacean Export from China With Building Resilient Food System Through China's Lens. *Frontiers in Sustainable Food Systems*, *7*, 1189526. https://doi.org/10.3389/fsufs.2023.1189526

Patunru, A., & Amanta, F. (2021). COVID-19 food security and trade: the case of Indonesia. Arndt-Corden Department of Economics, Crawford School of Public Policy, ANU College of Asia and the Pacific at the Australian National University, 114.

Pazir, M. K., Ahmadi, A., & Khezri, P. H. (2022). The effect of COVID-19 pandemic on the shrimp industry of Iran. *Marine Policy*, *136*, 104900. https://doi.org/10.1016%2Fj.marpol.2021.104900

Pollack, T.M., Thwaites, G.E., Rabaa, M.A., Choisy, M., Doorn, R.V., Luong, D.H., Tan, D.Q., Quang, T.D., Dinh, P.C., Nghia, N.D., Tu, T.A., Quang, L.N., Khanh, N.C., & Anh, D.D. (2020). Emerging COVID-19 success story: Vietnam's commitment to containment. Published online at OurWorldInData.org. Retrieved from: https://ourworldindata.org/covid-exemplar-vietnam-2020 [Online Resource]

Pongsakornrungsilp, S., Pongsakornrungsilp, P., Kumar, V., & Maswongssa, B. (2021). The art of survival: Tourism businesses in Thailand recovering from COVID-19 through brand management. *Sustainability*, *13*(12), 6690. https://doi.org/10.3390/su13126690

Samadi, Roghayyeh, Heli Marjanen, and Mohammad Taghi Razavian. (2022). "Consumers in Limbo: How the COVID-19 Pandemic Has Changed Local Food Consumption in Tehran." *Food Studies: An Interdisciplinary Journal* 13 (1): 1–23. https://doi.org/10.18848/2160-1933/CGP/v13i01/1-23

SEAFDEC (2021a). Fisheries Country Profile: Vietnam. Southeast Asian Fisheries Development Center. URL: http://www.seafdec.org/fisheries-country-profile-vietnam/ accessed 7.2.2024.

SEAFDEC (2021b). Fisheries Country Profile: Indonesia. Southeast Asian Fisheries Development Center. URL: http://www.seafdec.org/fisheries-country-profile-indonesia/ accessed 7.2.2024.

Schmidheiny, K., & Siegloch, S. (2023). On event studies and distributed-lags in two-way fixed effects models: Identification, equivalence, and generalization. *Journal of Applied Econometrics*, *38*(5), 695–713. https://doi.org/10.1002/jae.2971

Thammachote, P., & Trochim, J. I. (2021). The Impact of the COVID-19 Pandemic on Thailand's Agricultural Export Flows. PRCI Research Papers No 32070. Michigan State University, Department of Agricultural, Food and Resource Economics, Food Security Group, Michigan. URL: https://www.canr.msu.edu/prci/PRCI-Research-Paper-4-Thailand_updated.pdf

Thammachote, P., & Trochim, J. I. (2023). Thailand Seafood Trade Flow and Its Challenges. Research Papers No 16. Michigan State University, Department of Agricultural, Food and Resource Economics, Food Security Group, Michigan. URL: https://www.canr.msu.edu/prci/publications/ResearchPapers/PRCI%20Research%20Paper%20Seafood.pdf

The Jakarta Post (2020). Stay home, President says. The Jakarta Post, Jakarta. URL: https://www.thejakartapost.com/news/2020/03/16/stay-home-president-says.html

Thorbecke, W., & Atsuyuki, K. (2022). *Indonesia and Vietnam in Global Supply Chains and the Age of COVID: A Tale of Two Countries* (No. 22010). URL: https://www.rieti.go.jp/en/publications/nts/22e010.html

UNCTAD (2022). Review of maritime transport. Navigating stormy waters. Geneva: United Nations Conference on Trade and Development.

UNDESA (2020). 'World Economic Situation and Prospects as of Mid-2020', URL: https://www.un.org/development/desa/dpad/publication/world-economic-situation-and-prospects-as-of-mid-2020/

Van Duijn, A. P., R. Beukers, and W. Van Der Pijl (2012). *The Vietnamese seafood sector. A value chain analysis*, 88. The Hague: Centre for the Promotion of Imports from developing countries.

Verma, S., & Gustafsson, A. (2020). Investigating the emerging COVID-19 research trends in the field of business and management: A bibliometric analysis approach. *Journal of Business Research*, *118*, 253–261. https://doi.org/10.1016%2Fj.jbusres.2020.06.057

Virakul, B., Chiangmai, C. N., & Senasu, K. (2022). Thailand and COVID-19 pandemic: Lessons learned, challenges, and the silver linings. In *Community, Economy and COVID-19: Lessons from Multi-Country Analyses of a Global Pandemic* (pp. 505–530). Cham: Springer International Publishing. https://doi.org/10.1007/978-3-030-98152-5_24

Waiho, K., Fazhan, H., Ishak, S. D., Kasan, N. A., Liew, H. J., Norainy, M. H., & Ikhwanuddin, M. (2020). Potential impacts of COVID-19 on the aquaculture sector of Malaysia and its coping strategies. *Aquaculture Reports*, *18*, 100450. URL: https://ui.adsabs.harvard.edu/link_gateway/2020AqRep..1800450W/doi:10.1016/j.aqrep.2020.100450

World Bank (2020). Thailand Economic Monitor June 2020: Thailand in the Time of COVID-19. URL:https://www.worldbank.org/en/country/thailand/publication/thailand-economic-monitor-june-2020-thailand-in-the-time-of-covid-19

WHO (2023). Daily cases and deaths by date reported to WHO. World Health Organization. URL: https://covid19.who.int/WHO-COVID-19-global-data.csv

Wooldridge, J. M. (2021). Two-way fixed effects, the two-way mundlak regression, and difference-in-differences estimators. Working Paper, pp. 1–89. *Available at SSRN 3906345*.

WorldFish (2020). The impact of COVID-19 on the aquaculture value chain. Penang: Value Chain Report No. 2.

WTO (n.d.) *Understanding the WTO Agreement on Sanitary and Phytosanitary Measures*. Geneva: World Trade Organization. URL: https://www.wto.org/english/tratop_e/sps_e/spsund_e.htm

14 Challenges to SDG 2 on Zero Hunger

Becoming aware of the vulnerabilities of the global food system

Ana García-Juanatey and Ilaria De Vita

Introduction

At the halfway point in the implementation period of the 2030 Agenda, the prospects for meeting the second of the Sustainable Development Goals (hereafter SDGs), whose primary objective is the eradication of hunger, are very bleak. According to the report *The State of Food Security and Nutrition in the World 2023*, coordinated every year by the Food and Agriculture Organization of the United Nations (hereafter FAO), we are moving further and further away from the zero hunger goal: in 2022, around 2.4 billion people in the world (almost 30% of the entire world population) were moderately or severely food insecure, an increase of almost 10% in the last three years.[1] This increase, besides, does not appear to be simply a one-off spike, as since 2014 the trend shows a gradual increase in the number of hungry people. Consequently, if we continue on this path, approximately one in ten people will be hungry by 2030.

The reasons why millions of people continue to suffer from hunger are complex and reflect both cyclical phenomena and chronic problems within food systems. In addition to the old scourges, such as the impact of conflicts and the persistence of extreme poverty and national and global inequality, two crises have worsened global food security since 2020: the outbreak of the COVID pandemic and the Russian invasion of Ukraine. On the one hand, the aftermaths of the pandemic affected food-deficit states, leaving their health systems and many household economies in shatters; on the other, the war in Ukraine contributed to the upward trend in cereal prices, generating further disruptions in the global cereal supply chain as well as contributing to higher international prices for energy and agricultural inputs.[2] As a result, global food prices have soared, reaching their highest point in a decade in the first half of 2022[3] – which had a fatal impact on people who spend a high percentage of their wages on food. At present, the projections for 2024 look discouraging, with adverse El Niño weather, coupled with other factors like export restrictions and higher demand for biofuels.[4] Therefore, it seems that a new food crisis may be around the corner, a situation that normally triggers a 'productivist narrative' response within international institutions and donors, including calls for further industrialisation of food systems, pointing at increasing food production as 'the solution' to world hunger.[5]

DOI: 10.4324/9781032655857-18

However, at this point in time, the negative environmental and social consequences of the productivist approach inherent to the global industrial food system became impossible to ignore.[6] In fact, in addition to the COVID-19 pandemic and Ukraine crises, there is another challenge to global food security of a much greater magnitude and of chronic nature: the global environmental change in which our planet is immersed. As the 2019 IPCC 'Special Report on Climate Change and Land' states with high confidence, climate change has adversely impacted food security and terrestrial ecosystems as well as contributed to desertification and land degradation in many regions.[7] In a similar vein, FAO affirms in its 2016 report on 'Climate change and food security: risks and responses', that 'food security in the face of climate change is among the most daunting challenges facing humankind'.[8] Furthermore, the excess of carbon in the atmosphere is not the only limit that is being surpassed and impacting agriculture: the exceeding of other thresholds, such as the alteration of phosphorus and nitrogen cycles or the loss of biodiversity, is also hindering the proper functioning of food systems.[9] This global environmental change questions the productivist narrative deeply, as it is widely acknowledged that today's dominant industrial agricultural model greatly contributes to pushing these boundaries.[10]

In order to tackle the surpassing of planetary boundaries such as climate change, it is key to explore another vulnerability of the global industrial food system: its fossil fuel dependence.[11] In the case of agriculture, modern industrial systems developed in the post-war period are heavily dependent on these non-renewable resources. Both their direct use in agricultural operations and their indirect use in the manufacturing of fertilisers, pesticides and machinery, contributed to the significant increases in food production observed since the 1960s.[12] Nonetheless, together with such a surge in food production, came a rising dependence on fossil fuel resources, as well as greater environmental costs.

With these considerations in mind, the aim of this chapter is to examine two main structural and deeply connected obstacles that hinder the fulfilment of SDG 2: the overcoming of several planetary boundaries and the fossil fuel dependence of industrial food systems. In order to do that, it draws particularly on the experience of the 2008–2009 food crisis.[13] In this sense, a close look at that crisis would shed light on the link between food and fossil energy prices, and on the possible impacts of some of the measures oriented at reducing fossil fuel dependence, such as investment in biofuels[14]; additionally, it would also point at another key issue: how speculative practices may increase commodity markets uncertainty in inflationary contexts.[15] Understanding these factors would be crucial to prevent new global food crises, particularly in a context characterised by greater climate impacts. In this sense, it should also be considered that one of the main geoeconomic and geopolitical barriers that the transformation towards sustainable food systems faces, is overcoming the dominant productivist or 'feeding a growing planet' narrative – which is deeply embedded in international institutions. Taking these complexities into account, the first part of this chapter tries to draw some lessons from the

2008–2009 food crisis; the second part examines what is considered as the main challenge to the achievement of SDG 2: feeding the world within planetary boundaries. Finally, the conclusions delve into the difficulties of achieving SDG 2 in these circumstances, pointing at the urgent need for a radical change in food security thinking.

Food security and SDG2: lessons from the 2008–2009 crisis

According to the definition coined at the 1996 World Food Summit, for a food security situation to exist, its four pillars must be met: *food availability*, which refers to sufficient quantities of food of adequate quality to feed the entire population; *access to food*, which means that not only must there be enough food for everyone, but it must also be ensured that the most vulnerable people can access the resources necessary to produce or purchase food; *utilisation*, which refers to other factors related to adequate food consumption, such as access to safe water, sanitation and health care; and *stability*, which ensures that a population, household or individual has access to adequate food at all times, without the risk of running out of food or water as a result of sudden shocks or cyclical events.

In order to examine the main challenges facing global food security in the current context, we can simplify this conceptual model by referring to its two essential pillars: availability and access. These two are examined below, with a focus on the evolution of global food security until the adoption of the 2030 Agenda. In particular, special attention will be paid to the 2008–2009 time frame, when the previous food crisis unfolded, extracting valuable lessons in order to face current or future crises.

Food availability

This pillar refers to the necessary, but not sufficient, condition for overall food security: the existence of sufficient quantities of food of adequate quality. In this sense, it is hard to argue that this pillar is of paramount importance for food security: if there is not enough food, it is impossible to meet people's nutritional needs. Indeed, as Patrick Webb and his co-authors argue, there is an undoubtedly hierarchical component to the pillars of food security. It states that availability is a necessary but not sufficient condition for ensuring access, which in turn is necessary but not sufficient for effective utilisation.[16]

This truism, however, has often been confused with the idea that it is necessary to increase food production at all costs, without taking into account how much or what kind of food is needed to ensure healthy and sustainable diets. This has been referred to by some authors as the 'productivity trap', a dominant paradigm in international institutions that could be summarised in the assertion that the key to fighting hunger is to boost food production – prioritising the availability pillar over others, such as access to food.[17]

Indeed, increasing food availability has been the main concern of global food policies since the post-war period. In the years following decolonisation, low food production and the lack of mechanisation of agriculture were seen as the major obstacles to reducing hunger in the so-called 'Third World'. Consequently, the various green revolutions that took place in those years appeared to be the perfect solution: they promised to increase production by using high-yielding cereal varieties, a large amount of perceived abundant fossil resources, water, fertilisers and pesticides.[18] And they delivered on their promise: they brought unprecedented increases in land productivity, so they spread rapidly, from Western countries to Asia and Latin America.

Conversely, these agricultural revolutions did not solve the problem of global hunger,[19] and they also generated serious environmental problems, such as soil degradation, agrochemical and pesticide pollution, and loss of biodiversity.[20] As a result, since the mid-1990s, international institutions such as the FAO began to recognise the importance of ensuring the sustainability of supplies and taking into account the ecological impacts of agricultural practices,[21] yet without fundamentally questioning the predominant focus on production.

The productivist narrative was then reinforced during the 2000–2015 interval, particularly during the 2008 crisis and the years that followed. During this period, the need for a significant increase in agricultural production was a constant theme in reports published by international institutions, and in the proposals of other relevant actors, such as large multinational food companies, even though the causes of the crisis were not effectively related to a global food shortage.[22] Adding to this perception of food scarcity as a cause of hunger were reports from this era, such as the study 'How to Feed the World in 2050', produced by a High Level Expert Forum at the FAO. The study forecasted an important deterioration in the situation of global hunger and malnutrition, mainly due to the phenomena of population growth.[23] These forecasts brought back into vogue the Malthusian theories that point to the possibility that population will increase faster than food production, reinforcing the productivist discourse and focusing on the need for a 'new green revolution'.[24]

Without questioning the likely problems of food availability in the medium term, it should be noted that the productivist narrative hides fundamental aspects of the current food model, which should be rethought. For example, according to the former UN rapporteur for the right to food, Olivier De Schutter, the narrative based on the urgency of 'feeding a growing planet' neglects to consider central issues such as the impact of consumption habits in rich countries with significant environmental and social impacts.[25] A main issue related to diet habits is the issue of meat consumption: it has been argued that a global transition to a diet low in meat could generate a food surplus that would ensure food security for the world's population, without the need for an increase in arable land, and thus limiting pressure on resources.[26] Similarly, the abovementioned narrative neglects a fundamental aspect that we will examine below: the question of how the available food is distributed.

Access to food

The food security pillar emphasises the importance of people's access to adequate resources to acquire appropriate food and a nutritious diet. It was defined by the FAO as a food security pillar in the early 1980s,[27] largely as a result of the impact of Amartya Sen's influential essay *Poverty and Famines: An Essay on Rights and Deprivation*.[28] In this work, he challenged the idea that the main cause of hunger was the decline in the availability of food; according to him, the roots of the hunger problem do not lie in the lack of food but in the difficulties of accessing to available food by segments of the population, generally the poorest people. This pillar therefore emphasises the relevance of the political and redistributive component in the fight against hunger: it is not sufficient that there is enough food; it must also reach all people. As Sen's analysis shows, there can be famines in a country where there is enough food to feed the entire population, but where part of the population does not have access to it. Vulnerability to hunger therefore depends on the type of entitlements or rights that each person possesses, so Sen puts the individual at the centre of the hunger analysis.

It is nowadays widely accepted that lack of access to and control over the resources needed to produce or obtain food is the main cause of food insecurity.[29] Although this lack of access may be physical (insufficient quantity of food due to factors such as isolation or displacement of the population or lack of adequate infrastructure) or social (for example, in the case of women, who often suffer more from hunger as a result of discrimination), the main cause of food insecurity is generally the lack of economic access (lack of financial resources to buy food due to high prices or low incomes).

Globally, this was dramatically observed during the 2008–2009 crisis, when the lack of economic access to food rose rapidly in price and pushed millions of people into desperate hunger. In March 2008, maize prices increased by 31%, rice by 71%, soya by 87% and wheat by 130%, compared to the previous year.[30] This rise in global prices seriously affected the food security of many countries in the global South, especially in food-deficit countries, which are very sensitive to what happens in international markets. Although there is no agreement on what was the main cause of this price rise, two factors have been widely pointed out: *the increase in the price of oil* and the increase in speculation in the food market.[31] With regard to the first factor, during the first half of 2008, the cost of a barrel of oil reached historic highs, weighing down the world economy; this increase consequently pushed up the price of food, particularly cereals, since their production is highly dependent on inputs derived from fossil fuels. For instance, in the midst of 2008, there was a sudden and significant surge in the prices of N, P, K, and S fertilisers, causing reverberations across the globe.[32] In addition to directly affecting food prices, this rise also led to a rapid *increase in the production of biofuels* produced from feedstock such as sugar cane and maize, which worsened the inflationary situation of food prices.[33] This is because, when crops are used for biofuel production, the first direct effect is the reduction of their availability as food and feed and generates market competition, which ultimately leads to higher prices of these products.[34] Regarding the second factor, speculation in the food market was a consequence of the bursting of the housing bubble in the United States in early 2008 and the financial crisis that followed; thus, as the housing market collapsed, speculators began to invest in safer markets, including food, pushing food prices upwards.[35]

In recent years, there are some parallels with the 2008 crisis, such as the role of rising fossil fuel prices and speculation in food markets. As we indicated in the introduction, due to factors such as the impact of climate change and the war in Ukraine, world food prices have soared in 2022, reaching their highest point in a decade in the first half of the year. The causes of this rise are also closely related to the increase in the price of fossil fuels and their derivatives, such as fertilisers, the production of which requires large quantities of natural gas.[36] Similarly, as we saw in the 2008–2009 crisis, the rise in food prices is generating speculative tendencies. According to recent research, some of Europe's largest pension funds are investing in essential foodstuffs, which is increasing volatility in these markets.[37] Against this background, in the short term, it is essential to limit price volatility and transfer resources to the poor, enabling them to afford to buy food.

Still, in the medium term, it is also essential to take measures to reduce the dependence of agricultural production on fossil fuels and other non-renewable resources. On this issue, the High Level Panel of Experts on Food Security and Nutrition (HLPE), in its 2011 report on *Price volatility and food security*, already predicted the end of the cheap food era. According to this report, the world may be facing the end of a long period of structural overproduction in international agricultural markets that has been supported by the extensive use of agricultural subsidies in OECD countries, as well as by the massive use of cheap natural resources (e.g. oil, water, biodiversity, fertilisers, and land).[38] In regards to this, the increasing scarcity of crucial inputs, particularly fertilisers and fossil fuels, pose a considerable challenge to ensure food availability. On the one hand, in regard to fertilisers, even though global reserves and resources seem sufficient for the foreseeable future, the expenses associated with nutrients (such as nitrogen, phosphorus, or potassium) are expected to increase gradually as the most easily extracted materials are depleted.[39] On the other hand, something similar occurs with fossil fuels: while there is considerable variation in estimates regarding the remaining oil and natural gas reserves, there is a general consensus that the easily accessible, high-quality oil has been largely exhausted,[40] leaving behind the most challenging and environmentally damaging extraction prospects underground.[41] Moreover, the use of fossil fuels and an excess of fertilisers in global food systems is contributing to ecological overshoot, as will be explored in the next section.

Thus, it is crucial to transform food systems in the direction of significantly reducing the global use of inputs such as fertilisers and fuels. This is a very challenging endeavour, considering, for instance, that it is estimated that nitrogen fertilisers, made mainly out of natural gas, now support approximately half of the global population.[42] Moreover, this transformation will have to take place against the backdrop of unprecedented environmental change: the transgression of a series of planetary boundaries that are already threatening food production.

A main challenge to the achievement of SDG 2: feeding the world within planetary boundaries

As highlighted in the introduction, more than eight years after the launch of SDG2, we are moving further and further away from achieving it, in particular its target 2.1 – that sets the goal of 'ending hunger and ensuring access for all people, in particular the poor and people in vulnerable situations, including infants, to safe, nutritious and sufficient food all year round'. Thus, according to the 2023 report coordinated by the FAO on world food security, the number of people affected by hunger at the global level has increased steadily since 2014. Current estimates, based on 2022 data, indicated that about 735 million people suffered from hunger during that year, or 9.2 percent of the world's population, an increase of about 122 million people since 2019, before the global pandemic.[43] In this sense, the report concluded that the world is not on track to achieve the goal of zero hunger by 2030, since, if current trends continue, the number of hungry people will exceed 840 million by 2030, which will represent almost 10% of the world's population.

Against this backdrop, and also echoing target 2.4, this report pointed to what is undoubtedly one of the greatest challenges facing humanity today: the transformation of food systems to ensure food security based on healthy diets, while ensuring that food production and consumption contribute to environmental sustainability.[44] In order to achieve that, two main challenges lay ahead: the surpassing of planetary boundaries and the growing scarcity of fossil fuels.

Planetary boundaries and their implications for food security

The proposal for a set of planetary boundaries originated in a paper published in 2009 by a number of authors, led by Johan Rockström. The objective of this influential research is to define a safe space for human development, one that avoids irreversible disruptions to the fundamental processes that guarantee life in the biosphere.[45] To this end, nine limits are established for fundamental natural processes: (1) climate change; (2) ocean acidification; (3) alteration of the nitrogen and phosphorus cycles; (4) freshwater availability; (5) deforestation and changes in land use; (6) loss of biological diversity; (7) chemical pollution; (8) particulate pollution of the atmosphere; and (9) stratospheric ozone concentration.

One of the ideas underlying this proposal is that the processes referred to in these thresholds are interdependent, so that a disturbance in the balance of one of them can significantly alter the rest. Such alterations could therefore trigger abrupt global change that could jeopardise agriculture and other processes fundamental to human life. Indeed, at present, according to the latest research, it appears that six of these thresholds have already been exceeded due to human action: (1) the concentration of CO_2 in the atmosphere, which contributes to climate change; (2) the loss of biodiversity and the alteration of the biosphere as a whole, which pushes the planet towards its fifth species extinction; (3) the nitrogen cycle, which is already altered because of an excess of this compound in nature, due to processes such as the production and use of nitrogen fertilisers or the burning of fossil fuels; (4) land-use change, which implies a reduction of land dedicated to wildlife; (5) the introduction of novel entities into the biosphere, such as radioactive waste, organic pollutants and microplastics; and finally (6), the availability of freshwater.[46]

As has been made clear by the authors of this study, their research questions the current paradigm of economic growth,[47] reflected also in the productivist narrative. Indeed, it is widely acknowledged that today's dominant agricultural production model is pushing these boundaries; in fact, it plays a central role in destabilising the Earth system on a planetary scale, and contributes to pushing the entirety of the thresholds described in one way or another. In this sense, ambitious research published in 2017, points to the current dominant agricultural model as the main cause of the crossing of two planetary boundaries: the integrity of the biosphere, which mainly refers to the loss of biodiversity, and biogeochemical flows, that is, the alteration of the phosphorus and nitrogen cycles. It also plays an important role in contributing to the crossing of three other boundaries: land use change, freshwater use and, of course, climate change.[48]

It is therefore necessary to deeply consider how to feed the world's growing population without exceeding the above-mentioned thresholds. Along these lines, a 2020 study proposed the feasibility of feeding ten billion people without pushing the planetary boundaries any further.[49] This research focuses on the four thresholds most affected by the agricultural model's pressures: biosphere integrity, earth system change, freshwater use and nitrogen flows. Despite almost half of the world's current food production exceeding these boundaries, this study suggests that it would instead be possible to sustain 10.2 billion people while respecting them. This is only possible through a transformation towards more sustainable production and consumption patterns such as better distribution of cropland, improved water and nutrient management, and reduced food waste and dietary changes. Moreover, a change of narrative is also needed, moving from productivist towards narratives associated with regenerative agricultural systems, with proven social and environmental benefits.[50] Thus, a radical transformation of food systems is needed in order to achieve the goal of feeding the entire world's population without further pushing these limits, as discussed in the next section.

Dependence on fossil fuels in a context of energy decline

Nowadays, fossil fuels play a critical role in each step of food systems. Current agri-food systems account for a large part of global energy consumption – about 30% of it – most of which in post-harvest stages and in the form of fossil fuels.

In fact, this energy accounts for about 30% of agri-food systems' GHG emissions.[51] As mentioned previously, high-input food systems developed during the Green Revolution facilitated farm mechanisation, strongly increased fertiliser production, and reduced income instability while improving food security.[52] However, the dark side of this story is, on the one hand, contribution to climate change and overcoming planetary boundaries, and, on the other, fossil fuels dependence. In fact, today industrial food systems are highly dependent on fossil fuels, mainly in the forms of fertilisers (made with natural gas), pesticides (made with fossil oils), and hydrocarbon-fuelled irrigation.[53] In fact, beyond industrial production, today fossil fuels are everywhere in food systems: on the transportation of agricultural inputs and outputs, food processing, irrigation, and post-harvest storage – up to the fridges in people's houses.[54] Thus, as Pfeiffer (2006) argues: today, in a very real sense, 'we are literally eating fossil fuels'.[55]

Moreover, and despite its demand is meant to grow further in the next decades along with the need for sustaining or increasing current crop yields, as was already mentioned, the availability of cheap fossil fuels is expected to decrease. High-quality oil consumption has predominantly occurred, and the recent, widely adopted imperative of cutting emissions should also imply an energy transition in food systems. Thus, the end of 'cheap oil' presents a significant challenge for food security, such as increasing cost of transportation.[56] For these main reasons, future generations have an elevated risk of facing a scarcity of fossil fuel resources, and subsequently low probability of being able to give continuity to their current consumption.

Consequently, it is clear that a global shift away from fossil fuels is a first necessary step in order to make the agri-food system more sustainable, reliable and accessible for all. In fact, satisfying energy demand through fossil fuels raises issues in terms of resilience to supply, accessibility, affordability, other than in terms of environmental impacts. For example, the variability of energy availability highly affects food production. Family farms produce around 80% of the world's food in value terms,[57] while millions of people, as well as small and medium agri-food enterprises, are in lack of reliable and affordable energy. In this sense, a large proportion of the agricultural community, belonging mostly to emerging and marginalised communities, has been left behind when agri-food production shifted to fossil fuels use.

However, rapidly cutting this dependence without harming food security is a challenging endeavour. As we have seen in the previous 2008–2009 some of the measures proposed to cut this dependency, such as investment on producing biofuels, may have negative impacts on food security.[58] In this sense, the recent report of the Global Alliance for the Future of Food 'Power Shift: Why We Need to Wean Industrial Food Systems Off Fossil Fuel', published in November 2023, points at some relevant way to cut this dependence which will not harm food security, such as transition to regenerative and agroecological approaches and promote plant-rich diets and minimally processed foods; furthermore, this report also recommends to review fiscal policies to counter the negative externalities of bioenergy production.[59] In addition to that, cutting down unacceptably high post-harvest losses is another crucial way of increasing our food supply without further environmental impacts.[60]

In regards to that, this transformation towards more sustainable food systems faces considerable geoeconomic and geopolitical barriers, particularly the overcoming of the dominant 'feeding a growing planet' narrative. This narrative interprets food crises as indicative of a world still marked by economic divisions, urging for increased economic integration and perceives an opportunity in addressing long-standing food security issues by bridging the 'yield gap' between the highly productive regions of the North and the under-producing regions of the South.[61] Nevertheless, as we have already discussed, this 'feeding a growing planet' narrative leaves out of the equation central issues such as the impact of consumption habits, as meat consumption in rich countries, as well as the significant environmental and social impacts of the industrial food system.[62] In contrast, it is essential to advocate for alternative narratives that question a food system which commodifies food, privatises land, displaced rural communities, and perpetuates widespread food insecurity and environmentally harmful production and consumption practices.[63]

Conclusions

This paper has examined key vulnerabilities of the global food system that hinder the fulfilment of SDG 2. The surpassing of six planetary boundaries, as well as the approaching of risk thresholds in the remaining three, are already having observable impacts on food systems. Considering the climate emergency as a representative example, the occurrence of droughts, floods and other extreme phenomena linked to this crisis is hampering people's ability to feed themselves adequately. Moreover, the outlook is worsening in the coming years, as global emissions continue to rise and no significant measures are being taken to avoid further breaching other planetary thresholds that affect food security, such as the availability of freshwater or the extinction of many species. For all these reasons, preventing the crossing of these thresholds is one of the main challenges in meeting SDG 2.

On the other hand, the decrease in the availability of resources on which the current agricultural model depends, such as fossil fuels, is another key obstacle to achieving this goal. As already mentioned, the world may be facing the end of a long period of structural overproduction in international agricultural markets that was made possible by the abundance of cheap natural resources.[64] Therefore, the increasing scarcity of inputs will also have an impact on food systems, which will have to be able to ensure food availability with a decreasing amount of these resources; additionally, this growing scarcity will most likely push food prices up, making it more difficult for the most vulnerable people to access food.

Policymakers will be therefore in charge of prioritising action to reduce the dependence of agricultural production on fossil fuels, by fostering policies which support smallholders through access to resources for agroecological and regenerative practices, as well as promoting plant-rich diets and significantly reduce food losses.[65] However, while promoting policies to ensure the transition to an environmentally bettered food chain, it would be even more essential to include measures which improve economic access, limiting price volatility and providing safety nets, such as cash transfers to the poor, enabling them to afford to buy food. In this sense, recognising the challenges faced by economically disadvantaged nations in implementing robust safety net measures, which entail a significant rise in international humanitarian assistance, is also essential. Furthermore, it should be a priority to promote institutional reforms that ensure that all members of society – including rural and urban individuals, men and women, producers, consumers, and the vulnerable – are properly organised and represented in the policy process and receive necessary support and incentives throughout the value chain.[66]

As a final point, everything implies that we need to urgently move towards sustainable food systems. This objective is reflected in the 2030 Agenda and is often repeated by international institutions. However, these institutions and other actors involved need to recognise that we cannot achieve this goal without challenging the productivist narrative which is in the core of mainstream food security analysis. In the current context, the possibilities of a new Green Revolution are hardly realisable, due to the increasing scarcity of the fossil fuels that made it possible, as well as the crossing of planetary thresholds, which is taking humanity into an uncharted territory. Therefore, alternatives for transforming food systems, such as moving towards less meat-based and more local diets in the global North, as well as significantly reducing the use of energy inputs through the whole system, need to be urgently put at the centre of research agendas and policy-making. In parallel, food security narratives need to change accordingly, moving from productivism to regeneration and resilience.

Notes

1 FAO, IFAD, WHO, WFP and UNICEF, 'Summary version of The State of Food Security and Nutrition in the World 2023. Urbanization, Agrifood Systems Transformation and Healthy Diets across the Rural–Urban Continuum'. Rome: FAO, 2023.

2 García Juanatey, A., 'The deterioration of global food security', in M. Galceran, 'An urban perspective to basic goods and rights', CIDOB Report no. 10, July 2023.

3 According to the FAO Food Price Index, the price of maize has increased by 47% and wheat by 42% in 2022 compared to 2021.

4 Naveen Thukral, N., 'Global 2024 staple food supplies to be strained by dry weather, export curbs'. Reuters, 2024.

5 García Juanatey, A., 'Más allá del derecho humano a la alimentación: la aportación del principio de equidad y de la erradicación de la pobreza a la consecución del ODS 2 sobre el hambre cero'. In E. López-Jacoiste (1st ed.), Derecho internacional, los ODS y la Comunidad internacional, Dykinson, 2023.

6 Anderson, M. D., and Rivera-Ferre, Madrid, 'Food system narratives to end hunger: extractive versus regenerative'. *Current Opinion in Environmental Sustainability* 49, 2021, 18-25.

7 IPCC, 'Summary for Policymakers'. In Climate Change and Land: an IPCC special report on climate change, desertification, land degradation, sustainable land

management, food security, and greenhouse gas fluxes in terrestrial ecosystems, edited by P.R. Shukla et al., 2019.

8 FAO, 'Climate change and food security: risks and responses'. Rome: FAO, 2016.

9 Rockström, J. et al., 'Planetary boundaries: exploring the safe operating space for humanity'. Ecology and Society, no.14, 2009.

10 Campbell, B. M., et al., 'Agriculture production as a major driver of the Earth system exceeding planetary boundaries'. *Ecology and Society* 22, 4, 2017.

11 An exception was the publication of Dale Allen: Pfeiffer, D., 'Eating fossil fuels: oil, food, and the coming crisis in agriculture'. New Society Publishers, 2006. A more recent publication on this matter is the report of the Global Alliance for the Future of Food, 'Power Shift:Why We Need to Wean Industrial Food Systems Off Fossil Fuel', 2023.

12 Woods, J. et al., 'Energy and the food system'. Philosophical Transactions of the Royal Society B: Biological Sciences 365, no. 1554, 2010, 2991-3006.

13 HLPE, 'Price Volatility and Food Security'. No. 1. Rome: CFS-HLPE, 2011, p.10.

14 HLPE, 'Biofuels and Food Security'. No. 5. Rome: CFS-HLPE, 2013.

15 Morales, L., and Andreosso-O'Callaghan, B., 'Volatility in agricultural commodity and oil markets during times of crises'. *Economics, Management & Financial Markets* 12, no. 4, 2017.

16 Webb, P. et al., 'Measuring household food insecurity: why it's so important and yet so difficult to do'. *The Journal of nutrition* 136, no. 5, 2006.

17 Lambek, N., 'The UN Committee on World Food Security's break from the agricultural productivity trap'. *Transnational Legal Theory* 9, no. 3-4, 2018, 415-429.

18 Moore Lappé, F., 'Doce mitos sobre el hambre'. Barcelona: Icaria Editorial, 2005.

19 Jenkins, J. C., and Scanlan, S. J., 'Food Security in Less Developed Countries, 1970 to 1990'. American Sociological Review 66, no. 5, 2001, 718-744.

20 Moore Lappé, F., 'Doce mitos sobre el hambre'. Barcelona: Icaria Editorial, 2005, 87.

21 FAO, 'FAO Celebrates Its 50 Years'. Rome: FAO, 1995.

22 De Schutter, O., 'The political economy of food systems reform'. European Review of Agricultural Economics 44, no. 4, 2017, 705-731.

23 FAO, High-Level Expert Forum, 'How to Feed the World in 2050'. Rome: FAO, 2009.

24 García Juanatey, A., 'Alimentación Sostenible, Hambre y Transición Ecológica en el Derecho Internacional'. Madrid: Ed. Reus, 2022.

25 De Schutter, O., 'The political economy of food systems reform'. European Review of Agricultural Economics 44, no. 4, 2017, 705-731.

26 Wirsenius, S., Azar., C. and Berndes, G., 'How much land is needed for global food production under scenarios of dietary changes and livestock productivity increases in 2030?'. Agricultural Systems 103, 2010, 621-638.

27 FAO, 'Resolution 2/83 on World Food Security'. In FAO Conference Report, Rome: FAO, 1983.

28 Sen, A., 'Poverty and famines'. Oxford: Oxford University Press, 1983.

29 García Juanatey, A., 'Alimentación Sostenible, Hambre y Transición Ecológica en el Derecho Internacional'. Madrid: Ed. Reus, 2022.

30 BBC, 'The cost of food: Facts and figures'. BBC, 2008.

31 HLPE, 2011, 'Price Volatility and Food Security'. No. 1. Rome: CFS-HLPE, 2011, p. 10. Otro factor ampliamente señalado es el aumento en el consumo de carne. Weis, T., 'The meat of the global food crisis'. Journal of Peasant Studies 40, 1, 2013, 65-85.

32 Fixen, Paul E., and Johnston, Adrian M., 'World fertilizer nutrient reserves: a view to the future'. Journal of the Science of Food and Agriculture 92, no. 5, 2012, 1001-1005.

33 HLPE, 2011, 'Price Volatility and Food Security'. No. 1. Rome: CFS-HLPE, 2011, 10.
34 HLPE, 2013, 'Biofuels and Food Security'. No. 5. Rome: CFS-HLPE, 2013.
35 Human Rights Council, 'Report of the Special Rapporteur on the right to food, Olivier De Schutter. Turning the Crisis into an Opportunity: Strengthening Multilateralism'. A/HRC/12/31, 2009.
36 World Bank, 'Fertilizer Volatility and the Food Crisis'. [Podcast], 2022.
37 Lighthouse Reports, 'Pension Funds: Gambling with Savings and Fueling Hunger'. Lighthouse Reports, 2022.
38 HLPE, 2011, 'Price Volatility and Food Security'. No. 1. Rome: CFS-HLPE, 2011, 10.
39 Fixen, Paul E., and Adrian M. Johnston, World fertilizer nutrient reserves: a view to the future'. Journal of the Science of Food and Agriculture, 92, no. 5, 2012, 1001-1005.
40 Mohr, S. H., Wang, J., Ellem, G., Ward, J., & Giurco, D., 'Projection of world fossil fuels by country'. Fuel, 141, 2015, 120–135. Fustier, K., et al., 'Global oil supply'. London: HSBC Global Research, 2016.
41 Masnadi, M. S., & Brandt, A. R., 'Climate impacts of oil extraction increase significantly with oilfield age'. Nature Climate Change 7, n. 8, 551-556.
42 Smil, V., 'Enriching the earth: Fritz Haber, Carl Bosch, and the transformation of world food production'. MIT press, 2004.
43 FAO, IFAD, WHO, WFP and UNICEF, 2023, 'Summary version of The State of Food Security and Nutrition in the World 2023. Urbanization, Agrifood Systems Transformation and Healthy Diets across the Rural–Urban Continuum'. Rome: FAO.
44 FAO, IFAD, WHO, WFP and UNICEF, 2023, 'Summary version of The State of Food Security and Nutrition in the World 2023. Urbanization, Agrifood Systems Transformation and Healthy Diets across the Rural–Urban Continuum'. Rome: FAO, 9.
45 Rockström, J. et al., 'Planetary boundaries: exploring the safe operating space for humanity'. Ecology and Society, no.14, 2009.
46 Richardson, K., et al., 'Earth beyond six of nine planetary boundaries'. *Science advances* 9, no. 37, 2023.
47 Steffen, W. L., Rockström, J. and Costanza, R., 'How defining planetary boundaries can transform our approach to growth'. Solutions: For A Sustainable & Desirable Future, 2011.
48 Campbell, B. M., et al., 'Agriculture production as a major driver of the Earth system exceeding planetary boundaries'. Ecology and Society 22, no. 4, 2017.
49 Gerten, D., et al., 'Feeding ten billion people is possible within four terrestrial planetary boundaries'. *Nature Sustainability* 3, no.3, 2020, 200-208.
50 Anderson, M. D., and Rivera-Ferre, M., 'Food system narratives to end hunger: extractive versus regenerative'. Current Opinion in Environmental Sustainability 49, 2021, 18-25.
51 IRENA and FAO, 'Renewable energy for agri-food systems – Towards the Sustainable Development Goals and the Paris agreement'. Abu Dhabi and Rome, 2023.
52 IRENA and FAO, 'Renewable energy for agri-food systems – Towards the Sustainable Development Goals and the Paris agreement'. Abu Dhabi and Rome, 2023.
53 Pfeiffer, D., 'Eating fossil fuels: oil, food, and the coming crisis in agriculture'. New Society Publishers, 2006. A more recent publication on this matter is the report of the Global Alliance for the Future of Food, 'Power Shift: Why We Need to Wean Industrial Food Systems Off Fossil Fuel', 2023.

54 Smil, V., 'Traditional Farming. Energy and Civilization: A History'. The MIT Press, 2017, 49-126.
55 Smil, V., 'Traditional Farming. Energy and Civilization: A History'. The MIT Press, 2017, 49-126.
56 Peduzzi, P., and Harding Rohr Reis, R., 'The end to cheap oil: a threat to food security and an incentive to reduce fossil fuels in agriculture'. Environmental development, 2012, 3(1), 157-165.
57 FAO, 'Small family farmers produce a third of the world's food'. Rome: FAO, 2021. https://www.fao.org/news/story/en/item/1395127/icode/.
58 HLPE, 2013, 'Biofuels and Food Security'. No. 5. Rome: CFS-HLPE, 2013.
59 Global Alliance for the Future of Food, 'Power Shift: Why We Need to Wean Industrial Food Systems Off Fossil Fuel'. 2023, p. 3.
60 Smil, V., 'Improving efficiency and reducing waste in our food system.' *Environmental sciences*, vol. 1, n. 1, 2004, 17-26.
61 Sommerville, M., Essex, J., and Le Billon, P., 'The 'global food crisis' and the geopolitics of food security'. *Geopolitics*, 19., 2014, 239-265.
62 De Schutter, O., 'The political economy of food systems reform'. *European Review of Agricultural Economics*, 44, no. 4, 2017, 705-731.
63 Sommerville, M., Essex, J., and Le Billon, P., 'The 'global food crisis' and the geopolitics of food security'. *Geopolitics*, 19., 2014, p. 258.
64 HLPE, 2011, 'Price Volatility and Food Security'. No. 1. Rome: CFS-HLPE, 2011, p.10.
65 Lambek, N., 'The UN Committee on World Food Security's break from the agricultural productivity trap'. *Transnational Legal Theory* 9, no. 3-4, 2018, 415-429.
66 FAO, High-Level Expert Forum, 'How to Feed the World in 2050'. Rome: FAO, 2009.

Bibliography

Anderson, M. D., and Rivera-Ferre, M., 'Food system narratives to end hunger: extractive versus regenerative'. *Current Opinion in Environmental Sustainability*, 49, 2021, 18–25.

BBC, 'The cost of food: Facts and figures'. BBC, 2008.

Campbell, B. M., et al., 'Agriculture production as a major driver of the Earth system exceeding planetary boundaries'. *Ecology and Society* 22, no. 4, 2017.

De Schutter, O., 'The political economy of food systems reform'. *European Review of Agricultural Economics* 44, no. 4, 2017, 705–731.

FAO, IFAD, WHO, WFP and UNICEF, '*Summary version of The State of Food Security and Nutrition in the World 2023. Urbanization, Agrifood Systems Transformation and Healthy Diets across the Rural–Urban Continuum*'. Rome: FAO, 2023.

FAO, '*Climate change and food security: risks and responses*'. Rome: FAO, 2016.

FAO, '*FAO Celebrates Its 50 Years*'. Rome: FAO, 1995.

FAO, *High-Level Expert Forum, 'How to Feed the World in 2050'*. Rome: FAO, 2009.

FAO, 'Resolution 2/83 on World Food Security'. In FAO Conference Report. Rome: FAO, 1983.

FAO, 'Small family farmers produce a third of the world's food'. Rome: FAO, 2021. https://www.fao.org/news/story/en/item/1395127/icode/

Fixen, Paul E., and Johnston, Adrian M., 'World fertilizer nutrient reserves: a view to the future'. *Journal of the Science of Food and Agriculture* 92, no. 5, 2012, 1001–1005.

García Juanatey, A., 'Más allá del derecho humano a la alimentación: la aportación del principio de equidad y de la erradicación de la pobreza a la consecución del ODS 2

sobre el hambre cero'. In E. López-Jacoiste (1st ed.), Derecho internacional, los ODS y la Comunidad internacional, Madrid: Dykinson, 2023.
García Juanatey, A., 'The deterioration of global food security', in M. Galceran, 'An urban perspective to basic goods and rights'. CIDOB Report no. 10, July 2023b.
García Juanatey, A., *Alimentación Sostenible, Hambre y Transición Ecológica en el Derecho Internacional*, Madrid: Ed. Reus, 2022.
Gerten, D., et al., 'Feeding ten billion people is possible within four terrestrial planetary boundaries'. *Nature Sustainability*, 3, no. 3, 2020, 200–208.
Global Alliance for the Future of Food, 'Power Shift: Why We Need to Wean Industrial Food Systems Off Fossil Fuel' 2023.
HLPE, 'Biofuels and Food Security'. No. 5. Rome: CFS-HLPE, 2013.
HLPE, 'Price Volatility and Food Security'. No. 1. Rome: CFS-HLPE, 2011, 10.
Human Rights Council, 'Report of the Special Rapporteur on the right to food, Olivier De Schutter. Turning the Crisis into an Opportunity: Strengthening Multilateralism.'. A/HRC/12/31, 2009.
IPCC, 'Summary for Policymakers'. In *Climate Change and Land: an IPCC special report on climate change, desertification, land degradation, sustainable land management, food security, and greenhouse gas fluxes in terrestrial ecosystems*, edited by P.R. Shukla, et al., 2019.
IRENA and FAO, 'Renewable energy for agri-food systems – Towards the Sustainable Development Goals and the Paris agreement'. Abu Dhabi and Rome, 2023.
Jenkins, J. C., and Scanlan, S. J., 'Food Security in Less Developed Countries, 1970 to 1990'. *American Sociological Review*, 66, no. 5, 2001, 718–744.
Lambek, N., 'The UN Committee on World Food Security's break from the agricultural productivity trap'. *Transnational Legal Theory*, 2018, 9, no. 3–4, 415–429.
Lighthouse Reports, 'Pension Funds: Gambling with Savings and Fueling Hunger.' Lighthouse Reports, 2022.
Masnadi, M. S., and Brandt, A. R., 'Climate impacts of oil extraction increase significantly with oilfield age'. *Nature Climate Change*, 7, no. 8, 551–556.
Mohr, S. H., Wang, J., Ellem, G., Ward, J., & Giurco, D., 'Projection of world fossil fuels by country'. *Fuel*, 141, 2015, 120–135.
Moore Lappé, F., *Doce mitos sobre el hambre*. Barcelona: Icaria Editorial, 2005.
Morales, L., and Andreosso-O'Callaghan, B., 'Volatility in agricultural commodity and oil markets during times of crises'. *Economics, Management & Financial Markets* 12, no. 4, 2017.
Naveen Thukral, N., 'Global 2024 staple food supplies to be strained by dry weather, export curbs'. Reuters, 2024.
Peduzzi, P., and Harding Rohr Reis, R., 'The end to cheap oil: a threat to food security and an incentive to reduce fossil fuels in agriculture'. *Environmental Development*, 2012, 3(1), 157–165.
Pfeiffer, D., *Eating fossil fuels: oil, food, and the coming crisis in agriculture*. New Society Publishers, 2006.
Richardson, K., et al., 'Earth beyond six of nine planetary boundaries'. *Science Advances* 9, no. 37, 2023.
Rockström, J. et al., 2009, 'Planetary boundaries: exploring the safe operating space for humanity'. *Ecology and Society* 14, no. 2, 32.
Sen, A., *Poverty and famines*. Oxford: Oxford University Press, 1983.
Smil, V., 'Improving efficiency and reducing waste in our food system'. *Environmental sciences* 1, no. 1, 2004, 17–26.
Smil, V., *Enriching the earth: Fritz Haber, Carl Bosch, and the transformation of world food production*. MIT press, 2004.
Smil, V., 'Traditional Farming', in *Energy and Civilization: A History*. The MIT Press, 2017, 49–126.

Sommerville, M., Essex, J., and Le Billon, P., 'The 'global food crisis' and the geopolitics of food security'. Geopolitics 19, no. 2, 2014, 239–265.
Steffen, W. L., Rockström, J. and Costanza, R., 'How defining planetary boundaries can transform our approach to growth'. Solutions: For A Sustainable & Desirable Future, 2011.
Webb, P. et al., 'Measuring household food insecurity: why it's so important and yet so difficult to do'. *The Journal of Nutrition* 136, no. 5, 2006, 1404S–1408S.
Weis, T., 'The meat of the global food crisis'. *Journal of Peasant Studies* 40, no. 1, 2013, 65–85.
Wirsenius, S., Azar, C. and Berndes, G., 'How much land is needed for global food production under scenarios of dietary changes and livestock productivity increases in 2030?'. *Agricultural Systems*, no. 103, 2010, 621–638.
Woods, J. et al., 'Energy and the food system'. *Philosophical Transactions of the Royal Society B: Biological Sciences* 365, no. 1554, 2010, 2991–3006.
World Bank, 'Fertilizer Volatility and the Food Crisis'. [Podcast], 2022.

15 Geopolitics of Migration Management

Navigating sustainable development goals

Elena Sánchez-Montijano

Introduction

Throughout history, the management of migration, especially migration flows, has remained in the hands of nation-states, with migration characterized by a permanent movement from one state to another (Castles, 2010). Behind this nationalist logic was the desire of countries to control their borders and, especially, who could be part of the *demos* of a particular country (Pécoud, 2020). However, globalization, complexity, interconnectivity, and the massification of migrations lead countries to join forces to manage a phenomenon that a single country can hardly manage. Today, geopolitics plays a crucial role in its management (Hyndman & Mountz, 2008; Hyndman, 2012). Migration has shifted from a matter of national interest to the highest level of international dialogue and cooperation, leading to the generation of different development mechanisms, institutions, and responsibilities (Micinski & Lefebvre, 2024).

Lately, this way of managing migration has gained importance in several cases, especially in response to migration crises. The most significant example in the framework of the geopolitics of migration that includes, at the same time, the Sustainable Development Goals (SDGs) is the Global Compact for Safe, Orderly, and Regular Migration,[1] a non-binding agreement adopted in 2018 and signed by 193 countries within the UN framework (IOM 2018, 2020). The Compact recognizes throughout the document the complexity and challenges involved in international migration and that only a coordinated management among the actors involved will have an effective and safe solution (Micinski & Lefebvre, 2024; Solomon & Sheldon, 2018). Another good example is the approach developed in recent years by the European Union (Collyer, 2016; Parkes, 2015), especially in the face of the need to raise coordinated action in two cases: the Syrian refugee crisis in 2015 and the forced displacement of millions of Ukrainians as a response of the Russia's invasion in 2022 (Zardo, 2022). Managing geopolitics does not always put migrants' rights at the center or align with the SDGs. In fact, much of the literature analyzing the relationship between geopolitics and migration highlights the opposite. In many cases, the geopolitics of migration is significantly disconnected from the SDGs, as it is a nationalistic and security response (Hyndman & Mountz, 2008; Hyndman, 2012).

DOI: 10.4324/9781032655857-19

Considering the ongoing debate, this text delves into the potential of geopolitics as an effective tool for managing the migration phenomenon while also contributing to achieving the SDGs. It examines the intricate relationship between geopolitics, migration, and sustainable development, analyzing how geopolitical policies and strategies can shape migration patterns and, consequently, impact the achievement of the SDGs. Additionally, it scrutinizes recent instances where geopolitics has played a pivotal role in migration management and assesses its ability (or lack thereof) to align with the SDGs. Ultimately, the text poses the questions: What is the interplay between migration, geopolitics, and SDGs? To what extent can geopolitics effectively manage migration within the framework of the SDGs? Following an exploration of the relationship between migration, geopolitics, and SDGs, we aim to address: Under what conditions can geopolitics facilitate migration management within the SDGs framework?

The text, in its approach to the analysis of this interrelation between migration, geopolitics, and development objectives, focuses mainly on the migratory phenomenon. The review undertaken encompasses key academic publications (evaluated based on impact and citations) regarding the nexus between sustainable development goals, geopolitics, and migration. Methodologically, a systematic review (Denyer & Tranfield, 2009), from 2015 to now, of publications on Google Scholar (as of February 1, 2024) was conducted, yielding: 1) 60 results for "allintitle: migration, 'sustainable development goals'" and 2) 68 results for "allintitle: migration, 'geopolitical'". This search was complemented with a review in JSTOR, following the same parameters.[2] Notably, no literature was found that encompassed all three concepts simultaneously. Among these publications, only those centered on migration were analyzed; those focusing on specific themes (such as health, education, water) or countries (e.g., India, Thailand) were excluded; while regional studies were included.

The text presented is divided into the following sections. The first section reviews the relationship between the SDGs and migration. This is followed by an approach to the geopolitics of migration. The third section reviews the relationship between these three phenomena. It presents some cases in which geopolitical action has been the basis for managing the migration phenomenon within the framework of the SDGs. The chapter continues with a reflection on the conditions necessary for the sustainable management of the three elements under analysis. It ends with some brief conclusions.

Relationship between SDGs and Migration

As widely acknowledged, the SDGs, adopted by the United Nations General Assembly in 2015, constitute a framework aimed at tackling global challenges and fostering sustainable development across various domains including poverty eradication, gender equality, education, health, climate action, and peace and justice. While none of the 17 goals explicitly addresses migration, several of them encompass this phenomenon within some of the 169 associated targets.[3] Moreover, paragraph 29 of the 2030 Agenda states:

> The positive contribution of migrants for inclusive growth and sustainable development. We also recognize that international migration is a multi-dimensional reality of major relevance for the development of countries of origin, transit, and destination which requires coherent and comprehensive responses.

This statement is a recognition of the cross-cutting nature of migration and the need for this phenomenon to be addressed holistically from each of the development goals (Solomon & Sheldon, 2018). Similarly, it highlights the interconnection between the SDGs and the drivers of migration, as well as the challenges and consequences associated with it. Indeed, as demonstrated by Prada (2020), a significant proportion of the indicators used to demonstrate the success of the development goals also reflect an impact on the migration phenomenon.

The IOM (2020: 5) encapsulates the relationship between migration and the SDGs as follows:

> Migration can be a powerful driver of sustainable development for migrants and their communities in countries of origin, transit, and destination. However, as much as migration has an impact on development, migration is also affected by development.

This definition holds significance for two primary reasons. Firstly, it elucidates the connection between sustainable development across various stages and forms of countries involved in migration (origin, transit, and destination). Secondly, it asserts that migration influences, at the same time it is influenced by development; hence, there exists both an endogenous and exogenous impact between these two elements.

For example, SDG 1 (No Poverty) and SDG 2 (Zero Hunger) are related to the economic drivers of migration, as people are often forced to leave their home countries searching for better economic opportunities and food security. In addition, SDG 10 (Reduced Inequalities) and SDG 16 (Peace, Justice, and Strong Institutions) are linked to the conflicts and political instability that can trigger migration; but also, with the situations they find when settling in a particular country. However, these goals are not the sole ones directly linked to the migration phenomenon; others have indirect connections (Sivakumar & Rajan, 2021), particularly when considering the various phases of migratory mobility.At the country of origin, SDGs and migration share a clear relationship concerning the factors underpinning the causes of mobility. Sustainable development efforts can contribute to mitigating the root causes of migration, such as poverty, inequality, conflict, and the lack of economic and social opportunities (Gavonel et al., 2021; Hackl, 2018). By promoting equitable access to education, healthcare, and employment, living conditions in countries of origin can be improved, thereby reducing the imperative to migrate. Similarly, fostering sustainable development within migrant communities can help address issues related to climate change and access to natural resources.

The relationship between migration and the SDGs is particularly noteworthy in both transit context and types of mobility. Aligning migration management with development goals can help ensure safe, orderly, and regular migration (Toochi Aniche, 2020). Some of the possible effective schemes could be under labor mobility programs, both temporary and permanent, or return. Foresti and Hagen-Zanker (2017) highlight that SDGs related to peace, justice, and gender equality can influence the conditions and safety of migrants during the journey. Likewise, the SDGs can show access to basic services and protection of migrants on the journey. Similarly, the link between these two realities would contribute to addressing environmental challenges that may be related to mobility.

Likewise, this interaction becomes relevant in the host country, where the SDGs could serve as indicators of the successful integration of migrants into host communities. In this regard, Micinski and Lefebvre's (2024) analysis highlights that the SDGs focused on reducing inequalities, mitigating climate change, as well as promoting peace and justice, have the potential to shape the capacity of host communities to effectively receive and welcome migrants. In other words, these goals not only target sustainable development at the global level but also have direct implications for the capacity of receiving communities to provide decent living conditions and equitable opportunities for migrants arriving in their communities.

Finally, in the context of migrant return, the study by Foresti and Hagen-Zanker (2017) highlights the relevance of the SDGs in addressing poverty reduction, promoting gender equality, and ensuring decent work. These SDGs play a key role in influencing the ability of migrants to access economic and social opportunities upon return to their countries of origin. That is, policies and actions aimed at achieving these goals can have a direct impact on migrants' prospects for reintegration into their communities of origin, affecting their access to employment, basic services, gender equality, and other important dimensions of their well-being and development.

In essence, the interaction between sustainable development and migration is bidirectional and presents remarkable complexity (Adger et al., 2019, 2023). On the one hand, fostering sustainable development that is equitable and resilient to challenges can play a crucial role in mitigating the root causes of migration and effectively managing migration flows. On the other hand, migration itself can have substantial effects on both origin and destination communities in terms of sustainable development. That is, migration dynamics can significantly influence various economic, social, and environmental aspects of the regions of origin and destination, underscoring the complexity and interconnectedness between the two phenomena (Crush, 2019; Suliman, 2017).

What do we Understand by the Geopolitics of Migration?

Geopolitics refers to the study of the power relations that occur between states and global actors, as well as how these influence policies and strategies; focusing on the relevance that geography acquires (Tuathail, 1999; Flint & Mamadouh, 2015). In the context of migration, the geopolitics of migration is a field that addresses the interaction between migratory movements and the geopolitical interests of states (both of countries of origin, transit, and destination) and actors that interrelate in the international community (Borrelli et al., 2022; Hyndman, 2012). This area of study delves into how migration policies and international agreements related to migration are influenced by a variety of geopolitical considerations, such as national security and power projection (Hyndman & Mountz, 2008; Hyndman, 2012). Similarly, border security, migration management, and the influence of state and non-state actors on migration policies are key dimensions within the analysis of the geopolitics of migration (Micinski & Lefebvre, 2024).

Equally significant is the impact of migration on geopolitics. Literature suggests that states pursue their geopolitical interests through migration and the global agreements that are generated around it. States use diplomatic tools to manage cross-border population mobility, which influences the architecture of the global governance of migration (Micinski & Lefebvr, 2024). In parallel, global agreements become key institutions for migration diplomacy, where states pursue their geopolitical interests through consultations, thematic events, formal negotiations, and intergovernmental conferences.

Despite the emerging body of literature on this topic, a critical review of the relationship between geopolitics and migration has surfaced. Some authors, such as Micinski and Lefebvre (2024) or Campos-Delgado (2024), contend that the implementation of these agreements generates contradictory processes, as states exhibit a disparity between strategic commitments and practical actions. Consequently, geopolitics can act as a catalyst for migration-related phenomena, as states navigate migration management and global migration agreements driven by geopolitical interests, often failing to address the actual needs of migration.

Similarly, several authors highlight the rigidity with which geopolitics comprehends the migration phenomenon. Allen et al. (2017) and Borrelli et al. (2022) argue that migration cannot be fully understood within the analytical categories to which geopolitics seeks to respond through concrete actions. They contend that providing an effective solution from geopolitics to the migration phenomenon is challenging, as geopolitical responses often oversimplify the complexity and dynamic nature of migration. This, in turn, prompts consideration of the impact of this complexity on geopolitics itself (Allen et al., 2017).

In this same critical sense, some authors review the conflict that arises in this relationship between the geopolitics of migration and respect for human rights; insofar as it complies with a purely nationalist and securitization logic (Hyndman, 2012). In this framework, this author examines two levels of political management of migration: biopolitics and geopolitics. On the one hand, biopolitics comprises territorial control and, above all, the management of a community; it includes dynamics of power, surveillance, and discipline at the individual level. On the other hand, geopolitics is the influence of political and economic power on decision-making about territories and borders. In the context of migration, Hyndman (2012) highlights that the intersection of geopolitics and biopolitics is manifested in border security policies, the securitization of migration, and human mobility management practices. In short, in more restrictive measures, with stricter border controls and selective migration policies, in which mobility only responds to the needs and interests of host countries, and where neither the interests of migrants nor development objectives are recognized or respected.

Within this critical context, given the emphasis that geopolitics places on national and security interests, the question arises as to how geopolitics of the migration connects with development objectives. Is there any relationship between them and under what conditions might this connection occur? These questions will be addressed in the following sections.

Intersection between Geopolitics, Migration, and SDGs

The intersection between geopolitics, migration, and sustainable development is undeniably complex and multifaceted, presenting a challenge in terms of coordination. It involves considering numerous factors and dynamics at global, regional, and local levels, necessitating collaborative action that addresses the interests and needs of various stakeholders, including governments, international organizations, civil society, the private sector, and migrants themselves. Ultimately, geopolitical decisions can profoundly impact migration and, consequently, hinder countries' ability to achieve the SDGs.

Following the critical review of the geopolitics of migration (Hyndman, 2012; Micinski & Lefebvr, 2024: Campos-Delgado, 2024), it could be thought that the development of a series of restrictive policies designed from national interests may hinder migrants' departure from their countries of origin, as well as their transit or access to basic services at any stage of mobility, which in turn would hinder the achievement of the SDGs. However, against this backdrop, effective and coherent migration management based on geopolitics, framed within the framework of respect for human rights, can contribute significantly to the achievement of several development goals.

First, it would contribute to the reduction of inequalities (SDG 10) because it would understand the causes that motivate migration. States could implement policies to address these inequalities, which could benefit migrants and reduce the factors that lead to the expulsion of migrants for this reason. In short, as Goal 10.7 states: "Facilitate orderly, safe, regular and responsible migration and mobility of people, including through the implementation of planned and well-managed migration policies." Secondly, it would contribute to the goal of peace, justice, and strong institutions (SDG 16) because by incorporating these three dimensions into the State, the push factors that motivate migration are reduced. Third, decent work and economic growth (SDG 8) can be achieved if orderly migration is facilitated. States can foster fair job opportunities and sustainable economic growth for migrants and receiving communities. Finally, it would contribute to partnerships between actors to achieve the goals (particularly, SDG 17), as international cooperation in migration management based on a geopolitical analysis can strengthen partnerships between countries and organizations to provide joint responses. This is an opportunity to revitalize the global partnership for sustainable development through the geopolitical management of migration.

In any case, the effective integration of geopolitics, migration, and sustainable development requires a holistic and collaborative approach that considers the interests and needs of the different actors. In essence, the intersection between geopolitics, migration, and sustainable development has the potential to foster a more just, equitable, and sustainable approach to managing migration and achieving sustainable development goals. Yet, the question remains: Is this feasible in practice, and are there cases where the geopolitics of migration intersects with development objectives?

The answer is yes. There are several examples in which the migration phenomenon is treated from a geopolitical perspective, within the framework of development objectives. The most relevant case, according to the IOM (2020), of migration management from geopolitics and under a sustainable development logic is the Global Compact for Safe, Orderly, and Regular Migration. The Compact and the SDGs provide the necessary normative frameworks to coordinate migration at the individual, community, national, regional, and global levels. In doing so, the Compact furthers the achievement of the SDGs by encouraging: First, international, and regional cooperation in migration management, including the harmonization of migration policies and the promotion of safe and orderly labor mobility. Second, by incorporating migration considerations in the planning and implementation of sustainable development policies, recognizing the role of migration as a cross-cutting factor that can affect multiple areas of development. Third, by ensuring the protection of the human rights of all migrants, regardless of their migration status, and promoting the social and economic inclusion of migrants in host communities. Fourth, address the underlying causes of migration, including poverty, conflict, inequality, and climate change, through comprehensive approaches that combine prevention, mitigation, and adaptation measures.

Other regional examples could be, first, the management of the refugee crisis in the Mediterranean. The geopolitics of the region, marked by conflicts in countries such as Syria, Afghanistan, and Libya, has led to an intense flow of refugees to Europe. The response of the European Union has been variable, with some countries implementing more restrictive nationalistic policies, while others advocated for a more humanitarian and collaborative response, in which the SDGs were an important part of the actions taken (Collyer, 2016; Zardo, 2022). Second, the migrant crisis in Central America and the United States. Factors such as violence, poverty, and lack of economic opportunities in countries such as Honduras, El Salvador, and Guatemala have led to an increase in migration to the United States. The U.S. response, marked by restrictive policies such as "zero tolerance" and the construction of a border fence, has generated controversy and raised questions about the effectiveness and sustainability of these measures in the long term (Faret et al., 2021). But at the same time, dozens of meetings and encounters have taken place between the different countries to reach agreements for the management of migration flows and, especially, to respond to the causes of migration (Delgado Wise, 2022).

In addition to these global or regional responses, international and civil society organizations highlight the actions undertaken by some specific countries, such as Senegal, Armenia, and Ghana. First, Senegal is relevant as a country that expels migrants in Africa and, above all, because of its high repatriation rates. Three ongoing programs in the regions of Sédhiou, Diourbel, and Saint Louis seek to empower the local community and the repatriated migrant community through green jobs, and gender and youth policies through the Priority Action Plan. The objective is to implement policies that lead to the fulfillment of the 2030 agenda in the health, education, and employment sectors. In practice, it is a program that, through universities in the three regions, involves diasporas and the private sector in local sustainable development. In general, the program has been successful in strengthening the capacities of local authorities and enhancing the development of the migrant community (Migration for Development, n.d.).

Second, Armenia stands out because the government started a process of nationalization of projects related to SDGs and migration, with the support of IOM. This experience involved adapting national issues toward sustainable global goals, which led at the same time to the development of indicators to measure the impact of migration policies on the SDGs. The results include the identification of five targets relevant to the Armenian context: labor migration, labor rights, orderly and safe mobility of people, diaspora engagement, and improved capacity to collect quality migration data (IOM, 2018).

Third, the Government of Ghana, with the support of the IOM, developed the program "Integrating Migration into National Development Plans: Towards Policy Coherence and the Achievement of Sustainable Development Goals at National and Global Levels" in 2018. The Project, funded by the UN and China, aimed to support the government in integrating migration into national development policies and achieving policy coherence with the SDGs. To this end, they established an inter-agency Technical Working Group on migration, which conducted sensitization training for officials and developed a Migration Policy Action Plan. The importance of the program in Ghana lies in the integration of migration into national development plans from a sustainable perspective (IOM, 2018).

Under what conditions can the Geopolitics of Migration Operate within the Framework of the SDGs?

There is substantial potential for geopolitics to manage the migration phenomenon within the framework of development objectives. However, several challenges and obstacles may hinder this interaction. Firstly, geopolitics often prioritizes national interests, making it challenging to implement common strategies due to diverging priorities among states. Secondly, there may be a lack of interest in cooperation and coordination among international actors, hindering the adoption of collective actions aligned with development objectives. Thirdly, structural inequalities at regional and global levels, including disparities in economic development and access to resources, may impede the implementation of migration policies that promote sustainable development. Fourthly, geopolitical conflicts and national security concerns can lead to restrictive migration policies that do not prioritize development objectives or human rights. Fifthly, the absence of a human rights-centered approach to migration geopolitics may perpetuate human rights violations. Finally, internal, and external political resistance to SDG-based migration policies can hinder effective and equitable measures.

However, amidst these challenges, opportunities also abound. Firstly, the geopolitics of migration acknowledges the strategic implications of human mobility, influencing power dynamics between states and shaping international migration governance. When aligned with the SDGs, migration geopolitics can manage mobility in a safe and orderly manner, fostering the social and economic inclusion of migrants and contributing to the fulfillment of the 2030 agenda across countries of origin, transit, and destination.

Secondly, security geopolitics shows that migration management is an aspect of national or regional security with an emphasis on border control and prevention of security threats. Under this logic, the SDGs from a security perspective ensure that migration is managed in a safe and orderly manner by institutions. It would imply generating institutional responses based on international cooperation, promoting mechanisms that guarantee security and control of flows.

Thirdly, the geopolitics of development acknowledges global interdependence and advocates for international cooperation to address migration challenges comprehensively within the principles of sustainable development. Within the SDG framework, the geopolitics of development can promote migration policies that contribute to goal achievement by fostering the social and economic inclusion of migrants based on strategic interests.

Ultimately, each type of geopolitics approaches the relationship between migration and SDGs from a different and complementary perspective, reflecting the debate in the literature. As mentioned, geopolitics could help manage migration in the framework of the SDGs if geopolitics promotes safe, orderly, and regular migration programs (Foresti and Hagen-Zanker, 2017). Furthermore, Likić-Brborić (2018) explains that geopolitics could help manage migration under the SDGs if a perspective that recognizes global interdependence and promotes international cooperation is adopted. It would imply that the implementation of migration agreements and policies seeks sustainable and equitable solutions between states, as well as the participation of civil society and other actors in migration governance.

Conclusions

In conclusion, while none of the Sustainable Development Goals (SDGs) explicitly focus on migration, several incorporate it within their scope, advocating for the management of orderly, safe, and regular migration (Goal 10.7). This recognition underscores the relevance of migration to sustainable development, with a bidirectional relationship between migration and the SDGs. Sustainable development efforts can address underlying migration drivers and enhance living conditions across countries of origin, transit, and destination. Additionally, the SDGs can influence migrant safety during journeys and facilitate their successful integration into host communities. Consequently, the relationship between sustainable development and migration is intricate and mutually influential, impacting economic, social, and environmental aspects in both origin and destination regions.

Geopolitics in migration addresses how migratory movements are related to the geopolitical interests of states and international actors. But it also reviews the influence of national security and power projection on migration policies and international agreements. In this framework, from a geopolitical perspective, states are using diplomatic tools to manage migration, affecting their global governance. Despite these attempts, the complexity of the migration phenomenon defies effective responses from geopolitics. Much of the literature focuses on a critical review of the relationship between migration and geopolitics insofar as it is an approach based mainly on processes of migration securitization. Migration policies thus become restrictive actions, in which border controls and selective mobility prevail.

In this framework, the intersection between geopolitics, migration, and sustainable development is complex and multifaceted, involving considerations at global, regional, and local levels. Geopolitical policies can impact migration and thus the ability of countries to achieve the SDGs. For example, on the one hand, restrictive policies can hinder migrants' access to basic services, hindering the achievement of the SDGs related to these issues. On the other hand, effective migration management can contribute to several SDGs, such as ending poverty, health and well-being, and decent work and economic growth.

Examples such as the Global Compact and regional initiatives like those in the European Union demonstrate how migration can be managed sustainably, aligning with the SDGs. Additionally, programs in countries like Senegal, Armenia, and Ghana showcase efforts to integrate migration into national development policies, promoting policy coherence with the SDGs and fostering fairer and more equitable migration management.

Ultimately, while the interrelationship between geopolitics, migration, and SDGs is possible, it is not without significant challenges. The text identifies several obstacles, such as the prioritization of national interests, lack of international cooperation, structural economic inequalities between countries and in the region, as well as a series of long-lasting geopolitical conflicts, which hinder migration management aligned with the SDGs. But equally, there are opportunities for action, which could contribute to a more integrated and human rights-based migration management, promoting the social and economic inclusion of migrants and aligning with the SDGs. Thus, geopolitics that fosters international cooperation and recognizes global interdependence could facilitate the implementation of sustainable and equitable migration policies, involving diverse actors in migration governance.

Notes

1 Resolution adopted by the General Assembly on 19 December 2018 A/RES/73/195.
2 I would like to thank Yamileth Guido Gonzalez for her assistance in classifying and reviewing the literature.
3 Four targets include migration explicitly: Goal 8.8: "Protect labor rights and promote safe and secure working environments for all workers, including migrant workers, in particular women migrants, and those in precarious employment". Goal 10.7: "Facilitate orderly, safe, regular, and responsible migration and mobility of people, including through the implementation of planned and well-managed migration policies". Goal 10.c: "By 2030, reduce to less than 3 percent the transaction costs of migrant remittances and eliminate remittance corridors with costs higher than 5 percent". Goal 17.18: "By 2020, (…) to significantly increase the availability of high-quality, timely, and reliable data disaggregated by (…) race, ethnicity, migratory status (…).".

References

Adger, W. Neil, et al. 2019. "Migration transforms the conditions for the achievement of the Sustainable Development Goals." *The Lancet Planetary* 3(11): E440–E442, https://doi.org/10.1016/S2542-5196(19)30213-X

Adger, W. Neil, et al. 2023. "Migration and sustainable development." *Perspective* 121(3), DOI: https://doi.org/10.1073/pnas.2206193121

Allen, William, et al. 2017. "Who Counts in Crises? The New Geopolitics of International Migration and Refugee Governance." *Geopolitics* 23(1): 217–243. https://doi.org/10.1080/14650045.2017.1327740

Borrelli, Lisa et al. 2022. "Agency within Mobility: Conceptualising the Geopolitics of Migration Management." *Geopolitics* 27(4): 1140–1167, https://doi.org/10.1080/14650045.2021.1973733

Campos-Delgado, Amalia. 2024. "Euphemistic Rhetoric and Dysphemistic Practices: Governing Migration in Mexico." *Geopolitics*, 2(1): 64–89, https://doi.org/10.1080/14650045.2023.2185513

Castles, Stephen. 2010. "Understanding Global Migration: A Social Transformation Perspective." *Journal of Ethnic and Migration Studies*, 36(10), 1565–1586, https://doi.org/10.1080/1369183X.2010.489381

Collyer, Michael. 2016. "Geopolitics as a migration governance strategy: European Union bilateral relations with Southern Mediterranean countries." *Journal of Ethnic and Migration Studies* 42(4): 606–624, https://doi.org/10.1080/1369183X.2015.1106111

Crush, Jonathan. 2019. "The problem with international migration and sustainable development". In *Achieving the Sustainable Development*, 85–97. London: Routledge, eBook ISBN: 9780429029622.

Delgado Wise, Raul. 2022. "Unsettling the migration and development narrative. A Latin American critical perspective", *International Migration*, 60: 8–18. https://doi.org/10.1111/imig.12994

Denyer, David, & Tranfield, David. 2009. "Producing a systematic review". In *The Sage handbook of organizational research methods*, 671–689. Sage Publications Ltd., ISBN: 9781446200643.

Gavonel, María Franco et al. 2021. "The migration-sustainability paradox: transformations in mobile worlds", *Current Opinion in Environmental Sustainability* 49: 98–109, https://doi.org/10.1016/j.cosust.2021.03.013

Faret, Laurent, Téllez, María E. A., & Rodríguez-Tapia, Luz H. 2021. "Migration Management and Changes in Mobility Patterns in the North and Central American Region". *Journal on Migration and Human Security*, *9*(2), 63–79. https://doi.org/10.1177/23315024211008096

Flint, Colin & Mamadouh, Virginie. 2015. "The MultiDisciplinary Reclamation of Geopolitics: New Opportunities and Challenges". *Geopolitics*, 20(1): 1–3, https://doi.org/10.1080/14650045.2015.1014282

Foresti, Marta & Hagen-Zanker, Jessica. 2017. "Introduction". In *Migration and the 2030 Agenda for Sustainable Development*, 5–12. Switzerland: Swiss Agency for Development and Cooperation SDC.

Hackl, Andreas. 2018. "Mobility equity in a globalized world: Reducing inequalities in the sustainable development agenda." *World Development*, 112: 150–162, https://doi.org/10.1016/j.worlddev.2018.08.005

Hyndman, Jennifer & Mountz, Alison. 2008. "Another Brick in the Wall? Neo-Refoulement and the Externalization of Asylum by Australia and Europe." *Government and Opposition* 43 (2): 249–269, https://doi.org/10.1111/j.1477-7053.2007.00251.x

Hyndman, Jennifer. 2012. "The Geopolitics of Migration and Mobility." *Geopolitics* 17(2): 243–255, https://doi.org/10.1080/14650045.2011.569321

IOM 2018. *Migration and the 2030 Agenda*. Geneva: Swiss Agency for Development and Cooperation SDC. https://environmentalmigration.iom.int/sites/g/files/tmzbdl1411/files/documents/sdg_en.pdf

IOM. 2020. *IOM Institutional Strategy on Migration and Sustainable Development*. Geneva: IOM. https://publications.iom.int/books/iom.institutional-strategy-migration-and-sustainable-development

Likić-Brborić, Branka. 2018. "Global migration governance, civil society and the paradoxes of sustainability". *Globalizations* 15(6): 762–778, https://doi.org/10.1080/14747731.2018.1503841

Micinski, Nicholas & Lefebvre, Camille. 2024. "The Geopolitics in the Global Compacts: Sovereignty, Emerging Norms, and Hypocrisy in Global Migration Governance." *Geopolitics* 29 (1): 1–12. https://doi.org/10.1080/14650045.2023.2265321

Migration for Development. n.d., s.f. *Senegal - Making Migration Work for Sustainable Development*, https://migration4development.org/en/about/our-programmes/senegal

Parkes, Roderick. 2015. "European Union and the Geopolitics of Migration." In *UIPaper 1*. Swedish Institute of International Affairs.

Pécoud, Antoine. 2020. "Philosophies of migration governance in a globalizing world." *Globalizations*. 18(1): 103–119, https://doi.org/10.1080/14747731.2020.1774316

Prada, Elena M. 2020. "The Relationship Between Sustainable Development Goals and Migration. An EU-28 Perspective." *Journal of Social and Economic Statistics*, 9(1). https://doi.org/10.2478/jses-2020-0004

Sivakumar, P. & Rajan, S. Irudaya. 2021. "Contours of migration and development in the SDG agenda". In *Sustainable Development Goals and Migration*. Routledge, 1–20. eBook ISBN9780429346866.

Solomon, Michele Klein & Sheldon, Suzanne. 2018. "The Global Compact for Migration: From the Sustainable Development Goals to a Comprehensive Agreement on Safe, Orderly and Regular Migration." *International Journal of Refugee Law*, 30(4), 584–590, https://doi.org/10.1093/ijrl/eey065

Suliman, Samid. 2017. "Migration and Development after 2015." *Globalizations* 14(3): 415–431, https://doi.org/10.1080/14747731.2017.1281625

Toochi Aniche, Ernest. 2020. "Migration and Sustainable Development: Challenges and Opportunities". In *Migration Conundrums, Regional Integration and Development: Africa-Europe Relations in a Changing Global Order*, 37–61. Springer ISBN: 978-981-15-2477-6.

Tuathail, Gearóid Ó. 1999. "Understanding critical geopolitics: Geopolitics and risk society." *Journal of Strategic Studies*, 22 (2–3): 107–124. https://doi.org/10.1080/01402399908437756

Zardo, Federica. 2022. "The EU Trust Fund for Africa: Geopolitical Space Making through Migration Policy Instruments." *Geopolitics*, 27(2): 584–603. https://doi.org/10.1080/14650045.2020.1815712

Conclusions and Critical Thoughts

Bernadette Andreosso-O'Callaghan, Daniel Rajmil and Lucía Morales

Although, from the beginning of times, the world has always been under constant change, the frequency of crises, be they financial/economic, energy/environmental, health or else a combination of all these, has increased. This state of "permacrisis" has pushed international actors to consider new frameworks so as to increase the sustainability of our productive models that would reconcile economic activity with environmental constraints. An important element in this search has been the emergence of new geoeconomic and geopolitical dynamics derived from the polarization of wealth between and within countries and regions. In their quest for sustainability models, the international institutions aim, theoretically and ideally, at delineating new frameworks that could contribute to both equality and growth.

In this vein, the United Nations 2030 Agenda intends to extend the previous Millenium Development Goals (MDGs) to a reachable policy-setting agenda that would foster economic growth and development in an equitable manner. Halfway through the 2030 Agenda's ambitious goals and objectives, it can be seen that geoeconomic and geopolitical tensions arising from the complexity of the international scenario that embraces the Sustainable Development Goals (SDGs) are growing. A critical assessment of the International Political Economy of current political and economic leaders suggests that, far from bringing a peaceful path to growth and development, these actors are increasing the existing and new political and societal cleavages.

The different chapters contained in this book have, from different disciplines, looked at complementary issues such as economic diplomacy, education, SMEs' policies and large emerging countries' strategies as key to achieve: (i) the SDGs agenda (ii) the international diplomacy (political and economic) that pushes for the global balance of power that is needed to achieve the SDG's: (iii) the specific role of international organizations; and/or (iv) the sustainable concept per se. One important conclusion arising from the study is that the so-called "Global South" and "emerging economies", seem no longer to be willing to accept dictates from the North, without multilateral cooperation. Interestingly, this extends to the case of policies in the environmental area.

DOI: 10.4324/9781032655857-20

The book encompasses different chapters and case studies that highlight the strong interaction existing between geopolitical and geoeconomic implications lying behind the 2030 Agenda. The existing international conflicts and wars show evidence that current conflict scenarios go far beyond merely political and war calculations and involve economic factors and diplomacy strategies. There is compelling evidence that the synergy between financial/business endeavors and political strategies is imperative to avoid economic stagnation and crises Acknowledging this is paramount to the understanding of environmentally friendly growth models and political steadiness.

The sustainability goals set by the UN Agenda 2030 aim at being clear, measurable (therefore prone to evaluation; ideally by independent assessors) as well as incontestable, reuniting thereby all countries under the visible banner of the UN. As argued in the book, a thorough analysis of the epistemology of the concept of sustainable development in a historical setting demonstrates the many contradictions, ambiguities and limitations of the concept and its rapid evolution. Firmly based on the view that today's economic development is not "sustainable" (i.e. there is too much CO_2) because it is anthropogenic, the official view on "sustainability" fails to acknowledge that this may be so because of policy choices selected and driven by these same global institutions. In a way, it is as if the snake was biting its tail, to use a simple metaphor that could describe this self-perpetuating cycle.

Therefore, an inescapable conclusion of this volume is that there is a need to go one major step ahead and to re-assess the sustainability concept per se, which is, as discussed in some parts of the book a key concept in terms of economic growth and development. What are we (i.e. all the interested parties) aiming at? Is the aim a new energy transition that repeats failures from the past? Is it a new economic model that favors large multinational firms only (and a small number of investors therein), a model that leads to higher market concentration, to more social exclusion, to increased poverty levels and to more friction between and within countries? These are crucial questions that are seldom debated in these – top – international circles. We will argue that there is a need to set up measurable and achievable energy consumption and production goals combined with the need to rediscover manufacturing processes that balance economic growth and environment, by releasing for example the many suppressed technologies that would have an immediate positive impact on efficiency, growth, and environmental conservation. Another urgency is to revise thoroughly the chosen globalization framework, again designed and promoted by these same international institutions, and to reconsider for example the global supply chains known for their detrimental impact on the environment as major contributors in terms of greenhouse gas emissions. In this, new political economic assets are emerging as the coveted energy transition is encountering obstacles in the form of novel rare materials, echoing past crises and colonial styles of exploitation in Africa or Latin America for example.

Concluding on a positive note, this book has shown that it is only by engaging in more critical multidisciplinary research and in elaborating science-based multidisciplinary indicators/models (that work), bringing together scholars from the fields of political economy, political science, business/finance, data science, education, law and also physics/engineering that breakthrough advances can be made in the core area of sustainable development for a better future.

Index

Pages in *italics* refer to figures and pages in **bold** refer to tables.

For Product Safety Concerns and Information please contact our EU
representative GPSR@taylorandfrancis.com
Taylor & Francis Verlag GmbH, Kaufingerstraße 24, 80331 München, Germany

www.ingramcontent.com/pod-product-compliance
Ingram Content Group UK Ltd.
Pitfield, Milton Keynes, MK11 3LW, UK
UKHW020154200926
475702UK00016B/2706
9781032655840